REDISCOVERING
THE BRITISH WORLD

REDISCOVERING THE BRITISH WORLD

Edited by

PHILLIP BUCKNER &
R. DOUGLAS FRANCIS

CALGARY

AT THE UNIVERSITY PRESS

2005

Published by the
University of Calgary Press
2500 University Drive NW
Calgary, Alberta, Canada T2N 1N4
www.uofcpress.com

We acknowledge the financial
support of the Government of Canada
through the Book Publishing Industry
Development Program (BPIDP), the
Alberta Foundation for the Arts for our
publishing activities. We acknowledge
the support of the Canada Council for
the Arts for our publishing program.

Canada Council   Conseil des Arts
for the Arts   du Canada

Canada

Cover design, Mieka West.
Internal design & typesetting,
Jason Dewinetz.

∞ This book is printed on 60lb Rolland
Enviro Natural forest friendly paper.
Printed and bound in Canada by
AGMV MARQUIS.

LIBRARY AND ARCHIVES OF CANADA
CATALOGUING IN PUBLICATION:

Rediscovering the british world /
edited by Phillip Buckner &
R. Douglas Francis.

Selection of papers presented at the
British World Conference held on
July 10, 2003 in Calgary Alberta.

Includes bibliographical references
and index.

ISBN-10 1-55238-179-X
ISBN-13 1-55238-179-3

  1 Great Britain – Colonies
     – History – 19th century.
  2 Great Britain – Colonies
     – History – 20th century.
  3 Great Britain – History – 19th
     century.
  4 Great Britain – History – 20th
     century.
  I Buckner, Phillip A. (Phillip
     Alfred), 1942–
 II Francis, R. D. (R. Douglas),
     1944–
III British World Conference (2003:
     Calgary, Alta.)
IV Title.

DA16.R34 2005   941.081
C2005-905604-5

INTRODUCTION
Phillip Buckner & R. Douglas Francis 9

1 WHAT DID A BRITISH WORLD
MEAN TO THE BRITISH?
REFLECTIONS ON THE NINETEENTH CENTURY
Catherine Hall 21

2 THE RISE OF THE ANGLOWORLD:
SETTLEMENT IN NORTH AMERICA
AND AUSTRALASIA, 1784–1918
James Belich 39

3 INDIGENOUS PEOPLES AND
IMPERIAL NETWORKS IN THE
EARLY NINETEENTH CENTURY:
THE POLITICS OF KNOWLEDGE
Elizabeth Elbourne 59

4 LOYALTY AND REBELLION IN
COLONIAL POLITICS:
THE CAMPAIGN AGAINST CONVICT
TRANSPORTATION IN AUSTRALIA
Paul Pickering 87

5 FROM VICTORIAN VALUES
TO WHITE VIRTUES:
ASSIMILATION AND EXCLUSION IN
BRITISH RACIAL DISCOURSE, c.1870–1914
Douglas Lorimer 109

6 COLONIAL COMPARISONS:
RETHINKING MARRIAGE, CIVILIZATION
AND NATION IN THE NINETEENTH-CENTURY
WHITE SETTLER SOCIETIES
Bettina Bradbury 135

7 INTERLOCUTING EMPIRE:
COLONIAL WOMANHOOD, SETTLER IDENTITY,
AND FRANCES HERRING
Adele Perry 159

8 THE LONG GOODBYE:
ENGLISH CANADIANS AND THE BRITISH WORLD
Phillip Buckner 181

9 FABIAN SOCIALISM AND
BRITISH AUSTRALIA, 1890–1972
Frank Bongiorno 209

10 WAR AND THE BRITISH WORLD
IN THE TWENTIETH CENTURY
Jeffrey Grey 233

11 THE OTHER BATTLE:
IMPERIALIST VERSUS NATIONALIST SYMPATHIES
WITHIN THE OFFICER CORPS OF THE CANADIAN
EXPEDITIONARY FORCE, 1914–1919
Patrick H. Brennan 251

12 EMPIRE AND EVERYDAY:
BRITISHNESS AND IMPERIALISM IN WOMEN'S LIVES
IN THE GREAT WAR
Paul Ward 267

13 BRITISHNESS, SOUTH AFRICANNESS
AND THE FIRST WORLD WAR
John Lambert 285

14 THE MIGRANT'S EMPIRE:
LOYALTY AND IMPERIAL CITIZENSHIP
AT THE LEAGUE OF NATIONS
Satadru Sen 305

15 THE EMPIRE ANSWERS:
IMPERIAL IDENTITY ON RADIO AND FILM, 1939–1945
Wendy Webster 321

16 REHABILITATING THE INDIGENE:
POST-WAR RECONSTRUCTION AND THE IMAGE OF
THE INDIGENOUS OTHER IN ENGLISH CANADA
AND NEW ZEALAND, 1943–1948
R. Scott Sheffield 341

17 AUSTRALIA'S COLD WAR:
BRITISHNESS AND ENGLISH-SPEAKING WORLDS
CHALLENGED ANEW
David Lowe 361

18 HISTORY WARS AND THE IMPERIAL LEGACY
IN THE SETTLER SOCIETIES
Stuart Macintyre 381

19 WORLDS APART:
THREE "BRITISH" PRIME MINISTERS AT EMPIRE'S END
Stuart Ward 399

NOTES ON CONTRIBUTORS 421
INDEX 425

INTRODUCTION

Phillip Buckner & R. Douglas Francis

BEGINNING IN THE 1960S, A REVOLUTION took place both in the historiography of the British Empire and in the historiography of each of the colonies of settlement, as they used to be known, or the Dominions, as they were officially named in 1907. In the nineteenth century the colonies of settlement – Canada, Newfoundland, Australia, New Zealand, and South Africa – were defined as part of what Sir Charles Dilke called "Greater Britain."[1] Indeed, the Dominions, along with India, were seen as the core of the British Empire. "We are part of an Empire which in one Continent is the heir of great Oriental monarchies, in other Continents is one of a brotherhood of democracies," the soon-to-be Prime Minister of Great Britain, A. J. Balfour, declared in 1901.[2] This perspective persisted well into the twentieth century and was reflected in the *Cambridge History of the British Empire*, published in nine volumes between 1929 and 1959. The emphasis in the *Cambridge History* was on India and the self-governing Dominions, each of which was dealt with in a separate volume in the series (except for Newfoundland, which was included in the volume on Canada). The rest of what was described as the "dependent" Empire was examined in only one volume. Of course, the *Cambridge History* reflected a vision of imperial history that is quite unacceptable today. It viewed the British as an imperial people peacefully building colonies of British settlement in underpopulated and undeveloped parts of the globe or generously spreading British civilization to parts of the globe where there were large and irremovable non-European populations. The *Cambridge History* was also based on the assumption that the Empire would last, if not for a thousand years, at least for the foreseeable future and that it would be a very long time

9

before the colonies in the dependent Empire would be ready to achieve equality with the "independent partner nations" that had been created by British immigrants overseas.[3]

Ironically, by the time the last volume in the *Cambridge History* was published in 1959, the foundations of British imperial authority were rapidly eroding. The Dominions increasingly looked less and less like parts of a Greater Britain or even like "partner nations," India had become a republic with only loose ties to what was now called the Commonwealth, and the "winds of change" were sweeping across Africa and Asia. As the Empire receded into history, imperial historians began to distance themselves from an historiography that had been triumphalist, xenophobic, and overly optimistic about the Empire's durability. The earlier imperial historians – from Dilke to the authors of the *Cambridge History* – had stressed that the British Empire was unique among the European empires established in the nineteenth century, both in its willingness to create self-governing colonies overseas and in its benevolence toward the indigenous people brought under British rule. The new historians had little patience with these self-serving platitudes and saw the British Empire as little different from other European empires. The emphasis of the new imperial historiography was very clearly not on the benefits of bestowing British civilization on non-British peoples but on the exploitative nature of British imperialism and on the negative impact of British rule, particularly on the large number of Africans and Asians who had been incorporated into the Empire against their wishes. Partly because there was a strong belief in the materialist foundations of imperial expansion and imperial rule, the new historiography did not draw a clear distinction between the exploitation of those parts of the world that were formally under British rule and the so-called informal empire. There never was any real agreement about which parts of the world were part of this "informal empire" – a term that lacked any generally agreed-upon definition and so could be expanded to include large parts of Asia, the Middle East, and South America. From the new historiographical perspective, most notably associated with the writing of Ronald Robinson and John Gallagher, even the granting of responsible government to the colonies of settlement was interpreted not as an enlightened gesture designed to lead to the creation of self-governing and increasingly autonomous British communities overseas but as a method of maintaining informal control over those communities.[4] In fact, the colonies of settlement were essentially peripheral to the new imperial historiography as the focus shifted to Africa and Asia and the "informal empire." There was even limited interest in British migration overseas, since the vast majority of the migrants went either to the United States or to the colonies of settlement. Constitutional history, which focused on the development of responsible government and the evolution of the colonies of settlement into self-governing Dominions, had been a central theme in the older historiography, but it was virtually ignored in the new imperial historiography.[5]

One ironic side effect of viewing the empire from the perspective of the African and Asian colonies and of including a large "informal empire" was that the new historians downplayed the historical significance of the Empire to the inhabitants of the British Isles. They depicted the Empire as being run by a small inner core of politicians and civil servants in London who collectively formed the "official mind" of British imperialism. The members of this small elite were described as "reluctant imperialists" who were prodded into occasional activity by missionary lobbies or particular financial interests or by the men-on-the-spot overseas. The new historiography assumed that the mass of the British people knew little about and had little interest in Britain's overseas empire – a point of view contradicted by all of the studies in this collection, most directly in Catherine Hall's chapter at the beginning of the volume. Ironically, by denying the importance of the empire in British history, the new historians, in a curious (and unintended) way, allowed the British people to escape responsibility for what was done in their name overseas. Since empire was something that happened outside the British Isles and involved only small numbers of British men and even smaller numbers of British women, overseas exploitation could hardly be the fault of the British people. The new historiography also argued that the end of the Empire came with a whimper, not a bang, and had a relatively slight long-term impact on the culture and institutions of the mother country. Ironically, one of the consequences of the end of the Empire was not only the death of the conviction that the British people were an imperial race destined to spread around the globe but also growing doubt whether the inhabitants of the British Isles had ever formed a single people. Not only did the belief in a "Greater Britain" disappear but the concept of "Great Britain" itself came under attack. The Irish – or at least Irish Catholics – had long since distanced themselves from Great Britain, but now Scottish and Welsh nationalists also began to challenge the notion of a single British identity shared by all the inhabitants of the United Kingdom. A "nation" that had defined itself in imperial terms began to look less and less like a nation at all.

A turning point in British historiography was Linda Colley's *Britons: Forging the Nation, 1707–1837*, published in 1992.[6] Colley sought to re-affirm that there had been such a thing as a British identity and that the Empire had played an important part in defining what it was to be British. She also insisted that it was possible to hold multiple identities and to define oneself both as British and as English or Irish or Scottish or Welsh. Colley unleashed two debates. One was about the nature of British identity – whether it had ever existed and, if it did exist, how it was defined. This was essentially a debate among historians of the British Isles. It generated an enormous literature and continues to do so. Although British imperial historians were initially on the periphery of this debate, as they had been on the periphery of British historiography since the 1960s, they were gradually drawn back into the mainstream of British history as the Empire came to be seen as central in the creation of the British state and in the creation of a sense of British identity.

The second debate that Colley set off was over the question of whether the term "British" should be reserved for the inhabitants of the British Isles. Since the 1960s the historians of the old Dominions had also lost interest in the Empire. What had once been a central field in their own historiographies was now seen as essentially part of an alien subject – British history. Indeed, national historiography in the Dominions seemed to fragment into a series of sub-fields, as historians everywhere abandoned the search for national identities and began to focus on what in Canada were called the "limited identities" of race, gender, class, and region. Even those who continued to insist on the need to study the nation and national identity saw little value in studying the Empire. In the recent *Oxford History of the British Empire*, Doug Owram notes that by the 1960s the study of Canada and the Empire had become a specialized field of little interest to most Canadian historians, which, he argued, is as it should be since the true concern of Canadian historians should be not with imperial history but with "the origin of Canada."[7] Similar claims were made by nationalist historians in the other Dominions. In Australia, the term "cultural cringe" was used to condemn those who continued to believe in the importance of the imperial connection in Australian history and culture.

There were a few voices in the wilderness who cried out against this attempt to rewrite the history of the Dominions. The most influential was J.G.A. Pocock, the New Zealand-born historian whose area of specialization was seventeenth- and eighteenth-century British history. As early as 1974, Pocock pleaded for a new British history that would include the old Dominions (or what he called the neo-Britains overseas) and that would recognize that the history of the Dominions was an integral part of imperial history.[8] But the call met with a very limited response, partly because most national historians continued to believe that one could be either an Australian, a Canadian, a New Zealander, or a South African, or one could be British but not both. Colley's emphasis on multiple identities offered a way out of this false dichotomy. If one could be Scottish – or even Irish – and British at the same time, why could one not be Australian or Canadian and British at the same time? Not everyone accepted this conclusion but the issue of Britishness has slowly been put back on the agenda in the writing of the history of the former Dominions. Partly this was because many historians in the older Dominions were increasingly concerned by the marginalization of the Dominions in the new imperial historiography. There was also a growing number of younger historians who felt that the Dominions must confront the reality of their own imperial past and accept the responsibility for the part that they had played in extending and maintaining the Empire, both at home and abroad.

The British World conferences grew out of these debates. The concept of a British World is not a new one. The phrase was frequently used from the late nineteenth century until the 1950s to describe what Dilke termed "Greater Britain," although the latter quickly became the preferred term for describing collectively the British colonies of settlement overseas. Like the boundaries of Greater Britain, the boundaries of the British World were and are open to interpretation. Dilke originally included the United States as part of his Greater Britain. Obviously the Thirteen Colonies were at the centre of the first British Empire. Indeed, although the first British Empire was destroyed when the United States achieved independence in 1783, it could be argued that during the first half of the nineteenth century the newly created United States was still to some degree part of a British-dominated cultural and intellectual world. But in the nineteenth century the Americans also created an empire of their own as they expanded across the continent, and in the early twentieth century they even acquired overseas colonies. In the twentieth century, British politicians like Joseph Chamberlain and Winston Churchill might talk of the unity of "the English-speaking peoples," but this unity was more imagined than real. Dilke recognized this in 1899 when he declared in his study of the British Empire that the pressure to restrict the use of the term to territories that were part of the formal empire was "too strong to resist."[9]

Those parts of Asia and Africa that came under British rule – especially India – were more clearly part of the British World, and the theme of how non-British peoples in Africa and Asia responded and adapted to, and negotiated a place for themselves, in the larger British World is the subject of a number of the articles in this collection, most notably that by Satadru Sen. But British rule in Africa and Asia was transitory. The new nations that emerged in the aftermath of decolonization from the 1950s to the 1970s were run by indigenous peoples who eagerly jettisoned most of their imperial past. The small British populations in Africa, Asia, and the Caribbean, who had once formed an integral part of the British World, faded away, leaving few traces of their existence even in those parts of the world where they had once formed the dominant social class. Outside the formal Empire there were a few, even smaller, British enclaves – in places like Shanghai and Buenos Aires – which would once have been considered part of the British World, but they have disappeared even more quickly and completely. It is doubtful whether the rest of the informal empire was ever really part of the British World, a World held together by a sense of belonging to a shared British culture, not simply by ties of commerce and trade.

The migration of millions of British immigrants overseas in the nineteenth and twentieth centuries was obviously critical in the creation of this sense of belonging to a shared British culture. Yet while this was one of the largest voluntary movements of people in history, as James Belich points out in his article "The Rise of the Angloworld: Settlement in North America and Australasia, 1784–1918," its impact has been inadequately studied. This is partly because most of the British migrants in the nineteenth century went to the United States, where they formed but one immigrant group among many (though the largest for most of the nineteenth century). As Charlotte Erickson pointed out many years ago, English and Scottish immigrants were so easily absorbed into the dominant American culture, so easily Americanized, that they became "invisible immigrants."[10] But a significant minority – probably over a third – of the British migrants in the nineteenth century, and an even larger proportion in the twentieth century, stayed within the Empire, relocating mainly in Canada, Australia, New Zealand, and South Africa. The debate over whether one can talk about a British diaspora continues,[11] but call it what you will, the migration of waves of Britons overseas was fundamental in creating a series of new states, states that have survived and remain one of the most important and lasting legacies of the British Empire.

To talk about decolonization in most of these states is patently meaningless, since control over land and other resources that were taken from
the indigenous people has not been handed back to them and never will
be, except perhaps at some distant point in the future in South Africa,
the only former Dominion in which the indigenous people form a majority of the population. In the other Dominions, limited compensation
and reconciliation are certainly on the political agenda, but as Stuart
Macintyre points out in his article on the history wars, there is considerable disagreement over how much compensation should be given and
how far reconciliation should go. The populations of Canada, Australia,
and New Zealand are no longer as predominantly British as they once
were, and all the former Dominions have begun to redefine themselves
as multicultural communities with their own distinct national identities
rather than as neo-Britains. But the legacy of their imperial past cannot
easily be wiped away and consigned to the "dustbin of history."

Of course, the Dominions never were simple replicas of the mother
country. It is well known that the populations of the Dominions were
more Scottish and more Irish than the people of the United Kingdom,
but this emphasis on the Scots and the Irish is frequently exaggerated.
During the first half of the nineteenth century, Scottish and Irish immigrants to the Empire did outnumber the English, but during the even
heavier waves of migrations in the late nineteenth and early twentieth
centuries, the English overwhelmingly predominated, though the Scots
remained significantly overrepresented.[12] Certainly it is a myth that
the Scots created Canada or the Irish, Australia. The colonies of settlement drew upon all parts of the British Isles for their immigrants, their
institutions, their laws, and their cultures. And they frequently rejected
aspects of the law or culture of the mother country that they felt could
not or should not be transplanted in a new environment. They wished to
be "British," but increasingly on their own terms and in their own way.
It was "Better Britains" – not simply neo-Britains – that they sought
to create. The extent to which the Irish, the Scottish, the Welsh, and
even the English within the United Kingdom defined their identity as
British remains an ongoing subject of debate. But in Greater Britain
overseas, migrants from the British Isles rarely settled or worshipped in
self-contained enclaves, and intermarriage rates among the Protestant
immigrants were high in all of the colonies of settlement. Over time, a
sense of being part of a British community – while remaining Scottish,
Irish, Welsh, or English – grew stronger, probably much stronger than
among those who did not leave their ancestral homes in the British Isles.

To some extent this was not true for Irish Catholics, since they did worship separately and did have high rates of endogenous marriages, but gradually many, probably most, Irish Catholics were integrated into the British communities created in the Dominions. To a more limited degree, so too were the descendants of most non-British European immigrants, particularly those from northern Europe who assimilated fairly easily into the colonial cultures created by the British overseas. Most resistant to the pressures for cultural integration were the large French-Canadian minority in Canada and the Afrikaners who formed a majority of the population of European descent in South Africa. But most of the French-Canadian elite and a substantial minority of the Afrikaner elite were willing to accept British institutions and pledge allegiance to the British crown so long as this did not mean abandoning their own cultural identities.[13] Many non-whites throughout the Empire also saw the advantages of being accepted as British, though they frequently ran into a racial barrier when they attempted to define themselves as culturally British. Indeed, there is no simple answer, as a number of the papers in this collection show, to what it meant to be British, either at home or in the overseas colonies.

But clearly there were strong linkages between the British at home and the British immigrants and their descendants overseas. Millions of Britons in Britain saw relatives, friends, and neighbours migrate. Some of those who left became return migrants, either because they failed to create a better life for themselves overseas or because they were so successful that they could afford to return in style. During the late nineteenth and early twentieth centuries, as the costs of transport fell and the safety and comfort of travelling by sea improved dramatically, a growing number of British migrants moved repeatedly back and forth between Britain and the colonies. They were joined by many second- or third-generation colonials who were lured to Britain as tourists or for a variety of business, professional, or political reasons. Many of these Australian, Canadian, New Zealand, and South African migrants never returned to the colony that they continued to call home. Over time a growing and increasingly complex web of family, cultural, commercial, and professional networks linked the British in Britain with Britons overseas. For too long, imperial history has focused on the links at the top among the imperial elites; we need to dig deeper if we are to understand the vast array of networks that held the British World together.[14]

In the past, historians have too readily accepted some version of the colony-to-nation thesis. It is as if the Empire existed essentially to create a series of independent nations and that the process of making the transition was simple, uncomplicated, and linear. This teleological approach glosses over the fact that, while there was a continual process of renegotiating the status of the Dominions, at least until the Second World War, the Empire could and did act as a unit. Even after the war, the belief in the existence of a British World remained strong both in Britain and the Dominions. Certainly, as Jeff Grey argues in his article, participation in the wars of the twentieth century led to stronger dominion nationalisms and a growing sense that the strategic interests of Britain and the Dominions were not identical. But as several other articles make clear, notably those by Pat Brennan, John Lambert, and Paul Ward, the First World War strengthened rather than weakened a sense of imperial identity among those who served on both the overseas and the home front, and reinforced the belief in the existence of a British World. Even after the Second World War the sense of being part of a larger British World endured among many of those who lived in Britain and the Dominions.[15] It certainly was not self-evident in 1945 that within a quarter of a century the British Empire would be dissolved.

An attempt to explore and interpret the value of the British World as a concept and its meaning to those who were part of it began as an initiative of a small group of historians – John Darwin at Oxford University and Rob Holland and Carl Bridge at the Institute of Commonwealth Studies at the University of London – who were determined to break the mould in which imperial history was being written and to bring the Dominions back into the picture. They already had an Australian on board (Carl Bridge was Head of the Menzies Centre for Australian Studies), and they recruited Phillip Buckner from Canada (at that time teaching at the University of New Brunswick, although he too would shortly become a senior research fellow at the Institute of Commonwealth Studies), James Belich from New Zealand (shortly to move to the University of Auckland), and Bill Nasson from the University of Cape Town in South Africa to join an informal committee responsible for organizing the first British World Conference at the Institute of Commonwealth Studies in June 1998. Twenty-two papers were presented to an audience of seventy scholars drawn from across Britain and the old Dominions. So successful was the conference that the scholars involved decided to hold a series of conferences in the Dominions, the first of which took place in South Africa, at the University of Cape Town, in January 2002. More than fifty papers were given to an audience of at least a hundred, and a selection of the papers has subsequently been published in a special issue of the

Journal of Imperial and Commonwealth History, issued simultaneously as a book under the title *The British World: Diaspora, Culture, Identity*.[16]

The next conference was hosted by the Humanities Institute at the University of Calgary from 10–12 July 2003. The organizing committee (to which Douglas Francis of the University of Calgary was now added) invited six keynote speakers to address the "British World" theme from the perspective of their own speciality: James Belich of the University of Auckland, Phillip Buckner of the University of New Brunswick and the Institute of Commonwealth Studies, Sarah Carter of the University of Calgary, Jeff Grey of the Australian Defence Academy in Canberra, Catherine Hall of the University of London, and Stuart Macintyre of the University of Melbourne. The conference attracted over 120 papers and about twice as many participants. The articles contained in this volume form but a small proportion of the papers given at the British World conference in Calgary and we hope to produce a second volume of papers given at the conference dealing specifically with Canada and the British World.

Selecting the papers to include in this volume was a difficult task, not least because even the founders of the British World project were never unified in their interpretation of what should be included within the framework of the project. Certainly a key part of the agenda of the British World project was to bring the old Dominions back into the mainstream of imperial history and to examine their connections with the United Kingdom and with each other – and most of the papers in this collection do focus on that theme. But there was a feeling among a majority of those involved in organizing the British World Conferences that to focus simply on the Dominions would be to take too narrow a view of the concept of a British World. Indeed, the call for papers for the Calgary conference stressed the desire of the organizers to include papers that dealt with British minorities outside the Dominions, papers that dealt with the reaction of the host societies within the Dominions to the incorporation of non-British minorities, and the reaction of those minorities to their incorporation into the British World, and papers with a broad focus on issues of gender, race, and ethnicity throughout the wider British World. The programme at Calgary reflected this wider interpretation of the meaning of the concept of a British World, and so does the selection of papers chosen for this collection. We hope that the papers that follow do give some idea of the complexity and the importance of studying the British World. It should not be necessary to point out that the purpose of resurrecting the concept of a British

World is not an exercise in imperial nostalgia, a lament for a world we have lost. Scholars who study Britishness and believe in its historical significance do not necessarily identify with it or approve of imperialism in any form. Our goal is to re-examine a complex phenomenon and to understand how it shaped the world in which we now live.

{NOTES}

1 Sir Charles W. Dilke, *Greater Britain: A Record of Travel in English-Speaking Countries during 1866 and 1867*, 2 vols. (London, 1868).

2 Quoted in Ian Christopher Fletcher, "'Some Interesting Survivals of a Historic Past'?: Republicanism, Monarchism and the Militant Edwardian Left," in *Republicanism in Victorian Society*, ed. David Nash and Antony Taylor (Phoenix Mill: Sutton Publishing, 2002), 92.

3 The reference to "independent partner nations" can be found in volume one of *The Cambridge History of the British Empire* (Cambridge: Cambridge University Press, 1929), 20–21.

4 This is a key theme in what was probably the most influential article ever published in British imperial history: Ronald Robinson and John Gallagher, "The Imperialism of Free Trade," *Economic History Review*, 2nd ser., 1 (1953): 1–15. See also Ronald Robinson, "Non-European Foundations of European Imperialism: Sketch for a Theory of Collaboration," in *Studies in the Theory of Imperialism*, ed. R. Owen and B. Sutcliffe (London: Longman, 1972) and "Imperial Theory and the Question of Imperialism after Empire," *Journal of Imperial and Commonwealth History* 12, no. 2 (1984): 45–46.

5 On this point, see Robert Holland, "Britain, Commonwealth and the End of Empire," in *The British Constitution in the Twentieth Century*, ed. Vernon Bogdanor (Oxford: Oxford University Press, 2003), 631–61.

6 Linda Colley, *Britons: Forging the Nation, 1707–1837* (New Haven: Yale University Press, 1992).

7 D. R. Owram, "Canada and the Empire," in *The Oxford History of the British Empire: Historiography*, ed. Robin W. Winks (Oxford: Oxford University Press, 1999), 5:161. For a critique from a "British World" perspective of the whole Oxford History project, see Phillip Buckner, "Was there a 'British' Empire? *The Oxford History of the British Empire* from a Canadian Perspective," *Acadiensis* 32 (2002): 110–28.

8 J.G.A. Pocock, "British History: A Plea for a New Subject," *New Zealand Journal of History* 8 (1974): 3–21. See also his "The Limits and Divisions of British History: In Search of the Unknown Subject," *American Historical Review* 87 (1982): 311–36; "History and Sovereignty," *Journal of British Studies* 31 (1992): 358–89; and "The New British History in Atlantic Perspective: An Antipodean Commentary," *American Historical Review* 104 (1999): 490–500. From a Canadian perspective, see Phillip Buckner, "Whatever Happened to the British Empire?" *Journal of the Canadian Historical Association* 3 (1993): 3–32. It is another New Zealander, James Belich, who has most consistently sought to examine the extent to which the term "Neo-Britain" is a useful description of the Dominions. See his "Neo-Britains," unpublished paper

presented at the first British World Conference at the Institute of Commonwealth Studies, London, June 1998; his two-volume history of New Zealand, *Making Peoples: A History of the New Zealanders from Polynesian Settlement to the End of the Nineteenth Century* (Auckland: The Penguin Press, 1996); and *Paradise Reforged: A History of the New Zealanders from the 1880s to the Year 2000* (Auckland: Penguin, 2001).

9 Sir Charles W. Dilke, *The British Empire* (London, 1899), 9.

10 Charlotte Erickson, *Invisible Immigrants: The Adaptation of English and Scottish Immigrants in Nineteenth-Century America* (London: Wiedenfeld and Nicholson, 1972).

11 For a recent discussion of the usefulness of the concept of a diaspora, see Rosalind McClean, "'How We Prepare Them in India': British Diasporic Imaginings and Migration to New Zealand," *New Zealand Journal of History* 37, no. 2 (2003): 131–51.

12 For a discussion of why the migration from England has been comparatively neglected, see Phillip Buckner, "Introduction," *British Journal of Canadian Studies* 16, no. 1 (2003): 1–6. This issue is devoted to the theme of English migration to Canada.

13 See Donald Lowry, "The Crown, Empire Loyalism and the Assimilation of Non-British White Subjects in the British World: An Argument against 'Ethnic Determinism,'" in *The British World: Diaspora, Culture and Identity*, ed. Carl Bridge and Kent Fedorowich (London: Frank Cass, 2003), 96–120.

14 For a useful start, see Alan Lester, *Imperial Networks: Creating Identities in Nineteenth-Century South Africa and Britain* (London: Routledge, 2001) and Simon J. Potter, *News and the British World: The Emergence of an Imperial Press System* (Oxford: Clarendon Press, 2003).

15 This is one of the themes in Phillip Buckner, ed., *Canada and the End of Empire* (Vancouver: University of British Columbia Press, 2004).

16 See P.A. Buckner and Carl Bridge, "Reinventing the British World," *The Round Table* 368 (2003): 77–88, and Carl Bridge and Kent Fedorowich, "Mapping the British World," in *The British World: Diaspora, Culture and Identity*, 1–15.

CHAPTER I

WHAT DID A BRITISH WORLD MEAN TO THE BRITISH?

REFLECTIONS ON THE NINETEENTH CENTURY

Catherine Hall

THE QUESTION OF WHAT IT MEANT TO BE BRITISH in a British World is a bit like Pandora's box: it opens up multiple issues and possible lines of inquiry. My focus here is on the contested meanings in the nineteenth century of both Britishness and empire. I am taking "a British World" to mean a world dominated by the British; such a world could include both formal and informal empire but I will focus on sites of formal empire. The British World, I suggest, was never imagined as an undifferentiated whole, and there were always contestations as to what it meant and who it included and excluded. I aim to reflect on two different ways that nineteenth-century Britons constructed a British World. Rather than focusing on the colonies of white settlement, a relatively neglected subject for imperial historians in the last decades but now being rediscovered in part owing to the British World initiative, I will focus on the West Indies – those islands that were neither colony nor dependency – and on Britain itself.[1] One of my examples concerns the debate as to who West Indians were and in what ways they were a part of the British World. The other example focuses on Thomas Babington Macaulay, one of the key figures in the narration of the English (by which Macaulay meant British) nation in the mid-nineteenth century. What vision of a British World did Macaulay develop in the 1830s and 1840s? These two examples draw on my research in two different arenas: (1) the connections between England and the West Indies in the late eighteenth and early nineteenth centuries and (2) a particular figure who was critical to the redefinition of the nation in the mid-nineteenth century. With these examples, I hope to elucidate the shifting nature of the definitions of both what it meant to be a Briton and what constituted a British

World, the complexity of the questions addressed, the impossibility of simple answers, and some possible lines of future inquiry.

My starting point is that whatever the complexity of the relations across the web of empire, Britain itself always occupied a privileged place in that world. It was the seat of power and the centre of government, commerce, and finance – quite simply, it was the metropole. The gap between the metropole and any colonial site – whether a colony of white settlement, a dependency with a non-white majority population, a protectorate, or even the peculiarly metropolitan colony of Ireland – was the gap made by imperial power. That gap operated differently according to the site of empire, but some things remained the same: metropolitan Britons, to put it crudely, were always the colonizers. Ionians may have been white Europeans but they were still subject to forms of colonial discourse. White Australians and Canadians were constructed as young, adolescent perhaps, growing toward maturity and full self-government. Indians and Africans were consigned to what Dipesh Chakrabarty has called, in a felicitous turn of phrase, "the waiting-room of history."[2]

The gap between metropole and colony was fundamental to the maintenance of metropolitan power and to the idea of empire. "They" were over there, and "they" were different, and "they" were too young or too backward to be capable of ruling themselves. Metropolitan power, as Partha Chatterjee argues, was structured through "a rule of colonial difference" and "the preservation of the alienness of the ruling group."[3] This rule of colonial difference, I would suggest, operated in diverse ways across different imperial sites. But the gap was critical to the structuring of difference between the one place and the other – "at home" and "away." For all the criss-crossings of empire that were constantly taking place and the forms of hybridization and creolization that occurred, the gap continued to matter. It structured difference, between white Englishmen and women and Britons in other parts of the world, for example, as well as between white and brown and black. Britain and its imperial possessions were understood as incommensurable, not the same kinds of places. While parallels might be rhetorically drawn between subject peoples in the empire and the Irish in the Victorian city or the teeming "mob" of late nineteenth-century London, no one really thought they were talking about the same kinds of people. Evangelicals believed that the souls of "heathens" abroad were likely to take more winning than those of backsliders at home, especially if the former were entrapped by false gods. Abolitionists thought that the West Indian plantocracy, despite being white, were horribly corrupted by the unlimited power that slavery had given them. Liberals thought that working-class men in Lancashire or the Midlands were likely to prove their worth as citizens long before Indians or Africans. These were the hierarchies and the incommensurabilities of empire, and these were the hierarchies that partially influenced the manner of governance of subjects and institutions "at home" and that structured colonial rule. Although some colonists dreamed of making "little Englands" across the empire, they never could. In Cape Colony, freed Africans disrupted the vision of picket fences and cottages with roses around the doors. In India, the hill stations, designed as homes away from home for the British, became peopled with aspirant Indians. In Australia, the seasons, the vegetation, and Aboriginal labour defied the desire for sameness, for a return to "home" in the colony.

If Britain could never be Britain outside of the metropole, if one notion of home was always associated with the mother country, what happened to the Britons who settled across the Empire? The Scots and the Irish were, as we know, significant to the expansion and maintenance of the Empire; they may or may not have thought of themselves as Britons, but they were certainly heavily implicated in and may have been committed to the idea of the British Empire. They occupied an ambivalent location as both insiders and outsiders, colonized by the English and colonizing the sites of empire. This ambivalent location was characteristic of the colonists, as they came to be called, those English, Irish, Scots, and Welsh in the Caribbean, North America, Australia, or elsewhere who settled and over generations became something different – West Indians, Americans, Australians. Were they British or not? When were they Britons and when something else? And if they were Britons, what did this mean, what rights did it carry? Arguments as to the rights of freeborn Britons were key to the struggles between colonists and metropolitans in the late eighteenth century, most significantly in the American War of Independence. They recurred in the nineteenth century in the debates over the rights of white settlers in Canada, Australia, and New Zealand. Indeed, some of those white settlers achieved the rights of citizenship before their brothers and sisters at home. "British," in other words, had no fixed meaning – anymore than West Indian, American, or Australian. What happened to Britons born on sites of empire? What were the effects of the process of creolization on identity formation? Who claimed which identities, and when, where, why, and how, was always a matter of historical specificity and of relations of power.

The conception of identity with which I am working is one that is not essential or fixed. Rather, identities are brought into being through discursive or symbolic work that demarcates the self from the other. Identity is formed by "the outside": by the interconnections of the positive presence of the self and the negative and excluded dimensions distinguished as the other. Being English or British, or Australian or West Indian meant being some things and not others. This distinction between self and other, between included and excluded, carried with it a desire to mark the boundaries of social authority. But what is marked as outside an identity, different, other to it, is in fact constitutive of it. The fullness of identity depends on what it lacks. For example, the African's "excitability" in nineteenth-century metropolitan discourse was counterposed to the Englishman's rationality; excitability signalled an incapacity for both self-restraint and self-government. Excitability, a necessary element of emotional life, was repressed inside the Englishman and split off, projected as a negative element, onto the imagined African. Likewise, the African's "indolence" was contrasted with the Englishman's capacity for hard work. Thus, identities were always constructed in a process of mutual constitution – the making of self through the making of others.[4]

The identity of the West Indian provides us with a powerful example of this process.[5] According to the *Oxford English Dictionary*, the first recorded use of the term West Indian, in 1597, served both to describe the indigenous inhabitants of the islands and to condemn the acts of another colonizing power: "those cruelties that were practised by the Spanish nation upon the West Indians." By 1661, only a few years after Cromwell's forces had taken Jamaica, the term had come to mean "an inhabitant or native of the West Indies, of European origin or descent." In a dramatic, if largely unacknowledged, transformation, the West Indian had been whitened: he, and it is mainly he, is one of the settlers from England, Scotland, or Ireland, a fortune-seeker in the Wild West of the seventeenth century. Once Britons, these settlers had been renamed. This meaning held for many decades. As late as George Eliot's *Daniel Deronda* in 1876, the OED notes, the West Indian was a byword for fabled wealth brought back to the metropole. And, of course, those who had returned and lived off that wealth were still called West Indians. If we then turn to the OED for the meaning of "negro," we find it a term firmly tied to black skin. A negro signified "an individual belonging to the African race of mankind, which is distinguished by a black skin, black tightly-curled hair, and a nose flatter and lips thicker and more protruding than is common amongst white Europeans."[6]

By the 1960s, however, (according to the abbreviated OED etymology) the West Indian had become black. The arrival in Britain of large numbers of black migrants from the West Indies in the late 1940s and 1950s brought with it the recognition both by the British and by the black peoples of the Anglo-Caribbean islands that these migrants were West Indians. Once the British Caribbean islands became independent, however, nationalist identities superseded the colonial nomenclature. "West Indian" is now rarely used. People are Jamaicans, or Trinidadians, or Barbadians – and those born in Britain are described as of African-Caribbean descent. "West Indian," we might suggest, was first and foremost a colonial identity. But while the West Indian could be white or black, the negro stayed negro, locked in his or her skin and hair.

Englishness and West Indianness have always existed in relation to each other: they have been mutually constitutive over a long connected history. But that mutual constitution has not taken place in conditions of equality: the colonial relation has been one of power. The British were the colonizers – English, Scots, and Irish – while the majority inhabitants of the islands – Africans, and then, following emancipation, Indians brought in as indentured labour – were the colonized. Complicating that binary division of colonizer and colonized – and these were of course always gendered identities with their particular characterizations of masculine and feminine – was the ambivalent status of the white settlers, the creolized natives of the different islands, who became West Indians and claimed rights of self-government from the mother country. They were both colonizers and colonized, for at critical moments their power to govern themselves was overruled by the imperial parliament, most famously in the case of emancipation, which the planters opposed to the end. At such times the white West Indian creoles debated the virtues of separating from the mother country and aligning themselves with those who had thrown off colonial rule in the United States. But their white identity could never be secure, for sexuality was not confined to white-on-white, and the patterns of concubinage between white masters and enslaved women meant that a "coloured" or "mulatto" population, in contemporary parlance, was a feature of Caribbean societies from the beginning.

Since the moment of its "discovery," the West Indies, and particularly the island of Jamaica, has been one kind of inside/outside to Britain. In the seventeenth century Jamaica was imagined in the metropole as a frontier, a place of danger and adventure where fortunes could be made and few questions asked. Initially the destination of buccaneers and pirates, it became transformed into the sugar-bowl of Europe, part of the great plantation settlement that stretched from the southern regions of colonial America to Brazil. By the late seventeenth century, the sugar regime, dependent on the labour of enslaved Africans, was established in Barbados and Jamaica, and the West Indies became renowned as a site of slavery where fabulous wealth could be accumulated but where no white person – let alone a white woman – would care to live. It was an un-English kind of place. By the eighteenth century, historian Kathleen Wilson argues, the Caribbean was associated with "ineffable otherness." The wealthy planters represented forms of vulgarity, backwardness, and degeneracy that inverted the standards of English civility and culture. Wilson suggests that the Caribbean became "the secret underground self" of English society, and eighteenth-century representations of its rapacious and menacing characteristics circulated widely. Teresia Phillips, courtesan, memoirist, sexual predator, and possible murderer, known in Jamaica as "the Black Widow" and memorably invoked by Wilson, is only the most dramatic of the personalities of that time and place.[7]

Englishmen in the Caribbean, concerned to improve the reputation of their countrymen in the metropole, tried to delimit the particular characteristics that Britons developed on these tropical islands. They were preoccupied with questions of sameness and difference. Since Britain remained "home" for many, in the imagination if not in reality, the effects of exile were disturbing. What happened when Britons left one place and settled in another? What kind of people were they? What difference did the tropics, or a different way of life, make to them? These were questions that were to preoccupy all Britons who settled elsewhere. In Australia, white men and women watched themselves become "Australian"; they pondered on the ways in which a new country made new subjects, and they experienced the difference fully when they came "home."[8] Anglo-Indians experimented over generations with different ways of living their Britishness in India. Their very label registered the gap between themselves and both the English and Indians. Their habits, once they returned to the metropole, became sources of caricature and comedy.[9]

For Edward Long, the famed eighteenth-century writer on Jamaica and defender of slavery, creolized whites, those born on the island, had particular characteristics that distinguished them from Englishmen. The men were "tall and well-shaped," and the sockets of their eyes tended to be deeper than those of the English, guarding them from the glare of the sun. The effects of climate produced varieties of feature amongst Europeans, Long argued, but could not explain the distinction between black and white. Creole men and women were remarkable for their excellent character, apart from a regrettable lack of education and tendency to indolence. Both men and women generally had skins "of a fainter white" than in England and a "suffusion of red" from the sun, which gave them a healthy complexion. The mistaken notion that they tended to swarthiness, Long opined, was because the English could not recognize the mixed parentage of those illegitimate children of the rich who were sent to expensive schools in the metropole and passed as white. "The genuine English breed," he insisted, "untainted with these heterogeneous mixtures, is observed to be equally pure and delicate in Jamaica as the mother country."[10] Maintaining the "purity" of Englishness was to him a priority – the heterogeneous mixtures were a source of pollution. But purity, of course, could not be maintained, for sexuality and reproduction critically intervened. The presence of a population of free men and women of colour, many of them the children of white masters and enslaved women, became a significant political issue from the 1820s.

Bryan Edwards, writing in the 1790s, similarly insisted that white residents took on common characteristics, notably "an independent spirit and a display of conscious equality throughout all ranks and conditions."[11] What united West Indian whites was their whiteness. Lady Nugent, wife of the Governor of Jamaica in the early nineteenth century, recorded her impressions of the island. Unlike Long and Edwards, both of whom were planters, her sojourn on the island was for a fixed period. As an imperial wife, she was used to the idea of official stints in one residence or another and had no strong identification with the island or its peoples. She was shocked by the effects of climate, as she saw it, on the habits of the Britons. "In the upper ranks," she remarked, "they become indolent and inactive, regardless of everything but eating, drinking and indulging themselves, and are almost entirely under the dominion of their mulatto favourites." The women, meanwhile, were small-minded and deeply uninteresting to her. In "the lower orders," creoles were even worse, for "conceit and tyranny" were added to their vices, alongside their treatment of "negroes as creatures formed merely to administer to their ease, and to be subject to their caprice."[12]

Britons and white West Indians, in other words, were not seen as the same. Something happened to Britons when they left the island shores – something made them into somewhat different kinds of people. While Long and Edwards were inclined to a primarily climatic explanation for this, others were convinced that environment, or more specifically, slavery, might bear some of the blame. Zachary Macaulay, the father of Thomas Babington Macaulay, spent several years in Jamaica as a young man. He found that his initial horror at what he saw and heard, the sickening punishments and degraded conditions of the enslaved, soon lessened and he became unfeeling to the sufferings of others. "The air of this island must have some peculiar quality in it," he wrote to a friend, "for no sooner does a person set foot on it than his former ways of thinking are entirely changed." It was only when he returned to England that he realized that he had "contracted a boorishness of manner." He noted that, while absent from Europe, he: "had scarce seen a white lady; and among men in the West Indies, whatever be their rank, there is a total emancipation not only from the trammels of ceremony, but, notwithstanding a great deal of hospitality and even kindness, from the more necessary forms of good breeding."[13]

Nonconformist missionaries who went to Jamaica in the 1820s were deeply shocked by the behaviour of their fellow white men. They found them cruel, arrogant, and brutal. They did not deserve the name of Englishman. It was their conduct in the wake of the great rebellion of 1831 that particularly roused the ire of the missionaries. The planters blamed the missionaries for the revolt, assuming that Africans could not have thought for themselves: it was they who had taught the enslaved to think of freedom. Nonconformist chapels were burnt to the ground, and missionaries themselves were persecuted, threatened with lynching, tarred and feathered, and driven from the island. The missionaries were horrified by this, and in their appeal for help to the imperial government and the British public, they argued that it was the planters who were truly degraded and brutalized, more savage than those they enslaved. They had had the advantages of being Britons but had corrupted them: they could no longer claim that name. In the utopian years immediately following emancipation, some believed that once Africans were freed, they would learn to take on the characteristics of Englishmen and become black Britons.[14]

All these Britons had lived in the West Indies, and all of them constructed Britishness as intimately connected to those islands, and a British World as certainly encompassing those islands. There may have been a particularly symbiotic relation between Britain and the West Indies. As John Stuart Mill remarked, the West Indies were a kind of outpost of the metropolis, an extension or perhaps an excrescence of the British self rather than a place entirely separate. The islands were perceived as inside rather than outside, a place that could be milked for all its worth with no returns, a breast on which to feed. Mill characterized the trade with the West Indies as not really an external trade – more like the trade between town and country. "Our West Indian colonies," he wrote, "cannot be regarded as countries with a productive capital of their own... [but are rather] the place where England finds it convenient to carry on the production of sugar, coffee and a few other tropical commodities."[15] Other parts of the Empire were not imagined in quite the same way. Partly, perhaps, this had to do with the early settlement of the Caribbean; partly with the way in which the Caribbean economy and society was so heavily skewed to European and Western needs – first sugar, then bananas, then tourism; and partly with the diasporic nature of the populations on these islands. There were almost no indigenous peoples. There was no serious discussion of independence for the Caribbean in Britain until the twentieth century. Britain assumed that those islands were indeed part of their world – even if by the end of the nineteenth century few people wanted them or had much interest in them.   .

Let me now turn to my second example – Thomas Babington Macaulay – who provides us with a very different vision of the British and their world. I want to delineate the development of his thinking in the early 1830s, thinking that was to shape his *History of England*, the most popular history book of the nineteenth century. Macaulay's father, Zachary, would have been quite at home with the picture of intimate connections across the British World that I have been sketching out in relation to the West Indies. He had lived for a period in Jamaica and then in Sierra Leone. In Jamaica he was an overseer. On his return to Britain, he experienced conversion and became an enthusiastic evangelical, closely associated with Henry Thornton and William Wilberforce, members of the famous Clapham Sect. This association enabled him to go to Sierra Leone, where he initially worked for the company established by "the Saints," as the grouping around Thornton and Wilberforce was called, and subsequently became the governor of the settlement. In 1800 he returned permanently to England, married, and moved to Clapham to be close to his friends and fellow-workers in the anti-slavery cause. He established a business trading with Africa and the East Indies and devoted most of his time to the struggle for emancipation. Zachary was a stalwart of the anti-slavery movement for the rest of his life, collecting materials and tirelessly campaigning, first against the slave trade and then against slavery itself. He was known as "a friend of the negro," since he believed in the universal family of man, and in the responsibility of the privileged to care for the oppressed, and of English men and women to educate and guide their black "brothers and sisters." These beliefs guided his life. He retained very close links to Africa through his business and political interests. One of his sons, Henry, worked in Sierra Leone, and one of his brothers, Colin, was a soldier in India, where sundry nephews were also employed. His was a life permeated with imperial connections.[16]

Zachary Macaulay's first son, Thomas, born in 1800 and lauded as exceptionally clever from his earliest years, was of a rather different metal from his father. Brought up as a Tory in the heartland of conservative evangelicalism, Thomas Macaulay rejected many of the beliefs associated with the evangelical reaction to what were seen as the immoral practices of eighteenth-century English society and the French revolution. What Thomas learned from his Clapham childhood, however, was a love of family and domesticity, a love so deep that he was never able to leave his family of origin; he also inherited a fear of European-style revolution and an expectation of a place in the public world of politics, along with the confidence to claim acceptance among the political elite. While his father was renowned for his quiet, behind-the-scenes work in the anti-slavery movement, preparing and editing documents, and gathering statistics that were then presented to the world by his friends, Thomas liked to be in the limelight.

The children of "the Saints" were taught to feel pity for "the African." "Little black boys" from Sierra Leone were taken in and cared for, one aspect of what might be described as the tutelary complex. But there were always discordant notes. Africans did not always behave in suitably grateful or reformed ways. There were stories of baleful black preachers and administrators encountered by Thomas's father in Sierra Leone, which, according to George Otto Trevelyan, Thomas Macaulay's nephew and first biographer, left Thomas unable "to entertain any very enthusiastic anticipations with regard to the future of the African race." In private letters, even as early as 1833, Thomas was referring to Africans as "niggers" – a term that his father would not have used and that was not acceptable to abolitionists.[17] He was impatient of what he saw as the excessive "negrophilia" of the older generation. As he recorded many years later in his journal, "I hate slavery from the bottom of my soul; and yet I am made sick by the cant and the silly mock reasons of the Abolitionists. The nigger driver and the negrophile are two odious things to me."[18]

Sympathy was central to the evangelical abolitionist. The enslaved had souls that must be freed; they were victims of a wicked system and their more powerful "brothers and sisters" must act on their behalf, must represent them, since they could not represent themselves.[19] As Laqueur has argued, their humanitarian narratives, with their details of the suffering bodies of others, engendered a compassion that came to be understood "as a moral imperative to undertake ameliorative action."[20]

Macaulay reacted against what he saw as an excess of sympathy. The analytic he developed was not one of suffering: his preoccupations were not with the neglected and the oppressed. His interest, formed in the period between Peterloo and 1831, when it sometimes seemed that British society might indeed succumb to revolution, was in cohering the nation, making it whole and stable, and ensuring that internal divisions were resolved. His commitment to the removal of civil disabilities practised against the Jews, for example, was rooted in his conviction that Jews could be brought into the nation, could be Englishmen. Indeed, they should be, for since they owned substantial property, it was important that they should be patriots. They had wealth, and therefore power: they should also have the responsibilities and rights associated with citizenship. All men should have the right to practise their religious beliefs. "There is nothing in their national character," he argued, "which unfits them for the highest duties of citizens. Why not try what effect would be produced on the Jews by that tolerant policy which has made the English Roman Catholic a good Englishman, and the French Calvinist a good Frenchman?"[21] A Jew was not a "Musselman," or a "Parsee," or a "Hindoo who worships a lump of stone with seven heads."[22] This did not mean that he liked Jews or identified with their suffering, but he believed that the responsibility of rulers was to make men patriotic. "If the Jews have not felt towards England like children," he argued, "it is because she has treated them like a step-mother."[23] England must assimilate her potentially wayward children. From the beginning of his association with the Whigs and the *Edinburgh Review* in the 1820s, Macaulay began to develop a different kind of voice from that of his father and the Clapham Sect. His form of masculinity and his vision of political culture was not that associated with an evangelical sensibility, but rather that of a new kind of elitist reforming man, a rationalist, yet also a romantic, a patriot, very much an Englishman. Macaulay, I suggest, was critical to the formation of a newly defined manly English citizenship, an identity that was not open to women.

After studying at Cambridge, Macaulay began to make a name for himself in the 1820s as an essayist. He was taken up by Brougham, one of the most distinguished of the Whig statesmen, and enlisted in the older man's attempts to demarcate the Whigs as clearly as possible from the political radicalism of the Utilitarians. Macaulay's attacks on James Mill brought him much attention, and he was offered a seat in the Commons, just in time to engage in the great theatrical debates over reform that occupied both Lords and Commons in 1831 and 1832.

Macaulay became famous as a result of his oratorical triumphs, his capacity to thrill and enthrall the House by sheer force of argument and words. In his speeches on reform, he summoned up an imagined nation. This was a nation that was marked, in Macaulay's vision, as the most civilized in the world, separated from the "tattooed savages of the Pacific," from enslaved "negroes," from "Mohawks and Hottentots." It was also distinct from those others who were deemed closer in their level of development, yet far from the rational world of Englishmen – the backward Scots, the dangerous revolutionaries of France, and the desperate insurgents of Ireland. England was simply "the greatest, and fairest, and most highly civilised community that ever existed."[24] English superiority was marked by a belief in property, stability, and a capacity to renew the constitution. And this was done in a peculiarly English way, "without bloodshed, without violence, without rapine, all points freely debated, all the points of senatorial deliberation punctiliously observed, industry and trade not for a moment interrupted, the authority of law not for a moment suspended."[25] These were the special characteristics of the English and of a variety of Whiggish liberalism that Macaulay did much to define.

Following his great success in these debates, Macaulay became Secretary of the Board of Control for India and a valued member of the Whig cabinet. One of the first acts of the new government was to introduce a Coercion Bill for Ireland. The country was in turmoil, with claims being made for the repeal of the Act of Union. In his speeches on reform, Macaulay had referred many times to the mistake that had been made in not conceding Catholic emancipation earlier – the effect of this error had been to stir up a level of agitation in Ireland that had almost reduced the country to breakdown. The great characteristic of the English, he insisted, was the capacity to reform in a timely manner, to recognize the need for change and thus avoid revolution. This was the spirit that had marked the revolution of 1688 and the final successful passage of the 1832 Reform Act. The ability to read the signs of the times and to act with them rather than against them distinguished the English from all other races and nations. But reform, in Macaulay's mind, was for England; Ireland was not ready for it. Post-1832, the signs in Ireland were of Jacobinism and revolution. The only possible reading of that for Macaulay was forcible suppression. Ireland was not England. In the debates on reform he had eloquently reflected on this: Ireland could be governed by the sword, as under Cromwell, and as Wellington might have done. England, in his view a far more advanced country, could only be governed by popular opinion. In his defence of the Coercion Bill, which repealed habeas corpus and gave the police the right to search for arms, he declared that cholera was preferable to the moral pestilence that had engulfed Ireland and that he would rather live in despotic Algiers than Kilkenny. Ireland was in danger of polluting the body politic. Daniel O'Connell, the famed "Emancipator" who now led the call for repeal of the Union between Britain and Ireland, wanted a separate parliament for Ireland. For Macaulay, this was an impossible demand. O'Connell did not seek a local parliament as in Jamaica or Barbados or Antigua, one that recognized and bowed to imperial sovereignty. Rather, he wanted an independent legislature. But England and Ireland, Macaulay declared, were "parts of one empire.... I wish to see them joined as the limbs of a well-formed body are joined." They must not be "like Siamese twins – where one is a constant plague to the other."[26] For Macaulay, the body was England – the limbs, those parts of the British Isles that had been grafted onto England, brought entirely within its purview, subjected to its culture, absorbed into one. The Irish had been offered a place under the English sun and were not properly grateful. O'Connell had won the privileges of a British subject and thought he could claim more. Jews and Irishmen were allowed to be Englishmen if they fully accepted English supremacy: assimilation was the name of the game. This was the kind of nation, the fantasized homogeneous nation, that he developed.

Macaulay played a crucial part in steering the India Bill of 1833 through the Commons. While the East India Company was to continue to rule for the British, a stronger government presence was established in India's new Supreme Council. "We are trying," Macaulay argued, utilizing a telling set of metaphors, "to make brick without straw, to bring a clean thing out of an unclean, to give a good government to a people to whom we cannot give a free government." In Europe, he continued, "you have the materials of good government everywhere ready to your hands. The people are everywhere perfectly competent to hold some share, not in every country an equal share, but some share of political power. If the question were, What is the best mode of securing good government in Europe? The merest smatterer in politics would answer representative institutions." But in India this was utterly out of the question: an enlightened and paternal despotism was the only possibility. India was a dependency: the solution was "to engraft on despotism those blessings which are the natural fruits of liberty." "Our Indian Empire" was an extraordinary phenomenon. "A handful of adventurers from an island in the Atlantic…[had] subjugated a vast country."This was "a territory inhabited by men differing from us in race, colour, language, manners, morals, religion."The East India Company had established order where "petty dynasties" and "predatory tribes" had reigned. There was now a government "anxiously bent on the public good"; "bloody and degrading superstitions" were losing their hold, and there were signs that "the morality, the philosophy, the taste of Europe" were beginning to have a "salutary effect on the hearts and understandings of our subjects."The "higher classes of natives" were beginning to pay considerable attention "to those intellectual pursuits on the cultivation of which the superiority of the European race to the rest of mankind principally depends." It might be possible that eventually Indians themselves would be able to enter high office, but this could only be by slow degrees. If this were to come about, then Britain should be ready to let go of her power, for empire was not necessarily a good thing and England was at heart a trading nation. "It is scarcely possible," he argued,

> to calculate the benefits which we might derive from the diffusion of European civilisation among the vast population of the East. It would be, on the most selfish view of the case, far better for us that the people of India were well governed and independent of us, than ill governed and subject to us; that they were ruled by their own kings, but wearing our broadcloth, and working with our cutlery, than that they were performing their salaams to English collectors and English magistrates, but were too ignorant to value, or too poor to buy, English manufacturers. To trade with civilised men is infinitely more profitable than to govern savages…. As a people blessed with far more than an ordinary measure of political liberty and of intellectual light, we owe to a race debased by three thousand years of despotism and priestcraft. We are free, we are civilised, to little purpose if we grudge to any portion of the human race an equal measure of freedom and civilisation.[27]

For Macaulay, then, the task was to educate those subjects, to offer them enlightenment.

In the wake of his work on the revised charter for the East India Company, Macaulay was offered the newly created position of lay member of the Supreme Council that had been created to govern India. This was a highly paid and very responsible job that required him to be in India, and he left England in February 1834 to spend three and a half years in what he described as exile. While in India, he composed his infamous Minute on Education – an argument for the government ceasing to support the teaching of Arabic and Sanskrit and focusing resources on the teaching of English. If the Indian languages were the medium of learning, he declared, pupils would encounter "astronomy, which would move laughter in girls at an English boarding-school – history, abounding with kings thirty feet high, and reigns thirty thousand years long – and geography, made up of seas of treacle and seas of butter."[28] English must be the medium of instruction in India. The only way to bring that country out of degradation was through a system of education that aimed to produce, in the very long term, Indians who would think and act like brown Englishmen. Difference did not appeal to Macaulay. England represented the apex of civilization for him: the only hope for Indians was to become as English as possible. Only sameness was possible, the inevitable obverse being degradation.

Macaulay regarded his time in India as exile from the only place worth living – England. It was lost time. He had no desire to study Indian languages or to engage with Indian culture. He had no interest in the ancient civilizations of South Asia. He spent what time he had free from official duties continuing to study the classics, and books, he found, were his best companions. India was in no sense for him an outpost of Britain – it was an utterly foreign place and its future lay in taking on European mores. His reasons for taking the job had been financial, and the only thing that reconciled him to his banishment was the amount of money he was making. His fortune would allow him on his return to provide for himself and his family. "I have no word to tell you how I pine for England," he wrote to two of his sisters, "or how intensely bitter exile has been to me."[29]

Macaulay returned to England in 1838 with a secure income. While in India, he had been contemplating writing a history of England, giving up politics for literature. After a brief period in which he tried to combine the two, he decided to devote himself to his writing. His *History*, in six volumes, was a spectacular success – but that is another story. True to its name, it was indeed a history of England. It told of the successful assimilation of the Scots and the continued problem of the Irish. Its focus was almost exclusively on the making of the nation and a homogeneous Englishness. And this was a nation made by manly patriots, with women secured as a stable, dependent presence. For Macaulay, who wrote the most influential history of the nineteenth century, despite his time in India, despite his family connections with Sierra Leone, the British World was

England, and it was a world in which men acted and women, for the most part, simply were. His Indian experience was internalized – other peoples and places were relevant only insofar as they underpinned a particular understanding of the English nation and clarified its unique position. The English construction of the manly self depended on that of multiple and lesser others. The identity of an Englishman appeared in his text as positive precisely because it was always predicated on that which it was not. Embedded in Macaulay's enthusiastic mapping of Englishness were his prior imaginings of other peoples – the absent presence of his *History*.

Here, then, are two very different ways of conceptualizing Britons' relation to their world. While the West Indian story takes us directly into questions of creolization and connection, Macaulay's insistence on "the island story" reminds us of a long tradition of the forgetting of empire. While the very category "West Indian" evokes the contested and shifting nature of markers of identity, Macaulay's determined refusal to tell an imperial story can be reinterpreted as only possible because of his prior internalization of subjected and colonized others. The British World, I am arguing, is defined by its outsides: without the Empire there was no England, without barbarism there was no civilization. My two examples could be endlessly multiplied, illustrating the plurality of ways in which Britons thought about or denied their Empire in the nineteenth century. What we increasingly know, as more research is done, is how present empire was, even in its absence, in nineteenth-century thinking. What we need to know more about is how this worked on different sites of empire at different times, what the relative weight of these different knowledges was, how some were institutionalized and others not, how a common sense of a British World, if there ever was such a thing, was constructed. There is indeed an exciting field of work to be developed.

{NOTES}

1 Carl Bridge and Kent Fedorowich, "Mapping the British World," *Journal of Imperial and Commonwealth History* 31, no. 2 (2003): 1–15.

2 Dipesh Chakrabarty, *Provincializing Europe: Postcolonial Thought and Historical Difference* (Princeton: Princeton University Press, 2000), 9.

3 Partha Chatterjee, *The Nation and Its Fragments: Colonial and Postcolonial Histories* (Princeton: Princeton University Press, 1993), 10.

4 Catherine Hall, *Civilising Subjects: Metropole and Colony in the English Imagination 1830–1867* (Cambridge: Polity, 2002).

5 For a longer version of these arguments, see Catherine Hall, "What is a West Indian?" in *West Indian Intellectuals in Britain*, ed. Bill Schwarz (Manchester: Manchester University Press, 2003).

6 *Oxford English Dictionary*, 2nd ed. (Oxford: Clarendon, 1989).

7 Kathleen Wilson, *The Island Race: Englishness, Empire and Gender in the Eighteenth Century* (London: Routledge, 2003).

8 See, for example, Angela Wollacott, *To Try Her Fortune in London: Australian Women, Colonialism, and Modernity* (London: Oxford University Press, 2001).

9 See, for example, the memorable portrait of Joseph Sedley in William Thackeray's *Vanity Fair* (1848; repr., Harmondsworth: Penguin, 1968).

10 Edward Long, *The History of Jamaica* (1774; London: Frank Cass, 1970), 2:261, 274.

11 Bryan Edwards, *The History, Civil and Commercial, of the British Colonies in the West Indies* (Philadelphia: James Humphreys, 1806), 2:202.

12 Lady Maria Nugent, *Lady Nugent's Journal: Jamaica One Hundred Years Ago*, ed. Frank Cundall (London: West India Committee for the Institute of Jamaica, 1934), 131.

13 *Life and Letters of Zachary Macaulay*, ed. Viscountess Knutsford (London: Edward Arnold, 1900), 6–11.

14 For a longer account of this, see Hall, *Civilising Subjects*.

15 John Stuart Mill, *Principles of Political Economy* (1848), in *Collected Works of John Stuart Mill*, ed. J.M. Robson (Toronto: Toronto University Press, 1965), 3:693.

16 Very late in his life he planned to return to Sierra Leone to rescue his fortunes. See Thomas Pinney, ed., *The Letters of Thomas Babington Macaulay* (Cambridge: Cambridge University Press, 1974), 2:310.

17 Ibid., 283.

18 G.O. Trevelyan, *The Life and Letters of Lord Macaulay* (London: Longmans, Green and Co., 1881), 17.

19 Hall, *Civilising Subjects*.

20 T.W. Lacqueur, "Bodies, Details and the Humanitarian Narrative," in *The New Cultural History*, ed. Lynn Hunt (Berkeley: University of California Press, 1989), 176.

21 Thomas Babington Macaulay, *Speeches on Politics and Literature* (London: Dent, 1909), 93.

22 Ibid., 87.

23 Lord Macaulay, "Civil Disabilities of the Jews," in *Literary and Historical Essays Contributed to the Edinburgh Review* (London: Oxford University Press, 1913), Part 2, 90.

24 Macaulay, *Speeches*, 14.

25 Ibid., 26–27.

26 Ibid., 79.

27 Ibid., 103–26.

28 Cited in Trevelyan, *Life and Letters*, 291.

29 Ibid., 307.

THE RISE OF THE ANGLOWORLD:

SETTLEMENT IN NORTH AMERICA
AND AUSTRALASIA, 1784–1918

James Belich

WHAT WAS THE MOST IMPORTANT EVENT of the 1780s in the English-speaking world? The obvious answer is the American Revolution, which split that world into two flanks, British and American. There is another answer, however: the beginnings of a great Anglophone eruption. In the 1780s, three jets of human lava shot out from old America and old Britain. One, the first great spasm of trans-Appalachian settlement, founded the American West; the second, the settlement of Botany Bay, founded settler Australasia; and the third, by the United Empire Loyalists, founded Anglo Canada outside Newfoundland and Halifax.

The great Anglo eruption continued throughout the very long nineteenth century. In 1780 the total number of Britons, settler and metropolitan, loyal and rebel, was about twelve million – half the number of Spanish and Spanish Americans. Mexico alone was more populous than what became the United States, and Cuba than all of Canada.[1] By the 1920s, this ranking had reversed. The Angloworld had about two hundred million citizens, as well as five hundred million subjects, whereas the Spanish world had less than one hundred million of either. It was not that Spanish-speaking populations had stagnated: in fact, they had multiplied four-fold. It was that the Anglos had exploded, multiplying sixteen-fold. This rate of population growth dwarfed even that of Asia, Africa, and Latin America in the twentieth century. In the nineteenth century, it was the Anglos who bred like rabbits. Moreover, Anglo economies grew to match. It was the nineteenth century that gave Britain and the United States the economic and demographic muscle to provide the world's leading superpower for two centuries.

In the past, Anglo-Americans had no trouble explaining their meteoric rise. Their growth was a matter of heroic individual achievement; the will of God, Providence, or Manifest Destiny; and intrinsic collective superiority – environmental, institutional, cultural, biological, or all four. Legacies of this tradition persisted and generated, in understandable reaction, a reluctance to address the expansion of English-speaking peoples at all, lest one be suspected of Churchillian Anglocentrism. Historians talk about the multiplication of non-white subjects but not about the multiplication of white citizens. Yet the Anglo explosion was, surely, a gargantuan phenomenon. We do not have to like it, but we do have to understand it. Where then do we look for a coherent explanation for the dramatic nineteenth-century growth of the Anglophones, without resorting to Anglo-American triumphalism?

The first step in my own megalomaniacal attempt to answer this question, still very much a work-in-progress, is to reshuffle the Angloworld. Imagine a malleable map of the world, like those used by paleogeologists to illustrate the continental drifts of a hundred million years ago. Pick up Australia and New Zealand and place them in the Mid-Atlantic, and push Canada and the British Isles a little closer to them and each other. This is intended to suggest the actual close relationship between old and new Britains in the nineteenth century – so close that it transcended geographic distance: Canada and Australasia were the two flanks of a non-contiguous "British West." Now, insert your thumbs firmly below Florida, and your forefingers in the Great Lakes. Prise the United States apart along the line of the Appalachians. This conceptually splits old eastern Atlantic America, which in the nineteenth century was a metropolitan area or colonizer, from new America, the American West, where the colonizing actually took place. By the nineteenth century, old Atlantic America had joined old Britain as an Anglo "oldland." The Midwest and West were America's "dominions." They and the British Dominions, the American and British "Wests," were Anglo "newlands." Here we have the Angloworld – its unities and its divisions.

My second step posits a change in the nature of European settlement, occurring first in the Angloworld between 1790 and 1815. Before this, the maximum population increase in a substantial colony was doubling in a quarter century. Most colonies, let alone European homelands, grew very much more slowly. Malthus famously considered the Thirteen Colonies' eighteenth-century doublings every twenty-five years to be the fastest-ever rate of human increase. Yet the Anglo newlands of the nineteenth century grew faster than fast. Indeed, they typically doubled in a single decade, with economies expanding to match. In the fifty years 1810–60, the American Old Northwest's five states grew twenty-six-fold from just over a quarter of a million people to seven million, dwarfing the Malthusian growth rate of the Thirteen Colonies. American historians still tend to see the growth of the Northwest as exceptional. In fact, it also happened in the British West. Ontario grew fifteen-fold, 1825–60, to 1.5 million people; Eastern Australia more than twenty-fold, 1828–61, to well over one million. Economic historians underestimate the economic growth involved by anachronistically focussing on *per capita* incomes. But this was quite probably the most volcanic form of socio-economic reproduction in human history. Let us call it "explosive colonization."

Explosive colonization was part-bubble, and at some point the bubble always burst. A crash took place; growth collapsed. After a period of stagnation, a second, more modest, kind of growth began, based on the mass export of staples to an oldland metropolis. The technology linking oldland and new thickened from trade route into virtual bridge, along which agricultural staples flowed one way, and industrial and cultural staples the other. Bright futures faded. Prophecies of newland greatness and independence, "the great empire of the St Lawrence," were displaced by assumptions of permanent partnership, in some respects junior to the oldland, in others equal or even superior. Using notions of rural virtue, Midwesterners, Anglo Canadians and Australasians saw themselves as *Better* Americans and *Better* Britons. Links with the metropolis tightened, against the grain of expectations about development toward economic and cultural independence. Let us call this "recolonization."[2]

Recolonization meant that Anglo settlement in the nineteenth century was not just an explosion, but also a process of reintegration. Colonizing forces exploded outward with unprecedented velocity, but instead of fragmenting into the independent nations of Spanish American reality and British dominion mythology, the colonies were re-leashed, re-secured firmly to the metropolis, by recolonization. Together, explosive colonization and recolonization were a form of hyper-colonization, the supercharged creation of a new socio-economy followed by its tight reintegration with the old.

At the broadest level, explosive colonization dominated the Angloworld from 1815 to about 1860. Recolonization ran neck and neck with it to 1890, with recolonization dominating thereafter, but with some late spasms of explosive colonization, notably in the Prairie provinces of Canada. Within these very broad patterns, there were about fifteen overlapping but distinguishable rounds of Anglo hyper-colonization: six or seven in the United States, four in Australasia, and four or five in Canada. The cultural dimension of this process is crucial, but the economic dimension is more easily traceable. Let us explore the economic anatomy of a round of hyper-colonization in a little more detail. It was a matter of boom, bust, and "export rescue" – the last being the economic face of recolonization.

Before rail, one requisite for an Angloboom was water. The development of the North American west before 1860 was primarily waterborne, with the Mississippi River system, the Great Lakes, and the St. Lawrence standing in for the Tasman Sea in Australasia. Until 1825, the cheapest way to transfer bulk from Cincinnati to New York was down the Ohio and Mississippi Rivers to New Orleans by flatboat, and then up the east coast of the United States. Water transport not only provided vertical routes to oldlands, but also horizontal routes to other newlands. A water-linked constellation of newlands was the most explosion-prone, hence the very late explosions of isolated British Columbia and Western Australia, both dating from the late 1880s. Another requisite was the preexistence of some "normal" colonization in or near the exploding region. New South Wales spent forty years as a normal settlement, growing only incrementally, before exploding around 1830. It also acted as a base for booms in other newlands. A key factor here was that nineteenth-century transport was simply not up to the long-range mass transfer of animals. Livestock had to be built up to critical mass in a local reservoir. So it was sheep from New South Wales, not Britain, that stocked Victoria, New Zealand, and Queensland; horses from Ohio, not New York, stocked the Midwest.

Another requisite of booms was fresh land. Booms do seem to have occurred in the same place more than once, but I suspect this is more appearance than reality. Ohio, for example, boomed and busted three times before 1860, with the busts in 1819, 1837, and 1857. But each boom focused on a different region of the state: riverine Ohio before 1819, lacustrine Ohio before 1837, and various marginal regions before 1857.[3] The fresh land, of course, came from indigenous peoples and was usually taken by force. What is interesting here is that the relevant tribal peoples were very often a match for normal colonization; it was explosive colonization that was too much for them. Climactic, formidable, and often pan-tribal resistance correlated with Angloboom in Tasmania around 1830, Queensland and New Zealand in the 1860s, the American Midwest in the 1870s, and Manitoba in the 1880s. Prior to this, the relevant Aboriginal, Maori, Indian, and Métis groups had resisted and co-operated quite successfully for decades. Recognizing the human tsunami of explosive colonization, therefore, recontextualizes indigenous resistance in Anglo settler societies. Eventual subjugation was due not to the weakness of the defence but to the strength of the attack.

What was the key dynamic of the Anglobooms? Three obvious candidates are gold, steam, and staples, but none actually stacks up. The Anglobooms were sometimes associated with gold rushes but were seldom caused by them. Indeed, it may well have been the other way around. Western Georgia in 1830, Victoria in 1851, and Otago in 1861 were already booming when their gold rushes occurred. Even in California in 1848, mining began at Sutter's Mill, not milling at Sutter's Mine. Gold rushes obviously supercharged and extended booms, but they rarely caused them. Fully mature Anglobooms began in 1815, and this corresponds with the arrival of steamships in North America. But the reliable mass advent of steamships on the Mississippi River *postdates* United States Boom One, which ended in 1819. Nor were steamships at all significant in Australasian Boom One, 1828–42.[4]

The dominant existing explanation for Anglobooms is still Harold Innis's staples thesis, whereby booms were powered by the mass export of staples such as timber, cotton, wheat, and wool from newlands to old.[5] Yet, in the 1830s, the American Old Northwest boomed even more than the Old Southwest despite the former's lack of cotton, and despite still-modest wheat and meat exports. Auckland province in New Zealand outgrew some southern rivals in the 1860s and 1880s despite its paucity of sheep. In New South Wales, wool exports were modest until after the bust of 1842, and cattle, which had little export value, were at least as important as sheep until 1843. Canadian economic historians Marvin McInnis and Douglas McCalla have debunked the belief that wheat exports powered Ontario's boom in the 1830s.[6] Except for the Ottawa Valley, timber exports were not very significant to 1830s Ontario either. Throughout the Angloworld, recolonial historiography retrospectively backdated the centrality of exports. The assumption that staple exports were the original engine of growth is strangely persistent and consistent. A survey in 1995 showed that 84 per cent of a large sample of United States historians still believed that cotton was the primary stimulant of the antebellum American economy.[7] This is not only untrue, but obviously untrue. How did cotton create the mushroom cities of Cincinnati, St. Louis, and Chicago? It is as though historians operate under an unconscious cultural compulsion to retrospectively rationalize the Anglobooms.

So what did drive the Anglobooms? In my view, the key dynamic was a complex of activities that can collectively be called the "Progress Industry": the massive activity generated by the process of migration itself, and by the rapid creation of infrastructure, notably transport infrastructure. Organized immigration; settlement and land development schemes; the housing, clothing and feeding of immigrants; and the construction of towns, farms, and camps were all core parts of the Progress Industry. The supply of capital and credit; of draft animals and their feed; of food, clothing, and equipment; and of wood, the basic raw material and fuel, was another element. When the inflow of immigrants over five years equalled the original population, you did not need much other business. Explosive colonization was able to happen through the colony's own growth.

Public and private sectors converged in the Progress Industry, with the former specializing in transport infrastructure – roads, harbours, canals, and railways. This was known as "public works" in Australasia and "internal improvements" in the United States, but government borrowing or land subsidies featured large in both.[8] Rivalry and duplication enhanced the Progress Industry rather than diminished it. In the 1830s, three different Lake Erie towns succeeded in persuading the Ohio Canal Board to make them termini of the same canal.[9] This "waste" tripled the cost and cut efficiency by two-thirds, but it also tripled the Progress Industry – the farm, manufacture, and labour markets generated by canal construction. The classic Canadian case was the construction of three transcontinental rail systems before and during the great Prairie boom of the 1900s, when one or two would have been sufficient.

It is not easy now to appreciate the sheer scale of the Progress Industry. McCalla estimates that rail construction in Upper Canada in the 1850s may have directly occupied as much as 15 per cent of the male workforce – not counting the people who made their living by servicing and supplying the rail camps. In the earlier Upper Canadian boom of the 1820s and 1830s, the local government spent £2.75 million, while the British government spent £4 million. This spending – without counting the rest of the Progress Industry – substantially exceeded the total value of wool and timber exports combined.[10] Most of this money was poured into canals, and poured is the right word. "A mania for canalling seemed to possess the people," one contemporary noted.[11] "In the 1820s and 1830s canal fever struck Canada. The disease was not fatal, though it appeared to be at some stages; it left its victim weakened, scarred, deficient in strength to resist a similar disease soon to come – railroad fever." Contemporaries and historians alike were bewildered by the level of waste. According to one of the former, "economy and the Welland canal are as far apart as earth and heaven."[12] By 1848, according to one of the latter, "Canada had invested in a vast capacity for canal traffic – far more than the needs of its economy might reasonably justify."[13] As McCalla notes, "The Welland was not even remotely successful in commercial terms."[14] That's Progress for you.

Cities and farms boomed with the Progress Industry and were interlocked with it. A pervasive rush mentality extended to farming, where a "stocking rush" occurred during booms: older farms grew livestock and seed to stock newer farms. Another major market for explosive colonial farming was supply and support of the Progress Industry. The wandering male crews who staffed that industry were big consumers of meat, bread, liquor, and leather. Booms also produced high demand for work animals and their feed. We tend to forget that nineteenth-century farms had this extra role, performed by petrol refineries and vehicle factories in the twentieth. Supplying the wars and gold rushes sometimes associated with booms provided yet another market. Moreover, boom-phase farmers were often part-time, working in the lumber, transport, or Progress Industries in their off-season. Boom-phase farming was not export oriented, but it was not semi-subsistence either. Its market was massive, diverse, dynamic, and commercial, but local.

Normal colonization took a couple of centuries to produce substantial cities; explosive colonization took a couple of decades. Chicago grew from fifty people in 1830 to over one million sixty years later. Melbourne grew from zero to half a million in the same period. These precocious settler cities mushroomed as both bases for and sites of mass settlement and the Progress Industry. Many later became great export centres, and this was retrospectively assumed to have been their *raison d'etre* from the outset. In fact these towns spent their boom times as net importers, not exporters. They were gateway cities that opened primarily inward. Imports exceeded exports by value in Cincinnati as late as 1857, and Chicago as late as 1860.[15] My reading suggests the same was true of Toronto, at least until the 1850s.[16] Toronto also illustrates the fact that settler cities were not necessarily instant cities, but sometimes exploded after a long period of "normal" or incremental growth. Toronto, or York as it was then, only quadrupled in population between 1800 and 1825, but then exploded twenty-fold over the next quarter-century.[17]

Settler cities also specialized in what might be called "rehydration." In contrast to the virtual bridge of recolonization, newland links with the metropolis under explosive colonization were only of medium quality. As we have seen, they could not transfer livestock en masse, and the same applied to large manufactures such as mills or coaches. These were therefore transferred in "dehydrated" form: machine tools, manuals, complex parts, and human skills. They were then "rehydrated" in the workshops and small factories of the settler city, which was therefore precociously industrial. Take-off in settler cities was marked by the mushrooming of banks and newspapers, which "rehydrated" and adapted oldland money and information.

A classic crop of exploding cities was produced in Western Canada, the "Last Best West." The population of Calgary was static in the 1890s, then grew eleven-fold in the 1900s. Edmonton, Regina, and Saskatoon mushroomed likewise. They did so as part of the last great Angloboom, which boosted the population of Alberta and Saskatchewan almost five-fold to 850,000 people during the single decade of the 1900s. What some Canadian historians note, but do not emphasize, is that wheat exporting was not actually the main game in the Prairie provinces at this time. Major wheat exports were "only achieved long after the period of prosperity had begun."[18] Wheat exports from Alberta and Saskatchewan did not really rocket until 1909 at the earliest. The main business in the 1900s was farm-*making* not farming, together with a massive Progress Industry.

Booming required a curious ideology, exemplified in Prairie historiography's ritual humiliation of Saskatoon. "Saskatoon," according to its 1900s boosters, was "one of the most astounding of modern miracles," "the Centre of an Inland Empire," "the fastest growing city in the world," and a "City of Destiny and certain greatness." By 1912, it was "the greatest example of town and city building in the world's history," "the eight-year-old wonder of the British empire." "Is there, was there ever another Saskatoon?"[19] The answer is yes – hundreds, from Cincinnati to Marvellous Melbourne, from Denver to Dunedin. All boasted and boosted in their day. The Canadian Prairies were the culmination and apotheosis of explosive colonization. Does this make their history less interesting, or more?

In Saskatoon, as elsewhere, the bubble burst, the crash came, and grand dreams turned to dust. Historians argue over whether these busts constituted technical depressions, but they certainly decimated growth rates. Casualties were often very high. Some strong companies and large landowners scraped through to export rescue, but they lost millions. Companies in Winnipeg in 1883, Auckland in 1886, and Melbourne in

1893 died like flies, as did small farms. The bust phase lasted from two to ten years and created some of the preconditions for export rescue. Farmland was reshuffled from holdings that were too big or too small into more viable sizes. Processing and distribution, on the other hand, concentrated in the hands of larger and larger organizations. An over-supply of transport routes, bequeathed by active Progress Industries, led to cut-throat competition and the slashing of freight rates, as in the American West after the busts of 1873 and 1893. This, combined with technical developments such as improvements in hulls and engines, which enabled steamships to balloon in size, helped thicken the links between oldland and new, permitting a recolonial flow of staples from newland to old.

From the perspective of New York and London, recolonization was a matter of making distant territories virtual hinterlands, so permitting unprecedented growth. This involved two sets of variables: the technical defeat of bulk, distance, and decay for export staples; and the cultural achievement of reliability, efficiency, and optimal fit between supply and demand. Recolonial relations meant that a mega-city was not looking to its virtual hinterland merely for luxury or discretionary foods, or for top-ups in years of bad harvests, but literally for its daily bread – and meat. The supply had to be completely reliable and intimately attuned to demand. The two ends of the system had to dovetail perfectly, like the two halves of a neatly broken glass.

For wool, the wool press defeated bulk in the 1840s, while the clipper and later the iron-hulled sailing ship defeated distance. For wheat, silos and elevators defeated bulk and decay, and canals, rail, and giant steam-ers defeated distance. The rise of the urban carnivore had a particularly intimate relationship with recolonization. Demand for meat in London and New York grew rapidly, not only because of population growth but also because prime meat was a nutritional marker of status. New York's meat supply, and its recolonial relations with the Midwest, grew in four spurts of export rescue. From the 1820s, the mass advent of steamers on the Mississippi defeated decay by supplying quality marine salt to the first "Porkopolis," Cincinnati. They also defeated distance, not so much by carrying pork downriver themselves as by shipping flatboat crews back up, so saving them a three-month walk and slashing the costs of flatboating. The cured pork, which preserved better than beef, then went to New York via New Orleans. From the 1840s, live beef, which was preferred to pork, came to New York via rail, defeating both distance and decay. Railing dead meat was much cheaper, however, and from the late 1860s, it was achieved with the use of natural ice to extend the packing season and to chill railcars. Finally, mechanically assisted refrigeration cut in from the 1880s.[20]

London's meat supply went through comparable stages, apart from Londoners' taste for sheepmeat: the mass production of cured pork in Ireland and America, from the 1820s; the steam transport of livestock, from the 1840s; and the steam transport of dead meat preserved with natural ice, from the 1870s. Between 1880 and 1910, mechanical refrigeration then pumped 153 million frozen sheep and lambs into London's gaping maw.

It was this system, the explosive creation and then tight reintegration of virtual hinterlands, that allowed London and New York to grow so big so early; they were the first cities in the world to reach 2.5, then five, then ten million people. Export rescue solved the problems of distance and decay and also achieved optimal fit. Production, distribution, and consumption adjusted to suit each other – New Zealand spring lamb came in London's spring. Shared language, assumptions, habits, tastes, and experience lowered what economists would now call "transaction costs." This created a kind of transnational social capital that lubricated and buttressed economic interaction.

Anecdote best indicates the operation of this semi-tangible "Anglonet," even across the American-British divide. After the crash of 1837, several American states suspended payment on their British debts. Baring Brothers and other Anglo bankers mounted an expensive, sophisticated, and ultimately successful political campaign to persuade them to reconsider. The bankers could not, would not, and did not attempt something similar when fledgling Latin American nations reneged on their debts in the 1820s.[21] In 1842 an enterprising Hungarian entrepreneur established a canning plant in what is now Rumania that tinned beef and shipped it down the Danube to the Black Sea and thence via the Mediterranean to the British navy. All went well until 1846, when horrified British officers discovered offal in the tins. The "objectionable matter" was thought to have been "deliberately placed…by disgruntled workers." But this was an unlikely form of industrial action in the Ottoman Empire in the 1840s, where it was likely to incur severe penalties, such as death. I think it much more likely that a Moldavian worker would have thought: "It's only a bit of tripe, what's the problem?" Workers from the Angloworld were more familiar with middle-class British offal-phobia, and subsequent naval and military meat contracts went to Australia and the United States.[22] A recent business history of one New Zealand–British company, now the pharmaceuticals giant Glaxo, notes its management talking quite un-selfconsciously of "abroad" being outside *both* Britain and New Zealand, as the two were in fact linked by a recolonial bridge.[23]

I cannot enter into the full social and cultural implications of re-colonization in this paper, but I can briefly subject the thesis to the test of war. Linda Colley has noted that Welsh and Scots Britonism proved itself in eighteenth-century wars against France.[24] Dominion Britonism did likewise in the First World War, when New Zealanders, Australians, and Canadians fought like Britons because they thought they were Britons. The American Old Northwest's relationship with its northeastern oldland underwent an equivalent war test in the Civil War. Despite some pro-Confederate feeling in southern Indiana, Illinois, and Ohio, the contribution of these "recolonized" states to the Union war effort was even higher than that of the northeast in proportion to military population.[25]

Recolonization was a matter of shared collective identity and shared "social capital" as well as complementary economics, and each reinforced the other. Britain served as a second metropolis for the American West, pouring in migrants and money for its booms and providing export rescue after its busts. Between the 1870s and the 1890s, the Midwest fed London, as well as New York. In this period, America was to some extent "recolonized" by Britain. America at last returned the favour in the 1900s, when it acted as a supplementary metropolis for the explosive colonization of the Canadian Prairies. The Dominions were old Britain's replacement for America, and for a time, 1880s-1940s, they performed this function quite well. The concepts "British Empire" and "British Commonwealth" conceal a virtual nation, an ephemeral second United States, Britain-plus-Dominions, whose dominion citizens considered themselves co-owners of London, the Empire, and Britishness in general. Charles Dilke's "Greater Britain" did exist. Just as England and its "Celtic fringe" sometimes downplay their one-time unity and importance to each other, so Britain and its "dominion fringe" write each other out of history.

I do not wish to exaggerate the novelty of this approach. The busts or crashes on which my cycles pivot are well-known to economic history. Notions of cycles in history themselves date back beyond Kuznets and Kondratieff to the nemesis following hubris in Greek drama. I am happy to acknowledge convergences with the work of Harold Innis, Donald Denoon, Avner Offer, and others. But my approach does involve breaking three current rules of the historian's game. First, it requires economic and cultural history to take each other seriously: my booms are more dream-driven than those of conventional cycles of supply and demand. Second, it goes beyond national packaging, or even oceanic or macro-regional packaging, as in "the Atlantic World" or "North America." But it stops short of globalism, or even pan-Europeanness, instead focussing on a particular culture group to allow culture-specific factors a role. Finally, while I am deeply interested in the impact of the Anglo explosion on indigenous peoples, my focus here is unashamedly on white Anglo-Saxon Protestants. I am trying to explain how WASPS swarmed.

At least two obvious questions remain. First, was hyper-colonization exclusive to the Angloworld? My short answer is no. Something very like explosive colonization occurred in Siberia between 1890 and 1914, and in Latin American countries from the 1870s, especially Argentina. But Argentina, the great adopted neo-Britain, used Anglo money and markets, but not migrants. Moreover, it did not participate fully in either the costs or the benefits of recolonization. Hyper-colonization was not restricted to the Angloworld, but it did begin there, happen more often there, and work better there, for good and ill.

The second remaining question, of course, is what set off the Anglo explosion? Hyper-colonization, I suggest, explains *how* WASPS swarmed. It does not explain *why*. That the answer must work for both British and American Wests complicates it greatly. One thing seems clear: rational actor models, Adam Smith's economic man, or the steady march of Whig Progress are not going to take us very far. Booming, busting Anglos had more in common with coral insects than rational actors. Despite no less than fifteen lessons, the Angloworld was built on successive layers of financial corpses.

So what did trigger the Anglo explosion? Apart from obvious precon-ditions, such as industrial revolutions and mortality transitions, I have no more than guesses as yet. Let me prematurely expose two of them, centering around technology and ideology.

On the technological front, transport improvements were obviously important, but what we tend to overlook is that some were non-in-dustrial. In 1815 the end of over a century of endemic warfare suddenly eliminated privateers and greatly cheapened sailing ship transport by reducing crews, guns, insurance rates, and the need to convoy. Later, clipper ships and iron hulls further improved efficiency – all this without a steam engine in sight. In the newlands, work animals flourished as nowhere else and never before. New Zealand and Ontario each had one horse to every three people in the 1860s, about four times the British rate, and this was in bust-phase. Boom-phase New South Wales had even more in 1851 – about one horse to every 1.5 people.[26] Oxen and horses powered much of the Anglo explosion. Horses did not simply drag wagons and carry riders; they also powered mills, cranes, and other construction equipment, and even paddle-wheeled horse ferries. It has recently been calculated that in America in 1850 horses still provided over half of all work energy, with humans contributing 13 per cent and inanimate sources of power (wind, water, and steam) the rest.[27] Several authorities have observed that, against expectations, rail increased the demand for horse transport. As noted above, farming supplied the equivalent of gasoline and vehicles, as well as human food and clothing. Log rafts of twelve acres, seven-masted sailing ships, giant wagons with ten-ton loads hauled by twenty span are as much symbols of the Anglo explosion as steamships and locomotives.

Lewis Mumford's well-worn classification of technology is useful here: eighteenth-century eotechnic – water, wind, wood, and work animals; nineteenth-century paleotechnic – steam, coal, iron, and rail; and twentieth-century neotechnic – petroleum, steel, electricity, and automobiles.[28] We tend to assume that each new stage displaced the other, and it is true that neotechnic largely replaced paleotechnic in the twentieth century. But paleotechnic did not replace eotechnic in the nineteenth. The two actually flowered together, and they did so most in the Anglo newlands. Here, the abundance of land, wood, water, wind, and work animals created a *non*-industrial revolution, which co-existed with the early transfer of the industrial one. The use of two full suites of technology, eotechnic and paleotechnic, doubled the action. France and Belgium experienced early Industrial Revolutions but lacked vast settler newlands. Spain and Russia had vast settler newlands but not early Industrial Revolutions. Only the Angloworld had both.

On the ideological front, I am focussing on what my addiction to neologism tempts me to call "settlerism," part of which was a secular utopianism. Older utopianisms looked up to heaven, forward to the future, or back to an idealized past. Settler utopianism looked out – to the newlands. The formal theology of this creed was contained in the texts inadequately known as "emigrant guides" and "booster literature." These used a remarkably consistent set of paradise imagery: deserts became gardens, omelettes grew on trees, and pigs begged to be killed from the Midwest to Western Australia. There was an intriguing sideline in giant vegetables, symbols of natural abundance: fifty pound cabbages, proudly displayed, are to be found in the literature of both Wests, and were eventually satirized in Oklahoma around 1900 as "corn bigger than saw logs and watermelons bigger than whales."[29] It is easy to dismiss boosterism as overwrought advertising, but it worked, even on the middle-class boosters themselves. It worked best when formal versions converged with informal, populist versions.

The myths of settlement, of course, promised yeoman freeholds. They also offered many other paradises: for brides, workers, artisans, investors, and declining gentry. The populist version stressed the dignity of labour, the absence of deference and servility, and the opportunity to own one's own horse and house, and to hunt, holiday and eat prime cuts of meat like lords. These concepts pervade the letters of migrants to Canada in the 1830s and to New Zealand in the 1870s alike.[30] Settler utopianism could even prove resistant to contrary evidence. Kerby Miller has found that the Irish utopian image of America was surprisingly unaffected by realistic letters back because "the image served a number of practical functions in rural Irish society." He noted that "children learn from their childhood that their destiny is America."[31] The myths of settlement made another important promise: that you could migrate without ceasing to be metropolitan.

Until about 1800, emigration in both Britain and America was often seen as social excretion, very much a demoting experience. American officials repeatedly referred to frontier settlers in the 1780s and 1790s as "banditti" and "semi-savages." As late as the 1820s, it was said that "the people of the Atlantic States have not yet recovered from the horror inspired by the term backwoodsman."[32] In Britain at this time, emigration was seen as a mere "shovelling out of paupers," with Canada sarcastically known as "the prize of the Irish." Most eighteenth-century emigrants to new worlds went because they had little choice: they were political, religious, or economic refugees, or indentured servants, convicts, or slaves.[33]

In the 1820s, however, there was a marked shift in the nature and implications of emigration. Contemporaries spoke of "revolution in colonial thought."[34] Emigration burgeoned in scale, consisted mostly of free migrants, and came in part from the richest places on earth: England, Lowland Scotland, and the American Northeast. Emigration from Britain and from Atlantic America in the 1830s ran at between three and four times the level of the 1820s, and totalled over 1.5 million people.[35] It ceased to mean social and cultural demotion; denizens of the Wests saw themselves as metropolitan, fully British or American, even as Better British or Better Americans.

One source of this shift was the legacy of the United States Northwest Ordinance of 1787, foreshadowed in 1784, which made American new-lands and their inhabitants politically equal to the old. This form of reproduction, by the cloning of new polities rather than the extension of old ones, was not necessarily obvious; states such as Virginia might have been perfectly happy to extend themselves all the way to the Pacific. But through the fortuitous pettiness of those states without direct access to the West, the cloning system was adopted. Aspirants to statehood regularly claimed that autocratic governors "degraded" American "citizens" into "subjects."[36] To keep Canada British, the Northwest Ordinance was gradually leveraged into the British West in the form of separate polities and the doctrine of colonial self-govern-ment. The process began in 1784 with the formation of New Brunswick and other new provinces for the United Empire Loyalists, continued with the increasing assertiveness of Canadian representative assemblies in the 1820s, and culminated with the Durham Report of 1839. Thus the cloning system resulted not only from notions of self-government as the birthright of all Britons, but also from prosaic competition for settlers between Britain and the United States. As a British official put it in 1796, "Good policy…requires that we should leave as little for [Canadians] to gain by separation as possible."[37] Even very young neo-Britains acquired self-government after 1840 – New Zealand at the age of sixteen. Autonomous colonies or states, with common law and representative institutions, underwrote the metropolitanness of their denizens. In many cases, the prospect or reality of separation and representation seems to have helped trigger booms.

From the 1820s, in old Britain, a distinction was increasingly made between the "emigrant" and the "settler" or "colonist."[38] This partly reflected the Wakefieldian distinction between disorganized emigra-tion and organized colonization, but it may have had other resonances as well. An emigrant joined someone else's society, a settler or colonist remade his own. There may have been a tendency to prefer the latter for Anglos, and the former for non-Anglos. I have made a cursory test of this possibility in a full-text searchable run of *Blackwood's Magazine*, 1843–63.[39] It is no more than suggestive, but it is a step up on the pile of examples normally used to indicate mass attitudes. "Emigration" is the common word for the process of people leaving Britain, but they themselves are seldom called "emigrants." That dread word is used mostly for non-Britons, while the words "colonist" and "settler" are used to describe British emigrants.

This was not solely a matter of nationalism. "Settler" was sometimes used even for British emigrants to the United States. A migrationist London newspaper was called *The American Settler*.[40] The emigrant-settler transition reflected not only an enhanced portability of national identity, but also of pan-Anglo identity, and above all, perhaps, of virtual metropolitan status, a conceptual full citizenship, as against exile or marginality. This was by no means the least remarkable of the Angloworld's mass transfers.

{NOTES}

1 Peter Bakewell, *A History of Latin America: Empires and Sequels 1450–1930* (Oxford: Blackwell, 1997); John R. Fisher, *The Economic Aspects of Spanish Imperialism in the Americas, 1492–1810* (Liverpool: Liverpool University Press, 1997); J. V. Fifer, *The Master Builders: Structures of Empire in the New World* (Durham: Durham Academic Press, 1996).

2 For a fuller exposition of these concepts, see James Belich, *Making Peoples: A History of the New Zealanders from Polynesian Settlement to the End of the Nineteenth Century* (Auckland: Allen Lane, 1996) and *Paradise Reforged: A History of the New Zealanders from the 1880s to the Year 2000* (Auckland: Allen Lane, 2001).

3 John C. Hudson, *Making the Cornbelt: A Geographical History of Middle-Western Agriculture* (Bloomington: Indiana University Press, 1994); Malcolm J. Rohrbough, *The Trans-Appalachian Frontier: People, Societies, and Institutions, 1775–1850* (New York: Oxford University Press, 1978); R. Douglas Hurt, *The Ohio Frontier: Crucible of the Old Northwest, 1720–1830* (Bloomington: Indiana University Press, 1996); Andrew R.L. Cayton, *The Frontier Republic: Ideology and Politics in the Ohio Country, 1780–1825* (Kent, OH: Kent State University Press, 1986); Robert Leslie Jones, *History of Agriculture in Ohio to 1880* (Kent, OH: Kent State University Press, 1983); John G. Clark, *The Grain Trade in the Old Northwest* (Urbana: University of Illinois Press, 1966).

4 James Mak and Gary M. Watson, "Steamboats and the Great Productivity Surge in River Transportation," *Journal of Economic History* 32 (1972): 629–40; Erik F. Haites and James Mak, "Steamboating on the Mississippi, 1810–1860: A Purely Competitive Industry," *Business History Review* 45 (1971): 52–78; W. Wallace Carson, "Transportation and Traffic on the Ohio and Mississippi before the Steamboat," *Mississippi Valley Historical Review* 7 (1920): 26–38; Frank Broeze, *Island Nation: A History of Australians and the Sea* (St. Leonards: Allen and Unwin, 1998).

5 Harold Innis, *Essays in Canadian Economic History* (Toronto: University of Toronto Press, 1956); Harold Innis, *Staples, Markets and Cultural Change: Selected Essays*, ed. Daniel Drache (Montreal: McGill-Queen's University Press, 1995).

6 R. Marvin McInnis, *Perspectives on Ontario Agriculture, 1815–1930* (Gananoque, ON: Langdale Press, 1992); Douglas McCalla, *Planting the Province: The Economic History of Upper Canada, 1784–1870* (Toronto: University of Toronto Press, 1993). Also see William L Marr, "The Allocation of Land to Agricultural Uses in Canada West, 1851: A View from the Individual Farm," *Canadian Papers in Rural History* 10 (1996):

191–203; Frank D. Lewis and M. C. Urquhart, "Growth and the Standard of Living in a Pioneer Economy: Upper Canada 1826–1851," *William and Mary Quarterly*, 2nd ser., 56 (1999): 151–81.

7 Robert Whaples, "Where Is There Consensus among American Economic Historians? The Results of a Survey on Forty Propositions," *Journal of Economic History* 55 (1995): 138–54.

8 Albert Fishlow, "Internal Transportation in the Nineteenth and Twentieth Centuries," in *The Cambridge Economic History of the United States*, vol. 2, *The Long Nineteenth Century*, ed. S.L. Engerman and R.E. Gallman (Cambridge: Cambridge University Press, 2000); Ronald E. Shaw, *Canals for a Nation: The Canal Era in the United States, 1790–1860* (Lexington: Kentucky University Press, 1990); Albert Fishlow, *American Railroads and the Transformation of the Ante-Bellum Economy* (Harvard: Harvard University Press, 1965), 5.

9 Harry N. Scheiber, *Ohio Canal Era: A Case Study of Government and the Economy 1820–1861* (Athens: Ohio University Press, 1969), 121–23.

10 McCalla, *Planting the Province*, 207, 173.

11 Contemporary quoted in Gerald M. Craig, *Upper Canada: The Formative Years, 1784–1841* (Toronto: McClelland and Steward, 1963), 158.

12 P.G. Skidmore, "Canadian Canals to 1848," *Dalhousie Review* 61 (1981–82): 718–34.

13 Marvin McInnis, "The Economy of Canada in the Nineteenth Century," in *Cambridge Economic History of the United States*, 82.

14 McCalla, *Planting the Province*, 124.

15 T. S. Berry, *Western Prices before 1861: A Study of the Cincinnati Market* (Harvard: Harvard University Press, 1943), 478; Scheiber, *Ohio Canal Era*, 231; Clark, *Grain Trade*, 265.

16 R. Cole Harris and John Warkentin, *Canada before Confederation: A Study in Historical Geography* (Toronto: Oxford University Press, 1974); Peter G. Goheen, *Victorian Toronto, 1850 to 1900: Pattern and Process of Growth* (Chicago: University of Chicago Press, 1970).

17 Ibid., 49.

18 W.L. Marr and D.G. Paterson, *Canada: An Economic History* (Toronto: Gage, 1980), 344.

19 D.C. Kerr, "Saskatoon, 1910–1913: Ideology of a Boomtime," *Saskatchewan History* 32 (1979): 16–28; R. Rees, "The 'Magic City' on the banks of the Saskatchewan: The Saskatoon Real Estate Boom of 1910–1913," *Saskatchewan History* 27 (1974): 51–59; Alan F.J. Artibise, "City-Building in the Canadian West: From Boosterism to Corporatism," *Journal of Canadian Studies* 17 (1982): 35–44.

20 Mary Yeager, *Competition and Regulation: The Development of Oligopoly in the Meat Packing Industry* (Greenwich: JAI Press, 1981); Jimmy M. Skaggs, *Prime Cut: Livestock Raising and Meatpacking in the United States, 1607–1983* (College Station: Texas A & M University Press, 1986); Barry K. Goodwin, "Mechanical Refrigeration and the Integration of Perishable Commodity Markets," *Explorations in Economic History* 39 (2002): 154–82; R.A. Clemen, *The American Livestock and Meat Industry* (1923; repr., New York: Johnson Reprint, 1966); Margaret Walsh, *The Rise of the Midwestern Meat Packing Industry* (Lexington: University Press of Kentucky, 1982); John H. White Jr., *The American Railroad Freight Car* (Baltimore: Johns Hopkins University Press, 1993).

21 R.W. Hidy, *The House of Baring in American Trade and Finance: English Merchant Bankers at Work, 1763–1861* (Harvard: Harvard University Press, 1949).

22 Richard Perren, *The Meat Trade in Britain 1840–1914* (London: Routledge and Kegan Paul, 1978).

23 R.P. Davenport-Hines and Judy Slinn, *Glaxo: A History to 1962* (Cambridge: Cambridge University Press, 1992).

24 Linda Colley, *Britons: Forging the Nation, 1707–1837* (New Haven: Yale University Press, 1992).

25 Robert Dykstra, "Iowa," in *Radical Republicans in the North: State Politics during Reconstruction*, ed. James C. Mohr (Baltimore: Johns Hopkins University Press, 1976), 170.

26 G.T. Bloomfield, *New Zealand: A Handbook of Historical Statistics* (Boston: G. K. Hall, 1984), 181–82; Malcolm J. Kennedy, *Hauling the Loads: A History of Australia's Working Horses and Bullocks* (Melbourne: Melbourne University Press, 1992), 67. For British horse numbers, see F.M.L. Thompson, "Nineteenth-Century Horse Sense," *Economic History Review*, n.s., 29 (1976): 60–81.

27 Joel A. Tarr, "A Note on the Horse as an Urban Power Source," *Journal of Urban History* 25 (1999): 434–48; also see Dolores Greenberg, "Reassessing the Power Patterns of the Industrial Revolution: An Anglo-American Comparison," *American Historical Review* 87 (1982): 1237–61.

28 Lewis Mumford, *Technics and Civilization* (London: Routledge and Kegan Paul, 1934), 109–10.

29 Contemporary quoted in J.M. Powell, *Mirrors of the New World: Images and Image-Makers in the Settlement Process* (Folkestone: Archon Books, 1977), 82.

30 Wendy Cameron et al., eds., *English Immigrant Voices: Labourers' Letters from Upper Canada in the 1830s* (Montreal: McGill-Queen's University Press, 2000); Rollo Arnold, *The Farthest Promised Land: English Villagers, New Zealand Immigrants of the 1870s* (Wellington, NZ: Victoria University Press, 1981).

31 Kerby Miller and Bruce Boling, "Golden Streets, Bitter Tears: The Irish Image of America during the Era of Mass Migration," *Journal of American Ethnic History* 10 (1990–91): 16–36.

32 Timothy Flint, quoted in Francis S. Philbrick, *The Rise of the West, 1754–1830* (New York: Harper Torchbooks, 1965), 356.

33 Aaron S. Fogleman, "From Slaves, Convicts and Servants to Free Passengers: The Transformation of Immigration in the Era of the American Revolution," *Journal of American History* 85 (1998): 43–76.

34 Edward Brynn, "The Emigration Theories of Robert Wilmot Horton, 1820–1841," *Canadian Journal of History* 4 (1969): 45–65.

35 R. K. Vedder and L. E. Gallaway, "Migration and the Old Northwest," *Essays in Nineteenth-Century Economic History: The Old Northwest*, ed. D.C. Klingaman and R. K. Vedder (Athens: Ohio University Press, 1975), 161; W.A. Carruthers, *Emigration from the British Isles* (London: King, 1929), 305; Helen I. Cowan, *British Emigration to North America: The First Hundred Years*, rev. ed. (Toronto: University of Toronto Press, 1961).

36 Peter S. Onuf, *Statehood and Union: A History of the Northwest Ordinance* (Bloomington: Indiana University Press, 1987).

37 Quoted in Cowan, *British Emigration to British North America*, 11. Also see Craig, *Upper Canada*, 12.

38 See, for example, the proceedings of the Select Committee on Emigration 1827, noted in A.G.L. Shaw, "British Attitudes to the Colonies, ca 1820–1850," *Journal of British Studies* 9 (1969): 71–95.

39 *Blackwood's Edinburgh Magazine* in Internet Library of Early Journals, *www.bodley.ox.ac.uk/ilej*

40 Marjory Harper, "Abraham and Isaac Ride the Range: British Images of the American West," *Journal of the West* 40 (2001): 8–15.

CHAPTER 3

INDIGENOUS PEOPLES AND IMPERIAL NETWORKS IN THE EARLY NINETEENTH CENTURY:

THE POLITICS OF KNOWLEDGE

Elizabeth Elbourne

IN A GLOBALIZED WORLD in which historical interests have become increasingly transregional, historians of imperialism have become keenly aware of the value of an approach to the history of the British Empire that focuses not solely on metropole and colony, or on future nations as bounded entities, but also on the complicated communication networks that cut across the Empire as a whole.[1] A rich vein of writing on the black Atlantic is only one example. More recently, scholars have begun to argue for the value of a networked approach to the study of relationships between British and British-origin people and so-called indigenous or Aboriginal groups in the early white settler empire.[2] In the early nineteenth century, transregional networks and experience informed not only British policy toward indigenous peoples in particular colonies but also, more nebulously, ideas and debate about Aboriginal peoples, settlers, and the relationships between them that circulated through such sites as newspaper publications, parliamentary chambers, courtrooms, and family letters. This was a highly politicized struggle over "knowledge" that can only be fully understood in transnational perspective. Nonetheless, eighteenth- and nineteenth-century peoples now defined as Aboriginal have themselves tended to be studied as precisely "indigenous" or locally bounded. Using examples drawn primarily from the Cape Colony and from missionary sources, this essay explores the possibility that these imperial networks also affected indigenous interlocutors themselves, at least in some ways and at least at certain levels of society. Did, for example, struggles across colonial boundaries help to create conditions conducive to a sense of transregional Aboriginal identity, an early exemplar of the tension and interaction between the "local" and the "global"? Aboriginal identity, like the black/white colonial binary, also has its own history, intertwined with the history of global colonial expansion.

Let me first briefly recapitulate some ways in which networks mattered in the formation of imperial policy towards colonized groups in the white settler empire, using the example of capillary connections between New South Wales and the Cape Colony. Probably the best-known imperial debate over the status of indigenous peoples in the early nineteenth century, recently explored in a variety of different contexts by Alan Lester, Zoe Laidlaw, and myself, is the debate over the 1835–36 House of Commons Select Committee on Aborigines (British Settlements), which sat to examine the status of indigenous peoples throughout the British colonies.[3] "Aborigines" were the original inhabitants of British settlements, according to the report's parameters. The majority of the peoples considered – the Maori, Upper and Lower Canadian Aboriginal groups, Aboriginal people in New South Wales, and the Khoekhoe and San in southern Africa – have come to be considered indigenous or Aboriginal in modern parlance as well, although the Xhosa have not. As this implies, the concept of an "Aboriginal" group was arguably more capacious in the early nineteenth century than at present, being less tied to minority status and less frequently linked to pastoralism. At the same time, the committee's 1836 and 1837 reports clearly thought of people they termed "Aborigines" as standing in a particular external relationship to something called "civilization." "Aborigines" were also seen as intrinsically vulnerable to exploitation. Such changing uses and connotations of the term "Aborigine" suggest the historically contingent nature of the idea. The Committee's reports attacked what the authors saw as rampant settler sin and promoted the assimilation, protection, and Christianization of indigenous peoples as a prophylactic against settler vice. The report also urged that settlers and indigenous peoples be brought under a single legal system – an argument that was controversial from both settler and indigenous perspectives. The Committee's 1836 and 1837 reports met with a barrage of criticism from white settler communities across the Empire, forming part of a vigorous transimperial political debate in which settlers and their critics alike assumed that there was fundamental continuity across very diverse colonies. The Committee led directly to the formation of the Aborigines Protection Society, which would itself contribute to debates across the Empire about the relationships between so-called Aborigines and British-origin settlers.

These are, however, only the most evident examples of the importance of networks in the formation of policy. As Zoe Laidlaw will surely demonstrate further in her forthcoming book, personal networks were formed in the early years of the nineteenth century by British administrators of various kinds, from judges to governors, who moved between colonies.[4] Consider the links between the Cape Colony and New South Wales. Richard Bourke moved from being acting governor of the Cape Colony (1826-29) to being governor of New South Wales (1831-37). Judge William Burton, under Bourke at the Cape, became a judge on the supreme court in New South Wales, where he famously gave legal articulation to the doctrine of *terra nullius* in the Jack Congo Murrell case; a man who is perceived as a liberal in the Cape context for drafting Ordinance 50, which granted a degree of equality under the law to the Khoekhoe, is ironically perceived by historians as a conservative in the New South Wales context, in which equality under a single legal system denied Aboriginal sovereignty.[5] Sir George Grey is perhaps the most famous of the mobile administrators: he explored South Australia before becoming its governor, then governed New Zealand, and finally the Cape. The Eastern Commissioners of Inquiry moved from New South Wales to the Cape Colony; J.T. Bigge had a particularly tumultuous political impact in New South Wales before influencing the liberalization of the Cape economy. Such men tended to evolve ideas about Aborigines and their ideal relationship to the colonial state that they then applied in very diverse situations. These networks were largely male-dominated and professional. Imperial women developed networks that were less formal but also important. It seems symbolically apt, for example, that on her way from Van Diemen's Land to New South Wales Lady Jane Franklin, amateur botanist and controversial wife of the governor of Van Diemen's Land, John Franklin, threw clover seeds in her path, seeking to seed the alien Australian landscape with home. She also helped found a botanical society that had international links; several years later, she came to public prominence in Upper Canada as a bereaved wife after the failure of Franklin's doomed expedition to the Canadian arctic.[6] At the same time, self-described humanitarians in Britain, both male and female, evolved policies that they pressured the Colonial Office to put into effect in the Australian colonies, predicated on models derived from experience elsewhere in the Empire, especially the Cape. British-origin settlers in the Cape Colony and New South Wales made common cause, in the meantime, in their opposition to supposedly misguided "humanitarian" meddling. Such examples could be multiplied across imperial spaces.

One important aspect of the study of transnational networks that has received relatively little attention, however, is the way in which such networks enabled indigenous people to interact, whether in imagination or, more rarely, in person, both with the British at the imperial centre and also with one another. In other words, such networks not only contributed to the creation of British policy toward indigenous people, but also involved indigenous people directly. This argument does not seek to minimize the importance of other, often longer-standing regional networks that make it hard to see the globalization that accompanied colonialism as an entirely new phenomenon.[7] Nor do I wish to downplay the far greater importance of local struggles and local particularities. Nonetheless, it seems worth asking what the impact was of specifically colonial transregional networks on the indigenous peoples who were the subject of so much British debate. What structural opportunities and constraints did such networks present in the early nineteenth century and what intellectual vistas might they have opened?

This essay makes an initial rather than definitive foray into a very complicated subject in the hope of posing questions and laying out an agenda for future work. I want to explore to what extent a handful of indigenous people – in a variety of situations but mostly Christian converts – had access to information networks concerning the white settler Empire as a whole, and to what extent these information networks may or may not have affected local communities. I take the example of the networks and contacts developed by a group of British evangelicals who were involved in the London Missionary Society (LMS), the Aborigines Protection Society, and the 1835–36 House of Commons Select Committee on Aborigines. These were explicitly Christian networks, driven in the first instance by missionary propaganda. By the late 1820s and 1830s, a loosely linked group in Britain was centred around the British MP and leader of the parliamentary abolitionist forces, Sir Thomas Buxton, but it also included missionaries in a variety of places, most of whom never actually met. Indigenous participants were clearly much less tightly linked but included communities of converts in the Cape Colony, the Canadian colonies, and what would become New Zealand. Indigenous groups in New South Wales were the subject of discussion across these networks in this period but, still in the thrall of violent conquest, they did not tend to participate actively in such networks themselves. I would argue that at least a few indigenous people, including but not limited to a handful of visitors to Britain, tried to use global networks and even to mobilize the idea of being Aboriginal to defend their own material interests, against the background of vehement debates about indigenous-settler relationships. In this, they were part of a long history of interaction among indigenous peoples, colonialism, and globalization, which has in itself helped produce the very concepts "indigenous" and "Aboriginal."[8] Ironically, however, in order to participate in the international networks of this period with the partial aim of protecting local communities, indigenous people frequently needed to present themselves in print or in person on the British stage as, to some extent, disembodied actors with the concomitant ability to move between different cultural worlds. They also often needed to be Christian, or at least to present themselves as such. They had to present themselves, in sum, in ways familiar to the British, while posing as exemplars of the universal man posited by early nineteenth-century liberalism. This liberal subject was far from neutral, but rather implicitly male and implicitly possessed of many of the traits of the imagined ideal European, as many critics have pointed out.[9] Indigenous people very directly confronted this contradiction as they sought to use international languages about rights and property ownership.

The development of an international missionary movement was tightly tied to the growth and spread of print culture, as well as to the sheer capacity of evangelicals to reach a variety of different places as communication networks expanded and as empire shrank the world. Not surprisingly, in the 1790s and early 1800s, as the first British missionary societies organized themselves, missionary periodicals both kept pace with and helped fuel the rapid expansion of missions themselves. In Britain, new journals such as the *Transactions* of the London Missionary Society, the *Evangelical Magazine* also published by the LMS from 1793 onward, the *Proceedings of the Church Missionary Society*, and the *Periodical Accounts relative to the Baptist Missionary Society* complemented the existing Moravian journal, *Periodical Accounts*, which publicized Moravian missions in English. Such periodicals extended the international networks that characterized eighteenth-century Protestantism, in a complex interplay between local dynamics and an imagined international Protestant community of the godly.[10] The information conveyed in such periodicals potentially enabled convert communities to gain "knowledge" of sorts (however deeply mediated) about indigenous communities elsewhere.

Consider the example of the Cape Colony. Missionary periodicals dispatched there by the home society were some of the few texts that were available to missionaries on stations remote from centres of production of printed material and characterized by a chronic lack of cash. Just as in Britain, missionary periodicals were sometimes read aloud at church meetings, particularly at the mission support groups that often became a feature of community life. In the LMS, at the Cape as elsewhere, monthly prayers on the first Monday of every month for missions around the world provided an opportunity for connection with an imagined community that extended far beyond local bounds. International prayer was a key feature in other societies as well in helping to create imagined international Christian communities.

At the Moravian (Unitas Fratrum or United Brethren) station of Genadendal in the western Cape, the missionaries kept a diary in 1809, which was published in English translation in the *Periodical Accounts Relating to the Missions of the Church of the United Brethren Established among the Heathen*. In a self-referential process, the diary made claims about the influence of accounts of other missions on the local Khoekhoe community. At the "monthly prayer-day" of the United Brethren, the missionaries reported, they read aloud to their congregations reports from the *Periodical Accounts*, as well as reports from Greenland. They also included a private letter from a missionary in Labrador, Brother Hasting, "in which he desires us to give the love of the believing Esquimaux to their Brethren and Sisters at Genadenthal." According to the account published by J.A. Kuester and his fellows,

> this caused a general emotion throughout the whole
> congregation; and after the meeting was over, large parties
> came to thank us, and to request, that we would greet the
> Esquimaux believers in the most cordial manner and say, that
> they would pray for them, as they had done for the Hottentots
> [Khoekhoe]. Many came singly, both women and men, and
> expressed their love for the Esquimaux in the most affectionate
> terms; observing what a great blessing they enjoyed to have such
> a heart's-fellowship with children of God in remote parts of the
> world, and that they would, from this time forward, continually
> name them in their prayers.[11]

Similarly, from 1807 on, the LMS formed local Auxiliary Societies in various parts of the world. Converts made contributions to the world-wide missions of the society, and LMS publications were distributed and read.[12] These societies became important at the Cape. In 1834 the LMS missionary James Read, Sr. reported to his superiors in London that he had travelled to the impoverished Khoekhoe mission station of Bethelsdorp to be present at the anniversary of the formation of the Auxiliary Missionary Society. "To my great surprise I found they had subscribed out of their great poverty during the year upwards of £52 and at the doors the day of the meeting was collected upwards of £15. Many admirable speeches were made by the Hottentots and it was a time of refreshing from God's presence."[13]

Missionary periodicals, international prayer, and missionary society meetings were not, of course, the only ways in which indigenous communities gained knowledge about groups in structurally analogous situations. In the early nineteenth century, however, other routes also tended to be mediated by missionaries. The most significant sources of knowledge were probably Western-style education in schools run by missionaries and newspapers available most readily to those who had acquired literacy in European languages. In the letter quoted above, James Read commented on the burgeoning schools at the recent Khoekhoe settlement of Kat River in the eastern Cape and reported more particularly on the school run by his son, James Read, Jr.: "The children are in a state of forwardness in Dutch and English grammar, arithmetic, history and geography. The school wants a pair of globes very much but we do not know where to get them."[14] In his own account of the Kat River settlement, the younger Read reported that the community subscribed to two local newspapers, the more liberal *South African Commercial Advertiser*, published in Cape Town, and the pro-settler *Grahamstown Journal*. The *Advertiser* tended to publish information about missionary activity, among other things, while the *Journal* printed (as Alan Lester has pointed out) many letters and reports from settlers in other colonies.[15] "As it would have taken a long time to send the papers over the Settlement," Read noted, "a man was sent from each location to attend the Reading Society."[16] Here, presumably, newspapers were read aloud and their contents then reported back to local hamlets. By the early 1830s, people of Khoekhoe descent were contributing letters in Dutch to the (bilingual) *Grahamstown Journal*, while the speeches at an 1834 Philipton community meeting, held to write a petition to oppose the proposed renewal of vagrancy legislation, were reproduced in full in the pages of the *Commercial Advertiser*.

Although this type of evidence from Khoekhoe missions in the Cape Colony is suggestive rather than conclusive, it does suggest that more systematic study in different colonies might reveal that local convert communities were coming to see themselves not only as incorporated into a wider international Christian community but also into a world in which conceptual categories such as "white," "black," "Aboriginal," and "settler" had transnational as well as local bite. What, for example, are we to make of an Auxiliary Society meeting at the Khoekhoe mission station of Paarl in the western Cape in 1828 at which a Dutch-speaking minister of the Dutch Reformed Church

> spoke among other things of the prejudices which the people have here against the instruction of the blacks, which, as he expressed it, they had sucked in with their mothers' milk. Exhorted them to place themselves in the condition of an unhappy slave who had been sold without any consent of his own, and obliged to submit to the arbitrary will of different masters etc., and to think what would be their situation if in addition to this they were deprived of the gospel and its comforts, but how gospel tended to ameliorate the condition of the slave population etc.[17]

This was, of course, a local analysis, but it was also one that could be extended to other colonies with slavery and with "black" and "white" populations; the context of an Auxiliary Society meeting suggests the feasibility of wider application. The categories "black" and "white" were central to the dynamics of many different settler colonies, coming to the fore with particular force at moments of armed conflict. Clearly missionary networks were only part of a much more complicated picture in which violence played a critical role, and clearly Khoekhoe identity overlapped in complex ways with black identity. If, however, throughout the nineteenth century, conflictual colonial relationships were entrenching transnational binaries of whiteness and blackness, then it seems important to examine the transnational sources of information available to colonized peoples.[18]

There was a very complex interplay between local circumstances and the type of information that ended up in missionary and evangelical periodicals designed for international circulation. Most crucially, local communities did not have much control over what was said about them, even if converts did occasionally contribute polite letters to missionary periodicals. Although much of the information conveyed in missionary periodicals was relatively scattered, as well as shaped by the political presuppositions of particular missionaries, editors attempted to impose a schematic epistemological framework dictated by evangelical ideological presuppositions, including the inferiority of societies that were not Christian, as well as by the urgent need for success stories to drive fundraising. Despite these constraints, it was clear to many converts that international publicity could occasionally be powerful.

There were, however, distinct limits to the extent to which indigenous peoples could affect the narratives about them that reached Britain. I want to pause on a difficult example of the international circulation of competing "humanitarian" and "settler" narratives in the 1810s – the report of James Read, Sr. of the murder of the Ourson family. I and others have written about the frontier conflicts of which this report was part; I have also written about the impact in Britain of Read's complaints of what we might now call human rights abuses.[19] There is no need to reiterate that discussion here, so much as to revisit a story that turns out to have had more layers than I, for one, realized. My point is that stories were powerful and yet also very complicated. Effective political narrative demanded a starkness that did not always reflect reality. At the same time, the example illustrates the potential power of international information networks and the importance of the circulation of iconic stories.

In the late eighteenth and early nineteenth centuries, the eastern Cape frontier was enormously violent, as farmers incorporated dispossessed Khoisan peoples and war captives into their household economies.[20] At the tail end of the 1799 to 1803 Khoekhoe rebellion against their Dutch masters (probably in 1802 before the British departure), a Khoekhoe man named Ourson, his wife, and his young child were murdered at the behest of commando-leader Piet van Rooyen, at a time when settler commandoes were sweeping the eastern Cape. Ourson had earlier been employed as a wagon driver by Colonel Lemoyne, the British commander of Fort Frederick. Several years later, in 1808, Read described these murders, without mentioning the military context, in a letter to his superiors in London in which he detailed a range of atrocities perpetrated against Khoekhoe and enslaved people in the vicinity of his mission station, Bethelsdorp. This is how he described the murders:

> The Hottentot was one Ourson an excellent character who had been waggoner to our worthy friend Col. Lemoyne at Fort Frederick and was repairing peacefully from Graaff Reinet to our Institution – They were met…by number of Affrican [sic] Peasants [i.e., white farmers] – After they had conversed some time with him friendly; his hands were tied to knees on which he was placed, and shot dead, after 8 balls had been fired at him. The Infant was then taken from the mother's arms by the leggs [sic] & the brains beaten out against a small hill. When the tears were seen to fall from the mother's eye a savage Boor [Boer] now living in our neighbourhood (and who has been appointed

Heemraad for this District) drew his knife and threatened if he saw another tear he would cut her eyes out of her head that moment – as soon as the child was dead the mother was thrown upon her back and her throat cut.[21]

This letter, which included several other examples of violent atrocities, entered into international networks under evangelical sponsorship and took on a life of its own once extracts from Read's descriptions of violence were published in London in the LMS's *Transactions*. The letter was read at the highest levels of the British government, including by the Prime Minister. It sparked a government investigation but no fundamental change in the unfree status of the Khoisan. The testimony of grave violence provided in this letter and in further notes furnished by Read helped precipitate the establishment of a circuit court system in the eastern Cape. The circuit court system enabled British officials to claim that they had established the rule of law, despite the fact that the Khoekhoe continued to be treated differently in law and coerced into labour.

Read's account of the Ourson murders is not the only written narrative of these horrific events available to the historian. Read told a story about extreme cruelty that led white farmers to attack Khoekhoe people in a random manner. This dovetailed with the concerns of British evangelical activists about the immorality of settlers, the vulnerability of indigenous peoples, and more broadly, the inevitability of human sin. In 1810, after the publication of Read's letter, the governor at the Cape, the Earl of Caledon, instructed the landdrost of Uitenhage, Jacob Cuyler, to investigate Read's complaints.[22] Not surprisingly, Cuyler attempted to clear himself and his colleagues of the charge of complicity in atrocities. Cuyler's investigation was deeply flawed, as might perhaps be expected of a man whose own relatives were named in the charges and whose own professional reputation was at stake; even Deputy Secretary Christopher Bird informed Cuyler that his investigation was "unsatisfactory and incomplete."[23] Some of the additional information about the Ourson murders is nonetheless revealing about the horrific environment in which so many were forced to live.

At first, the key witness to the Ourson murders, Read's own uncle-in-law, Willem Valentyn, rescinded his testimony, claiming that he knew of the murder only by hearsay, and denying that he knew "of any Hottentots being ill used or murdered by any of the Inhabitants, nor recollect having mentioned anything of that kind to any of the members of the Institution [Bethelsdorp]."[24] Read would later argue that witnesses were deeply afraid for their own safety and refused to participate. Other witnesses told a murkier, although no less horrific, story. The Khoekhoe man Jantje Michels testified:

> I was on the Commando of Piet van Rooyen, and the camp
> lay at the Zwartkops River, and the Hottentot alluded to was
> brought to the camp by spies of Hottentots sent out, with
> his wife and a child, and I heard that he had been taken at
> Zandfontein. I was sitting at the fire cooking for my master
> Barend Marais, who was sick, when the Hottentot Class Meyer
> came to the place where I sat and was cleaning his knife, when I
> asked him what he had done with his knife, he answered he had
> cut the throat of Ourson's child, and told me that his brother
> Paul had cut the Hottentot woman's throat. The same Class
> Meyer informed me that Ourson was shot.[25]

Read confirmed this broad account in a written deposition: "Willem Booy and Willem Meyer declared that a certain Hottentot named Ourson, with wife and child, coming to the Bay, had by consent of Piet van Rooyen been shot, but the Hottentots missing him, he had further knocked him down and cut his throat off, and further cut the woman's throat, and cut the child to pieces."[26] Local official Ignatius Muller, who was present in the camp at the time and who was accused of threatening Ourson's wife with cutting out her eyes, testified that Ourson's wife had been shot by a patrol under his command, without his knowledge, while she was trying to run away. On October 17, Read asked Cuyler to call Andries Pretorius, who testified that Valentyn had indeed seen the murder and that Read had overheard him talking about it. Read was thus forcing a member of his wife's family to bear witness against his will. Finally, Valentyn was recalled and testified at last that

> he was at the Commando of Piet van Rooyen at Zwartkops
> River, and he saw a Hottentot together with his wife and
> child brought in by spies of Hottentots, among which was one
> Magerman, a Hottentot of Piet van Rooyen's; that they were
> taken on one side and shot, and that the next day passing by he
> saw the three bodies lying at a little distance, but cannot say that
> he saw any mangling or cutting upon them. That he mentioned
> this to Mr. Read, and that he further said that he heard Ignatius

Muller say when the woman was crying she must not cry or that he would put his fingers in her eyes, but did not hear him say anything about cutting out her eyes.[27]

Read also submitted notes in which he listed atrocities and the names of the witnesses from whom he had garnered information. According to the notes, "Stout," an older daughter of Ourson, had testified that she saw the Khoekhoe man Hendrik Platje "cut to pieces alive by [settler Thomas] Ferreira, assisted by his sons and Lucas the son of Van Rooyen."[28]

The balance of information revealed in Cuyler's inquiry suggests that the murders were, in fact, a targeted political assassination rather than a random act of violence, although it is more than clear that there were many random acts of violence perpetrated against Khoisan dependents by settlers. It may be pertinent that in November 1801 three Khoekhoe men led by rebel leader Klaas Stuurman had assassinated Piet van Rooyen's kinsman, C. J. van Rooyen. The 1810 inquiry also underscores, if the accounts of testimony are even partially accurate, that Khoekhoe dependents (at least some of whom might reasonably be described as enslaved) served on commandoes during the 1799–1803 war and killed for their masters. This was not material that entered international information networks. Possibly Read wasn't given the full story about how Ourson was killed. Possibly, also, the testimony that Cuyler reported was false because he wanted to spread guilt.

Be that as it may, both Cuyler in 1810 and the local officials who investigated the case again in 1811 claimed that because the murder had occurred during a period of military conflict, it should not be treated as an ordinary murder and, by implication, that those who had ordered it should be exempt from punishment. Indeed, the Batavian governor from 1803 to 1806, J.W. Janssens, made the assumption buried in this argument explicit. He told the missionary Johannes Theodorus Van der Kemp that it was politically essential to forgive the past and that Van der Kemp should show affection to both settlers and indigenes, "for love had good and hate nothing but bad results"; Van der Kemp responded that he was happy to be hated by murderers.[29]

In Britain, evangelical activists continued to use the story in an iconic fashion as an argument for the re-establishment of an imagined moral order and proof of the need for protection of "Aborigines" on an international scale. William Wilberforce, the parliamentary leader of the abolitionist forces, argued that the exemplary capital punishment of "two or three of ye most powerful and savage of ye Boors" would break the pattern of systematic "abominations."[30] The theme of Afrikaner violence conveniently dovetailed with the arguments implicitly made by contemporary British officials such as John Barrow that Afrikaner violent abuses of indigenous peoples justified the imposition of British control.[31] In order for this to be a useful story in Britain, it needed to be about one-sided atrocities carried out on individual bodies. Indeed, Thomas Lacquer has highlighted the importance for humanitarian discourse in the late eighteenth and early nineteenth centuries of the suffering individual body, in an essay in which he convincingly argues for the importance of what he calls the "humanitarian narrative" to the politics of reform at the turn of the nineteenth century.[32] On the frontier and in certain Cape administrative circles, in contrast, it was tacitly understood by whites that killing was necessary to maintain white control and that murder was in that sense political and indeed systematic. Although this is a large and sensitive topic, it is arguable that some blacks needed to be implicated in the killings in order for the system to work. Knowledge of the participation of Khoekhoe and San dependents in killing was part of that frontier knowledge: intimacy and violence were closely bound together.

In the different ways in which the story of the murder of the Ourson family was used, one might see reflected competing white ideas about knowledge and virtue. On violent frontiers, whites "knew" that killing was acceptable, and indeed inevitable, in the pursuit of ethnic domination. In Britain, activists "knew" that Britain ruled only because of her supposedly superior virtue; white settlers (whether of British origin or not) were supposedly out of control, and non-virtuous, and in that sense threatened the very basis of British rule. These were narratives that transcended the boundaries of particular areas of the British Empire, despite the tensions between the British and Afrikaners. Indigenous people could only with difficulty shape these narratives in the form that reached Britain, although they were frequently the ultimate source of information that found its way into such accounts. At the same time, the potential utility of internationally circulating narratives could also be discerned, despite their costs.

There were, however, several more direct ways in which indigenous individuals and groups could try to influence information reaching Great Britain in the early nineteenth century. Direct appeals to the monarch or to British supporters by indigenous visitors to Britain were the most direct and the most visible means of influencing British opinion. More routine methods included appeals to local representatives of the Crown in particular colonies, appeals to missionaries to act as intermediaries, letters to the British public or to British missionary societies, or appeals to the courts. But small numbers of indigenous people from Africa, the Canadian colonies, New Zealand, and New South Wales were also brought to Britain for a variety of purposes. In most of these cases, individuals were taken as, or presented themselves as, representative of their particular group, even as they also needed to interact in some way with British expectations about assimilation, "civilization," and the possibility or not of the Christianization of so-called primitive peoples. Sponsorship was usually necessary for such visits, given the high cost and logistical obstacles involved in travelling to Britain. In the early nineteenth century, a small number of British individuals with links to missionary and other Christian organizations were particularly active in providing such sponsorship. But they were not alone, for the display of indigenous people for commercial purposes co-existed with political, educational, and religious visits, however much the agency of people displayed to commercial ends might be called into question.[33]

The historian needs to pay attention not only to the individual visits that have loomed large in accounts of particular areas and peoples, but also to the circuits and procedures that emerged to accommodate such visits in the late eighteenth and early nineteenth centuries. It is also important to consider to what extent participants saw themselves as part of an international project that transcended local circumstances. Circuits were perhaps most easily created for educational purposes – an example that immediately raises complicated issues of freedom and coercion. Children could be easily transported from colonies to Britain, and they presented tempting targets for attempted assimilation. Several evangelicals brought African children, often of high social status, to Britain for an education in the early to mid-nineteenth century in the hope that they would return and spread Christianity and civilization to their communities. In these cases, the hoped-for flow of "knowledge" was to be primarily from Britain to Africa. At the same time, a number of evangelicals clearly anticipated that Africans educated in Britain would demonstrate to the skeptical the very capacity of Africans (and by extension of other "primitive" people) to become "civilized"; Africans were thus to convey "knowledge," but through their persons and through their performance of civilization rather than through any parallel conveyance of African knowledge to the British.

Consider the case of John Campbell. At the turn of the nineteenth century, Campbell, a member of the Board of Directors of the Edinburgh Missionary Society and future inspector of the London Missionary

Society's mission to southern Africa, attempted to sponsor the children of Sierra Leonean chiefs for education in Scotland. British evangelicals had founded the colony of Sierra Leone not only as a homeland for formerly enslaved people returning to Africa but also as a hoped-for beacon of enlightenment to its neighbours. It was on similar grounds that Campbell organized the visit of twenty-four children (twenty boys and four girls) of African chiefs from Sierra Leone to Edinburgh for education in what was clearly seen as an experiment. As an advocate for the conversion of Africa to Christianity by Africans, Campbell required indigenous agents of Christianization.[34] Scottish revivalist Robert Haldane, who had travelled on preaching tours with Campbell, financed the project to the tune of six to seven thousand pounds. An anonymous biographer of Campbell later recounted the story from Campbell's perspective:

> Whilst the African children were still in the hospital, some difference of opinion arose among the patrons about their education. This annoyed Mr. Campbell much; but a society was formed in London, which took them off his hands, and he returned to Edinburgh without them. Thus failed an experiment which he had much at heart, and which promised, by the Divine blessing, to prove a signal benefit to poor, enslaved, degraded Africa.[35]

Some years later in southern Africa, during his second voyage of inspection to the LMS African mission, Campbell tried to make up for the loss by persuading a Khoekhoe family to send a young boy to Scotland to be educated. "Various friends of the missionary cause having expressed regret after my first visit to Africa, in 1812, that I had not brought home some Hottentot or Bushman youth, to try what effect might be produced by an European education; on revisiting that country, in 1819, I resolved, if I could meet with a suitable Hottentot boy, whose parents were willing to entrust him to my care, I would certainly bring him to England."[36] Interestingly, one of Campbell's false starts was a boy whom Campbell changed his mind about taking once he realized that the boy was "a half-cast Hottentot, his mother only being a Hottentot."[37] Ultimately, Campbell brought back to Scotland a young boy called Paul Dikkop, whose deceased father had been a minor chief who, during Campbell's previous visit, had invited missionaries to settle at his homestead, Hooge Kraal (later the mission station of Pacalt). The boy's mother was enormously reluctant to send her son to Britain and initially refused, fleeing from the mission house, Campbell reported, as though it were on fire;

later, however, she changed her mind. In Scotland, Paul Dikkop went first to the Kingsland day-school, in the town in which Campbell was a minister. Later, Dikkop was sent to the Borough-road boarding school, in company with boys from Madagascar who were similarly in Britain to be educated. Dikkop would write to Campbell that he was "very sorrow" when the two Malagasy boys went to Manchester to learn Latin and Greek. Clearly the school was quite international, for Dikkop continued: "I have saw in the newspaper that the Portuguese hath beaten the French; although the Portuguese are a little city, they hath beaten them. We have one French man and one Portuguese man in our school."[38] A year later Dikkop would be dead at the age of thirteen from a mysterious illness that began as a pain in his side; when asked on his deathbed if he would rather live or die, he replied that he preferred to die. John Campbell never returned to Africa, but he spent much of the remainder of his life promoting the evangelization of Africa – including writing an odd little book for children in which he struggled to memorialize Paul and perhaps in some way to make sense of his death. Paul Dikkop's brief and tragic sojourn in Scotland was a small, unnoticed event from the perspective of world history, but his interactions with Campbell do underscore some constant themes. These include an evangelical assumption that indigenous people would be grateful to be remade and to enter the new family of the church, albeit at the cost of cutting for long periods personal ties with their biological families. The implications in a variety of imperial contexts would be enormous for many indigenous children. Many of the same pressures and entry costs would be exerted on adults who sought to use imperial networks.

Evangelicals and missionary supporters continued to sponsor the visits of Africans for educational purposes throughout the nineteenth century. For example, Anna Gurney, the main author of the 1836 and 1837 reports of the House of Commons Select Committee on Aborigines (British Settlements) participated in the education of visiting Africans. In 1849 she reported to her brother on a group of Sierra Leoneans whom she was obviously teaching. "They certainly are very steady & intelligent & *enquiring* young men – of their real mental caliber one can hardly judge – but they seem to me to be taking pains in the right direction – anxious to learn things that may be of use to their people – I think their capacities are good, but I doubt their *enduring long mental effort* – but then perhaps I *do keep them at their work* 'long hours.'"[39] Although these men were young adults, the point of their education was again to facilitate the Christianization of Africa by Christian Africans. Anna

Gurney also knew Samuel Crowther, the Nigerian who became the first black African bishop and who participated in the disastrous Niger expedition of 1841 organized by Sir Thomas Fowell Buxton, former MP and lynchpin of the Gurney-Buxton circle. Crowther was sponsored by evangelicals for education and ordination in Britain in 1843 before his return to Africa. Reflecting in 1850 on a letter from Crowther in which he apparently discussed threats on his life, Gurney declared, in a moment of self-consciousness comparatively rare among such sponsors: "We should not feel the missionary work a *light* concern at all events, for what is *as* play or ease to us may result in death to those upon whom we are acting – I do not mean that I wd shrink from sending them the gospel – even 'with persecutions' it wd in the long run, be even a *temporal* boon to these [-?] people, whom are exposed to be murdered anyway in sacrifices and slave raids – but this letter does make me feel *how* thoroughly prayerfully we shd stir in so serious a business."[40]

Such educational sponsorship merged into political sponsorship. Anna Gurney also hosted Africans in Britain for other purposes, for example. "Who dost thou think were our guests yesterday," exclaimed Anna's younger female relative, also Anna Gurney (née Backhouse) to her father-in-law, " – The two Ashantee princes, who have been in England some time, Uncle Cunningham did not know Aunt was out and sent them to be taken care of for a day – They came about 11 yesterday, so I had to entertain them – they can talk English pretty well – & one of them was quite agreeable – a nice intelligent *black*."[41] As this account suggests, visiting Africans were often drawn into the family networks of their sponsors at a time when they were cut off from their own networks. Such encounters were marked by some degree of social unease, presumably on both sides. They also, however, inserted the visitors into particular social and family worlds in which they became the clients of overlapping religious, political, and family networks.

Perhaps not surprisingly, patterns derived from educational visits and some of the same assumptions about tutelage informed the reception by these same networks of individuals who came to Britain to make more overtly political claims. Dyani Tshatshu, the mission-educated son of a minor Xhosa chief, and Khoekhoe convert Andries Stoffels travelled to London from the Cape Colony in 1835 in company with LMS envoys John Philip and James Read, Sr., as well as James Read, Jr., Read's son by his Khoekhoe wife. They all came to testify before the Select Committee on Aborigines, in the establishment of which Philip himself had played a major role. Tshatshu and Stoffels evidently had their own agendas in the wake of the brutal 1834–35 frontier war. Stoffels asked for the return to the Kat River settlement of the LMS missionaries (the Reads) who had been banned as dangerous agitators, but he also eloquently described the oppression of the Khoekhoe before the advent of at least putative equality under the law. Tshatshu requested the return of lands to his community.[42] At the same time, Stoffels and Tshatshu were presented as proof of the possibility of redeeming "savages," as they quite literally sang for their supper at evangelical dinner parties.[43] All the members of the party crisscrossed the country to be presented and to speak at a wide variety of frequently packed church and missionary society gatherings.[44]

I see such visits as a form of attempted alliance-building for the participants. Tshatshu, for example, consciously tried to build alliances with the "English nation," as he put it, over the heads of British settlers in southern Africa. As he informed a public meeting held at Exeter Hall in August 1836, at which he, Philip, and Stoffels were featured speakers: "When we signed the treaty with the British Government at the Buffalo River, a paper was read, which told us that we then became the children of England, and if one with yourselves, let us enjoy the privileges of Britons. Many Englishmen in the colonies are bad, but I will hardly believe that these Englishmen belong to you. You are a different race of men – they are South Africans – they are not Englishmen." He went on to remark that he had travelled in England and had met with "a friendly reception wherever I have gone; and I can say you are now my friends. I know my friends. Do not forget us."[45] Tshatshu spoke in Dutch (translated by the younger Read) and this speech was furthermore transcribed from his oral version. Yet despite the mediated nature of these words, the gist is clear. If Tshatshu did see his visit as a form of alliance-building, then he was following in the footsteps of his father, who many years before had entrusted his son to the missionaries at the LMS station of Bethelsdorp to raise. Read, Sr. had in fact acted *in loco parentis*, although it is significant that he had permitted Tshatshu to return temporarily to his own community to go through the circumcision ceremonies that Read recognized were essential to his later claim to the chieftaincy. The elder Tshatshu's placement of his son with the missionaries probably reflected the Xhosa practice of placing children out to be fostered in order to create alliances between groups. Some years later, when Dyani Tshatshu returned as a missionary to his father's lands with a British LMS agent, Williams, the elder Tshatshu averred that he would not try to change his son's customs. Williams wrote that "he said, 'he had not sent his son for an education and then to return and conform to them; but to teach him, his children, and people, how they were to act. He might build, cultivate, dress, &c &c as he pleased.'"[46] Ironically, despite (or perhaps because of) his close alliances of various kinds with British people, the younger Tshatshu became disaffected with the Cape administration on his return from Great Britain and fought against the colony in the 1846 war between the Xhosa and the British.[47] In Tshatshu's case, alliances and the knowledge they brought created not the expected deference but, seemingly, a greater ability to resist.

Both alliance-building and the politics of display were important in the multi-generational visits to Britain of members of what would become known as the Brant family, of Mohawk descent, from British North America. A member of this family was possibly one of the so-called "four Indian kings" who travelled to England during the reign of Queen Anne and received widespread publicity while masquerading to political ends as members of the Iroquois aristocracy.[48] One of his putative descendants (although the exact relationship is unclear), Koñwatsiātsiaiéñni, Mary or Molly Brant, became the sexual partner and "housekeeper" of the Indian agent William Johnson, bearing him nine children and acting as the director of his household and public hostess. Johnson was a critical go-between in alliances between the Iroquois and the British and exercised important patronage networks. Molly Brant's brother Thayendanega, or Joseph Brant, fought on the British side during the American revolution and was later granted lands in Upper Canada after the American conquest of Mohawk lands. Thayendanega visited Britain twice in 1775–76 and 1785–86. In the first case his visit was initially ancillary to that of Sir Guy Johnson and Daniel Claus, Sir William Johnson's sons-in-law, in quest of reinstated jobs, but it enabled Brant to discuss terms of alliance with the British in the aftermath of William Johnson's death and the outbreak of hostilities between the British and settlers in modern-day New York State. In the second instance Brant came on his own initiative to protest the post-war cession of Mohawk lands to the Americans without compensation, and to gain a more secure title to lands then recently granted to the Six Nations along the Grand River in modern-day Ontario. In particular, he wanted to be allowed to sell land.[49]

Thayendanega's own son Ahyouwaighs, or John Brant, went back to Britain in 1821 in a last-ditch effort to prevent the further erosion of lands in the face of the onslaught of white settlers. In conjunction with the Duke of Northumberland (whose father had supported the elder Brant on his own trip to Britain), Saxe Bannister, a later activist on Aboriginal issues, took up Ahyouwaighs' cause, and wrote "several papers" for the consideration of ministers. Brant was apparently promised redress by Colonial Secretary Lord Bathurst, but the Upper Canadian government thwarted metropolitan intentions.[50] Interestingly, Bannister also helped John Brant defend his father's reputation against what he saw as the calumnies of a British poet, Thomas Campbell. Campbell had written a poem called "Gertrude of Wyoming," in which he alluded to an American tradition that Brant had led a British-Iroquois massacre of American settlers and pro-American Oneidas at Wyoming. The younger Brant successfully confronted Campbell and demanded that he retract his negative portrayal.[51]

There is a great deal that could be, and has been, said about this fascinating and important family and the role of its members in the intricate fabric of Iroquois diplomacy. The point I want to make here is, more narrowly, that like many intermediaries, the Brants participated in family networks that shaded into high political networks. Such family politics required close attention to appearance and reputation. John Brant and his sister Elizabeth displayed their well-maintained Western-style house near modern-day Toronto, for example, in a manner that proclaimed their capacity to act as agents of "civilization" and thus to maintain alliances.[52] John Brant's defence of his father's reputation was an important part of these politics of display.

Although indigenous people were for the most part used by white interlocutors with their own agendas, they also took advantage of transnational networks to gain knowledge of other groups and to attempt to negotiate within tight limits with powerful settler states. A significant point about the 1835–36 Committee is that it represented an organized effort by Fowell Buxton and his allies to make systematic claims about settler-indigenous relations across the empire as a whole. For all the report's paternalism and its promotion of what might now be typed as assimilation, the report testified to systematic settler violence that it saw as a product both of moral choice and also (to a more limited extent) of the very conditions of colonialism. This was an agenda that helped prompt a variety of people to pass information on to the organized advocates of Aboriginal rights who emerged in Britain in the 1830s, or to seek redress through their auspices, despite the rapidly declining influence of such groups and their increasingly less radical outlooks.

It was against this background that the Aborigines Protection Society was formed in Britain in 1837 under the aegis of members of the Buxton-Gurney circle. It inherited many of the evangelical networks pioneered by missionary societies. The APS published annual reports from 1838 onwards that were circulated across the British empire. Local societies were rapidly founded in a number of British settlements. The society made expert use of print culture. By 1847, "The Aborigines' Friend" supplemented the society's annual reports. By the 1840s, in sum, the notion of an international network of Aboriginal people was being adroitly publicized and was available to literate converts in indigenous communities: the local meanings of this network need to be further interrogated.

There remain a number of future areas for investigation. Let me close with some possible items for a further research agenda. A first broad point is that there was more unease and indeed uncertainty among British policy-makers of various stripes in the 1820s and 1830s about the justification for British "ownership" of land in the white settler colonies than an account from the late nineteenth century backwards might suggest, and this at a time at which notions of liberal citizenship for whites were increasingly at odds with the imperial denial of indigenous "rights." The type of unease expressed in the 1836 and 1837 reports of the Select Committee on Aborigines about what was plainly portrayed as the British theft of Aboriginal lands was not, however, an expression of relatively uniform official opinion (in contrast to the way in which Henry Reynolds and the judges in the 1992 Mabo decision arguably read this report), but rather one side in a complicated, passionate, and shifting debate with transnational dimensions.[53] Judges tend to look for certainty in combing the past for precedents. This is not possible in this period. At the same time, the flip side of this observation is that the British sense of their right to rule was not firm across all sectors of society, or even all policy-makers. The decline of status relationships such as chattel slavery posed real conceptual problems for some, however much imperial realities over-rode the scruples of most. The implications of this for Aboriginal interlocutors deserve further investigation: what possibilities seemed, however momentarily, to open in the 1820s and 1830s?

A second critical point is that humanitarians in Britain itself, notably Thomas Fowell Buxton and his allies on the Select Committee on Aborigines, urged the Colonial Office to incorporate indigenous people across the British Empire as subjects in order to protect them from indiscriminate violence (in the context of the Australian colonies) and from de facto enslavement (drawing on the example of the Cape Colony and of debates about the aftermath of slavery). For some humanitarians, this represented a pulling back from previous outright opposition to colonial expansion. Be that as it may, this stance required the denial of Aboriginal peoples' right to govern themselves through their own law and customary behaviour when these conflicted with British laws. This dovetailed with the concern of certain administrators and judges, such as Judge Burton of New South Wales, to put British rule on a firmer footing at a time of some anxiety and debate over the British right to rule. British humanitarians recognized indigenous ownership of the land but not indigenous legal custom. In the Jack Congo Murrell case in New South Wales, and in subsequent cases, this distinction proved impossible to maintain, with important implications for the British consolidation of a degree of control over indigenous polities. Transimperial concerns created transimperial policies that had unexpected local ramifications. It might be worth thinking about how politics in one colony (such as Khoekhoe support for equality under the law) influenced politics in another (white humanitarian downplaying of Australian Aboriginal unease about the loss of legal sovereignty, for example).

Third, the (temporarily influential) British "friends of the Aborigine" urged in the 1830s that settler treaties with indigenous peoples not be recognized, in order to prevent fraud, and that the Crown oversee all treaties and dispose of all land in particular colonies, again on the basis of what were perceived to be transnational patterns. This suggested prohibition drew in particular on evangelical language about the sinfulness of (mostly lower-class) settlers, traders, and sailors across the British World, and the consequent need for close metropolitan oversight of settler-indigenous relationships; this drew in turn on evangelical conventional narratives of sin and redemption. Treaties were overruled in Port Philip and in New Zealand as a result. This placed indigenous groups in a direct relationship with the Crown that raised promises that would for the most part fail to be fulfilled as Crown land passed rapidly into settler hands. The Khoekhoe in the Cape Colony, for example, petitioned unsuccessfully in 1829 that all unallocated Crown land in the colony be returned to them. How aware were indigenous interlocutors of broad imperial patterns in debates about land ownership?

Fourth, the space opened up by transimperial networks was exploited by a few indigenous individuals who travelled to Britain to make political claims of various kinds. In order to make these claims, individuals such as Andries Stoffels, Dyani Tshatshu, or James Read, Jr. of the Cape, or Peter Jones, John Brant, John Sunday, or Catherine Sutton of British North America needed to present themselves as "civilized" in order to have access to the international resources of humanitarian networks, or indeed to speak on the British political stage. The promise of diplomatic contact doubtless increased the attraction of Christianity for indigenous converts across the Empire (despite the great complexity of reasons for conversion). Did it also increase the appeal of a transnational Aboriginal identity, as the wording of petitions in the Cape Colony suggests? This remains for me an important topic of investigation.

Finally, British-sponsored networks used a different understanding of the nature of land ownership than did many members of indigenous societies, in a variety of contexts. For example, Buxton had little knowledge of, say, Australian Aboriginal views of land as sacred space, defined by the stories told in particular places and the sacred uses to which land was put. The denial of non-Christian spirituality made a variety of land uses impenetrable. This is not to mystify indigenous land use of various kinds, but rather to observe that indigenous people who tried to use these networks needed to code switch to some extent, speaking a language about alienable freehold property that might not have reflected their own initial conceptions. For British interlocutors, land as private property had its own sacred commitments; it drew the uncivilized into the ranks of the civilized, for example, as the desire for accumulation created complex societies. These were very complicated narratives on all sides that are difficult to capture in discussions of land rights. At the same time, British humanitarian networks did ultimately draw on a view of land ownership as based in some sense on prior possession, which contrasted with classic settler defences of their own land ownership as based on use. This was an important transnational debate that would only grow in importance down to the present day.

{NOTES}

1 Among many examples, Alan Lester, "Historical Geographies of Southern Africa," introduction to *Journal of Southern African Studies* 29, no. 3 (January 2003): 595–614; Richard Grove, *Green Imperialism: Colonial Expansion, Tropical Island Edens and the Origins of Environmentalism, 1600–1860* (Cambridge: Cambridge University Press, 1996); Richard Drayton, *Nature's Government: Science, Imperial Britain, and the Improvement of the World* (New Haven: Yale University Press, 2000). This is, of course, one of the animating principles behind the "British World" series of conferences, of which the current volume is one product: Carl Bridge and Kent Fedorowich, eds., *The British World: Diaspora, Culture and Identity* (London: Frank Cass, 2003). From diverse theoretical perspectives, see also Paul Gilroy, *The Black Atlantic: Modernity and Double Consciousness* (Cambridge, MA: Harvard University Press, 1992); Antoinette Burton, "Who Needs the Nation? Interrogating 'British' History," in *Cultures of Empire*, ed. Catherine Hall (Manchester: Manchester

University Press, 2000), 137–53; Homi Bhabha, "DissemiNation: Time, Narrative and the Margins of the Modern Nation," in *The Location of Culture* (London: Routledge, 1994), 139–70.

2 Cf. the forthcoming special issue of *The Journal of Colonialism and Colonial History*, "Indigenous Women and the Colonial Encounter," December 2005, edited by Pamela Scully; Scully, "Sara Baartman's Atlantic World," North American Conference of British Studies Annual Metting, Philadelphia, October 29–31, 2004; Tolly Bradford, "Networkings: Perspectives on the History and Historiography of Nineteenth-century British missions in South Africa and Canada," African Studies Association/Canadian Association of African Studies Annual Meeting, New Orleans, November 11–14, 2004; Alan Lester, "Introduction: Historical Geographies of Southern Africa," *Journal of Southern African Studies* 29, no. 3 (2003): 595–613.

3 Elizabeth Elbourne, "The Sin of the Settler: The 1835–36 Select Committee on Aborigines and Debates over Virtue and Conquest in the Early Nineteenth-Century British White Settler Empire," *Journal of Colonialism and Colonial History* 4, no. 3 (Winter 2003), muse.jhu.edu/journals ; Alan Lester, "British Settler Discourse and the Circuits of Empire," *History Workshop Journal* 54, no. 1 (Autumn 2002): 24–48; Zoë Laidlaw, "'Aunt Anna's Report': The Buxton Women and the Aborigines Select Committee, 1835–37," *Journal of Imperial and Commonwealth History* 32, no. 2 (May 2004): 1–28.

4 Zoë Laidlaw's forthcoming book, based in part on her PhD dissertation from the University of Oxford, will be entitled *Colonial Connections 1815–1845: Patronage and the Information Revolution in Colonial Governance*.

5 I develop this argument further in Elbourne, "The Sin of the Settler."

6 Penny Russell (ed.). *This Errant Lady: Lady Jane Franklin's Overland Journey to Port Phillip and Sydney, 1839* (Canberra: National Library of Australia Press, 2003).

7 Compare Terence Ranger, "The Local and the Global in Southern African Religious History," in *Conversion to Christianity: Historical and Anthropological Perspectives on a Great Transformation*, ed. Robert W. Hefner (Berkeley: University of California Press, 1993), 65–98.

8 Compare Claire Smith, Heather Burke, and Graeme K. Ward, "Globalization and Indigenous Peoples: Threat or Empowerment?" in *Indigenous Cultures in an Interconnected World*, ed. Claire Smith and Graeme K. Ward (St. Leonards, NSW: Allen & Unwin, 2000), 1–24.

9 E.g., Carole Pateman, *The Sexual Contract* (Cambridge: Polity Press, 1988), 1–4 and *passim* argues that classic seventeenth- and eighteenth-century contract theorists in the liberal tradition overlooked the "sexual contract" that necessarily preceded any other form of contract making; in consequence, the stories of theorists about an imagined "social contract" that formed the basis for the creation of civil society took for granted the maleness of contract makers who alone were capable of being "individuals" in a legal and political sense. A similar analysis could be extended to the ways both the vestiges of contract theory and Scottish enlightenment theories of social change were applied to indigenous peoples in the eighteenth and nineteenth centuries, in my opinion. Elbourne, "Domesticity and Dispossession: British ideologies of 'home' and the primitive at work in the early nineteenth-century Cape", in Wendy Woodward, Patricia Hayes and Gary Minkley (eds.), *Deep Histories: Gender and Colonialism in Southern Africa* (Amsterdam: Rodopi, 2002), 27–54.

10 On transnational Protestantism, among many possibilities, W.R. Ward, *The Protestant Evangelical Awakening* (Cambridge: Cambridge University Press, 2002).

11 J.A. Kuester, J.G. Bonatz, H. Marsveld, D. Schwinn, and I.C. Kuehnel, "Diary of the Mission of the United Brethren, at Gnadenthal, Cape of Good Hope, 1809," in *Periodical Accounts Relating to the Missions of the Church of the United Brethren Established among the Heathen* 5 (1810): 28–29.

12 Basil le Cordeur and Christopher Saunders, eds., *The Kitchingman Papers: Missionary Letters and Journals, 1817 to 1848 from the Brenthurst Collection, Johannesburg* (Johannesburg: Brenthurst Press, 1976), 103n12; Richard Lovett, *History of the London Missionary Society* (London: Oxford University Press, 1899), 1:81–82.

13 James Read to William Ellis, Philipton, 3 July 1834, in *Kitchingman Papers*, 141.

14 Ibid., 144.

15 Lester, "British Settler Discourse."

16 James Read junior to John Philip, Bethelsdorp, 16 November 1835, in *Kitchingman Papers*, 159.

17 James Kitchingman's journal, 21 February 1828, in *Kitchingman Papers*, 102.

18 Zine Magubane, *Bringing the Empire Home: Race, Class and Gender in Britain and Colonial South Africa* (Chicago: University of Chicago Press, 2004), 129–52, raises the issue of the views of whiteness held by black South Africans.

19 Clifton Crais, *White Supremacy and Black Resistance in Pre-industrial South Africa: The Making of the Colonial Order in the Eastern Cape, 1770–1865* (Cambridge: Cambridge University Press, 1992). On Read's letter and its political aftermath, Elizabeth Elbourne, *Blood Ground: Colonialism, Missions and the Contest for Christianity in Britain and the Eastern Cape, 1799–1853* (Montreal: McGill-Queen's University Press, 2002), 158, 200–203.

20 Susan Newton-King, *Masters and Servants on the Cape Eastern Frontier 1760–1803* (Cambridge: Cambridge University Press, 1999); Elbourne, *Blood Ground*, 156–60 and *passim*.

21 Council for World Mission Archives (cwma), School of Oriental and African Studies, University of London, London Missionary Society papers, South Africa (lms-sa), incoming correspondence, 3/5/b, James Read to lms directors, 30 August 1808.

22 C. Bird to J.A. Truter, Cape Town, 27 November 1810, in *Records of the Cape Colony*, ed. G.M. Theal (London: William Clowes and Sons, 1905), 7:434–35.

23 Christopher Bird to Jacob Cuyler, Cape Town, 28 February 1811, in ibid., 496.

24 Enclosure no. 4, J. Knobel, record of examination of Willem Valtyn, 9 October 1810, in J. Cuyler to the Earl of Caledon, 25 October 1810, in ibid., 405.

25 Enclosure no. 6, J. Knobel, record of examination of Jantje Michels, 15 October 1810, in J. Cuyler to the Earl of Caledon, 25 October 1810 in ibid., 406–7.

26 Enclosure no. 2, J. Read, deposition, in J. Cuyler to Earl of Caledon, Uitenhage, 25 October 1810, in ibid., 412.

27 Enclosure no. 10, J. Knobel, report of the examination of Andries Pretorius and Willem Valtyn, 17 October 1810, in J. Cuyler to Earl of Caledon, Uitenhage, 25 October 1810, in ibid., 412.

28 Enclosure no. 2, J. Read, deposition, in J. Cuyler to Earl of Caledon, Uitenhage, 25 October 1810, in ibid., 412.

29 Hendrik Kraemer Institute, Oegstgeest, Netherlands: Diary of J.T. van der Kemp, "Dag Verhaal," 1805.

30 CWMA, LMS-Home 2/5/B, Wilberforce to Burder, 3 August 1811. I discuss both the British debate and Van der Kemp's discussions with Janssens further in Elbourne, *Blood Ground*, 198–209.

31 John Barrow, *An Account of Travels into the Interior of Southern Africa in the Years 1797 and 1798*, 2 vols., (London, 1801, 1804). In volume two, published after Britain had ceded the Cape Colony to the Batavian Republic after a short period of ownership, Barrows argues for the importance to Britain of re-incorporating the Cape Colony into the British empire: 3–4, 438–39 and *passim*. He also argues throughout that the inferior economic arrangements of the Dutch East India Company, the economic ease and the lack of education of the Dutch inhabitants in the eastern Cape region led to the extreme indolence of what he calls the peasantry, as well as their enormous cruelty to the indigenous Khoekhoe, which superior British economic measures would ameliorate, essentially by civilizing the Dutch: vol. 2, 95–106, 430–37. Barrow also suggests that the "sanguinary character of many of the African colonists" may have stemmed from their having been soldiers in German regiments serving abroad, characterized by cruel punishments: again, education and civilization were needed and could be provided by the British: vol. 2, 101.

32 Thomas Laqueur, "Bodies, Details and the Humanitarian Narrative," in *The New Cultural History*, ed. Lynn Hunt (Berkeley: University of California Press, 1989), 176–204; see also Alan Lester, "Obtaining the 'Due Observance of Justice': The Geographies of Colonial Humanitarianism," *Environment and Planning D: Society and Space* 20, no. 3 (2002): 278.

33 Robert Altick, *The Shows of London: A Panoramic History of Exhibitions, 1600–1862* (Cambridge: Bellknap Press, 1978) describes a number of such commercial exhibitions, including the well-known example of Sara Baartman, exhibited in London under the name the "Hottentot Venus" in 1810–11.

34 Campbell's advocacy of a self-directing African church and the spearheading of conversion attempts by Africans (as opposed to long-term reliance on white missionaries) emerges clearly from his correspondence with the LMS directorship during his first voyage of inspection to southern Africa in 1812, during which the creation of an African ministry and the self-limiting nature of white missionary activity were topics of heated debate. Elbourne, *Blood Ground*, 225–26; CWMA, LMS-SA, 5/2/C, John Campbell to W. Tracey, 7 April 1813.

35 Anon., "Preface," in John Campbell, *African Light Thrown on a Selection of Scripture Texts. Second Edition with a Biographical Sketch of the Author* (Edinburgh: John Johnstone, 1842), 27.

36 John Campbell, *Hottentot Children; with a Particular Account of Paul Dikkop, the son of a Hottentot Chief, who died in England, September 14, 1824* (London, n.d.), 6.

37 Ibid., 14.

38 Campbell reproduces this single 1823 letter from Paul to himself in ibid., 43.

39 Friends' House Library, London, Gurney Papers, temporary ms 434, Anna Gurney to Hudson Gurney, 9 August 1849.

40 Ibid., 2/16, Anna Gurney to Hudson Gurney, 20 April 1850.

41 Ibid., 3/88, Anna Gurney [née Backhouse] to J.J. Gurney, Earlham, 17 September 1838.

42 "Special General meeting of the London Missionary Society," in the *Evangelical Magazine and Missionary Chronical,* September 1836:422; Evidence of John Tshatshu, British Parliamentary papers, *Report from the Select Committee on Aborigines (British Settlements) with the minutes of evidence, appendix and index: Imperial Blue Book,* 538 of 1836.

43 Elbourne, *Blood Ground,* 288.

44 James Read, Senior, to James Kitchingman, 2 August 1836 and 4 September 1836, in *The Kitchingman Papers,* 164–70.

45 *Evangelical Magazine and Missionary Chronicle,* n.s., 14 (September 1836): 422.

46 *Missions in Caffraria: From their Commencement to the Present Time* (Dublin: Religious Tract and Book Society for Ireland, 1833), 89–90.

47 Le Cordeur and Saunders, eds., *Kitchingman Papers,* 53, no.3, citing CWMA, LMS-SA 16/3/A, Brownlee to Ellis, 14 February 1839.

48 Eric Hinderaker, "The 'Four Indian Kings' and the Imaginative Construction of the First British Empire," *William and Mary Quarterly,* 3rd series, 20 3, no. 56 (1996): 487–526; Daniel Richter, *The Ordeal of the Longhouse* (Chapel Hill: University of North Carolina Press, 1992), 227–29.

49 John S. Hagopian, "Joseph Brant vs. Peter Russell: A Re-examination of the Six Nations' Land Transactions in the Grand River Valley," *Histoire Sociale* 30, no. 60 (1997): 300–33; William L. Stone, *Life of Joseph Brant – Thayendanegea,* 2 vols. (Buffalo: Phinney, 1838); Isabel Kelsay, *Joseph Brant, 1743–1807: Man of Two Worlds* (Syracuse, NY: Syracuse University Press, 1986), 157–75, 379–94.

50 Stone, *Life of Jospeh Brant,* 2: 527–29; Saxe Bannister, *Remarks on the Indians of North America in a Letter to an Edinburgh Reviewer* (London: T. & G. Underwood, 1822).

51 Stone, *Life of Joseph Brant,* 2:529.

52 Stone, *Life of Joseph Brant,* 2:523–25, citing James Buchanan, *Sketches of the History, Manners and Customs of the North American Indians* (London: Black, Young and Young, 1824). I explore the politics of family and gender among the Brant family more fully in a paper forthcoming in the *Journal of Colonialism and Colonial History,* special issue on "Indigenous Women and the Colonial Encounter," December 2005.

53 Henry Reynolds, *The Law of the Land* (Ringwood, Victoria: Penguin, 1987); *Mabo and others v. Queensland,* 175 CLR 1 F.C. (1992). On British unease over the doctrine of *terra nullius;* see also Stuart Banner, "Why *Terra Nullius?* Anthropology and Property Law in Early Australia," *Law and History Review* 23, no. 1 (Spring 2005): 95-132.

CHAPTER 4

LOYALTY AND REBELLION
IN COLONIAL POLITICS:

THE CAMPAIGN AGAINST
CONVICT TRANSPORTATION IN AUSTRALIA [1]

Paul Pickering

ON MONDAY EVENING, 25 August 1851, the streets of Hobart Town
in Tasmania were the scene of an extraordinary episode in the political
history of the young colony. Earlier in the year, what had been regarded
as the first political assembly in Tasmania's history had taken place,
but this late winter evening saw what was claimed to be the first public
meeting of those described as "native-born Tasmanians." According to
their own account, the organizers described the purpose of the meeting
as twofold: to testify to their loyalty to the Queen and, at the same time,
to demonstrate their "repugnance" at the system of convict transportation. In this enterprise they had "invited the co-operation of their fellow
citizens." Seven o'clock was the hour appointed for "gathering" in front
of the Treasury Building at the corner of Murray and Macquarie Streets
in central Hobart. "Shortly before that hour," reported the *Colonial
Times*, "the street began to fill with eager crowds of people, who were
marshalled in order by the committee." At a few minutes after seven the
Trades' Union marched down Macquarie Street, preceded by a musical
band. As they arrived at the Treasury Building, three cheers were given
"for Her Majesty" while the band struck up "God Save the Queen."
Before the procession moved off, a member of the organizing committee,
Edward Kemp, addressed the crowd on the need for order. At the head
of the parade were the "native-born" – women as well as men – followed
by members of the Trades' Union and "a large number of respectable
citizens." Four "beautiful" banners belonging to the local branch of an
organization called the Australasian League Against Transportation were
carried by the Tasmanians at the front and, the *Colonial Times* report

continued, "throughout the line torches were borne, throwing a vivid light along the whole procession. The effect was very striking."[2]

The retinue proceeded along Macquarie Street past Government House, where, the report noted, a "burst of groans" showed "the popular feeling." Proceeding up Murray Street through the commercial hub of the city, three groans erupted at a group of official buildings that included the police office, the gaol, and the colonial secretary's office,[3] followed by three cheers at the premises of Richard Cleburne, a merchant and Hobart city commissioner (and later a member of the Tasmanian parliament) who was a prominent opponent of convict transportation. The procession marched along Liverpool Street – pausing for three groans at the Emporium, the premises of William Purkiss, a draper and pro-transportationist – and then Hartington Street, Warwick Street, and Lansdowne Crescent, halting intermittently to cheer or groan. Having passed beyond the town, the retinue marched into the foothills that overlooked it. "Ascending to the summit," commented the *Hobart Town Courier*, "was a work of considerable difficulty – the path was rough and rugged; but success crowned the efforts of the persevering." At the top a large pile of wooden faggots over twenty feet high had been built and saturated with pitch. "The heavens bore a dark aspect," continued the report, "and the greatest impatience was manifested" by the crowd.[4] According to the *Colonial Times*, the delay was "due to the absence of the most important personage of the occasion – his Lordship Earl Grey," the British secretary of state for colonial affairs.

Why were the citizens of Hobart impatient to incinerate the colonial secretary in effigy in the hills overlooking their town? The short answer is for his role in promoting the reintroduction of convict transportation to the Australian colonies. Shortly after taking office as part of Lord John Russell's Whig administration in 1847, Earl Grey had, despite statements made while in opposition, indicated that he was considering a resumption of transportation to mainland Australia. Transportation to the mainland had been ended in 1840 (by Russell himself), but those holding conditional pardons were still being sent to the Port Phillip district and a steady flow of convicts continued to arrive in Van Diemen's Land at the time that Grey took office. Grey's determination to recommence transportation proper drew an angry response across the Antipodes, leading to the formation of the Australasian League Against Transportation.[5] John West, one of the leaders of the campaign, was not exaggerating when he argued in 1852 that convict transportation was "the most important colonial agitation of modern times."[6]

Before too long, Grey's effigy arrived and was "duly installed upon a tar barrel on top of the pile." "His Lordship was dressed," the report in the *Colonial Times* continued with meticulous detail, "in the highest style of fashion: with a star on his left breast" and "holding a bunch of dispatches in his right hand." An effigy of Sir William Denison, the governor of Tasmania, was also "thrown up by the crowd" and "reclined at the foot of his Lordship." Denison was wearing the uniform of an engineer – which he was – but here the gesture was an unmistakable sneer due to the lesser status of engineers within British military hierarchy. Once the effigies were in position, three cheers were "unanimously" given for Her Majesty, and while the band played "God Save the Queen," the bonfire was lit. According to the report in the *Colonial Times*, the pile burst into flame, "casting a radiance far around the neighbouring hills and over the town." "The glare of the fire," continued the report, "revealed the vast multitude which covered the hill," including "a large number of influential citizens." The reporter concluded that there "must have been three and four thousand persons present," which was a sizeable minority of the town's total population of about twenty-four thousand at this time. The reporter for the *Hobart Town Courier* did not offer an estimate of the size of the crowd: it was a "countless multitude."[7]

As the ritual continued, three cheers were given for the Australasian League and for its founder, the Reverend John West, and its president, Charles Cowper; three for the "neighbouring colonies," the "native youths," and the "native girls and their parents," as well as three for "the colony," "the working classes," and the "Trades' Union." Three groans were given for transportation before the cheering resumed: three cheers to "free labour"; the League Secretary, Gilbert Wright; Mr. Kemp, "the father of the people"; and Mr. Gregson as well as to the anti-transportation candidates at the forthcoming election, the first under a system of partial self-government. Once this "ceremony," as it was called, was complete, the "mass, preceded by the band and banners, moved down the hill, and reformed at the top of Upper-Goulburn Street [and] marched back through the town to Victoria Street, where they were again addressed by Mr. Kemp, who congratulated them upon the order and regularity of their proceedings, and counselled them to depart to their homes in peace." Before the crowd took his advice and dispersed, there was time for another rendition of "God Save the Queen" and three more cheers for Her Majesty. In this way, the episode ended in the way that it had begun.[8]

Following E.P. Thompson's long-standing dictum – that history is made up of episodes that we must seek to "get inside" if we are to "get inside history at all"[9] – the essay that follows will explore the cultural infrastructure of the Hobart "ceremony." It will attempt to do more than this. By "hopping back and forth, between the whole conceived through the parts that actualise it and the parts conceived through the whole that motivates them,"[10] the aim is also to shed some of the light from the bonfire on the wider campaign against "convictism" and on the development of popular politics on the periphery of the British World.

The first historian of the campaign, John West, himself an active participant in it, suggested that opposition to the transportation of convicts to the Australian colonies "opened up a new world of political thought."[11] For the student of demotic politics in the British World, however, the cultural infrastructure of the Hobart episode had many familiar elements – from the use of emblematic banners and flags to the orderly parade along a symbolically significant route, providing ample opportunities for ritualized expressions of approbation and disapprobation; from the evocative use of torch-light, an unmistakable reminder of the famous Chartist parades that had caused a frisson of alarm in Britain during 1839, to the apogee of plebeian ritual, the burning of effigies.

The "ceremony" as a whole was an elaborate piece of counter-theatre of the type that had become an established feature of public life during the long eighteenth century in Britain.[12] Earlier in the day, Sir William Denison had been given an official welcome back to Hobart, "the seat of Government," following a lengthy tour of the north of the island ("hunting and electioneering," according to his opponents). With understandable exaggeration, a favourable newspaper described the event as "for ever worthy of association with the proudest epochs of Tasmanian history."[13] Friend and foe agreed that the streets of the town had been thronged with spectators – men, women, and children – who watched the lieutenant governor ride through a series of triumphal arches (inscribed with "V.R. in variegated letters") that had been specially erected for the occasion, and followed by an ever-increasing train of riders and carriages. Near the Guard House in Elizabeth Street, the retinue passed beneath a "Triumphal Arch." Over twenty feet high and supported by the jaws of a whale, bales of wool, and sheaves of wheat (the staples of the Australian economy), the arch was topped with the Royal Standard and the word "Welcome." By the time Denison had reached Government House, near to where the counter-demonstration would commence later that day, the crowd had swelled into a "vast concourse" of people. According to the *Hobart Town Advertiser*, their "enthusiasm was extreme"; Denison received an "ovation so complete in all its details" from a crowd that comprised "true British subjects."[14] Not surprisingly, Denison recorded the warmth of his reception during the day but made no mention of the warmth of the fire that incinerated his effigy that night.[15]

The wider campaign against the policy that Denison was promoting on behalf of the British government was also based on explicitly British models. For Henry Parkes, a former Chartist and future premier of New South Wales, the struggle to "stop the black tide of convictism from rolling on to the shores of Australia" was not unlike that which "put an end to the scarcely bleaker system of Negro slavery."[16] Parkes also felt that the Political Unions formed during the struggle for the Reform Act of 1832 provided a useful "example" for colonial radicals.[17] It is not difficult to understand why: sitting alongside Parkes at meetings of the New South Wales Constitutional Association (an organization that in 1849 put all other business aside to concentrate on the struggle against convictism[18]) and the anti-transportation association itself were veterans of the Political Unions such as Richard Hipkiss and Isaac Aaron.[19] Like Parkes himself, these men provided a flesh-and-blood link to British reform movements.

Other commentators saw a template for political action in the campaign for Catholic Emancipation. John Dunmore Lang, the irascible Presbyterian minister who was well known to radical audiences in Britain and Australia as an advocate of immigration, democratic reform, and Australian independence, used the "language of O'Connell" to urge his listeners to organize against the curse of transportation. Lang also showed that he appreciated the value of experience in political organization when he quoted from Byron's *The Giaour*:

> Freedom's battle once begun,
> Bequeathed from bleeding sire to son,
> Though baffled oft, is ever won.[20]

Edward Hawksley, the editor of Sydney's only Chartist newspaper, also found much to emulate in O'Connell's campaign, even though the Liberator might not have agreed with the assessment. "It may be said that Catholic Emancipation was obtained simply by a demonstration of moral force; but this we deny," Hawksley wrote. "O'Connell himself, said to the British Government, if you do not give us emancipation we will take it."[21] A contributor to the British radical press, Hawksley was undoubtedly familiar with the catch-cry of early Chartism – "Peaceably if we may, forcibly if we must"[22] – and would have liked to see a similar policy adopted in New South Wales.

Pre-eminently, however, the Australasian League Against Transportation was modelled on the Anti-Corn Law League, an organization that, it was widely held, had forced the Britain's landed aristocracy to repeal the corn laws that buttressed their social and economic power. As Charles Gavan Duffy, a future premier of Victoria, noted, the League had defeated "the aristocracy of England in their fiercest contest."[23] "It must be remembered, and it cannot be too often repeated," editorialized Hawskley, "that the united mass of the Corn Law League overthrew the most powerful and influential interest in England – that of the wealthy and titled agriculturalists, and that what can be done in England can be done here."[24] The influence of the Anti-Corn Law League on colonial politics has been largely overlooked by historians.[25] It is no accident that the nascent campaign against convict transportation at the other end of the British World called itself a League. As early as 1843, George Wilson, the president of the Anti-Corn Law League, had recognized that the League's political machinery had broken new ground. "They were anxious that when the League should have been dissolved they should leave a record of their labours," he told an audience at London's Drury Lane Theatre, a record that would guide and instruct "others in that path of usefulness which they had opened up."[26] Here was a spectre to frighten even the most hardened Tory back-bencher. "If Ministers…yield to the clamour of the League," George Finch, the Tory member for Rutland, had warned the House of Commons on the eve of the League victory in 1846, "they would have plenty of other leagues."[27]

It is doubtful that Finch had the Australian colonies in mind, but his prophecy was soon fulfilled there. Formed in 1851 and bringing together New South Wales, Victoria, Tasmania, and South Australia, as well as New Zealand, the Australasian League Against Transportation was Australia's first national political movement. The initial impetus for a united movement had come from Tasmania. As the delegates departed from Launceston for an inaugural national conference in January 1851 to the strains of "Rule Britannia" and with three cheers for Queen Victoria ringing in their ears, one spectator noted that within a "few weeks the Australasian League will be a great fact."[28] The deliberate appropriation of *The Times*'s famous description of the Anti-Corn Law League as "a great fact" of British public life is significant as evidence of a common assumption among colonial radicals.[29] "Let the same boldness of purpose, the same undying energy, the same earnest and steady perseverance, characterise our League," editorialized Henry Parkes in May, "as distinguished…the Corn Law Repealers."[30] By June the promise had been fulfilled: the Australasian League had become a "great fact," according to the *Colonial Times and Tasmanian*.[31] Again the corporeal links to the Anti-Corn Law League were important. In New South Wales, reformers could draw on the experience of Richard Windeyer, who had been a branch secretary in the League; Richard Hipkiss had been, by his own estimation, a personal associate of Joseph Parkes, one of the League's leading political strategists; and the peripatetic Dunmore Lang was in personal communication with numerous British radicals, including the iconic leaders of the League, Richard Cobden and John Bright.[32] Later when Henry Parkes (no relation to Joseph) visited England, he enjoyed the company of Abraham Paulton, a prominent League official and publicist, and Cobden himself.[33]

With hindsight, one commentator described the Australasian League as "perfect in organisation," but it is important to remember that it had a good model in the Anti-Corn Law League's "engine of political warfare."[34] "Our League" (to borrow Parkes's words) adopted an almost identical set of strategies to its eponymous forerunner. Indeed, the Australasian League's campaign was very much a colonial version of the "pressure from without" that the Anti-Corn Law League had developed in both form and scale during the previous decade. Take, for example, the use of petitioning. The earlier League regarded petitioning as the "constitutional artillery of public opinion,"[35] and between 1839 and 1843 it was the most persistent petitioner of the House of Commons. Over the five sessions there were 16,351 petitions for repeal tabled in the House (containing an average total of 1,153,690 signatures every session).[36] For the League, as for the Chartists, petitioning required considerable organizational effort and produced significant dividends, both in mobilizing public opinion and in promoting the spread of the organization. Signature collectors scoured the four corners of Britain, even penetrating dark corners of the nation that were "almost beyond the reach of bell, book or candle."[37] There were many dark corners in colonial Australia also. As West recalled, collecting signatures against transportation "in a scattered population was attended with much difficulty and expense."[38] Despite the difficulties, the results speak for themselves. Between 1851 and 1853 the House of Commons received over fifty petitions containing nearly twenty thousand signatures from New South Wales and Tasmania.[39] As the Hobart "ceremony" made clear, the campaign was not only aimed at convincing the government, but was also concerned with enlisting the sympathy of the monarch (another feature shared with the earlier League). Taking memorials sent directly to Queen Victoria into account, it was estimated that by April 1852 petitions containing approximately thirty-six thousand signatures had been sent to Britain.[40]

As with the Anti-Corn Law League (and the Chartists), petitioning against transportation gave women an opportunity for political activism and expression that was often denied to them in other circumstances. In Sydney, Parkes told a crowd in April 1851, a petition against transportation had been signed by no less than twelve thousand "daughters, wives and mothers of that city." Rising to his task, Parkes continued by ascribing a role to women not only as signatories but also as advocates: "He trusted that a time would soon arrive when no man would dare to raise his voice to advocate transportation in the presence of a daughter of Australia." The similarity to the pivotal role played by the "petticoat politicians" of the Manchester League can hardly have escaped attention.[41] It was no accident that the involvement of women was emphasized in the reports of the Hobart "ceremony."

Other strategies employed by the Australasian League provide further evidence of the pervasive influence of the Anti-Corn Law League on oppositional politics in the Australian colonies. The Anti-Corn Law League was a self-consciously national movement, but its heartland was in the English provinces, in the industrialized cities and townships of Lancashire, Cheshire, and Yorkshire, with Manchester at the apex.[42] Provincial radicals knew well that sooner or later they would have to take their case to the metropolis, which they did by holding large national conferences on parliament's doorstep and by undertaking countless delegations. One London Leaguer even found the arrival of "the main body of Goths and Vandals" from Manchester a daunting prospect.[43] The need to make the case in London was understood in the colonies too, and in this sense it is important to regard their activities as merely an extended form of provincial radicalism. To the metropolitan governing class, there was probably very little difference between "Goths and Vandals" from Lancashire and from Launceston.

The first act of the newly formed national League had been to empower London delegates to (in West's words) "agitate the colonial cause beneath the walls of parliament...to weary ministers into justice – to conquer their obstinacy by a perpetual coming."[44] Richard Cobden could not have put it better. The delegates also assiduously cultivated the metropolitan press.[45] The delegation was headed by John King, the former town clerk of Melbourne, and their mission was aided by the pen of Robert Lowe, a former member of the New South Wales parliament, who had recently begun to write for *The Times* on colonial affairs.[46] The League also sought to recruit allies among the ranks of British radicalism; they even canvassed the possibility of enlisting the support of the former Chartist and Complete Suffragist, Henry Vincent, and of Richard Cobden himself.[47]

Admittedly, expectations were low. "The British public have little political affinity to us, we are too distant for our grievances and struggles to do more than arouse in them a secondary interest," lamented Parkes in May 1851; the delegates had met with "indifference," reported the *Colonial Times* four months later.[48] They were not, however, without some successes; several MPs took up the cause, presenting petitions and bringing on a parliamentary debate in July 1851; and some British businessmen (the backbone of the Anti-Corn Law League) responded to calls for assistance.[49] The discovery of gold in eastern Australia dramatically raised the level of interest in the colonies, and King was well placed to take advantage of this. Soon articles on the evils of transportation appeared in the liberal and radical press from the *British Banner* and the *Nonconformist*, to *Reynolds' News* and the *Glasgow Sentinel*.[50] So convinced was the Whiggish *Morning Chronicle* by the agitation that it reported that a petition bearing fifty thousand signatures was on its way.[51] The report went on to note that a motion against transportation had been counted out in the House of Commons; what it did not make clear was that this was a standard tactic – known as "burking" – that was often employed by an incumbent government (regardless of its stripe) to silence debate in parliament. The League itself had often suffered this fate; it was a sign not of failure but of success. By mid-1852 even its critics accepted that the Australasian League had "opened the eyes of many staunch men in England."[52]

A campaign of this magnitude was expensive. Here too the Australasian League emulated the Anti-Corn Law League's efforts at fundraising. In 1842–43, for example, the Manchester League had raised (and spent) a £50,000 "fund"; in each of 1844 and 1845, a "fund" of £100,000 was collected and expended, and late in 1845, the League commenced a £250,000 "fund," of which only part had been collected when the Corn Laws were repealed.[53] The Australasian League adopted a more modest target, £20,000, but used the same language to describe it: a "fund."[54] Soon contributions began to come in: by June 1851, £7,000 had been subscribed in Melbourne; by August the combined total had reached £15,000.[55] Membership (with voting rights) was open to all who subscribed one shilling but, like the earlier League, in practice the leadership of the movement was controlled by the large subscribers – those dubbed the "hundred guinea patriots."[56] This caused resentment, as it had done in the ranks of the Manchester League. "We hope every member of our community will join the League," editorialized Hawksley, "but we are almost afraid that if the Committee or the Council do not take some immediate steps in showing that the poor labourer can become a member as well as the rich man, it will not take so wide a range as it otherwise would."[57] Despite the efforts to represent itself as the voice of the nation, Cobden did not shy away from describing the League as a "middle class set of agitators."[58] The Australasian League – particularly in Sydney – was dominated by professionals, "merchants and business men" (the characterization is Parkes's) who, in many respects, were engaged in a colonial version of the nineteenth-century bourgeois revolution against a lingering *ancien régime* represented in New South Wales and Van Diemen's Land by the squatters who depended on convict labour to support their social and political power. "The only aristocracy of Australia," sneered Parkes, "are the advocates of transportation." The events of 1851 in New South Wales, Victoria, and Tasmania were not the same as those of 1848 in Europe, but it is easy to imagine how they might have seemed to be. At the height of the campaign, Parkes reprinted an article from the *Economist*, the journal of the Manchester School that had been established with funds from Cobden's Anti-Corn Law League, which identified the decline of aristocratic power as the most significant development of the nineteenth century.[59]

If the strategies and cultural forms of the campaign are recognizable even across what has been called the "tyranny of distance," what about the ideas? Ostensibly it is tempting to highlight the participation of native-born Tasmanians in the Hobart "ceremony" as evidence of a profound shift in early colonial politics, the humble beginning of the path to independence. "It is impossible," recalled Parkes in 1892, "to overvalue the importance of that first popular movement.... A public spirit was awakened never more to be lulled to rest."[60] The famous Southern Cross flag was first flown, not over the palisades of the Eureka Stockade on the Victorian Gold fields in 1854, but at meetings of the League in 1851. When a ship flying the flag sailed into San Francisco harbour in 1852, it left no doubt to American eyes that the Australasian colonies "will before long be a free and independent confederacy like our own."[61]

Moreover, there were few commentators in either Britain or in the colonies who believed that dispute was limited to a simple issue of crime and punishment. Occurring at the same time as the granting of limited self-government and the separation of Victoria from New South Wales, and against a backdrop of the discovery of gold in southeastern Australia, the campaign against "convictism" came at a crucial moment in Australia's national development. Opposition to convict transportation became a metaphor for the demand of greater local independence and redefined the relationship of the Australian colonies to Britain. In *The Times* Robert Lowe insisted that the League had "in it the germ of a development which, under the fostering care of Lord Grey, will probably grow up into a regularly organised confederacy, never to be dissolved until the last right has been extracted from the reluctant hands of the Colonial Office."[62] The theme was taken up by Gilbert Wright, the secretary of the League, who had been cheered in Hobart. "When they had subdued the old dragon Transportation," he told a massive public meeting in Sydney, "they would be in a position to merit, as well as accomplish, if not the concession, the conquest of all their constitutional rights and liberties."[63] For a radical reformer such as Hawksley, the opportunity could be easily squandered. "It is not a thing to our liking to say merely what we will *not* have," he argued. Posing the question, "Should the League continue as a mere Negation?," Hawksley offered a resounding no: "The colonies have but one interest.... Let their one banner unfold to every eye its one description – FREEDOM, INDEPENDENCE, PROSPERITY."[64]

Hawksley was a republican, a follower of Dunmore Lang, who had recently been elected as the member for Sydney in the New South Wales parliament at the top of the poll. Lang had subsequently made several speeches, both inside the House and out, advocating an Australian republic. He would consolidate his views in *Freedom and Independence for the Golden Lands of Australia*, a foundational republican text published later in 1852, and would found another "League" to promote the republic early in 1853. Lang's words, like those of Hawksley and others who advocated an Australian republic at the height of the campaign against transportation, constitute a beacon – brighter than the Hobart bonfire – that has been followed by many historians. In his recent history of Australian democracy, John Hirst, for example, recognizes the almost universal desire to replicate the institutions of the mother country, but he insists that Australian democrats "took their democratic principles seriously, which meant they were in principle republicans. Democracy and republicanism were then closely connected. If you believed that political rights should be equally shared you could not agree that one person should be monarch by right of birth.... A British constitution simply could not be thoroughly democratic."[65] Similarly, John Gascoigne has recently written that "those advocating a more democratic model of society were driven to concepts such as 'the rights of man' – concepts replete with overtones of Enlightenment theory." "It was a programme," he argues, that "went beyond the traditional and often rather misty appeal to historic rights."[66]

In this essay, however, I want to suggest that the Hobart episode, and the wider campaign of which it was part, marked a formative Australian manifestation of a colonial form of popular constitutionalism, a set of ideas that set the Australian colonies on a path not to independence in the form of republican separatism, but to a "comfortable" constitutional monarchism that gained an almost hegemonic dominance over the mind of the populace.[67] A number of recent historians have drawn attention to the central place of a popular interpretation of the British Constitution in nineteenth-century political discourse in Britain,[68] an insight that needs to be extended throughout the British World. Here I will argue that the "rather misty appeal to historic rights" has too often been discounted: "popular constitutionalism" provided a uniquely British beginning for Australia's democratic experiment.

The terms of the debate are worthy of careful attention. The language of the campaign was, with few exceptions, couched in terms of popular constitutionalism. What exactly is meant by this? Students of British radicalism will be familiar with the generous parameters of the libertarian interpretation of the rights of the free-born Briton. There were few Chartists, for example, who could not find ample justification for their program (with the possible exception of the secret ballot) under the aegis of the venerable Constitution, as well as the right to bear arms, the right of free speech, the right to trial by jury, protection from arbitrary arrest, and so on, but two points are particularly germane to the colonial situation.

First was the assertion that British rights were, to quote the renowned Irish political orator, John Curran, "consummate with and inseparable from British soil...no matter under what Sun."[69] In other words, a Briton's rights travelled with them even to the end of the earth. The "natives of Australia," declared the League in April 1851, "are entitled to the rights and privileges of British subjects." More particularly, native-born Australians claimed the right of self-government as a fundamental British freedom. The first Australian-born man to represent Sydney in the New

South Wales parliament, a radical merchant named Robert Campbell, put the case succinctly from the chair at a massive demonstration against transportation in Sydney in 1849: "Responsible government was what every Briton expected to have on leaving his native shore," Campbell stated, "and it was with feelings of pride that he attended that meeting to claim for his native land the right of responsible government.... They had assembled on that day to ask for their rights as Britons." Lang was also adept at speaking the language of popular constitutionalism. Speaking after Campbell at a later meeting, Lang moved the first resolution calling for self-government, which he defined as "ministers chosen from, and responsible to, the colonists themselves, in accordance with the principles of the British Constitution."[70] It was thus no accident that the effigy of Grey in Hobart held a bundle of dispatches – the point is that it was not only the content of Grey's orders that was at issue: the issuing of dispatches itself was condemned. This was arbitrary government; Grey was "the dictator of Downing Street," "a treacherous Whig." How easily these words came to the lips of British radicals.

Notwithstanding the stridency of these views, the second element of popular constitutionalism was its loyalty. In her important study of the forging of British identity up to 1837, Linda Colley has put loyalty back on the agenda of British history.[71] Loyalty was a powerful force in the colonies also. The colonial authorities and their supporters were quick to point the finger of disloyalty. Those who opposed government policy, charged the *Hobart Town Advertiser*, were an "insignificant minority" committed to supplanting "the institutions dear to the hearts of all true British subjects" with a heinous mixture of "demoralising and levelling socialism" and "mob-law of American origin." Those who had engaged in "the midnight orgies of last Monday" when "the effigy of the Queen's representative" had been incinerated, "accompanied by expressions of fiendish delight," the editor continued, had "evinced the depravity of their natures, and the brutality of their feelings."[72] The leading politician in New South Wales, William Charles Wentworth, used his platform appearances to repudiate what he saw as a pernicious trinity of "Socialism, Chartism [and] Republicanism" that had emerged during the campaign against transportation.[73] Moreover, the governors of New South Wales and Tasmania (Sir Charles Fitzroy and the hapless Denison) had been quick to characterize the opposition to Grey's policy as the work of "designing and disaffected persons" (Fitzroy's words) "whose object under the pretext of agitating the question of transportation, is to instil sentiments of disloyalty into the minds of the lower orders of the country, and to render them discontented with the government of the mother country."[74]

Although the Leaguers angrily repudiated accusations of disloyalty when the contents of Fitzroy's dispatch became public, the campaign against transportation did give rise to expressions of qualified allegiance similar to those that historians of Ireland have referred to as "conditional loyalty."[75] "The affection and allegiance of these colonies," West told a meeting in Sydney, "could only be retained by England on the principle of reciprocal benefits." In the Legislative Council, John Lamb, a former British naval officer and a prominent member of the Australasian League, was even clearer than West. He "did not believe that there was any class in this community that was anxious for separation," he told the House. "But the manner in which their petitions and memorials had been treated by the Colonial Minister was sufficient to alienate the affection of any people in the world." Although "he would yield to no man in point of loyalty," Lamb continued, if "the flag which now waved over them was only the emblem of misrule and oppression, it would soon be removed." Parkes agreed. "We are no advocates for violence, for steel and gunpowder, and such like things," he insisted, but "if it be wrong to breach the peace of a community, it must be wrong to excite, by unjust conflict, such disorder." They were confronted with nothing less than "Official Provocation."[76]

A couple of points must be made. First, liberals and radicals believed that the aegis of popular constitutionalism sanctioned their right to rebel against tyranny. Although Parkes recognized that he had skated close to the edge of sedition, he denied that he had engaged in either "wanton defiance" or "anti-British" rhetoric. On the contrary: "If they were loyal to their British privileges they would assert…that the continuance of convictism was incompatible with the possession of those privileges."[77] Expounding the right to loyal dissent also had the added advantage of bringing the American revolution within the compass of the British Constitution. For many radical commentators in the Australian colonies, what the Americans had done was assert their rights as Britons. "It was this kind of treatment from Downing Street," suggested Lamb, "which first alienated the affections of the American colonies, and eventually drove them to rebellion." Others, including Parkes and Lang, were also struck by the "remarkable analogy" to the United States of America.[78]

Second, it is crucial to remember that the language of conditional loyalty was not peculiar to colonial radicals. The basis of the "mass platform" that characterized demotic politics in Britain after 1830 was what the *Manchester Examiner* (edited by Abraham Paulton) would later call a "salutary terrorism...that convinces spiritual and temporal Lords that concession is much more safe and more salutary than repression."[79] The Chartists were undoubtedly the best known exponents of this strategy, but it was by no means exclusive to them. Richard Cobden believed that the Anti-Corn Law League needed to build a mass movement to "frighten the aristocracy"; the leading parliamentary spokesman for repeal, C. P. Villiers, also believed that "the *brickbat argument* is the only one that our nobles heed."[80]

Nevertheless, for Chartists, Corn Law repealers, and anti-transportationists alike, whether in Manchester or Melbourne, the object of their ire was the government, not the Crown. Indeed the most striking feature of the debate about transportation is not the first resonances of separatism or republicanism, but the attachment to monarchy that it reveals. Inevitably there was a tinge of ambiguity. The memorial to Queen Victoria that was collected in 1851, for example, called on her to end transportation and to "censure" Earl Grey "in order to continue the happy connexion of these Colonies with Great Britain, and to secure the present affectionate allegiance of the Colonists to your Majesty's Person and Government."[81] Similarly there was a debate whether a gift to the Queen – a diadem of Australian gold – ought to be accompanied with a demand that she dismiss Earl Grey from "her Councils."[82]

It is dangerous to read too much into the reference to the Queen's "Person"; in fact, more often than not the monarch was entirely exculpated. Although he had suggested that strings be attached to the gift, Gilbert Wright had made it clear that he "yielded to no man in loyalty to the Queen, and in the deep conviction that the monarchical form of government, as constituted in Great Britain, was the best form of Government."[83] The president of the Australasian League, Charles Cowper, went further: "Whatever constitutional grievances we had to complain of were not attributable to her Majesty.... They were rather the fault of her advisers." Even Sydney's leading Catholic priest could find no fault with the monarch. The "greatest enemies of the Crown of Great Britain were to be found in Her Majesty's Ministers themselves," he stated. "If only he could get to the Queen," he told a meeting against transportation, he "had no doubt...she would place the question of Colonial Administration on a basis which would be acceptable to all."[84] At Hobart, as we have seen, Earl Grey was consumed in flames to the strains of "God Save the Queen."

It is important to note that these conceptions often went beyond mere formulaic professions of loyalty to call for direct intervention by the Crown. Only recently have historians of British reform movements begun to recognize the frequency with which they called for an interventionist monarchy.[85] Apart from Alan Atkinson, who ascribes a role to what he calls the "energetic Crown" in the development of Australia's "muddle-headed republic," popular monarchism has been virtually ignored by historians of Australia.[86] In Mark McKenna's eloquent history of Australian republicanism, we have the history of the tail rather than the dog. Far from being republicans (however defined), many British radicals and liberals – in Britain and in colonial Australia – were attracted by the notion that royal power could be exercised in their favour. For many opponents of transportation, the final court of appeal was Queen Victoria. They "had only to make their remonstrances known to her respectfully, perseveringly, and firmly to obtain redress," predicted Charles Cowper. For some, the independent appeal to the monarch was an important step on the road to nationhood: by "appealing to the Throne direct," one anti-transportationist argued, "the colonists of Australasia would be recognised as free subjects of the British Crown."[87]

Of course, Queen Victoria had no more interest in altering Grey's policy in relation to transportation than she had in repealing the Corn Laws or enacting the People's Charter by royal decree, but it would be a mistake to underestimate the residual popular belief in the benevolent role of monarchy. The "republic" was "captured," to invoke McKenna's memorable phrase, all too easily. An important benchmark of colonial attitudes at almost the same time as the Hobart "ceremony" was provided by John Mitchel, the Irish rebel who had been transported for fourteen years for his part in the abortive uprising of 1848. Mitchel arrived at Cape Town on his journey into exile and was delighted to find the colony in an uproar over Grey's proposal to send convicts there. "I drunk tonight, with enthusiasm, in red wine of Cape vines, the health of the future South African Republic," he wrote.[88]

Mitchel was equally thrilled when he reached his destination to find the citizens of Van Diemen's Land up in arms over transportation. "I delight in the fact that these colonists are growing accustomed to regard Downing-Street as a den of conspirators and treacherous enemies, accustomed to look for nothing but falsehood and insolence from that quarter." There was, however, a crucial difference, as he soon discovered when it became apparent that these same colonists were busily engaged in collecting a petition to the Queen praying for his release. Not considering himself "to be a British subject," he wrote to the *Colonial Times*, "I must take the 'Comparative liberty' of requesting...that my name may be excepted from the prayer of it. I have no idea of begging pardon, or of permitting anyone to beg pardon for me, if I can help it."[89] The fact that Mitchel's new countrymen could make such a blunder speaks volumes. Here was something new – republican separatism – that they could not comprehend. In an important recent essay, Donal Lowry has argued that the "retreat of active British governmental interference in the politics of the dominions" later in the century left the Crown resembling "the proverbial smile on the face of the Cheshire cat" and making "it very difficult for republicanism to flourish."[90] The only issue that needs to be taken with Lowry's assessment is that he finds this development surprising. After all, Mitchel's fellow rebel, Charles Gavan Duffy, became premier of an Australian colony and accepted a knighthood, as did Henry Parkes, the former Chartist. At the brink of open rebellion in 1851, the citizens of Hobart cheered as effigies of the colonial secretary and their governor were consumed by fire to the strains of "God Save the Queen." The Crown was already smiling like the Cheshire cat. Not until we recognize the centrality of popular constitutionalism, including its undoubted monarchism, will we begin to properly understand the later political history of the Anglophone societies across the British World.

{NOTES}

1 The research for this essay was funded by the Australian Research Council.

2 *Colonial Times and Tasmanian* (Hobart), 26 August 1851.

3 Ibid.; *The Hobart Town Directory and General Guide* (Hobart: J. Moore, 1852), 28, 68.

4 *Hobart Town Courier*, 27 August 1851.

5 For a detailed account of the campaign, see J.M. Ward, *Earl Grey and the Australian Colonies 1846–1857* (Melbourne: Melbourne University Press, 1958); C.S. Blackton, "Earl Grey and Australia's First National Movement, 1846–1852," *Pacific History Review* 10 (1941): 297–309.

6 John West, *The History of Tasmania* (1852; repr., Sydney: Angus and Robertson, 1971), 209. See also William Westgarth, *Personal Recollections of Early Melbourne and Victoria* (Melbourne: Robertson and Company, 1888), 144.

7 *Colonial Times and Tasmanian*, 26 August 1851; *Hobart Town Courier*, 27 August 1851.

8 *Colonial Times and Tasmanian*, 26 August 1851.

9 E.P. Thompson, "The Peculiarities of the English," in *The Poverty of Theory and Other Essays* (London: Merlin Press, 1979), 65. See also Inga Clendinnen, "Understanding the Heathen at Home: E.P. Thompson and His School," *Historical Studies* 18 (1979): 435–41.

10 Clifford Geertz, "From the Native's Point of View: On the Nature of Anthropological Understanding," in *Local Knowledge* (New York: Basic Books, 1983), 69. I am grateful to Dr. Jonathan White for this reference.

11 Thomas McCombie, *The History of the Colony of Victoria from Its Settlement to the Death of Sir Charles Hotham* (Melbourne: Sands and Kenny, 1858), 176.

12 See E.P. Thompson, "Patrician Society: Plebeian Culture," *Journal of Social History* 7 (1974): 383–405.

13 *Hobart Town Advertiser*, 26 August 1851; *Colonial Times and Tasmanian*, 26 August 1851.

14 *Hobart Town Advertiser*, 26 August 1851; *Hobart Town Courier*, 27 August 1851. West claimed that an effigy of him had been publicly gibbeted during the official welcome. See West, *History of Tasmania*, 240.

15 Sir William Denison, *Varieties of Vice-Regal Life* (London: Longmans, Green & Co, 1870), 1:164–65.

16 *Empire* (Sydney), 15 February 1851.

17 Ibid., 17 September 1851.

18 *People's Advocate* (Sydney), 21 April 1849.

19 For Hipkiss, see *People's Advocate*, 16 December 1848; 24 March 1849; 30 April 1853. For Aaron, see *People's Advocate*, 24 February 1849; 16 June 1849; 17 August 1850; *Empire*, 10 June 1851; 6 October 1851; Carlos Flick, *The Birmingham Political Union and the Movements for Reform in Britain 1830–1839* (Connecticut: Archon Books, 1978), 119, 178.

20 *People's Advocate*, 24 August 1850; Lord Byron, "The Giaour: A Fragment of a Turkish Tale" (1813), in *The Complete Poetical Works*, ed. J.J. McGann (Oxford: Oxford University Press, 1981), 3:39–82, lines 123–25.

21 *People's Advocate*, 24 April 1852. For Hawksley, see M. Diamond, "Edward Hawksley: A Catholic and a Radical," in *Disreputable Profession: Journalists and Journalism in Colonial Australia*, ed. Dennis Cryle (Rockhampton: Central Queensland University Press, 1997), 41–54; A. Messner, "Contesting Chartism from Afar: Edward Hawksley and the People's Advocate," *Journal of Australian Colonial History* 1 (1999): 62–94.

22 See Dorothy Thompson, *The Early Chartists* (London: McMillan, 1979), 19.

23 *Cork Examiner*, 23 November 1849.

24 *People's Advocate*, 26 April 1851.

25 An exception, albeit unpublished, is Terry Irving, "The Development of Liberal Politics in New South Wales 1843–1855" (PhD diss., University of Sydney, 1967), chap. 8. Dunmore Lang's Australian League and the Ballarat Reform League are other examples of the influence of the Anti-Corn Law League that deserve further attention.

26 *Anti-Bread-Tax Circular* (Manchester), 4 April 1843. See Paul Pickering and Alex Tyrrell, *The People's Bread: A History of the Anti-Corn Law League* (London: Leicester University Press, 2000), chap. 1.

27 *Hansard* (House of Commons), 23 February 1846, col. 173.

28 Cited in West, *History of Tasmania*, 232. See also *Empire*, 4 July 1851.

29 *The Times* (London), 18 November 1843.

30 *Empire*, 5 May 1851.

31 Quoted in *Empire*, 4 July 4 1851.

32 *People's Advocate*, 24 March 1849; 10 December 1853; *Star* (Sydney), 11 October 1845; Irving, "Development of Liberal Politics," 97; *John Dunmore Lang: Chiefly Autobiographical, 1799–1878*, ed. A. Gilchrist (Melbourne: Jedgarm Press, 1951), 2:536–37; D. W.A. Baker, *Days of Wrath: A Life of John Dunmore Lang* (Melbourne: Melbourne University Press, 1985), 348–49. I have work in progress on Lang's links with the League.

33 Henry Parkes, *Fifty Years in the Making of Australian History* (1892; repr., New York: Books for Libraries Press, 1971), 167–69. For Paulton, see Pickering and Tyrrell, *People's Bread*, 20–21.

34 James Fenton, *A History of Tasmania from Its Discovery in 1642 to the Present Times* (Hobart: J. Walsh and Sons, 1884), 200.

35 *Anti-Corn Law Circular*, 10 December 1839; 6 February 1840.

36 *British Parliamentary Papers, Reports of the Select Committee of the House of Commons on Public Petitions*, vol. 110 (1839), 820–25; vol. 116 (1840), 1023–29; vol. 125 (1841), 847–52, vol. 126 (1842), 36; vol. 130 (1843), 728–34; vol. 135, 1755–61. See also Pickering and Tyrrell, *People's Bread*, 26; P.A. Pickering, "'And Your Petitioners &c': Chartist Petitioning in Popular Politics 1838–1848," *English Historical Review* 466 (2001): 368–88.

37 *Anti-Corn Law Circular*, 5 March 1840.

38 West, *History of Tasmania*, 226.

39 See *British Parliamentary Papers, Report of the Select Committee of the House of Commons on Public Petitions*, no. 71 (1851), 1193; no. 45 (1852), 622–23; no. 83 (1852–53), 1552–53.

40 *Empire*, 8 April 1852.

41 *Empire*, 5 April 1851; Parkes, *Fifty Years*, 19. See also Pickering, "And Your Petitioners," 381–83; Pickering and Tyrrell, *People's Bread*, chap. 6.

42 See Pickering and Tyrrell, *People's Bread*, chap. 2.

43 Quoted in R. Garnett, *The Life of W.J. Fox* (London: John Lane, 1910), 268.

44 West, *History of Tasmania*, 238.

45 *Empire*, 5 February 1852; 13 February 1852, 18 February 1852; 7 April 1852.

46 See ibid., 19 March 1851, 16 June 1851; *The Times*, 6 October 1851, 15 October 1851. See also Paul A. Pickering, "'The Finger of God': Gold and Political Culture in Colonial New South Wales," in *Gold: Forgotten Histories and Lost Objects of Australia*, ed. Iain McCalman (Cambridge: Cambridge University Press, 2001), 21–43.

47 *Empire*, 16 April 1852.

48 Ibid., 5 May 1851; *Colonial Times and Tasmanian*, 23 September 1851. See also *People's Advocate*, 22 June 1850; *Empire*, 17 November 1851; *The Times*, 15 October 1851.

49 *Empire*, 8 April 1852.

50 *People's Advocate*, 13 September 1851; 18 October 1851; *Reynolds' Weekly Newspaper* (London), 22 December 1850; *Reynolds' Newspaper*, 20 July 1851.

51 *Morning Chronicle* (London), 31 July 1851.

52 *People's Advocate*, 31 July 1852.

53 See Pickering and Tyrrell, *People's Bread*, 33.

54 *Empire*, 7 April 1851.

55 Ibid., 26 May 1851; 9 August 1851. During 1851 the New South Wales Branch raised £2505/7s. See also the Branch's 1852 Balance sheet, which provides an overview of the activities on which funds were expended. *Empire*, 7 October 1851; 10 July 1852.

56 Ibid., 18 June 1851.

57 *People's Advocate*, 12 April 1851. See also 14 May 1853. For the League see *Manchester Times*, 8 December 1838; 17 April 1841; 22 October 1842; *Anti-Corn Law Circular*, 16 July 1840; F.A. Montgomery, "Glasgow and the Movement for Corn Law Repeal," *History* 64 (1979): 366.

58 *Anti-Bread-Tax Circular*, 8 September 1842.

59 See *Empire*, 25 April 1851; 1 July 1851; Parkes, *Fifty Years*, 18. See also Pickering and Tyrrell, *People's Bread*, chap. 10; Irving, "Development of Liberal Politics," 334, 337.

60 Parkes, *Fifty Years*, 19. Ward noted that inadvertently Grey had provoked a union of the colonies that he had earlier advocated. See Ward, *Earl Grey*, 215–26.

61 *San Francisco Herald* reprinted in *People's Advocate*, 30 October 1852. See also H.W. Stewart, *Rhymes and Ramblings* (Melbourne: Alexander McCubbin, n.d [1921]), 21–22; John Mitchel, *Jail Journal: or Five Years in British Prisons* (1854; Dublin: Jane Corrigan, 1864), 149.

62 *The Times*, 6 October 1851.

63 *Empire*, 8 April 1852.

64 *People's Advocate*, 3 July 1852.

65 John Hirst, *Australia's Democracy: A Short History* (Sydney: Allen and Unwin, 2002), 38, 57. "Of course the democrats," Hirst continues in an unconvincing passage, "could not be too open about their republicanism because most colonists were very loyal to the Queen."

66 John Gascoinge, *The Enlightenment and the Origins of European Australia* (Cambridge: Cambridge University Press, 2002), 35, 47.

67 I am here invoking the oft-quoted desire of Prime Minister John Howard, a monarchist, to make Australians "relaxed and comfortable."

68 See James Vernon, *Politics and the People: A Study in English Political Culture, c. 1815–1867* (Cambridge: Cambridge University Press, 1993), 296; James Epstein, "The Constitutional Idiom: Radical Reasoning, Rhetoric and Action in Early Nineteenth-Century England," *Journal of Social History* 23 (1990): 553–74; *Re-reading the Constitution: New Narratives in the Political History of England's Long Nineteenth Century*, ed. James Vernon (Cambridge: Cambridge University Press, 1996). See also P.A. Pickering, "'The Oak of English Liberty': Popular Constitutionalism in New South Wales, 1848–1856," *Journal of Australian Colonial History* 3 (2001): 1–27.

69 Quoted in *Argus* (Melbourne), 15 July 1854.

70 *People's Advocate*, 23 June 1849; 17 August 1850; *Empire*, 8 April 1851.

71 Linda Colley, *Britons: Forging the Nation 1707–1837* (London: Vintage Books, 1996). See also W.K. Hancock, *Australia* (Brisbane: Jacaranda, 1961), 51; M. Harris, "Monarchy and Australian Character," in *Australia and the Monarchy: A Symposium*, ed. G. Dutton (Melbourne: Sun Books, 1966), 107–18. In a review of *Britons*, E.P. Thompson noted that Colley had put loyalty on the agenda.

72 *Hobart Town Advertiser*, 26, 29 August 1851.

73 *Empire*, 16 September 1851.

74 Ibid., 4 October 1851. See also Denison, *Varieties of Vice Regal Life*, 159; Earl Grey, *The Colonial Policy of Lord John Russell's Administration* (London: Richard Bentley, 1853), 2:47–48, 84–85.

75 *Empire*, 14 October 1851; A.T.Q. Stewart, *The Narrow Ground: Aspects of Ulster 1609–1969* (London: Faber and Faber, 1977).

76 *Empire*, 1 May 1851; 1 November 1851; 25 March 1852.

77 *People's Advocate*, 3 July 1852; Pickering, "Oak of English Liberty," 19–21.

78 *Empire*, 1 November 1851; 29 December 1851; 8 April 1852; Pickering, "Oak of English Liberty," 21–22.

79 *Manchester Examiner*, 18 March 1848.

80 Manchester Public Library, Ms. J.B. Smith Papers, R. Cobden to J.B. Smith, 4 December 1841; Pickering and Tyrrell, *People's Bread*, 143–44.

81 *Empire*, 28 July 1851.

82 Ibid., 7 July 1851.

83 Ibid.

84 Ibid., 5 April 1851; 8 April 1852; *People's Advocate*, 10 April 1852.

85 See Alex Tyrrell with Y. Ward, "God Bless Her Little Majesty: The Popularising of Monarchy in the 1840s," *National Identities* 2 (2000): 109–25; Pickering and Tyrrell, *People's Bread*, 128–29; Paul Pickering, "The Hearts of the Millions: Chartism and Popular Monarchism in the 1840s," *History* 88 (2003): 227–48.

86 Alan Atkinson, *The Muddle-Headed Republic* (Melbourne: Oxford University Press, 1993), chap. 2.

87 *Empire*, 5 April 1851; 1 August 1851.

88 Mitchel, *Jail Journal*, 111.

89 Ibid., 146, 155. Mitchel had taken the same attitude in his discussions with the Chartists. See Paul Pickering, "'Repeal and the Suffrage': Feargus O'Connor's Irish Mission, 1849–50," in *The Chartist Legacy*, ed. O. Ashton and S. Roberts (London: Merlin Press, 1999), 124, 133–34.

90 Donal Lowry, "'These Colonies are Practically Democratic Republics' (James Bryce): Republicanism in the British Colonies of Settlement in the Long Nineteenth Century," in *Republicanism in Victorian Society*, ed. David Nash and Antony Taylor (Stroud: Sutton Publishing, 2000), 139.

CHAPTER 5

FROM VICTORIAN VALUES TO WHITE VIRTUES:

ASSIMILATION AND EXCLUSION IN BRITISH RACIAL DISCOURSE, c.1870–1914

Douglas Lorimer

WHILE RECENT CRITICAL, LITERARY, and historical studies of the images of race constructed by the Victorians have added greatly to our understanding of nineteenth-century racism, there is a danger that these studies underestimate the sophistication, the complexity, and therefore the power of Victorian racial discourse and its legacy for our post-colonial present. Although there is a recognition that the identities of nation, class, gender, and race are cultural constructions founded out of competing visions, full of ambiguities and contradictions, and subject to change over time, we are still vulnerable to the genetic fallacy of trying to define essences by origins. In recent years, the centre of scholarly attention has moved backward from the nineteenth to the eighteenth century. Here scholars find the origins both of modernity and of a modern British identity shaped internally by Protestantism and a parliamentary constitutional monarchy with its associated liberties, and externally by success in imperial wars and by commercial ascendency in the world economy. The defining external "other," both foreign and colonial, existed in part to confirm the superiority of Britons and their rightful place as world leaders. Once established, the rest is history, for what remains for the nineteenth and twentieth centuries is the unfolding of a narrative of identities that fit uncomfortably, even anachronistically, in the present. This form of narrative serves the useful purpose of collapsing the distinction between British domestic and imperial history and of recognizing the interdependence between the metropole and the periphery.[1] Nonetheless, the narrative needs to address the unanticipated, even radical, departures from the eighteenth-century genesis of modernist constructions of identity.

Whether we are sympathetic or hostile to the new cultural history and its postmodern and post-colonial inclinations, we need to take seriously the claim that decolonization is more than a political process. As Catherine Hall has observed, decolonization is also a cultural process.[2] We are engaged in a process of the decolonization of the historical inheritance and culture of the descendants of colonized subjects (peoples coming under British rule by force or conquest), of the colonials (voluntary migrant settlers largely from the British Isles), and of the colonizers (agents and consumers of imperial culture in the metropolitan society). The issue scholars face is how to represent the Victorians. Under the influence of Edward Said and less subtle exponents of critical theory, we have focused our attention on how the Victorians represented the colonial other, but we have paid less careful attention to how we represent the Victorians. While Said has been wrongly charged with essentializing the Occident, less subtle and skilful practitioners of his method may be colonizing the Victorians. We may be constructing a racist Victorian other as a means to define our implicit non-racist Self.[3] If we see ourselves engaged in a project of decolonizing the culture of the colonized, the colonialist, and the colonizer, we would do well to recognize that racism is alive and well in the twenty-first century. Rather than construct Victorians who are our defining others, we should pay more attention to the similarities between our racism and that of our Victorian predecessors.

For the long nineteenth century, the discourse of race can be characterized as a contest between voices for the assimilation of colonial others and those advocating forms of separate development or racial exclusion. In the early and mid-nineteenth century, the voices for assimilation were best represented by the anti-slavery movement and advocates of the civilizing mission. Between 1830 and 1865, a complex set of changes in the colonial periphery and in the metropolitan culture, most recently explored by Catherine Hall in her *Civilizing Subjects*, saw the creation and erosion of the original utopian, radical, and bourgeois vision of remaking the world's peoples – including the freed slaves of the West Indies, the peoples of India and Africa, and the indigenous peoples of British North America and Australasia – into British, civilized, and therefore modern subjects. Especially in the 1850s and 1860s, there were signs of an alternative exclusionary and racist vision. Prior to 1870, and even before the 1890s, this new exclusionary vision had not matured sufficiently to articulate how new forms of racial subordination would be institutionalized in law, in administrative practice, and in social conventions within British imperial jurisdictions and the metropolitan society. But by the beginning of the twentieth century, the assimilating vision of Victorian values had been superseded by the exclusionary language of white virtues.

By 1865, marked by the ending of American slavery and the Morant Bay Rebellion in Jamaica, the optimistic hopes for the emancipation of black slaves and the philanthropic visions of a just settlement of the competing claims of colonial settlers and Aboriginal peoples had proven to be illusionary. The trials of the West Indian sugar economy after emancipation and free trade, and the failure of the Niger expedition in 1841 dashed abolitionist confidence in a speedy and thorough conversion of freed slaves and African heathen into civilized British subjects. In addition, new voices in the 1850s and 1860s expressed a more strident, unabashed racism. Thomas Carlyle's intervention in 1849, as Catherine Hall rightly emphasizes, gave licence to speak the unspeakable – to challenge the abolitionists' moral vision, to denigrate Africans and their New World descendants, and to disparage philanthropic optimism as foolish, unrealistic sentiment. Carlyle's prejudices were given more formal expression by new studies in ethnology, which now separated science from religion and philanthropy, and articulated a new, strident racism best exemplified by Robert Knox's *Races of Man*, published in 1850 and reissued in 1862.[4]

For studies that bring the examination of Victorian racial attitudes to a conclusion in the 1860s – for example, Philip Curtin's *Image of Africa* – Knox and his follower James Hunt, with his newly named science of anthropology, provide a fitting conclusion to a narrative of the decline and disintegration of the abolitionist and philanthropic visions of the civilizing mission. The 1860s have attracted a great deal of attention because of the intersection of the constructions of identities of race, nation, class, and gender evident in responses to events such as the American Civil War and the Jamaica Insurrection, Fenianism in Ireland, the beginnings of a concerted campaign for female suffrage, and the passage of the Second Reform Act of 1867.[5] Yet, while the 1860s exposed with particular clarity how class, gender, and race operated as interdependent categories, there is a danger that our new appreciation of the role of culture may lead us to reinvent the simpler constructions of an older history of ideas, attributing too straightforward an influence to specific ideas or authors.

The most significant measure of the transformation of identities in the 1860s was the redefinition of what constituted knowledge. As T.W.

Heyck has ably argued, the emergence of the modern intelligentsia and its authority through the growth of the sciences and the professionalization of intellectual endeavour in the institutions of the academy limited the older free market in ideas.[6] Within this new institutional context, science and knowledge, like citizenship, were more sharply defined within the masculine sphere. Although anthropologists appear to remain attached to the disciplinary myth that the birth of their science liberated reason from religion, in the 1860s the advocates of their newly named "science of man" established their innovative stance by being anti-philanthropic and anti-humanitarian. They did so by taking the exceptional stance of supporting the Confederacy and slavery, defending Governor Eyre, and attacking missionary societies. The anthropologists also excluded women, claiming that they needed to be able to explore, along with Captain Richard Burton, peculiarly masculine subjects such as phallic worship.[7]

In contrast, promoters of the civilizing mission and past causes such as anti-slavery were now identified as promoters of "sentiment," not knowledge. The active participation of women in these causes, as well as the general association of philanthropy as part of the female domestic domain, meant that these endeavours were "feminized." This feminization, as Susan Thorne has demonstrated for the London Missionary Society and the missionary movement in general, also applies to the Anti-Slavery Society and Aborigines Protection Society. Women had played an important role in the heroic years of the anti-slavery campaign, and they continued to be important local organizers and supporters throughout the century. Although the executive committees of both societies remained exclusively male until the end of the nineteenth century, women constituted about 40 per cent of their subscribers, and that proportion increased as both societies faced a decline in membership.[8] For Thomas Carlyle, the centre of misguided philanthropy and weak and equally misguided female sentiment was Exeter Hall, the assembly off the Strand where anti-slavery and missionary societies held their annual meetings. Carlyle's language stuck, for in the imperial enthusiasms of the 1890s, journalists like George Steevens of *The Daily Mail* called for a "new humanitarianism," unlike the old female sentimentalism of abolitionists and missionaries, and based on the exertion of real masculine knowledge and power.[9]

This kind of change in sensibility may be difficult to document precisely, but it serves as a better measure of change than do the unsubstantiated assertions of influence, down to 1914 or even to the 1950s, of a rather eccentric group of extremists like Knox, Hunt, and the Anthropological Society of London. A more detailed examination of the post-1870 period suggests that race remained a disputed territory and that the memory of abolitionist achievements, if not the substance of their reforming vision, persisted after 1870 and was far more central to imperial ideology than the new anthropology of the 1860s. In fact, it is difficult to trace by direct reference the influence of Knox or Hunt in the proceedings of the Anthropological Institute after the 1870s. Like Carlyle in 1849, Knox, Hunt, Richard Burton, and other advocates of a newer, more strident racism depict themselves as outsiders, even as self-conscious eccentrics, at war against the respectable, Biblical, moral orthodoxies of abolitionism and monogenesis. Hunt probably has had more readers among researchers in the last thirty years than among Victorians in the last three decades of the nineteenth century. Under the new Darwinian evolutionary synthesis, and despite the dramatic debates of the 1860s, British biological science, unlike its French or American counterparts, was thoroughly orthodox in its monogenesis.[10] By the 1890s, the rare reference to Knox associated him with the American school of polygenists; thus he was not only at odds with orthodox science, but also tainted as a defender of slavery. In his emphasis on the diverse cultural roots of evolutionary social thought, J.W. Burrow best captures the significance of the scientific debate on race in the 1860s in describing Knox, Hunt, and the Anthropological Society of London as a kind of cul-de-sac, a dead end or a turn not taken.[11]

Beyond their role in undermining what Graham Wallas called the "optimistic ethnology of Exeter Hall," the debates on race of the 1860s, as distinct from the crises of the Indian Mutiny and the Jamaica Insurrection, had little direct influence on colonial policy.[12] In terms of colonial race relations, the Aborigines Protection Society (APS), the principal lobby group for persons of colour, was politically far more important than the Anthropological Society or its successor, the Anthropological Institute. Although the philanthropists and the anthropologists could both trace their origins back to the Parliamentary Committee on Aborigines in 1837, the two societies appealed to two quite distinct constituencies divided by social status, gender, and religion. By the 1870s, unlike the 1840s and 1850s, no active members belonged to both societies. Although the anthropologists frequently claimed that their science had profound lessons for the administration of a multiracial empire, their first serious proposal for an Imperial Bureau of Ethnology in 1907 was initially greeted with scepticism even by Liberal imperialists such as Asquith.[13] In sum, mid-Victorian science, and mid-Victorian polygenesis in particular, was not the seed from which the racism of empire sprouted. The Victorian discourse on race, especially the discourse of racial exclusion, relied less upon the science of racial stereotypes than upon a new language of race relations.

The development of a dominant discourse of racial exclusion occurred in the later nineteenth century within the context of the administration of the government of India, the partition of Africa, the achievement of responsible government and dominion status by the colonies of settlement with jurisdiction over indigenous populations and immigration, and the extension of the franchise and rise of a gendered and racialized conception of British citizenship within the metropolitan society. This crude list grossly simplifies the profound changes within the larger historical context of the world economy, imperial relations, and the metropolitan society and culture that occurred between the 1860s and 1914. The obvious point is that constructions of race and race relations changed as the historical context changed. Our histories of racism run the risk of stressing continuities when more can be learned about the construction and reconstruction of race by paying attention to how the language of race changes over time. At present, our constructions of the historical narrative may explain the racism that suffered a retreat between the 1930s and 1950s, but as Foucault so aptly observed, we need not a history of the past but a history of the present. In probing the Victorian legacy of racism for the twenty-first century, we need to focus less on images of race, which display a distressing continuity over time, and to pay more attention to the new language of race relations that developed after the 1870s.[14] It is on this language of race relations that new forms of racial subordination and new doctrines of racial exclusion were constructed. Just as the interplay between Jamaica and the metropole had a key part in the reconstruction of race around questions of slavery, emancipation, and the problem of freedom between 1830 and 1865, the context of southern Africa and late Victorian and Edwardian Britain informed the new language of race relations and its attendant forms of racial subordination and exclusion prior to 1914. It was in this context that Victorian values were transformed into white virtues, though not quite so directly as my title might suggest.

In order to represent the disputed territory of Victorian constructions of race, I have endeavoured to trace the fault lines between a discourse of assimilation and a discourse of racial exclusion in the period 1870–1914. The discourse of assimilation enshrined the Victorian values of respectability as the source of truth, morality, civilization, and character, and claimed that while these values were the particular result of the British historical inheritance and experience, they were of universal significance and could be transplanted to all peoples and to all quarters of the globe. What I have termed a discourse of assimilation is similar to what Peter Mandler has termed a "civilisational perspective," which he sees as distinct from continental forms of organic nationalism resting upon fixed, distinct characteristics. This "civilisational perspective," the dominant strain of thought in elite liberal culture, viewed British political culture and institutions as a product of long historical development and as uniquely suited to change, progress, and leadership in the modern world. The civilizing mission, originating in the evangelical revival, included the spreading of this superior British way to other peoples and cultures. Such a vision assumed that all peoples shared a common nature and capacity, though from the Scottish enlightenment and its intellectual offshoots, various cultures were placed in stages of development, as in the conventional designations of savage, barbarian, and civilized. Over time, peoples had the capacity to evolve in progressive stages toward the British civilized ideal. The Victorian encounter with other cultures, principally in India and then in Africa, dampened early optimism for a sudden conversion in either religious or secular terms. With the development of an evolutionary synthesis both in Darwinian biology and in social theory, there was a great extension of the sense of historical time in which this progressive evolution could work itself out. Consequently, various cultures could be viewed as further apart both spatially and temporally, and the time for the civilizing process extended further and further into the future. In this way, the process of assimilation or the civilizational perspective, with the confident assumption of progress by evolutionary stages toward the British ideal, accommodated a ranking of cultures without needing to rely upon the biological determinism or the fixed racial types of the comparative anatomists.[15]

The capacity to receive and exercise the benefits of full participation in British political life, with the exercise of the franchise being the litmus test, rested, as Stephan Collini has pointed out, upon that mysterious ether the Victorians called "character." In the definition provided by the *Oxford English Dictionary*, cited by Collini, character applied both to the assessment of individuals and of races. When arguing for an extension of the franchise for a greater proportion of men and on the same terms for women, J.S. Mill still argued for significant exclusions based upon persons – paupers, tax delinquents, bankrupts – displaying deficiencies of character. Though the Second Reform Act was more generous than either the Liberals or Tories originally intended, it put into law the test of character according to the liberal slogan of manliness and independence, and thus excluded by gender all women and by class those less-than-respectable males who were not heads of households and were made unmanly by dependency or poverty.[16]

Under the criteria of the Second Reform Act, how did this test of citizenship apply when translated to the colonial sphere? The criteria of manliness and independence seems to fit with the first test applied to colonized subjects, namely the duty to labour. The principal deficiency of British colonized subjects of African, South Asian, or other non-European descent was the lack of an appetite for work or industry, and from this deficiency most other deficiencies followed, including a want of self-discipline or thrift in the use of time or money, and the absence of a sense of purposefulness or duty, together with the lack of willpower to achieve some higher end. Yet even the satisfaction of this test of respectability or manliness and independence would not match characteristic English traits defined within a colonial context. The unique qualities of the "English" were conventionally listed as the qualities needed for governing others. The prized qualities were those associated with the leadership of English gentlemen, including physical courage, unquestioned integrity, capacity to inspire loyalty in others, and a disinterested judgment that put the greater good over narrow self-interest.[17] These qualities of gentlemanly leadership, learned on the sports field, were what Lord Rosebery looked to find in the "imperial race" of male graduates at Glasgow University in 1900. Benjamin Kidd looked for the same qualities as he called upon his countrymen to take on the task of controlling the tropics and their development through the labour of the coloured races. In this call, he specifically rejected the racial typologies and biological determinism of the scientists. He depicted the English capacity for government and for leadership as a result of social evolution, and even though it was a long way in the future, eventually other peoples and cultures would develop the "social efficiencies" that justified Britain's imperial mission.[18]

One suspects, though, that for Kidd's readers, his social evolution confirmed a sense of British leadership and superiority and helped clarify the defining difference of the colonial other. Consequently, these treatments may not stand in sharp contrast to more exclusionary viewpoints. The discourse of exclusion incorporated the same values of Victorian respectability, emphasized the same traits of national character, saw them derived from the same unique features of British historical experience, but denied that these values could be transplanted to other climes and other peoples, especially those newly designated as "non-Europeans." In this sense, Victorian values, established as a universal creed in the early and mid-Victorian periods, became the exclusive property of whites as the discourse of racial exclusion became the dominant, though never singular, discourse by the end of the long nineteenth century.

This nineteenth-century dialogue between assimilation and exclusion was not a case of a non-racist perspective being replaced by a racist perspective. Both discourses, assimilation and exclusion, rested upon a confident belief in the superiority of British civilization and both incorporated forms of racial inequality, though that inequality was conceptualized in different ways. In part, the discourse of race in the nineteenth century was a way of addressing the phenomenon of globalization in which peoples of differing cultures and identities, including differing visible features such as skin colour, were brought within newly constituted colonial societies, polities, and cultures by the powerful engine of imperialism. This new global reality became more apparent as the nineteenth century advanced. We tend to underestimate the novelty of this new world order of the late nineteenth century and to overlook that the Victorians themselves felt they were living in circumstances without clear historical precedents. Under these circumstances, they developed a new vocabulary of race relations.

This construction of Victorian racial discourse as a dialogue between notions of assimilation and exclusion within the context of a new unprecedented global order has the advantage of recognizing not only that race was a constructed identity but also that it was disputed ground. This description also attempts to avoid colonizing the Victorians, for rather than making the Victorians into our racist other, we need to recognize that the nineteenth-century construction of racial discourse is uncomfortably similar to our own. The contradictory tension between assimilation and exclusion, or separate development, is still with us. It is there in our discussions of multiculturalism and the place of history in the school curriculum. It is there in the tension between universalism and particularism in Kenan Malik's enquiry into *The Meaning of Race* (1996), or in Paul Gilroy's search for a way out of the politics of race and ethnicity in *Against Race* (2002). Rather than seeing the Victorians as the authors of racial fictions now refurbished for the deconstruction of modern scholars, we may learn more from realizing that the Victorian discourse on race, like our own, contained within it contradictory tendencies of universalism and particularism out of which our own racism and anti-racism developed.[19]

Although precedents for ideas of racial exclusion or separate development can be found in the eighteenth century, the Victorian discourse on race, including a discourse of exclusion, arises out of and in response to the discourse of assimilation that was dominant in the period from at least the 1780s to the 1860s. This discourse of assimilation, enshrined in the ideology of the civilizing mission and most extensively promulgated by the anti-slavery and missionary movements, rested on the assumption that the most advanced and most civilized values and practices were those of the British and Christian nation, and that it was Britain's ordained role to extend the benefits of its governance and civilization to the rest of humanity. For imperial advocates, the success of the anti-slavery movement stood as the defining symbol of the uniquely humanitarian motivation and quality of Britain's international role, both in its diplomacy with other European nations and its relations with all peoples, regardless of race, within the Empire.[20] For those groups caught up in the moralizing objectives of the imperial mission, their own British identity was in part defined by the conduct of imperial agents overseas. Thus these groups, best represented by adherents to anti-slavery and missionary causes, were both supporters of imperialism and potential critics of the exercise of colonial authority.[21]

This discourse of assimilation rested upon an assumption that the diverse peoples of the world had the willingness and capacity to convert to Christian, Victorian forms of modernity. While there was widespread agreement on the universal application of Victorian values and on the moral and humanitarian inspiration of the British imperial mission, there was far less agreement about the nature of the colonizing process and about the forms of replication of British society in its diverse and far-flung Empire. Even though the discourse of assimilation rested upon an assumption of a common human nature, rooted in Biblical authority, the forms of replication of British society and culture, itself containing unequal divisions by class, gender, and ethnicity, was the subject of an ongoing dialogue, even dispute, the terms of which changed over the course of the nineteenth century. Therefore, this assimilating discourse readily accommodated forms of social and racial hierarchy in its colonial reconstructions of Victorian values.

Of course, the process of colonization, whether conceptualized as a form of assimilation or of modernization, never went as smoothly as advocates of the civilizing mission or colonial development envisaged. The Victorian discourse on race from the 1830s through the 1850s – including the question of West Indian slave emancipation and the problem of freedom; evangelical and utilitarian visions of reform in India; the development of legitimate commerce in Africa; and relations between Aboriginal peoples and British emigrants in colonies of settlement – focused on the management of the transition of various peoples and cultures to this new global, modern, imperial order. The old imperial ways of unregulated freebooting conquest and plunder with no respect for the lives or morality of the peoples subject to imperial intervention – whether at the hands of East India Company nabobs, West Indian planters, or land hungry settlers and profiteering traders in colonies of settlement – could no longer be tolerated in the new moralized order of the Victorian metropolitan and imperial culture.

The immorality of the old Empire as distinct from the newer conception of the imperial mission was clearly articulated in 1837 by the abolitionist-sponsored Parliamentary Committee on Aborigines. It began with a strident critique of the destructive and evil consequences of European colonialism upon Aboriginal peoples. It also set out both a doctrine of Aboriginal entitlement and the ethical grounds for British interventions into Aboriginal life and culture. This statement of principles became the founding charter of the Aboriginal Protection Society (APS).[22] The APS adhered to its founding ideas of human brotherhood and Aboriginal entitlement until its demise in 1909. It became the principal lobby group for Aboriginal peoples and for colonial subjects of colour in general, but suffered a marked decline in public esteem as the century advanced. Subject to the criticism of colonial settlers and imperial advocates such as Flora Shaw, and an annoyance to colonial secretaries such as Joseph Chamberlain, the APS has been equally subject to the dismissive judgement of imperial historians who, from the perspective of the Colonial Office files, see it as politically ineffective and naïvely utopian in its simplistic morality of Aboriginal entitlements and equality of all persons before the law.[23]

The principal parliamentary spokesperson for the APS from 1892 to 1910 was Sir Charles Dilke, once a leading Liberal touted as a possible successor to Gladstone until a sensational divorce scandal ruined his political prospects. Dilke expressed dismay at the decline in the public's concern for racial oppression and in its sympathy for persons of colour. Ironically, historians have identified the youthful Dilke's best-selling travelogue, *Greater Britain* (1869), as one of the important sources of a more vigorous Anglo-Saxon racism. Out of Dilke's confused use of race and culture – especially his strident advocacy of the special global role of English-speaking peoples sharing a common political heritage, which he attributed to the Saxon race – his readers in Britain and America, and subsequently historians, may have misunderstood or missed altogether his principal message. In 1869 Dilke was a young radical, ready to advocate republican sentiments at a time when Victoria had not yet assumed the public persona of a modern monarch. He was also radical in his defence of grants of land and the franchise to the recently emancipated slaves in the United States, and he extended the same political rights to former slave populations of the West Indies. He helped coin the modern meaning of imperialism, extending the concept of authoritarian rule from Napoleon III's France to British rule in India. Having little regard for the cultures of Aboriginal peoples, he envisaged a new world order in which whites would become a kind of global bourgeoisie and persons of colour a global proletariat.[24]

Consequently, one of his chief concerns was the abuse of colonial labour, most evident in his later political role as parliamentary spokesperson for the APS and for E.D. Morel's Congo Reform Association. He speculated that larger continental states – such as the United States and Australia, with English-speaking peoples and a "Saxon" political inheritance, both in culture and in institutions – would come to dominate the world. Consequently, a smaller territorial state such as the United Kingdom could only compete through its cultivated kinship with these emerging states and through its leadership of the Empire's diverse populations, a majority of whom were persons of colour. Britain's imperial destiny was to extend the benefits of this Saxon political inheritance to all peoples regardless of race and in the process save the inhabitants of the British Isles from a narrow, insular provincialism. While admitting the enormity of this imperial mission in 1869, especially in regard to India, and more reserved in his optimism in his sequel, *The Problems of Greater Britain* (1890), Dilke focused his last twenty years in parliament defending his assimilating vision by championing the rights of persons of colour who were now subject to the new and objectionable language of racial exclusion.[25]

The mid-Victorian who best anticipated the form of racial discourse of the later nineteenth and early twentieth centuries was Herman Merivale, Oxford political economist and Colonial Office undersecretary, who first published his *Lectures on Colonies and Colonization* in 1841 and reissued them with substantial revisions in 1861. Drawing on the experience of conflicts between European settlers and Aboriginal peoples in North

America and southern Africa, and most specifically between whites and Maoris in New Zealand, Merivale identified three possible outcomes of the colonial encounter – extermination, insulation, or amalgamation. In his view, extermination was the result of allowing destructive conflicts to run their course without policy. In his 1861 revisions, he identified specific causes of Aboriginal decline – warfare, disease, and despair – and specifically rejected the application of the new Darwinian natural selection as some form of natural law. The second policy, the insulation of Aboriginal people through treaties creating reserved land, he also saw as doomed to failure. Citing the experience of the United States, where the actions of settlers and the duplicity of the American government had violated treaties and led to the forced removal of Native Americans from reserved land, he thought that the third option of amalgamation was the only real alternative. He defended, similar to later advocates of colonial tropical development, the right of settlers to occupy and develop lands and put them to productive use, but he also understood that the resultant amalgamation or assimilation to modern, Victorian values and practices would be under conditions of unequal, inferior status. For Merivale, the most complete and effective amalgamation would occur through intermarriage. Such unions between white males and Aboriginal women secured inequality through gender and resulted in offspring more thoroughly assimilated by culture to British ways. For Merivale, the emphasis was on culture, not biology, and he pointed to the Métis community of the Red River settlement as a positive example of such unions.[26]

Merivale recognized that in most instances amalgamation would be a cultural process necessitating the education of Aboriginal peoples in Victorian values, especially through the skill and discipline of industrial work. Assuming that social relations between white settlers and Aboriginal peoples would be unequal by race and by class, Merivale offered a critique of philanthropic agencies such as the APS. He perceptively observed that Native peoples could not be given effective equality before the law simply by declarations of principle that the law applied equally to settler and Native alike. Although he realized that Natives had to be in a position to make their standing in the law effective, he did not see that recourse to the law in itself assumed some measure of acculturation, nor did he take the further step of spelling out how such legal equality might be created. Instead he opted for the creation for Aboriginal peoples of a special, protected, unequal status before the law. It would be the particular role of the Colonial Office to develop such a protected legal status and to enforce its provisions, often in opposition to the desires of colonial legislatures representing settler interests. Even here, Merivale was a realist, for he recognized that settler-dominated legislatures establishing greater autonomy made the overseeing role of the Colonial Office less and less effective.[27]

Merivale's assessment of the development of colonial plural societies relied more on culture than on race. Similarly, when he applied his political economy to the West Indies, his analysis of the balance of land, capital, and labour provided an explanation, which modern historians still accept, for the more successful transition from slavery to free wage labour in Barbados than in Jamaica.[28] Like his contemporaries, Merivale had little respect for Aboriginal cultures, and there was no doubt an element of chauvinism in his recognition of the power of modernizing forces unleashed by colonial conquest. At the same time, he had the insight to see that assimilation of diverse peoples to Victorian modernity created new conditions of social and legal inequality that exposed colonized peoples to exploitation and abuse. He also understood that the management of the transition to these new modern and multiracial conditions was among the most complex and difficult challenges for future makers of colonial policy.

When the advocates of the "New Liberalism" such as James Bryce or Gilbert Murray addressed questions of racial conflict and the construction of racial inequality and segregation in the law, they reiterated many of the concerns originally advanced by Merivale. They did so, however, in a different historical context and had available a much richer language of race relations for constructing forms of racial inequality within modern multiracial colonial and self-governing societies. They also looked forward to the new twentieth century, which they anticipated would be unlike the nineteenth century. In 1902 Bryce advised his readers that they faced a world crisis and stood before an new era, just as Columbus had stood before a new world. Not only was this new era constituted by white citizens with elected legislatures keen to defend their privileges by writing racial exclusions in the law, but the new century would also face demands by peoples of African and Asian descent for an equal share in the entitlements of democratic citizens and even self-government in colonies where they constituted majorities. As W.E.B. Du Bois famously observed in the Address of the Pan-African Conference in London in 1900, these imperial advocates understood that "the problem of the twentieth century is the problem of the colour line." The difference was that the assembled pan-Africanists wished to obliterate it, whereas most, though not all, imperial advocates wished to defend the colour line to maintain racial inequality and exclusion against what they correctly anticipated would be the more assertive demands of persons of colour.[29]

Compared to Merivale's observations in the 1840s and 1860s, or more notably compared to the language of Granville Sharp or Edward Long on slavery and race in the late eighteenth century, or compared to the competing constructions of abolitionists and anthropologists in the 1860s, the late Victorians and Edwardians had a new and far richer vocabulary of race and race relations out of which to construct forms of racial exclusion and subordination. These constructions, most evident in the discussion of the new South Africa following the South African War of 1899–1902, but also part of the discourse on policies affecting Aboriginal peoples and immigration in the self-governing Dominions, applied in the main to modern, industrializing capitalist economies with legislative assemblies elected by white male citizens. The commentaries and policy makers assumed that conflict was endemic in multiracial and multi-ethnic societies, and the aim was to construct provisions in law and administrative practice that would achieve the impossible – namely, an orderly, stable polity in which racial exclusion and subordination would be made legitimate in the law and receive the consent not only of privileged whites, but also of the racial others excluded or placed in a unequal, subordinate position.

To describe the roots of the racial conflicts assumed to be endemic to these societies, and to describe the legal and other strategies for the management of these conflicts, a new language of race relations developed between the 1890s and 1914. The term with the longest history was "colour prejudice," which originated in the abolitionist critique of slavery and racism in the 1820s and 1830s. Seen as an unwarranted, irrational dislike or contempt for persons of colour and derived from a past of racial slavery or comparable forms of colonial oppression, colour prejudice, in the discourse of assimilation, was viewed as fundamentally in contradiction to British standards of equality before the law. These standards seemed best exemplified in Queen Victoria's proclamation to the peoples of India in 1858 following the Mutiny and most clearly violated in the Ilbert Bill in 1883. The Ilbert Bill controversy involved the defence of European privileged status in law through the stereotyping contrast of white female virtue and the sensual and unmanly character of Indian men. A comparable discourse developed over the discriminatory immigration policies enacted by self-governing legislatures representing white settlers. As R.A. Huttenback has shown, this language of race, including the terms "native," "coloured person," or "non-European," was the subject of extensive discussion and negotiation between the Foreign and Colonial Offices, as well as between colonial and dominion legislatures and administrations, in the development of an acceptable, non-racial language in which to frame exclusive immigration restrictions.[30]

In the new language of race relations, colour prejudice was normalized: it was viewed as irrational but as a natural, biologically inherited xenophobia, evident in white reactions and probably shared by all peoples in response to persons of a visibly different physical appearance. Consequently, various analogues to colour prejudice developed to describe this construction of a normalized natural or xenophobic response, including "colour" or "race antipathy," "race hatred," "repugnance," or "race instinct."[31] In his Romanes Lectures for 1902, entitled *The Relations of the Advanced and the Backward Races of Mankind*, James Bryce developed the case for the psychological roots of racial conflict. He was particularly inventive in developing substitutes for the older terminology of colour prejudice, referring to an "aversion to colour," "repulsion," "race-antagonism," "race-pride," and "race-rivalry."[32] This construction of naturalized and normalized responses placed biological limits on notions of equal status under the law and on rights of citizenship. Consequently, forms of segregation and discrimination were in accordance with this constructed natural order, which no successful politician and only utopian ideologues would challenge.[33]

The terminology of "segregation" and "discrimination" – and even the more critical expression, "racialism" – came into use during this period. Segregation, a term originating in the American South, had a liberal origin as a way to protect persons of colour against this inborn white chauvinism. British usage of the term appears to be borrowed from the United States, for the earliest uses of "segregation" occurred in British commentaries on the implementation of Jim Crow legislation in the South.[34] The analogous term, "discrimination," was used less frequently and had an ambiguous application. It retained its original, general meaning of an accurate, exact, or discerning judgment, and thus when applied to race, it was not necessarily prejudicial. Sir Charles Lucas of the Colonial Office contrasted "colour discrimination," an appropriately drawn distinction between racial groups, from "colour prejudice," an irrational and unwarranted attitude or action.[35] The terms "racialism" and "anti-racialism," originating in 1907 and 1911 respectively, predated the more familiar term "racism" by thirty years. Ironically, "racialism" originated among British settlers in the Transvaal protesting against the Afrikaner nationalist and linguistic preferences. While protesting against Afrikaner "racialism," these advocates of the rights of British settlers supported white solidarity against any extension of civil liberties to blacks. As the new union came into being, these same advocates for British migrants somewhat prematurely predicted the death of "racialism" in South Africa.[36]

Of more extensive and more generic application was the term "non-European," which came into use in the 1890s to describe all persons of colour. The invention of the term "non-European" as a primary division of the world's peoples, and the later and less frequently used term "non-white," ran counter to the multiplication of more and more finely defined racial types by the racial scientists. This new generic vocabulary depicted a more starkly drawn world order divided unequally in wealth and power between Europe and the "others."[37] In such a world, a colour-blind Empire was an anachronistic Victorian illusion. John Seeley's *Expansion of England* (1883) contrasted an empire of settlement for whites embodying "ultra-English" customs and practices with an empire of rule for colonial others with distinctly "unEnglish" authoritarian institutions. The peoples of these two empires were to be kept apart even within single colonial or dominion jurisdictions with the provision of a newly named "colour bar," which spread back, not without controversy, to the metropolis of London itself.[38] In the course of this discourse from the 1890s to 1914, the cluster of conflicts and issues raised by what was called the "Native question" or the "colour question" or the "race problem" came to be identified initially as "race relationships" or "inter-race relationships," or by 1910 as "race relations."[39]

Within this newly invented discourse of race relations, the contending visions of assimilation or exclusion and separate development were still evident, but the exclusionary voice was dominant. In December 1907, Sir Charles P. Lucas prepared a *Confidential Print on the Native Races in the British Empire*. A long-serving member of the Colonial Office with special responsibilities for dealing with the dominion governments and the thorny issue of exclusionary immigration legislation, Lucas had to address the new pressures for constructing in policy and in law forms of racial exclusion and subordination. Upon the initiative of Lord Elgin, the colonial secretary, he drafted his report in preparation for parliamentary discussion of the new constitutional arrangements in South Africa and their implications for imperial policy, especially as they affected "Natives" or "persons of colour."[40] Lucas still defined what he termed the traditional "English" view as one in which the law was colour-blind and the goal should be the assimilation of peoples regardless of race to an equality of citizenship. But he agreed that colonial policy needed to address the transition of non-European peoples to modern conditions and recommended the creation of reserve lands and a protected inferior status in law to facilitate this transition to modern and equal citizenship. What he feared was that such policies might become fixed and permanent, and separation and exclusion would be extended over time. The outcome, he rightly predicted in the case of South Africa, might be a permanent, subordinate, vulnerable status with little or no possibility of equality of citizenship.

While Lucas trusted colonial administrators under the watchful eye of the Colonial Office to manage this transition, he believed the main obstacle lay in the forces of democracy, which he identified with white working-class labour movements fearful of competition from African and coloured migrant workers. He rejected the idea that prejudice was a product of ignorance or a lack of familiarity with other races, since those communities with the longest history of racial subordination – for example, the United States – were the societies with the most intense conflict and prejudice. The advance of democracy, with a fusion of class and race antagonisms expressed most forcefully by working-class colonial whites, liberated new, narrow, self-interested passions. For Lucas, democracy with its assertive racism contradicted an older civilizing and assimilative morality, and thus did not represent a conversion of Victorian values into white virtues.[41]

A voice more sympathetic to democracy, Graham Wallas, in *Human Nature in Politics* (1908), also probed whether democracy and citizenship was limited by the biological inheritance of race. As a journalist and new kind of political scientist more interested in behaviour than theory, Wallas recognized that the old assimilating cultural imperialism of abolitionists and missionary advocates was no longer credible, but at the same time he thought that imperial policy and the complex array of colonial laws and regulations had no coherence and no underlying principle or objective. They were simply a cluster of pragmatic responses to local pressures, and for colonized subjects the contradictions and inconsistencies were bound to create a sense of the hypocrisy and inequity of British rule. What Wallas termed the "humanitarian" policy was the only option, for the advance of democracy would not be limited to whites. In a future of increased imperial rivalry between nation-states, Asians, Africans, and other colonized peoples would be expected to serve their imperial overlords, and from this military service they would inevitably demand the rights of citizenship.[42]

With the new twentieth century, the assertion of democratic rights by British subjects of non-European origin confronted newly created but nevertheless more substantial obstacles than the constructed stereotypes found in travel literature and fiction, and made authoritative by anthropology and its associated sciences. There were diminished possibilities for the lobbying for the rights of persons of colour through the past alliance with radicals and liberals in the anti-slavery movement or in agencies such as the APS. In 1900 the Pan-African Conference's Address to the World attempted to appeal to a historical consciousness of such an alliance that went back to Granville Sharp and the origins of the anti-slavery movement. As rich as that historical association had been, under the conditions of the new century, the political and intellectual basis for such an alliance of British radicals and colonial nationalists scarcely existed. In 1909, with the resources of its members and finances exhausted from pressing the case of the rights of Africans and coloureds in South Africa, and with the death of its secretary, H.R. Fox Bourne, the APS reluctantly amalgamated with the British and Foreign Anti-Slavery Society. The APS members were divided on whether they should support colonial nationalist demands for the vote and for self-government. The Anti-Slavery Society was much more cautious, reluctant to move beyond the well-defined sphere of its special mission on slavery and the slave trade, and forced by events to address various forms of coerced labour as they arose in South Africa or in plantation production in West and East Africa.[43]

Under Fox Bourne's leadership, the APS had championed the legal rights of Western-educated Africans. Once the models of a positive British influence in Africa, these professional doctors, lawyers, clergy, and teachers were now increasingly subject to denigration as "mimic-men" by colonial administrators, cultural relativists like Mary Kingsley, and racial supremacists who denied that Africans and other non-European peoples could assimilate to the values and conventions of Western civilization. Under the leadership of Rev. John Harris, an associate of E.D. Morel, the newly amalgamated Anti-Slavery Society looked with favour upon Lord Lugard's indirect rule and helped redefine humanitarian goals under the separate, unequal, and protected terms of colonial trusteeship. When the amalgamated society ventured into more contentious political territory in daring to offer a critique of the labour practices of the new Union of South Africa, it soon paid a political price. As a result, in 1911 George V resigned as royal patron and severed the royal connection with anti-slavery philanthropy that had been established by his grandmother.[44]

The assertion of equality before the law and the right to vote for persons of colour also confronted more substantial intellectual challenges. The new language of race relations, built in part upon the historical continuities of racial oppression and conflict, constructed a more powerful defence of racial subordination and exclusion. Of particular importance was the use of the psychology of prejudice, best and most influentially exemplified by James Bryce, for it rooted racial conflict not in a past inheritance subject to change or in competing economic or other rational interests in the present, but in a construction of human nature fixed by inborn instincts, including a xenophobia that determined that races must be separate and unequal. This construction of human nature defined political possibilities, for in the new age of democratically elected governments, the instinctive xenophobia of white males ruled.[45] A minority dissenting voice still existed, however, best exemplified by Sydney Olivier's effort to apply his Fabian socialism, Colonial Office experience, and knowledge of Jamaica to the analysis of what he called "race relations." He drew a parallel between race and class relationships and argued that racial conflict, racial prejudice, and theories of racial inequality were largely a product of conflicts between white capital and coloured labour.[46]

With a trendy Edwardian interest in the occult and paranormal psychology, Olivier also took an interest in the psychology of race. Indulging in the bipolar contrast of black and white and showing some measure of cultural relativism, Olivier saw some attractions in the construction of an African primitivism having a closer affinity to nature, greater spirituality, and a more natural sexuality in contrast to European civilization with its excessive intellectuality, aggressive materialism, and emotional repressions.[47] Unlike their Victorian predecessors, some Edwardian commentators were prepared to explore the emotional and sexual roots of racial attractions and prejudices. For example, William Archer, drama critic and English translator of Ibsen, in his account of his travels in the United States with the innovative title *Through Afro America* (1910), tried to explain the intensity of the anti-black feelings of white Americans, most evident in the horrific, ritualized murders of the lynch mobs. He denied the commonplace allegation of black male sexual aggression against white women. Like Ida B. Wells, the African-American civil rights activist and anti-lynching campaigner who toured Great Britain in the 1890s, Archer claimed that the root of these outrages lay in white males' guilt about their sexual attraction to and exploitation of black women. Unlike Wells or Olivier, however, Archer's analysis confirmed the insights of James Bryce that racial prejudices and conflicts were deeply rooted in human nature. Consequently, legislated inequality and exclusion was a necessary and legitimate political response to the dictates of white instincts.[48]

We need to know much more about British racial discourse after the 1870s, and especially from 1890 to 1914, when a new and, to our ears, familiar language of race relations became commonplace. Such a focus will also necessitate a reconsideration of our received narrative of the history of racism. The familiar racial typologies of scientific racism have come to define racism itself as a form of biological determinism. This scientific construction of racial types had its origins in the eighteenth century, gained academic institutional credibility in the mid-nineteenth century, and suffered a retreat from the 1930s through the 1950s. Sometimes this retreat is misconstrued as the demise of racism as an ideology, when it in fact represents the dismantling of a temporary scaffold, leaving intact what has been variously termed structural or systemic or institutional racism.[49]

Cultural studies that focus on origins and identities to construct a Victorian racist other run the risk of overlooking a more potent legacy of Victorian racial discourse for our own time. To understand the historical ancestry of the racism that persists in the twenty-first century, we need to go back to the late Victorians and Edwardians who coined our language of race relations. This language, originating in a discourse of assimilation, constructed forms of racial exclusion and subordination under modern conditions for colonized subjects of British rule, for self-governing colonials, and for the colonizers in the imperial culture of the metropolis. This discourse on race was contemporaneous with the founding of the modern social sciences and helped establish a language suited to describe the conditions of modernity and its defining contrast to "primitive," "traditional," or "premodern" conditions. This language of race relations also informed the discourse on race and the metropolitan context of colonial students and other coloured residents in the United Kingdom in the 1920s and 1930s, and it shaped the debate on post-1945 immigration of British colonial subjects from the distant reaches of the Empire.[50] This late Victorian and Edwardian dialogue of assimilation and exclusion still shapes our discourse on the meaning of human rights and multiculturalism, on the nature of globalization and world inequality, and even on that persistent colonial and post-colonial theme of imperialism and democracy.[51]

{NOTES}

1 Linda Colley, *Britons: Forging the Nation, 1707–1837* (London: Vintage, 1996) and "Britishness and Otherness: An Argument," *Journal of British Studies* 31 (1992): 309–29; Kathleen Wilson, *The Sense of the People: Politics, Culture and Imperialism, 1715–1785* (Cambridge: Cambridge University Press, 1995); Shula Marks, "History, the Nation and Empire: Sniping from the Periphery," *History Workshop Journal* 29 (1990): 111–19; Catherine Hall, "Thinking the Postcolonial, Thinking the Empire," in *Cultures of Empire: A Reader* (New York: Routledge, 2000), 1–33.

2 Catherine Hall, *Civilising Subjects: Metropole and Colony in the English Imagination, 1830–1867* (Cambridge: Polity, 2002), 1–22.

3 Edward Said, *Orientalism* (Harmondsworth: Penguin, 1978); "Orientalism Reconsidered," *Race and Class* 27 (1985): 1–15, and *Culture and Imperialism* (New York: Knopf, 1993); Patrick Brantlinger, *Rule of Darkness: British Literature and Imperialism, 1830–1914* (Ithaca: Cornell University Press, 1988); Robert J.C. Young, *Colonial Desire: Hybridity in Theory, Culture and Race* (London: Routledge, 1995); H.L. Malchow, *Gothic Images of Race in Nineteenth-Century Britain* (Stanford: Stanford University Press, 1996). Douglas Lorimer, "Restructuring Victorian Racial Discourse: Images of Race, the Language of Race Relations, and the Context of Black Resistance," in *Black Victorians/Black Victoriana*, ed. G. Gerzina (New Brunswick: Rutgers University Press, 2003), 187–89.

4 Robert Knox, *The Races of Man: A Fragment* (London: Henry Renshaw, 1850) and *The Races of Man: A Philosophical Enquiry into the Influence of Race over the Destinies of Nations* (London: Renshaw, 1862); Evelleen Richards, "The 'Moral Anatomy' of Robert Knox: The Inter-Play between Biological and Social Thought in Victorian Scientific Naturalism," *Journal of the History of Biology* 22 (1989): 373–436.

5 Philip Curtin, *The Image of Africa: British Ideas and Action, 1780–1850* (London: Macmillan, 1965); Christine Bolt, *Victorian Attitudes to Race* (London: Routledge & Kegan Paul, 1972); Douglas Lorimer, *Colour, Class and the Victorians* (Leicester: Leicester University Press, 1978); Catherine Hall, Keith McCelland, and Jane Rendall, *Defining the Victorian Nation: Class, Race and Gender and the Reform Act of 1867* (Cambridge: Cambridge University Press, 2000).

6 T.W. Heyck, *The Transformation of Intellectual Life in Victorian England* (London: Croom Helm, 1982).

7 Douglas Lorimer, "Science and the Secularization of Victorian Images of Race," in *Victorian Science in Context*, ed. B. Lightman (Chicago: University of Chicago Press, 1997), 212–35; George Stocking, *Victorian Anthropology* (New York: Free Press, 1987).

8 Susan Thorne, *Congregational Missions and the Making of an Imperial Culture in Nineteenth-Century England* (Stanford: Stanford University Press, 1999); Clare Midgley, *Women against Slavery* (London: Routledge, 1992), and "Anti-Slavery and the Roots of 'Imperial Feminism,'" in *Gender and Imperialism*, ed. C. Midgley (Manchester: Manchester University Press, 1998), 161–79; estimate of female subscribers from my analysis of lists of donors in *The Anti-Slavery Reporter* and *The Aborigines' Friend* (1870–1909).

9 Lorimer, *Colour*, 129–30; H. John Field, *Toward a Programme of Imperial Life: The British Empire at the Turn of the Century* (Westport, CT: Greenwood, 1982), 187–89.

10 George Stocking, "The Persistence of Polygenist Thought in Post-Darwinian Anthropology," in *Race, Culture and Evolution* (Chicago: University of Chicago Press, 1982), 42–68 is often cited, but his principal examples are American or

European, not British, scientists; see Douglas Lorimer, "Theoretical Racism in late Victorian Anthropology, 1870–1900," *Victorian Studies* 31 (1988): 405–30, and "Nature, Racism and late Victorian Science," *Canadian Journal of History* 25 (December 1990): 369–85, and "Science and Secularization," 214–18.

11 A.H. Keane, *Ethnology* (Cambridge: Cambridge University Press, 1896), 165–66; J.W. Burrow, *Evolution and Society* (Cambridge: Cambridge University Press, 1966).

12 Graham Wallas, *Human Nature in Politics* (1908; repr., London: Constable, 1948), 288.

13 Lorimer, "Science and Secularization," 217; "Mr. Asquith and Anthropology," *The Times*, 12 March 1909.

14 Lorimer, "Race, Science and Culture: Historical Continuities and Discontinuities, 1850–1914," in *Victorians and Race*, ed. Shearer West (Aldershot: Scolar Press, 1996), 12–33; Elazar Barkan, *The Retreat of Scientific Racism* (Cambridge: Cambridge University Press, 1992).

15 Peter Mandler, "'Race' and 'Nation' in mid-Victorian Thought," in *History, Religion and Culture: British Intellectual History*, ed. S. Collini, R. Whatmore, and B. Young (Cambridge: Cambridge University Press, 2000), 224–44.

16 Stephan Collini, *Public Moralists: Political Thought and Intellectual Life in Britain, 1850–1930* (Oxford: Clarendon, 1991), 91–118; John S. Mill, "Representative Government" [1861], in *Utilitarianism, Liberty, Representative Government* (London: J.M. Dent, 1910), 280–84.

17 These stereotypes were commonplace in Victorian travel literature and popular science: see Lorimer, "Science and Secularization," 218–28; the popular works of J.G. Wood, *The Natural History of Man; Being an Account of the Manners and Customs of the Uncivilised Races of Men*, 2 vols. (London: George Routledge, 1868, 1870); and Robert Brown's multi-volume series, *The Races of Mankind*, 4 vols. (London: Cassell, Petter and Galpin, 1873–1876), *The Peoples of the World*, 6 vols. (1881–1886), and *The Countries of the World*, 6 vols. (1884–1889).

18 R. Huttenback, *Racism and Empire: White Settlers and Colored Immigrants in the British Self-Governing Colonies, 1830–1910* (Ithaca: Cornell University Press, 1976); Lord Rosebery, "Questions of Empire," in *Miscellanies: Literary and Historical* (London: Hodder and Stoughton, 1921), 2:229–63; Benjamin Kidd, *Social Evolution* (New York: Macmillan, 1895), 283–308, 325–49.

19 Kenan Malik, *The Meaning of Race: Race, History and Culture in Western Society* (New York: New York University Press, 1996); Paul Gilroy, *Against Race: Imagining Political Culture beyond the Color Line* (Cambridge, MA: Harvard University Press, 2000); Etienne Balibar, "Paradoxes of Universality," and David Goldberg, "The Social Formation of Racist Discourse," in *Anatomy of Racism*, ed. David Goldberg (Minneapolis: University of Minnesota Press, 1990), 283–94, 295–319.

20 At the golden jubilee meeting for the abolition of slavery in 1884, leading Liberal and Conservative politicians all emphasized not only the place of abolition in the nation's history but their families' participation in this still celebrated event. *The Anti-Slavery Reporter*, 4th ser., 4 (1884), special jubilee number.

21 H.R. Fox Bourne, *The Aborigines Protection Society: Chapters in Its History* (London: P.S. King, 1899); Thorne, *Congregational Missions*, 155–70.

22 *Report of the Select Committee on Aborigines (British Settlements)* (1837; repr., Shannon: Irish University Press, 1968), 3–6, 74–81; British and Foreign Aborigines Protection Society, *Regulations of the Society and Address* (London, 1837); Bourne, *Aborigines*

Protection Society; "The Claims of Uncivilised Races," *The Aborigines' Friend*, n.s., 5 (1896–1900), appendix (December 1900): 1–12.

23 Public Record Office (PRO), CO 96/284 Aborigines Protection Society to Chamberlain, 19 February 1896; CO 96/284, APS to Chamberlain, 2 March 1896; Flora Shaw, "Dry-Nursing in the Colonies," *Fortnightly Review*, n.s., 46 (1889): 367–79; Andrew Porter, "Trusteeship, Anti-Slavery and Humanitarianism," in *Oxford History of the British Empire* (Oxford: Oxford University Press, 1999), 3:198–221.

24 Charles Dilke, *Greater Britain: A Record of Travel in English-Speaking Countries during 1866 and 1867* (New York: Harper & Brothers, 1869), 27–35, 200–27, 314–20, 332–36, 520–34, 545–46; S. Gwynn and G.M. Tuckwell, *Life of Sir Charles Dilke* (London: J. Murray, 1917), 2:368–86; Richard Koebner and Helmut Dan Schmidt, *Imperialism: The Story and Significance of a Political Word, 1840–1960* (Cambridge: Cambridge University Press, 1964), 87–91; Roy Jenkins, *Sir Charles Dilke: A Victorian Tragedy* (London: Collins, 1965); Reginald Horsman, *Race and Manifest Destiny: The Origins of American Anglo-Saxon Racism* (Cambridge, MA: Harvard University Press, 1981). Horsman interprets Dilke from the viewpoint of his impact on American racism and overlooks Dilke's interest in propagating liberal "Saxon" political institutions and culture to the "non-Saxon" world; Lorimer, "Race, Science and Culture," 16–17.

25 Charles Dilke, *Greater Britain*, 545–46; *Problems of Greater Britain* (London: Macmillan, 1890); "Remarks of Sir Charles Dilke to the Annual Meeting of the Aborigines Protection Society," *The Aborigines' Friend*, n.s., 6 (April 1901): 3–5.

26 Herman Merivale, *Lectures on Colonization and Colonies* (1861; repr., New York: Augustus Kelly, 1967), 487–523, 536–40, 544–52; David McNab, "Herman Merivale and the Native Question, 1837–61," *Albion* 9 (1977): 359–84.

27 Merivale, *Lectures*, 518–23, 536–52.

28 Ibid., 314–19, 336–48.

29 James Bryce, *The Relations of the Advanced and the Backward Races of Mankind* (1902; repr., Ann Arbour, MI: University Microfilms International, 1979); Gilbert Murray, "The Exploitation of Inferior Races in Ancient and Modern Times," in *Liberalism and Empire*, ed. Francis W. Hirst, G. Murray, and J.L. Hammond (London, 1900); "Address to the Nations of the World by the Pan-African Conference in London, 1900," in *Ideologies of Liberation in Black Africa, 1856–1970: Documents on Modern African Political Thought from Colonial Times to the Present*, ed. J. Ayodele Langley (London: R. Collings, 1979), 738–39; Alistair Bonnett, "Whiteness in Crisis," *History Today* 50, no. 12 (2000), www.historytoday.com

30 Lorimer, "Reconstructing Victorian Racial Discourse," 194–95; Thomas R. Metcalf, *Ideologies of the Raj* (Cambridge: Cambridge University Press, 1995), 199–214; Mrinalini Sinha, "Chathams, Pitts, and Gladstones in Petticoats: The Politics of Gender and Race in the Ilbert Bill Controversy, 1883–1884," in *Western Women and Imperialism: Complicity and Resistance*, ed. Nupur Chaudhuri and Margaret Strobel (Bloomington: Indiana University Press, 1992), 98–116.

31 Leonard Alston, *The White Man's Work in Asia and Africa: A Discussion of the Main Difficulties of the Colour Question* (London: Longmans Green, 1907), 4–8, 16–18, 91–92; William Archer, *Through Afro-America* (1910; repr., Westport, CT: Negro Universities Press, 1970), 7–9, 71; Sir Charles P. Lucas, *Greater Rome and Greater Britain* (Oxford: Clarendon, 1912), 107–8; Murray, "Exploitation," 142–43; Newton H. Marshall, "Empires and Races," *The Contemporary Review* 96 (September

1909): 314–16. Wallas, *Human Nature*, 55–58, and Sydney Olivier, *White Capital and Coloured Labour* (1910; repr., Westport, CT: Negro Universities Press, 1970), 36, 38–39, were critical of the idea but used the term "race instinct" to describe the position of authors they criticized.

32 Bryce, *Relations*, 7–20, 27–29, 46.

33 Murray, "Exploitation," 151.

34 John W. Cell, *The Highest Stage of White Supremacy: The Origins of Segregation in South Africa and the American South* (Cambridge: Cambridge University Press, 1982); *The Anti-Slavery Reporter*, 4th ser., 11 (1891): 31; "The Negro Problem in America," *The Spectator*, 26 October 1901, 595–96.

35 Lucas, *Greater Rome*, 99–100; for use of discrimination in older sense and in new sense as applied to racial discrimination, see *The Anti-Slavery Reporter*, 4th ser., 21 (1901): 170–71.

36 *Daily Chronicle*, 12 January 1907; "South Africa's Future – Problems to be Solved – The Death of Racialism," *The Westminster Gazette*, 11 April 1910. A Transvaal Correspondent, "Racialism in South Africa," *The Empire Review* 20 (January 1911): 400–405.

37 Benjamin Kidd, *Social Evolution*, 60; PRO, CO 886/1, Dominions No. 1. Confidential. The Self-Governing Dominions and Coloured Immigration. C.P.L. July 1908, 52–53; Sir Charles Bruce, *The Broad Stone of Empire: Problems of Crown Colony Administration, with records of personal experience* (London: Macmillan, 1910), 1:382; Wallas, *Human Nature*, 6–10, 281–83, 288–89.

38 J.R. Seeley, *The Expansion of England* (1883; Chicago: University of Chicago, 1971), 140–42; on colour bar: *The Aborigines' Friend*, n.s., 8 (May 1909): 257–62; *The Anti-Slavery Reporter and Aborigines' Friend*, 5th ser., 2 (October 1911): 106–7; Bruce, *The Broad Stone*, 1:378. On the anti-imperial London of radicals and colonized subjects of colour, see Jonathan Schneer, *London 1900: The Imperial Metropolis* (New Haven: Yale University Press, 2001), and on the experience of black residents and visitors, see Jeffrey Green, *Black Edwardians: Black People in Britain, 1901–14* (London: Frank Cass, 1998).

39 The term "inter-racial" gained currency in the reports of the Universal Races Congress, which met in London in July 1911, whereas the phrase "race relations" initially applied to white-black relations in the United States and probably had an American origin, though among British sources it was first used by Sydney Olivier: G. Spiller, ed., *Papers on Inter-Racial Problems Communicated to the First Universal Races Congress* (1911; repr., Miami, FL: Mnemosyne, 1969); Lord Avebury, "Inter-Racial Problems," *Fortnightly Review*, n.s., 90 (July-Dec. 1911): 581–89; *Review of Reviews* 42 (1910): 335; H.H. Johnston, "Racial Problems," 237–42; Wallas, *Human Nature*, 269, 288–90; Olivier, *White Capital and Coloured Labour*, 172–73; R.P. Brooks, "A Local Study of the Race Problem: Race Relations in the Eastern Piedmont Region of Georgia," *Political Science Quarterly* 26 (June 1911): 193–221; Archer, *Through Afro-America*, x.

40 PRO, CO 885/19 Miscellaneous No. 217 Confidential. *Native Races in the British Empire* [C.P.L.] (31 December 1907); Ronald Hyam, *Elgin and Churchill at the Colonial Office, 1905–1908: The Watershed of the Empire-Commonwealth* (London: Macmillan, 1968), 367–68.

41 PRO, CO 885/19. *Native Races*, 6–17, 26–31, and *Greater Rome and Greater Britain*, 102–7.

42 Wallas, *Human Nature*, 8–10, 282–94.

43 Rhodes House Library, British Empire E2/11 British and Foreign Anti-Slavery Society Minute Book, #932 4 May 1900; *The Anti-Slavery Reporter*, 4th ser, 21 (January 1901): 3–13; cf. lobbying by APS, *The Aborigines' Friend* 20 (1900) and 21 (1901).

44 Rhodes House Library, British Empire, S20: British and Foreign Anti-Slavery and Aborigines Protection Society Minute Book, #1798, 5 August 1910, and #1811, 7 October 1910; Lorimer, "Reconstructing Victorian Racial Discourse," 202–3; T.C. McCaskie, "Cultural Encounters: Britain and Africa in the Nineteenth Century," *Oxford History of the British Empire*, 3:665–89; Bernard Porter, *Critics of Empire: British Radical to Colonialism in Africa* (London: Macmillan, 1968).

45 Bryce, *Relations*, 31–46.

46 Olivier, *White Capital*, 126–31, 160–75.

47 Olivier, *White Capital*, 147–49; Francis Lee, *Fabianism and Colonialism: The Life and Political Thought of Lord Sydney Olivier* (London: Defiant Books,1988); Norman and Jeanne MacKenzie, *The First Fabians* (London: Quartet, 1979), 58–60, 268–74; Anne McClintock, *Imperial Leather: Race, Gender, and Sexuality in the Colonial Context* (London: Routledge, 1995) presents the most ambitious effort to explore the interconnections of race, gender, and sexuality in this period.

48 Archer, *Through Afro-America*, 213–23; on Wells, see Vron Ware, *Beyond the Pale: White Women, Racism and History* (London: Verso, 1992), 173–97; Nicole King, "A Colored Woman in Another Country Pleading for Justice in Her Own: Ida B. Wells in Great Britain," in *Black Victorians*, 88–109.

49 F. Barkan, *The Retreat of Scientific Racism* (Cambridge: Cambridge University Press, 1992); F. Furedi, *The Silent War: Imperialism and the Changing Perception of Race* (New Brunswick: Rutgers University Press, 1998).

50 Barbara Bush, *Imperialism, Race, and Resistance: Africa and Britain, 1919–1945* (London: Routledge, 1999); Shompa Lahiri, *Indians in Britain: Anglo-Indian Encounters, Race and Identity, 1880–1930* (London: Frank Cass, 2000); Laura Tabili, *"We Ask for British Justice": Workers and Racial Difference in Late Imperial Britain* (Ithaca: Cornell University Press, 1994).

51 Some recent works attempt to link the narrative of past racism to the present: for example, Malik, *The Meaning of Race*, and more directly in an American context, Thomas Holt, *The Problem of Race in the 21st Century* (Cambridge, MA: Harvard University Press, 2000). But other efforts bear a distressing similarity to their late Victorian and Edwardian predecessors, such as T.H. von Laue, *The World Revolution of Westernization: The Twentieth Century in a Global Perspective* (Oxford: Oxford University Press, 1987) and Samuel P. Huntington, *The Clash of Civilizations: Remaking of the World Order* (New York: Touchstone, 1997).

CHAPTER 6

COLONIAL COMPARISONS:

RETHINKING MARRIAGE, CIVILIZATION AND NATION IN NINETEENTH-CENTURY WHITE SETTLER SOCIETIES*

Bettina Bradbury

WHEN MALE POLITICIANS IN Australia, New Zealand, and other British colonies debated changing the rules of marriage, they, like politicians addressing similar issues elsewhere, grappled with the complicated details of marriage law and with marriage's inextricability from understandings of civilization, nation, identity, gender, and race. Marriage in the colonies and in the politics and discourses of empire was a powerful signifier of stability, respectability, and successful colonization. It was understood both as a civilizing force and as a measure of civilization. To contemplate changing marriage law was to tamper with an institution widely understood to have "a great deal to do with framing the national character," with laying the "foundation for the nation's happiness and strength."[1] This paper explores debates about changing married women's property rights; it draws largely on the arguments made by colonial politicians during the 1870s and 1880s and focusses mainly on New Zealand, New South Wales, Queensland, and South Australia.[2] Feminist historians have examined the nineteenth-century changes to married women's property rights in diverse jurisdictions for several decades now. Most studies, however, focus on only one country, and many on one state, province, or colony. The vast majority of studies have

* This project is currently funded by an SSHRC grant, for which I am grateful. Many graduate students have helped with the research drawn on here and in the broader project of which it is part. I would particularly like to acknowledge the work of Lisa Chilton, now in the History Department at the University of Prince Edward Island; Rebecca Waese, who copied many of the Australian debates for me; and Lori Chambers of Lakehead University, who shared the material she had collected for her book *Married Women and Property Law in Ontario* (Toronto: Osgoode Legal Society, 1997).

dealt with either England or American states;[3] less attention has been paid to similar debates in British colonies.[4] Here I read these debates as part of broader colonial culture, as moments when politicians articulated understandings about their place in the Empire at the same time as they made claims for the distinctiveness of their own colonies.[5]

Recent research by feminist scholars highlights the significance of marriage between Europeans as a central component of the "colonial project." In colonial British Columbia, as Adele Perry has argued, marriage was invested with the possibility of turning European males away from the rough, homosocial culture of the gold fields and from liaisons with First Nations women.[6] In the early days of British rule in all these colonies, intimacy between European men and local indigenous women offered the men more than sexual gratification. For many, it opened up links to broad networks of kin that frequently helped them in their work as fur traders, whalers, and so on. In most of the colonies that became white settler societies, however, the period of cross-racial mixing through European marriage, indigenous marriage, or casual liaisons was relatively brief. Changing ideas of race combined with decreasing need for the support of indigenous peoples, changing economic realities, and colonial projects to shift the focus of reformers and colonial officials to marriage among Europeans.[7] The Colonial Office and colonial legislatures readily granted a range of Christian denominations the power to marry their parishioners in order to make legitimate marriage as readily available as possible. Marriages between British migrants would, as Alan Lester has argued for the Cape, increase the local population, forge a "British settler identity," and maintain settlers' social and sexual distance from indigenous peoples. Colonial Australian politicians saw fostering formal, legal heterosexual marriages among freed convicts as a critical element in cleaning up Australia's tainted image as a convict colony. Settlement promoter Edward Gibbon Wakefield argued that women's moral authority would cultivate civilization on colonial soil. Ideal immigrants, he argued, were childless married couples.[8] Married women immigrants would provoke less anxiety about morality than shiploads of unmarried women did on so many occasions.[9]

Within the broader relations of empire, the reputation of colonies as destinations for immigrants, capital, and colonial favour was seen to rest on projecting the image of a place where sexuality was contained in heterosexual, patriarchal marriage between Europeans.[10] At the same time, legal, Christian marriage was also a critical component of attempts to contain and civilize indigenous peoples and emancipated slaves throughout the Empire.[11] The promotion of marriage was always articulated through languages of sexuality, race, class, and gender that accentuated the differences between respectable European colonizers and those of other races, classes, and sometimes religions.[12]

Marriage as panacea in these colonial projects has an abstract, though thoroughly gendered, quality. The marriages in which so much faith was placed bore most resemblance to the idealized middle-class relationships of the Western world and were increasingly normalized in ways that naturalized gender difference and hid their foundations in class and racial privilege.[13] Men would provide. Women would oversee the domestic realm and raise children. Women would tame and civilize, act as "God's police," through their superior moral virtues.[14] The realities of most colonial marriages were more diverse.

In the political economy of occupation and settlement, the significance of marriage is clear. Heterosexual marriage requires male and female bodies. Hence the significance of European female migration into colonies where men outnumbered women, in some cases dramatically. Marriage transferred the material fruits of wives' labour and the wealth of all but a canny, elite few to husbands. The English common law determined the rights and obligations of husbands and wives in all the increasingly white settler colonies except South Africa and Quebec.[15] Thus in most of Canada, Australia, and New Zealand, women lost the ownership of their wages, of all their property except land, and of any other cash they generated once they married. Profits from any land wives owned at the time of the marriage or inherited during the marriage also became the property of husbands, except among the small and usually wealthy minority whose family had made a marriage settlement designating their property as separate. Marriage law thus served as a powerful instrument of male accumulation.[16] Furthermore, men gained more than ownership of their wives' earnings and property at marriage: the law made them owners of their wives bodies – and hence gave them the right to all that those bodies produced, including domestic labour, sex, and children.[17]

In return, men were expected to provide for their wives during the marriage and afterwards. In the early years of some of these colonies, women whose husbands died might have expected to profit from dower rights during their widowhood. But this "old hidden right," which had ensured that widows received the use of a third of their husband's property in compensation for their loss of property during marriage, was quickly circumscribed in legislation dealing with conveyancing, inheritance, will making, and dower.[18] All colonies found their own ways of institutionalizing the liberal principal of clear title through land registries. As the nineteenth century advanced, land that might once have been used by First Nations, Aboriginies or Maori, and then been subject through marriage to a widow's dower, was liberated of such historic and gendered claims. Men were free to buy, sell, and bequeath property in the clear knowledge that earlier claims had been extinguished. For married women, who in most of these colonies could not write a will, freedom of willing meant, as the Australian legal historian, Bruce Kercher, explains with brutal simplicity, "freedom for men alone."[19] The link between attracting immigrants, the importance of stable male land holding, and marriage can be expressed no more directly than in the words of an aspiring politician from Victoria, Australia, Archibald Boyd, published in the *Port Phillip Herald* in 1845. Reminding readers of their competition with other nations for immigrants, he argued that uncertain and short land tenure had "in all countries been found to paralize [*sic*] industry and prevent expenditure, and are especially injurious in a young community, by checking marriage with its consequent morality and civilization."[20] That European women were expected to convey the morality and civilization of which he spoke was so common sense, it needed no mention.

Life in the colonies accentuated the challenges to stable marriages. In New Zealand and most of the Australian colonies, as in Canada, the earliest attempts of legislators to grapple with women's claims on property centred on the problem of desertion. Starting in the 1840s in New South Wales and Queensland and continuing throughout the century in the other colonies, politicians debated what to do about men who left their wives or failed to provide. The responses to the problems posed by such men – referred to as "drunken and spendthrift," or "careless, dastardly, spongers or sluggards" in New South Wales; "brutal, cruel husbands" in South Australia; "good for nothing loafers," "vicious husbands, with debased appetites and inclinations," or "reckless, improvident drunken husbands" in New Zealand – were similar. Early acts provided protection orders so that such men could not return, take money their wives had earned or property they had purchased through their own labour, and leave again. By the 1870s, however, feminist critiques of marriage under the common law were spreading. Politicians in New Zealand and most Australian and Canadian colonies began to propose giving wives greater rights to keep their own property separate from that of their husbands. Many of the bills went beyond the provisions made in the English Married Women's Property Act of 1870. After the passage of England's Married Women's Property Act of 1882, those colonies that had not yet passed legislation mandating that all wives' property would remain separate as their own after marriage, including monies earned as wages and in other ways, scrambled to do so. In England there was evident concern about the need for unity in the laws throughout those parts of the Empire peopled by British emigrants. In the colonies, politicians expressed fear that women might not migrate and marry if they realized they would have fewer rights as wives than at home.

Colonial politicians wove many threads into their deliberations about changing the law of husband and wife. Some of these were colonial versions of arguments identified by historians who have studied similar debates in American states and in England. Some liberal politicians drew on feminist analyses of the links between slavery and marriage and explicitly identified themselves as strong supporters "of women's rights," or as familiar with the arguments of John Stuart Mill.[21] Others expressed concern about the possibilities of collusion and fraud between spouses that such a law would open up. They evoked colonial variants of the melodramatic tales about bad husbands who drank, deserted, or simply failed to provide. Invariably, these husbands were represented as part of the "labouring classes," and in the colonies as elsewhere, such tales of manhood gone awry were a crucial element in legitimating the idea that all men should be deprived of automatic ownership of their wives' property. These were colonial strands in the broader nineteenth-century, middle-class thrust to reshape the masculinity of other classes. Yet many colonial politicians also made it quite clear that they themselves were only too familiar with neglectful husbands among their social peers as well.[22] By exposing the worst kinds of husbands, they highlighted the qualities of good husbands.

A further thread in these colonial debates was the conviction, professed by many politicians both for and against proposed bills, that in changing women's rights within marriage they were effecting radical social change not just in families, but in the nation. Arguing for change in New South Wales in 1875, Charles Pilcher was explicit. He "was endeavouring to effect a radical change in the law, as it had existed for ages, and which had had a great deal to do with forming the national character." He parried the critique that it would upset "peace and happiness of domestic life."

On that front, their existing law was "a gross injustice upon women and a disgrace to a civilized country."[23] Similarly in an 1883 speech in South Australia, Richard Baker argued that

> this question underlays the whole foundation of national life, for nations become great, not because of any peculiarity of climate or of country...but because of the national character of people within them.... The marriage system and the lessons it inculcated was one of the greatest, if not the greatest, factor, in the formation of national character.[24]

Marriage and the gender relations it embodied were, in these formulations, inseparable from the health of society and the character of the nation.

In their public reimagining of relations between husbands and wives, colonial politicians situated marriage in the history and anthropology of civilization, drawing "webs of comparison" across time and cultures.[25] Their arguments drew upon contemporary understandings of anthropology and history as well as on the hardening understandings of biology, which were racializing meanings of civilization.[26] Those wanting to change the law linked existing legislation to feudalism or barbarism to underline its inappropriateness to a modern society. Those seeking the status quo stressed the long tradition of Christian marriage and the superiority of English law. Whether they supported or opposed change, politicians struggled with one central conundrum. Anglo-Saxon claims to be the most advanced civilization rested in part on the understanding that the treatment of women was a key indicator of civilization. Yet the common law treated wives less fairly than other bodies of law.

In making his case for change in New Zealand in 1870, James Richmond stressed the exceptional nature and barbaric origins of the common law in Europe with a brief lesson in legal history drawn directly from Judge Story's *Treatise in Equity Jurisprudence*. Arguing that the European civil law derived from the Romans was superior, he pointed to the embarrassing roots of the common law of England among the Saxons. "Civilization," he lectured,

> had not reached those parts of Europe from which English people obtained their law. The Saxons brought with them the barbarous customs of their forests...and became the dominant race in England, their law becoming the common or the unwritten law of England. The root of the common law of

England could be seen in a very recent barbarism, whereas the root of the civil law was in an ancient civilization. Under that law wives were under the control of their husbands, but had still large powers over her property.[27]

Supporters like Richmond could thus exploit the paradox of British claims to represent the most advanced civilization when their law denied women liberal rights within marriage. Knitting the common law closely back to its roots in barbarism served Richmond's case for a more civilized law without denying that England was the world's most civilized nation.

South Australian Conservative politician, Richard Baker, took pains to critique such versions of legal history. Under Saxon law, he proposed, "the wife did not merge in the husband.... When the Roman priests first went to Ireland they were astonished at the great power the wives claimed over property after marriage." Since existing marriage laws had "formed the moral life of Great Britain and that race to which we were all proud to belong – the Anglo-Saxon race," he would therefore support only the most careful changes to existing law.[28] On both sides, such rooting of current marriage law in Saxon times served, as Benedict Anderson has argued, to forge a "conception of modernity, explicitly juxtaposed to" the past that was central to the subjective idea of the nation.[29] The diverse claims about the links between marriage and civilization echo Bederman's suggestion that the concept of civilization was deployed in many different ways so as to "legitimate different sorts of claims to power."[30] Positioning current laws within the broad history of civilization effectively underlined the European, Christian, and Anglo-Saxon origins of marriage law in the colonies. By reaching back into European history, colonial politicians staked claims to a place within Western civilization despite their geographical locations on the periphery. They claimed a shared British heritage and distanced themselves, their history, and their marriage customs from those of the peoples whose lands they had recently occupied and settled.

Such appeals to the ancient roots of marriage law, however, did little to forge any sense of colonial specificity and difference. Here, more recent history played a role. Across these colonies, politicians advocating change sought to locate their young and vigorous colonies ahead of the metropole in legislation as well as on the civilization ladder.[31] When George Waterhouse introduced a new Married Women's Property Bill in New Zealand in 1881, a bill that was very similar to the one then being considered in the "Imperial Parliament," he expressed concern that previous legislation in that colony had been ahead of England but that since the 1870 Act in Great Britain, New Zealand had fallen behind. Linking marriage law to New Zealand's desire for female immigrants, he further suggested that "women would not want to come and settle in New Zealand if they were going to lose rights, so recently won in England."[32] A year later, Premier Frederick Whitaker argued that New Zealand was behind "almost all the civilized world in its legislation" and that "a new country like this should set an example to older" ones.[33] "Are we to be dragging at the heels of the mother country in matters of reform?" asked another member in 1884.[34] In South Australia in 1882, where legislation had not yet been passed, Attorney General John Downer similarly played on this construction of antipodean identity: we "who prided ourselves that we were as a rule in the van of civilization had let all other portions of the world distance us in legislating in this particular."[35] A year later, Commissioner of Public Works J.G. Ramsay again stressed that the law of property for married women "was in an unsatisfactory state which was not creditable to South Australia."[36]

Direct comparison with the mother country was one central thread in the development of distinct colonial identities in these British, white settler societies.[37] In 1872, when the House in New South Wales was debating a bill that was pretty well a copy of the English Act of 1870, several members suggested modifications. The English bill restricted the property a wife could keep to £200 worth of inherited property, as well as any personal property, including all kinds of earnings. William Forster proposed that wives in New South Wales be allowed to own the full amount of their real and personal property because the circumstances of England and the colony were totally different. He argued strongly against allowing a colonial mentality to prevent them going "in advance of England."[38] Three years later he tried again, contrasting the rigid class structure of "the home country, where real estate was handed down from generation to generation," with the situation of hundreds of men in the colony who "spend the whole of their savings in allotments of land for the benefits of their wives and children."[39] Arguments like Forster's directly linked the greater availability of land and the absence of a rigid and old class structure to women's rights and claims in the colonies.

Opponents of change were equally likely to use comparisons with England to suit their purposes. In Queensland in 1872, George Thorn opposed the first bill that was introduced, arguing that "England and the colonies were two very different places." Playing on the argument, repeated in each colony, that giving wives separate property would lead men and women to collude against creditors, he and others suggested that the population was so scattered and sparse and so mobile that detecting and pursuing those guilty of fraud would be difficult.[40] Copying English acts was always contested. Those who disliked particular bills decried the colonial impulse as "slavish copying."[41] Those who proposed legislation based largely on English acts stressed the advantages of a law well framed and the possibility of drawing on English decisions. This took its most subservient form in suggestions like that of G.W. Cotton in South Australia in 1883, who argued for copying English legislation exactly because "one of the greatest misfortunes of living in a new country" was lack of experience: "Hon. members could only expect to come in for some share of ridicule if they tried to improve on the English Act."[42]

After 1881 politicians in South Australia, New South Wales, Ontario, and British Columbia were all debating near carbon copies of the English Act introduced that year and passed in 1882. For supporters, the legitimacy of English legislation became a weapon to convince conservative opponents to support the measure.[43] This could hardly be a revolutionary measure, when "the most conservative nation in the world" had passed it "with the approval of the House of Lords," suggested Prime Minister Stout in New Zealand in 1884. Arguing that it was not a "socialistic bill," as some suggested, but "individualistic," giving perfect freedom to individuals to deal with their own property and so allow the world to progress, Stout justified copying because the law was well written and would allow ready recourse to English decisions.[44]

Distinguishing their colony from the metropole was one of a range of comparisons that colonial politicians made with other contemporary societies as they framed their arguments for or against change.[45] Who the "other" was ranged across the globe, encompassing European nations, especially France, other British colonies, the United States, Orientalist interpretations of Muslims, formerly enslaved blacks, and, in New Zealand, the local indigenous peoples. Together, these comparisons wove a world map of the sociology and anthropology of marriage, imbued with social and moral judgements elaborated in huge leaps from marriage law to social life.

Colonial politicians supported or objected to whole bills or particular clauses by describing the impact of similar laws in the American states, Canada, England, and sometimes, India. Citing experts from those countries was a favourite device. Across the colonies, members drew liberally from the evidence given at Select Committee hearings in

England in 1870 to conclude that similar regulations had been working for many years with great success in "Canada and the United States."[46] In moving the second reading of a New South Wales bill in 1875, Charles Pilcher cited a range of American and other experts to dispel the idea that the law would create "dissensions in domestic life" and depose "the husband from the position of head of the household." Dudley Field of New York was cited as claiming that "scarcely any of the great reforms which have been effected in this State has given more satisfaction than this"; also cited was Mr. Fisher's statement that no one in Vermont "wanted to go back to the old law." And, in case fellow members might be leery of American examples, Mr. Rose, a Canadian minister described as "among our own fellow-countrymen," had made it known that neither "men or women" in his province wanted to return to "the old law."[47]

Citing experts was a favourite legitimating device, but colonial politicians drew readily on vaguer generalizations about marriage rules or national character to make their case. Deplorable marital relations in societies understood to have laws that gave wives too much power were a favourite device of opponents of change. South Australian conservatives stand out for their representations of France as an example to be avoided. In their earliest debates in the 1870s, one member clearly explained that the Napoleonic code meant that marriage created community property administered by the husband but shared jointly by husband and wife. This, he explained, could be avoided by making a marriage contract and opting for separate property for each spouse.[48] In the 1880s debates, politicians spoke as if marriage contracts always separated the partners' assets. This was not necessarily so.[49] And, though such men usually saw contracts as the basis of civilized exchange and the rule of law, here contracts were incorporated into a representation of French marriages as loveless, monetary arrangements resulting from bargains made between the heads of families. Richard Baker cautioned that marriage in France "brought about a state of morality which we ought not to be anxious to emulate, while it also had a deterrent effect upon the increase in the population, which in a young country like ours was not at all desirable."[50] Separate property and women's role as reproducers were thus woven together as a warning of the dangers to national life and natural increase that changing the marriage law might produce in the colony. Supporters of the bill did not contest this construction of the French as immoral. Their counter arguments simply found different ways to explain French immorality. Passing such a law in South Australia, argued one politician, would not have the same effect among "Anglo-Saxons."[51]

In other colonies, in contrast, politicians argued that French and other European civil law offered an example of a better way to organize property in marriage. In Queensland, New Zealand, and Upper Canada, the possibilities of marriage creating shared property that recognized women's contribution and claim on assets acquired during marriage, and the option of deciding by contract whether and how to separate husband and wife's property if desired, were presented as serious alternatives to the common law. "The French law was better," suggested the eloquent Queensland supporter and trained solicitor, Charles Lilley, "for it preserved to the wife the whole of her separate property and gave her control over it."[52] Similarly, James Richmond outlined what he saw as the fairer provisions of European civil law when he introduced his bill in New Zealand in 1870, while another member opposed the bill by arguing that one problem was that it did not make provisions for women's separate earnings to become part of the "community of interest," an issue they had heard about in other countries.[53] Eleven years later, George Waterhouse introduced an unsuccessful bill by arguing that the principle of the bill was recognized in "many other, indeed, he thought he might say, in almost all civilized countries," and went on to name all the countries of "Latin descent," France, Italy, Spain, and colonies like the Cape of Good Hope and Lower Canada that had been "acquired by conquest."[54] Such appeals to the justice of European civil codes or the Custom of Paris/Civil Code in Quebec entered dangerous territory, for they challenged the hierarchy of moral, racial, and economic superiority that located Anglo-Saxon laws and institutions as the world's most advanced commercial civilization and the English as superior to the French.

The United States, like France, was an example that evoked contentious debate. Against the argument that the United States was very advanced in such legislation and that their laws had been working well since the 1840s or 1850s,[55] opponents advanced the problem of uppity women and divorce. One New Zealand politician liked to refer to married women's property legislation as "a Californian bill" and an important example of what to avoid. "He could imagine the necessity for such a law in California, where it was well known and even boasted by some people that men and women came together and got married with the intention of staying together only just so long as it suited...and then got divorced on the ground of incompatibility of temper." Were such a law passed in New Zealand, he suggested, men, "instead of marrying as now, would, as in California, keep mistresses."[56] Adding the authenticity of individual experience, Menzies assured members of the Council a year later that "he had visited California himself" and "that the state of society in California was not such as they should wish to see in this colony."[57] In South Australia in 1882, A. Hay argued that the bill they were debating "created two separate interests," and so would lead to a division between man and wife. He suggested that a similar measure was in operation in some parts of America, and that it had worked so badly by causing strife and division between married people that divorces represented one in every ten or twelve marriages celebrated.[58]

Seldom did either proponents or opponents of bills compare their colony with only one other jurisdiction. Comparisons could be made in one speech that ranged from "civilized" countries to "uncivilized" groups. Most frequently, such comparisons invited opponents to see the injustice of a situation where women in backward cultural or religious groups had greater rights within marriage than British women. "Among a great many uncivilized and semi-civilized nations the wife had control of her property," the South Australian MP Richard Baker reminded his fellow politicians, explaining that "under Mohammedan law the wife retained the whole of her property, and she could acquire property after her so-called marriage."[59] Another reference to Muslim wives keeping their own private property produced great hilarity when one member intervened to remind his fellow members that "they have two or three wives, though," which led Baker to retort: "Each had her own property, and there should be the same law here."[60]

Such references to wives among the "uncivilized" or non-Christian were never elaborated upon, as was the case in discussions of French or American marriage, for they were not introduced to provide potential models for change. A brief mention was sufficient to evoke the kinds of Orientalist understandings that led to the South Australian men's laughter and to underline the injustice of Muslim women having greater rights to property after marriage than British women settlers. In several jurisdictions during the 1880s, reference was made to the new law with regard to the property of married women being prepared by "eminent lawyers of the day" for India. Chief secretary and premier of South Australia, the liberal William Morgan, had only to add that existing law in his colony "was a disgrace to any civilized community" to make his meaning clear and to solicit hearty "hear, hears" from some of his peers.[61] India was thus cast squarely among the uncivilized. If colonial powers were going to write such a law for an uncivilized country like India, surely South Australians could use their parliamentary institutions to devise their own. As in the appeals made to the history of the law and of civilization, this cartography of marriage regimes served to position these white settler societies, with their systems of participatory government, against those under direct rule and inhabited by "uncivilized" racial, ethnic, and religious groups. It built on the understanding that a major measure of civilization was the place of women. And, as with the shifting claims of imperial feminists, it served to legitimize new rights for civilized women of the British Empire because imperial claims to supremacy rested in part on women of the Empire enjoying greater rights than those less "civilized."[62]

While male politicians frequently joked that the laws proposed would incite men to avoid marriage, supporters contributed examples where the barbarities of the common law encouraged women to avoid marriage. Their examples were seldom English women, despite contemporary concern about the large numbers of "spinsters" in England.[63] "It was a well-known fact," argued Richard Baker in South Australia, that in some parts of the world, such as the West Indies and the southern United States, some women chose "to lead a life of immorality rather than the one of practical slavery which marriage without protection of the property and earnings would entail."[64] Colonial audiences would have immediately understood the references to emancipated slaves in these regions and connected them to constructions of ex-slave women as promiscuous, involved in "illicit forms of sexuality which transgressed racial and social" boundaries.[65] George Waterhouse evoked similar "information" about Jamaica in New Zealand a year later. Prior to emancipation, he suggested, some slave men and women had been allowed by their masters to hold property in their own right. "But when they found after emancipation that by marrying they subjected themselves to the laws related to property they protected their property by refusing to marry at all and lived in a state of concubinage." He then drew a direct parallel much closer to home, reporting having heard that Maori women in Hawke's Bay were refusing to marry because when they did, their land would become subject to European law and they would lose control of it.[66]

In New Zealand, male, Pakeha (Maori for Europeans) politicians made explicit contrasts between the rules of marriage law among the Maori and in the English common law. I have found no similar references in Australian debates to Aborigines. The absence of comment is at first glance glaring, given their penchant for comparisons with less civilized societies and the ways anthropologists were constructing the Aboriginal peoples of Australia as representing the earliest stages of evolution. Yet perhaps it was the very idea that there was "no such thing as marriage, in the proper sense of the word" among Aboriginals that continued to inform such silence. Their exclusion from this debate parallels the broader logic of elimination in the Australian colonial project and the accompanying discourse of exclusion that denied claims to land and half-caste claims to Aboriginal identity.[67]

In New Zealand, Maoris were harder to exclude because of their greater visibility, the understanding that they were superior to many other "savages," the recent "Maori wars," and their customs regarding property and marriage. From early in the history of the colony, politicians had argued that common-law marriage rules were discouraging Maori women from legal marriage, especially with Europeans.[68] In his introduction of a new bill to change married women's property rights in the New Zealand Legislative Council in 1881, Waterhouse explained that a Maori woman "held property in her own right, without being in any way subject to her husband." This, he suggested was "right and proper." He professed "astonishment that a highly-civilized nation like Great Britain should have allowed such a length of time to elapse" before their own women had the rights being proposed.[69] A year later Mr. Oliver suggested that the Maori race was an exception among those races "not far advanced in civilization" because their women were permitted to hold land. "European interference with Maori custom by the establishment of English law was simply retrograde so far as the natives were concerned." In the same debate, Fraser repeated that under existing law a Maori woman who married "a bad white man or Maori might lose every acre of her land that passed through the Land Court." Because the bill would have an impact on the Maori, he wanted the bill postponed until it could be printed up in their language.[70] In debates about marriage law, only New Zealand politicians acknowledged that indigenous people in their colony had different and fairer marriage laws. Such debates were part of the much wider process of carving out "different kinds of British identities...in relationship to the cultures of Indians, Maoris, Aborigines and West Indian slaves, to name but a few."[71]

Between the 1850s and 1890s, colonial, male politicians in the white settler societies of Australia, New Zealand, and English Canada all embarked on reshaping the local contours of patriarchy by changing married women's claim to their own property. Early laws were frequently attempts to suit local conditions and particular problems, and prior to 1870, most of those dealt only with desertion. By the 1880s, most colonies were passing acts that were pretty close copies of English law, despite some sensitivity about the colonial mentality behind "slavish copying."

Local statutes meant that at the end of the nineteenth century, married women in all the common-law, self-governing, settler societies had the right to retain ownership and control of their own property, real or personal. Other continuing disabilities varied. *Coverture* – the common-law rule that fused man and wife into one person, the husband – had been reshaped, patriarchy in marriage relandscaped. Wives had new legal powers if they had any property of their own. Men's control over their bodies and their labour power, however, remained.[72]

The debates about changing the marriage contract in the colonies that have been examined most closely here – New Zealand, New South Wales, Queensland, and South Australia – suggest that the similarity of the outcome resulted from something larger than the mere copying of English legislation, from something more rooted in culture than the utilitarian arguments for the advantages of sharing jurisprudence might suggest. Reimaging the marriage contract pushed male colonial politicians to consider seriously the potential social impact of reordering relations between husbands and wives. In attempting to rethink gender relations within marriage in their own colony, they drew on a shared colonial culture, a set of understandings and information that circulated throughout the Empire. Rethinking marriage was an occasion to articulate claims about the place of their colony in the Empire, in history, and in the world. They drew on imperial culture and history to do so, borrowing stories and arguments from British publications, debates, and committees, but they domesticated these in a variety of ways and took pains to explain what was different about their particular colony.

By the time of the 1870s and 1880s debates about marriage and property, these colonies had all established their difference from colonies of direct rule by acquiring some form of responsible government. Laws clearly established ways to purchase lands from indigenous peoples and to avoid or eliminate widows' potential claims to dower. Across the Empire, some experts and producers of popular culture were confidently predicting the disappearance of Australia's Aboriginals, New Zealand's Maori, and Canada's eastern First Nations peoples.[73] And women were demanding new rights in part on the basis of their moral superiority over men and their cultural superiority over other races. As male politicians struggled to rethink the link between marriage and society in these relatively new and geographically distant colonies, they made meaning of marriage law by comparisons across time and across the cultures of the Empire and the wider world. They drew on the evolutionary concepts of contemporary history, the law, anthropology, and science, building on and fuelling contemporary understandings of racial difference. They proclaimed their heritage as Christian, civilized, and advanced. In their arguments and examples, colonial politicians elaborated historical cartographies and social anthropologies of marriage law to distinguish their civilized heritage from ancient barbarians, contemporary "heathens," and other peoples whom they characterized as uncivilized. They also took pains to disassociate their own future from what they represented as the dangerous results of marriage regimes in some other Western societies: France and the United States, especially California, were usually the examples to avoid.

The universal decision in these colonies to embrace separate property rather than the different logic of the rules that created shared property in European civil codes, combined with the dilution or elimination of dower, left most married women in all the colonies without any claim on their husband's properties and hence dependent on men's wills.[74] This was entirely consistent with the liberal logic of the law. Each individual would control their own property. Many women had little chance of accumulating property or earning a significant income. According wives rights to their own property also resolved a fundamental conflict between imperial claims to be the most advanced civilization and the provisions of the common law. If Maori or Muslim women could hold property in their own right, why could English women not do so without a marriage settlement?[75] The arguments are familiar. Middle-class feminists in the colonies, as in England, would continue to make them as they claimed greater rights for themselves as civilized and as white. Feminist critiques of marriage had changed the ways the place of women could be measured. Subordination and protection within marriage had been destabilized as a measure of women's protection. There were also many material reasons to allow wives to control their own property.[76] Discursively the change was part of the construction of a new stage of civilization in which a limited degree of fiscal autonomy for wives, and later the vote for women, could constitute new measures of progress. As colonial politicians debated and enacted these changes, they were transforming local marriage laws and also making claims for their colonies/nations as more advanced, and as British, white, and civilized.

DATES OF MAJOR LEGISLATION TOUCHING ON MARRIED WOMEN'S PROPERTY RIGHTS IN NEW ZEALAND, NEW SOUTH WALES, QUEENSLAND AND SOUTH AUSTRALIA, AND ENGLAND, 1840–1901.

New Zealand

1860 Married Women's Property Protection Act
1870 Married Women's Property Protection Act
1880 Married Women's Property Protection Act – Consolidation
1884 Married Women's Property Act

New South Wales

1836 Dower
1840 An Act to Provide for the Maintenance of Deserted Wives and Children 4 Vic 5
1850 Dower, Amendment
1862 Married Women's Property Act 42 Vic 11
1879 Act to amend the Law relating to the Rights and Liabilities of Married Women
1876 Act to Enable Married Women to Dispose of Reversionary Interests in Personal Estate
1886 Married Women's Property Act, Amendment
1889 Matrimonial Causes Act, 1899
1893 Married Women's Property
1901 Deserted Wives and Children Act
1901 Dower – repeal
1901 Married Women's Property

Queensland

1840 The Deserted Wives and Children Act
1858 The Deserted Wives and Children Act, Amendment
1864 The Matrimonial Causes Act, 1864
1875 Matrimonial Causes Jurisdiction Act, Amendment
1890 Law Relating to the Property and Contracts of Married Women, Amendment
1897 Married Women's Property Act of 1890, Amendment
1897 Matrimonial Causes and Jurisdiction Act of 1864, Amendment

South Australia

1852 Real Property, Amendment
1884 Married Women's Property Act
1898 Married Women's Property Act, Amendment
1902 Married Women's Property Act, Amendment

England

1833 Dower Act
1870 Married Women's Property Act
1874 Married Women's Property Act, Amendment
1877 Married Women's Property, Scotland
1881 Married Women's Property, Scotland
1882 Married Women's Property Act
1884 Married Women's Property Act, Amendment
1886 Married Women (Maintenance in Case of Desertion)
1893 Married Women's Property Act
1908 Married Women's Property Act

Sources

Bettina Bradbury, "From Civil Death to Separate Property: Changes in the Legal Rights of Married Women in Nineteenth Century New Zealand," *New Zealand Journal of History* 29, no. 1 (1995); Judy Mackinolty and Heather Radi, eds. *In Pursuit of Justice: Australian Women and the Law, 1788–1979* (Sydney: Hale & Iremonger, 1979), 251–54; Lee Holcombe, *Wives and Property: Reform of the Married Women's Property Law in Nineteenth-Century England* (Toronto: University of Toronto Press, 1983), 257; and local Statutes.

{NOTES}

1 *Sydney Morning Herald* (SMH), 15 December 1875, citing Charles Pilcher in the New South Wales House of Commons; *Argus*, 28 April 1900, cited in Katy Holmes, "'Spinsters Indispensable': Feminists, Single Women and the Critique of Marriage," *Australian Historical Studies* 29 (April 1998): 68.

2 Marriage laws in the colonies covered four main areas: the rights of different denominations to legally perform marriage or the mechanics of the registration of marriages; divorce; miscegenation in some colonies; and married women's property rights. Here I concentrate on the latter.

3 Early work on this topic in England includes Lee Holcombe, *Wives and Property: Reform of the Married Women's Property Law in Nineteenth-Century England* (Toronto: University of Toronto Press, 1983); Mary Lyndon Shanley, *Feminism, Marriage, and the Law in Victorian England, 1850–1895* (New Jersey: Princeton University Press, 1989); Mary Poovey, *Uneven Developments: The Ideological Work of Gender in Mid-Victorian England* (Chicago: University of Chicago Press, 1988). In the United States, Norma Basch, *In the Eyes of the Law: Women, Marriage and Property in Nineteenth-Century New York* (Ithaca: Cornell University Press, 1982); Marylynn Salmon, *Women and the Law of Property* (Chapel Hill: University of North Carolina Press, 1986); Carole Shammas, Marylynn Salmon, and Michel Dahlins, *Inheritance in America from Colonial Times to the Present* (New Brunswick: Rutgers University Press, 1987); Françoise Basch, "Women's Rights and the Wrongs of Marriage in Mid-Nineteenth-Century America," *History Workshop Journal* 22 (Autumn, 1986): 18–40. More recent studies of links between marriage law and other bodies of law and of marriage and nation in the United States include Amy Dru Stanley, *From Bondage to Contract: Wage Labor, Marriage and the Market in the Age of Slave Emancipation* (Cambridge, MA: Cambridge University Press, 1998); Hendrik Hartog, *Man and Wife in America: A History* (Cambridge, MA: Harvard University Press, 2000); and Nancy Cott, *Public Vows: A History of Marriage and the Nation* (Cambridge, MA: Cambridge University Press, 2000).

4 There have been fewer studies of marriage law in Australia, Canada, New Zealand, and the South African colonies. On Canada, see Lori Chambers, *Married Women and Property Law in Ontario* (Toronto: Osgoode, 1997); Constance B. Backhouse, "Married Women's Property Law in Nineteenth-Century Canada," *Law and History Review* 6, no. 2 (Fall 1988): 211–57; Philip Girard, "Married Women's Property, Chancery Abolition, and Insolvency Law: Law Reform in Nova Scotia, 1820–1867," in *Essays in the History of Canadian Law, III, Nova Scotia*, ed. Philip Girard and Jim Phillips (Toronto: University of Toronto Press, 1990); Philip Girard and Rebecca Veinott, "Married Women's Property Law in Nova Scotia, 1850–1910," in *Separate Spheres: Women's Worlds in the Nineteenth-Century Maritimes*, ed. Janet Guilford and Suzanne Morton (Fredericton: Acadiensis Press, 1994). On New Zealand, see Bettina Bradbury, "From Civil Death to Separate Property: Changes in the Legal Rights of Married Women in Nineteenth-Century New Zealand," *The New Zealand Journal of History* 29, no. 1 (April 1995): 40–66; Janine Paver, "'Two Separate Purses': The Passage of the Married Women's Property Act of 1884" (bachelor's honours paper, Victoria University of Wellington, 1991); and on Australia, John Mackinolty, "The Married Women's Property Acts," in *In Pursuit of Justice: Australian Women and the Law, 1788–1979*, ed. Judy Mackinolty and Heather Radi (Sydney: Hale & Iremonger, 1979); Diane Kirkby and Hilary Golder, "Marriage and Divorce Law Before the Family Law Act, 1975," in *Sex, Power and Justice: Historical Perspectives on*

Law in Australia, ed. Diane Kirby (Melbourne: Oxford University Press, 1995); and, for a truly Australian story, Diane Kirkby and Hilary Golder, "Mrs. Mayne and Her Boxing Kangaroo: A Married Woman Tests Her Property Rights in Colonial New South Wales," *Law and History Review* 21, no. 3 (2003).

5 This paper builds on the growing literature that seeks to understand the workings of gender across the British Empire, as well as that which seeks to explore wider networks and circuits of ideas, laws, and influence. Catherine Hall, *Civilising Subjects: Metropole and Colony in the English Imagination, 1830–1867* (Chicago: University of Chicago Press, 2002); Ann Laura Stoler, "Tense and Tender Ties: The Politics of Comparison in North American History and (Post) Colonial Studies," *Journal of American History* 88, no. 3 (2001): 882–87; Alan Lester, *Imperial Networks: Creating Identities in Nineteenth-Century South Africa and Britain* (New York: Routledge, 2001); Lauren Benton, *Law and Colonial Cultures: Legal Regimes in World History, 1400–1900* (Cambridge: Cambridge University Press, 2002); Claire Midgely, *Gender and Imperialism* (Manchester: Manchester University Press, 1998); Mrinalini Sinha, "Mapping the Imperial Social Formation: A Modest Proposal for Feminist History," *Signs: Journal of Women in Culture and Society* 25, no. 4 (Summer 2000): 1077–82.

6 Adele Perry, *On the Edge of Empire: Gender, Race, and the Making of British Columbia, 1849–1871* (Toronto: University of Toronto Press, 2000).

7 Sylvia Van Kirk, *"Many Tender Ties": Women in the Fur-Trade Society in Western Canada, 1670–1870* (Winnipeg: Watson & Dywer, 1980); Erik Olssen, "Families and the Gendering of European New Zealand in the Colonial Period, 1840–80," in *The Gendered Kiwi*, ed. Caroline Daley and Deborah Montgomerie (Auckland: Auckland University Press, 1999), 39–40.

8 Lester, *Imperial Networks*, 49; Patricia Grimshaw *et al.*, *Creating a Nation, 1788–1990* (Victoria: Penguin, 1994); Anne Summers, *Damned Whores and God's Police* (Victoria: Penguin, 1975), 296–99; Rita Farrell, "Women and Citizenship in Colonial Australia," in *Women as Australian Citizens: Underlying Histories*, ed. Patricia Crawford and Philippa Maddern (Melbourne: Melbourne University Press, 2001), 123–25; Olssen, "Families and the Gendering of European New Zealand," 39–41; Charlotte Macdonald, "Too Many Men and Too Few Women: Gender's 'Fatal Impact' in Nineteenth-Century Colonies," in *The Gendered Kiwi*, 26; Jean-Jacques Van-Helten and Keith Williams, "'The Crying Need of South Africa': The Emigration of Single British Women to the Transvaal, 1901–10," *Journal of Southern African Studies* 10, no. 1 (October 1983): 29.

9 Perry, *On the Edge*, 155–58; Charlotte Macdonald, *A Woman of Good Character: Single Women as Immigrant Settlers in Nineteenth-Century New Zealand* (Wellington: Bridget Williams Books, 1990), 492–93.

10 Grimshaw, Lake *et al.*, *Creating a Nation*; Summers, *Damned Whores*, 296–99; Rita Farrell, "Women and Citizenship in Colonial Australia," in *Women as Australian Citizens*, 123–25.

11 Pamela Scully, *Liberating the Family? Gender and British Slave Emancipation in the Rural Western Cape, South Africa, 1823–1852* (Oxford: James Curry, 1997); Hall, *Civilising Subjects*, 135, 166, 189; Stanley, *From Bondage to Contract*.

12 Kathleen Jamieson, "Sex Discrimination and the Indian Act," in *Arduous Journey: Canadian Indians and Decolonization*, ed. Rick J. Ponting (Toronto: McClelland and Stewart, 1986); Patrick Wolfe, *Settler Colonialism and the Transformation of*

Anthropology: The Politics and Poetics of an Ethnographic Event (London: Cassell, 1999). James Belich suggests that the "heyday of interracial sex" and "marriage alliance" was likely between 1820 and 1850. This parallels the timing in British Columbia and many other colonies. *Making Peoples: A History of the New Zealanders from Polynesian Settlement to the End of the Nineteenth Century* (Auckland: Penguin Press, 1996), 251–53; Perry, *On the Edge of Empire.*

13 Leonore Davidoff and Catherine Hall, *Family Fortunes: Men and Women of the English Middle Class, 1780–1850* (Chicago: University of Chicago Press, 1987). Helen Bradford argues cogently about what South African historians of the colonial period have missed by not taking women and gender into account, and hence, misunderstanding the significance of marriage, in "Women, Gender and Colonialism: Rethinking the History of the British Cape Colony and Its Frontier Zones, c.1860–1870," *Journal of African History* 37, no. 3 (1996): 351–70.

14 Summers, *Damned Whores.*

15 There the British allowed Afrikaaners and Québecois to retain the laws rooted in Holland and France that governed marriage and other civil matters. This is a different story, which I am exploring separately.

16 Rosalind Atherton, "Expectation without Right: Testamentary Freedom and the Position of Women in Nineteenth-Century New South Wales," UNSW *Law Journal* 11, no. 1 (1988): 133–57.

17 Sara L. Zeigler, "Wifely Duties: Marriage, Labor, and the Common Law in Nineteenth-Century America," *Social Science History* 20, no. 1 (Spring 1996): 63–96.

18 English historians have shown the gradual whittling away of dower leading up to the amendments made in the 1833 Dower Act. Dower retained importance longer in the Americas, where land, the usual basis of dower, was more plentiful, though conveyancing law minimized its hold. See especially Susan Staves, *Married Women's Separate Property in England, 1660–1833* (Cambridge: Harvard University Press, 1990); Shammas *et al., Inheritance in America.*

19 Bruce Kercher sets out the broad contours of the Australian legislation in *An Unruly Child: A History of Law in Australia* (Sydney: Allen & Unwin, 1998), 142. Men's freedom of willing combined with inheritance laws that placed wives far behind a large range of relatives, to ensure that husbands could, if they wished, readily leave their wives close to penniless.

20 *Port Phillip Herald*, 5 August 1845.

21 *New Zealand, Debates* (NZD), 23 June 1870; *Queensland, Debates,* (QD), Assembly, 3 July 1872, 478; *South Australia Debates* (SAD), 1 October 1872, 2099; SAD, 16 October 1872, 2320.

22 SMH, 14 December 1875; James A. Hammerton, *Cruelty and Companionship: Conflict in Nineteenth-Century Married Life* (London: Routledge, 1992); Davidoff and Hall, *Family Fortunes*; Ben Griffins downplays the shared class interests of feminists and middle-class men in controlling male working-class behaviour in "Class, Gender and Liberalism in Parliament, 1868–1882: The Case of the Married Women's Property Acts," *The Historical Journal* 46, no. 1 (2003): 59–87.

23 SMH, 15 December 1875.

24 SAD, 10 July 1883, 411.

25 Benedict Anderson argues that this way of using history was intimately tied into the emerging ideas of nation during the late eighteenth and early nineteenth centuries. *Imagined Communities: The Origin and Spread of Nationalism* (London: Verso, 1983), 68.

26 Such "webs of comparisons," to use the words of Clare Midgley, were of course central to the diverse ways languages of civilization worked in this period, as were the "protean," multiple ways it was used. Claire Midgley, "Anti-Slavery and the Roots of 'Imperial Feminism,'" in *Gender and Imperialism*; Gail Bederman, *Manliness and Civilization: A Cultural History of Gender and Race in the United States, 1850–1917* (Chicago: University of Chicago Press, 1995), 23.

27 NZD, 29 June 1870, 141. England's early "savage" stage was compared by some contemporaries ascribing to the theory that societies passed through a series of stages from barbarism to civilization with that of the Maori at the time of colonization. Pat Moloney, "Savagery and Civilization: Early Victorian Notions," *New Zealand Journal of History* 35, no. 2 (2001): 157–58.

28 SAD, 10 July 1883, 412–13.

29 Anderson, *Imagined Communities*, 68, 44.

30 Bederman, *Manliness*, 23.

31 In this they share with the feminists of a later period "their construction of a New World identity and politics marked by difference from, and temporal advancement beyond, both the feudal oppressions of the European Old World," and the primitiveness of Aboriginals or Maoris, as Marilyn Lake argues in "Australian Frontier Feminism and the Marauding White Man," in *Gender and Imperialism*, 126. And they drew on existing constructions of the colonies as healthier and more progressive. Belich, *Making Peoples*, 301–8.

32 NZD, 21 June 1881, 134.

33 NZD, 6 June 1882, 296.

34 NZD, 23 September 1884, 495.

35 SAD, 10 October 1882, 1187.

36 SAD, 27 June 1883.

37 Catherine Hall, "Histories, Empires and the Post-Colonial Moment," in *The Post-Colonial Question: Common Skies, Divided Horizons*, ed. Iain Chambers and Lidia Curti (London: Routledge, 1996), 71.

38 SMH, 8 December 1871. On the passage of this Act in England, see Holcombe, *Wives and Property*, 166–83.

39 SMH, 7 December 1871.

40 QD, 3 July 1872, 476–83. Lori Chambers takes the concern with fraud rather at face value in *Married Women*. It seems to me that this near obsession constitutes a representation of marriage and husband-wife relations that demands closer analysis.

41 NZD, 9 September 1884, 197; QD, 1872, 42.

42 SAD, 31 July 1883, 610.

43 QD, 10 January 1871, 455, 456; 3 July 1872, 478; NZD, 21 June 1881; 9 September 1884; SAD, 31 July 1883.

44 NZD, 9 September 1884, 202.

45 Anne McClintock, *Imperial Leather: Race, Gender and Sexuality in the Colonial Context* (New York: Routledge, 1995).

46 SAD, 22 June 1880, 171; SMH, 15 December 1875; 8 July 1871.

47 SMH, 15 December 1875.

48 SAD, 16 October 1872, 2322.

49 On the ways French men and women adapted to this law imposed on all regions

after the revolution, see Margaret Darrow, *Revolution in the House: Family, Class and Inheritance in Southern France, 1775–1825* (Princeton: Princeton University Press, 1989).

50 *SAD*, 3 August 1882, 546.

51 *SAD*, 17 July 1883, 477.

52 *QD*, 3 July 1873, 479.

53 *NZD*, 20 June 1870, 141–42. This was not what the Napoleonic code provided. Separate property had to be chosen explicitly in a marriage contract in Frane.

54 *NZD*, 21 June 1881.

55 *NZD*, 29 June 1870, 143; *SAD*, 22 August 1882, 699; 24 July 1883, 534.

56 *NZD*, 21 June 1881, 136.

57 *NZD*, Council, 1 June 1882, 204.

58 *SAD*, 8 August 1882, 551.

59 *SAD*, 10 July 1883, 412.

60 *SAD*, 5 September 1882, 824.

61 *SAD*, 22 June 1880, 171.

62 Of course, this argument had a long history by this point. See Midgley, "Anti-Slavery and Imperial Feminism," in *Gender and Imperialism*, 169, where she talks about this argument in William Thompson's 1825 *Appeal of One Half of the Human Race* and Marion Reid's 1843 *A Plea for Woman*.

63 Sheila Jeffreys, *The Spinster and Her Enemies: Feminism and Sexuality, 1880–1930* (London: Pandora Press, 1985); Carmen Faymonville, "'Waste Not, Want Not': Even Redundant Women Have Their Uses," in *Imperial Objects: Victorian Women's Emigration and the Unauthorized Imperial Experience*, ed. Rita S. Kranidis (New York: Twayne, 1998); Katie Holmes, "Spinsters Indispensable."

64 *SAD*, 22 June 1880, 172.

65 Hall, *Civilizing Subjects*, 72.

66 *NZD*, Council, 21 June 1881, 136.

67 Patrick Wolfe, *Settler Colonialism*; R. B. Smyth, *The Aborigines of Victoria* (1876), cited in Patricia Grimshaw, "Maori Agriculturalists and Aboriginal Hunter-Gatherers: Women and Colonial Displacement in Nineteenth-Century Aoteoroa/New Zealand and Southeastern Australia," in *Nation, Empire, Colony: Historicizing Gender and Race*, ed. Ruth Roach Pierson and Nupur Chaudhuri (Bloomington: Indiana University Press, 1998), 333.

68 *NZD*, 13 July 1854, 221, for example.

69 *NZD*, 21 June 1881, 135.

70 *NZD*, 6 June 1882, 295–96.

71 Lester, *Imperial Networks*, ix.

72 On men's claim on wives' labour power in the United States, see Sara L. Zeigler, "Wifely Duties: Marriage, Labor, and the Common Law in Nineteenth-Century America," *Social Science History* 20, no. 1 (Spring 1996): 63–96.

73 John Stenhouse, "'A Disappearing Race before We Came Here': Doctor Alfred Kingcome Newman, the Dying Maori, and Victorian Scientific Racism," *New Zealand Journal of History* 30, no. 2 (October 1996).

74 Atherton, "Expectation without Right." Women in New Zealand and Australia would seek support as widows later by fighting for Testator's Maintenance Acts. See Kercher, *An Unruly Child*, 144; Summers, *Damned Whores*, 358.

75 These are similar arguments to those made by English feminists. Antoinette Burton, *Burdens of History: British Feminists, Indian Women and Imperial Culture, 1865–1915* (Chapel Hill: University of North Carolina Press, 1994).

76 These included limiting the effects of men's bankruptcy on family goods; absolving governments of the need to support wives of men who deserted them, or drank up earnings; and ensuring that wives had some money to feed themselves and their children if husbands did not hand over their wages.

CHAPTER 7

INTERLOCUTING EMPIRE:

COLONIAL WOMANHOOD, SETTLER IDENTITY, AND FRANCES HERRING[1]

Adele Perry

SETTLERS OCCUPIED A STRATEGIC, curious, and contested place within the conduits of power that constituted the British World. Settlers were undeniably colonizers of African, Australasian, Asian and North and South American space. They alienated indigenous territory, exploited local labour, and reaped tangible benefits from colonial states that rewarded them for their simple existence. At the same time they were themselves colonized. The British World was fragmented by the lived practice of rule and by settler self-government, but it remained governed by the metropole that gave it its name. Settlers thus occupied what we might call a doubled place within the Empire: they experienced being colonized and colonizing in simultaneous and seemingly contradictory ways.

The ambiguities of settler colonialism had special resonance for women. Imperial rhetoric and policy bestowed a literally pregnant mission on settler women, defining them and their reproductive work as essential to – and constituent of – settler regimes. Yet backwoods experience of work, motherhood, and daily patriarchies fragmented and profoundly challenged settler women's relationship to the Empire they putatively served. In this paper I explore the curious politics of being a settler and more particularly a settler woman by focusing on the literary work of Frances Elizabeth Herring, an author, feminist, and mother who lived in and wrote about late nineteenth- and early twentieth-century British Columbia. Approaching literature as a window into the social relations of nineteenth-century colonialism, as Antoinette Burton has recently argued, necessitates challenging historians' conventional dichotomization of primary and secondary sources.[2] It also demands that we not treat literature as simply mimetic, but instead approach it as we would any other source – as a necessarily problematic and narrative fragment of the past that both reflects and constitutes the social world. As Misao Dean argues, literary texts do not either reveal or obscure the reality of women's lives since they constitute historically specific versions of femininity.[3] Herring's literary work positions herself and settlers more generally as imperial interlocutors, liminal or in-between subjects who stood critically between the colony and the metropole and could speak the truth of each to the other. Herring did this especially through the figure of the settler woman, a character-type she imagined as produced by the so-called new world and empowered by her special role in the inseparable histories of colonialism and nation-building.

In imagining settler women in these ways, Herring's work throws light on a question that has long vexed historians of imperialism: namely, where settler colonialism fits in global analyses of empire.[4] Patrick Wolfe correctly notes that "for all the homage paid to difference, postcolonial theory in particular has largely failed to accommodate such basic structural distinctions" like those between colonies of settlement and colonies of occupation or exploitation.[5] But one of the enduring lessons of what is being dubbed the "new imperial history" is surely the importance of the local and the particular. And the local reminds us that the "basic structural distinctions" of empire were often lived in unexpected ways. Colonial history is full of examples of societies that stood outside or between the usual categories, including British Columbia.[6] Conceptualizing these places as colonies of settlement and minimizing the significance of Indigenous exploitation and settler insecurity accords their colonizing projects a stability and an eventual outcome that was, as Cole Harris has suggested, far from clear in the nineteenth century.[7] Drawing hard and fixed lines between colonies of settlement and colonies of occupation or exploitation ultimately does historiographical violence to the fact that all colonies are ones of occupation, but rarely in an uncomplicated fashion.

Settler identities and politics thus can be chimeras, ones that historians have too often taken at face value. The imperialist hyperbole that marked 24th of May celebrations across the British World speaks to a profound uncertainty about the place of settlers and settler societies within empire rather than the opposite. The very fact that colonial history troubles clean tripartite distinctions between settlers, Natives, and colonizers rendered settlers' need to define themselves and their place within empire all the more urgent. Settlers had (and continue to have) a profoundly ambiguous and deeply unsettling relationship to the societies they inhabit and claim. This is a relationship defined vis-à-vis both indigenous and migrant groups. Settler colonies like Canada, Australia, and New Zealand worked both to dispossess indigenous peoples and to incorporate them within a reconstituted society and polity ordered along principles and practices of European hegemony. Settler colonialism is thus not, as Wolfe has argued elsewhere, a "zero-sum conflict" where settlers simply replace Natives. Settler colonialism is rooted in two over- lapping social relations: the dispossession and assimilation of indigenous peoples and the ranking and ordering of migrants into "undesirable" and "desirable" categories, principally along the axes of race.[8]

Settler women were accorded a special role in this layered relationship. Anna Davin's germinal 1978 argument acknowledged the centrality of reproduction to imperialism, an insight sustained and complicated in recent work by Ann Laura Stoler and, in a different vein, by Nancy Rose Hunt.[9] Settler regimes were distinguished as much by their reproductive regimes as they were by their policies and practices of migration and settlement. Settler colonies were defined by the fact that the non-indige- nous population was reproduced not through migration (either voluntary or involuntary) but through local reproduction. Imperial women were thus positioned as the definitive political subjects of settler regimes, the oft-noted "mothers of the Empire."

But settlers and settler women could trouble empire as well as act on its behalf. Nicholas Thomas includes settlers in his discussion of the many historical actors who troubled the lines between colonized and colonizer.[10] This ambivalence has continued long after the demographic *realpolitik* of settler regimes in the British World of Australia, Canada, and New Zealand took root in the late nineteenth century. The discourse that positions white settlers as heirs to Canada, as Sherene Razack ex- plains, consigns Aboriginal peoples "forever to an earlier space and time" and scrips people of colour as "late arrivals, coming to the shores of North America long after much of the development has occurred."[11] But the pervasiveness of this set of connections in both scholarly and popular discourse is consistently complicated by a social experience of colonial space that routinely queries claims to white-settler hegemony. We are told that our relationship to Canada is authentic and profound, but the simple fact of Aboriginal persistence and the unavoidable presence of Aboriginal resistance reminds us that the relationship between newcomer and Native will never be so simple. The putative "whiteness" of settler colonies is queried by multiracial and multicultural patterns of migra- tion and settlement even in the face of vigorous anti-migrant activity and restrictive legislation. At the same time, the stubborn assertion of metropolitan snobberies and the simple fact of metropolitan distance remind us that we can never really go "home" and disturbingly suggest that maybe we never had one. Settlers are again and again reminded that we sit in a curious and particular place in the complicated circuits that made up the British World.

Herring occupied one such curious spot. Born to a middle-class English family in 1851, Herring immigrated to British Columbia as a single woman in 1874. According to family oral tradition, Herring's migration was motivated by complicated webs of family antagonism and obligation, and especially by conflict with her stepfather. She married her first cousin, Arthur May Herring, soon after arriving in British Columbia. He had been married the year before in California, suggesting that his bond with Frances was a response to more than one familial crisis.[12] They established a home and Frances, who had trained and worked as a teacher in England, soon took over the schoolroom at the old fur-trade community of Fort Langley, where she taught sewing, music, and religion as well as academic subjects to her largely First Nations students. In 1878 the family relocated to New Westminster, where Arthur operated a successful pharmacy business, acquired significant holdings in real estate, and was active in local government.[13]

Frances mothered eight children, four of whom lived to adulthood. The usual burdens of motherhood were mitigated by her relative wealth and privilege and by the status she derived from belonging to a respectable, white-settler family. The Herrings had sufficient income to always employ a domestic servant, either a Chinese man or a young white woman, and Frances pursued a rich life outside of the domestic sphere. Some of her time was devoted to the first wave of the Canadian women's movement, which emphasized women's moral authority, sought change through constitutional means, and worked within an ideological framework that emphasized white women's racial mission.[14] Herring worked within professional and reform organizations, giving papers to the British Columbia Teachers' Convention and assuming the presidency of the Royal Columbian Hospital Women's Auxiliary, an organization that she eventfully brought into the National Council of Women. Her firm support for suffrage earned her a reputation for having been "very active in support of equal rights for women" and "woman suffrage."[15]

The Herrings witnessed the solidification of British Columbia's settler regime in the nineteenth century. Arthur May Herring arrived in the colony in 1858 as a child of the Royal Engineers, the troops sent to both literally and symbolically shore up Britain's newly asserted claim to the territory. The brute presence of colonial power did not entirely mute the fact that this remained very much an Aboriginal society, where non-indigenous people's presence was small and profoundly insecure. British Columbia's entry into Canadian confederation in 1871 did not unto itself shift this dynamic, but the cumulative impact of indigenous depopulation, slow but meaningful settler migration, and, after 1886, British Columbia's integration into mainstream North American society via the arrival of the Canadian Pacific Railroad did. The result was an early twentieth-century British Columbia that was significantly different than its mid-nineteenth-century incarnation. As a married couple, Arthur and Frances thus witnessed British Columbia's transition from an isolated, racially diverse, and sparsely settled colonial society to an increasingly assured white-settler society ensconced within the Canadian nation-state.

Writing assumed more and more importance in Herring's life as she and British Columbia's settler colonialism aged. Between 1890 and 1900, she edited a column in the local newspaper, the *British Columbia Commonwealth*, that focused on recipes, household hints, and garden advice, interspersed with inspirational tales of career women and assertive wives and mothers.[16] She also worked as a correspondent for the Toronto *Globe* and published a number of short stories with national magazines. After the turn of the century, Herring increasingly focused on the novel, and between 1900 and her death in 1916 she published six full-length novels, five of them popular romantic works set in British Columbia in the last half of the nineteenth century.[17] Far from centres of literary production, Herring no doubt relied on herself for inspiration and succour. She also relied on her own enterprise, peddling her books from her home for a discounted price of one dollar.[18] While of questionable literary quality, her novels were reasonably popular in their day: at least three of her novels, *Canadian Camp Life* (1900), *Among the Peoples of British Columbia: Red, White, Yellow, and Brown* (1903), and *In the Pathless West with Soldiers, Pioneers, Miners, and Savages* (1904), went into subsequent editions. Her five books set in British Columbia are a curious combination of melodrama and travel literature,[19] organized around short narratives with a greater or lesser relationship to a central theme. Like the Strickland sisters, Herring relied heavily on the "sketch" as a literary device.[20] It was a form of writing that was perhaps uniquely able to convey colonial experience to a metropolitan audience.

Most of Herring's adult life was lived within the context of urban British Columbia's emergent middle class, but only *Canadian Camp Life,* a story of a family summer vacation, dwells in that world. The bulk of her work conjures up the exotic, multiracial world of the nineteenth-century backwoods. As a professional white woman who did not arrive in British Columbia until 1874, Herring's direct personal experience of much of the society or many of the events about which she wrote was obviously limited. In this sense, she cannot really be seen as what Jean Barman, in her fine work on Constance Lindsay Skinner, calls an "experiential historian."[21]

The undeniable gaps between Herring's experience and her subject matter did not lead either Herring or her publishers to question her reliability as an authentic repository of colonial experience with valuable inside knowledge of the lived experience of empire. *Nan, and Other Pioneer Women of the West* was marketed as the work of one who had "been a pioneer in British Columbia."[22] In 1913 Judge F.W. Howay, a prominent British Columbia personage and popular historian, shored up these claims with the endorsement that "the local color which is necessary to make that strange, rough, yet gentle, life, understood by those of to-day, can only be given by one who has lived and moved in that time and amongst that people."[23] While the travel writers studied by Karen Dubinsky emphasized their difference from what they witnessed at Niagara Falls, Herring marketed herself as part of the story.[24] This was a literature of the settler, not of the Native or the traveller. Herring defined her literary mission as that of imperial interlocutor capable of speaking for the periphery in the language of the metropole. She explained that she "sent out" her first novel, *Canadian Camp Life*, "from this far corner of civilization" to "the writers of the great world."[25]

Whether putatively historical or contemporary, Herring's work promised its readers an authentic vision of the British Columbia backwoods. Ample photographic illustrations accompanied each of her books, and while they bore little direct relation to the text, they did impart an ethnographic gloss. Herring plainly called her work "fact."[26] Her later books, including *Nan*, were presented as historical works. Howay explained that her sketches were "the result of many reminiscences of which careful note has been kept by the writer for at least thirty years."[27] Elsewhere, Herring shored up her writing's status as fact – and, by implication, not as fiction – as historians continue to: namely, by linking it to the usual representatives of institutionalized, Western knowledge and authority, most notably missionaries and government agents.[28] "All I tell of the Indian life, careless in some respects as it is, cruel in others," Herring explained in one Preface, "can be verified by those who care to write to any of the Indian Agencies or Missionaries Along the Coast."[29] This is both a characteristically feminine denial of authorial status and a characteristically Western view of who possesses the "truth."

Choice bits of local knowledge further substantiated Herring's claim to tell British Columbia's truth to those who had not lived it like herself. Herring especially used her knowledge of Chinook Jargon to provide readers with a digestible taste of hybrid, backwoods culture and to shore up her authority over it. Chinook Jargon was the trade language used to communicate between First Nations and settlers and different Aboriginal nations. It emerged in the nineteenth century and survived as a meaningful lingua franca into the twentieth.[30] Herring wrote dialogue in Chinook, accompanied by her own bracketed translations. In positioning herself as a literal translator, Herring entrenched her claim to be an interlocutor or cultural intermediary who interpreted British Columbia in ways knowable to metropolitan readers.

To some extent Herring wrote for a local audience, one that, as Howay put it, "will recognise, even through the veil, many of the incidents she mentions."[31] Yet a local audience would not likely have needed the Chinook translated. Her aesthetic was one that meshed local knowledge with the transnational increasingly global language of European hegemony, including words like "squaws," "bucks," and "wigwams." Herring's is a literature of settler imperialism, where direct and extensive local knowledge sits in uneasy equilibrium with the traveller's tendency to see one thing where there are many. This was a version of what literary scholar Mary Louise Pratt calls "creole self-fashioning," the complex process whereby colonials balanced their experience of local space with the broad tropes of empire.[32] Herring's self-fashioning was especially expressed in her image of the settler or pioneer woman.

This vision of settler womanhood recycled and fed what can seem to be a giant, international mill churning out hackneyed images of European femininity across the colonial and Anglo-American world in the nineteenth and early twentieth centuries. Any reader of the first two decades of feminist analyses of the history of imperialism will be familiar enough with the various incarnations of this image, which circulated in only slightly variant guises in North America, the Antipodes, Africa, Asia, and the Pacific.[33] In each of these contexts, European women stood for morality, civilization, and racial separation, a set of articulations made operable by concomitant ideas of indigenous peoples and European men.

The settler women depicted in Herring's work shared much in common with this suspiciously omniscient image, but its circular logic was complicated if not broken by its refraction through the settler perspective. Herring articulated a vision of a resilient, capable colonial womanhood in obvious contrast to the delicate, dependent femininity associated with bourgeois metropolitan culture. She disapproved of women who were overly concerned with gossip and clothes, and singled out for scorn white women who put on "french and frills." This choice of metaphor is not incidental, and clearly labels this style of womanhood not only bourgeois but metropolitan.[34] Settler women reaped their status not by commanding the details of the metropole, but by their ability to navigate the hostile territory of colonial space. Ishbel proves herself in uniquely new world adversity. It is only when her husband is disabled and her family is forced to move and live by Ishbel's washing and mending that her status as a pioneer woman is guaranteed. "Here her true womanliness showed itself," writes Herring, "and her steadfast heart never failed."[35]

The quotidian work of colonization both makes settler women and liberates them. Like Australian feminists, Herring constructed the new world as a special place of opportunity for women. "As colonized and colonizers," Marilyn Lake writes, "Australian feminists shaped their New World identity in opposition to the 'Old World barbarism' of Britain and the older 'primitive barbarism' evident to them in Aboriginal society."[36] Agnes, the narrator of *Among the People of British Columbia: Red, White, Yellow, and Brown*, is the starkest example of the transformative promise of colonization for women. At the beginning of the novel, she is isolated, fearful, and full of resentment, deeply victimized by the double misogyny of her natal family and native Britain. Her mother has died, her sister has migrated to British Columbia, and her father "who wanted a son, never quite forgave me my sex." Agnes "used to wonder why I was not born a boy, and whose fault it was."[37] Colonial migration transforms the status of Agnes's womanhood. In British Columbia she is loved by her family, valued by friends, and courted by a local young doctor.

In representing the settler woman, Herring is, in large part, representing the white woman. Yet the relationship between whiteness and settlement was not uncomplicated in Herring's work or in British Columbia. Non-Native migration to British Columbia was always multicultural and plural, and from the 1850s onward, Chinese people formed a significant settler minority. The anti-Asian movement that began in the 1870s took off in the next few decades, and Chinese people were increasingly the primary racial other against which whites defined themselves. Much of the imagery here, as in the San Francisco context studied by Nayan Shah, was highly gendered, pivoting on ideas of feminized men, prostituted and bound women, and deviant or absent domesticity.[38] Herring traded in these ideas of the people she called "yellow," using Chinese men as stereotypical foils for a superior white domesticity.[39] Yet she also suggested that Chinese migrants, like European ones, were reshaped by their acquaintance with British Columbia's soil. Sing owns a wash-house, sequesters his wife, and speaks of the lesser value of his daughter's labour. Yet his patriarchy, like that of English migrants, was waning in the new ground of British Columbia. "All the children," she writes, "had a British name as well as Chinese, and strange for a Chinaman – Sing seemed as proud of his two little girls as of his boys."[40]

This simultaneous affirmation and abrogation of race suggests the particular trajectory of Herring's racial imaginary. The title of *Among the Peoples of British Columbia: Red, White, Yellow and Brown* makes obvious what she saw as the primary division among humanity. Yet for all their obvious social purchase, racial categories were not, for Herring, strictly immutable. She suggests that the social experience of the new world cut across race, blunting, as in the case of Sing and his daughters, what she sees as the division between yellow and white. What about the line between white and red? It is obviously not mediated by the new world experience, and in fact it draws its definition from it. But Herring does suggest that this line is breached by the powerful and common bond of mother-love. When Nan, the key character in *Nan and Other Pioneer Women*, is beaten and broken, it is only Kitty, her First Nations neigh-bour, who comes to her aid, affectionately calling her "tenas tecoup klootchman," or little white woman in Chinook. In childbirth, Nan tells Kitty: "You're the only one hes bin good to me."[41]

This is primitivist discourse, where primitivism, as it often could be, emerges as superior to "civilization."[42] For Herring, primitive mother-hood is more emotive, more loyal, and ultimately more capable of pro-tecting the vulnerable. Kitty is not the only character who is abandoned by the settler society and saved by the nurture of a First Nations woman. *In the Pathless West* revolves around the story of Billy, a young white boy who arrives with the Royal Engineers and thus symbolizes the beginnings of British Columbia's settler colonialism. To what extent Billy's story mirrors that of Herring's husband's is not clear, although the overlap in biographical details seems far from coincidental. Billy's mother dies in passage, leaving him with his drunken, violent, and neglectful stepfather. Finding no support in the white community, Billy flees to a family of the "Northern Tribe," where he is renamed Bee-lee.

In what we might consider a counter-captivity narrative, Billy is emotionally and physically restored by his relationship with the mother of the family, Hai-dah, whose name suggests she is a mother not only to Billy/Bee-lee, but also to the Nation. Herring describes Billy/Bee-lee's first meeting with Hai-dah and her family:

> "Car mica clattawa?" (Where are you going?)
> "Clattawa nica illehee!" she replied. (I am going home.) On looking at the squaw he remembered she had tried to entice him to go with her before by offering him some sticks of red and white peppermint candy. So he settled himself in the bottom of the canoe, and was soon sound asleep. The klootchman grunted her approval of his good sense, and covered him with her blanket. He felt secure from Billings [his stepfather] anyway, and his sleep lasted till the canoe grated on a shingly beach miles up the coast.[43]

That the settler child opts to remain with Hai-dah and her family confirms the superiority of First Nations nurture above white neglect. Herring writes that "Bee-lee could see no likelihood of his return to civilisation. This scarcely troubled him, for he was growing in stature and in health as he had never done before."[44] Billy/Bee-lee was ultimately enriched by his time with Hai-dah and her people. *The Gold Miners: A Sequel to the Pathless West* finds an adult Billy empowered by his ability to speak Chinook Jargon and his abilities at "handling the Indians."[45] Bee-lee/Billy is a uniquely capable and distinctly hybrid subject who could navigate both colonial and indigenous worlds and, importantly, has no connection to Britain. This story has all the makings of a classic narrative of colonial and personal progress, but Herring uses them to unsettle colonial knowledge about both settlement and indigenousness.

Herring's stress on the liberating transracial effects of new world migration and the universality of motherly love signal some of the profound ambivalences produced by settler colonialism, but her work does not constitute a serious challenge to colonialism and racism's refraction through gender. The new world may weaken what Herring sees as inherent Asian sexism, but Asian women never emerge as full-fledged subjects in her work. Herring's stress on Aboriginal women's mother-love sits in uneasy juxtaposition with her unwillingness to accord them the same capacity for agency as she gives settler women. Aboriginal patriarchy is inescapable in a way that European, and to a lesser extent Asian, patriarchy is not. Herring, like the authors analyzed by Sarah Carter and others, relies heavily on the image of the "squaw drudge."[46] Women's hardship was an inherent component of Aboriginal culture, just as it was of British culture. Herring describes the indignities suffered by elderly women:

> Their lot is hard enough while their lords are alive, but some consideration has to be shown them, especially if he is a good hunter.... When her "man" is dead, the squaw had a hard time of it, she has to work for son or daughter, friend or foe, as desired. The older and more feeble she grows, the more ridicule she excites; and the less work she can accomplish, the less is she desired in any wigwam.[47]

Here is a patriarchy analogous to that of Britain but made absolute and intransigent by the fact that colonialism and migration cannot offer the same escape. The new world territory that offers escape for women like Agnes is the very ground that demeans the women of the "Northern Tribes."

Herring's vision of womanhood and liberation owed much to a transnational first-wave feminist politics that was deeply rooted in notions and practices of European racial specificity and superiority but was given particular meaning by the local context of British Columbia. Settlement there was racially diverse and comparatively slow: the province did not register a non-Aboriginal majority until the final decades of the nineteenth century.[48] By the first years of the twentieth century, Aboriginal depopulation and restrictive and, after 1923, overtly prohibitive immigration legislation cumulatively put British Columbia's diversity on the retreat. Yet British Columbia remained more Aboriginal, more Asian, and more British than other Canadian provinces.[49] Outside of the indigenous population, it remained less female. This discourse reflected, in part, females' relative rarity. White women made up a tiny portion of settler society during British Columbia's years as a separate colony.[50] As late as 1911, only about 30 per cent of British Columbia's adult population was female, and the 50-per cent mark would not be in sight until the post-war period.[51]

This demography reflected a pattern common to settler colonies whose economy was based on resource extraction and in turn helped to foster a rough, homosocial culture of young, largely working-class men.

Revolving around migration and seasonal wage-labour, this was a culture of rough sociability and to some extent protest that, as Angus McLaren notes, erupted easily into violence.[52] In his 1908 novel, *Woodsmen of the West*, M. Allerdale Grainger evoked the overlap among masculinity, class, and rough culture in Vancouver. In the working-class part of town, "you see few women. Men look into the windows; men drift up and down the street; men lounge in groups upon the curb."[53] This special brand of masculine sociability and its imprint on the fabric of British Columbia challenged first-wave feminism's foundational values of self-control, sobriety, and nurture just as the place of white women in discourses on colonialism nurtured it. British Columbia, like the American west or the Australian bush, provided feminists like Herring with fertile ground for what historian Peggy Pascoe has aptly dubbed "the search for female moral authority."[54]

This search for female moral authority is obviously contingent on romantic views of women, and less obviously but no less importantly, upon a deeply pessimistic view of white men, especially young and working-class ones, as fundamentally oversexed and rapacious. For Herring, it is indeed men's profoundly flawed character that necessitates – and will continue to necessitate – feminism. "Women's rights," she argues, "are only a need created by fallen manhood, which is apt to run to sensuality, and so to abuse the 'weaker vessel.' When manhood has learned self-control, there will be no necessity for any 'protection' for women; but when that time arrives, the millennium will be at our door."[55] Like Australian feminists of the early twentieth century, Herring's views "came from, and spoke to, the historical experience of women for whom heterosexuality was equated with violation and degradation."[56]

Colonial contexts intensified male vice in Herring's mind. Her work conjures up a place of instant community, weak social bonds, social mobility, and cultural pluralism played out on a backdrop of continuing First Nations presence. This context facilitates white men's fundamentally licentious character and presents women with particular and heavy burdens. "In a new country as in a savage one," intones Herring, "the burden and heat of the day falls as a rule, more heavily on the 'weaker vessel.'"[57] Herring's female characters suffer regular and serious abuse at the hands of their husbands, fathers, uncles, and lovers, who frequently escape community sanction and "move on." Mrs. Chester's husband seduces and absconds with her adolescent daughter Marguerite,[58] who is also sexually abused by her adoptive father. The gold-mining community where they live is unable to mount a meaningful challenge to the incest: "Stormy meetings were held, and rousing speeches made, but as so often happened in those days, it ended in much talk, but nothing doing."[59] African-American Big Bertha is seduced, robbed, and forced into the sex trade. When her morality is questioned, Bertha responds with a critique of women's "sex slavery." "I was driven by one man to get my living through many men," she says. "Most women get their living, in the same way by one man."[60]

Herring parks the blame for women's suffering firmly at the door of "fallen manhood" and the backwoods. Yet it is in this very predicament that the settler woman finds her political role and social efficacy. Herring positions white women as able, even destined, to constrain the rough, violent, and amoral activities of white men allowed to run amok without their collective better halves. Keeping fallen men away from their natural tendencies of sensuality and violence is indeed white women's particular mission, and one rendered particularly significant on the edges of British colonialism, where settler women hold the potential to redeem both individual white men and the backwoods as a whole. "A man without a wife is like a mariner tossing at sea without a rudder. Every wind catches him, and turns him this way and that; when he has a good wife, he has anchor and ballast and rudder," says a character in *Canadian Camp Life*.[61]

In restraining men, pioneer women not only improve colonial society and individual men, but also find their deepest calling and satisfaction. Herring's acknowledgement of the difficulties of motherhood and heterosexual coupling for women sits uneasily beside her sense that the family is the place where the true pioneer women finds her ultimate sphere of action. These are not examples of the "new women" who, like Skinner, found subjectivity outside of marriage and motherhood.[62] Herring's mothers are satisfied and agentic. "Mother-love," she writes, "is the deepest and holiest of mortal passions."[63] Unlike her Australian contemporary, Rose Scott, Herring did not sever the connections between wifehood and motherhood.[64] One young female character named Josie threatens to remain a "lady bachelor" at the beginning of *Canadian Camp Life*. By the end of the book, she is married, having seen the truth of her mother's belief that "no amount of success in other ways could ever content the inner heart of a true woman or compensate to her for the home life."[65] It is easy to say that Herring is dogged by romantic conceptions of heterosexuality and maternity, but it is more revealing to note that she raises a tension that continues to undergird Western feminist thinking: namely, how motherhood can be simultaneously the seat of women's oppression and the source of their most profound power and joy.[66]

The reproductive work of settler women is empowering personally and politically. Herring describes the young white women who displaced First Nations women in the 1860s as literal mothers of the Empire, as "the happy mothers of large, healthy families, the very backbone of a new country." Their reproductive work served high imperial conflict like the Boer war and settlement alike. The same mothers of pioneer families bore and raised sons who "proved their mettle in the cause of their beloved country on the veldt and kopjes of South Africa."[67] Reproduction and colonialism are here a single political act, and one the white woman is uniquely responsible for.

If settler women represent the potential of empire, First Nations women signify the vicissitudes of colonialism. This dichotomous pairing is articulated most clearly around marriage and more particularly interracial marriage. Partnerships between settler men and indigenous women were a common feature of British Columbia's social life.[68] For Herring, hybrid relationships are, as they were throughout much of the nineteenth-century Anglo-American world, inherently pathological,[69] the antithesis of the egalitarian new world gender relations of the pioneer woman and her restrained mate. While Herring is willing to credit indigenous women with superior mother-love, she is unwilling to accord them the capacity for controlling men. One white man's time in the chain gang is chalked up to his Aboriginal mate. Had he "some strong-minded, high-tempered woman," he would have been kept on the right track.[70]

Rather than a symbol of his reform, the First Nations woman represents the white man's immorality. The only First Nations women who reverse this connection to exert positive influences over white men, according to Herring, are those under the firm direction of Catholic missionaries.[71] Herring employs disease, a powerful symbol of moral degradation in turn-of-the-century discourse, to symbolize the degeneracy of mixed-race households. Consumption, she intones, "almost invariably" strikes even "the most rugged white man who marries or lives with a squaw."[72] She uses the racialized term "squaw-man" to further indicate that a white man's claim to identity is eroded by relations with Aboriginal women. "No one was more despised than the squaw-man, even by the Indians themselves," writes Herring.[73] Conversely, scorn for First Nations women indicates proper white male character.[74]

These discussions are more about white men and white women than First Nations women, who function as little more than foils for white morality or identity in Herring's texts. This manoeuvre denies Aboriginal women agency but, ironically, empowers Herring to acknowledge some of the violence and degradation suffered by indigenous women. *In the Pathless West* offers the story of two Northern women who "scorned the vile white men," but are abducted and brutally raped, beaten, and injured by a gang of white men.[75] Herring sees these dynamics at work everywhere. One character explains mixed-race relationships: she speaks of "young women who had been taken from their tribes, and supposed they were the proud possessors of white husbands, only to find themselves ruthlessly put aside when occasion or fancy dictated the dastardly action, and sent back to their tribes with perhaps a large family of half-breed children for that tribe to bring up and care for in their own haphazard fashion."[76]

Janice Acoose/Misko-Kìsikàwihkwè (Red Sky Woman) suggests that the image of the passive and constantly abused First Nations woman is a resonant one that continues to shape Canadian literature.[77] Herring occasionally reckons with the implications of representing white and First Nations women in these ways. She knows that in casting First Nations women as signs of colonialism gone awry and white women as the symbols of correct imperialism, she pits them against each other. *In the Pathless West* tells the story of a white man who abandons his First Nations wife, Marie, and children for an unnamed young white woman, an "ailing, complaining wife."[78] Marie and her mother conspire to poison the white wife but inadvertently kill "her former lord." Both women are left bereft. To Herring, this is more than a story of love gone awry. "Is it any wonder," writes Herring, "that under Marie's tuition her children grew up to hate the white man, and still more despise the white woman, or that more than one of them expiated their crimes upon the scaffold? Whose fault was it?"[79]

Here Herring acknowledges gender's centrality to racism and critiques women's role in the construction and maintenance of white supremacy. Yet this exploration of white women's relationship to colonialism comes at the expense of Herring representing Marie – weak, whining, and vindictive – as undeserving of the status of settler womanhood. Ultimately, First Nations women, like white men, serve as a convenient foil for Herring to construct the settler woman in opposition to. Burton argues that the existence of an "apparently less civilized female Other" allowed feminists to argue that custom, and not nature, was responsible for gender and its oppression. Yet in the process, non-Western women were consigned to being passive victims of patriarchy or equally passive objects of white female benevolence.[80] Herring's relational positioning of Aboriginal and settler women was thus a small part of a larger turn-of-the-century project whereby feminists hitched their political cart to that of empire and in doing so, gained political legitimacy at the cost of an enduring legacy of racially exclusive thinking and practices.[81] That Herring read this set of overlapping connections through the particularities of settlement complicated her imagining of gender and race, but it did not remove them from this fraught ideological terrain.

The settler woman whom Herring depicted in print and to some extent in life was an interlocutor and a translator. She explained the backwoods, with its plurality, its apparent savagery, and its irreparable cultural difference, to the metropole. In doing so, the settler woman commented on the curious place of settlers, and more especially settler women, within the webs of imperial power, knowledge, and control. Her vision of settler womanhood was hewn from the particular experience of British Columbia and pivoted on a not uncomplicated but ultimately dichotomous view of settler and indigenous women. Herring hoped that her fiction would illustrate the work of settler women to those separated from British Columbia by space and those separated from the nineteenth century by time. She introduced one of her books with the comment that

> in this period of the emancipation of our sex, from the over-
> thraldom of men, and the recognition of our rightful place in
> the economy, not only of the household but of the national life,
> it will surprise some of our younger sisters to look back upon
> the pioneer life of a comparatively new country, as is this "Last
> West" of ours, and see for themselves the snares which beset
> the footsteps of men when they lack the restraining force of the
> "Motherhood of Women."[82]

But who can claim membership in Herring's motherhood and who is excluded from it? It is worth noting that Herring represented the "Last West" and women's place in it through print, a medium deeply constituent of the divide between indigenous and European. Herring's work did indeed find a place between centre and margin from which the settler woman could speak, and her voice was powerful, limited, and premised on the silence of others.

{NOTES}

1   I have been working intermittently on this project for some time, and would like to thank Brenda Austin-Smith, Jean Barman, Carole Gerson, Phillip Herring, Marion Herring, Don Stewart, Veronica Strong-Boag and participants at the Calgary "British World," BC Studies, and International Federation for Women's History and Women and History at Manitoba meetings for their feedback, assistance, and interventions along the way. This work has been funded, at various times, by a SSHRC doctoral fellowship, a SSHRC postdoctoral fellowship, and the Canada Research Chairs Program.

2   See Antoinette Burton, *Dwelling in the Archive: Women Writing House, Home, and History in Late Colonial India* (New York: Oxford University Press, 2003), 28.

3   Misao Dean, *Practising Femininity: Domestic Realism and the Performance of Gender in Early Canadian Fiction* (Toronto: University of Toronto Press, 1998).

4   See, for a recent discussion, Fiona Paisley, "White Settler Colonialisms and the Colonial Turn: An Australian Perspective," introduction to *Journal of Colonialism and Colonial History* 4, no. 3 (Winter 2003), *muse.jhu.edu/journals*

5   Patrick Wolfe, "History and Imperialism: A Century of Theory, from Marx to Postcolonialism," *American Historical Review* 102, no. 2 (April 1997): 418.

6   Adele Perry, *On the Edge of Empire: Gender, Race, and the Making of British Columbia, 1849–1871* (Toronto: University of Toronto Press, 2001); Trever Burnard, "A Failed Settler Society: Marriage and Demographic Failure in Early Jamaica," *Journal of Social History* 28, no. 1 (Fall 1994): 63–82. This point is also made in Daiva Staisulis and Nira Yuval-Davis, "Beyond Dichotomies – Gender, Race, Ethnicity and Class in Settler Societies," in *Unsettling Settler Societies: Articulations of Gender, Race, Ethnicity and Class* (London: Sage, 1995), and, in a sustained fashion, by Penny Edwards in "On Home Ground: Settling Land and Domesticating Difference in the 'Non-Settler' Colonies of Burma and Cambodia," *Journal of Colonialism and Colonial History* 4, no. 3 (Winter 2003), *muse.jhu.edu/journals*

7   Cole Harris, *The Resettlement of British Columbia: Essays on Colonialism and Geographical Change* (Vancouver: UBC Press, 1997).

8   Patrick Wolfe, *Settler Colonialism and the Transformation of Anthropology: The Politics and Poetics of an Ethnographic Event* (London: Cassell, 1999), 3.

9   Anna Davin, "Imperialism and Motherhood," *History Workshop* 5 (1978): 9–66; Ann Laura Stoler, *Carnal Knowledge and Imperial Power: Race and the Intimate in Colonial Rule* (Berkeley: University of California Press, 2002); Nancy Rose Hunt, *A Colonial Lexicon of Birth Ritual, Medicalization, and Mobility in the Congo* (Durham, NC: Duke University Press, 1999).

10   Nicholas Thomas, *Colonialism's Culture: Anthropology, Travel, and Government* (Princeton, NJ: Princeton University Press, 1994).

11   Sherene H. Razack, "When Place Becomes Race," in *Race, Space, and the Law: Unmapping a White Settler Society* (Toronto: Between the Lines, 2002), 3.

12   "Marriage," *Mainland Guardian*, 18 June 1873.

13   Author's interview with Philip and Marion Grace Herring, 21 December 1994. Herring's life is explored in more detail in my "Frances Elizabeth Herring," *Dictionary of Canadian Biography* (Toronto: University of Toronto Press, 1998), 14:485–86. For contemporary biographies, see Henry James Morgan, *The Canadian Men and Women of the Time: A Hand-book of Canadian Biography of Living Characters,*

2nd ed (Toronto: William Briggs, 1912), 529; John William Leonard, *Woman's Who's Who of America: A Biographical Dictionary of Contemporary Women of the United States and Canada 1914–1915* (New York: American Commonwealth, 1914), 383–84; F.W. Howay and E.O.S. Scholefield, *British Columbia from Earliest Times to the Present* (Vancouver: S.A. Clarke, 1914), 232–36. My thanks to Carole Gerson for sharing some of this with me.

14 See Mariana Valverde, "'When the Mother of the Race Is Free': Race, Reproduction, and Sexuality in First-Wave Feminism," in *Gender Conflicts: New Essays in Women's History*, ed. Franca Iacovetta and Mariana Valverde (Toronto: University of Toronto Press, 1992); Carole Bacchi, *Liberation Deferred? The Ideas of the English-Canadian Suffragists, 1877–1918* (Toronto: University of Toronto Press, 1983), chap. 7.

15 See "Fifth Annual Report of the Superintendent of Education, 1875–76," *British Columbia Legislative and Sessional Papers* (Victoria: Richard Wolfenden, 1877), 90; "Sixth Annual Report on the Public Schools of British Columbia, 1876–77," *British Columbia Legislative and Sessional Papers* (Victoria: Wolfenden, 1877); National Council of Women of Canada, *Yearbook* (Toronto: Parker and Sons, 1912), xiv; Leonard, *Woman's Who's Who of America*, 238; Howay and Scholefield, *British Columbia*, 232; Leonard, *Woman's Who's Who of America*, 384.

16 See "Tact in the Home," *British Columbia Commonwealth*, 22 October 1892; "Some Women," *British Columbia Commonwealth*, 15 August 1892.

17 Frances E. Herring, *Canadian Camp Life* (London: T. Fisher Unwin, 1900); *Among the People of British Columbia: Red, White, Yellow, and Brown* (London: T. Fisher Unwin, 1903); *In the Pathless West: With Soldiers, Pioneers, Miners, and Savages* (London: T. Fisher Unwin, 1904); *Nan and Other Pioneer Women of the West* (London: Francis Griffiths, 1913); *The Gold Miners: A Sequel to the Pathless West* (London: Francis Griffiths, 1914).

18 "Brief Local Items," *Vancouver Province*, 3 September 1900.

19 I am grateful to Brenda Austin-Smith for this way of characterizing Herring's work.

20 Carole Gerson, "Nobler Savages: Representations of Native Women in the Writings of Susanna Moodie and Catherine Parr Traill," *Journal of Canadian Studies* 32, no. 3 (Summer 1997): 5–21.

21 Jean Barman, "'I Walk My Own Track in Life & No Mere Male Can Bump Me off It': Constance Lindsay Skinner and the Work of History," in *Creating Historical Memory: English-Canadian Women and the Work of History*, ed. Beverley Boutilier and Alison Prentice (Vancouver: UBC Press, 1997), 129; Jean Barman, *Constance Lindsay Skinner: Writing on the Frontier* (Toronto: University of Toronto Press, 2002).

22 See the advertisements at the back of Herring, *Gold Miners*.

23 Judge F.W. Howay, "Preface," in *Gold Miners*, Herring, 11.

24 Karen Dubinsky, "Vacations in the 'Contact Zone': Race, Gender, and the Traveller at Niagara Falls," in *Nation, Empire, Colony: Historicizing Gender and Race*, ed. Ruth Roach Pierson and Nupur Chaudhuri (Bloomington: University of Indiana Press, 1998). Also see Sara Mills, *Discourses of Difference: An Analysis of Women's Travel Writing and Colonialism* (London: Routledge, 1991); Nancy Pagh, *At Home Afloat: Women on the Waters of the Pacific Northwest* (Calgary: University of Calgary Press, 2001).

25 Herring, *Among the People*, v.

26 See Herring, *Among the People*, vi–vii.

27 Herring, *Nan*, "Preface," n.p.

28 For a discussion of such authorities and history, see Dipesh Chakrabarty, *Provincializing Europe: Postcolonial Thought and Historical Difference* (Princeton: Princeton University Press, 2000).

29 Herring, *In the Pathless West*, v.

30 See Jean Barman, *The West Beyond the West: A History of British Columbia* (Toronto: University of Toronto Press, 1991), 169–70.

31 Howay, "Preface," in *Gold Miners*, Herring 12.

32 Mary Louise Pratt, *Imperial Eyes: Travel Writing and Transculturation* (London: Routledge, 1992), chap. 8.

33 See, for instance, Elizabeth Jameson, "Women as Workers, Women as Civilizers: True Womanhood in the American West," in *The Women's West*, ed. Susan Armitage and Elizabeth Jameson (Norman, OK: University of Oklahoma, 1987); Margaret Strobel, *European Women and the Second British Empire* (Bloomington: Indiana University Press, 1991); Napur Chaudhuri and Margaret Strobel, eds., *Western Women and Imperialism: Complicity and Resistance* (Bloomington: Indiana University Press, 1992); Helen Callaway, *Gender, Culture, and Empire: European Women in Colonial Nigeria* (Urbana, IL: University of Illinois Press, 1987); Claudia Knapman, *White Women in Fiji, 1835–1930: The Ruin of Empire?* (Sydney: Allen and Unwin, 1986); Syliva Van Kirk, *"Many Tender Ties": Women in Fur-Trade Society in Western Canada, 1670–1870* (Winnipeg: Watson and Dwyer, 1980).

34 Herring, *Gold Miners*, 13; Herring, *In the Pathless West*, 123.

35 Herring, *Nan*, 55.

36 Marilyn Lake, "Colonised and Colonising: The White Australian Feminist Subject," *Women's History Review* 2, no. 3 (1993): 377–86. Also see her "Between Old World 'Barbarism' and Stone Age 'Primitivism': The Double Difference of the White Australian Feminist," in *Australian Women: Contemporary Feminist Thought*, ed. N. Grieve and A. Burns (London: Oxford University Press, 1994).

37 Herring, *Among the People*, 2.

38 Nayan Shah, *Contagious Divides: Epidemics and Race in San Francisco's Chinatown* (Berkeley, CA: University of California Press, 2001).

39 Herring, *Canadian Camp Life*, 48–49.

40 Herring, *Among the People*, 42.

41 Herring, *Nan*, 41, 40.

42 On this, see Maria Torgovnick, *Gone Primitive: Savage Intellects, Modern Lives* (Chicago: University of Chicago Press, 1990); Gail Bederman, *Manliness and Civilization: A Cultural History of Gender and Race in the United States, 1880–1917* (Chicago: University of Chicago Press, 1995); Joy Dixon, "Ancient Wisdom, Modern Motherhood: Theosophy and the Colonial Syncretic," in *Gender, Sexuality, and Colonial Modernities*, ed. Antoinette Burton (New York: Routledge, 1999).

43 Herring, *In the Pathless West*, 118–19.

44 Herring, *In the Pathless West*, 170.

45 Herring, *Gold Miners*, 21.

46 Sarah Carter, *Capturing Women: The Manipulation of Cultural Imagery in Canada's Prairie West* (Montreal: McGill-Queen's, 1997), chap. 5; Ranya Green, "The Pochahantas Perplex: The Image of Indian Women in American Culture," in

Unequal Sisters: A Multi-Cultural Reader in U.S. Women's History, ed. Ellen Carol DuBois and Vicki L. Ruiz (New York: Routledge, 1990).

47 Herring, *In the Pathless West*, 165.

48 See Harris, *Resettlement of British Columbia*, esp. chap. 5 and 9.

49 See Barman, *The West*, Table 9.

50 See Perry, introduction to *On the Edge of Empire*.

51 See Barman, *The West*, Table 2, 369.

52 Angus McLaren, "Men, Migrants and Murder in British Columbia, 1900–1923," in *On the Case: Explorations in Social History*, ed. Franca Iacovetta and Wendy Michinson (Toronto: University of Toronto Press, 1999); Robert A. Campbell, *Sit Down and Drink Your Beer: Regulating Vancouver's Beer Parlours, 1925–1954* (Toronto: University of Toronto Press, 2001).

53 M. Allerdale Grainger, *Woodsmen of the West* (1908; repr., Toronto: McClelland and Stewart, 1964), 13.

54 Peggy Pascoe, *Relations of Rescue: The Search for Female Moral Authority in the American West, 1874–1939* (New York: Oxford, 1990). On Australia, see Marilyn Lake, "Frontier Feminism and the Maurading White Man: Australia, 1890s to 1940s," in *Nation, Empire, Colony*.

55 Herring, *Nan*, 40.

56 Marilyn Lake, "The Inviolable Woman: Feminist Conceptions of Citizenship in Australia, 1900–1945," *Gender and History* 8, no. 2 (August 1996): 203.

57 Herring, "Preface," *Nan*, n.p.

58 Herring, *Gold Miners*, 94–99.

59 Herring, *Nan*, 95.

60 Herring, *Gold Miners*, 34.

61 Herring, *Canadian Camp Life*, 7.

62 See Barman, *Constance Lindsay Skinner*.

63 Herring, *Nan*, 40.

64 See Judith Allen, "'Our Deeply Degraded Sex' and 'The Animal in Man': Rose Scott, Feminism, and Sexuality, 1890–1925," *Australian Feminist Studies* 7/8 (Summer 1988): 65–91.

65 Herring, *Canadian Camp Life*, 70 and 158.

66 For what remains a powerful innovation of this mire of contradictions, see Adrienne Rich, *Of Woman Born: Motherhood as Experience and Institution* (New York: Norton, 1986).

67 Herring, *In the Pathless West*, 86.

68 See Jean Barman, "Invisible Women: Aboriginal Mothers and Mixed-Race Daughters in Rural Pioneer British Columbia," in *Beyond the City Limits: Rural History in British Columbia*, ed. Ruth Sandwell (Vancouver: UBC Press, 1998).

69 See Robert C. Young, *Colonial Desire: Hybridity in Theory, Culture and Race* (London: Routledge, 1995), chap. 4.

70 Herring, *Among the Peoples*, 22.

71 See Herring, *Nan*, 24; Herring, *Canadian Camp Life*, 66.

72 Herring, *In the Pathless West*, 135. On disease as metaphor, see Mariana Valverde, *The Age of Light, Soap, and Water: Moral Reform in English Canada, 1885–1925* (Toronto:

McClelland and Stewart, 1991), chap. 3; Frank Mort, *Dangerous Sexualities: Medico-Moral Politics in England Since 1830* (London: Frank Cass, 1987), especially part 1.

73 Herring, *Gold Miners*, 21.

74 See Herring, *Nan*, 121–22, 129.

75 Herring, *In the Pathless West*, 210–16.

76 Herring, *Among the Peoples*, 142.

77 Acoose/Misko-Kìsikàwihkwè (Red Sky Woman), *Iskwewak – Kah' Ki Yaw Ni Wahkomakanak: Neither Indian Princesses Nor Easy Squaws* (Toronto: The Women's Press, 1995), 39.

78 See Herring, *In the Pathless West*, 90–92.

79 Ibid., 87–93.

80 Antoinette Burton, *Burdens of History: British Feminists, Indian Women, and Imperial Culture, 1865–1915* (Chapel Hill: University of North Carolina Press, 1994), 94.

81 See Valverde, "When the Mother of the Race Is Free"; Vijay Agnew, *Resisting Discrimination: Women from Asia, Africa, and the Caribbean and the Women's Movement in Canada* (Toronto: University of Toronto Press, 1996), chap. 2.

82 Herring, "Preface," *Nan*, n.p.

CHAPTER 8

THE LONG GOODBYE:

ENGLISH CANADIANS
AND THE BRITISH WORLD

Phillip Buckner

OVER TEN YEARS AGO, in my presidential address to the Canadian
Historical Association, I asked the question: "Whatever happened to the
British Empire?" My concern was to address the issue of why Canadian
historians had locked themselves into a teleological framework that was
obsessed with the construction of a Canadian national identity, one that
"downplayed the significance of the imperial experience in shaping the
identity of nineteenth-century Canada." In that paper I attempted to
show that during the nineteenth century the majority of English-speaking Canadians defined themselves as British and shared many of the
same myths, prejudices, and enthusiasms as the British did in the mother
country. My emphasis was on the nineteenth century, for I accepted as
a given that this "sense of a shared identity would grow weaker in the
twentieth century."[1] Ironically, I have increasingly realized that in making
this last comment, I remained a prisoner of the very colony-to-nation
framework that I criticized in my address. In essence, the colony-to-nation approach posited a misguided moment of imperial enthusiasm in
the late nineteenth century, symbolized by Canadian participation in the
South African War, and then a gradual weakening of a sense of British
identity among English-speaking Canadians and a parallel growth in
a sense of being distinctively Canadian. This whole approach, which
remains embodied in most recent general histories of Canada, assumes
that imperialism and nationalism were antithetical concepts and that
as support for one – Canadian nationalism – grew stronger, support
for the other – British imperialism – inevitably grew weaker (or vice
versa). The problem is that while the way in which English-speaking
Canadians defined their national identity was undoubtedly transformed

in the twentieth century, the sense of being part of a British World did not dissolve in the linear fashion implied in this framework. Until the 1960s, a majority of English-speaking Canadians continued to embrace the notion that Canada was essentially part of a family of British nations. It seems to me that the question we need to focus on is not how this sense of a shared identity dissolved in the twentieth century but why it persisted for so long.

The book that I blame (perhaps unfairly) for leading me and many other Canadian historians down the wrong path is Carl Berger's *The Sense of Power: Studies in the Ideas of Canadian Imperialism, 1867–1914*. Berger's book was a brilliant reappraisal of those intellectuals who supported some form of imperial federation in the years before the First World War. The fundamental thesis of the book was that the leading advocates of imperial federation in Canada had been unfairly portrayed by their opponents as "misguided colonials who showed an obsequious deference for everything British and disparaged colonial things." Berger disputed this stereotype and argued that "Canadian imperialism was one variety of Canadian nationalism – a type of awareness of nationality which rested upon a certain understanding of history, the national character, and the national mission."[2] Berger's attempt to rehabilitate the imperial federationists was never accepted by all Canadian historians. His most trenchant critic was Doug Cole, who argued that Berger had confused nationalism with patriotism. Nationalism is "the consciousness of being an ethnically differentiated people and expresses itself as loyalty to an ethnic nation." It is "based upon a self-conception, self-awareness, and self-assertion of an ethnically circumscribed group of people." Patriotism, on the other hand, is "a loyalty, not to an aggregate of people but to a political state and the geographic territory circumscribed by that state." Cole accepted that the imperialists were Canadian patriots who sought to "promote Canadian interests," but he denied that "Canadian imperialism" was "a variety or extension of Canadian nationalism" because Canadian imperialists "had no intention of creating a separate Canadian culture, ethnic identification, and nation."[3]

While Berger's argument has become embodied in Canadian historiography, Cole's critique is rarely discussed. Interestingly, Cole's views have received greater attention in Australia, where there has been an increasingly bitter debate over the issue of Australia's British identity.[4] The lack of a similar debate in Canada partly reflects the near total disinterest of most Canadian historians in the whole issue of the imperial relationship and its significance in the twentieth century. Indeed, the only recent theoretical contribution to this debate came from an imperial historian, David Cannadine. Cole defined the Canadian imperialists as "Britannic nationalists," but Cannadine prefers to talk about "Imperial Canadians." He argues that for these Canadians "imperialism was not the denial of Canadian independence; it was something better, something bigger, enabling Canada to participate in the greatest global community the world has ever seen." But, like Cole, he argues that, so long as Canadians clung to their imperial loyalties, they could never have a sense of complete nationhood, which explains why "Canada lacks national monuments, national myths, national heroes and national traditions. It has never come alive or taken off or achieved credibility as one of Benedict Anderson's 'imagined communities.'"[5]

Since the publication of Berger's book, there has been an enormous outpouring of literature on the subject of nationalism and national identity. I cannot even attempt to deal at length with this literature here, but I think one can draw from it some general conclusions. The first is that the nation, in Benedict Anderson's felicitous phrase, is indeed an imagined community: all national identities are socially constructed and based upon invented traditions, and the nation can be imagined by its members in a variety of different – sometimes even contradictory – ways. If this is true, then Berger was correct to insist that Canadian nationalism can come in a variety of forms and that no one form is more legitimate or superior to another. The second general conclusion to be drawn from the recent literature is that it is impossible to maintain the distinction between "patriotism" and "nationalism." Most students of nationalism would now find more relevant the distinction between ethnic nationalism and civic nationalism (which is territorially based). But even this distinction has its difficulties since most nations are constructed out of a jumble of pre-existing historical materials and mix together notions of territoriality and ethnicity. As Colin Kidd points out, the "English" nation, as it was defined between 1600 and 1800, was "neither indisputably ethnic nor exclusively civic-territorial."[6] Nor was the concept of the British nation as it emerged in the eighteenth and nineteenth centuries. And nor was the concept of a Canadian nation as it emerged in the late nineteenth century. In fact, the distinction between civic and ethnic nationalism was so blurred and so confused in the late nineteenth century, both in Britain and in Canada, that it makes no sense to distinguish between them.

The third conclusion I would draw from the literature on nationalism is that people can hold more than one national identity at a time. J.M. Winter has written that "the most striking feature of pre-war discussions of national identity [in Britain] is their vagueness." The volume of migration from Britain to areas of white settlement and back again helped "to obscure distinctions between the English and the other, especially the imperial other." Many young British-born people emigrated to Canada before 1914; some returned to Britain and some of them re-emigrated back to Canada for a second or even a third time. "What was their nationality? Canadian? British? The distinctions were on the whole blurred before 1914."[7] If such distinctions were vague and blurred in Britain, they were even less clear in late nineteenth-century Canada among those British subjects who were born in Canada of British parentage or descent and who considered themselves just as good Britishers (a term frequently used before the First World War) or Britons as those born in the British Isles. At public events they sang "Rule Britannia" just as heartily as they sang "The Maple Leaf Forever," the two national songs of English-speaking Canadians in the late nineteenth century. Indeed, the Empire in the late nineteenth century was a remarkably fluid place in which to live. Emigrants from the British Isles frequently crossed the Atlantic several times before settling permanently on one side or the other with wives and children born on either or both sides of the Atlantic. The flow of migration was not just one way. Many Britons born in Canada found military and civil positions for themselves throughout the Empire or went abroad as missionaries.[8] English-speaking Canadians in the late nineteenth century had a strong sense of belonging to an extended British community. Sir Donald Mackenzie Wallace, who visited Canada in 1901, noted that English-speaking Canadians had a "feeling of affectionate tenderness for the old country, akin to the love which every one feels for the place endeared to him by early associations." It was a sentiment that could be experienced even by one who had been born overseas since even "though he may never have seen the old home, he has heard of it from his infancy, is almost as familiar with it as if he had spent there a good proportion of his life."[9]

Although an affectionate attachment for the "old country" did not necessarily mean a commitment to the Empire, in the vast majority of cases a strong sense of British identity was inseparable from a strong commitment to the British Empire. *What is my Country? My Country is the Empire. Canada is my home.* was the title of a book published by Percy Machell in 1912. Machell attributed the quotation to an unnamed Canadian cabinet minister, but the purpose of his book was to remind his countrymen in Britain that "these Islands are only a parish of the Empire, any part of which may be our Home."[10] This was a common feeling among Canadians, Australians, New Zealanders, and South Africans of British ancestry in the late nineteenth century, who saw the Empire as their creation. This sense of imperial identity was a source of pride to most English-speaking Canadians. After visiting Canada in 1905, John Foster Fraser concluded: "Beyond his scoffing the Canadian has a genuine affection for what he calls the 'old country' although maybe neither he nor his sires were British-born. He is proud of the British Empire, he loves the Union Jack – though he usually mistakes the sheet of the mercantile marine for it – and when the man of the States 'blows' about America, and suggests it could eat Canada any morning before breakfast, the Canadian points to a red-splashed map of the world, and asks him what America has to show alongside the British Empire."[11] A Canadian put it more succinctly when he welcomed the Duke of Cornwall and York to Canada in 1901 waving a banner that declared: "We are Proud to be Canadians God Bless the British Empire."[12]

Today we accept as normal that immigrants to Canada and their descendants can easily negotiate between the identity of their home country and of their adopted country. Why then should it be so difficult to accept that most British immigrants and their descendants were able to hold onto more than one national identity? Most English-speaking Canadians were proud to be a part of the world's largest global community, but it is nonsensical to say that English-speaking Canadians lacked "national monuments, national myths, national heroes and national traditions." Berger shows how Canadians in the late nineteenth century set about resurrecting the Loyalists and reinterpreting the War of 1812 to provide themselves with indigenous heroes and indigenous myths, albeit ones that were compatible with their belief that Canadians – or at least English-speaking Canadians – were also the heirs of British traditions and British history. English-speaking Canadians would continue to "invent" indigenous national traditions of this kind, extolling the superiority of Canadian volunteers over those from Britain in the South African War and the First World War and establishing the myth that Canadians invented the concept of responsible government and the idea of dominion status. They also would invent "national heroes" like Laura Secord, Sam Steele, and Billy Bishop, who were, of course, also imperial heroes. And one does not have to travel very far in Canada before one trips over monuments to the "pioneers" who settled Canada or to the gallant "Canadians" who gave their lives in the South African War or the First World War. John Rickard has written that "the Australian mythology both competed with and depended on the mythology of

Britishness."[13] The same was true of the English-Canadian mythology. A sense of being part of an extended British community – a Greater Britain – lay behind the decision of English-speaking Canadians to create the Dominion of Canada in 1867 (as it did behind the Australian decision to create their federation three decades later). But this belief also co-existed and competed with the desire to create a Better Britain. When John A. Macdonald and the other Fathers of Confederation talked about building a "new nationality," they had in mind the creation of a new national identity, one that would embody the best of British culture and traditions but that was modified to meet the requirements of life in North America. They wanted to create a nation that would remain essentially British but also free to evolve its own national identity while remaining permanently allied with the mother country under the same crown. Most imperial federationists shared these goals, and in that sense Berger was correct to see them as one variety of Canadian nationalists.

My problem with Berger is not that he turned Canadian imperialists into Canadian nationalists but rather with his limited definition of imperialism and his failure to recognize that the vast majority of Canadian nationalists were imperialists, even if they did not share the goals of the imperial federation movement. At the beginning of *The Sense of Power*, Berger declares that "in the context of Canadian history imperialism means that movement for the closer union of the British Empire through economic and military co-operation and through political changes which would give the dominions influence over imperial policy."[14] Because Berger defines imperialism in this narrow way, it is not surprising that he sees the Imperial Federation League and the British Empire League, which succeeded it in 1896, as the voice of imperialism in Canada, even though the membership of both organizations was small. In fact, imperial enthusiasm in late nineteenth-century Canada went well beyond the small group of intellectuals and politically active males, drawn from the upper social classes, who joined the Imperial Federation League. For example, no organization in Canada was more dedicated to the preservation of the Empire and the British way of life than the Orange Lodge. By the late nineteenth century, the Orange Lodge had expanded far beyond its original Protestant Irish roots and had become a truly "Canadian" organization, drawing its members from every social class and every Protestant ethnic group in the country, including some First Nations. At its peak in the late nineteenth century, one in three of all English-speaking Protestant adult males belonged to it. Nobody, however, has ever accused the Orange Lodge of being composed of intellectuals and so its influence has been largely ignored, as has the influence of the host of fraternal and friendly societies that extolled the virtues of the imperial connection. Branches of the Sons of England, for example, spread rapidly across Canada in the late nineteenth and early twentieth centuries, and yet there is not a single scholarly study of the impact of one of the largest voluntary associations in Canada. Nor was imperialism purely a male enthusiasm. Until the founding of the Imperial Order Daughters of the Empire (IODE), there was no women's organization devoted solely to the promotion of the Empire, but the Orange Lodge and the Sons of England had women's auxiliaries. Moreover, most women's organizations, such as the Girls' Friendly Society and the local church groups that raised money to send missionaries overseas, saw Canada as an integral part of a wider Empire.

These organizations are usually seen (rather like the imperial federation movement used to be) as organizations run by misguided colonials who showed an obsequious deference to everything British, but this is clearly nonsense. Most Orangemen were devoted to the principle of local self-government, and the Orange Lodges in Canada would co-operate with the lodges in Britain only on their own terms. Similarly, "colonial female imperialism was its own creation with its own historical roots and its own sense of organizational identity," and the Canadian women who ran the IODE and the other female imperialist organizations were only prepared to co-operate with British female organizations in Britain – like the Victoria League – on their own terms.[15]

By defining as imperialists only those who supported the movement for greater imperial unity, Berger implies that those who fought for Canadian autonomy were, by implication, anti-imperialists. In English-speaking Canada, however, there was widespread enthusiasm for the Empire and few real anti-imperialists. It does not follow that most English-speaking Canadians wanted some form of closer imperial union. Many, if not most, were liberal imperialists who believed in a decentralized Empire. Canadian historians have had difficulty in coming to grips with the liberal imperialists, perhaps because they have difficulty in seeing liberalism and imperialism as compatible doctrines. They have therefore eagerly seized upon the term "colonial nationalism," a term used by Richard Jebb in his 1905 book. After touring Australia and Canada, Jebb returned to Britain convinced that in both countries a "new nationalism" had taken root, one which urged that "the interests of the territory as a unit of progressive civilization should be considered by its own inhabitants before the interests of the far-flung race to which they belonged, if the two happened to be in conflict." If the Empire was to survive, Jebb argued, it could only be by substituting the concept "of alliance for federation…as the guiding principle of closer coherence between the Mother Country and the self-governing colonies."[16] In understanding that the primary loyalty of Canadians would increasingly be to the emerging Canadian nation, Jebb showed great insight, but the term "colonial nationalism" was an ambiguous one, and so far as I am aware, was never used by Canadian nationalists (or nationalists in the other self-governing colonies) to describe themselves.

One of the first Canadian historians to make use of this term was Ramsay Cook in his 1963 biography of John W. Dafoe.[17] Cook pointed out that Dafoe was opposed to any efforts at imperial centralization and that as early as 1902 he proclaimed: "Let us develop our own resources, defend our own interests, and build up here a puissant Commonwealth which, in times of peril, will voluntarily place at the disposal of the Motherland her entire available resources. To ask for more than this, is to risk the chance of getting less."[18] Cook declared that "this doctrine, labelled Liberal imperialism by Dafoe, was really colonial nationalism" and that what made "colonial nationalism, different from later nationalism was that the strengthening of the autonomy and the internal development of Canada was not an end in itself. The ultimate objective was the strengthening of the Empire, which was conceived of as a unity, though an undefined unity, based on sentiment rather than legal ties and political commitments." Dafoe certainly did believe that the Empire could be a force for the spread of liberal institutions and liberal values in the world. He was also deeply committed to the notion of Canada as an essentially British nation that would embody those liberal institutions and values for which the British Empire stood. But I do not see that the "ultimate objective" of the policies of autonomy and national development that he espoused was simply the "strengthening of the Empire," for Dafoe believed in the evolution of a strong and autonomous Canada, within the Empire if possible but without it if necessary. He was, in short, both a liberal imperialist and a Canadian nationalist and in his mind these objectives were perfectly compatible within a decentralized Empire. For Dafoe and the liberal imperialists, the objective was the transformation of the Empire into a community of self-governing British nations who would come together in times of peril to defend the liberal institutions and values in which they all believed.[19] Liberal imperialists like Newton W. Rowell believed that for the Empire to survive, "the people of Great Britain" would have to accept that "they were dealing, not with subjects, but with fellow citizens." They interpreted Sir Wilfrid Laurier's repeated refusal, expressed at a series of imperial conferences, to endorse any form of centralized institutions not as leading to the collapse of the imperial relationship but as laying "the foundations broad and secure for the future of the Empire."[20]

Canadian historians have underestimated the strength of liberal imperialism in the pre-1914 period, partly because they have overestimated the influence of the imperial federationists. They have, for example, too often taken at face value the claim (made by the imperial federationists themselves) that Canada decided to participate in the South African War because of the pressure that the imperial federation lobby was able to exert on the Laurier government. Carman Miller has drawn a distinction between what he calls the "patriotic" – that is, Canadian nationalist – response to the war and the "loyalist" – that is, imperialist – response.[21] But most English-speaking Canadians saw no contradiction between their nationalism and their imperialism. Indeed, the vast majority had no doubt that the war in South Africa was a just war that would result in more liberal institutions in South Africa, and that Canada ought to assist Britain in her hour of need.[22] If there was a division among English-Canadians, it was between the imperial federationists who hoped that the war would lead to centralized imperial institutions in which Canada would participate and those liberal imperialists who believed – like Dafoe – that it would show that no such institutions were necessary for the Empire to function as a unit in times of crisis.

In a variety of ways, the South African War strengthened Canadian enthusiasm for the Empire. Those who had served in South Africa formed veterans' associations dedicated to keeping alive the memory of those who "laid down their lives in South Africa in the cause of the British Empire," gathered together in Ottawa each year to celebrate Paardeberg Day, and marched with the veterans of the Fenian Raids and the Northwest Rebellion in Decoration Day ceremonies, held annually in a number of Canadian cities.[23] One of the most popular military figures to emerge out of the war was Robert Baden-Powell. In 1910 Baden-Powell toured Canada, promoting the Boy Scout movement, and in 1911 a special edition of *Scouting for Boys* was published, including a letter "To Every Canadian Boy" telling them that "Canada can be a very big nation in a few years if each one of you determines to do his bit in making it so."[24] By 1913 there were over forty thousand Boy Scouts in Canada, a disproportionately larger number than in Britain, and the Girl Guides, founded in 1912, was growing rapidly.[25] Another imperial figure whose popularity derived from the war was Winston Churchill, who visited Canada in 1901, lecturing to "magnificent audiences." The government of Prince Edward Island even named a post office and the settlement that gathered around it after him.[26] The South African War also created the first imperialist organization in Canada run by women. Founded in February 1900 and originally called the Federation of British Daughters of the Empire, it became the Imperial Order of the Daughters of the Empire (IODE) and moved its headquarters to Toronto in October 1901. By 1910 it had 137 chapters across Canada with over ten thousand members.[27] In the early years of the twentieth century, the cultural, social, and economic ties between Canada and Britain grew stronger in a variety of ways, and an ever-denser web of associational networks linked Britons in Canada and Britons in the mother country. Much has been made of the "alliances" formed by constructive imperialists in Britain and in Canada who sought to strengthen the imperial connection through formal institutions, but links were also formed between liberal imperialists in both countries whose ideal was greater decentralization.[28]

Given his limited definition of imperialism, it is not surprising that Berger declared that in "its central ambition, Imperialism failed. It was a victim of its own zeal; in another sense, it was a casualty of the First World War."[29] Like Berger, most Canadian historians tend to see Canadian imperialism as a casualty of the First World War. Yet the most detailed study of the participation of an English-Canadian community in the Great War is Ian Miller's recent study of Toronto. Miller argues that the degree of enthusiasm for the First World War among Torontonians has been underestimated, and he paints a picture of a community – men and women, the labour movement, and virtually every ethnic group in the city – united "in a remarkable testament to the social cohesion that characterized the city during the Great War."[30] Miller's account has not convinced everyone: his critics point out that even if this was true for Toronto, it may not have been true for the rest of the country. Yet it was certainly true in the Maritimes, where, as Ian McKay points out, "almost everybody – workers, employers, Acadians, Blacks, Catholics, Protestants, Liberals, Conservatives, men, and women – supported the Empire in its struggle against the Germans."[31] In short, Miller and McKay, looking at two very different areas of Canada, reach very similar conclusions.

In another recent study, Jonathan Vance argues that in the aftermath of the war Canadians were demoralized but set out to make sense of the losses they had suffered by erecting a myth that gave meaning to their experience.[32] Miller, however, takes issue with the argument that the war demoralized Canadians. He insists that Canadians "did not need to take refuge in myths; they took comfort in their shared memory of sacrifice." In his view it was not the war but the post-war world that led to disillusionment and despair.[33] Regardless of which interpretation you prefer, it is clear that both would agree that the war did not lead to widespread disillusionment with the Empire, though it did greatly increase a sense of Canadian national consciousness. In a paper written in 1917 to celebrate the fiftieth anniversary of the creation of the Canadian federation, George M. Wrong declared that since 1867 "we have made the transition from an imported to a native culture."[34] While many English-speaking Canadians still thought of themselves as essentially British and when asked their nationality by British visitors were "as likely to say 'British' as Canadian,"[35] a declining number spoke of Britain as "home." The distinguished Canadian historian, W.L. Morton, wrote about his own childhood in Manitoba in the interwar years in these terms: "British we were, but English in the sense of southern English we never were. On the contrary every English-Canadian in my childhood milieu disliked an English lord, an Oxford accent, and English style.... Our Britishness, then, was not Englishness, but a local brew which we called Canadian."[36]

This attitude was shared even by many of the British-born. Take, for example, the case of Arthur Hawkes. Born in Aylesford, Kent in 1871, at the age of 14 Hawkes migrated to the Canadian West, where he worked on a farm. He returned to England to work as a journalist for several county papers and then for the *Daily Mail* and the *Manchester Guardian*. He crisscrossed the Atlantic at least nineteen times before settling with his family in Toronto in 1905.[37] In 1911 he established a newspaper aimed specifically at the British-born and their offspring in Canada and at those in Britain with relatives in Canada. Initially the paper was called *British News in Canada*, then *The Canadian and British News in Canada*, and finally simply *The Canadian*. The title reveals Hawkes's intellectual odyssey. From the beginning, he identified himself as both British and Canadian, and his paper's masthead read: "For those Who Love the Old Land and the New." In 1911 Hawkes campaigned vigorously against reciprocity on the grounds that it would destroy the imperial connection, but in 1912–1913 he campaigned equally strongly against Borden's naval bill on the grounds that Canada ought to have its own navy. Hawkes resented being called a colonial, and he objected to those Englishmen who continued to refer to "the Old Country" as "home," insisting that his family members "do not want to go back to the land of their birth. We do not speak of England as 'home.' This is our home. We want no other." Hawkes was resolutely opposed to the imperial centralists and he believed in the need to develop a set of Canadian symbols, supporting the campaign to make the red ensign Canada's official flag: "We are Canadians as well as Britishers, and our flag must correctly represent us."[38] In his 1919 book, *The Birthright*, Hawkes went even further, declaring that "primarily, fundamentally, finally, Canada must be the first in whatever we say, and think, and perform." But Hawkes rejected the claim that his views had fundamentally altered since he had campaigned against reciprocity, pointing out that the full title of his 1911 anti-reciprocity pamphlet had been "An Appeal to the British-born to Promote the Sense of Canadian Nationality within the British Empire." Hawkes – like most liberal imperialists – insisted that this remained his goal: the promotion of a sense of Canadian nationality within a "Britannic Alliance of free and equal nations."[39]

During the Second Imperial Press Conference, held in Ottawa in 1920, Lord Burnham, the proprietor of the London *Daily Telegraph*, declared that "the British World is a world of its own, and it is a world of many homes." I was very pleased to find this quotation, only to discover that Simon Potter had beaten me to it and used it as the take-off point for his recent article entitled "Communication and Integration: The British and Dominions Press and the British World, *c.*1876–1914." Potter makes a convincing case that "the relationship between Britain and the Dominions transcended policy decisions about defence and private calculations regarding investment and migration" and that it is time to reconstruct the "complex webs of communication" that linked not just core and periphery but the various settler colonies. This reconstruction, he argues, "is essential if we wish to improve our understanding of a British world that interacted through friendship, acquaintance, travel, business, correspondence, and, crucially, the sharing of news."[40] The consolidation of the press into fewer and larger papers after 1901 and the concentration of ownership in fewer hands drew even tighter the links between the colonial and British press. Individual journalists also crossed the Atlantic (both ways) in increasing numbers and the First Imperial Press Conference, held in London in 1909, brought together journalists from Britain and the Dominions and helped to reinforce the sense of a shared imperial identity.

A second conference was planned for Ottawa in 1915 but had to be delayed until 1920. Many of the same people who had attended the 1909 conference were in Ottawa in 1920, although their ranks had been thinned by the war since many journalists had enlisted while others had served as war correspondents. But for the survivors, the war had strengthened their sense of a shared British identity. In his speech opening the conference, Lord Burnham declared to a round of applause: "We can never forget that time after time during the war the Canadian corps saved the situation on the day – 400,000 men drawn from the life-blood of your body politic." The man who led the Canadian Corps, Sir Arthur Currie, stressed in his speech that it was possible to be both "thoroughly loyal to British institutions, to British traditions and to the British Empire" and at the same time "intensely Canadian." Currie declared that "Canada can render the greatest possible service to the Empire and to the world at large by developing...Canadian institutions, Canadian ideals, and a Canadian national spirit." Only one person was slightly off-message. During the opening remarks to the conference, William Lyon Mackenzie King, the leader of the Opposition in the Canadian parliament, queried why the conference was described as an "Imperial" Press Conference rather than a "British" Press Conference: "I cannot but feel that the word 'Imperial' carries with it...an idea of centralization, and...an idea of aristocracy as contrasted with democracy." In measured tones, Lord Burnham responded: "In spite of what Mr. King has been kind enough to say to us, we intend to stick to our title of Imperial Conference [Applause.]....We are proud of the name of Britain; but we are not ashamed of the British Empire [Hear, hear]." The applause of the delegates did not mean that they wanted imperial centralization (though that may have been how King interpreted it), for they also applauded John W. Dafoe when he declared that the British Empire is composed of nations of equal status, "united in a partnership of consent."[41]

The one hundred delegates from abroad travelled across Canada and were met and entertained by leading Canadian newspapermen. The *Manitoba Free Press* declared that "our visitors are merely members of the family who have come from the Old Land and the far corners of the world to see how we Canadians are getting along in our home." In Toronto the delegates were told by Premier E. C. Drury that "in Ontario we are Canadians, and, for the benefit of our friends from Great Britain, I say that we are not colonials. We are a nation in thought and feeling, if we are not a nation technically." Sir James Akins, the lieutenant governor of Manitoba, declared that although it "was the desire of Canada to be essentially British," it must acquire the only remaining power of "a nation, a sovereign state" – the power to declare war – and that the

Empire should be transformed into "some kind of league of nations." It is easy to see how the trip convinced Lord Burnham that "there is a passionate Canadian patriotism and an equally passionate devotion to Empire" and that "our Imperial Press Conference is surely a part, and an essential part of a co-operative commonwealth."[42]

This concept of a "co-operative commonwealth" swept the field in the post-war period. In this sense Berger is correct to say that imperialism as he defined it was a casualty of the First World War. After 1918 the idea of imperial federation was dead, as successive imperial conferences made clear. But the liberal imperialist ideal of an Empire composed of autonomous British nations joined by sentiment and culture did not die.[43] John Boyd undoubtedly reflected the views of a majority of English-speaking Canadians in 1919 when he declared: "We are Canadians and we intend to remain Canadians, first and foremost proud of our native land and its great history, attached to our institutions and jealous of our rights, our interests and our autonomy." But, he insisted, "whilst we are Canadians and whilst such are our sentiments," we also "rejoice in the power, the prestige and the greatness of the British Empire" and are proud to be members of "that great Empire."[44] It is true that during the interwar years Canada did become increasingly North American in orientation. By 1939 the United States had already become the major source of capital investment in Canada and it was rapidly overtaking Britain as a market for Canadian goods, while Canadian culture was increasingly feeling the impact of American cultural penetration. The movies Canadians watched, the radio programs they listened to, the popular fiction they read, the sports they played were largely American in origin. Increasingly, Canadians worked in American branch plants and joined American unions. This does not mean that they automatically suspended their own beliefs and sense of identity. During a meeting of the International Barbers' Union in Buffalo, New York in 1919, one delegate from New England foolishly referred to the British flag as a symbol of "oppression," leading to an outcry from the Canadian vice-president, H. J. Halford of Hamilton, Ontario, who declared: "That uncalled for reference is an insult to the Canadian delegates and we won't stand for it. The Canadian delegates are proud of the British flag."[45] Indeed, the increasing influence of American culture probably led Canadians to cling even more tightly to what most clearly distinguished them from their neighbours, and a large part of the appeal of the imperial connection was the fact that it was associated with the definition of Canada's national identity. During a lengthy coast-to-coast tour of Canada in 1929, Winston Churchill recorded in his journal that "the sentimental feeling towards England is wonderful. The United States are stretching their tentacles out in all directions, but the Canadian national spirit is becoming so powerful and self-contained that I do not think that we need fear the future."[46]

In interwar Canada a whole host of political, educational, and cultural institutions and formal and informal groups reinforced this identification of Canadian nationalism with loyalty to the Empire and to British institutions. The largest and most important group, John Dafoe noted in 1941, was the veterans of the First World War, who "had made their way to key positions in almost every field of Canadian activity: in business, great and small; in the learned professions, in national organisations of all kinds, in the universities, the banks, the churches, the newspapers, in the civil service; in the political parties, the governments, federal and provincial."[47] Undeniably, the veterans had come home with a clearer and stronger sense of their own national identity. But this did not mean that most harboured anti-British or anti-imperial sentiment (though a few certainly did). Sir Arthur Currie noted in a speech given in Liverpool on the day before he sailed for home : "One thing which has struck me more than any other is that the Canadians and English understand each other better than they did before, and that surely tends for the solidarity of the Empire."[48] At the very least, service overseas must have broken down the distinction between the native-born and the British-born in Canada since the Canadian forces overseas were composed almost equally of the two groups. Moreover, an estimated fifty thousand Canadian soldiers married English, Scottish, or Irish women while serving overseas.[49]

The commitment of the veterans was shown in the post-war period in the activities of the Canadian Legion of the British Empire Service League. Between 1917 and 1925 there were some fourteen or fifteen veterans' organizations in Canada, but in 1925 Field-Marshal Earl Haig visited Canada as part of a lengthy international tour encouraging the creation of an Empire-wide league. Haig, who was greeted with demonstrations of popularity everywhere (particularly by Scottish-Canadian organizations), seems to have had little difficulty in persuading the Canadian veterans to unite in a Canadian branch of that league. The *Legionary*, the official organ of the Canadian Legion, declared in its first editorial that the purpose of the Legion was to "promote loyalty to the Empire and to Canada." The central motif of the badge adopted by the Legion reflected this symbolism: it contained a Union Jack on which was superimposed a maple leaf. By the time the Canadian Legion held its first national convention in Winnipeg in January 1927, it already had eight hundred branches with twenty thousand members. While its primary activity was to lobby the government on behalf of the veterans, it also established a number of committees, including one on Empire Relations. In its first report, accepted unanimously by the convention, this committee recommended the promotion of Empire settlement and trade and the development of Empire markets, as well as "the suppression of foreign literature and films whose influence was antagonistic to British ideals," a demand that textbooks used in schools be of British composition and manufacture, and in general, the development of a "spirit of Empire."[50]

The Legion led the campaign to put an end to the celebration of Thanksgiving and Armistice Day on the same day, a campaign that succeeded in 1931 when Armistice Day became Remembrance Day. The Legion also took control of the services held on November 11th to ensure that it became "a day to pay tribute to the men and women who had laid down their lives in a just cause and to reflect upon the nobility of the sacrifices for Christianity and Western civilization."[51] In 1936 the Legion "conceived, sponsored and organized" the Vimy Pilgrimage. No fewer than 10,300 Canadian veterans went to France to participate in the unveiling of a monument by Edward VIII to the Canadians who had died at Vimy. In the aftermath of the pilgrimage, the Legion issued a 225-page souvenir book, *The Epic of Vimy*, which quickly went into a second printing. On 9 July 1937 a filmed record of the pilgrimage, *Salute to Valour*, had its premiere at Shea's Hippodrome Theatre in Toronto to sell-out crowds. The *Legionary* pointed out with pride that the Vimy Pilgrimage "had made history for the British Empire.... For the first time, a British monarch acted in a foreign country as the King of one of his Dominions. For the first time, through a symbolism which attracted the attention of the world, the true meaning of the Statute of Westminster was publicly demonstrated in a manner hitherto unattempted."[52] As David Lloyd points out, "The Vimy Pilgrimage combined a strong attachment to the King and the British Empire with a growing sense of Canadian identity."[53]

The Legion was probably the most influential of the organizations upholding the imperial relationship, but what is sometimes forgotten is the large number of patriotic organizations that had promoted the war on the home front and that continued to promote a sense of imperial identity after the war was over. The IODE, for example, had played a very active part in providing material and moral support for the war effort, and its membership had soared during the war to an all-time high of fifty thousand. In the interwar years its numbers inevitably dropped, to a low of twenty thousand during the 1930s.[54] But it continued to preach the gospel of Canadian imperialism and to pressure schools and other public bodies to incorporate that gospel into their activities. So did the Orange Lodge. During the First World War, Orange Halls across the country were frequently used as recruiting depots, and it is estimated that fifty-five thousand Orangemen enlisted. In 1922 the Orange *Sentinel* claimed that over half a million Canadians belonged to the Orange Order.[55] A recent study of the lodges in Ontario indicates a rapid growth during the war and then a decline – a fairly rapid one during the 1930s – until 1939.[56] But even at its low point in the 1930s, the Lodge continued to be one of the largest voluntary organizations in Canada. In Toronto, the Orange parade on 12 July 1937 took more than five hours to pass a single point.[57]

The pattern of the Boy Scouts was similar. Membership soared during the First World War, as the Scouts were mobilized to guard telephone lines and railway bridges and to act as fundraisers and security guards at public rallies. In 1916 a new organization for boys too young to be Scouts was also formed – the Cubs. In 1919 Baden-Powell made another of his periodic visits to Canada and praised the movement in Canada for the "valuable amount of war work" it had carried out. In 1924 a substantial contingent of Canadian Scouts travelled to a jamboree held during the Empire Exhibition in Wembley Stadium, an event that was "entirely successful in its purpose of bringing together the Scouts of the Empire."[58]

If we are to understand the continuing strength of imperial sentiment in interwar Canada, we desperately need more studies not of the handful of Canadian intellectuals and their debates but of the popular organizations that shaped the opinions of ordinary English-speaking Canadians at the local level and made them rally around the flag in 1939. The educational system played a part in this process. So did a popular culture that promoted the notion that the Empire was a force for universal good. Not all English-speaking Canadians shared this enthusiasm. A few – a very few – wanted Canada to cut the imperial connection and remain neutral in 1939. But the majority of English-speaking Canadians clearly did not agree, and they once again responded to the Empire's call to arms. Men like Walter Thompson, who served in the Canadian Air Force during the Second World War, admitted that he was not entirely clear what motivated him: "It was some kind of intellectual thing. It came from *Mort d'Arthur, Hurrah for Merry Sherwood* and *Ivanhoe*. It came from

Chum's and *Boy's Own Annual*. It came from my maternal grandparents and later from Russell's introduction to *Mathematical Philosophy*."[59]

There has been a rather acrimonious debate over why Canada went to war in 1939. Terry Copp argues that "the British connection was a central fact of Ontario life in the 1930s," that Ontario did not hesitate to give its support to the British war effort, and that it did have some sense of what it was fighting for. Ian Miller puts even greater emphasis on the latter point. He argues that although enthusiasm for the war was limited because of memories of the First World War, the war was perceived to be "necessary" and Canadians "wholeheartedly supported it." Jack Granatstein, on the other hand, believes that Canadian opinion was more deeply divided than Copp and Miller claim and that from the outset, enthusiasm for the war was "limited to those Liberals and Conservatives who, by class and attitude, harked back to an allegiance that was already starting to fade." In a vitriolic attack on Ian Miller, Granatstein recently proclaimed that Miller should tattoo on his forehead the maxims that "Toronto is not Canada," that "the press is not public opinion" and that "Canada went to war in 1939 because Britain went to war – until proven otherwise." No one in favour of war, he claims, "mentioned Canadian interests or even appears to have thought very much about them."[60] Pleased as I am to discover that Professor Granatstein has discovered the virtue of regional studies, I only wish that he had read some of those that do exist. If he had even glanced at *The Atlantic Provinces in Confederation*, he would have learned that "the spirit of total war pervaded all levels of society" in the Maritimes and that "no Canadian region appreciated the imperatives of national defence more than the Maritime provinces; and no one could fault the region's generous response to the war's demands."[61] And if we are not going to use the press as a barometer of public sentiment, what are we going to use? Granatstein would seem to prefer that we rely on the opinions of Mackenzie King and his cronies in the Prime Minister's Office, but King remained heavily dependent on Quebec for his support and his views were not really in line with those of the English-Canadian majority, probably not even with the majority of English-Canadian Liberals. Granatstein may consider the Canadian sense of obligation to Britain as "misplaced," but most English-speaking Canadians took it as a given in 1939 that the British Empire was worth defending and that the survival of Britain as a liberal, democratic power in Europe was a vital Canadian interest. Granatstein presents no convincing argument to show why they were wrong to hold such views and no evidence at all to justify his claim that such views were only held by those who had "a Tory attitude in Ontario." In 1939 the response of most English Canadians to the crisis in Europe was an instinctive reaction; it does not follow that it was an irrational one.

Canadian historians usually assume that the Second World War ended the sense of belonging to a wider British World, and in retrospect it does seem clear that by the end of the war Britain lacked the ability to hang onto its Empire. Yet we must be careful not to let hindsight becloud our understanding of what Canadians thought at the time. Canadians did emerge out of the war with a greatly strengthened sense of national identity, but at the same time "World War II fuelled imperial sentiment where it remained vibrant, renewed interest in the Commonwealth where it had lapsed, and generated new enthusiasm for the Commonwealth among those who had little interest in it."[62] David B. Harkness's 1945 book, *This Nation Called Canada*, captures this ambiguity. Harkness believed that the war had led to "our self-realization as a Canadian people," and he called for a Canadian constitution and the dropping of the word "dominion" to describe the "nation" of Canada. But he believed nonetheless that the British nations – including Canada – were still "bound together by sentiments, ideals and heritage which are more potent than legislation and more binding than treaties" and that "on all such levels Canada is a British nation and proposes to continue to be a British nation."[63] In 1949 the British Commonwealth of Nations became simply "the Commonwealth," but as Frank Soward noted in 1950, Canadians continued to talk about the Empire, for "the older name, invested with the lustre of a great tradition declined and still declines to give way" to the title of Commonwealth.[64] The post-war Commonwealth was a very different creature from the pre-war Commonwealth. Francine McKenzie points out that whereas the pre-war Commonwealth had consisted of an imperial centre in Britain and a series of colonial pe-ripheries that responded to British initiatives and sought to influence British policies, in the post-war Commonwealth the Dominions were determined to establish their status as completely independent nations with their own independent foreign policies and to become "as central to the Commonwealth as the metropole." Yet there remained among dominion policy-makers "an enduring attachment to Britain." McKenzie concludes that there was a future for the Commonwealth, but only "as long as it proved its worth to its members. Practical utility and mutual benefit replaced sentiment, history, loyalty and tradition as the forces holding the Commonwealth together."[65]

While this may have been true for the officials in the Canadian Department of External Affairs, it is less clear that it was true of Canadian public opinion, for it is easy to exaggerate the speed with which Canadian attitudes changed in the aftermath of the Second World War. As late as 1963, 47 per cent of the Canadian population (and undoubtedly a much higher proportion of English-speaking Canadians) believed that "Britain's status as world power is not over," and between 60 and 70 per cent of English-speaking Canadians continued into the 1950s and early 1960s to indicate their support for maintaining the existing relationship with Britain and the Commonwealth.[66] This is not entirely surprising since Canada changed rather slowly during these years. Between 1945 and 1970 three million immigrants entered Canada, but 28 per cent of the total – over nine hundred thousand – were from the United Kingdom. Except in Quebec, people of British origin still outnumbered all the rest. Though their numerical predominance was waning, their political power was still entrenched. In 1944 a bitter debate ensued in the Canadian press over the question "How British is Canada?" when the *Winnipeg Free Press* pointed out that just over 50 per cent of the population was now of non-British origin. The *Ottawa Journal* responded by stressing that even if this were the case, the "leading peoples" in Canada were still of British origin, and it undertook a rather crude (but probably fairly accurate) survey of the Canadian House of Commons to show that of the 179 non-French Canadian MPs, only ten could not be identified as British by origin or name and four of those ten had been born in the United States.[67] During the 1950s, the balance of ethnic power changed very slowly, and the British predominance outside of French Canada was still very marked at the end of the decade.

Moreover, the same institutions that had supported the British connection in 1939 were still there throughout the 1950s. Indeed, there was new wave of veterans. Half a million Canadians had spent a considerable part of the war stationed in Britain. Their wartime experience "made them more consciously Canadian that they had been before; but their particular experience in England…brought them close to the British people and gave a new reality to the Commonwealth connection."[68] By 1959 the Legion had close to a quarter of a million members, and for the first time – but not the last – a Legion convention was opened by the prime minister.[69] In 1958 the organization changed its name to the Canadian Legion and in 1960, with the Queen's consent, added the word "Royal." During the 1950s and early 1960s, the Royal Canadian Legion repeatedly debated the question of adopting a Canadian flag, but they could not decide between the red ensign and a red ensign modified by replacing the coat of arms with a maple leaf. However, the Legion did make very clear during the flag debate of 1964 that one thing it did not want was a new flag without the Union Jack on it. Neither did the Orange Lodge, nor the IODE. The membership of the Orange Lodge grew during the war and peaked around 1950, then began a slow decline throughout the 1950s and 1960s. But Orangemen continued to march every July and the Lodge remained an important political force in municipal politics into the 1960s. The IODE, which had dropped to a membership of twenty thousand during the Great Depression, rose again to a membership of nearly thirty-five thousand in 1945. Though there was a slight decrease after the war, its membership fluctuated at around thirty-one or thirty-two thousand until 1960, when it began a slow but steady decline.[70] Since both the Orange Lodge and the IODE had trouble attracting youth, the average age of members grew steadily older. Nonetheless, in the 1940s and 1950s, and even in the early 1960s, the Orange Lodge and the IODE remained important upholders of the British connection and its symbols.

This lingering sense of a shared identity seems to have vanished remarkably quickly in the 1960s.[71] Imperial historians tend to see this as a direct result of the final collapse of Britain's economic and military power, symbolized by the British decision to seek entry into the EEC. There is a danger, however, in overemphasizing the imperial side of the equation. The commitment of the British government and people to the Empire was certainly a necessary condition for its survival, but that commitment was never a sufficient basis for the survival of imperial sentiment in the Dominions. What this also required was a desire on the part of the people who inhabited the Dominions to remain part of a British World. In Australia and New Zealand, there was a strong material basis to imperial loyalty, but this had ceased to be the case in Canada by the 1950s. Rather, emotional ties were the basis of Canadian loyalty to the Empire. These ties were partly based on a lingering sense of "kith and kin" among Canadians whose forebears had migrated from the British Isles. Fundamental changes were taking place in the composition of the Canadian population in the post-war period, but Britain remained the most important country of origin of immigrants and only in the 1960s did many (but certainly not all) of Canada's ethnic leaders begin to demand equal recognition of their ethnic identities in the Canadian mosaic. By the 1960s, other fundamental changes were also taking place in Canada, changes that had little do with the decline of Britain's international status but that weakened the attachment of Canadians to the British connection. The decline of the mainstream Christian churches and the growing strength of American popular culture in Canada weakened any lingering sense of being part of a British World among younger English-speaking Canadians, and the Quiet Revolution ended forever the passive acceptance by French-speaking Québecois of the notion that Canada was "essentially British."[72]

Indeed, it was the spectre of Quebec separatism – not the Suez crisis – that led Lester B. Pearson to decide that it was time to have a new Canadian flag devoid of British symbolism. For a time Pearson even toyed with the idea of changing the role of the monarchy. In June–July 1967 the Queen visited Canada as part of Canada's centennial celebrations. Although the Queen received "a warm, and often enthusiastic reception," Harry Lintott, the British High Commission in Canada, warned the British Commonwealth Office that a growing number of Canadians viewed the monarchy as a "relic of British imperialism" and felt that Canada had "come of age" and "deserves its own institutions"; he proposed that this feeling was bound to grow stronger as "the opinions of the young generation and particularly of Canadians who neither have British connections nor have fought side by side with the British in the war, will increase in weight." In November Lintott warned the Commonwealth Office that Pearson now "believes that the days of the monarchy in Canada are numbered." Lintott believed that Pearson's change of heart was due to "the recent increase in tempo of the debate about French Canada, and in particular the prospect of negotiations about the constitution" but that it also reflected the belief that "the monarchy is no longer suitable to Canada, that it has no appeal for the younger generation, and that it has a divisive rather than a unifying influence in the country as a whole." Pearson, Lintott warned, intended to raise this issue with the Queen on his forthcoming visit to London.[73] The Queen was therefore not unprepared when a few months later Pearson suggested that it might be time to abandon "the fiction that the Queen was Queen of Canada" and that Canada become a republic with a Canadian head of state.[74]

For better or worse, the fiction was not abandoned, whether because Pearson did not have the stomach for it (he had after all been a committed monarchist all his life and he liked and admired the Queen) or because he recognized that the attempt to abolish the monarchy was a step too far and would deeply divide Canadians along ethnic lines. But my point is that it was changes in Canada – not events in Britain – that precipitated the final disentanglement with Empire. Jack Granatstein is partially right: there was no plot either by Mackenzie King nor his successors to destroy the imperial relationship. But contrary to what Granatstein argues in *How Britain's Weakness Forced Canada into the Arms of the United States*, it was not simply British weakness that forced Canadians out of the British embrace, though that was undoubtedly an important factor.[75] Support for the British connection in Canada survived well into the twentieth century because the imperial relationship had real meaning to a majority of English-speaking Canadians and fed into their sense of national identity. The nature of that relationship certainly changed over time. In the years before the First World War, few English-speaking Canadians believed that Canada should leave the Empire, but the role that the emerging Canadian nation should play in the Empire was contested. The First World War ended the debate over the merits of imperial federation and ensured the victory of the liberal imperialist vision of how the Empire should function. But the war and its aftermath also persuaded some English-speaking Canadians that Canada should withdraw from membership and participation in the Empire, even an Empire reorganized on liberal imperialist principles. The majority of English-speaking Canadians, however, continued to take pride in Canada's membership in "the greatest monument ever devised by man to justice, tolerance, liberality, freedom and true democracy."[76] English-speaking Canadians showed in 1939–45 that they were committed to being part of a British World with shared cultural values. After 1945 this sentiment persisted among the generation that had fought the war, but in the 1960s and 1970s fundamental changes in Canadian society made the British connection seem less and less meaningful. A growing number of native-born Canadians of all ethnic backgrounds – including younger Canadians with British forebears – no longer had the sentimental attachments necessary to preserve the connection with a wider British World and the symbols of Canada's imperial past increasingly seemed to be a source of division that threatened rather than reinforced Canadians' sense of national identity. In the 1960s and 1970s, a vigorous rearguard action was fought by those who believed that the Canadian national identity was – and ought to be – defined by the British connection. The majority of English Canadians, however, no longer shared these views and at last were willing to say goodbye to the British World.

{NOTES}

1 Phillip Buckner, "Whatever Happened to the British Empire?" *Journal of the Canadian Historical Association* 3 (1993): 3–32.

2 Carl Berger, *The Sense of Power: Studies in the Ideas of Canadian Imperialism 1867–1914* (Toronto: University of Toronto Press, 1970), 8, 9–10.

3 Doug Cole, "The Problem of 'Nationalism' and 'Imperialism' in British Settlement Colonies," *Journal of British Studies* 10 (1971): 172.

4 See Deborah Gare, "Britishness in Recent Australian Historiography," *The Historical Journal* 43, no. 4 (2000): 1145–55, and the Symposium on "Britishness and Australian Identity," *Australian Historical Studies* 32, no. 116 (April 2001): 76–136.

5 David Cannadine, "Imperial Canada: Old History, New Problems," in *Imperial Canada 1867–1917*, ed. Colin M. Coates (Edinburgh: University of Edinburgh, 1997), 10, 4.

6 Colin Kidd, *British Identities before Nationalism: Ethnicity and Nationhood in the Atlantic World 1600–1800* (Cambridge: Cambridge University Press, 1999), 75.

7 J.M. Winter, "British National Identity and the First World War," in *The Boundaries of the State in Modern Britain*, ed. S. J. D. Green and R. C. Whiting (Cambridge: Cambridge University Press, 1996), 263, 265.

8 In 1891 J. Hampden Burnham even published a study entitled *Canadians in the Imperial Naval and Military Service Abroad* (Toronto: Williamson & Co., 1891).

9 Sir Donald Mackenzie Wallace, *The Web of Empire: A Diary of the Imperial Tour of Their Royal Highnesses The Duke and Duchess of Cornwall and York in 1901* (London: Macmillan, 1902), 452.

10 Percy Machell, *"What is my Country? My Country is the Empire. Canada is my home": Impressions of Canada and the North-West* (London: Sifton, Praed & Co., 1912), 3, 44.

11 John Fraser Foster, *Canada As It Is* (London: Cassell & Co., 1905), 7–8.

12 Printed Ephemera from the Metropolitan Public Library, Canadian Institute for Historical Microreproductions, microfiche no. 4329.

13 John Rickard, "Response: Imagining the Unimaginable," *Australian Historical Studies* 32, no. 116 (April 2000): 130.

14 Berger, *Sense of Power*, 3.

15 Julia Bush, *Edwardian Ladies and Imperial Power* (London: Leicester University Press, 2000), 83.

16 Quoted in John Eddy and Deryck Schreuder, "The Making of the Idea of Colonial Nationalism, 1898–1905," *The Rise of Colonial Nationalism: Australia, New Zealand, Canada and South Africa First Assert Their Nationalities* (London: Allen & Unwin, 1988), 74, 84.

17 Eddy and Schreuder clearly see the concept of colonial nationalism as a transitional doctrine that can only be applied to the pre-war period.

18 Ramsay Cook, *The Politics of John W. Dafoe of the Free Press* (Toronto: University of Toronto Press, 1963), 24.

19 John Clifford, *God's Greater Britain: Letters and Addresses* (London: J. Clarke & Co., 1899), 19, 20–21.

20 N. W. Rowell, *Liberals and the Empire* (Ottawa: Central Information Office of the Liberal Party, [1912]), 13, 29.

21 See Carman Miller, "Loyalty, Patriotism and Resistance: Canada's Response to the Anglo-Boer War, 1899–1902," paper delivered at the conference "Rethinking the South African War," University of South Africa, Pretoria, August 3–5, 1998.

22 The argument that I present in this paper is a condensed version of my chapter entitled "Canada" in David Omissi and Andrew Thompson, eds., *The Impact of the South African War* (Houndmills: Palgrave, 2002), 233–50.

23 *South African Association of Nova Scotia* (Halifax, 1904), 1; Paul Maroney, "'Lest We Forget': War and Meaning in English Canada," *Journal of Canadian Studies* 23, no. 4 (Winter 1988): 188–204.

24 Sir Robert Baden-Powell, *The Canadian Boy Scout: A Handbook for Instruction in Good Citizenship* (Toronto: Morang and Co., 1911), vii and xvii.

25 *Canadian Annual Review for 1910*, 594–95; *for 1911*, 615; *for 1913*, 738; *Canadian Boy Scouts: Reports of the Contingent at the Coronation* (Montreal, 1912), 7.

26 John Ramsden, *Man of the Century: Winston Churchill and His Legend Since 1945* (London: Harper Collins, 2002), 374.

27 Emily P. Weaver *et al.*, *The Canadian Women's Annual and Social Service Directory* (Toronto, 1915), 49–52.

28 See Simon J. Potter, "The Imperial Significance of the Canadian-American Reciprocity Proposals of 1911," *The Historical Journal* 47, no. 1 (2004): 98–100.

29 Berger, *Sense of Power*, 5.

30 Ian Hugh Maclean Miller, *Our Glory and Our Grief: Torontonians and the Great War* (Toronto: University of Toronto Press, 2002), 49, 79, 104–5, 176.

31 Ian McKay, "The Stillborn Triumph of Progressive Reform," in *The Atlantic Provinces in Confederation*, ed. E. R. Forbes and D. A. Muise (Toronto: University of Toronto Press, 1993), 203, 210, 212.

32 Jonathan Vance, *Death So Noble: Memory, Meaning, and the First World War* (Vancouver: University of British Columbia Press, 1997), 266.

33 Miller, *Our Glory and Our Grief*, 199–200.

34 George M. Wrong, "The Creation of the Federal System in Canada," in *The Federation of Canada 1867–1917*, ed. George M. Wrong et al. (Toronto: Oxford University Press, 1917), 23.

35 So Alastair Buchan reported when he visited Canada in 1935. See Alastair Buchan, "A Memoir," in *Britain and Canada: Survey of a Changing Relationship*, ed. Peter Lyon (London: Frank Cass, 1976), 34.

36 *The Globe Magazine* (Toronto), 24 September 1964.

37 *The British News of Canada* (Montreal), 30 March 1912.

38 Ibid., 6 April, 6 July, 24 August 1912; 1 March, 7 June 1913.

39 Arthur Hawkes, *The Birthright: A Search for the Canadian Canadian and the Larger Loyalty* (Toronto: J.M. Dent & Sons, 1919), xvi, 16, 121.

40 Simon J. Potter, "Communication and Integration: The British and Dominions Press and the British World, c.1876–1914," in *The British World: Diaspora, Culture and Identity*, ed. Carl Bridge and Kent Fedorowich (London: Frank Cass, 2003), 190–206.

41 Robert Donald, *The Imperial Press Conference in Canada* (London: Hodder and Stoughton, [1921]), 6, 30, 34, 147, 156, 158, 206.

42 Ibid., 2–3, 27, 32, 50–51, 55, 60, 66, 83, 104, 132–33, 137, 147.

43 John Darwin describes this as the "Dominion idea." See his "The Dominion Idea in Imperial Politics," in *The Oxford History of the British Empire*, vol. 4, *The Twentieth Century*, ed. Judith Brown and W.R. Louis (Oxford: Oxford University Press, 1999).

44 John Boyd, *The Future of Canada: Canadianism or Imperialism*. (Montreal: Librairie Beauchemin, 1919), 76.

45 *Canadian Annual Review for 1919* (1920), 117–18.

46 Quoted in Ramsden, *Man of the Century*, 375.

47 J.W. Dafoe, "Why Canada Is at War," in *Canada Fights: An American Democracy at War*, ed. J.W. Dafoe (Toronto: Farrar and Rinehart, 1941), 80.

48 *Daily Post* (Liverpool), 9 August 1919, in *Canadian Annual Review for 1919* (1920), 41.

49 See *Canadian Annual Review for 1919* (1920), 26.

50 Clifford Bowring, *Service: The Story of the Canadian Legion* (Ottawa: Canadian Legion, 1960), 9, 42, 44, 48, 53, 60.

51 Vance, *Death So Noble*, 219.

52 Bowring, *Service*, 101; James Hale, *Branching Out: The Story of the Royal Canadian Legion* (Ottawa: The Royal Canadian Legion, 1995), 52–55.

53 David W. Lloyd, *Battlefield Tourism: Pilgrimage and the Commemoration of the Great War in Britain, Australia and Canada, 1919–1939* (Oxford: Berg, 1995), 215.

54 Katie Pickles, *Female Imperialism and National Identity: Imperial Order Daughters of the Empire* (Manchester: Manchester University Press, 2002), 26. See also Lisa Gaudet, "Nation's Mothers, Empire's Daughters: The Imperial Order Daughters of the Empire, 1920–1930" (M.A. thesis, Carleton University, 1993).

55 *Sentinel*, 14 November 1922.

56 I have taken the figures on Lodge membership in western Ontario here and elsewhere from Eric P. Kaufmann, "The Demise of Dominant Ethnicity in English Canada? Orange Order Membership Decline in Ontario, 1918–1980" (unpublished paper presented at the conference "Canada and the End of Empire," Institute of Commonwealth Studies, April 2001).

57 *Toronto Telegram*, 12 July 1937.

58 E. K. Wade, *Twenty-One Years of Scouting: The Official History of the Boy Scout Movement from Its Inception* (London: C. Arthur Pearson Ltd., 1929), 179, 234, 273–74.

59 Walter R. Thompson, *Lancaster to Berlin* (Wilmslow, Cheshire: Crécy Publishing, 1997), 209.

60 This debate can be followed in Terry Copp, "Ontario 1939: The Decision for War" and the "Commentary" by Jack Granatstein in *A Country of Limitations: Canada and the World in 1939*, Norman Hillmer et al. (Ottawa: Canadian Committee for the History of the Second World War, 1996), 269–78, 290–91, and in Ian Miller, "Toronto's Response to the Outbreak of War, 1939," *Canadian Military History* 11, no. 1 (Winter 2002): 5–23 and J.L. Granatstein to the editor, ibid., 11, no. 2 (Spring 2002): 4.

61 Carman Miller, "The 1940s: War and Rehabilitation," in *The Atlantic Provinces in Confederation*, 307, 308.

62 Francine McKenzie, *Redefining the Bonds of Commonwealth, 1939–1948* (Houndmills: Palgrave Macmillan, 2002), 27.

63 David B. Harkness, *This Nation Called Canada* (Toronto: Elliott Press, 1945), 23, 11, 56.

64 F. H. Soward, *The Adaptable Commonwealth* (London: Royal Institute of International Affairs, 1950), 5, 18.

65 McKenzie, *Redefining the Bonds of Commonwealth*, 226–27, 266.

66 Mildred Schwartz, *Public Opinion and Canadian Identity* (Berkeley: University of California Press, 1967), 64, 74, 76.

67 The exchange is discussed in an editorial in *The Telegraph-Journal* (Saint John), c.May-June 1944, which is partially reproduced in James G. Allen, *Editorial Opinion on the Contemporary British Commonwealth and Empire* (Boulder: University of Colorado Studies, 1946), 521–22.

68 C. P. Stacey and Barbara M. Wilson, *The Half-Million: The Canadians in Britain, 1939–1946* (Toronto: University of Toronto Press, 1987), 92.

69 Hale, *Branching Out*, 128.

70 Pickles, *Female Imperialism and National Identity*, 26.

71 This argument is developed in my introduction to *Canada and the End of Empire*, ed. Phillip Buckner (Vancouver: University of British Columbia Press, 2004).

72 On the significance of religion and its decline in English-speaking Canada, see Gary Miedema, "'For Canada's Sake': The Re-visioning of Canada and the Restructuring of Public Religion in the 1960s" (PhD diss., Queen's University, 2000).

73 Public Record Office, FCO 49/68, Harry Lintott to Sir Saville Garner, personal and confidential, 15 July 1967, and FCO 49/107, Lintott to Garner, secret and personal, 15 November 1967, with "secret and personal" minute by Garner to Secretary of State, 17 November 1967.

74 See *Mike: The Memoirs of the Right Honourable Lester B. Pearson* (Toronto: University of Toronto Press, 1975), 3:300–301.

75 J.L. Granatstein, *How Britain's Weakness Forced Canada into the Arms of the United States* (Toronto: University of Toronto Press, 1989).

76 Boyd, *Future of Imperialism*, 76.

CHAPTER 9

FABIAN SOCIALISM AND
BRITISH AUSTRALIA, 1890–1972

Frank Bongiorno *

IN A LECTURE AT THE LONDON SCHOOL OF ECONOMICS in April 1899, Sidney Webb, the English Fabian socialist, gave his impressions of the Australian federal movement, gathered on a recent visit. He reported that

> great credit was due to Australian statesmen and the public for the way in which, without the consolidating force of foreign war or external pressure, they had hammered out a basis of agreement.... The long and patient discussions on all these points had proved a most beneficial education to the Australian statesmen, with the result that at this moment these statesmen were... actually superior to our own in their acquaintance with both the theory and practice of political science.

Sidney admired Australia, not least because he found it so unlike the United States. In particular, he was impressed by the lack of corruption in politics and by the fact that Australian premiers died poor. He noticed a habit in Australia – especially among the wealthy – of running down politicians, but he could see little justification for this attitude of contempt. The politicians and newspapers, he believed, were Australia's very best produce. All that was really lacking in them was intellectual leadership.[1] Similarly, Beatrice Webb – rather less inclined to mince words – wrote in a private letter to her sister that Australian politics revealed "the British genius for democratic self-government," which

* I would like to thank Nicole McLennan, Race Mathews, Ken Inglis, and Barry Smith for their helpful comments on the text, as well as Jim Jupp for his recollections.

she contrasted with "the low level of manners and general cultivation in all other departments of colonial life – *it would be intolerable to live here except as a politician.*"[2]

Fabian influence in Australian politics and culture from the 1890s until the mid-1960s was essentially a function of Australia's place in the British World. Fabian socialism was attractive to socialists in Australia not simply because it was socialism but because it was recognized by Australians as a peculiarly British (or English) form of socialism associated with internationally famous British names such as Webb, Shaw, Wells, and Cole. As late as 1961, briefing notes for Fabian interviewers in a Melbourne survey advised that "if any person you approach wants to know more about who you are and who you represent, explain that the Fabian Society was formed in England late last century by Bernard Shaw and others."[3] British emigrants to Australia contributed to the Fabian presence in Australian life, but their role cannot alone explain its influence: many native-born radicals also found much to admire in Fabian socialism over the last century. The story of Fabianism is thus not merely a chapter in the history of Australian socialism, but also in the larger history of British imperial identity in Australia. Paradoxically, however, the decline of Britishness in Australia in the 1960s was accompanied by the rise of the Fabian Society as a nationally significant factor in Australian political and intellectual life. In the 1960s, Australian Fabianism was both internationalized and indigenized.[4] The change was dramatized when Australia's leading Fabian, Gough Whitlam, arrived in Britain on his first visit as prime minister. "It's good to be home," said Gough. "Is that what you were expecting me to say?"[5]

Fabianism was a part of the ferment of ideas that contributed to the reconstruction of the Australian polity in the years around the turn of the century. New radical political ideas were in the air. Women's organizations were clamouring for the vote. Secularists condemned religion and royalty as founded on superstition, while republicans directed their antipathy at the monarchy and advocated the separation of the Australian colonies from the Empire. Anarchists declared that the real problem with modern society was that the state usurped the freedom of the people, and socialists rejected capitalism as wasteful and unjust; both looked forward to a new order that would avert the looming social catastrophe.[6]

Small socialist organizations, inspired by the ideas of socialist authors such as Edward Bellamy, William Morris, Robert Blatchford, the Webbs, and Karl Marx, were formed in the various colonies in the late 1880s and early 1890s. Although American socialist and populist writers such as Bellamy, Laurence Gronlund, and Ignatius Donnelly were significant, British influences were arguably the most potent for Australian socialists. Fabian literature was available in Australia, as were the writings of English socialists such as Hyndman, Morris, and Blatchford.[7] Indeed, Fabian Societies were actually established in Adelaide and Melbourne in the 1890s. Another organization formed in Melbourne in 1905, called the Social Questions Committee, has been described by Race Mathews as "Fabian-in-all-but-name," and a Fabian Society re-emerged in Melbourne in 1908.[8]

These short-lived organizations were part of a plethora of socialist organizations that came to life in the years between 1885 and the Great War. Doctrinally, most were eclectic, and in constructing their programs and ideologies, they often drew on an extraordinary and incongruous combination of authorities that might include Jesus Christ, Karl Marx, and Otto von Bismarck in the same breath. Ruskin, Carlyle, and Tolstoy were particular favourites: Marx, far from having a privileged place in the Australian socialist pantheon, simply took a seat alongside a wide array of critics of capitalism. Accordingly, W. G. Higgs, a member of the Australian Socialist League in Sydney, emphasized his debt to Marx, Shaw, the Webbs, and Bismarck – and, as Raymond Markey reminds us, "with no apparent embarrassment."[9] When considering the influence of Fabianism in Australia, therefore, we need to go beyond its formal manifestations in Fabian Societies to consider the various forms of radical thought that drew on one or another Fabian idea. For example, there was great interest among some socialists in the "gas and water" socialism of the Fabians. It was one of the impulses behind Labor's municipal socialism in Australia.[10]

Two Melbourne Fabians' ideas and activities provide something of the flavour of Fabian socialism in *fin de siècle* Australia. The first, Henry Hyde Champion, founded the short-lived Melbourne Fabian Society in 1895 and was also a member of the later Fabian Society of Victoria before the First World War. Born at Poona in India in 1859, Champion came from a privileged social background. A military career was followed by conversion to socialism and a few stormy years as one of the Marxist-leaning Social Democratic Federation's leading agitators in the 1880s. Champion eventually found himself accused of colluding with the Tory Party, and British historian Henry Pelling has emphasized the differences between Champion's peculiar Tory-influenced brand of socialism and the "Little England" ideas of the Manchester school, as well as the overwhelming majority of British socialists.[11] Champion arrived in the colonies at a crucial moment in the history of the Australian labour movement: during the maritime strike of 1890, which led to the formation of the Labor Party. Although he was initially welcomed by unionists for the international celebrity he was, Champion soon became involved in a bitter brawl. In a Melbourne newspaper article, he memorably described the union rank-and-file as "lions led by asses." The strike ended in a humiliating defeat for labour, and unionists denounced Champion as a traitor. While the Victorian labour movement lacked cohesion during the depression of the 1890s, one matter on which most activists could agree was that Champion needed to be kept at arms' length. At least until the end of the decade, few would have anything to do with him, although this might also have been related to the complications of his personal life in Melbourne at that time, for he was involved in an affair with a married woman.[12]

Champion's emigration to Australia in 1894 has usually been explained in terms of the decline of his fortunes in the British socialist movement. Discredited among socialists by his scheming with the Tory Party, Champion supposedly sought to rebuild his career in the colonies on the principle that "it is better to run a cabbage garden than to spend one's prime knocking round the porticos of literature & politics in the centre of the world."[13] Yet Champion's letters to his friend Morley Roberts indicate that there were additional reasons for his departure. Champion was heavily in debt and probably already involved with a wealthy married woman he had met in Melbourne in 1891 during his earlier troubled visit. She was Adelaide Hogg, a leading Melbourne theosophist and a niece of Sir Thomas Elder (1818–1897). Elder was an immensely rich business-man and pastoralist from whom Adelaide stood to inherit a vast sum of money. When the old man died, leaving an estate valued at £615,573, she inherited (according to Champion's testimony) £25,000, sufficient to give her an annual income of £1,500-£2,000. To a man on the verge of bankruptcy, this sort of money would have been very useful, although it is also evident that Champion loved the woman.[14]

Champion ran, edited, and largely wrote the modestly titled newspa-per, the *Champion*, between 1895 and its demise in 1897. He also sought a seat in the Victorian parliament almost from the moment his ship arrived in the colonies. The condition of the colony would not improve, he wrote to Roberts in April 1896, "until I, or some one built on my plan comes along to boss the country." Champion believed he would be a member of parliament within the year, and that after a further year, he could "shove [his] pals in wholesale." He therefore suggested that Roberts might consider coming to the colonies and that after five years, if all went well, they could take "it in turns to be Premier of this twopenny halfpenny microcosm."[15] Verity Burgmann has correctly observed that visiting "socialist celebrities had to behave very badly" indeed "in order to deter the adoration of the colonials."[16] Champion had managed to perform this feat. There was nobody in Melbourne, he remarked in a letter, but "provincials of the most banal type – dear good people no doubt many of them, but, dear Lord!, not companions."[17] To English socialist Edward Carpenter, one of his creditors, Champion wrote that Australians were "Italianized by the sun & run to surface emotions on a basis of gross materialism. They don't read & have to be taught from the beginning."[18] Blaming the barbarians was a convenient explanation for failure, although the complaint that colonials did not read was exposed as ludicrous when Champion later managed to make a living by running a library and literary journal.

Champion's condescending attitudes to colonials contributed to his unpopularity among many socialists and trade unionists. The opinions of one activist, Jack Phillips, were not unusual. In October 1894, Phillips advised Bernard O'Dowd, a fellow radical, that Champion "may be useful yet." By April 1895 he had changed his mind: "Discard Champion from anything that you take in hand[.] He only promised to be a very poor crutch a[t] the best and his terms as stated to us were essentially autocratic and I think he over rates himself."[19] We should not underestimate this hostility: O'Dowd claimed that a Victorian scheme of Labor Party organization formulated in 1896 was specifically designed with the intention of preventing an unnamed individual – obviously Champion – from using the machinery to get into parliament![20] Mathews suggests that Fabianism was unfortunate in having the "overbearing" Champion as its Australian spokesman.[21]

Bernard O'Dowd was another early Australian Fabian. He was born in 1866, the son of Irish-Catholic immigrants from Ulster. After his father's death, which forced him to abandon his university studies, and an unsuccessful attempt to earn a living as a schoolteacher, Bernard moved permanently to Melbourne in the mid-1880s and was for many years assistant librarian in the Supreme Court, during which time he completed degrees in arts and law at the University of Melbourne. In 1913 he became Victorian assistant parliamentary draughtsman and was promoted to the chief's position in 1931. At various times a spiritualist, secularist, and socialist, O'Dowd published several books of verse between 1903 and 1921, establishing a reputation as one of Australia's leading poets. He contributed prose and poetry to a large number of newspapers and magazines, and was active in many political and religious organizations and movements. Some prominent younger writers rated him a significant influence on their careers. He refused the offer of a knighthood in 1934 and died in 1953.[22]

In 1905 O'Dowd was an active member of the Social Questions Committee (SQC), a Fabian-style body established in Melbourne by the visiting English socialist, Tom Mann, and a radical Melbourne businessman, J.P. Jones. The SQC, of which the young John Curtin (prime minister, 1941–45) was also a member, conducted a house-to-house canvas in order to gather information on underfed children and unemployment. Some of the results of their research were published in the *Socialist* newspaper.[23] Unfortunately, the Committee also attracted the hostility of Victorian Labor Party officials, who saw it as a potential rival. They tried to limit co-operation between the Labor Party and the SQC, although common action between Labor and the SQC continued at the local level and there was great sympathy within local Labor Party branches for the SQC's activities.[24] Inspired by the information gathered from the research of the SQC, O'Dowd wrote a poem, "Victoria 1906," also published in the *Socialist*. In introducing his verse, O'Dowd remarked that so bad were many of the cases exposed by the Committee, that "until these undertones cease, Art dare not continue to be for Art's sake only, but must be for man's sake mainly." The poem, not one of Bernard's better efforts, alternates its stanzas between visions of peace, joy, and prosperity and reports of the horrific cases of poverty uncovered by the SQC.[25] In 1908 O'Dowd was involved in the Fabian Society of Victoria, which announced its aim as "the reorganization of Society on a more equitable basis by the emancipation of land and industrial capital from private ownership, so that such land and capital may be administered for the general benefit of the community."[26] When this new body soon launched an investigation into the cost of living, O'Dowd's wife, Eva, played Beatrice to Bernard's Sidney, for she was one of the principal investigators.[27] The Fabian Society did not last long – but its formation is a testament to the desire of some of Melbourne's radical intellectuals for a body devoted to the investigation of social questions.

O'Dowd has usually been seen by historians as a representative of the radical nationalist tradition in Australian politics and culture.[28] Yet he also came to identify strongly with Britishness. In the late 1880s, he had been a republican and an advocate of Australian separation from the British Empire. He soon lost interest in separation, however, and directed his energies into other causes, such as socialism and theosophy. He was hostile to British aggression in the South African War, but along with many other Australian pro-Boers of 1899–1902, he supported the Allied cause in 1914 as necessary resistance to the German bully.[29] O'Dowd's position caused dismay among some of his comrades in the Victorian socialist movement: one was horrified that "a man of the stamp of Bernard O'Dowd" was "siding with the jingoes."[30] The young Esmonde Higgins, a nephew of the Arbitration Court judge, H. B. Higgins, was similarly shocked, and he told his sister, literary critic and poet Nettie Palmer, that "finding…Bernard O'Dowd & lots of decent people had become violently anti-Germany or else flag-waggers, I did my honest best to see if I could be either, but I couldn't."[31] The imperial government's brutal suppression of the 1916 Easter uprising in Dublin soured O'Dowd's attitude to the Allied cause,[32] but he was still able to admire Great Britain:

> Whatever her other sins in the past & present may have been or may be, the nation that, against her material interests and ignoring the call of the Teutonic blood which she shares with the Germans, leaped without hesitation into the awful storm to honour her treaties & to save a small people from arrogant & wanton annihilation, may wait the ultimate verdict of history on her action with perfect confidence. Although national force was used by her, the motive certainly, in our darkness as to what is right and wrong in such matters, appears not only to make her entry into the war consonant with the highest Christian principles, but any other action on her part would have been cowardice of a particular mean type.[33]

O'Dowd's socialist comrades ought not to have been surprised by his response to the war, for he had made his identification with the ideal of British liberty very clear for some years. In the late 1890s, his case against the draft federal bills (the basis for federated Australia's constitution) was founded, to some extent, on their betrayal of British constitutional tradition.[34] Moreover, in 1912 he had written an article in the Melbourne *Socialist* contrasting two types of Australian socialist, the "Marxite" and the "British." The "Marxite," he said, was "somewhat doctrinaire, as a rule, given to an almost fetishistic belief in the efficacy of hard and fast rules and doctrines, intense in its devotion to what sometimes seem narrow ideals, but as intense in its hatred and repudiation of all Socialists who do not subscribe to its set doctrine." The British type of socialists, on the other hand, while believers in the common basis of all socialism – the democratic socialization of the means of production, distribution, and exchange – were a varied lot:

> Some of them are almost, if not quite, Anarchists; others are Communists; others believe in the possibilities of the Labor Party, and think it worth permeating; others are Fabians; others are industrial unionists; many are advocates of art, literature, and religion, as necessary levers to a Socialism worth having; others, again, believe in the "materialistic basis"; others believe, and others, again, don't believe, in Class war. Some are anti-militaristic, and believe in a democratically organised citizen army; others are anti-militaristic, and don't believe in any form of defence at all.

It was this eclectic socialism, thought O'Dowd, that dominated the Victorian Socialist Party (VSP), of which he was a member. The achievement of Tom Mann, the British socialist who had spent the years 1902–1909 in Australia as one of the leading lights in the VSP, was that he had "gathered together, from the solitudes into which unwise doctrinaire tactics and undigestible ultra-Marxism had driven them, the very cream of the most advanced and varied ability in Victoria." O'Dowd left his readers in no doubt that his own allegiances were to the British, Fabian, and undoctrinaire variety of Australian socialism.[35] There is a straight line between this reasoning and O'Dowd's belief in 1914 that Britain was on the side of liberty in the Great War. Both positions were an expression of O'Dowd's allegiance to an Australia that was securely embedded in a British World.

Fabianism was a continuing influence on certain Australian intellectuals in the first few decades of the century, without succeeding in spawning an Australian Fabian Society. Influential friends and acquaintances of O'Dowd with Fabian affiliations included John Latham, a barrister, politician, diplomat, and, eventually, chief justice of the High Court; Edward Shann, an economic historian; Fred Eggleston, a solicitor, politician, and diplomat; Walter Murdoch, a literary critic, essayist, and academic; and Ernest Scott, a *Hansard* reporter and later professor of history at the University of Melbourne. All of these men had been members of an elite Melbourne dining club called the Boobooks in the early years of the century; all had, at the very least, Fabian leanings at some point in their lives. All, moreover, combined their Fabian orientation with membership in the Melbourne Round Table group. Here, they combined British race patriotism with the pursuit of Australia's interests, as they understood them, within an imperial framework.[36]

There were also antipodean expatriates prominent in English Fabianism in this period. William Pember Reeves, a New Zealander, was a presence in English Fabianism from the mid-1890s. Having been an innovative labour reformer as a minister in the New Zealand Liberal government, Reeves later became director of the London School of Economics and Political Science. His brilliant daughter, Amber, had a child by H. G. Wells.[37] Another Fabian expatriate was Dr. Marion Phillips, an Australian historian. Phillips later became the British Labour Party's chief woman officer. She served briefly in the House of Commons between 1929 and 1931, and was probably, in fact, the first Australian woman to win a seat in a national parliament.[38] Fabian traffic therefore travelled in more than one direction.

Fabian Societies appeared in all Australian state capitals in the years following World War II, but enjoyed a continuous existence only in Melbourne. The relative weakness of Fabianism in Sydney is probably connected with differences in the political and intellectual cultures of the two cities. Fabianism in Melbourne was congruent with that city's traditions of liberalism and civic humanism, which have their origins in the ideals of the gold rush generation of emigrants of the mid-nineteenth century. Fabianism, like Victorian colonial liberalism, expressed a reform-ist belief in the possibility of state action to effect social improvement. Melbourne, for example, had since the 1860s been a bastion of tariff protectionism, which was integral to its peculiar brand of liberalism, in contrast with free-trade Sydney, whose more *laissez-faire* liberal traditions would have been less confusing to a British observer.

It is not that Fabianism was absent from Sydney. There had been a Fabian-style body, the Social Democratic League, formed in 1917[39] and an active New South Wales Fabian Society in the late 1940s and early 1950s. There was also a Fabian presence at the University of Sydney in the 1960s, with Jim Spigelman, now chief justice of the Supreme Court of New South Wales, as a leading figure. Nevertheless, many of Sydney's intellectuals in the post-war period were influenced by the combination of Freudianism (or Reichianism) and anarchism associated with the libertarian Sydney *Push*, which in turn owed much to the influence of Professor John Anderson of the philosophy department at the University of Sydney.[40] The strength of this Sydney libertarian tradition, especially at the university, must have reduced opportunities for Fabian activity in Sydney. Moreover, Sydney refugees from the Communist Party after

1956 formed a group that coalesced around the magazine *Outlook*. It had connections with the Melbourne Fabians, but the existence of a staunchly anti-communist section within the Victorian Fabian Society was unpalatable to some Sydneysiders, and there was conflict between the two groups. Melbourne remained the "nurse and tutor" of Australian Fabianism, but Sydney would produce Australian Fabianism's messiah, Gough Whitlam.[41]

By the time Whitlam won office in December 1972, Fabianism had become an expression of middle-class political mobilization in urban centres across the nation. Nevertheless, the Victorian Fabian Society, formed in 1947, was by far the strongest, and it operated as a *de facto* national organization with members in every state in the post-war years.[42] As many historians have pointed out, the ideal of a British Australia remained very much alive in these years, so we should not be surprised to find it thriving in the Australian Fabian Societies. Moreover, the apparent Fabian ascendancy in Britain during the period of the Attlee government gave force to British sentiments among Australian democratic socialists. When the Victorian Fabian Society was founded, its provisional chairman, Frank Crean, a member of the Victorian parliament, announced that it had "adopted the attitude and aims of the English Fabian Society.... The founders believe there is an outstanding need for such a body in the Australian Labor movement, a body which might help to lay the educational and propagandist foundations for a transition to democratic Socialism such as is occurring in Britain."[43] Crean was a member of the Round Table group for twenty years: his investment in the idea of a British Australia seems clear enough.[44] Yet his sentiments found many echoes elsewhere. Geoffrey Serle, the Melbourne historian, has often been seen as a left-nationalist.[45] Nevertheless, in the late 1940s and early 1950s, his attachment to the British World is at least as apparent as his specifically Australian nationalism. In an article written for *Australian Observer* in 1948, while on a Rhodes Scholarship, Serle celebrated Britain's traditions of liberalism and humanitarianism. Britain had evolved "a method of change in society which rests on consent," which was integral to its national traditions and history. It was absurd for Ernest "Bevin and his cohorts to be horrified at the new states of eastern Europe.... To expect democratic socialism to be a thriving force in Bulgaria is just as ridiculous as the Communists expecting to Sovietise Britain or Australia. It is an historical impossibility." The lessons for "Australia, with its dominant ties to British thought and philosophy," seemed clear to Serle. Australia "must express its socialism democratically, or that socialism will not flourish."[46]

Yet, despite echoes of O'Dowd, in an important respect there had been a clear shift in Australian socialists' relationship to Britain. In 1898 the Webbs had visited Australia and New Zealand because of the antipodes' reputation as a social laboratory, and many British and European visitors to Australasia were interested in what a French sojourner, Albert Métin, called an antipodean "socialism without doctrines."[47] Notwithstanding Beatrice's condescension toward colonials, the Webbs believed that British socialists might be able to learn something from the social experimentation of Australia and New Zealand. Yet by the 1940s, it was supposedly backward Australia that had to learn from Britain. For Fabian socialists, a more conventional colonial relationship with the mother country appears to have been restored: hence Crean's belief that Australia might emulate Britain's path to democratic socialism and Serle's opinion that insufficient capitalist development and "intellectual preparation" had occurred for Australia to make much progress toward separate nationhood and democratic socialism. Serle, who served as chairman of the Victorian Fabian Society in the first half of the 1950s, noted that "this is the one very obvious thing we can learn from British socialism, where the many years of unceasing labor by the Fabian Society are now bearing fruit." By contrast, in Australia, the Labor Party was dominated by an "anti-intellectual outlook" and "intellectually the party is 25 years behind our British comrades."[48]

In another article, Serle proclaimed British success in socialist planning as "the only hope of any alternative to a world dominated by either eastern or further western ruthlessness." Here, Serle was subscribing to a widely held belief on the left that British (and, by implication, Australian) democratic socialism offered a Third Way between Soviet socialism and the unbridled capitalism of the United States.[49] Interestingly, the view that Australia should lend its support to Britain as a third force in world affairs survived the defeat of the British Labour government – surely further evidence of the strength of British patriotism among Australian Fabians in this period. In the Fabian publication *Policies for Progress* (1954), the editors, Serle and political scientist Alan Davies, commented that "as members of a small nation, we can do little but offer as much support as we are able to the principles and authority of the United Nations and, more important perhaps, support policies which will build up Britain's strength for, whether Churchill, Eden, Attlee or Bevan is

Prime Minister, British policy is one of the few restraining influences in the world today."[50] Similarly, another historian and Fabian, Ken Inglis, used the *Fabian Bulletin* in 1952 to criticize the American orientation of Australian foreign policy under the Menzies government. The ANZUS Treaty, said Inglis, had "gained Australia publicity" and "put us on the map – the American map": "We have only rumours to tell us that Britain is annoyed at her exclusion, but it is important that people all over the world have found the rumours credible."[51] The tenor of Inglis's criticism only makes sense in the context of a British Australia in the 1950s.

Inglis would, later in the decade, travel to Oxford to carry on his doctoral studies, a familiar path for Australian academic Fabians in the 1950s. Jim Cairns, another 1950s Fabian and, like Crean, a member of the Round Table in Melbourne, spent a year in Oxford in 1951–52 under the supervision of G.D.H. Cole.[52] Cairns would later become deputy prime minister of Australia and also succeed Crean as treasurer in the Whitlam Government. Michael Roe, later professor of history at the University of Tasmania, was a Melbourne Fabian before his departure for postgraduate study at Cambridge, a path also followed by another Fabian historian, F. B. Smith, at the end of the 1950s. The expatriation of young Australian Fabians for postgraduate study in Britain, combined with established academics' sabbaticals in the United Kingdom, were a drain on Australian Fabianism in the 1950s, yet they also helped to bring the antipodeans into closer touch with British developments. It was from Oxford, for example, that political scientist Jamie Mackie wrote for the *Fabian Bulletin* in 1952, exploring recent developments in British socialist thought, such as Nye Bevan's *In Place of Fear* and the *New Fabian Essays*.[53] Indeed, Australian Fabian discussions of socialism in the 1950s were, to some extent, framed by the terms of contemporary British debates over the future of socialism. Australian Labor had lost office in 1949, British Labour in 1951; a general weariness among electors with post-war austerity seemed to be at the heart of both defeats. It appeared that the forward march of democratic socialism had been halted, and no obvious paths for a resumption of the journey presented themselves in the thickets of the conservative hegemony and relative affluence (compared, at least, to the hungry 1930s) in both countries. Moreover, the easy assumption that Australian Labor could learn from her British counterpart now seemed less valid than in 1947 or 1948. For example, the first issue of the Victorian Fabian Society's *Fabian Bulletin* quoted G.D.H. Cole to the effect that "we have drifted into a position in which nobody feels any enthusiasm for further nationalization, and nobody knows what to do about the major part of industry that is left under capitalist ownership and control."[54] In Australia, where Section 92 of the Constitution appeared to rule out a large-scale program of nationalization, this opinion had a particular force.

As Paul Smyth has suggested, the revisionism of Crosland and others gained little acceptance among Australian Fabian socialists of the 1950s.[55] The British revisionists were arguing that democratic socialists should place less emphasis on nationalization of industry than on the development of the welfare state and the use of "selective state intervention" to achieve a more just society. With "the rise of an ever more influential managerial class," nationalization would not solve the problem of "labour relations," nor would it achieve the desirable goals of "decentralisation" and "consumer control".[56] On the other hand, the writings of Nye Bevan, usually seen as the leader of the traditionalists, seemed to some Australian Fabians to offer a way forward. Serle called *In Place of Fear* "probably the most important statement of political principles for many years."[57] Another Fabian, John Button, recalled the influence Bevan had on his political development as a young student of law and politics at Melbourne University in the 1950s:

> The leading political figures on the left of British politics
> seemed erudite and articulate compared with most of their
> Australian counterparts. Prominent amongst them was Aneurin
> Bevan, a former Welsh coalminer. Intelligent, self-educated,
> a persuasive orator, and the spirited leader of the British left,
> Bevan had been health minister in Clement Attlee's postwar
> Labour government. I read a review of his book *In Place of Fear*
> in the *New Statesman* in 1952 and arranged for it to be sent to
> me from London. It arrived in my study like a breath of fresh
> air. With its mixture of idealism and commonsense, it seemed to
> contain the key to rational political endeavour.

In 1957 Button would travel to Europe and Britain, where he worked for a time as a researcher for the Trades Union Congress.[58] After his return to Melbourne two years later, he would become a leading Fabian activist. He was elected to the federal Senate in 1974, and was a leading minister in the Labor governments for ten years (1983–93).

British emigration to Australia was another way in which Fabianism can be seen as a manifestation of Australian Britishness in the 1950s. Dave Preston, an English emigrant to Australia in the late 1940s, who had been a member of the British Labour Party, became a student at the Victorian Labour College and a member of the Australian Labor Party (ALP). "I am a keen student of Socialism and its application by the British Labour Party," he remarked in a letter to Victorian Fabian Society official John Reeves, "but what I have seen so far by the Victorian Labour movement trade union and political, fills me with some thing short of contempt, if not disgust, at the ignorance of Socialist principles (or disregard) displayed by its leaders." But Preston hoped that "perhaps somehow, some time the Australian Fabian Society can help in the great work of stirring towards a Socialist Society here in Australia."[59] Among emigrants to the antipodes, Preston was not alone in making such a judgment. Academic emigrants to Australia from the United Kingdom such as Jim Jupp, a political scientist, and Heinz Arndt, an economist, also complained, not unjustly, about the anti-intellectual tenor of the Australian labour movement.[60] While an intellectually or ideologically distinctive immigrant contribution to post-war Fabianism in Australia is hard to discern, there is abundant evidence that the Australian Society did benefit from the massive flow of British migrants into Australia in the 1940s, 1950s, and 1960s. In February 1961, the secretary of the Australian Society, Race Mathews, wrote to Shirley Williams, his London counterpart, asking if she would resume "the practice followed some years ago of notifying this society of the names and addresses of British Fabians who migrate" to Australia. "In this way," explained Mathews, "we once gained a number of extremely useful new members, but the idea seems to have lapsed lately."[61] Happily, Williams was immediately able to draw Mathews's attention to Jack Blitz, an active member of the Society in England for twenty years, who was on his way to Melbourne, and she agreed to place a notice in the *Fabian News* asking anyone going out to Australia to get in touch with Mathews. "I quite agree with you," she said, "that it seems a great shame to lose Fabians simply because they move."[62]

Almost moribund by the late 1950s, the Victorian Fabian Society was revived in the early 1960s and quickly gained a membership of several hundred. Nevertheless, an attempt in 1963 to gain "some form of recognition" from the British Society failed. Tom Ponsonby, the acting general secretary of the British Fabians, had been commissioned by the London executive to see if a "formula could be drawn up which would enable us to establish some definite form of relationship." He felt it "should be a relationship between equals and not a relationship between one organisation affiliating to another."[63] Mathews was disappointed, and he commented in a letter to the British Fabian Society president, Tony

Crosland, who was due to visit Australia shortly, that he hoped some relationship could be established "as, if only for the sake of the tradition involved, we would wish to bind ourselves to the parent body in the closest practicable manner."[64] Crosland's visit, which was arranged by the strongly anti-communist – and CIA-funded – Australian Association for Cultural Freedom (AACF), might not have assisted this endeavour, for the English Fabian MP is supposed to have reported back to Williams on his return to London that the Victorian Fabians "were all mad except for Race Mathews."[65] Meanwhile, Richard Krygier, the organizer of the tour on behalf of the AACF, told Crosland that the Victorian Fabian Society was "under the control of nuclear disarmers and a few fellow-travellers." He doubted whether Crosland would qualify for admission![66]

Before Crosland's arrival in Australia, Mathews commented in a letter to him that "the controversies within the British Labour Party have been closely followed here."[67] Andrew Scott has presented the Crosland visit as a significant moment in the evolution of post-war Labor Party thought in Australia.[68] Certainly, there was great interest within Australia at this time in what was happening in British socialism: this was, to some extent, a consequence of the intellectual vacuum in Australia, and especially in Victoria. Nevertheless, by 1963 this vacuum was being filled, a change to which the Victorian Fabians, in partnership with Gough Whitlam, were contributing.[69] The direct influence of British revisionism on this process is not entirely clear. When asked by Scott about what influence Crosland's ideas had on him, Whitlam replied "bugger all" (Australian English for "none"!). Mathews, however, has partly contradicted this point and Crosland's revisionism did exercise some influence over Australian labour thought in the 1960s.[70] It would also have been odd if, at a time when the ALP had been out of office for well over a decade, Australian democratic socialists of this period had not turned their attention to the Wilson Labour government. Unsurprisingly, there is no shortage of evidence that they did so.[71] Nevertheless, this interest seems of a rather different order to the earlier preoccupation with the Attlee government's deeds, or with turn-of-the-century interest in the work of the Webbs. It arguably has much more in common with recent Fabian interest in possible Australian applications of a Blairite Third Way, which, while more than tinged with Anglophilia, cannot be presented as a simple by-product of it.

Labour's victory under Wilson came just after the crisis in British-Australian relations provoked by Britain's unsuccessful application for entry into the European Economic Community (EEC) in 1961–63. For

Stuart Ward, this was the "key symbolic event" in the process by which "British race patriotism" in Australia came to grief because the United Kingdom's reorientation provided a fundamental challenge to the idea of an underlying mutual interest between Australia and Britain, an assumption that had dominated Australia's relations with the Empire for decades. The "deep sense of attachment to a wider British community" that was critical in the history of Australian Fabianism rapidly became obsolete, and new ways of thinking about national identity emerged. Whether or not one accepts Ward's claims about the fundamental significance of the EEC issue to this process, his account of the timing of Australia's reluctant emergence from the British embrace seems sound enough.[72]

Australian Fabianism in the second half of the 1960s should be seen in this context, but the Fabians' role was not simply reactive. On the contrary, Fabian intellectuals and activists contributed significantly to the debate about national identity, as they had contributed intellectually and politically to the development and maintenance of a British Australia in the three quarters of a century beforehand. In 1966 the Fabian Autumn Lectures, organized by Button, were entitled "The Blurred Image: The Australian Identity at Home and Abroad." The series, which involved speakers such as author and publisher Geoffrey Dutton, historian Noel McLachlan, and eminent architect Robin Boyd, examined British and American influences in Australian society and the effect of these on Australia's relations with Asia. Dutton used the opportunity to preach republicanism, which McLachlan, not long back in Australia after many years in London as a postgraduate student and then a lead writer for *The Times*, thought utterly irrelevant. Meanwhile, Button, as chairman, took pleasure in pointing out the irony that Dutton's message that Australia no longer needed British bootstraps was being delivered in the Kew Town Hall, "the launching pad for One [Prime Minister Robert Menzies] who did so much to strengthen the ties that bind us to Britain."[73]

It is not hard to make a case for the importance of Fabians such as Phillip Adams, an advertiser and film producer who played an instrumental role in the revival of the Australian film industry in the late 1960s, and Gough Whitlam, a cultural hero and prime minister (1972–75), in the promotion of the new nationalism. Yet the case for a creative Fabian role in the making of the new nationalism does not rest merely on such prominent and influential Fabian activists. For example, it is not well known that Henry Reynolds was president of a Townsville branch of the Fabian Society in the late 1960s.[74] Reynolds is now Australia's leading historian of race relations and a direct influence on the landmark Australian High Court decisions of recent years that have recognized Native title; in 1968 he was an obscure lecturer at James Cook University College, Townsville, in remote northern Queensland. His membership in the Fabian Society was part of a broader set of political involvements of Reynolds and his wife, Margaret, later a Labor Senator: these include the North Queensland branch of the Australian Institute of International Affairs, which Reynolds formed in 1966; an anti-Vietnam War Peace Committee, which Henry and Margaret joined; and a local branch of the Save Our Sons Movement, formed by Margaret. The Reynoldses were also engaged in activities aimed at improving the lot of Aboriginals and Torres Strait Islanders. Before long, Henry was also researching the history of frontier violence between settlers and Aboriginal people.[75]

In his memoir *Why Weren't We Told?*, Reynolds provides an account of his personal discovery of the violent history of Australia's frontier, yet at every step along the way his personal journey is connected to that of Australia, from racism to reconciliation, from white semi-colonial outpost to a mature nation increasingly willing and able to face the truth about its violent past. The undergraduate education Reynolds received at the University of Tasmania in the 1950s contained very little Australian subject matter, although those interested in Australian history could "pursue a few local topics in a subject on the British Empire and Commonwealth." As an honours student, he began to read some Australian history, and in 1959 he wrote a thesis that explored, as it celebrated, the democratic, egalitarian, and radical nationalist tradition in Australian history. He read Russel Ward's influential study of this tradition in *The Australian Legend*: it had been published in the previous year, and despite Ward's focus on the bushmen of the frontier, it had little to say about Aboriginal people or violence. When as a masters student Reynolds taught history at Hobart Technical College in the early 1960s, the set text was *A Short History of Australia* (1916) by Ernest Scott, who had been involved with the Melbourne Fabian Society in the mid-1890s. According to Reynolds, Scott's story was of how "Australia began with a 'blank space on the map' which was progressively filled in as a result of European endeavour." The book contained only four references to Aboriginal people:

> In the only passage of any substance [about Aboriginal people] Scott dealt with frontier conflict. It was perfunctory but it did not disguise the brutality involved. The tragedy of the process

was, he wrote, very grim and hateful. Scott assumed that the indigenous story was almost completed, the end both known and in sight. The Aborigines were not a people who could be absorbed or who could adapt to civilised life, and in the more populated parts of the country they were "fading out of existence very rapidly, and within the present generation will probably cease to exist."

Reynolds confessed that "although we used the book for months, referring to it constantly, none of the students found the treatment of the Aborigines insufficient, dismissive or racist. Nor did I."[76]

Reynolds then spent a couple of years in Britain and Europe, where the radical nationalism he had embraced as a student seemed to smack of isolationism and provincialism. Nevertheless, as much as Reynolds "was delighted by English landscape and English light," he "never felt really at home." He came to believe that "there was no longer any way back to Europe other than to live as a visitor, a sojourner, an outsider." The time in England itself seems to have been critical to Reynolds's development as a political activist, a historian of race relations, and an Australian. He recalls listening to an African man speaking at Hyde Park Corner. The man was being heckled by a group of young Australians, who told him there was no racial prejudice down under. The African knew better, "and launched a tirade about Australia's treatment of the Aborigines.... He scorned the hecklers for being ignorant about their own history." It was in England that Henry and Margaret decided they would "do something for the Aborigines" when they returned to Australia.[77] A decade and a half later, in the book that made his reputation, Reynolds wrote that if Australians were "unable to incorporate the black experience into our national heritage we will stand exposed as a people still emotionally chained to our nineteenth century British origins, ever the transplanted Europeans." He ended *The Other Side of the Frontier* by contrasting the neglect of the Aboriginal dead with the ways in which the white Australian casualties of the European wars had been commemorated in memorials across the continent. Aboriginal people had died defending "their own soil and not half a world away furthering the strategic objectives of a distant Motherland whose influence must increasingly be seen as of transient importance in the history of the continent."[78]

Ernest Scott, English emigrant, Fabian socialist, and Round Tabler, would have rejected this startling adaptation of the Australian radical nationalist tradition, and Reynolds, too, in later work, came to view the relationship between imperial Britain and the Australian colonist in rather more subtle terms.[79] Nevertheless, the respective loyalties of these two Fabians provide a useful counterpoint on which to end this chapter, for they are emblematic of the shifting relationship of Fabian socialism to imperial and national identity in Australia. In Scott's Australia, the nation's place in the Empire was largely taken for granted, and the essential complementarity of Australian and British interests regarded as a given. In Reynolds's Australia of the late 1960s and beyond, the country's destiny as a separate nation seemed no less evident. Reynolds was by no means a leading Fabian of the 1960s, but his intellectual and political development is, in many respects, emblematic of the way in which the meaning of Australian Fabianism shifted in the 1960s. Certainly, Reynolds's hostility to the White Australia Policy and his concern with racial issues were very typical of Fabian concerns of the 1960s.[80] An organization that had once been emblematic of Australia's Britishness now became an expression of Australian national sentiment and an international outlook concerned with how Australia might adapt to a post-colonial world order.

{NOTES}

1 *Manchester Guardian*, 22 April 1899; *Echo* (London), 30 December 1898. I am indebted to F. B. Smith for these quotations, which were contained in a typescript in his possession, and now in mine. See also Sidney Webb to Graham Wallas, in *The Letters of Sidney and Beatrice Webb*, vol. 2, *Partnership 1892–1912*, ed. Norman MacKenzie (Cambridge: Cambridge University Press, in co-operation with the London School of Economics and Political Science 1978), 88–89.

2 Beatrice Webb to Catherine Courtney, [17 September 1898], in *Letters*, 82–83.

3 State Library of Victoria (SLV), Race Mathews Papers, MS 9967, Box 4, "Victorian Fabian Society – Survey 1961. Briefing for Interviewers," typescript, 1961.

4 Jim Davidson, "The De-dominionisation of Australia," *Meanjin* 38, no. 2 (July 1979): 139–53.

5 Deane Wells, *The Wit of Whitlam* (Collingwood, Victoria: Outback, 1979), 23.

6 The best survey of the full range of these movements in this period is Bruce Scates, *A New Australia: Citizenship, Radicalism and the First Republic* (Melbourne: Cambridge University Press, 1997). Excellent, but with a slightly narrower focus, is Verity Burgmann, *"In Our Time": Socialism and the Rise of Labor, 1885–1905* (Sydney: George Allen & Unwin, 1985).

7 Bruce Mansfield, "The Socialism of William Morris: England and Australia," *Historical Studies* 7, no. 27 (November 1956): 285–90; Frank Bongiorno, "Love and Friendship: Ethical Socialism in Britain and Australia," *Australian Historical Studies* 32, no. 116 (April 2001): 1–19, and "Marxism and the Victorian Labour Movement,"

1870–1914," in *The Point of Change: Marxism/Australia/History/Theory*, ed. Carole Ferrier and Rebecca Pelan (St. Lucia: Australian Studies Centre, Department of English, University of Queensland, 1998), 64–74.

8 For early Fabianism in Australia, see Race Mathews, *Australia's First Fabians: Middle-Class Radicals, Labour Activists and the Early Labour Movement* (Melbourne: Cambridge University Press, 1993).

9 Raymond Markey, *The Making of the Labor Party in New South Wales 1880–1900* (Kensington: New South Wales University Press, 1988), 243.

10 Frank Bongiorno, *The People's Party: Victorian Labor and the Radical Tradition, 1875–1914* (Carlton: Melbourne University Press, 1996), 150.

11 H.M. Pelling, "H.H. Champion: Pioneer of Labour Representation," *Cambridge Journal* 4, no. 4 (January 1953): 236. For Champion's career, see also Mathews, *Australia's First Fabians*, especially chap. 3; Burgmann, *"In Our Time,"* 117–19; Peter Kellock, "H.H. Champion: The Failure of Victorian Socialism" (bachelor's thesis, Monash University, 1971); Geoffrey Serle, "Henry Hyde Champion," in *Australian Dictionary of Biography*, ed. Bede Naim and Geoffrey Serle (Carlton: Melbourne University Press, 1979), 7:603–5; Bongiorno, *People's Party*, 141.

12 *Age* (Melbourne), 4 May 1896; Kellock, "H.H. Champion," 43–44.

13 Walter H. & Leonore Annenberg Rare Book & Manuscript Library of the University of Pennsylvania, Morley Roberts Collection, Box 1, Champion, H.H. 1896–1923, 4811, H.H. Champion to Morley Roberts, 6 April 1896. All subsequent references to letters from Champion to Roberts are at the same location.

14 Ibid., 22 August 1897, 3 July 1898, 23 December 1898, 26 October 1896. See also Fayette Gosse, "Sir Thomas Elder," in *Australian Dictionary of Biography*, ed. Douglas Pike (Carlton: Melbourne University Press, 1972), 4:133–34.

15 H.H. Champion to Morley Roberts, 6 April 1896.

16 Burgmann, *"In Our Time,"* 8.

17 H.H. Champion to Morley Roberts, 6 April 1896.

18 Sheffield City Archives, Carpenter Papers, MSS 386-60, H.H. Champion to Edward Carpenter, 8 December 1895.

19 SLV, Bernard O'Dowd Papers, MS 6133 Box 227/1a, Jack Phillips to Bernard O'Dowd, 1 October 1894, 10 April 1895.

20 *Tocsin* (Melbourne), 23 August 1900. See also *Champion*, 23 May 1896, where Champion himself made the same claim.

21 Mathews, *Australia's First Fabians*, 229–30.

22 Victor Kennedy and Nettie Palmer, *Bernard O'Dowd* (Carlton: Melbourne University Press, 1954); Hugh Anderson, *The Poet Militant Bernard O'Dowd* (Melbourne: Hill of Content, 1968).

23 Mathews, *Australia's First Fabians*, chap. 4.

24 Bongiorno, *People's Party*, 155.

25 *Socialist*, 19 May 1906.

26 SLV, J.P. Jones Papers, Box 1266/1, "Rules of the Fabian Society of Victoria: adopted at a general meeting of the Society held on Saturday August 22, 1908."

27 Ibid., Fabian Society of Victoria, Minutes, 14 September 1908.

28 See, for example, W.H. Wilde, *Three Radicals* (Melbourne: Oxford University Press, 1969), 3.

29 *Socialist*, 2 October 1914.

30 Ibid., 23 October 1914.

31 National Library of Australia (NLA), Palmer Papers, MS 1174/1/1259, Esmonde Higgins to Nettie Palmer, 3 October 1914. See also Gavin Souter, *Lion and Kangaroo: The Initiation of Australia* (Sydney: Sun, 1992), 213, where this letter is quoted, and NLA, Palmer Papers, MS 1174/1/1287, Esmonde Higgins to Nettie Palmer, 25 October 1914.

32 Kennedy and Palmer, *Bernard O'Dowd*, 158.

33 SLV, Sam Merrifield Papers, O'Dowd, Folder 3, O'Dowd, unpublished manuscript, n.d. [c.1918].

34 Frank Bongiorno, "From Republican to Anti-Billite: Bernard O'Dowd and Federation," *New Federalist* 4 (December 1999): 49–57.

35 *Socialist*, 26 January 1912.

36 Mathews, *Australia's First Fabians*, chap. 5 and 6; Stuart Macintyre, *A History for a Nation: Ernest Scott and the Making of Australian History* (Carlton: Melbourne University Press, 1994); Leonie Foster, *High Hopes: The Men and Motives of the Australian Round Table* (Carlton: Melbourne University Press in association with The Australian Institute of International Affairs, 1986).

37 John Child, introduction to *State Experiments in Australia & New Zealand*, by William Pember Reeves (1902; repr., Melbourne: Macmillan of Australia, 1969), 1: ix–xv; Norman and Jeanne MacKenzie, *The First Fabians* (London: Weidenfeld and Nicolson, 1977), 363, 370–72.

38 Beverley Kingston, "Marion Phillips," in *Australian Dictionary of Biography*, ed. Geoffrey Serle (Carlton: Melbourne University Press, 1988), 11, 216–17.

39 Ian Turner, *Industrial Labour and Politics: The Dynamics of the Labour Movement in Eastern Australia 1900–1921* (Sydney: Hale & Iremonger, 1979), 191n.

40 For a history of the "Push," a very loosely organized group of Sydney intellectuals and bohemians in the period between the 1940s and the 1970s, see Anne Coombs, *Sex and Anarchy: The Life and Death of the Sydney Push* (Ringwood, Victoria: Viking, 1996). For the differences between Sydney and Melbourne intellectual traditions, see John Docker, *Australian Cultural Elites: Intellectual Traditions in Sydney and Melbourne* (Sydney: Angus and Robertson, 1974).

41 Frank Bongiorno, "Origins of the Present Crisis? Fabianism, Intellectuals and the Making of the Whitlam Government," in *It's Time Again: Whitlam and Modern Labor*, ed. Jenny Hocking and Colleen Lewis (Armadale, Victoria: Circa/ Melbourne Publishing Group, 2003), 311–38.

42 It is striking that although Australian historians are now turning to the intellectual history of the post-war decades, the Fabians remain absent from most accounts. An exception is Paul Smyth, *Australian Social Policy: The Keynesian Chapter* (Sydney: University of New South Wales Press, 1994).

43 *Australian Observer* (Canberra), 31 May 1947, 45.

44 Foster, *High Hopes*, 69.

45 For an expression of Serle's radical nationalism in the late 1940s, see his letter to the *Listener*, 29 January 1948, 184.

46 A. G. Serle, "Conditions of Democratic Socialism," *Australian Observer*, 3 April 1948, 377–78.

47 Albert Métin, *Socialism without Doctrine*, trans. Russel Ward (Chippendale, NSW: Alternative Publishing Co-operative, 1977).

48 Serle, "Conditions," 377–78.

49 A. G. Serle, "Why Europe Must Unite," *Australian Observer*, 6 March 1948, 349.

50 Introduction to *Policies for Progress: Essays in Australian Politics*, ed. Alan Davies and Geoffrey Serle (Melbourne: F.W. Cheshire, 1954), xv.

51 K.I. [Inglis], "Our New Foreign Policy," *Fabian Bulletin* 1, no. 9 (August 1952): 7.

52 Paul Strangio, *Keeper of the Faith: A Biography of Jim Cairns* (Carlton South: Melbourne University Press, 2002), 76–78. For his membership in Round Table, see Foster, *High Hopes*, 39.

53 Smyth, *Australian Social Policy*, 165–66. The original article was J.A.C.M. [Mackie], "New Steps to Socialism," *Fabian Bulletin* 1, no. 10 (October 1952): 4–7. Smyth fails to identify Mackie as the author.

54 G.D.H. Cole, "Shall Socialism Fail?" *Fabian Bulletin* 1, no. 1 (n.d. [*c.*June 1951]). The same quotation appears in *Fabian Bulletin* 1, no. 5 (December 1951): 12.

55 Smyth, *Australian Social Policy*, 154–55.

56 C.A.R. Crosland, "The Transition from Capitalism," in *New Fabian Essays*, ed. R.H.S. Crossman (London: Turnstile Press, 1952), 63–64; Strangio, *Keeper*, 104; Andrew Scott, *Running on Empty: "Modernising" the British and Australian Labour Parties* (Annandale, NSW: Pluto Press, 2000), 55–60.

57 The review is signed "G. S." *Fabian Bulletin* 1, no. 9 (August 1952): 8.

58 John Button, *As It Happened* (Melbourne: Text Publishing, 1998), 62–63, 104–6.

59 NLA, John Reeves Papers, MS 9475/2/3, Box 10, Dave Preston to John Reeves, 25 August [*c.*1949].

60 H.W. Arndt, "Three Times 18: An Essay in Political Autobiography," *Quadrant* 59, 13, no. 3 (May–June 1969): 33; James Jupp, *Australian Labour and the World* (London: Fabian Society, Fabian Research Series 246, 1965), 8, 11.

61 SLV, Race Mathews Papers, MS 9967, Box 4, Race Mathews to Shirley Williams, 14 February 1961.

62 Ibid., Shirley Williams to Race Mathews, 24 February 1961. See also J.F. Blitz to Race Mathews, 28 August 1961.

63 Ibid., Tom Ponsonby to Race Mathews, 9 May 1963.

64 Ibid., Race Mathews to C.A.R. Crosland, n.d. [May 1963]. See also Scott, *Running on Empty*, 163–64.

65 Jim Jupp to Frank Bongiorno (e-mail message), 24 October 2002.

66 Scott, *Running on Empty*, 164–65.

67 SLV, Race Mathews Papers, MS 9967, Box 4, Race Mathews to C.A.R. Crosland, 5 March 196[3].

68 Scott, *Running on Empty*, 65–68, 165–66.

69 Bongiorno, "Origins of the Present Crisis?"

70 Scott, *Running on Empty*, 67–68, 166; Mathews, *Australia's First Fabians*, 233.

71 The *Fabian Newsletter* for the period 1964–70 provides abundant evidence of the Australian Fabian interest in the Wilson Labour government.

72 Stuart Ward, *Australia and the British Embrace: The Demise of the Imperial Ideal* (Carlton South: Melbourne University Press, 2001), 2, 4, 10.

73 Noel McLachlan, *Waiting for the Revolution: A History of Australian Nationalism* (Ringwood, Victoria: Penguin Books, 1989), biographical note on author; Jean Battersby, "Against and for UK Bootstraps," *Canberra Times*, 20 April 1966, in SLV, Race Mathews Papers, MS 9967, Boxes 2 and 3, "1966 Autumn Lectures, Press Cutttings." All other information about this series comes from the collection of material at this location.

74 *Fabian Newsletter*, October 1968, 1.

75 Henry Reynolds, *Why Weren't We Told? A Personal Search for the Truth about Our History* (Ringwood: Viking, 1999), chap. 6 and 7.

76 Ibid., 14–15, 126–33, 15–16.

77 Ibid., 22, 23, 61.

78 Henry Reynolds, *The Other Side of the Frontier: Aboriginal Resistance to the European Invasion of Australia* (1981; Ringwood, Victoria: Penguin Books, 1990), 200, 201–92. See also Peter Read, *Belonging: Australians, Place and Aboriginal Ownership* (Melbourne: Cambridge University Press, 2000), 184–91.

79 Henry Reynolds, *Law of the Land* (Ringwood, Victoria: Penguin, 1987).

80 A 1967 survey of Society members found that education was rated by members as the most important issue facing the Society, followed by race and ethnic relations – the latter, presumably, reflecting the hostility of many students and young graduates to the White Australia Policy and growing awareness of the plight of indigenous Australians. SLV, MS 1478/4, Victoria Fabian Society Minutes, VFS Research Committee, "Membership Questionnaire – Some Results."

CHAPTER 10

WAR AND THE BRITISH WORLD IN THE TWENTIETH CENTURY

Jeffrey Grey

IN HER SEMINAL STUDY OF THE CREATION of British national identity in the eighteenth century, Linda Colley shows that the two key determinants in the process were war and Protestantism. Religion shaped the ways in which people "approached and interpreted their material life [and] viewed their politics," while recurrent war with "an obviously hostile and alien foreign power" from the age of Marlborough to that of Wellington was "the making of Great Britain." As Colley tells us in the conclusion to the book, "War played a vital part in the invention of a British nation after 1707." None of this, of course, was unique to the United Kingdom: religion (and Protestant religion at that) was a central determinant in the national definition of early modern Sweden, and subsequently of the newly created United States of America, while war and military activity have frequently provided vehicles for the creation of a common national sentiment (the function of the French Army in the nineteenth century was famously to turn "peasants into Frenchman"). In England's case, the long series of wars with Catholic France provided an outlet for those aggressive tensions that had resulted in civil conflict in the second half of the seventeenth century; assured the Protestant stamp of British national identity with all the ensuing social, cultural, and economic consequences; broadened the talent base on which the ruling classes drew to admit elites and aspirants from the Celtic peripheries (and this was especially noticeable in the military); and led to the creation of a mass British patriotism "transcending the boundaries of class, ethnicity, occupation, sex and age."[1]

Colley also reminds us that "ordinary" people asserted their membership in a British nation individually and collectively because they saw benefit in doing so, that patriotism was a political act, and that a simple equation between patriotism and conservatism is simply wrong. Inferring the conclusions of Andreski's theory of the military participation ratio,[2] she compares the political reforms that followed Waterloo with the "slow rate of political reform" after the 1830s and suggests that the absence of major external threats until 1914, and the concomitant absence of need to mobilize the nation, meant that the political demands of "ordinary Victorian Britons" could be more easily ignored (the same might be said of the process of military reform in this period, and for much the same reason).[3] Nor did "Britishness" exclude continuing identification with region or locale. Colley quotes tellingly the observation of a correspondent to *The Times* in 1887: "An Englishman has but one patriotism, because England and the United Kingdom are to him practically the same thing. A Scotchman has two, but he is sensible of no opposition between them."[4]

If the process of defining Britishness had been concluded more or less satisfactorily by the beginning of Victoria's reign, that of sorting out the relationship between British identity and membership in a wider British World outside Britain had yet to begin, and it is this, and especially the role of war in the process, that is the main concern of this paper. If war defined the British nation, it also fundamentally defined the relationship between the British World and Britain in the course of the twentieth century. In particular, there are three aspects of the interactions among war and military activity, Britain, and that part of the British World constituted as the Dominions that demand attention: what we might term the constitutional and higher policy dimensions that followed from dominion status; military activity, behaviour, and characteristics, especially during the two world wars; and the forms of public commemoration of that activity in the aftermath of conflict. Taking a lead from Colley's work, I suggest that war both created and frustrated the impetus toward a Greater Britain; that as it laid the basis for greater identification with, and attachment to, Britain among the settler societies of the Dominions, it simultaneously undermined that process.

The place of military history within a broader context of British and Empire history is now an uncertain one. In his opening remarks at the first of the British World conferences, in Cape Town in January 2002, John Darwin expressed a hope to see imperial historians grazing "alongside the sleek herds of social, cultural, gender and military historians."[5] Few military historians would recognize themselves in that characterization. Where once imperial history was a prominent subset of the "drum and trumpet" genre of military historical writing, the military dimension of imperial history has been thoroughly eclipsed by healthy growth in Darwin's other "herds" and by a more general decline in both military and diplomatic history within university history departments throughout the English-speaking world over the last forty years.

A generation ago, some of the most interesting comparative work on Anglo-Dominion relations was being written about the imperial strategic relationships forged between Canadian confederation in 1867 and the outbreak of the First World War.[6] In the 1970s, this was succeeded by a second wave of scholarship, focused on the interwar period and organized around Anglo-Dominion co-operation over the Singapore strategy and the defence of Britain's possessions in the Far East.[7] But the older conception of imperial and Commonwealth history was dead on its feet by this time (symbolized by the closure of the Commonwealth studies program at Duke University), and more methodologically conservative and less theoretically inclined fields (such as military and diplomatic history) suffered accordingly in ensuing decades. Military historians continued to write, of course, and to write on imperial and Commonwealth subject matter. But much of the comparative dimension has been lost, and imperial military history as practiced in the former Dominions now tends either to be relentlessly mononational or exclusively bipolar in its concerns, either treating the national experience more or less in isolation or else in terms of the imperial connection with Britain. There is little sense of comparison *across* the Empire/Commonwealth, very few attempts to look sideways and inform discussion of, say, Anglo-Australian relations during the First World War with extrapolations from the Anglo-Canadian or Anglo-New Zealand experience.[8] Although we tend to assume that, at least until the 1960s, the armed forces of the Dominions developed along British lines as "British-pattern" militaries, there has been little attempt to test this assumption through hard comparative work. The same applies to the development of defence industries and the relationship with both public and corporate Britain in the realm of capital equipment acquisition, the growth of systems of military education, and much else besides.

The military context of early settlement and expansion in the colonies of settlement differed widely in the course of the eighteenth and nineteenth centuries, and this, at least as much as derivation from British models, explains the form and nature of the military development of the

British World during the twentieth century. Put simply, the military challenges faced by British administrations in the colonies, and then by their self-governing colonial successors, did much to shape the ways in which "overseas Britons" thought about war and the organizational responses to it. In Canada, New Zealand, and southern Africa, colonists formed militias to supplement the regular forces of the Crown and were employed against enemies both internal and external. The long struggle with the French for colonial possession in Canada was succeeded by a strong militia involvement against the Americans in 1812–14, the Fenian threat after the end of the American Civil War, and the expedition to suppress internal revolt at the Red River Colony. In New Zealand, the second of the New Zealand wars in the 1860s, coinciding with the deliberations of the Mills Committee and a general push to minimize the imperial military presence in the self-governing colonies, required the New Zealand colonial authorities to shoulder a much larger proportion of the organizing, fighting, and supplying than had been the case during the war of the 1840s.[9] In southern Africa, of course, white settlement prospered from a seemingly continuous series of conflicts with various African groupings and with the Boers, each determined to assert and protect their own vision of a tribal future.

Only in the Australian colonies was this experience of serious, formal military activity lacking: although the Australian colonists apprehended a succession of external threats in the nineteenth century, none came to fruition, while the struggle with indigenous people was not waged by colonial militaries – nor even very much by the imperial military – but largely by police, their "Native" auxiliaries, and white settlers. This absence of formal military involvement in the dispossession of the Aborigines, it has been suggested, contributed to the very considerable violence on the Australian frontier, but it also deprived Australian colonists of any frontier military myth on which to build a wider conception of themselves as soldiers.[10]

The movement to self-governing and then to dominion status in the second half of the nineteenth century was accompanied by gradual efforts in London to regularize and codify the basis of the defence of the Empire. Like great imperial powers in other times faced with diverse responsibilities on a global scale, Britain sought to shift the costs of defence to those dependencies able (though not always or necessarily willing) to share in them. The problem for London remained the same one, essentially, that had confronted George III's ministers in dealing with the American colonies after the Seven Years' War: to utilize local resources in pursuit of imperial policy while retaining control at the local level and persuading the colonists that all this was for their own good.

What historians categorize, a little too neatly, as the "doctrine" of Imperial Defence in fact evolved slowly and incompletely until the turn of the century. The removal of the remaining garrisons in 1870 had been intended to force the hand of colonial governments to provide for their own landward defences from their own resources; serious colonial military forces quickly became the exception rather than the rule, and even then, they were usually only prompted by the exigencies of the moment. The capacity of external war scares to concentrate colonial attention on defence was limited; internal threats were more compelling but equally short-lived in their effect. The formation of the Colonial Defence Committee in 1885 was intended to impose central direction on defence planning in the colonies but the Committee had no power to compel colonial governments to submit their plans, and many duly did not. The earlier system of utilizing retired imperial officers or those on half pay (often much the same thing) to advise colonial governments was of limited utility since these men, however well intentioned, were usually no longer current in military matters and were often of limited ability in any case. The shift in policy in the 1890s, by which London posted active duty officers as commandants to the colonial forces, did not necessarily fare any better: officers of the first rank avoided the duty because there were few opportunities to shine in, say, the Australian colonies, where the expectation of active service was non-existent, while the impact of forceful imperial officers with hard-edged imperial agendas – E.T.H. Hutton being the best example – prompted negative reactions in colonial politicians and thus to some extent undercut London's intentions.[11]

The South African War at the turn of the century seemed to promise much.[12] The colonies dispatched a regular succession of contingents. Strong public support, after the reverses of "Black Week" in December 1899 had appeared to suggest that Britain could lose the war after all, certainly confirmed a union of sentiment throughout the Empire such as to delight the hearts of imperial federationists. But public support was less than it seemed. The British raised many of the later contingents directly or through the efforts of private individuals – Lord Strathcona's Horse being a prime example – and colonial governments became less and less willing to underwrite the costs of involvement. Nor were the numbers impressive. The other British colonies fielded a total of about

30,000 men, less than the southern African colonies, which contributed 50,000, and a small proportion of the total of 450,000 who fought there, most of them dispatched from Britain.

Nor were Her Majesty's colonial governments as wholehearted in support of imperial means to imperial ends as they might have appeared or, at times, proclaimed. The government of Sir Wilfrid Laurier in Canada was lukewarm in its ardour for the war because francophone Canada was, at best, indifferent to it. Even that "ardent imperialist," "King Dick" Seddon of New Zealand, had suggested at the war's outbreak that commitment would lead to greater New Zealand participation in imperial decision-making, reflecting the strong, if self-interested, sentiment for imperial federation in that colony.[13] This notion of reciprocity was a strong one in virtually all the colonies. Colonial and dominion governments placed increasing emphasis on being partners in Imperial Defence to the point of asserting a role in the policy process but were usually reluctant to meet their own commitments in turn by developing their forces or making them available for deployment outside their own boundaries. This latter situation was reversed during the Great War, with the Dominions raising, fielding, and maintaining large armies placed at the disposal of the British high command. Membership in the Imperial War Cabinet as conceived by Lloyd George in 1917–18, however, fell well short of providing the Dominions with a real voice in the conduct of the war effort.[14]

Although the Dominions would contribute much larger expeditionary forces to the Empire's war effort in the two world wars than had been the case in South Africa, the notion that they would function merely as an imperial military reserve at British behest and direction was in slow but steady retreat even before the outbreak of the Great War. Laurier had insisted that the initial Canadian contingent for South Africa should serve together as a unit under Canadian command, while the small Australian colonial contingents were quickly formed into an Australian regiment, anticipating the creation of that national entity by about twelve months. Such a move found favour with the troops themselves "because nationalism was already a vigorous growth even among those imperially minded colonials who had volunteered for service."[15] Although a more conspiratorial slant has been placed upon it, the meetings between senior officials at the War Office and the dominion defence ministers that occurred during the Imperial Conference of 1911 underpin the point.[16] The British government had already accepted privately that a declaration of war on behalf of the Empire did not actually bind the Dominions to contribute anything at all to the British war effort if they so chose: "whether the Dominions should or should not furnish naval and military contingents outside their territories...is a matter which they can decide for themselves."[17]

It had been agreed in principle in 1907 that the armies of the Dominions (there were as yet no navies) should pursue standardization along British lines in the interests of efficiency and to encourage a capacity to operate together in war (although Lord Esher described such agreements as "pious aspirations and somewhat vague generalities").[18] These principles were reaffirmed at the 1911 meeting, suggesting that little had actually been done about them in the intervening period. All that really came out of the deliberations in 1911 was agreement on joint contingency planning, because under the Australian Defence Act and the Canadian Militia Act, the forces of the Dominions could not be sent for service outside the Dominion's borders. Both George Foster Pearce (the Australian defence minister) and Wilfrid Laurier (the Canadian prime minister) were at pains to emphasize this in their remarks, and when the British suggested that the minutes of the discussions might be published, Laurier, in particular, expressed vehement opposition.[19]

When war came, of course, large numbers of men from the Dominions enlisted in the expeditionary forces raised to fight. As in 1899, there is evidence to suggest that the main influx of volunteers did not come forward until disaster seemed to face British arms, in this case with the retreat from Mons (the same appears to hold true in Britain itself). In both Canada and Australia, the first contingents included large numbers of men who were in fact of British birth and, in many cases, only relatively recently arrived in the Dominion concerned; over the entire course of the war, only 51 per cent of total enlistments in the Canadian Expeditionary Force (CEF) were Canadian born.[20] In South Africa the war in Europe was always "English business," and the great majority of those who volunteered for the South African Infantry Brigade were "English" rather than Afrikaners. Canada and New Zealand both followed Britain's lead and introduced conscription in the course of the war. The South African government did not dare to introduce conscription for service overseas, especially in the light of the Afrikaner rebellion that had greeted the war's outbreak in 1914. Australia, which of course rejected conscription in successive referenda in 1916–17, had in fact broken with British practice before the war by introducing compulsory military training in peacetime, but Australians could not be induced to extend that principle to service overseas. Conversely, Britain had rejected peacetime conscription before 1914 only to introduce it in wartime when the voluntary system proved insufficient to meet the war's voracious manpower needs (and many of the arguments, and much of the literature, used in Australian pre-war debates on the subject were derived directly from their British counterparts, such as the National Service League). Whatever the moral or political arguments about it at the time or since, conscription enabled the Canadian Corps and the New Zealand Division to field full-strength (at times over-strength) units and formations right through to the armistice, while the Australian units were increasingly "hollow" and the South African Brigade was attenuated almost to the point of extinction by the end of the war.[21] This had important consequences for casualty rates incurred in the final six months of the fighting.

The Great War posed some fundamental challenges for the British World. Significant groups in Australia, Canada, and South Africa rejected the war outright or came to harbour very mixed views of its purpose and conduct as the war progressed. That these were mainly non-British groupings (francophones and Afrikaners) or others estranged from a mainstream, Protestant Anglo-Celtic establishment (the Irish-Catholic working class in Australia) makes their opposition less surprising. That opposition should not be regarded as uniform and undifferentiated, however. The proportion of Catholics in the Australian Imperial Force (AIF) mirrored their proportion in the population as a whole, and Catholic enlistment held up at the same rate as enlistments overall, and fell away at the same time and, one must surmise, for the same reasons. This realization limited the options available to His Majesty's governments overseas and made it more difficult to present the Dominions' war efforts as undifferentiated from each other, or from the metropolitan centre itself. In Australia, the divisions over conscription fed sectarianism and charges of "disloyalty" (to Australia, or to Britain? – the distinction was often intentionally unclear), to the extent that by the last year of the war, Catholic clergy and many involved in industrial labour refused further involvement with recruiting efforts for the AIF. Francophones were under-represented in the CEF, and this too fed charges of "disloyalty" from English Canada that were to have implications for the future.

At the front, British military authorities became gradual enthusiasts for dominion formations and the commander-in-chief, Sir Douglas Haig, initially lukewarm in his appreciation of "colonials," became a strong advocate of supporting the dominion divisions through, for example, the ready exchange of officers on higher staff formations, a faint resonance perhaps of the attempts to form an Imperial General Staff before 1914.

Initially, the Dominions relied heavily on the British and Indian armies for senior officers in both command and staff positions, since the rapid expansion of the expeditionary forces very quickly exhausted the limited supply of such men available from domestic sources. Some British senior officers such as Lieutenant General Sir William Birdwood, Lieutenant General Sir Alexander Godley, and Lieutenant General Sir Julian Byng – commanding the Australian, New Zealand, and Canadian forces, respectively – did very well in terms of promotion and advancement from their association with the dominion armies. But by the middle of the war, if not before, a willingness to defend dominion rights and perceived dominion interests began to assert itself, unevenly and by no means across the board, but identifiably so, for all that. The Canadian prime minister, Sir Robert Borden, told Lloyd George toward the war's end that "the idea of nationhood has developed wonderfully of late in my own Dominion; I believe the same is true of all the Dominions."[22]

The most obvious manifestation of this was the creation of the Canadian Overseas Ministry, an initiative followed by no other Dominion, to their likely disadvantage. Its genesis, of course, lay in the domestic political struggle in Ottawa over Sam Hughes's mismanagement of mobilization and continual interference with the running of the Canadian Corps, but it symbolized a willingness on the part of Canada to see its relationship with Britain as no longer merely "colonial" and dependent.[23] The replacement of British staff officers – especially senior ones on divisional headquarters – by dominion officers, or at least by officers holding commissions in the dominion forces, took time, but the selection of commanders was addressed more directly. In Australia in 1916, as the AIF expanded from two infantry divisions to five, the Defence Minister, Pearce, overruled Birdwood in the selection of commanding generals for the new divisions and insisted that Australians should be preferred wherever possible. In the CEF the impetus for "nationalizing" the corps came from the senior British officer, Byng, who resolved that when he handed over command of the Canadians, it should be to a Canadian, with Sir Arthur Currie, of course, the beneficiary. The New Zealand Expeditionary Force remained under the command of an Englishman, Godley, for the war's duration, but since Godley had been in New Zealand since the end of 1910 as commandant of the New Zealand Military Forces, he counted perhaps as an honorary colonial. There were other examples, such as Major General E. G. Sinclair-Maclagan, who ended the war commanding the 4th Australian Division and who had been on the staff at RMC Duntroon in 1914.

The war helped to etch an enhanced sense of nationalism into many of those who fought in it, and not simply or only through episodes such as Gallipoli or Vimy Ridge, in which so much was invested by subsequent generations. Many Australians, for whom England was the "home" of the imagination, found the reality of wartime leave in the United Kingdom sobering. Not only did Australian soldiers on leave become increasingly unpopular in parts of the country because of their spending power and behaviour, but some found the way things were done not to their liking: the sight of women engaged in non-traditional trades and occupations certainly offended some men, who resolved not to allow such practices to take root in Australia.[24] It is premature to suggest that as a result of their war service Australian soldiers rejected their British identities in favour of an Australian one (although in some individual cases that undoubtedly was so), but there seems little doubt that a process of differentiation was certainly underway – as indeed it had been in South Africa during the Boer War. This process also involved a breaking down of older state/colonial loyalties in favour of a less ambiguously national one, something that Alfred Deakin had hoped would occur in 1908 when he began the process of acquiring a national navy. Like Australians, New Zealanders also began to differentiate themselves from their English counterparts, at the same time consciously rejecting an "Australasian" tag and with it any sense of being "honorary Australians."[25]

The Great War was a watershed in Anglo-Dominion relations at both an official and a popular level. The great material, financial, and human cost of the war left Britain temperamentally disinclined to continue shouldering a global defence burden in those parts of the world where an alternative might present itself, much as the Mills Committee had concluded in 1862. The Statute of Westminster (1931) needs to be seen in this light, and so too does the response to it on the part of the Dominions. Canada and South Africa embraced it eagerly, not least for domestic political consumption by their non-British communities. Australia did not enact it until 1942, by which time Britain's capacity to meet the defence needs of the Pacific Dominions had been exposed as hollow to the core. New Zealand did not enact it until after the Second World War, in 1947, for a number of reasons. Among these were a conservative antipathy to any measure thought to jeopardize "imperial unity" and Labor concern for possible electoral consequences from too avid support for constitutional reform in a period of high domestic unemployment and social dislocation.[26] The Pacific Dominions, much more so than the others, threw themselves into the interwar programs of Imperial Defence out of conviction and with enthusiasm that should, on occasions, have been seasoned with a little more scepticism than such programs usually attracted. The one group within official circles that consistently questioned what became the "Singapore strategy," from the late 1920s until the outbreak of war, was the Army, or rather a succession of its senior officers. (The Singapore strategy used the construction of a modern naval base on the island, and the provision of a fleet from Britain to be based there in the event of a crisis, as the basis of the defence of Britain's Empire in the Far East.) It is possible, and permissible, to see Australian Army opposition to such a navalist basis to interwar Australian defence as professionally and perhaps personally self-serving. But it is equally true that the Australian Army emerged from the Great War experience with a far stronger sense of an Australian identity than permeated the other services – especially the Royal Australian Navy – and that the process of differentiation between imperial and national interests that had arisen during the war carried through for this group into the interwar years. It is worth mentioning here in passing that the Australian prime minister who approved involvement in the Singapore strategy at the 1923 Imperial Conference, Stanley Melbourne Bruce – the only interwar prime minister to have seen active service – had served throughout the war in the British Army.

The Second World War again saw enormous contributions by the Dominions to the Empire, and subsequently Allied, war effort, and the process of differentiation and the fracturing of a single common position between them developed even further. The automatic assumption that a declaration of war by the King-Emperor bound the Dominions as well no longer applied as a result of the Statute of Westminster, and thus Canada declared war in its own right after Prime Minister Mackenzie King had placed the matter before the Canadian parliament. In Australia, on the other hand, Menzies broadcast to the nation that as a result of the declaration in London, "Australia is also at war." The legacy of the Great War now made itself felt. In Canada, King's government initially declined to send an expeditionary force overseas because it was worried by the political implications of heavy casualties and the resultant pressures that would build to reintroduce conscription.[27] Canada's emphasis was to be placed on the defence of Canada and on contributions to the newly agreed upon Empire Air Training Scheme (although Canadians called it the British Commonwealth Air Training Plan). In South Africa, with many Afrikaner nationalists ideologically disposed toward Nazi Germany rather than Britain,[28] the government resolved that its armed forces would not serve outside the African continent unless they volunteered to do so, and it maintained this position until late in the war. In Australia, there was initial hesitation over the raising and dispatch of an expeditionary force too, but here the motivation was concern that Japan would take its opportunities in Southeast Asia while the European colonial powers were distracted in Europe. While the government continued to express confidence in the Singapore strategy in public, in private Menzies began to press London for assurances that the fleet would be dispatched to the base (completed only in February 1938) should the need arise. Assurances were given, but they were meaningless, as the British chiefs of staff knew full well.

The Second World War was more truly a global conflict than the First had been, and this placed new pressures upon the major components of the Empire and confronted them with new and difficult choices. Canada's ground force contribution went to Britain and, with the exception of the raid on Dieppe in 1942, took no part in the war until the invasion of Sicily in 1943, to their intense and growing frustration. In the Middle East and the Mediterranean, South Africans, New Zealanders, and Australians fought Italians, Germans, and the Vichy French as part of an imperial army that included soldiers from the metropolitan centre as well as India and various of the colonies. The outbreak of the Pacific War posed few problems for Canada, which, the tragic and token commitment to Hong Kong in 1941 notwithstanding, had no interest in the Asia-Pacific region, but it presented difficulties for the Pacific Dominions in their relations with Britain. Folk memory "recalls" that the Labor prime minister, John Curtin, withdrew Australian forces from the Mediterranean to bring them back for the defence of Australia against Japanese attack. In fact, it was Churchill who offered to return them – albeit to the Far East for, he hoped, service in Burma to defend the gateway to India. In this Churchill received support from President Franklin Delano Roosevelt, who was not pleased by perceived Australian truculence in insisting that the troops return to Australia, not India. It was at this point that Curtin asserted the prerogative of small powers in great power coalitions to refuse the use of their resources and insisted on the return of Australian forces to fight in the Australian territory of Papua. Even then, the Australian government agreed to leave one of its three divisions, the 9th, with Montgomery's 8th Army until after the German defeat at El Alamein, and this formation did not return until early 1943.

New Zealand chose to leave its division in the European theatre, after consultation with London and Washington. Although Wellington raised a small division, the 3rd, for service in the Solomons with U.S. forces in 1943, the fight against the Japanese in the Southwest Pacific was left to the Americans and the Australians. Here was a clear expression of the bifurcation of national interests among the Dominions: Canada was an Atlantic nation, and its focus on the war in Europe – given the coterminous border with the United States – made perfect sense; Australia was increasingly beginning to see its future in terms of Asia and the Pacific, although that process would be a gradual, even at times a glacial, one; New Zealand, though a Pacific nation, chose to act like an Atlantic one for constitutional, economic, and sentimental reasons.

The Second World War was the last great war of the Empire/ Commonwealth (although arguably the last great British Imperial Army was the 14th Army in Burma, in which the Dominions had very little representation). Once again, the war emphasized the process of differentiation rather than providing any great and dramatic fissuring of relations between Britain and the Dominions. During the war, the Australian government viewed the wartime relationship with the United States as fortunate, expedient, and strictly temporary, and the alliance with the United States on which Australia (and New Zealand) were to embark in the 1950s was still some way off. The post-war military relationships, conducted in the context of the Cold War, often used traditional British military structures in the pursuit of better relations with Washington, not London. The formation of the Commonwealth Division in Korea in 1951 was an example whereby small forces contributed by the Dominions and India could maximize their military utility by combining within a larger common structure, but all the contributing nations, without exception, fielded their forces within a United Nations context and under overall American command.[29] Canada's long-running commitment to the North Atlantic Treaty Organization likewise was more about relations with the United States, not the United Kingdom, and an attempt to give meaning to the concept of a "middle power," while Australian and New Zealand involvement in SEATO was in pursuit of greater access to American resources, planning, and decision-making.

Within Southeast Asia, Britain remained a major power militarily and economically, despite the decline in its post-war global fortunes, but even here the relationship with Australia and New Zealand was increasingly one between contracting parties in pursuit of their own interests. In 1954, during the "United Action" crisis over Indochina, Canberra indicated that it was not prepared to join an American-led coalition to intervene on behalf of the French unless Britain took part. In 1961 Canberra decided that it would contribute forces to an American-led coalition to resolve the Laotian crisis, despite the fact that Britain declined to be involved.[30] Senior British officers were appalled to be told by Australian Cabinet ministers in 1955 that Australia increasingly would look to the United States in defence matters because 1942 had demonstrated that Britain could not be relied on – the legacy of Singapore ran deep even among Australian conservatives whose belief in Britain might once have been assumed automatically.[31] The world, and especially the British World, had moved on. South Africa, of course, took itself out of the Commonwealth altogether in 1961, but from the time of the Nationalist electoral victory in 1948, resurgent Afrikaner nationalism was intent on a conscious and thorough repudiation of the nation's "English" heritage, a process embodied in the Afrikanerization of the South African Defence Force and the purges of officers with British backgrounds or sympathies.

The ways in which British societies overseas remember and commemorate involvement in the great wars of the century once again draws attention to the process of differentiation between the Dominions, and between the Dominions and Britain, that has characterized the military relationship over the last 150 years. The impetus to national memorializing of shared military endeavour comes out of the Great War experience. Contemporaries memorialized involvement in the South African War, often in quite substantial form, as in Toronto, where the imperial monument, erected at a cost of $38,000, remains the largest in the city.[32] But such memorials were usually imperial in form and symbolism; the memorial erected to the New South Wales volunteers at Bathurst, for example, varies little if at all in form, content, or purpose from the one erected to the Royal Dublin Fusiliers in Dublin – they are both conventional regimental monuments of an entirely traditional kind, exciting little interest. But as a symbol of new nationhood and national endeavour, the Boer War just did not work, as Ken Inglis has noted, at least in the Australian context;[33] in Australia and elsewhere, it was soon overshadowed by involvement in the Great War and came to be seen quite differently in retrospect than it had been by contemporaries.

The Great War, on the other hand, did "work," in often tragic ways. For Australia and New Zealand, commemoration focused on Anzac Day; in Canada it was Vimy Day, while South Africans – or at least English ones – could focus on Delville Wood Day. Ulster Protestants, another British World overseas, focused on the first day on the Somme and the "martyrdom" of the 36th Ulster Division, a memory shared by the tiny Dominion of Newfoundland but virtually unknown and unobserved in

Ireland outside Ulster.[34] All, of course, observed Remembrance Day in November. In the interwar period, and into the 1950s, all of these occasions were observed publicly with religious services, marches of veterans' groups, speeches by dignitaries, and other commemorative activities. Vimy Day and Delville Wood Day are now distant memories, historical curiosities. The Great War functioned as a symbol of fundamental national disunity in these societies as much as it represented involvement in the Empire war effort, and as the generation of men who had taken part in the war died away, observance of these occasions died with them. As Bill Nasson has observed, in South Africa there was not one Great War experience, but four, and these could never be combined.[35] The same, perhaps a little less starkly, held true in Canada as well. In Australia and New Zealand, Anzac Day has long since moved beyond its association with Britain and Empire, which goes some way toward explaining why it remains a vibrant and central occasion in the national life of those increasingly non-British societies. Ideas of national identity in Canada and South Africa, too, have long outstripped their British heritage, diminishing the memory and commemoration of the Great War.[36] But as in Eire more recently, new generations may yet rediscover them anew and put them to their own purposes, as has occurred in the Pacific Dominions in the last decade of the twentieth century.

Colley notes that Britain is "a culture that is used to fighting and has largely defined itself through fighting."[37] In the course of the twentieth century, the Dominions, too, acquired much experience of fighting. Much, by no means all, of the history of Anglo-Dominion relations was defined by or at least sharply influenced by participation in the Empire's wars and military efforts, and a desire to regulate and control military resources shaped the evolving constitutional relations between London and those other British governments overseas. A shared colonial inheritance was gradually differentiated in the minds of overseas Britons through participation in war and the opportunities this presented to define and redefine the relationship with Britain, and with each other.

{NOTES}

1 Linda Colley, *Britons: Forging the Nation, 1707–1837* (New Haven: Yale University Press, 1992), 18, 53, 322, 367, 365.
2 Andreski's work deals with the impact of war service and military organization on inequality and social stratification, utilizing the proportion of individuals within a

given national population utilized in military activities. Stanislav Andreski, *Military Organisation and Society* (London: Routledge and Kegan Paul, 1968), especially 33–34. For suggestive work that builds on Andreski's basic premises, see Arthur A. Stein, *The Nation at War* (Baltimore: Johns Hopkins University Press, 1978).

3 Colley, 371

4 Ibid., 413n18.

5 P.A. Buckner and Carl Bridge, "Reinventing the British World," *The Round Table* 368 (2003): 82.

6 D.C. Gordon, *The Dominion Partnership in Imperial Defense, 1870–1914* (Baltimore: Johns Hopkins Press, 1965); Richard A. Preston, *Canada and "Imperial Defense": A Study of the Origins of the British Commonwealth's Defense Organization, 1867–1919* (Durham: Duke University Press, 1967). The latter ranges much more widely geographically than its title suggests.

7 The literature here is extensive and of high quality. Notable contributions include John McCarthy, *Australia and Imperial Defence 1918–1939: A Study in Air and Sea Power* (St. Lucia: University of Queensland Press, 1976); James Neidpath, *The Singapore Naval Base and the Defence of Britain's Eastern Empire 1919–1941* (Oxford: Clarendon Press, 1981); I.C. McGibbon, *Blue-Water Rationale: The Naval Defence of New Zealand 1914–1942* (Wellington: Government Printer, 1981); W. David McIntyre, *The Rise and Fall of the Singapore Naval Base, 1919–1942* (London: Macmillan, 1979).

8 A partial and not entirely successful effort in this direction is provided by F.W. Perry, *The Commonwealth Armies: Manpower and Organisation in Two World Wars* (Manchester: Manchester University Press, 1988). The book demonstrates one of the problems of this sort of large-scale comparative work – lack of access to the archives across the Commonwealth – and is written very largely from secondary sources, which then leads the author into error when writing about the Dominion armies.

9 The key modern work here is James Belich, *The New Zealand Wars and the Victorian Interpretation of Racial Conflict* (Auckland: Auckland University Press, 1986).

10 Very little has been written about black-white conflict in Australia in the context of military history (rather than race relations). A recent and important exception is John Connor, *The Australian Frontier Wars 1788–1838* (Sydney: University of New South Wales Press, 2002).

11 Little has been written on the colonial commandants. An excellent study, limited to the Australasian colonies, is Stephen Clarke, "Marching to Their Own Drum: British Army Officers as Military Commandants in the Australian Colonies and New Zealand 1870–1901" (PhD diss., University of New South Wales, 1999). There is still no study of E.T.H. Hutton, despite his importance as commandant in Australia and Canada and despite the richness of his private papers.

12 The centenary of the South African War has produced a number of new works on the subject, but few of these examine the colonial contributions from a comparative perspective. See Craig Wilcox, *Australia's Boer War: The War in South Africa 1899–1902* (Melbourne: Oxford University Press, 2002); Peter Dennis and Jeffrey Grey, *The Boer War: Army, Nation and Empire* (Canberra: Army History Unit, 1999); John Crawford and Ian McGibbon, eds., *One Flag, One Queen, One Tongue: New Zealand, the British Empire and the South African War* (Auckland: Auckland University Press, 2003). The standard work on Canadian involvement is Carman Miller, *Painting the Map Red: Canada and the South African War 1899–1902* (Montreal: McGill-Queen's

University Press, 1993). The best short overview, incorporating much recent South African work, is Bill Nasson, *The South African War, 1899–1902* (London: Arnold, 1999).

13 Gordon, *Dominion Partnership*, 230–31; Preston, *Canada and "Imperial Defense,"* 263.

14 Margaret MacMillan, "Sibling Rivalry: Australia and Canada from the Boer War to the Great War," in *Parties Long Estranged: Canada and Australia in the Twentieth Century*, ed. Margaret MacMillan and Francine McKenzie (Vancouver: University of British Columbia Press, 2003), 18, makes the point that before the Great War, "Australia and Canada were like adolescents: comfortable at home but grumbling at the mother country and threatening to leave one day."

15 Preston, *Canada and "Imperial Defense."*

16 John Mordike, *An Army for a Nation: A History of Australian Military Developments, 1880–1914* (Sydney: Allen & Unwin, 1992); *"We Should Do this Thing Quietly": Japan and the Great Deception in Australian Defence Policy 1911–1914* (Canberra: RAAF Aerospace Centre, 2002).

17 Public Record Office (PRO), CAB 17/79, minute, Foreign Office, 24 February 1911.

18 Quoted in Jeffrey Grey, "Defending the Dominion 1901–1918," in *Between Empire and Nation: Australia's External Relations from Federation to the Second World War*, ed. Carl Bridge and Bernard Attard (Melbourne: Australian Scholarly Publishing, 2000), 27.

19 PRO, WO106/43, "Proceedings of a Committee of Imperial Defence conference convened to discuss questions of Defence (Military) at the War Office, 14 June 1911." The older literature dealing with the conference, especially Gordon and Preston, appears not to have utilized this lengthy document.

20 J.L. Granatstein, *Canada's Army: Waging War and Keeping the Peace* (Toronto: University of Toronto Press, 2002), 74–75.

21 Jack Granatstein has written extensively on the conscription issue in Canadian history and has recently modified his earlier, critical stance in light of the manpower and force structure implications on the Western Front in the last year of the war. See his "Conscription and My Politics," *Canadian Military History* 10, no. 4 (Autumn 2001): 35–38.

22 MacMillan, "Sibling Rivalry," 20.

23 See Desmond Morton, "'Junior but Sovereign Allies': The Transformation of the Canadian Expeditionary Force, 1914–1918," *Journal of Contemporary History* 8, no. 1 (October 1979); and *A Peculiar Kind of Politics: Canada's Overseas Ministry in the First World War* (Toronto: University of Toronto Press, 1982). Administration generally receives much less coverage than command – what in military terms is known as "G" snobbery. A useful analysis of the administrative problems faced by the 1st AIF is provided by Bruce Faraday, "Half the Battle: The Administration and Higher Organisation of the AIF 1914–1918" (PhD diss., University of New South Wales, 1997).

24 Michael McKernan, *The Australian People and the Great War* (Melbourne: Nelson, 1980), 129–30. McKernan provides an illuminating discussion of Australians' reactions to Britain while on leave from the front. E.M. Andrews, *The Anzac Illusion: Anglo-Australian Relations during World War I* (Melbourne: Cambridge University Press, 1993), 165–89 provides an extensive discussion of the mutual admiration and antipathy between the British and Australians.

25 James Bennett, "'Massey's Sunday School Picnic Party': 'The Other Anzacs' or Honorary Australians?" *War and Society* 21, no. 2 (October 2003): 23–54. He declares that "after their initial stand-off in Egypt, soldiers from both New Zealand and Australia worked together cooperatively for the most part, learned to trust each other and, at times, even sang each other's praises. While Bean and some other Australians felt the kiwis to be a pale imitation of the Australian digger, the kiwi nonetheless did not see himself as an honorary Australian."

26 Angus Ross, "New Zealand and the Statute of Westminster," in *The First British Commonwealth: Essays in Honour of Nicholas Mansergh*, ed. Norman Hillmer and Philip Wigley (London: Frank Cass, 1980), 136–58.

27 Granatstein, *Canada's Army*, 176–78.

28 Brian Banting, *The Rise of the South African Reich* (1964; new ed., London: International Defence and Aid Fund, 1986), 56. "During the thirties many Nationalist Party leaders and wide sections of the Afrikaner people came strongly under the influence of the Nazi movement."

29 Jeffrey Grey, *The Commonwealth Armies and the Korean War: An Alliance Study* (Manchester: Manchester University Press, 1988).

30 Peter Edwards, *Crises and Commitments: The Politics and Diplomacy of Australia's Involvement in Southeast Asian Conflicts 1948–1965* (Sydney: Allen and Unwin, 1992), 120–38, 208–28.

31 Jeffrey Grey, *"Up Top": The Royal Australian Navy and Southeast Asian Conflicts, 1955–1972* (Sydney: Allen & Unwin, 1998), 20–21.

32 Phillip Buckner, "Canada," in *The Impact of the South African War*, ed. David Omissi and Andrew S. Thompson (London: Palgrave, 2002), 240–41.

33 Inglis has written extensively on the issues surrounding commemoration. See in particular *Sacred Places: War Memorials in the Australian Landscape* (Melbourne: Miegunyah Press, 1998); see as well "Anzac, the Substitute Religion," in *Observing Australia 1959 to 1999: Ken Inglis*, ed. Craig Wilcox (Melbourne: Melbourne University Press, 1999), 61–70.

34 I am grateful to Professor Keith Jeffery, University of Ulster at Jordanstown, for this latter observation.

35 Bill Nasson, "A Great Divide: Popular Responses to the Great War in South Africa," *War and Society* 12, no. 1 (May 1994): 47–64. See also Albert Grundlingh, "Black Men in a White Man's War: The Impact of the First World War on South African Blacks," *War and Society* 3, no. 1 (May 1985): 55–81; N.G. Garson, "South Africa and World War 1," in *First British Commonwealth*, 68–85.

36 While some important work has been done on war memorials and the physical commemoration of war in Australia and New Zealand, much less work has been done on the forms and development of ceremonial commemoration and its place in the broader national and popular cultures. Anecdotal evidence suggests, for example, that there are subtle but important differences in Anzac commemoration in Australia and New Zealand. This area cries out for a comparative cross-cultural analysis of commemoration across the Dominions in the aftermath of 1914–18.

37 Colley, *Britons*, 9.

THE OTHER BATTLE:

IMPERIALIST VERSUS NATIONALIST SYMPATHIES WITHIN THE OFFICER CORPS OF THE CANADIAN EXPEDITIONARY FORCE, 1914–1919

Patrick H. Brennan

IN A FAREWELL MESSAGE to his 1st Brigade troops on 6 February 1919, Brigadier-General William Griesbach told the men that they would "return [home] with a wider vision and finer conception of Canada, its opportunities and destinies, than they ever had before." Amid the strongly "Canadianist" tone of his comments, however, he also proudly reminded them that "you have seen something of the might and power of the great Empire to which we belong, and you will return to Canada persuaded that this great Empire is an instrument of righteousness, and a safe-guard of the life, property and liberties of the whole world."[1] Griesbach was Canadian born, of British descent, a Conservative politically, and an unabashed Anglophile – in all respects, attributes shared by most of the senior officers of the Canadian Corps, approximately three-quarters of whom were Canadian appointments and Canadian by birth or im-migration.[2] His own sense of Canadianism was well developed before the war, and three and a half years at the front appeared to have only strengthened it. But the Brigadier also remained intensely loyal to the concept of Empire and the inherent British character of Canada, and saw the Dominion's future inextricably linked to the maintenance of a strong imperial link. Clearly, he had no difficulty reconciling what on the surface might appear to be two allegiances. In this he was also typical.

In the decades since the Great War, most English-Canadian histo-rians have been bent on fighting other "battles." Scouring the historical record to find evidence of an emerging English-Canadian nationalism, they have freely invoked the nation-building experience of that conflict to prove their case. Thus, the soldiers who battled up Vimy Ridge as British, they have assured us, came down Canadian.[3] Still, in their search for evidence that the Canadian Expeditionary Force was the centrepiece of a nascent wartime nationalism, historians have focused more on the attitudes of civilian leaders like Prime Minister Robert Borden, various other Unionist politicians, some intellectuals, and even Sam Hughes[4] than on military leaders.[5] In contrast, this paper examines the ideas, sentiments, and actions of the senior officers of the Canadian Corps, a group of men who by any measure should have been in the forefront of any nationalist experience during the First World War.

It is not the purpose of this paper to refute the impact of the Canadian Corps's bloody struggles in creating and deepening Canadian national sympathies among the tens of thousands of officers and men who passed through its ranks,[6] or the assumption that such sympathies played a central role, as Jonathan Vance has eloquently argued, in the creation of an explanatory myth of the war.[7] After all, there is abundant evidence, both anecdotal and scholarly, to buttress both conclusions. But the so-called nationalism of the senior Canadian commanders can best be understood in the context of the sentiments of "imperialist-nationalism" held by many English Canadians in pre-war Canada. Imperialist sentiments, after all, "were characterized by a profound emotional attachment to Canada," and far from denigrating Canada, as Carl Berger has pointed out, Canadians holding such views were unfettered optimists who exaggerated both their country's potential and its achievements – in other words, they looked at least superficially nationalist.[8] Furthermore, in the British World, of which these senior officers were a thoroughly integrated element, "the rise of colonial national identities did not contradict or undermine imperial Britishness."[9] It was quite possible for one person to have a number of concurrent identities – for example, to be both a Canadian and a Briton – and not see them in conflict at all. Indeed, there is solid evidence that the power of this conception was growing throughout the British World during the immediate pre-World War I years, not the least among English Canadians. In the Australian experience, which offers many parallels to the English-Canadian one, nationalism, rather than being thwarted by or in conflict with British imperial sentiment, "was based on a local patriotism which saw itself as part of a pan-Britishness."[10] In the end, much of the evidence put forward by post-Great War Canadian historians in building their nationalist case has simply been taken out of that proper context – the context whose elements define the British World of the late nineteenth and early twentieth centuries.[11]

Among the bulk of the senior officers in the Canadian Corps, the national sentiments that had undoubtedly been enhanced by their wartime experiences remained inextricably – and in their minds, logically

– tied to pro-British Empire sentiment. Wartime relations between the Canadian and the British military had generally been warm, and at the time, much of the nationalist friction in evidence had more to do with the growing collective pride of these officers in the Canadian Corps and their individual accomplishments than with the emergence of any full-blown nationalist identity built upon disillusionment with imperialism.

The struggle to establish the principle of a significant measure of Canadian control over her overseas forces was largely a civilian effort directed from Ottawa and has been well documented. Senior Canadian officers fully sympathized with this development, both for practical administrative reasons and because of their growing sense of identity with the Corps, the latter as much a reflection of their increasing military professionalism as of national sentiment. During the first two years of the war, Canadianization – the organized practice of replacing senior British officers with suitably trained Canadians – was partly driven by an emerging sense of Canadian identity but also very much by personal career considerations. Sam Hughes embarked on a crude form of Canadianization from the outset, though it did not always assume forms compatible with the best interests operationally of the forces in the field.[12] Indeed, the Canadian officers committed to merit-based promotion and professionalization were not ungrateful that Lieutenant-General Julian Byng, the Corps's British commanding officer during the last months of the Hughes regime, with the sometime support of General Headquarters and the War Office, was determined and increasingly able to shield the Expeditionary Force from the deleterious effects of Hughes's cronyism.[13] As Byng confided to a British friend:

I presented a sort of ultimatum the other day saying I did not think I could carry on unless promotions and appointments were in my hands. The men are too good to be led by politicians and dollar magnates.... I don't want Imperial officers but I want to shove on the Canadians who have proved their worth and get rid of the Bumstunts.... If [the Canadian government and the British military authorities] refuse, I shall offer my resignation as I feel too strongly about it.... [The senior Canadian officers] are (I think) all with me but powerless to do anything. Having no axe to grind of my own I can face it with equanimity and am only trying to do my best for these men.[14]

A growing measure of British intervention in 1916–17, by facilitating the professionalizing of the Canadian Army, effectively saved it. As Andy

McNaughton, then a promising young artillery officer, succinctly put it, "you can have an entirely civilian army [but] its members will be dead before they are good."[15] The gratitude of the Canadian officers whose rise Byng had assisted was sincere. Forty-five years later, Alex Ross, who began the war as a company commander and ended it in command of a brigade, offered this appraisal:

> [Byng] did a great deal for us. He revolutionized a lot of our organization and made it much more sensible.... We always got along very well together.... We all respected him and we always found him fair and found him sound according to our common sense ideas.[16]

After 1916, with the departure of Hughes, the whole process of Canadianization was as much (or more) about military efficiency than nascent nationalism. All Canadians agreed on the merit of giving Canadians as many opportunities as possible and not unnecessarily relying on British professionals.[17] In practice, Canadianization pitted two reasonably well-defined Canadian factions – the "Currie reformers" and the "old guard" – against each other,[18] with the British merely facilitating the ascendancy of the former. Through 1917, British officers had to occupy many of the key staff positions at the Corps and divisional levels, and the two most senior staff positions, the Brigadier-General General Staff and the Deputy Adjutant and Quarter-Master General, were still in the hands of British officers in the closing days of the war. Once appointed Corps commander in June 1917 (an instance itself of Canadianization), Arthur Currie relentlessly pressed for the training and appointment of competent Canadians, following the practice inaugurated under his British predecessor, Byng. Nevertheless, Currie accepted the necessity of retaining key British officers for military efficiency's sake. Neither Currie nor his senior Canadian commanders seemed to have any problem, nationalist or otherwise, with this situation.[19] It helped that most of the British officers so employed were of a high quality and that those who did not accommodate to the "Canadian style" were speedily returned to a British unit.

While there is much anecdotal evidence in the popular histories of British regulars treating "colonials" condescendingly as little more than frontier woodsmen,[20] concrete evidence of friction or lack of respect between senior British and Canadian officers who worked together intimately within the Corps or on training courses is hard to find. Indeed, familiarity seems to have bred respect, not contempt. Understandably,

Canadian officers wanted respect, and as their military proficiency improved, they generally seemed to receive it.[21] Of course, if they encountered old stereotypes, they were resentful. When Currie learned in the spring of 1918 that his British superiors felt his men "were very stout fighters [and] good on the…limited objective offensive, though they shake their head at what we might do in open warfare owing to the absence of regular officers," he grumbled in his diary that "they forget that our [officers] have seen more war in the last three years than the British Army did in the previous one hundred."[22] Overall, however, relations appear to have been congenial, a situation hardly surprising when one bears in mind that senior Canadian officers remained steadfastly pro-Empire and were participating in a common endeavour with their imperial colleagues, and, to all intents, were doing so as part of a single army. As Currie himself put it some years later when speaking of his mentor, Byng, Canadians had no trouble with British officers who "knew, respected and believed in them."[23]

It needs to be remembered as well that even during the later stages of the war, Canadian officers utilized the principle of Canadianization, on at least some occasions, as leverage to advance their own careers. In 1918, when Canadian Headquarters in London showed no sign of pressing for the replacement of the British commander of the Canadian Cavalry Brigade, Brigadier-General Jack Seeley, his Canadian second-in-command pressed the matter – and his own case – successfully, at least in part by invoking the "time-for-a-Canadian" argument.[24]

When Anglo-Canadian friction did occur, it was the senior officers' growing pride in and collective identity with the Canadian Corps – in other words, *esprit de corps*[25] and the desire for collective recognition by British military leaders and the public alike – *as well as* a measure of national identity that seems to have driven them. There is no question that the failure of the London press to give specific credit to the Canadian Corps for its hard-won victories during the Last Hundred Days grated on Currie and his subordinates. When Canadian troops broke through the Hindenburg Line and captured the vital German Army rail centre of Cambrai in early October, official reports credited the neighbouring British 3rd Army – ironically now commanded by General Byng – with the action. At Valenciennes, captured by the 4th Canadian Division less than a month later, General Horne, the commander of the 1st Army, to which the Canadians were then attached, reversed the local population's plans and offered the Canadian Corps only a token role in official ceremonies marking the city's liberation. The 4th Division's commanding officer,

David Watson, angrily noted that Horne's action was much resented by everyone, while Currie, who only attended after Horne ordered him to do so, characterized the ceremony with understatement as "a frosty affair."[26] Tellingly, at Mons, a site pregnant with symbolism for the British Expeditionary Force and its leaders, Currie ensured Canadian pride of place in the staging of the official ceremonies.

General Currie and his commanders deemed the victories of the Last Hundred Days their greatest achievement, one bought at great price in Canadian blood and treasure, and they were frustrated by the lack of recognition that was given them. Particularly galling was the failure of the English press to highlight – or indeed, to mention at all – the substantial role of the Canadian Corps in the series of dramatic British offensives that had ended the war, for it was acknowledgement of their part in the British Empire effort that they wanted. Understandably frustrated, a suspicious Currie explained the situation to Prime Minister Borden:

> It has been intimated to me that a certain section of the
> American press is seeking to belittle the work of the Canadians,
> intimating that what we call the "Imperial" troops have done
> the bulk of the fighting. If this is the case, it may be Boche
> propaganda, but I am inclined to think that the English press
> are the people to blame, for it [is] a fact that their reports on the
> operations since August 8th have in very few cases been fair or
> just to the Canadians.... As they [the *Times*] give evidence of a
> willingness to differentiate [between "British" and "Canadian"]
> sometimes, it has struck me that it would be fair to differentiate
> always. We are British, certainly, and proud to be called
> such, but a certain section of the English press are evidently
> determined on a policy to ignore the word "Canadian".... Mr.
> Livesay, our correspondent, has, on many occasions represented
> our views at Censor Headquarters, only to be asked what
> objections the Canadians had to the use of the word "British." I
> believe the papers have the policy I speak of, and I believe they
> receive their instructions from the highest military authorities.[27]

Currie was concerned about the reputation of his soldiers, clearly conscious of his Canadian identity, but also worried about how the Canadian public, unaware of the savage battles their countrymen had been engaged in and groaning under the weight of heavy casualty lists, might judge his leadership.[28]

So determined was the Corps commander to get the "true" story out that at Ottawa's request (for they, too, were feeling the pressure), he ordered the compilation of a comprehensive list of every German unit that the Canadians had "engaged or defeated" in their victorious advance from Amiens. It seems that his intelligence and staff officers took their orders literally – and interpreted "engaged" liberally – so that if even a handful of prisoners of war were taken or German bodies recovered on the battlefield, their unit appears to have been counted in these statistics. Nor was any mention made of the pitifully under-strength state of many of the German divisions encountered, some of which could barely muster the numbers of a Canadian battalion. Given the organizational chaos in the collapsing German army, any totalling of units by Currie's criteria of "engaged or defeated" was bound to yield exaggerated numbers. Nevertheless, with absolute conviction, Currie proudly informed Ottawa, and anyone else who would listen, that the Canadian Corps had defeated no fewer than forty-seven German divisions – one-quarter of all those known to be on the Western Front. Generated in the emotion of the moment, this claim was preposterous; nevertheless, it gave rise to the understandably popular and lasting myth among Canadians that the Corps had practically demolished the Kaiser's legions single-handedly during the Allies' final push.[29] "One does not dare to publicly say so," Currie wrote Sir Edward Kemp, the minister of the Overseas Military Forces of Canada, in a self-congratulatory tone the day before the capture of Valenciennes, "but it would appear that the Germans concluded that if they could stop the Canadian Corps, they would stop the others."[30]

During the 1920s, with the draft volumes of the much anticipated British official history beginning to appear, the sensibilities of Canadian officers were again aroused. Not only national myths but personal reputations were at stake. The efforts of General James Edmonds, the British Army's senior historian, to provide a fair account "of the none too brilliant early performances of the Canadians"[31] at Ypres and St. Eloi were met with outrage and thinly veiled accusations of anti-colonial prejudice from Canada.[32] Major-General Frederick Loomis acidly observed that

the outstanding feature of the...chapters appears to me to be the Anti-Canadian atmosphere or spirit which permeates the narrative. I am not alone in this conclusion [and this] unfair, unfriendly and ungenerous treatment may prove to be the cause of far-reaching results which all loyal British subjects will regret.[33]

Major-General James MacBrien also predicted darkly that the impact of "any inadvertent misrepresentation [of early Canadian performances] would be correspondingly far-reaching in its effect on inter-imperial relations."[34] For his part, Currie concluded bitterly that Edmond's account

> seem[s] to disclose…[a] deplorable yet consistent tendency to disparage every effort of the Canadian commanders and troops alike. The frequent recurrence of such passages drives one to the conclusion that the use of this method of disparagement is deliberate. He appears to be determined that, so far as it lies within his power to influence their judgment and imagination, future generations must not be allowed to think that Dominion troops were comparable in any degree with their brothers-in-arms recruited in the Old Country. I know that at the first reading this account will be a sad blow to Canadian pride, but it will be resented, because it is ungenerous and untrue.

Currie went on to add that some of his best wartime comrades had been British officers, and he fully trusted that their fair-mindedness would lead them to protest. He pointedly concluded: "I recall with pardonable pride that throughout the war the reputation and tradition of British arms did not suffer at [our] hands."[35] Haig and other British commanders had rightly felt that for "political" reasons, they had necessarily intervened to shield from the public eye the early failings of Canadian commanders – not the least of which was Currie himself at Ypres – thus saving the latter's careers. Thus, the complaints of the Canadian commander and those officers like Loomis, MacBrien, and Fortescue Duguid, the Canadian official historian, who were considered to be part of Currie's personal "faction," elicited little sympathy in Britain.[36] A harassed Edmonds was not prepared to whitewash the Canadian performance. "It seems to me," he confided to a senior colleague, "that if the [Canadians want] a vainglorious account [they] better write [their] own as the Australians have done. I am afraid nothing I can write will satisfy them."[37] Eventually, a resolution was reached that went some way toward meeting the Canadian objections, a compromise that, as the official Canadian historian observed with understatement, avoided "what would otherwise have been a nasty mess."[38]

A nascent national spirit was one – but only one – of the factors contributing to a growing awareness on the part of senior officers of the

Canadian Corps's identity as a separate entity within the BEF (British Expeditionary Force). Stephen Harris has concluded:

> All the available evidence suggests that the Canadian contingents developed an *esprit de corps* significantly stronger than would have been the case had they been dispersed throughout the British army, and once it was formed the Canadian Corps was widely regarded as an entity greater than the sum of its parts.... The Canadian commanders and staffs had the opportunity to work together over a relatively prolonged period which furthered a special spirit of co-operation and community, and by the end of the war produced a cohesive and well-oiled military machine. But the boost to morale resulting from the rule that the Canadians would serve together was probably the most important factor in developing the Corps' sense of destiny about which Canadian veterans talked so much after the war.[39]

Rooted in unit pride as well as an emerging dominion identity, Canadian commanders wanted to be acknowledged favourably by the British professional soldiers who were, after all, both their mentors and partners in the greatest enterprise of their lives. It mattered what the British thought, not only because the Canadians were beginning to see themselves rather proudly as somewhat more than simply British North Americans, but because they also still saw themselves – and proudly so – as part of the British family. When an irritated Currie questioned how in one British official history draft the same artillery that was "Canadian" on one page could be referred to only paragraphs later as "British," was his nationalism offended or did he desire appropriate recognition for his army's participation within a collective British Empire effort?[40] Likely, it was a mixture of both.

Throughout the war, it is worth pointing out, nascent national feeling certainly did not hold back Canadian officers – Currie included – from seeking and accepting appropriate British honours, for KCMGs, CBs, and CMGs were plentiful and their awarding much delighted in.[41] Major-General Henry Burstall, born in Canada and a pre-war regular soldier, even went so far as to retire to England and the life of an country gentleman shortly after the war.

Much has been made of Sir Arthur Currie's willingness to stand up to British General Headquarters (that is, Field Marshall Haig) and the

War Office on various occasions in 1918 when "Canadian interests" were supposedly at stake. His actions, backed as they were by the Borden government, have been held up as manifestations of an emerging Canadian nationalism.[42] Currie's refusal to allow the use of the Corps as a "fire brigade" for the hard-pressed BEF during the German spring offensives in 1918,[43] or diluting infantry strength to produce two extra divisions,[44] a second Canadian Corps, and a Canadian Army he would undoubtedly have commanded, are two commonly invoked examples.[45] It can be argued, however, that in these situations the Canadian commander was motivated as much or more by practical military considerations such as preserving the fighting power of Canadian formations – for the common cause – and ensuring adequate reinforcements, as well as a personal sense of responsibility for his soldiers. Canadian interests in any narrow national sense appear to have been distinctly secondary in his considerations. Furthermore, the testy relationship between Currie and Haig was mostly the product of personal and professional differences between two strong-willed generals. The national identity of the Canadian Corps that *enabled* Currie to disagree with his British superiors – giving him the right and the power[46] – did not make him *want* to do so.

There is, in fact, plenty of evidence to show that the Canadian high command was impressed with the British Army's doctrinal thinking and, with the exception of Passchendaele (which many senior British officers also questioned), with its operational planning. After all, the Canadian Corps remained a fully integrated component of the British Expeditionary Force, and to diverge from basic British practice would have made no sense. As much as the Canadians innovated tactically, through their policies of institutionalizing and universalizing what had been learned from combat experience,[47] the Corps's tactical doctrine remained firmly based on and compatible with BEF practices, a state of affairs with which its ablest field commanders remained fully satisfied.[48] Furthermore, the Canadian Corps relied heavily on the augmentation of BEF resources to pave the way for its victories in 1917–18, a military dependency that one might have expected an exaggerated nationalism would have driven it to address.[49] Finally, for proof that the Canadian command respected, and indeed sought to emulate British military practice, one need look no further than their continued and exclusive use of British programs in the training of promising middle-ranking and senior Canadian officers right up to the armistice.[50] "Most Canadian historians," as Phillip Buckner has correctly pointed out, "would prefer simply to ignore the whole issue [of widespread imperialist sentiment in Canada] and to focus on the gradual evolution of a distinct and separate Canadian national identity with its own separate and distinct national symbols."[51] The accounts of the Great War written by Canadian military historians have uniformly emphasized the Canadianness of the story. All elements distinguishing the Canadian experience from the larger British Empire experience have been duly noted as proof of the wartime growth of a national consciousness and its inevitable concomitant, the erosion of confidence in previously held imperialist convictions. Even if exaggerated, this persistent emphasizing of nationalism was not wrong, *per se*, since it highlighted a basic truth – that the war did significantly accelerate the emergence of a sense of English-Canadian national identity, and nowhere was it more clearly displayed than in the senior ranks of the Canadian Corps. However, the nationalist focus of this writing – itself clearly driven by nationalist sympathies and a nationalist agenda – made its point at the expense of properly factoring in the prevailing imperialist sentiment[52] and the continued compatibility of the two conceptions in the minds of senior Canadian military men. Thus, it has skewed our understanding of what the leaders of the Canadian Corps believed and practiced. In fact, the "other battle" – the supposed struggle between imperialist and nationalist sentiments – was fought in the mind of each officer. There were no nationalist and imperialist camps in the way there had been "reformers" and "anti-reformers," "professionalizers" and "militia myth" adherents. As a group, senior Canadian army officers were successful products of pre-war British Canadian society – and of the larger British World. During the war, they saw the Empire's leadership at both its best and worst. And unlike most of their countrymen at home, they endured the condescension and earned the praise of the British elite first-hand. They seem to have emerged from the experience more confidently Canadian and yet with an unshaken faith in the British Empire and a certainty that Canada would – and should – continue to make common cause with the British World. Britishness, in other words, remained central to their sense of Canadian national identity.

In the draft of a forward he had been asked to write for a history of Nova Scotia's 85th Battalion shortly after the war, Arthur Currie talked at length about the Canadian "nation," but justified the country's participation in the conflict by arguing that "we were fighting for our personal and moral liberty, so that every tradition which goes with the British flag should be upheld and allowed to endure."[53] The fact that the senior officers of the Canadian Corps would play only a minor role in the postwar intellectual and political life[54] of their country may reveal something about the direction English Canada subsequently took in the ongoing battle over the potential coexistence of imperialism and nationalism in Canada's identity.

{NOTES}

1 Edmonton Archives, William Griesbach Papers, misc. documents file, "Farewell to the 1st Brigade."

2 Utilizing as a base the thirty-four senior positions in the Canadian Corps, namely the Corps commander (and his two principal staff officers), four Divisional commanding officers (and their four principal staff officers), twelve Infantry Brigade commanding officers, five Divisional artillery commanding officers, the Corps artillery and heavy artillery commanding officers (and their two principal staff officers), the Machine Gun Corps commanding officer, and the Engineer commanding officer, fifty-two officers held these positions from June 7, 1917, when Arthur Currie took command of the Corps from Julian Byng, its last British commander. Of those fifty-two officers, some of whom held more than one of the posts during the period in question, thirty-one were Canadian-born Canadian officers, nine were British-born Canadian officers, eleven were British regulars (of whom one was Canadian born), and one was an ex-French regular who had immigrated to Canada. In other words, 77 per cent were "Canadians" and 21 per cent "British." Only four were francophones (one of those French by birth), and all but six were Protestants. Sources for this data include G.W.L. Nicholson, *Canadian Expeditionary Force: 1914–1919: The Official History of the Canadian Army in the First World War* (Ottawa: Queen's Printer, 1964), Appendix A, as well as selected files in the National Archives of Canada (NAC), Department of National Defence Papers, RG 24 and the Personnel Records of the Canadian Expeditionary Force, RG 150.

3 One of the earliest, and often quoted, is D.J. Goodspeed, *The Road Past Vimy: The Canadian Corps, 1914–1918* (Toronto: Macmillan, 1969), 93.

4 For instance, Robert Craig Brown, *Robert Laird Borden: A Biography*, vol. 2, *1914–1937* (Toronto: University of Toronto Press, 1980); John English, *The Decline of Politics: The Conservatives and the Party System, 1901–1920* (Toronto: University of Toronto Press, 1977); Ronald Haycock, *Sam Hughes: The Public Career of a Controversial Canadian* (Waterloo: Wilfrid Laurier University Press/Canadian War Museum, 1986); and Desmond Morton, *A Peculiar Kind of Politics: Canada's Overseas Ministry in the First World War* (Toronto: University of Toronto Press, 1982).

5 Only two senior officers have been the subject of biographies. There are three of Currie, including Daniel G. Dancocks, *Arthur Currie: A Biography* (Toronto: Methuen, 1985); A.M.J. Hyatt, *General Sir Arthur Currie: A Military Biography* (Toronto: University of Toronto Press/Canadian War Museum, 1987); and Hugh M. Urquhart, *Arthur Currie: The Biography of a Great Canadian* (Toronto: J.M. Dent, 1950). There is one on McNaughton: John Swettenham, *McNaughton*, vol. 1 (Toronto: Ryerson, 1968). McNaughton was portrayed by his biographer, John Swettenham,

as the wartime Canadian nationalist *par excellence*. Currie would probably rank second, though there is universal acceptance in the historiography that his defence of Canadian military interests was rooted in his Canadian "nationalism."

6 As with most scholars who write on the subject, the author struggles to find the appropriate term to use for "Canadian sentiment" or "national sympathies." Without question, nationalism – the common cultural (and other) characteristics that bind a people – exaggerates, or perhaps better, distorts what prevailed in Great War English Canada. Similarly, the "patriotism" of the time was not rooted in a singular devotion to Canada. Some have invoked the term "Dominionism" to represent this complicated brew of Anglo-imperial and local-national sentiments and identities holding sway in British Dominions. In this paper, "nationalism" has often been employed, but the reader should be aware of the constraints that the author attaches to its meaning.

7 Jonathan Vance, *Death So Noble: Memory, Meaning, and the First World War* (Vancouver: University of British Columbia Press, 1997).

8 Carl Berger, *The Sense of Power: Studies in the Ideas of Canadian Imperialism, 1867–1914* (Toronto: University of Toronto Press, 1970), 260–61.

9 Kent Fedorowich and Carl Bridge, "Mapping the British World," *Journal of Imperial and Commonwealth History* 31, no. 2 (May 2003): 6.

10 Neville Manley, "Britishness and Australia: Some Reflections," *Journal of Imperial and Commonwealth History* 31, no. 2 (May 2003): 121.

11 Fedorowich and Bridge, "Mapping the British World," 10–11.

12 Morton, *Peculiar Kind of Politics*, chap. 1–3.

13 NAC, David Watson Papers, MG30 E69, diary, 4 February 1917.

14 House of Lords Record Office, Ralph Blumenfeld Papers, BR-BY file, BY.15, Byng to Blumenfeld, 1 June 1916. Byng's predecessor, British general Edwin Alderson, attempted to do the same but with less success. British Library, Edward Hutton Papers, Add. Ms. 50088, Alderson to Hutton, 20 September 1915.

15 Swettenham, *McNaughton*, 1:174. For a good insight into how dependent the Canadian Corps was on British staff expertise, see Liddell Hart Centre for Military Archives (LHC), King's College, General Alan Brooke Papers, 5/2/1, notes for memoirs, 87–89.

16 NAC, CBC Records, RG41 BIII 1, *Flanders Fields* transcripts, vol. 21, Ross interview, tape 1.

17 NAC, George Perley Papers, MG27 II D12, Perley to Borden, 3 March 1917.

18 Kenneth Eyre, "Staff and Command in the Canadian Corps: The Canadian Militia 1896–1914 as a Source of Senior Officers" (master's thesis, Duke University, 1967), 118–34.

19 Stephen Harris, *Canadian Brass: The Making of a Professional Army, 1860–1939* (Toronto: University of Toronto Press, 1988), 118–29.

20 The precedent was the South African War. See Carmen Miller, "The Unhappy Warriors: Conflict and Nationality among the Canadian Troops during the South African War," *Journal of Imperial and Commonwealth History* 23, no. 1 (January 1995): 75–100, especially 97–99.

21 NAC, RG41, BIII 1, *Flanders Fields* transcripts, vol. 21, John Clark and Alex Ross interviews, and vol. 22, Duncan McIntyre interview.

22 NAC, Arthur Currie Papers, MG30 E100, vol. 43, personal diary, 3 May 1918.

23 House of Lords Record Office, Lloyd George Papers, LG/F/60/4/14, Currie to Geddes, undated (c.1925).

24 NAC, Richard Turner Papers, MG30 E46, vol. 11, file 79, Paterson to Turner, 22 April 1918.

25 On the development of *esprit de corps*, see Harris, *Canadian Brass*, 106.

26 NAC, Currie Papers, MG30 E100, vol. 43, personal diary, 7 November 1918; NAC, David Watson Papers, MG30 E69, diary, 7 November 1918.

27 NAC, Currie Papers, MG30 E100, vol. 1, General Correspondence, 1915–18, A–F file, 26 November 1918.

28 Ibid. Fully 20 per cent of all Canadian wartime losses were incurred from 8 August onward.

29 Ibid. On the repetition of the "one quarter of the German army" myth, see Daniel G. Dancocks, *Spearhead to Victory: Canada and the Great War* (Edmonton: Hurtig, 1987) and Shane Schreiber, *Shock Army of the British Empire: The Canadian Corps in the Last 100 Days of the Great War* (Westport, CT: Praeger, 1997), 132.

30 NAC, Currie Papers, MG30 E100, vol. 1, General Correspondence, 1915–18, G–L file, Currie to Kemp, 1 November 1918.

31 Public Record Office (PRO), Cabinet Records, CAB 103/210, Edmonds to Daniel, 9 January 1929.

32 Ibid., CAB 45/155, Macphail to Amery, 25 April 1926.

33 Ibid., CAB 45/156, Loomis to Duguid, undated.

34 Ibid., MacBrien to Lord Cavan, 24 November 1925.

35 Ibid., CAB 45/155, Currie to MacBrien, 1 June 1926.

36 Ibid., CAB 103/210, Edmonds memo, undated. See also CAB 45/130, Haldane to Edmonds, 28 January 1929.

37 Ibid., CAB 45/155, Edmonds to Milne, 30 April 1926.

38 LHC, General James Edmonds Papers, VI/9/163, Duguid to Edmonds, 13 August 1926.

39 Harris, *Canadian Brass*, 106.

40 PRO, CAB, 45/147, Currie memoire: Mount Sorrel, undated (1926).

41 LHC, Brooke Papers, 2/1/11, Radcliffe to Brooke, 8 January 1918; NAC, Currie Papers, MG30 E100, vol. 1, General Correspondence, 1915–18, A–F file, Currie to Bristol, 16 May 1918, and Currie to Carson, 20 February 1918; and NAC, Watson Papers, MG30 E69, diary, 27 January 1916.

42 Harris, *Canadian Brass*, 110 and 135–36. See also Hyatt, *General Sir Arthur Currie*, chap. 6.

43 Something the Australians agreed to do.

44 The BEF had adopted this measure in order to keep the same number of divisions in the field, while easing their reinforcement crisis. The Australians would follow suit later in the year. The Canadians were spared by the arrival of the first conscripts.

45 NAC, Edward Kemp Papers, MG27 II D9, vol. 132, file c-25, Currie to Kemp and Currie to General Lawrence, 27 March 1918. Hyatt, *General Sir Arthur Currie*, 98–102.

46 Harris, *Canadian Brass*, 143.

47 Patrick Brennan and Thomas Leppard, "How the Lessons Were Learned: Senior Commanders and the Moulding of the Canadian Corps after the Somme," in *Canadian Military History Since the 17th Century*, ed. Yves Tremblay (Ottawa: National Defence, 2001), 135–44. On the tactical innovation within British doctrine, see also Ian Brown, "Not Glamorous, but Effective: The Canadian Corps and the Set-Piece Attack, 1917–1918," *Journal of Military History* 58, no. 3 (July 1994): 421–44; Tim Cook, *No Place To Run: The Canadian Corps and Gas Warfare in the First World War* (Vancouver: University of British Columbia Press, 1999); and William Rawling, *Surviving Trench Warfare: Technology and the Canadian Corps, 1914–1918* (Toronto: University of Toronto Press, 1992).

48 For example, see NAC, Griesbach Papers, MG30 E15, vol. 5, file 34, Griesbach memo to 1st Division HQ, 12 August 1918 and vol. 3, file 16b, Macdonell to 1st Division, "Lessons Learnt from Recent Fighting," 1 September 1918.

49 British artillery comprised seven-ninths of the Canadian medium and heavy artillery at Vimy Ridge, for example, a situation that had changed little by the Last Hundred Days campaign.

50 NAC, RG 150, personnel files for Lt. Col. E.S. Doughty, Lt. Col. R.A. MacFarlane, Lt. Col. R. H. Palmer and Lt. Col. J.G. Weir. During the fierce fighting of the Last Hundred Days, these four officers, although serving as commanders of the 31st, 58th and 49th Infantry Battalions and the 2nd Machine Gun Battalion, respectively, were nonetheless permitted by Lt. Gen. Currie to leave their posts in order to attend the BEF's three-month-long senior officers course at Aldershot.

51 "Casting Daylight upon Magic: Deconstructing the Royal Tour of 1901 to Canada," *Journal of Imperial and Commonwealth History* 31, no. 2 (May 2003): 159.

52 This is a phenomenon widespread in the historiographies of the Dominions. See Fedorowich and Bridge, "Mapping the British World," 11.

53 Currie Papers, v.6, misc. correspondence, undated draft.

54 Only a handful of the fifty-two officers referred to in note 2 held national public office after the war. Brigadier-Generals Griesbach (who had been elected as a Unionist MP in 1917) and A.H. Macdonell were both made Conservative senators in 1921. Brigadier-Generals Robert Rennie and Victor Odlum ran unsuccessfully as Liberal candidates in the 1921 federal election. Brigadier-General J.A. Clark was elected as a Conservative MP in 1921, 1925, and 1926 and then retired, while Brigadier-General James Stewart was elected to parliament as a Conservative in 1930 but defeated in 1935. Most of these men returned to their pre-war business or profession after the war, and they may well have exercised a measure of political influence behind the scenes. Whether actively involved in politics or not, the great majority certainly held Conservative, pro-Empire sympathies.

CHAPTER 12

EMPIRE AND THE EVERYDAY:

BRITISHNESS AND IMPERIALISM
IN WOMEN'S LIVES IN THE GREAT WAR

*Paul Ward**

THE WORLD WARS WERE DRAMATIC EVENTS for women as well as men. Men of military age were expected to join the armed forces, fulfilling the supreme duty to the nation of being prepared to kill and die for their country. In their absence, young, active women were encouraged to contribute to the war effort by entering the workforce. Historians have focused on the roles of these active women – those who entered the munitions factories, the transport services, and the auxiliary paramilitary forces. During the Great War, in the United Kingdom, upwards of five million women workers contributed to the war effort in such ways. These women are seen as being let out of the cage, breaking the constraints of separate spheres and emerging into public spaces, even if only for the duration of the war, after which they were forced back to home and duty.[1] Such public activism, undertaken for a variety of motives, has been seen as having a profound effect on women's consciousness.[2] The impact of war, therefore, is seen as dramatic, changing women's lives, taking them out of the ordinary into the extraordinary. Susan Kingsley Kent argues that "the language of traditional femininity, of separate spheres for women and men, could not adequately articulate the experience and requirements of a war that failed to respect the boundaries between home and front, between civilian and soldier."[3] Antonia Lant makes a

* David Taylor and Sarah Bastow offered valuable comments on drafts of this paper. Thanks are owed also to Hilary Haigh, the University of Huddersfield archivist who drew my attention to the microfilms of the Colonies files in the Women at Work collection at the Imperial War Museum. I am grateful to the history division at the University of Huddersfield for enabling my research through time, funding, and a congenial atmosphere.

similar point about the "clashes between domestic ideals and women's wartime lives" during the Second World War, arguing that "wartime ideology, the discourse that explains mobilization, recruitment, fighting and killing, runs up against the peacetime ideology of separate spheres for men and women and the clear differentiation of men's and women's cultural, economic, and political contributions."[4] The majority of British women in the Great War, however, did not go into munitions factories or the auxiliary forces, or any other form of paid war work. Many were too young or too old, or continued to be housewives and mothers. Many middle- and upper-class women did not face the economic imperative to work but chose to participate voluntarily in the war effort, and it is possible to examine their ideological motives for doing so.

Aristocratic women, in particular, had a pre-war tradition of organizing voluntary effort and continued to play a role of social leadership during wartime. In Ireland, Lady Aberdeen, wife of the viceroy, was central to the voluntary patriotic war effort. In Australia, Lady Helen Munro Ferguson, wife of the governor-general, organized the Red Cross; in New Zealand, Lady Liverpool, wife of the governor, set up her own patriotic fund; and in Canada, the Imperial Order Daughters of the Empire was led by women of privileged social position.[5] But voluntary effort also spread far down the social scale because most women in the Empire did not undertake paid work during the war. As Martin Pugh points out, "Even in 1918 when some 6 million women were officially in paid employment, the substantial majority of women still remained at home."[6] This was recognized across the Empire during the war. Mrs. George McLaren Brown, in her wartime account of the Canadian War Contingent Association, is worth quoting at length:

> When, nearly two years ago, the call to arms first sounded, the
> men in Canada, like men of British birth all the world over,
> at once gave up their usual occupations and hastened to offer
> themselves in defence of the Empire they loved so well. But the
> breach they left behind in the body politic was enormous and
> immediately there arose and went humming round the globe
> the question: "Who will fill this breach – who will carry on the
> work and duties our men perforce have had to lay aside?" And in
> Canada, as in all parts of the Empire, with one voice the women
> cried, "We can and we will." Right loyally they have proved
> that this claim was no idle boast. Everywhere, in factories,
> warehouses and shops, in hospitals, schools and offices, in the

City and on the land, the women have stepped in and shouldered the burden. But behind those splendid women were thousands and thousands of others – no less eager, no less willing, but who for many reasons were unable to leave their homes and go outside to take up the men's work. "We cannot make munitions nor till the land," they said, "nor go into the offices or the schools, but right here in our homes there are many other things we can do to help our men."[7]

In this essay, I turn my attention to the women who did not leave the home and examine their social, cultural, individual, and emotional responses to the war. I examine the women for whom war did not challenge their traditional gender roles, and I look at the everyday, private lives of women to discuss the impact of war on their sense of themselves as British. As Michael Billig comments, "National identity in established nations is remembered because it is embedded in routines of life, which constantly remind, or 'flag,' nationhood."[8] In wartime, women were integrated into the nation by the routine events of their lives, not just the dramatic and extraordinary. Women in the home confronted the realities of war at their breakfast, lunch, and dinner tables and in their leisure time. The banal, passive acts of eating margarine and knitting became part of "being British" and implied a demand for recognition of women's citizenship. This was frequently seen as an imperial Britishness, since the war enhanced the sense of the Empire's common purpose. This imperial, British, and domestic role did not necessarily entail the demand for the vote in Britain since war enabled many women to gain citizenship within the domestic sphere.[9] Citizenship entailed patriotic participation, which enabled membership in the national community for women in the home. I will also make some comparative comments on "British" women in the Dominions, tentatively suggesting that the domestic setting of participating in the war effort contributed to a sense of Britishness across the white Dominions, even where the distinctive national identities of the Dominions were developing. Women in Britain and Greater Britain saw the bonds of Empire and Britishness augmented by the war, not only because they went into the factories but also because they stayed in the home and made patriotic meals.

Themes such as margarine and knitting sound remarkably flippant when discussing a war in which one million men, as well as around one thousand women, of the British Empire were killed. A "pervasiveness of death" invaded everyday life.[10] Seventeen thousand men from

New Zealand died, 60,000 from Canada, about 60,000 from Australia, and around 7,000 from South Africa. Three million people in Britain suffered the loss of a close family member, and such losses reinforced familial identities, as mothers, wives, sisters, aunts, and cousins (and as fathers, brothers, uncles, too). Because the war effort was imperial, and because the British-born in the Dominions were more likely to enlist than the non-British-born, war casualties often brought home the imperial context of the war. For example, Florence Lockwood, a British Liberal and suffragist, listed her male relatives who were serving in the forces. As well as nephews and cousins in the local Yorkshire territorial force, she had relatives in the Royal Irish Rifles, Gordon Highlanders, and Australian fleet.[11] Grief often invaded every waking moment of the bereaved.[12] This was not, however, the only experience of the war that imperial Britons had. Miss E. Airey of Norfolk, whose three brothers joined the armed forces in 1914, experienced several war years without personal grief. She wrote in her memoir of the war: "In the Spring of 1918 came the news that my brother had been killed in France. This was a great tragedy for us *and the first real sorrow that I had known.*"[13] In order to appreciate the full and varied impact of the Great War on identity, we need to examine the experiences of people before, as well as after, grief and sorrow entered their lives.

Nina MacDonald expressed well the concurrence between the public and domestic aspects of patriotism:

> Sing a song of War-time,
> Soldiers marching by,
> Crowds of people standing,
> Waving them "Good-bye."
> When the crowds are over,
> Home we go to tea,
> Bread and margarine to eat,
> War economy![14]

Such verses draw attention to the construction of the notion of the "home front" in the Great War. This was a war to be fought not only on the battlefields but in the houses (homes) of the citizens (subjects) of the United Kingdom and the Empire. Home and nation became synonymous terms. The *Win the War Cookery Book* exhorted: "The British fighting line shifts and extends and now *you* are in it. The struggle is not only on land and sea; it is in *your* larder, *your* kitchen and *your* dining room. Every meal *you* serve is now literally a battle."[15] This meant that the routine activities of people uninvolved in the war in any other way took on national significance. Viola Bawtree, living at home in Sussex with her parents and two sisters, was too young to play an active role; nonetheless, she "did her bit" for the nation, as she explained in her "war diary": "We three girls eat margarine now instead of butter. Sylvia says we do it because we can't afford butter, but I like to imagine we're doing it because every patriotic person does so, and because we're loyal Britons – it goes down easier that way."[16] While this quotation suggests a consolatory purpose, that patriotism made margarine less distasteful, it also shows how in wartime the most commonplace activities brought people face to face with their membership in the nation.

Sometimes children were not entirely free agents in having their membership in the nation and Empire brought to their attention. The Boys' and Girls' League of South Africa encouraged "a sacrifice of a child's personal property" through regular collections "for the relief of distress occasioned by the war." This was imposed patriotism.[17] Viola Bawtree's actions, however, indicate the willingness of many of those who could not participate in the war except from within the home. Viola felt that she could make some contribution to the financing of the war through her pocket money by initiating her War Savings Card: "It's a great treat to feel you're doing something for your country. To get my first [6d] stamp I've gone without a pot of Glycola and shan't mind chapped and rough hands a bit for the cause."[18] Here Viola reinforced precisely the nature of the nation as "imagined community." She felt her membership in that community not only in the abstract but also in the day-to-day of pocket money and chapped hands. We see this again in the war memoir of Annie Purbrook, forty-nine years old in 1914 and married to the owner of a small printing works:

> My maid has like hundreds of others, gone to munition work. Of course, they earn more.... So, to-day, many ladies who had hitherto only planned and supervised the work of the home are perhaps doing a great part or even the whole [of the housework], and sometimes the washing also. They carry on cheerfully on the whole and feel that they too are taking their share in this huge enterprise.[19]

This experience of war being brought down to the level of the prosaic and mundane often occurred within an imperial context. Empire Day of 1917, for example, was used to read King George V's proclamation on food economy from the town halls of the United Kingdom.[20] Throughout the Empire, a similar turn to food economy was being emphasized. In Canada, women were urged to "eat fish as a patriotic duty"; the food controller explained that "all persons in ordering their food ought to consider the needs of Great Britain and her Allies…for wheat, beef, bacon, and fats, and the Canada Food Board desires the public to do everything possible to make these commodities available for export by eating as little as possible of them."[21] The activities of daily life were being accommodated to the desire to serve the nation and Empire in wartime. Such necessities were sometimes taken a step further by portraying the sacrifices being made as heroic. In February 1916, *The Times* published a letter from a middle-class household in which the male writer explained that he and his wife had agreed to aid the nation in its time of need. The first pledge was unlikely to cause undue hardship to the family, since it stated that "the servants must take 25 per cent less wages." The other nine pledges imposed a range of minor restrictions on the family, such as "no casual entertaining," "if any golf, no caddies," and "rigid economy in food: no soups, entrees, sweets…or fruit except from our own garden; only joints, plain puddings, and simplest food." The letter further explained what this meant in practice: "At breakfast we have come to a sort of Continental breakfast with porridge and marmalade added. Only on Sundays do we now make the acquaintance with the friendly kipper or eggs and bacon."[22] Again here the breakfast table had come to symbolize patriotic commitment. And that the breakfast table existed in every household had the effect of making easier the imagining of the nation. Of course, such themes were the subject of wide-scale propaganda. Even before the war, the British Women's Patriotic League had answered the question "How can I show my patriotism?" with the command: "By *always* buying British or Empire made goods" and "By bringing up children to do the same."[23] In wartime, when frugality was called for from all ranks in society, the most famous breakfast table in the nation became the source of example as the royal family called on the nation to eat less bread.[24]

As the war continued, food shortages caused considerable annoyance but they enabled many women to feel that they were contributing to the war effort even without leaving their routine domestic spaces. Helen Harpin, living at home with her parents, wrote to her fiancé on the Western Front, "No, the rationing is *not* very nice tho' we are bearing up remarkably well." To stress her continuing commitment to the war effort, she congratulated him on his military achievements: "Your enterprise on the 28th must have been very successful. I'm particularly glad about the prisoners & I hope you have killed lots more (Yes war isn't good for natures)."[25] In this case, the domestic hardship of war (this was limited in her case, since Helen had also written of the degrading nature of looking for servants) was not translated into opposition to the war effort but was borne, stoically, alongside a continuing patriotic commitment. This too could be displayed with food and drink. The Reverend Andrew Clark, in rural Essex, noted the patriotic activities of the Trittons, the most prominent of local families. One of the daughters, Lucy, recruited in the local villages; another, Marjorie, collected novels to send to the front; and a third, Annette (Nettie), compiled a roll of honour to place in the church porch. Their mother, meanwhile, invited soldiers to tea in her home: on one occasion Rev. Clark counted sixty-one men.[26] The soldiers were fighting for home, and most women, by remaining in their domestic setting, made more real the images of home, and therefore the nation.[27] In 1915 the *Spectator* considered housewives to be succeeding in their domestic patriotism, arguing that "it is a splendid reflection on the influence of family life that it is the married men who measure and accept their responsibilities with conspicuous readiness. They have learned that a home is a thing worth fighting for."[28] These women were doing more than committing themselves to the war effort; they were reinforcing the commitment of the soldiers. The passive patriotism of the table had developed into active patriotism, by which women could show their commitment to the war effort in the routine activities of their lives. Entertaining soldiers in the home, whether in Britain, Australia, or Canada, gave such women a role in defining the British World, and though that role may have been limited by ideas associated with what was acceptable for a woman to do, it still bestowed citizenship by enabling membership in the imperial nation.

Women's patriotism in the home extended into their leisure time, into areas where they were able to make choices about their participation in the war effort. Much of this was done without breaking out of accepted gender roles. Mrs. McLaren Brown, in emphasizing the role played in the war effort by non-employed Canadian women, described how their domestic patriotic activities brought them out of the home but kept them within separate spheres:

> We can knit socks and mufflers and mittens, we can sew shirts
> and pyjamas and underwear, we can make cakes, sweets and
> jam, we can give tobacco, gum, candles and soap, and a hundred
> other things; and we can organise committees and centres to

collect them, pack them up, and send them overseas as comforts for our fighting men, who have little time and opportunity to find comforts for themselves.[29]

Perhaps the most widely undertaken patriotic act by women in wartime was knitting. The *Saturday Review* described Britain in September 1914 as "a vast knitting machine."[30] This activity was widely mocked, both at the time and subsequently. It did not receive the hostility provoked by the practice of giving out white feathers, but it certainly attracted ridicule.[31] Two *Punch* cartoons serve to show this apparently affectionate ridicule. The first, from 1914, shows a young woman struggling to learn how to knit to produce a pair of mittens, which leave the British soldier in the trenches baffled as to their use, but by applying his ingenuity he discovers a way to keep his face, feet, and hands warm while he smokes his pipe.[32] The second has an officer holding up a sock while his auntie sits in her armchair knitting another. "Do you know, Aunty, I can get both my feet into one of these socks you've made for me?" he says. "But surely, my dear," she replies, "it's not so easy to walk that way?"[33] Arthur Marwick reports that "it was said that many men in the trenches used these unwanted, and often unsuitable, items for cleaning their rifles and wiping their cups and plates."[34] Other representations of knitting were much kinder. Jessie Pope, the most renowned wartime British female patriotic verse writer, established the important emotional connection over geographical distance between the knitter and the soldier:

> Shining pins that dart and click
> In the fireside's sheltered space
> Check the thoughts that cluster thick –
> *20 plain and then decrease …*
>
> Never used to living rough,
> Lots of things he'd got to learn;
> Wonder if he's warm enough –
> *Knit 2, catch 2, knit 1, turn …*
>
> Wonder if he's fighting now,
> What he's done an' where he's been;
> He'll come out on top some how –
> *Slip 1, knit 2, purl 14.*[35]

The Ladies' Working Part of the Good Hope Red Cross Society recorded how none of the clothing, pillowslips, or comforts they had sent to South African soldiers had been ready-made but that "every article supplied…has been a labour of love."[36] Bruce Scates shows that, in the Australian case, "enormous emotional labour was invested in even the most prosaic commodities."[37] Susan Kingsley Kent notes that the outbreak of war reconfirmed traditional gender roles, which had been under threat from the feminist activity of the suffragettes and suffragists in Edwardian Britain. The war brought the expectation that men would join the army, and this in turn had consequences for women's roles. One of the few acceptable forms of active patriotism for women was knitting. As Caroline Playne remarked in her 1931 history of the war, "The great era of knitting set in; men should fight but women should knit."[38] Mrs. C.S. Peel in her late 1920s history recalled how

we knitted socks (some of them of unusual shape), waistcoats, helmets, comforters, mitts, body belts. We knitted at theatres, in trains and trams, in parks and parlours, in the intervals of eating in restaurants, of serving in canteens. Men knitted, children knitted, a little girl promoted to four needles anxiously asked her mother, "Mummie, do you think I shall *live* to finish this sock?"[39]

The reference to men knitting is worth a brief comment. The 1870 Elementary Education Act had made it compulsory for girls to learn to knit, but it had also encouraged boys to learn.[40] Peel also recorded how during wartime women donned uniforms in public as "the outward and visible sign of their patriotism," visually announcing their entry into the public sphere, whatever the limits.[41] Female tram and bus conductors in Britain often encountered hostility, yet trams and buses were parts of the public sphere where women could be seen conducting acts of domesticity, such as knitting, for patriotic purposes. Florence Lockwood, for example, saw it as worth recording in her diary: "Ladies knitting in the tram car, on our way to Slaithwaite…. Territorials want warm clothes – sleeping helmets & gloves."[42]

Barbara McLaren, in a propagandist book published in 1917, suggested that "if the complete history ever comes to be written of the work of women with their needles during the war, it will reveal an outstanding record of patient, loyal, skilful achievement, and an output of which the figures can only be described as phenomenal."[43] The Queen Mary's Needlework Guild, for example, produced 15,577,911 articles during the war. It had branches throughout the Empire.[44] Other patriotic women specialized: Lady Smith-Dorrien organized the sewing of brightly coloured small bags for wounded soldiers to safeguard their valuables. By May 1917, 1,833,194 bags had been sent.[45] Katherine, Duchess of Atholl, a Scottish aristocrat, organized the knitting of a garment that could be worn under the kilts of the Highland regiments. Within three weeks of making her appeal, fifteen thousand had been sent.[46] South Africa had a veils fund "for the purpose of supplying veils for the men going to German sw [Africa] where the torment of flies & desert made life without them intolerable.... A C'ttee of ladies bought the stuff & volunteers made up the veils."[47] In New Zealand, Miria Woodbine Pomare, wife of the MP for Western Maori, spun wool yarn for sea-boot stockings.[48] The recording of the numerical achievements of this voluntary knitting and sewing effort suggests that it was felt necessary to validate the worth of such organizations.

But these organizations were made up of individuals, all of whom had their own motives for participating. Mrs. Peel remarked that knitting "was comforting to our nerves...and comforting to think that the results of our labours might save some man something of hardship and misery, for always the knowledge of what our men suffered haunted us."[49] In addition to being patriotic, the act of knitting could close the distance between women at home and men at the front. Helen Harpin sent her fiancé socks as a mark of her affection for him, though that did not preclude patriotic motivations.[50] Others joined knitting circles for social purposes.[51] Ada McGuire, though, revealed the meaning of knitting to her. "I am busy knitting woollen helmets for the soldiers," she wrote to a friend in the United States in the midst of a letter that explained her attitude to the war. Expressing her patriotism, she continued: "It is hard to realise what a love one has for one's country till that country is threatened and threatened by such a foe! We cannot underestimate Germany's power – we will need to strain all our resources to crush their hateful arrogance." She wished that she were a man so that she could enlist, but noted that "of course it is easy to say so when it is impossible." She was restricted to knitting, but that was an expression of her integration into the nation and the Empire: "We are all tremendously eager to show how loyal we are. We all think *imperially* now."[52]

Knitting was banal, but it included women in the war effort; it "flagged" the nation to them. Given its banality, other banalities intervened. Ada McGuire expressed her boredom with the task in hand: "I have been making socks & helmets but I cannot get a great amount done as I have not much time & it takes a long time knitting a pair of socks. If only *one* sock would do."[53] In those days of the dismembering of the male, others had solutions to the "technical" problems of knitting socks.[54] Miss G.M. West, working in a Red Cross hospital, recorded in her diary in 1915: "Aunt Maggie has sent me a sock. Enclosed was a note saying that she had meant to make a pair but all the wool got used up on one, but perhaps there was some poor fellow who had lost one leg & would find it useful."[55]

Examination of almost any aspect of daily life would show how the war intervened to bring the nation and Empire into women's lives.[56] This intervention included tensions between the language of traditional femininity and the encouragement to enter the public sphere. Women were pulled by contradictory pressures to leave the home to participate in the war effort and to stay home because the soldiers were fighting for homes with women within them. Many women resolved this contradiction by remaining within the home *and* participating in the war effort. The Great War did disrupt the private sphere, but it did not destroy it. It transformed even the home into part of what Denise Riley calls the "social" sphere.[57] It became an arena where women could engage in the war effort. The home front meant not only Britain and the Dominions but literally incorporated the home. Women were able to express their citizenship within the domestic sphere. Nicoletta Gullace argues that during the war, citizenship became defined by service to the nation and not by the male body.[58] Many women did give service to the nation outside of the home, in paid employment and in auxiliary military services, but when women's suffrage came to be discussed in Britain, it was women over thirty, those least likely to have entered the munitions factories and auxiliary military forces, who were granted the vote. As Lord Selborne argued, such women would be a "steadying influence" amidst an enlarged electorate.[59] In Canada, too, some women were granted the vote as recognition of their patriotism. The Military Voters Act granted the vote to women in the armed forces, but the Wartime Elections Act gave the vote to the female relatives of servicemen – the women most likely to have knitted and put together parcels of comforts.[60]

Most historians recognize that the Great War played a profound part in the development of distinctive dominion nationalisms. The place of Gallipoli in the formation of Australian and New Zealand identities is rightly emphasized, and Marilyn Lake argues convincingly that at Gallipoli men gave birth to the Australian nation, rendering women invisible.[61] However, one Australian schoolteacher showed the way in which some women did share in the strengthening of Australian national identity at Gallipoli. She wrote: "DEAR AUSTRALIAN BOYS,

Every Australian woman's heart this week is thrilling with pride, with exultation, and while her eyes fill with tears she springs up as I did when I read the story in Saturday's *Argus* and says, 'Thank God, I am an Australian.'"[62] Dominion differences could also be identified at the day-to-day level. Sister MacAdams, a dietician at the Ontario Military Hospital in Orpington, Kent, who was standing for the Alberta legislature from afar, became more aware of her difference from the English during her service in England. This difference was expressed through a woman's proper realm when she was interviewed by the *Weekly Dispatch*. "'We Canadians,' she said with a smile lighting up her face, 'will be glad to get a good meal when the war is over!' She says English people have different ideas about the kind of food that is required," the paper reported.[63] Edith Woods described South African women's patriotic activities in relation to those of women in Britain, noting how [South African] "women held street collections, concerts, entertainments and sales.... This was much the same as in England, except that at our sales there are fewer pictures & objets de vertu & more pumpkins & produce."[64]

Stuart Ward points out that "successive generations of historians have set out to identify the earliest sprouting of youthful, assertive national-ist behaviour and, having done so, to explain why these signs of early promise failed to achieve the full bloom of national independence."[65] The expression of Australian, South African, Canadian, and New Zealand national identity was not incompatible with the expression of a "British race patriotism" or "Britishness." As Scotland used the war to emphasize its distinctive role in the war effort through the building of a separate Scottish war memorial in Edinburgh castle, so too did the Dominions through their commemoration of the war dead.[66] Phillip Buckner and Carl Bridge have pointed out that national identities in the Dominions were frequently associated with building "Better Britains" rather than with repudiating Britishness.[67]

It has sometimes been said that parts of the British population re-mained indifferent to the British Empire because their material needs remained paramount.[68] A similar argument might be used to explain how women, confined to the home, could also remain indifferent to the nation and Empire.[69] Yet in wartime, the distance between the material and the ideological was narrowed considerably. Hence, in the Great War, everyday actions such as eating margarine and knitting brought the British World into the home. British women came face to face with their Britishness at the breakfast table and with their knitting needles, wherever they were in the Empire. They fulfilled their role with an understanding of the imperial context of their actions. At the beginning of the war, Mrs. Arthur Morrison, organizer of the first Union Jack Flag Day, held in Glasgow to raise money for the war effort, explained how she hit upon the idea:

> It occurred to me that if a street collection was held it would raise a large sum of money in the least possible time with a minimum of expense and from the magnificent manner in which the whole Empire had responded to the call of the Motherland I decided that no more suitable emblem could be sold than the Union Jack.[70]

At the end of the war, Queen Mary, patron of imperial knitters around the world, thanked "the women of the Empire," who had formed a "sisterhood of suffering and service." Women, she said, had "proved their courage, steadfastness, and ability." The reward for this service was that "plans are afoot for bringing to an end the existence of such bad and crowded housing as makes home life almost impossible."[71] The impact of the war, therefore, confirmed the traditional and "British" role of women in a context of domesticity.

{NOTES}

1 Gail Braybon and Penny Summerfield, *Out of the Cage: Women's Experiences in Two World Wars* (London: Pandora, 1987); Deidre Beddoe, *Back to Home and Duty: Women between the Wars, 1918–1939* (London: Pandora, 1989).

2 Angela Woollacott, *On Her Their Lives Depend: Munitions Workers in the Great War* (Berkeley: University of California Press, 1994), 5: "Not all women experienced greater gender consciousness during the war, but the evidence suggests that, at least for some women, wartime work created gender-related growth in esteem and self-assertiveness."

3 Susan Kingsley Kent, *Making Peace: The Reconstruction of Gender in Interwar Britain* (Princeton: Princeton University Press, 1993), 36.

4 Antonio Lant, *Blackout: Reinventing Women for Wartime British Cinema* (Princeton: Princeton University Press, 1991), 17.

5 Eileen Reilly, "Women and Voluntary War Work," in *Ireland and the Great War: "A War to Unite Us All?"* ed. Adrian Gregory and Senia Paseta (Manchester: Manchester University Press, 2002), 49–72; Melanie Oppenheimer, "'The Best PM for the Empire in War?': Lady Helen Munro Ferguson and the Australian Red Cross Society, 1914–1920," *Australian Historical Studies* 33 (2002): 108–24; Heather Nicholson, *The Loving Stitch: A History of Knitting and Spinning in New Zealand* (Auckland: Auckland University Press, 1998), 79–80; Katie Pickles,

Female Imperialism and National Identity: Imperial Order Daughters of the Empire (Manchester: Manchester University Press, 2002), chap. 2.

6 Martin Pugh, *Women and the Women's Movement in Britain 1914–1959* (Basingstoke: Macmillan, 1991), 12.

7 Imperial War Museum, London (IWM), Colonies Files, Women at Work Collection, Mrs. George McLaren Brown, "Canadian War Contingent Association," in *Women of the Empire in War Time* (microfilm).

8 Michael Billig, *Banal Nationalism* (London: Sage, 1995).

9 Anne Summers explores the way in which women asserted their citizenship as military nurses in *Angels and Citizens: British Women as Military Nurses, 1854–191*, 2nd ed. (Newbury: Threshold, 2000).

10 *Authority, Identity and the Great War*, ed. Frans Coetzee and Marilyn Shevin-Coetzee (Oxford: Berghahn 1995), xix.

11 Kirklees Archives, Huddersfield, KC329, Florence Lockwood, unpublished diary, vol. 1, September 1914. Lockwood marked their names in red as they became casualties.

12 See, for example, Bob Bushaway, "Name upon Name: The Great War and Remembrance," in *Myths of the English*, ed. Roy Porter (Cambridge: Polity, 1992); J.M. Winter, "Communities in Mourning," in Coetzee and Shevin-Coetzee, eds., *Authority, Identity*, 325–55; *The Politics of War, Memory and Commemoration*, ed. T.G. Ashplant et al. (London: Routledge, 2000).

13 IWM Department of Documents (DD), London, 81/9/1, Miss E. Airey, typescript memoir (my italics).

14 *The Virago Book of Women's War Poetry and Verse*, ed. Catherine Reilly (London: Virago, 1997), 69. The tune is the children's nursery song, "Sing a Song of Sixpence."

15 Quoted in Pugh, *Women and the Women's Movement*, 13.

16 IWM, DD, 91/5/1 "Episodes in the Great War 1916 from the Diaries of Viola Bawtree," 23 February 1916. Rationing of foodstuffs was not introduced until January 1918. Margarine and butter were rationed in February in London and the Home Counties. Many women "monumentalized" the war through writing war in diaries; see Paul Ward, "'Women of Britain Say Go': Women's Patriotism in the First World War," *Twentieth-Century British History* 12 (2001): 27.

17 IWM Colonies Files, Unattributed press cutting (microfilm). See Jonathan F. Vance, *Death So Noble: Memory, Meaning and the First World War* (Vancouver: University of British Columbia Press, 1997), 234–41, for children and patriotism in Canada.

18 IWM, DD, 91/5/1 "Episodes in the Great War 1916," 5 March 1916.

19 IWM, DD 97/3/1, Annie Purbrook, memoir, 8.

20 Kirklees Archives, Lockwood diary, 24 May 1917.

21 Quoted in Robert Craig Brown and Ramsay Cook, *Canada 1896–1921: A Nation Transformed* (Toronto: McLelland and Stewart, 1974), 238.

22 *The Times*, 2 February 1916, quoted in *Human Documents of the Lloyd George Era*, ed. Royston Pike (London: George Allen and Unwin, 1972), 229.

23 IWM DD, B05/3/14, British Women's Patriotic League.

24 Pike, *Human Documents*, 211–12.

25 IWM DD, CON SHELF, H. M. Harpin, letters, 8 March 1918, 3 May 1918.

26 *Echoes of the Great War: The Diary of the Reverend Andrew Clark 1914–1919*, ed. James Munson (Oxford: Oxford University Press, 1985), 43, 78, 79, 66, 98, 145.

27 One of the roles of those women who left Britain's shores to serve in France in the WAAC was to create "home from home" for the men. Mrs. Grace Curnock explained in 1917 how "British women have a wonderful power – a power which is the keynote of the nation's worldwide greatness, they carry Home wherever they go. At Christmas the men will be made happier from the knowledge that in WAAC camps and YMCA huts, British women are keeping the great festival with all the traditions of home." Elizabeth Crossthwait, "'The Girl behind the Man behind the Gun': The Women's Army Auxiliary Corps, 1914–18," in *Our Work, Our Lives, Our Words: Women's History and Women's Work*, ed. Leonore Davidoff and Belinda Westover (Basingstoke: Macmillan, 1986), 167.

28 Quoted in Nicoletta F. Gullace, *"The Blood of Our Sons": Men, Women and the Renegotiation of British Citizenship during the Great War* (New York: Palgrave Macmillan, 2002), 114.

29 IWM, Colonies Files, Mrs. McLaren Brown, "Canadian War Contingent Association" (microfilm).

30 "Women in War Time," *Saturday Review*, 27 March 1915.

31 Nicoletta Gullace, "White Feathers and Wounded Men: Female Patriotism and the Memory of the Great War," *Journal of British Studies* 36 (1997): 178–206.

32 "The History of a Pair of Mittens," *Punch*, 18 November 1914, in Richard Rutt, *A History of Hand Knitting* (London: Batsford, 1987), 140.

33 *Punch*, 23 January 1918, in Cally Blackman, "Handknitting in Britain from 1908–39: The Work of Marjory Tillotson," *Textile History* 29 (1998): 187.

34 Arthur Marwick, *Women at War 1914–1918* (London: Fontana/Imperial War Museum, 1977), 35.

35 Jessie Pope, "Socks," in Reilly, *Virago Book of Women's War Poetry*, 89.

36 IWM Colonies Files, The Good Hope Red Cross Society, report (microfilm).

37 Bruce Scates, "The Unknown Sock Knitter: Voluntary Work, Emotional Labour, Bereavement and the Great War," *Labour History* 81 (2001): 31.

38 Kent, *Making Peace*, 15.

39 Mrs. C.S. Peel, *How We Lived Then 1914–1918: A Sketch of Social and Domestic Life during the War* (London: John Lane/The Bodley Head, 1929), 60.

40 Blackman, "Handknitting in Britain," 179.

41 Susan R. Grayzel, "'The Outward and Visible Sign of Her Patriotism': Women, Uniforms and National Service during the First World War," *Twentieth-Century British History* 8 (1997): 178–206.

42 Kirklees Archives, Lockwood, diary, 14 October 1914.

43 Barbara McLaren, *Women of the War* (London: Hodder and Stoughton, 1917), 85.

44 *Queen Mary's Needlework Guild: Its Work in the Great War* (London: n.p., n.d. [1919?]). See also file IWM Department of Printed Books (DPB), B.O. 2/2. An example of a local variant is the Queen's Appeal for Socks Fund founded in Johannesburg in August 1914.

45 IWM DPB, B.O. 2/19.

46 Sue Bruley, *Women in Britain since 1900* (Basingstoke: Palgrave, 1999), 43. There was

also a "Kingswear Fund for Trawlers' Seaboot Stockings for the Fleet." Marwick, *Women at War*, 143.

47 IWM Colonies Files, Edith Woods to WE Dowding, 19 June 1916 (microfilm).

48 Nicholson, *The Loving Stitch*, 84.

49 Quoted in Blackman, "Handknitting in Britain," 188.

50 IWM DD, Harpin, Letters, 22 March 1918.

51 For example, IWM DD, Purbrook, "Memoir," 3.

52 IWM DD, 96/31/1, Ada McGuire, letter, 28 August 1914.

53 Ibid., 22 September 19[16?].

54 Joanna Bourke, *Dismembering the Male: Men's Bodies, Britain and the Great War* (London: Reaktion, 1995).

55 IWM DD, 77/156/1, Miss G.M. West, diary, 10 June 1915.

56 Motherhood was a central aspect of women's lives that was made patriotic in wartime; see Gullace, *Blood of Our Sons*, 53–69 and Joy Damousi, "Private Loss, Public Mourning: Motherhood, Memory and Grief in Australia during the Inter-War Years," *Women's History Review* 8 (1999): 365–78. See also Scates, "The Unknown Sock Knitter," for women's role in the process of others' mourning.

57 Denise Riley, *"Am I That Name?" Feminism and the Category of "Women" in History* (Basingstoke: Macmillan, 1988).

58 Gullace, *Blood of Our Sons*.

59 Quoted in John Turner, *British Politics and the Great War: Coalition and Conflict 1915–1918* (New Haven: Yale University Press, 1992), 120. See also Kent, *Making Peace*, chap. 4, and Martin Pugh, *Women's Suffrage in Great Britain 1867–1928* (London: Historical Association, 1980).

60 Brown and Cook, *Canada 1896–1921*, 271. For a discussion of women and citizenship in Australia, see Marilyn Lake, "The Inviolable Woman: Feminist Conceptions of Citizenship in Australia, 1900–1945," *Gender and History* 8 (1996): 197–211.

61 Marilyn Lake, "Mission Impossible: How Men Gave Birth to the Australian Nation: Nationalism, Gender and Other Seminal Acts," *Gender and History* 4 (1992): 305–22. See also Jeff Kershen, "The Great War Soldier as Nation Builder in Canada and Australia," in *Canada and the Great War*, ed. Briton C. Busch (Montreal: McGill-Queen's University Press, 2003).

62 Quoted in W. F. Mandle, *Going It Alone: Australia's National Identity in the Twentieth Century* (Harmondsworth: Allen Lane, 1978).

63 *Weekly Dispatch*, 29 July 1917.

64 IWM Colonies Files, Edith Woods to WE Dowding, 19 June 1916 (microfilm).

65 Stuart Ward, *Australia and the British Embrace: The Demise of the Imperial Ideal* (Melbourne: Melbourne University Press, 2001), 6.

66 National Library of Scotland, Acc. 4714, Scottish National War Memorial folder 1923, *Report of the Committee on the Utilisation of Edinburgh Castle for the Purpose of a Scottish National War Memorial*, Cd 279, HMSO, 1919. The London war museum became the Imperial War Museum.

67 P.A. Buckner and Carl Bridge, "Reinventing the British World," *The Round Table* 368 (2003): 79.

68 For example, Richard Price, *An Imperial War and the British Working Class: Working-Class Attitudes and Reactions to the Boer War* (London: Routledge and Kegan Paul, 1972).

69 For example, Virginia Woolf, *Three Guineas* (New York: Harcourt Brace, 1938).

70 IWM, Women at Work Collection, BO 2/52/16, Flag Days.

71 *Morning Post*, 5 December 1918.

CHAPTER 13

BRITISHNESS, SOUTH AFRICANNESS, AND THE FIRST WORLD WAR

John Lambert *

THE FIRST WORLD WAR WAS A DEFINING EVENT in the history of South Africa's English-speaking community. Over a hundred thousand white South African men, mostly of British stock, served in South African regiments, while many enlisted in imperial units, the Royal Navy, and Royal Flying Corps.[1] The war, and particularly the Somme offensive at Delville Wood in July 1916, gave English-speakers an intense pride in the role played by the Union of South Africa. Until the 1950s, the legend of the "Springboks on the Somme" retained as potent a memory for English-speakers as did Gallipoli for Australians and New Zealanders, and Vimy Ridge for Canadians. The bravery of the 1st Infantry Brigade and the losses it suffered on the Somme became etched into their consciousness and helped shape the way in which they perceived themselves as South Africans.

This chapter examines how English-speaking South Africans experienced the war and how it contributed to their image of themselves both as British and as South African. Most of them, even those who were second- and third-generation South Africans, regarded themselves and South Africa as an integral part of the British World and, when war broke out in 1914, accepted that, as British subjects, it was their duty to support the mother country. Their experiences during the war, however, and the camaraderie and dangers they experienced as soldiers, and which they shared with Afrikaners, also nurtured a deep pride in

* I gratefully acknowledge the financial assistance of the University of South Africa and of the National Research Foundation. I am indebted for advice and criticisms from Burridge Spies, Alex Mouton, and Bridget Theron.

being South African. In this way, the war was pivotal in encouraging the development among English-speakers of South Africanism, an ideology that had its origins earlier in the century. Espoused by the former Boer leaders, Louis Botha and Jan Smuts, and given political expression in their South African Party (SAP), South Africanism aimed at reconciling and uniting both white language groups in a South Africa that was an integral part of the British Empire.[2]

As was evident in the Calgary British World conference, while there is ongoing interest in the other "old Dominions" in the way in which the First World War was pivotal in shaping their national identities within the British World, South Africa's English-speakers tend to suffer a collective amnesia when it comes to the way in which it shaped their South African identity. This reflects the fact that the war failed to shape popular perceptions about a *national* identity embracing both white groups and that whereas Gallipoli continues to arouse emotions in Australia, Delville Wood retains little resonance in South Africa.[3]

On 4 August 1914, Germany's failure to reply to Britain's ultimatum to withdraw her troops from Belgium involved not only the United Kingdom but also the self-governing Dominions in the First World War. In Canada, Australia, and New Zealand, with their predominantly British populations, there was widespread support for Britain. Patriotic feelings ran high, with the dominion governments offering troops and assistance. The Australian minister of defence summed up majority sentiment in these Dominions in his response that Australia was prepared to offer freely "the vigour of her manhood, the bounty of her soil resources, her economic organization, all she possesses, to the last ear of corn and drop of blood... to maintain the glory and greatness of the Empire, and to battle in the righteous cause wherein she is engaged."[4]

The South African government could not make a similar response. Here, too, the outbreak of war saw scenes of great excitement: enormous crowds demanding the Union's participation packed out public meetings throughout the country. These were, however, overwhelmingly English-speaking crowds whose exuberant renderings of *God Save the King* and patriotic songs struck few chords in Afrikaner breasts, and Afrikaner rather than English South Africans dominated parliament. Louis Botha's SAP government had a majority of Afrikaner members of parliament (MPs), most of whom opposed sending troops to Europe. Botha was also very sensitive to the fact that former Cabinet Minister General Hertzog had only a few months earlier established the National Party, which opposed the imperial connection. The South African War had ended only twelve years earlier, and there was a fear that Afrikaners would use Britain's involvement in Europe to try to regain their independence. The great majority of blacks within the Union's borders was also a potential source of danger while there were German troops in South West Africa. With a small white male population of military age of about 360,000,[5] South Africa could not realistically consider sending troops to Europe until its internal security had been ensured and the German menace neutralized.

War could not have come at a worse time for the government. Union was only four years old and a national sentiment had yet to evolve among whites. In addition, instead of healing the divisions between the two groups, Union seemed to have emphasized disunity. The year 1914 witnessed not only the establishment of the National Party, with its implications for Afrikaner as well as white unity; it also saw social and industrial unrest culminating in the general strike of 1914, during which the newly created Active Citizen Force had to restore order on the Rand.

There was therefore little chance of a united white South African approach to the war. Despite this, most English-speaking South Africans saw the war as "emphatically 'our war.' ... We may well be proud of the high privilege of being called upon to play our part in the struggle."[6] Because they believed that Britain had only reluctantly abandoned her neutrality to honour her commitment to Belgium, they equated patriotism with morality: they accepted that the Empire, "this great confederacy of free peoples of which we here in South Africa are, thank God, an integral part," was fighting for honour and justice.[7] Their pride was summed up by Francis Carey Slater:

> Steadfast England, sheltering tree
> Rooted in the northern sea,
> In your strong boughs' security
> The hunted wildbird, Liberty,
> Found, long since, a place of rest
> And builded an abiding nest.

> Raked by war's hell-driven blast
> Your cherished leaves are falling fast
> Fresh sap to agéd roots they give
> And proudly die that you may live
> To win for wounded Liberty
> The world and immortality.[8]

Many would have agreed with the editor of the Police journal, *The Nongqai*, that the "immediate duty of all of us who wear the King's uniform and owe allegiance to one sovereign is clear. The hour of trial…is with the Empire whose honour is in our keeping, in the deep and enduring virtues of whose freedom, protection and privileges we of the Great Union of South Africa so richly share."[9] With sentiments such as these, it is understandable that many English-speakers found it outrageous that South Africa's contribution might have to be the "spontaneous unofficial display of loyalty by the people of the sub-continent as distinct from the official act of the Government."[10]

The South African government could not ignore its obligations, however, and undertook to defend the Union's coastline and to maintain internal security, allowing the approximately seven thousand imperial troops in the Union to be withdrawn. But Botha was unwilling to accede to a British request to seize Luderitzbucht and Swakopmund, and neutralize German wireless facilities in South West Africa without parliamentary approval. He summoned a special session of parliament for 9 September.

Botha moved an address to the King assuring him that the Union would take all measures necessary to neutralize the German threat in South West Africa. Speaking to his motion, he said that the Union had to choose between "faith, duty and honour" and "dishonour and disloyalty."[11] While Hertzog's twelve Nationalist members voted against the motion, the sturdily imperialist Unionist Party and even the seven Labour MPs voted with the SAP.

The Unionist leader, Sir Thomas Smartt, pledged his party's wholehearted support to Botha in prosecuting the war.[12] Colonel Creswell also promised the Labour Party's support, but a small section of the party broke away to form the International Socialist League committed to fight "War-on-War." The League gained little support; working-class English-speakers proved to be every bit as jingoistic as their social "betters," and many even deserted the Labour Party. In the 1915 general election, only four Labour candidates were elected. Even Creswell was defeated, despite having fought in South West Africa.[13]

The patriotic societies threw their weight behind the war effort. There was a wide variety of such societies, including the British Empire League, the Navy League, the Victoria League, and the Patriotic League. Other societies catered to ethnic allegiances, such as the Irish Association, the Cambrian Society, the Sons of England, and numerous Caledonian Societies. These societies were often South African branches of Empire-wide societies, and, as their names indicate, their interests were essentially British and imperial rather than South African. While they did much good work, especially in raising funds for the war and for various charities such as the Governor-General's Fund, in tone they were jingoistic, often even racist. Their emphasis on Britishness and their determination to uproot any form of unpatriotic or seditious behaviour among South Africans made them deeply offensive to most Afrikaners. The British League, founded in 1915, was particularly racist and was in the forefront of anti-German campaigns in the Union.[14]

As in Britain and the other Dominions, anti-German sentiment was rife and was fanned by an English-language press that was virulent in its attacks on all things German. Although enemy aliens were interned, the Union had a large population of naturalized Germans, and, as the war settled into stalemate on the Western Front, anti-German newspaper propaganda became more vicious. The sinking of the passenger liner *Lusitania* in May 1915 saw widespread hysteria and rioting throughout the country. German-owned buildings were burned and wrecked, and German families long naturalized in South Africa were targeted. Supporters of the British League, sailors and soldiers, old men and youngsters were part of a mixed bag of rioters, many of whom used the opportunity for looting. There were strident demands, often from competitors, that the businesses of naturalized Germans be confiscated.[15]

Anti-German sentiments continued for the remainder of the war. The atmosphere in Durban, where all German music was banned, was described in 1917 as redolent of "the molten hate of the Hun and his works."[16] News of the treatment received by prisoners of war – forced labour, starvation rations, and so on – also contributed to keeping anti-German sentiment alive even after the war.[17]

English attitudes to Afrikaners were more ambivalent. Their respect and admiration for General Botha grew during the war. They appreciated the courage that it had taken for him to go against Afrikaner sentiment in choosing "faith, duty and honour." "General Botha has responded nobly to the call," said Vere Stent, the editor of the *Pretoria News*, "and Englishmen cannot be too grateful to him."[18]

Although the commandant-general of the Union Defence Force, General Christiaan Beyers, and a number of senior officers were Afrikaners, the upper echelons were predominantly English-speaking, and the ethos and structures of the force were essentially British. Under the 1912 Defence Act, all able-bodied men between eighteen and sixty were liable for military service in either an "English" regiment or an

"Afrikaner" commando. In August, in anticipation of parliamentary approval, the regiments and commandos were mobilized and an appeal was made for an extra seven thousand volunteers.[19]

Many senior Afrikaner officers opposed intervention in South West Africa. Beyers resigned his commission, and in early October, he and a number of other senior officers rebelled after a commando at Upington, under Colonel Manie Maritz, defected to the Germans. The Rebellion threatened to pit Afrikaner against English, but, while the rebels tended to be drawn from the Afrikaner poor white class, most members of the commandos remained loyal to Botha, as did most Afrikaner civil servants and policemen.[20] Botha also tried to minimize conflict between the two groups by using the commandos to crush the rebels. The widespread nature of the Rebellion, however, meant that he had to call out the Imperial Light Horse and the Transvaal Scottish to assist the commandos. In addition, the commandos were not composed entirely of Afrikaners, as in country districts English-speakers often joined their local commando. An estimated nine thousand English troops took part in putting down the Rebellion,[21]

Fighting side by side with Afrikaners made the English realize how difficult it was for them to fight against their kith and kin.[22] Although they demanded that the rebels be severely punished (a demand that Botha sensibly ignored), they saw the loyalty of most Afrikaners as evidence of a growing unity between the two groups. To Vere Stent, "everyone believed that now at last the English-speaking and the Dutch-speaking South Africans would come together and fight side by side…and that they would cement forever a great alliance of the races."[23]

The South West African campaign also impressed English South Africans with what the "loyal Dutch" were doing for the Empire.[24] This was the only campaign during the war where a dominion army operated independently of the imperial army and under its own command. As during the Rebellion, Afrikaners provided most of the troops fighting in the campaign. The editor of *The Nongqai*, as staunch a proponent of the new Union of South Africa as he was an ardent imperialist, enthused: "In the field of conflict, history now sees the first united entry shoulder to shoulder of the two great races that live in South Africa. … Under one common flag of liberty [they] are entered on a conflict on behalf of the Union of South Africa." At the conclusion of the campaign, he wrote that "people have seen a vision of what a united South Africa may accomplish, and will press steadily forward to that end."[25]

English admiration for Afrikaner loyalists was, however, counterbalanced by their anger at rebel actions and their hostility to the Nationalists, whom they blamed for encouraging sedition. Anti-nationalist feelings ran particularly high after the general election of 1915 revealed that Hertzog had more Afrikaner support than did Botha.[26]

By mid-1915, with the Rebellion crushed and South West Africa conquered, English-speakers again demanded that Union troops be sent to Europe.[27] Faced with the continuing slaughter on the Western Front, the imperial government was urging the Dominions to provide more troops. With the failure of the Gallipoli campaign, Australians and New Zealanders joined Canadian troops already in Flanders, while South Africa was asked to send troops to East Africa and Europe. The government agreed to raise the South African Field Artillery and two brigades of infantry, the 1st for service in Flanders as part of the Imperial 9th (Scottish) Division, and the 2nd for service in East Africa. South Africa would also provide mounted units, medical, ambulance, and a whole range of ancillary service corps. The troops were to fall under imperial command, with the soldiers having the status of British regular troops. In the case of the 2nd Brigade, however, overall command of the imperial army was vested first in General Smuts and later in General van Deventer.[28]

As the Defence Act of 1912 stipulated that members of the Active Citizen Force could serve only in southern Africa in defence of the Union, volunteers had to be recruited for the units. Each brigade was to consist of four regiments, those of the 1st Brigade being the 1st Cape of Good Hope, 2nd Natal and Orange Free State, 3rd Transvaal and Rhodesia, and 4th South African Scottish. The 2nd Brigade was to be made up of the 5th Cape of Good Hope; 6th Natal, Orange Free State, and Eastern Cape; 7th Transvaal; and 8th South African Railways and Workers.

As the members of the regiments were unhappy at losing their identity, the military tried to place men from particular regiments together.[29] Thus men from the Kimberley Regiment formed the Kimberley Company of the 1st Regt. while no. 1 platoon of A Company, 3rd Regt., comprised men from the Imperial Light Horse, and C Company men from the Rand Light Infantry. The 4th (Scottish) Regt. was largely drawn from the Transvaal Scottish and the Cape Town Highlanders.[30]

In practice, the spirit of camaraderie that grew up among the members of the 1st Brigade in France saw regimental affiliations lose their importance. As P. Hunter of the Imperial Light Horse said after the war,

"We lost our identity as ILH men and were simply men of the 3rd South African Infantry and proud of it."[31] The decision to raise new regiments for the imperial campaigns therefore reinforced South Africanism within the army and contributed to the development of a South African military tradition, even if it remained one that enshrined British traditions.

During the second half of 1915, great recruiting campaigns were organized, with cities, towns, and country areas vying with each other to raise the most men. There was little difficulty finding officers (who were required to be gentlemen with military experience and able to lead their men in the field),[32] but there were complaints that other ranks were coming forward too slowly.[33] Despite this, both brigades were raised within the required time, many of the volunteers having already fought in South West Africa.[34] The difficulty of raising men was to be a recurrent theme during the rest of the war, reflecting the fact that with her white population divided, South Africa had only a small reservoir of men from whom recruits could be drawn. Recruiting for Flanders was also hampered by the fact that the imperial government paid dominion soldiers. Imperial rates were one shilling a day compared to the Union rate of three shillings, which men in East Africa received. The Afrikaner majority in Botha's cabinet who opposed troops fighting in Europe refused to make up the difference, and it was only in late 1916 that the British matched the South African wages.[35]

Few Afrikaners volunteered to serve in Europe. Bearing in mind Afrikaner antipathy to sending troops to Europe, it is reasonable to assume that most Afrikaner volunteers would have gone to East Africa, where there was also more chance of serving under Afrikaner officers. The evidence suggests that while Afrikaners were well represented in the East African Brigade, only 10 to 15 per cent of the 1st Brigade were Afrikaans-speaking.[36]

There were also accusations that English men were reluctant to fight, and frequent attempts were made to shame them into volunteering.[37] This verse, in The Nongqai, was an early warning to "shirkers":

> Where will you look, Sonny, where will you look
> When your children yet to be
> Clamour to learn of the part you took
> In the war that kept men free?
> ...
> But where will you look when they give the glance
> That tells you they know you funked?[38]

Attacks on "unmitigated shirkers" and "loathsome slackers" became more strident as the need for men became more urgent. English women were enthusiastic supporters of the war effort, and from 1914 organized fundraising and other activities in support of the troops.[39] By late 1915, on the grounds that "a pretty woman, a persuasive woman, an insistent woman, is the best recruiting sergeant in the world," women were drawn unofficially into the recruiting campaign, with Vere Stent urging that it would be better for them to send a man "to his death than keep a dishonourable slacker at home."[40] Fear of social ostracism became more pronounced as the anti-shirker campaign grew, particularly after South African women began copying the British practice of presenting white feathers to civilians.[41]

Accusations that English-speakers were reluctant to rally to the colours are not borne out by the figures of those who volunteered. In August 1914, many volunteered to serve in South West Africa and in the imperial armed forces.[42] The various patriotic societies were at the fore in encouraging enlisting, and their members served in all theatres of war.[43] In April 1915, fifty-three members of the Sons of England were in South West Africa, where they opened an Expeditionary Lodge. By July 1918, 208 members of the Sons of England had enlisted from Pretoria alone, of whom thirteen had been killed.[44] There were approximately 160,000 English-speaking men of military age in the Union, and a calculation of those who fought indicates that about 43 per cent of them served in the Union or British forces, a number that compares very favourably with the other Dominions.[45]

English and parallel-medium (English and Dutch) private and government schools also provided fertile recruiting grounds. Schoolboys were exposed to military service as cadets, and when war broke out, masters and old boys (alumni) enlisted. To a large extent, the honour of the schools came to be identified with the number of old boys serving at the front. Many schools ended the war with proud records inscribed on rolls of honours and memorials. To give two examples: over 800 Diocesan College old boys served, of whom 112 were killed; 800 old boys of Maritzburg College fought, with 96 fatalities.[46]

The realization that the survival of the Empire would be decided in Europe and a popular belief that the only "proper" fighting was in the trenches[47] encouraged many South Africans to enlist in British regiments, particularly in 1914 and early 1915 when there was no other way of serving in Flanders.[48] The number who did so cannot be ascertained, but it was large enough to affect recruitment for the infantry brigades in 1915.[49]

It was estimated in 1918 that twelve thousand officers had fought in imperial units, the Royal Navy, or Royal Flying Corps.[50] While this number seems excessive, it reflects the fact that many men went to England to get commissions, as the British Army was extremely short of junior officers. For example, 221 old boys of Johannesburg's King Edward VII School served in British units, of whom only six were not officers.[51]

There would have been as many reasons for men volunteering as there were volunteers. A desire for excitement and adventure would surely have played a part, as would a need to escape from poverty, unemployment, or uncongenial work or home conditions. The twin forces of comradeship and the need to prove one's masculinity to one's peers would also have played an important role, particularly in the close-knit world of old boys' associations and patriotic societies. Patriotic enthusiasm would also have been an important factor, particularly in 1914.

The churches, patriotic societies, and civilians generally continued throughout the war to express patriotic sentiments and extol the virtues of fighting and dying for the Empire, or for "King and Country." After the initial flush of enthusiasm, soldiers seldom did so, although this is not to deny that patriotism was a motive for enlisting. J.G. Fuller, in his work on troop morale and popular culture in the British and dominion armies, argues that British reticence about patriotism reflects the fact that in the Dominions, as much as in Britain, the British were sure enough of their own superiority to feel no need to refer to patriotism.[52]

In South Africa, soldiers often considered duty as important as patriotism and conflated the two with idealism. Many policemen, for example, who were not permitted to volunteer, sacrificed their service and pension rights to do so.[53] J. Levyns enlisted because he was "moved by the same spirit of idealism that caused so many thousands of my doomed generation to offer their lives to their country. I believed with them that... Great Britain had taken up arms to defend the noblest ideals of democracy."[54] Some enlisted despite hating the idea of soldiering. Eric Wentzel's obituary mentioned that he "did not love soldiering, but fell doing what he knew to be his duty."[55] Few were as forthright as Father Eustace Hill, who served as an Anglican chaplain in South West Africa and Flanders. He came to hate the war, referring to it as "utterly damnable and should be a method only heathens use for settling disputes." But, convinced of the rightness of Britain's cause, he was prepared to serve and to encourage others to serve.[56]

As was the case in Britain and the other Dominions, many English-speaking South African clerics conflated religion and patriotism, arguing that the war encouraged virtues of service and self-sacrifice.[57] In August 1914, the Dean of Pretoria gave biblical justification for the British decision to go to war, while Rev. Macmillan of Pretoria's Presbyterian Church pronounced that there "was nothing in the world so cleansing, so purifying, as war."[58] To the "Fighting Bishop," Michael Furse of Pretoria, there was no conflict between loyalty to the Empire and his Christian conviction, and he visited all three of the main theatres of war in which South Africans fought. In 1915 he wrote that it was "one of the most difficult things I have ever had to do to tear myself away from the company of those splendid fellows.... Again and again I long to be back with them."[59]

All of the major English-speaking churches provided military chaplains, stretcher bearers, and members of ambulance corps. Many shared the dangers of the soldiers to whom they were ministering. At Delville Wood they worked unceasingly. The Wesleyan chaplain, Capt. Cook, was killed assisting stretcher bearers, while Father Hill received the Military Cross for fearlessly attending the wounded.[60] "During the whole time we were in action he worked among the wounded, regardless of himself; in shell fire, machine-gun fire, or snipers, he unceasingly worked like a Trojan, and if ever a man deserves a V.C. he does...one of the best men that ever lived."[61] A few months later Hill was hit at Butte de Warlencourt while rescuing wounded men in no man's land and lost his right arm. He returned to the front and in early 1918 was taken prisoner.[62]

The 1st SA Infantry Brigade, 160 officers and 5,648 other ranks, embarked from Cape Town between August and October 1915. After training in England, they were sent to Egypt in December, where they served until April 1916.[63] They arrived in France in late April and after training in trench warfare, began moving into the trenches in early July to hold the line between the French and British forces.

On 14 July, Brigadier-General Henry Lukin was ordered to capture Delville Wood and hold it at all costs. The following day, the infantry charged at 0500 hours and drove the entrenched Germans from most of the wood before being raked by German artillery and machine-gun fire from the surrounding heights. They dug themselves in and, despite strain and exhaustion, hunger, and limited ammunition, held the wood. On the 18th, after a seven-hour bombardment, three German regiments attacked, and after fierce hand-to-hand fighting, drove the South Africans back into the southwest corner of the wood. They held this position until relieved at 1800 hours on 20 July, the remnants withdrawing to the pipes of the 4th Regt.[64] Of 121 officers and 3,032 other ranks who went into battle, 29 officers and 751 other ranks were present at roll call on 21 July.

As news of the carnage of Delville Wood reached South Africa, there was both horror at how much holding the wood had cost and intense pride in the achievement. While many expressions reflected intensely British sentiments ("Thank God they held the wood! And thank God! they kept up the traditions of our race!"),[65] others showed how Delville Wood became an integral part of South Africanism. To quote a few: "Delville Wood! What a name that will be in the history of South Africa! ... How fine they were, and how proud we are of them, and oh! how glorious it is to feel South Africa has at last taken her place among the other Dominions"; "They have added a glorious page to the proud story of South Africa's part in the War. It is a page upon which both races in South Africa can look with equal pride."[66] B. M. Bromley of Kalk Bay expressed the following sentiment:

> O little wood in far-off France!
> By what strange ways their feet were led,
> Our sons, of differing tongue and race
> Who there upon your pathways red,
> Once in true-hearted fortitude,
> Forged living links of brotherhood.
>
> And the deep wounds of Delville Wood
> For ever on our Scroll shall flame,
> With sacrificial light that fades
> Old scars of by-gone grief and shame;
> So for all time shall Delville Wood
> Stand unto us as Holy Rood.[67]

The soldiers themselves were often more laconic. L. Arrons wrote home, "Well, we have made our name, and that is all we care about. We had orders to hold the wood whatever happens – and we held it."[68]

Delville Wood was the pinnacle of South Africa's First World War experience. The war continued for another two weary years, and during this time, the Springboks distinguished themselves in other actions on the Western Front, as well as in East Africa and Palestine. But, as the slaughter of British and dominion troops continued unabated, so the need for new recruits became ever more urgent, especially in 1917 and 1918 when Germany seemed to be gaining the initiative. While Britain and Canada introduced conscription to solve the problem, Afrikaner opposition ruled it out as a solution in the Union, although there were suggestions that either English-speaking South Africans or those born in Britain should be conscripted.[69] Instead, the "Legend of the Wood" was used to encourage enlisting – "the call went up from Delville Wood for further men" – and wounded soldiers were used to shame men into volunteering.[70] The anti-shirker campaign became so vicious that in late 1916 a "Services Rendered for King and Empire" badge was introduced to distinguish those who had served.[71] The National Party, encouraged by German successes, was coming out ever more strongly in favour of establishing a republic outside the Empire. This was used by loyalists to brand those who did not volunteer as rebels and traitors to the Empire. In early 1918, when it seemed that the lack of recruits could imperil the continuation of the 1st Brigade, Vere Stent warned: "If South Africa is not to stand down for ever damned and disgraced and dishonoured we must maintain in the field this brigade of ours."[72] The existence of the brigade was only secured by temporarily adding battalions of Cameronians and Royal Scots Fusiliers to it. Its reputation was so high, however, that it retained the name "South African Brigade."[73]

South Africa was neither damned, disgraced, nor dishonoured, and on 11 November 1918 the 1st Brigade's 1st Regt. was still in the lines. "The fighting continued right up to 11:00 when the enemy stood up in his trenches and then came towards our line and wanted to fraternize but our troops ordered them back to their lines."[74] The war had ended; in helping bring about its end, South Africa had sacrificed 12,452 men, of whom 8,551 were white. A further 10,399 white men were wounded.[75]

There has been considerable literature on whether the war experience alienated Australians from Britain and the Empire.[76] There is little evidence of a major change in English-speaking attitudes in South Africa: this despite the fact that with their relatively small community, few would have been untouched by the war. About 43 percent of English-speaking men of military age fought and about 9 per cent of those did not return. Their loss impacted on the community and on the future of South Africa, especially as those who did not return included some of their youngest, fittest, and most intelligent men.[77]

Yet even when long casualty lists began to touch them directly and films of the slaughter on the Western Front showed them the horrors of battle,[78] most English-speakers appear to have maintained their faith in the Empire and in the justice of the imperial cause. Civilians continued to use imperial rhetoric to express their perceptions. At Delville Wood,

South Africa's young men had responded "as all British soldiers do"; "their glorious gallant lads had paid the price and were still offering their lives as sacrifices in the cause of the Empire and for the Empire."[79] Whether graves and memorials proclaimed that the fallen had died "For King and Empire" or "For King and Country," England was implicit in both.[80]

Memorial inscriptions do not necessarily reflect the sentiments of those they commemorate. Yet despite experiencing the horrors of battle, great war-weariness, and, particularly in East Africa, malaria and other diseases, English-speaking soldiers remained remarkably loyal to Britain and the Empire. After fighting in both South West and East Africa, and ill with malaria, my father still saw himself as a "British Soldier fighting Britannia's Cause."[81]

Attitudes to the British Army and military hierarchy were more critical. In most campaigns, South African soldiers fought side by side with troops from all over the Empire. Like their dominion fellows, many felt contemptuous of English tommies, but they learned to respect the dominion and colonial troops and, particularly on the Western Front, came to have a lasting admiration for the Jocks, "the flowers of the armies, the devils of the North."[82] Relations between British and South African soldiers on the Western Front seem to have been as friction-free as were those between the British and Canadians.[83] Some were, however, disgusted by the incompetence of the British military staff,[84] while others were bitter after Delville Wood, as they felt that British troops would have been relieved earlier than was the 1st Brigade.[85] Yet there is little evidence of troops becoming mutinous, other than in East Africa, where the ravages of disease meant that it could be difficult to persuade men to return after having been on leave in the Union.[86]

The end of the war left English-speaking South Africans with an intense sense of pride. Their Springboks had maintained their own alongside British and dominion soldiers, and, despite the Rebellion and the growth of Afrikaner nationalism, South Africa had been found wanting neither in loyalty nor valour and could hold her head up among the Dominions. At the same time, they were aware of the extent to which the war had changed the relationship of the Dominions with Britain, making nations of them.[87]

Yet, like their dominion fellows,[88] English-speaking South Africans accepted that South Africa remained a nation within the Empire. Despite their growing South Africanism, their nationalism remained essentially subsumed in imperialism, in stark contrast to the republican nationalism of the National Party. Fighting, and dying, alongside Afrikaners, many believed that their vision of an imperial, South Africanist nationalism would triumph after the war; that

> the day will come when forty thousand South Africans, Dutch-speaking and English-speaking, who have been winning undying glory at the front, will return to this country to take their part in its life and to promote its material and spiritual progress. They will bring back with them the seeds of a real Nationalism and the "nationalism" which seems to draw vertical lines of division in our political life will be discredited.[89]

Speaking at a recruiting meeting in Durban in 1918, Lt. Forbes, who had been wounded at Delville Wood, said that the "makers of the new South African nation were now moulding it in France."[90] The editor of the *Cape Times* concurred: "The South African Brigade...has been and will be in all future time a living emblem of the triumph of the principle of Union in this country."[91] The war would thus have given South Africans a chance to achieve that which Union had not done, a national identity.[92] As John Buchan wrote, "The Brigade was a microcosm of what South Africa may yet become if the fates are kind. It was a living example of true race integration."[93]

In a poem in memory of her son, Kenneth, Nellie Howard expressed the sentiments of many English-speakers:

> You have given us traditions,
> You have writ your country's name
> Upon a mighty pinnacle
> Set on the domes of fame.
>
> (*refrain*)   Ah Springboks! Gallant Springboks!
> May your country prove as true,
> May she render herself worthy
> May she give you nought to rue.
>
> You are welding us together
> Where war's mighty anvils ring,
> By each noble, loyal sacrifice
> For country, God and King.[94]

For English-speaking South Africans, the war had thus strengthened South Africanism, making it take on a more distinctively national or dominion character. Their South Africanism, however, remained subsumed within the wider imperial and British context, and they continued to regard themselves first and foremost as British subjects, part of the wider British World of which the Union was an integral member. Yet, as a minority in the political nation, many, possibly most, English-speakers must have had serious apprehensions about the future. They were aware of the dangers posed to their position and to the imperial connection by Afrikaner nationalism. This could be why they placed such stress on the importance of co-operation between English and "loyal" Afrikaners, co-operation that was to see the merger of the SAP and Unionist parties in 1920. For, as was to be borne out from the 1920s, unless they worked with "loyal" Afrikaners, neither their vision of South Africanism nor their position as British subjects within the British Empire was secure.

{NOTES}

1   Union of South Africa, *Official Year Book of the Union... No. 4, 1921* (Pretoria: Government Printing and Stationery Office, 1921) gives a total of 146,515 white men but calculates the number by adding together those who served in South West Africa (67,237), Europe and Egypt (30,719), East Africa (43,477), and the Union establishment (5,082). This ignores the fact that many men served in more than one campaign, with over half of those who fought in South West Africa re-enlisting for other theatres.

2   I have discussed South Africanism in "South African British? or Dominion South Africans? The Evolution of an Identity in the 1910s and 1920s," *South African Historical Journal* 43 (2000): 197–222. South Africanism has also been discussed by, *inter alia*, Saul Dubow, "Colonial Nationalism, the Milner Kindergarten and the Rise of 'South Africanism,' 1902–10," *History Workshop Journal* 43 (1997): 53–85, and Andrew Thompson, "The Language of Loyalism in Southern Africa, *c.*1870–1939," British World Conference, University of Cape Town, January 2002.

3   Comparatively little has been published in South Africa on the war. Works that have appeared are Peter Digby, *Pyramids and Poppies: The 1st SA Infantry Brigade in Libya, France and Flanders, 1915–1919* (Rivonia: Ashanti, 1993); Ian Uys, *Rollcall: The Delville Wood Story* (Johannesburg: Uys Publ, 1991). Louis Grundlingh examined the English-speaking response to the outbreak of the war in "Die Engelssprekende Suid-Afrikaners se Reaksie op die Uitbreek van die Eerste Wereldoorlog, 1914–1915" (master's thesis, University of the Orange Free State, 1978). Articles and chapters include Noel Garson, "South Africa and World War I," *Journal of Imperial and Commonwealth History* 8, no. 1 (October 1979): 68–85; Kent Fedorowich, "The Weak Link in the Imperial Chain: South Africa, the Round Table and World War One," *The Round Table: The Empire/Commonwealth and British Foreign Policy*, ed. A. Bosco and A. May (London: Lothian Foundation Press, 1997); Bill Nasson, "A Great Divide: Popular Responses to the Great War in South Africa," *War and Society* 12, no. 1 (1994): 47–64, and "Springboks at the Somme: The Making of Delville Wood, 1916" (University of the Witwatersrand, Institute for Advanced Social Research,

1996). James Ambrose Brown has written on East Africa in *They Fought for King and Kaiser: South Africans in German East Africa, 1916* (Johannesburg: Ashanti, 1991). Earlier works include *Union of South Africa and the Great War, 1914–1918: Official History* (Pretoria: Government Printer, 1923); John Buchan, *The History of the South African Forces in France* (London: Thomas Nelson, n.d.); F. B. Adler *et al.*, *The South African Field Artillery in German East Africa and Palestine, 1915–1919* (Pretoria: Van Schaik, 1958). For the equally neglected blacks during the war, see Albert Grundlingh, *Fighting Their Own War: South Africa's Blacks and the First World War* (Johannesburg: Ravan Press, 1987); Ian Gleeson, *The Unknown Force: Black, Indian and Coloured Soldiers through Two World Wars* (Rivonia: Ashanti, 1994).

4 *The British Empire* 66: 1824.

5 Just over 50 per cent of the total white male population of 717,742 were of military age, Union of South Africa, *Official Year Book of the Union... No. 4, 1921*, 143.

6 *S. Michael's Chronicle* 3, no. 9 (October 1914): 1.

7 "The Bishop's Sermon," *Pretoria News*, 21 September 1914. See also Editorial, *Rand Daily Mail*, 5 August 1914; Editorial, *Potchefstroom Herald*, 7 August 1914.

8 *The Collected Poems of Francis Carey Slater* (Edinburgh: William Blackwood, 1957), 287.

9 *The Nongqai* 2, no. 2 (August 1914): 73. See also Editorial, *Grahamstown Journal*, 1 September 1914.

10 Editorial, *The Grahamstown Journal*, 4 August 1914. See also "Ready to Help," *Rand Daily Mail*, 7 August 1914; Editorial, *Natal Mercury*, 10 August 1914.

11 Tommy Boydell, *"My Luck Was In": With Spotlights on General Smuts* (Cape Town: Stewart, 1948), 102–3.

12 Editorial, *Pretoria News*, 19 January 1915.

13 Boydell, *"My Luck Was In,"* 123–24; Editorial, *Pretoria News*, 10 August 1914; "War-on-War," 12 April 1915,

14 See *Pretoria News*, 7 May 1915, 11 February 1916.

15 See *Pretoria News*, 17 May 1915; *Natal Mercury*, 18 May 1915; Boydell, *"My Luck Was In,"* 107.

16 *The Nongqai* 8, no. 2 (August 1917): 72.

17 Defence Force Documentation Centre, Pretoria (DFDC), WO 1 Box 4, 1st SAI Brigade, statements by returned Allied prisoners, 1916–1918.

18 Editorial, *Pretoria News*, 13 November 1914.

19 "Union Defence Force Orders," *Cape Times*, 8 August 1914; "Natal and the War," *Natal Mercury*, 19 August 1914.

20 Kent Fedorowich, "'Sleeping with the Lion?' The Loyal Afrikaner and the South African Rebellion of 1914–15," British World Conference, University of Cape Town, January 2002, 8–9.

21 DFDC, SA Citizen Force, 1914–1918, 1, Box 93, List of Commando Officers on Active Service: Deneys Reitz, *Trekking On* (London: Faber & Faber, 1933), 91.

22 See Editorial, *Pretoria News*, 21 December 1914.

23 "Botha's Failure," *Pretoria News*, 23 April 1917. See also Editorial, *Grahamstown Journal*, 15 October 1914; Editorial, *Potchefstroom Herald*, 30 October 1914.

24 Editorial, *Pretoria News*, 24 May 1915.

25 *The Nongqai* 2, no. 4 (October 1914): 218; 3, no. 5 (May 1915): 266.

26 B. M. Schoeman, *Parlementêre verkiesings in Suid-Afrika, 1910–1976* (Pretoria: Aktuele Publikasies, 1977), 67.

27 Editorial, *Cape Times*, 29 May 1915; Editorial, *Pretoria News*, 1 June 1915.

28 DFDC, Diverse GPI, Box 64, Union Defence Force, South African Overseas Expeditionary Force, 120; Union East Africa Expeditionary Force, 136.

29 Ibid., South African Overseas and Imperial Service Contingent, Circular no. 1/1915, 1, 2.

30 H.H. Curson, *The History of the Kimberley Regiment* (Kimberley: Northern Cape Printers, 1963), 162; H. Klein, *Light Horse Cavalcade: The Imperial Light Horse, 1899–1961* (Cape Town: Howard Timmins, 1969), 90; Digby, *Pyramids and Poppies*, 19; Neil Orpen, *The Cape Town Highlanders, 1885–1970* (Cape Town: Cape Town Highlanders, 1970), 81.

31 Klein, *Light Horse Cavalcade*, 90.

32 DFDC, Diverse GPI, Box 64, South African Overseas and Imperial Service Contingent, Circular 1/1915, 2.

33 See "For God and King," *Pretoria News*, 27 November 1915.

34 *Rand Daily Mail*, 27 October 1915; *The Nongqai* 5, no. 1 (January 1916): 1.

35 D. Waley, *Sydney, Earl Buxton, 1853–1934: Statesman, Governor-General of South Africa* (Newtimber: Newtimber Publications, 1999), 275–78.

36 Estimate based on the regimental roll calls, see DFDC, Diverse GPI, Box III, 1st Infantry Brigade, Nominal Roll, 21 January 1917; WOID, SA Infantry Brigade, Box 1, 3rd Regt, SA Infantry, miscellaneous information; WW1 – Diverse, Box 21, 1st Regt SA1 Brigade. Buchan estimated the number in France at 15 per cent, rising to 30 per cent by 1918 (*South African Forces in France*, 15). Digby, *Pyramids and Poppies*, concurs, but neither indicate where their information comes from. The roll calls do not suggest an increase.

37 See Editorial, *Pretoria News*, 26 August 1914; "How to Get the Men," *Natal Mercury*, 19 April 1915.

38 *The Nongqai* 2, no. 6 (December 1914): 362.

39 For a discussion of the work done by women, see Paul Ward, "Empire and Everyday: Britishness and Imperialism in Women's Lives in the First World War," British World Conference 11, University of Calgary, July 2003. See article in this volume.

40 "Open Letter to the Women of South Africa," *Pretoria News*, 13 November 1915.

41 "Girls and the Recruiting Campaign," *Pretoria News*, 29 April 1916; "Women Make War on Rand Slackers," *Cape Times*, 25 July 1916. In Britain women tried to shame men into volunteering by offering white feathers to men in civilian clothes.

42 "Awaiting Orders," *Rand Daily Mail*, 8 August 1914; "A South African Contingent," *Cape Times*, 26 August 1914; DFDC, SA Citizen Force 1914–1918, 1, Box 14, Volunteers' Applications; Box 37, Applications for Service.

43 "Ready to Serve the Empire," *Cape Times*, 13 August 1914; Editorial, *Pretoria News*, 31 August 1914; "The War," 22 September 1914.

44 "SOE," *Pretoria News*, 4 May 1915; "Sons of England Active Service List," 1 July 1918.

45 The 1918 census shows about 390,000 men of military age (Union of South Africa, *Official Year Book of the Union... No. 4, 1921*, 158). Approximately 40 per cent of these were English-speaking. A calculation of English-speakers who fought in the various campaigns and imperial units, taking into account the reservations in note 1 above,

suggests that approximately seventy thousand English-speakers served. About 32 per cent of the total white male population of military age served. For statistics for the other Dominions, see M. Kitchen, *The British Empire and Commonwealth: A Short History* (New York: St. Martin's Press, 1996), 61.

46 J. Gardener, *Bishops 150: A History of the Diocesan College, Rondebosch* (Cape Town: Juta, 1997), 235; Simon Haw, *For Hearth and Home: The Story of Maritzburg College, 1863–1988* (Pietermaritzburg: MC Publications, 1988), 214.

47 Nasson, "Springboks at the Somme," 2.

48 *The Durban High School Magazine* 7 (September 1915): 1; Neville Lewis, *Studio Encounters: Some Reminiscences of a Portrait Painter* (Cape Town: Tafelberg, 1963), 19; *The Selbornian* (October 1918): 7.

49 "The Women's Duty," *Pretoria News*, 16 August 1915.

50 "Britain and the Dominions," *Natal Mercury*, 15 November 1918.

51 Digby, *Pyramids and Poppies*, 315.

52 J.G. Fuller, *Troop Morale and Popular Culture in the British and Dominion Armies, 1914–1918* (Oxford: Clarendon Press, 1990), 36–37.

53 "To Departing Comrades," *Pretoria News*, 30 August 1915; *The Nongqai* 7, no. 1 (January 1917): 6.

54 J.E.P. Levyns, *The Disciplines of War: Memories of the War of 1914–18* (New York: Vantage Press, 1984), 27.

55 *S. Andrew's College Magazine* 41, no. 1 (March 1919): 2.

56 K. C. Lawson, *Venture of Faith: The Story of St. John's College, Johannesburg, 1898–1968* (Johannesburg: Council of St. John's College, 1968), 126, 128.

57 "Diocesan synod," *Pretoria News*, 6 October 1914. See M. Moynihan, *God on Our Side: The British Padre in World War I* (London: Secker & Warburg, 1983).

58 "War and Christianity," *Rand Daily Mail*, 10 August 1914; "Preaching in St. Andrew's," *Pretoria News*, 25 August 1914.

59 *The Nongqai* 4, no. 6 (December 1915): 321.

60 *The Nongqai* 6, no. 2 (August 1916): 121; DFDC, WOIDA, Box 5, 1st SAI Brigade, operations on the Somme.

61 *The Story of Delville Wood: Told in Letters from the Front* (Cape Town: Cape Times, n.d.), 20.

62 Lawson, *Venture of Faith*, 127–28, 131.

63 DFDC, WOIDA, Box 4, 1st SAI Brigade War Diary, 26 September, 13 October–15 December 1915; "Springboks for the Front," *Pretoria News*, 3 December 1915.

64 DFDC, WOID, Box 7, Report by Brig-Gen Lukin, 4 August 1916; Diverse GPI, Box 13, DC1140/3, The Somme, 15–22 July 1916, 29; *The Nongqai* 6, no. 2 (August 1916): 120–21.

65 *Story of Delville Wood*, 46.

66 "Letters of Betty," *Pretoria News*, 29 July 1916; "The Casualties," *Cape Times*, 29 July 1916.

67 *Story of Delville Wood*, 61.

68 Ibid., 20.

69 Editorial, *Pretoria News*, 6 March 1917; "Conscription Impossible," 6 February 1918.

70 "Delville Wood Day," *Natal Mercury*, 18 July 1917.

71 *The Nongqai* 6, no. 5 (November 1916): 371.

72 "Come Over and Help Us," *Pretoria News*, 12 April 1918.

73 Digby, *Pyramids and Poppies*, 344.

74 DFDC, WOIDA, Box 2, 1st Regt. SAI War Diary, 11 November 1918.

75 Union of South Africa, *Official Year Book of the Union... No. 4, 1921*, 230.

76 J. Beaumont, ed., *Australia's War, 1914–1918* (St. Leonards: Allen & Unwin,1995).

77 See Buchan, *South African Forces in France*, 17–18, 280.

78 "Battle Pictures at the Opera House," *Pretoria News*, 31 October 1916.

79 Nasson, "Springboks at the Somme," 17; "Onward March to Victory," *Natal Mercury*, 5 August 1916.

80 See "Ceremony at Queen's Statue," *Cape Times*, 25 May 1917.

81 Billie Lambert was serving with the 6th Regiment of the 2nd South African Infantry Brigade. He wrote the words on a piece of khaki he sent to his mother at the end of 1916.

82 2nd Lieut. C. Keogh, *The Durban High School Magazine* 16 (November 1918); see also Fuller, *Troop Morale*, 161.

83 Patrick Brennan, "Imperialism versus Nationalism among Senior Officers of the Canadian Corps," British World Conference 11, University of Calgary, July 2003. See chapter in this volume.

84 See Levyns, *Disciplines of War*, 58, and William Macmillan, ed., *A South African Student and Soldier: Harold Edward Howse, 1894–1917: A Study* (Cape Town: n.p., n.d.), 53.

85 *The British Empire* 66:1843.

86 Leslie Blackwell, *African Occasions: Reminiscences of Thirty Years of Bar, Bench, and Politics in South Africa* (London: Hutchinson, 1938), 71.

87 This was realized even as early as 1916: see "Inter-imperial relations," *Pretoria News*, 29 December 1916.

88 Brennan, "Imperialism versus Nationalism"; Beaumont, "The Anzac Legend," in *Australia's War*, ed. J. Beaumont, 171; J. Phillips, "75 Years since Gallipoli," in *Towards 1990: Seven Leading Historians Examine Significant Aspects of New Zealand History* (n.p.: n.p., 1989), 110.

89 "True Nationalism and False," *Cape Times*, 15 September 1916. See also Editorial, *Grahamstown Journal*, 13 August 1918; "Reply to Fichardt," *Potchefstroom Herald*, 18 October 1918.

90 "New South African Nation," *Natal Mercury*, 30 May 1918.

91 Editorial, *Cape Times*, 31 May 1918.

92 See Editorial, *Natal Mercury*, 18 November 1918.

93 Buchan, *South African Forces in France*, 261.

94 *Grey College School Magazine* 9, no. 34 (August 1918): verses 5, 6, 9, 65–66.

CHAPTER 14

THE MIGRANT'S EMPIRE:

LOYALTY AND IMPERIAL CITIZENSHIP AT THE LEAGUE OF NATIONS

Satadru Sen

THE FIRST INDIAN TO become a celebrity athlete was a man of staggering contradictions. At various points in a public career that stretched between the 1890s and the 1930s, he was the definitive upper-class Englishman as well as the authentic Oriental. He was the stalwart defender of the Empire on the cricket fields of Australia and in the trenches of France, but he was also acutely aware of the racial hierarchies of British colonialism and could be a scathing critic of imperial policy. The individual in question was Kumar Shri Ranjitsinhji, or, as the British renamed him, Ranji. This renaming of the man is not insignificant. The contrast between the long, "exotic" name and short Anglicized nickname represents the discursive tensions that surrounded Ranjitsinhji during his long career as an athlete, a politician, a celebrity, and a legend. These tensions reveal a great deal about the ideologies of race, gender, and political identity in colonial India and the contemporary Empire. When we look closely at how Ranjitsinhji represented himself, and at how he was represented by others, we find that the fluctuating discourses of colour, manhood, and loyalty served a dual function. On the one hand, they served to restrict his mobility in an Empire that was defined in terms of race, gender, and political allegiance. On the other hand, because these discourses were not fixed but subject to transformation and manipulation, they could serve as enormous assets – to the man himself, as well as to those who clutched at his image.

As a teenager in the 1880s, Ranjitsinhji left Nawanagar, a small princely state in western India, and went to England. There, in the 1890s, he became a famous cricketer. In 1907 he returned to India and became the ruler of the state he had left behind. He became highly critical of the colonial authorities, although not consistently so. In the 1920s, he became an Indian representative at the League of Nations, where he became remarkably critical of British imperialism as it was practiced. Yet he felt compelled to reiterate periodically his allegiance to the Empire and the Crown. There were, in fact, strong connections between transgressive metamorphoses of identity and the persistence of rebellion in the political life of a loyal subject of the British Empire. As a migrant, Ranjitsinhji existed in a particular kind of liminal space between Empire and nation, a space where such apparently conflicted postures were possible and rewarding. His frequent protestations of loyalty to the Empire and his simultaneous declarations of sympathy for anti-colonial positions might be seen as attempts to outline the contingencies of imperial cosmopolitanism: that is, the articulation of conditions under which an Indian who was also British might participate in Empire, nation, and colony, and in a wider world of empires, nations, and colonies.

Obviously, the context of the rebellion and the loyalty is important. As John McLeod notes, the political proximity between the colonial regime and the princely states tended to fluctuate with British assessments of the threat posed by organized Indian nationalism.[1] The relationship between prince and Empire also evolved in response to the prince's reading of the relative strength of colonial and anti-colonial forces. As the Congress and its allies became powerful contenders in Indian and imperial politics, Ranjitsinhji drifted closer to the positions of Indian nationalism, embracing much of its rhetoric and its animus toward British policy even as he insisted that Congressmen were dangerous radicals who represented nobody.[2]

Ambivalent political affiliations were ubiquitous and perhaps inevitable in an era when English-educated Indians became increasingly radicalized in their attitudes toward British rule. Partha Chatterjee has suggested that in the decades before independence, a "secret" decolonization of Indian society was already far advanced, as closet nationalists emerged from the domestic state of the household and quietly took over public institutions such as the judiciary and the civil service.[3] Can Ranjitsinhji's appearances on the cricket field and the arena of princely politics, in the First World War and the League of Nations, be viewed as acts of infiltration? If so, then who was infiltrating what? In other words, where did the infiltrator's loyalties lie?

The problem of loyalty was especially acute for migrant Indians who came of age at the heart of the Empire; who travelled back and forth between Britain, India, and other parts of the contemporary world;

and who sought to redefine themselves with reference to their multiple and unequal worlds. The responses could vary tremendously, of course, depending upon the social and professional trajectory of the individual: the evolution of Aurobindo's "disloyalty" manifested itself quite differently from Gandhi's.[4] Cornelia Sorabjee's years in England made her a remarkably durable imperial loyalist, although hers was not an uncomplicated loyalty either.[5] Ranjitsinhji's outlook on his place in the Empire took its own course, determined by his early careers as a princely aspirant, a Cambridge man, and an England cricketer, and by his subsequent lives as a soldier in France, a delegate at the League of Nations, and a beleaguered ruling prince in a state of middling importance coming to terms with the British on the one hand and the forces of Indian nationalism on the other.

We can construct a reasonably coherent diagram for Ranjitsinhji's political evolution. As a student and then as a cricketer, he represented both England and Empire, and to the extent that he was accepted as an insider in Cambridge, Brighton, and Lord's, he became loyal. At the risk of veering too far toward an instrumentalist vision of loyalty, it is fair to assert that it paid him to be loyal. This is not to say simply that frequent declarations of passion for the Empire helped Ranji achieve his ambition of becoming the "jam" of Nawanagar. Ranji was loyal because from his location in England, the Empire was an exciting structure to be loyal to: a bigger, more adoring, and more rewarding stage than either England or India, well-stocked with useful identities, a geographical and discursive space where an enterprising and talented migrant could actually move and reinterpret himself with relative freedom. The cosmopolitan network of political connections and friendships that Ranjitsinhji cultivated after his Cambridge years worked to his benefit in that they made him famous, powerful, and wealthy, and allowed him to remain so long after the end of his career as an athlete.

Ranjitsinhji understood that the Empire was not an arena of limitless opportunity and mobility. Its ideologies of racial and national hierarchy that contained the conglomeration of peoples and migrants also contained what Ranjitsinhji liked to call his "aspirations."[6] These aspirations – that is, political identities – were inseparably tied to the fantasy of an Empire that was essentially a fraternal federation of elites for whom race was significant as a pedigree and an ornament but not as a barrier. This notion of imperial citizenship was not the delusion of a confused immigrant; reading Cannadine against the grain, it was a fantasy that the Empire actively encouraged.[7] Ranjitsinhji believed that because he had been accepted as a member of the fraternity of imperial elites, he could return to India as a ruling prince without also having to return as a native. In practice, this meant that he expected Nawanagar and India to have a moral status in the Empire that was not fundamentally dissimilar from that of Australia, South Africa, and England itself. He expected, specifically, to be recognized as an autonomous player in India and the world: to be left alone in his "domestic" affairs and to be actively involved in the "international" theatre of imperial and global politics. Beyond that, he expected the Empire to reward him for his loyalty by protecting him from those Indian critics who saw him an unreconstructed despot and a poodle of British imperialism.[8]

In an Empire undergirded by the separateness and non-equality of racialized "nations" and their component individuals, this imperial cosmopolitanism was inherently disloyal. Peter Robb observes that projects that involve the imagining of universal brotherhood typically cherish the extension of the normative community, rather than diversity.[9] That assertion might be amended. Diversity is immensely valuable to imperial ideologies, because it is critically important to the pleasure of possession. The pleasure is contingent upon the assumption that the possessed will accept the right of the possessor to order the imperial menagerie. This is where Ranjitsinhji balked, albeit inconsistently. It is not always clear whether he was disputing the organization of race and power in the Empire or insisting only on being counted among the organizers. In either case, and in spite of his repeated declarations of fidelity, he was seen by the imperial government and, after 1907, by the English press[10] as a subversive agent whose aspirations stretched what was permissible and who was difficult to dismiss (and hence all the more subversive) because as an insider in England, he had stretched the boundaries already.

The tortured nature of Ranjitsinhji's attachment to the Empire is thus partially indicative of a broad dynamic of the colonial relationship – the Oedipal conflict between Macaulay and his unwanted children – and a reflection, in part, of a split that had been a part of Ranjitsinhji's identity from his early years as an athletic celebrity. At the height of his membership in English and imperial society, he had been the invited outsider: a carefully constructed and maintained Indian, who was sometimes a partner and at other times a trophy of the British Empire. He may have seen himself as an imperial citizen, but he discovered, as the moderate nationalists had discovered, that there was always a gap between the imperial state and the black "citizen."[11] Within this gap lay the imperfectly transcended status of a colonial subject. Ranjitsinhji had come closer to Englishness than any moderate, and for him, at times, the gap had been deceptively small. In the years after the First World War, this distance between Ranjitsinhji and the Empire widened, and it was now manifested as the contingency that underlies any political partnership. In other words, Ranjitsinhji came to see his relationship with the Empire in terms of a contingent loyalty toward an entity that was separate but equal and that had political obligations toward him. His identities as an Indian, as a ruling prince, and as a subject of the Empire were now expressed consistently in terms of this contingent loyalty, in which princely self-interest, Indian nationalism, and a nostalgic affection for the fantasy-empire of elite solidarity could co-exist. This was a redeployment of the subject self with its obligation of loyalty: that is, having discovered that his position "inside" the Empire was necessarily disloyal, Ranjitsinhji sought to locate himself as an autonomous partner, whose insistence on autonomy was itself an act of loyalty.

The contorted, yet coherent, nature of Ranjitsinhji's loyalties as he emerged from wwi and began his first decade as a "returnee" ruling prince come into focus when we examine his performance as a delegate to the League of Nations. Ranjitsinhji served in Geneva three times: in 1920, 1922, and 1923. The question, of course, is whom he served. Sifting through the issues he chose to take up and the positions he created or defended, it is apparent that by this stage of his lives and careers, and in this specific forum, Ranjitsinhji saw himself as an Indian national representative. He was quite conscious of the political context within which this affiliation operated: he understood that he represented a colonized nation and that colonialism as a set of attitudes and hierarchies had relevance beyond the British-Indian relationship. He understood also that he had a second affiliation, which was with the British Empire. What he attempted to do in Geneva was to use the League to critique the Empire while being careful never to disavow it and to use his sheltered position and his privileged past within this Empire to articulate an anti-colonial political stance. In other words, at the League, Ranjitsinhji functioned as a kind of double agent: an imperial insider who had left the colony, ideologically speaking, and then infiltrated back in. At the same time, his "true" loyalties remained ambiguous and ambivalent. They certainly did not lie with the Congress, although there were broad areas of common interest. They did not lie squarely with the Indian princes either, because although there was overlap there as well, Ranjitsinhji's identity and concerns were broader. What we have, then, is a nostalgic double agent, and a lonely double agent, representing a nation that was not particularly interested in being represented by him.

Ranjitsinhji became a delegate to the League of Nations largely on account of the active role he played in creating a lobby of the middling princes that could approach the British (or provincial ministries) as a bloc. His status as a man who was well known in the wider Empire from his days as a cricketer also played a role.[12] It might be argued, in addition, that his eventual position as chancellor of the Chamber of Princes was itself due to a combination of his glamour as an imperial celebrity and his energetic and articulate support of England during the war, both of which were useful to the princes as a group. The idea that a prince be included in the Indian delegation to Geneva had come from Edwin Montagu, the secretary of state for India. It was intended as a gesture of gratitude toward the princes for their co-operation during the war, but it was also made clear by the India Office that Ranjitsinhji represented all of India in Geneva and not just the princely states.[13]

Ranjitsinhji's presence in Geneva was immediately contentious, and this was part of a larger problem, for Britain, of where colonial subjects stood in the world of international relations, and what they stood for. The India Office acknowledged that there was an "anomaly" in India, a colony and by no means a certain candidate for dominion status, having its own delegation and a "quasi-independent" rank at the League. This anomaly was perceived to have generated unforeseen problems in Geneva: embarrassing clashes between the Indian and British positions and unpredictable behaviour by Indian delegates, as well as American complaints that a separate Indian delegation was simply a ploy to boost the size of the British bloc in the League.[14] The American charge was certainly valid as far as British intentions were concerned, but the benefits of such "stacking" could be ensured only if Indian delegates consistently toed the imperial line, which, apparently, they did not.

The India Office had hoped that the structure of the three-man Indian delegations would be enough to prevent the problem from getting out of hand. The usual format was for two Indians to be balanced and controlled by a senior British official, such as William Meyer (former finance minister in the government of India) in 1920, Lord Chelmsford in 1922, and Lord Hardinge in 1923.[15] (In 1920, Ranjitsinhji was also accompanied by C. B. Fry and C. Berthon, the senior British administrative supervisor in Nawanagar.[16]) Thus, the framework of the delegation was itself a test of loyalty for the delegates. The Indians were carefully selected: Ranjitsinhji, in spite of his frequent clashes with the colonial authorities, had an established record of Anglophilia and loyalty as far as the Empire itself was concerned, and others, such as Sir Sivaswamy Ayer and Sir Imam Ali (the latter was a former diwan to the Nizam), were also expected to refrain from making waves. The guiding principle behind the structure was that "there must be limits, and independent action on first-class questions of foreign and inter-imperial policy could not be allowed."[17] Sometimes the plan worked reasonably well. When Ayer tried to criticize the British and South African governments for collusion in the administration of South West Africa, he was silenced by Chelmsford, who on a separate occasion managed to divert Ranjitsinhji from initiating a discussion of British activities in Kenya. Nevertheless, the fact that Chelmsford and the India Office found it necessary to intervene more frequently than they had anticipated indicates that the Indians in the delegation had a different idea of their identities and responsibilities from what their managers had in mind. I shall focus here on two issues – opium and immigration – on which Ranjitsinhji indicated where his loyalties lay at this time.

Ranjitsinhji became embroiled in the opium debate during his 1923 stint in Geneva, when the League became the forum for acrimonious discussions of the international trade in narcotics. Special delegations from the United States were inclined to blame India and China for generating in America the various social problems associated with narcotics, and they demanded strict controls against the production and export of opium. Ranjitsinhji was acutely sensitive to the cultural critique of "the Orient" that was implicit in the American position and went about mounting a defence, not of Britain or the British Empire, but explicitly of "Indian culture" and "Eastern peoples." He adopted a two-part defensive strategy. On the one hand, he argued economics; on the other, he talked culture. He talked about the financial importance of opium cultivation to India and Indian peasants, and declared that Indian opium-producers had already made significant monetary sacrifices by reducing exports to appease the anti-drug crusaders abroad. The colonial exchequer had forfeited forty million pounds in revenues, he announced, and the common cultivator had forfeited a basic source of livelihood.[18] It is worth noting that Ranjitsinhji had a personal stake in this debate about revenue. Nawanagar was a producer of opium, and the state monopoly on the sale of the drug ensured that Ranjitsinhji benefited directly from maximizing production and export. Between 1911 and 1920, Nawanagar's collections from opium production had grown steadily, from about

Rs. 16,000 annually to over Rs. 20,000.[19] Given his chronic need for liquid assets, Ranjitsinhji would have been loath to see any significant source of revenue diminished. Twenty thousand rupees, however, was a miniscule portion of the state's tax base of about four million rupees, and the prospect of a fall in opium earnings cannot fully explain why Ranjitsinhji waded so energetically into battle on this issue. It can be argued, of course, that he was doing the dirty work of defending the imperial treasury (which was considerably more invested in opium than Nawanagar[20]) from American attacks, while British delegates remained discreetly silent. However, the terms in which he staged his defence of "Indian culture" from critics of opium production were also an implicit rebuttal of colonial assumptions about the colonized and could not have been especially comforting to British, Australian, Canadian, or South African delegates in Geneva.

Ranjitsinhji complained that "India and China are lumped together as 'opium countries'" and denied that Indians were "an opium-smoking people."[21] Opium in India, he declared, was regarded "not…as a detrimental product, but as a natural product." The drug *was* used in India, he conceded, but primarily as veterinary medicine and a folk remedy, and secondarily "as a sedative by hard-working and poor people."[22] Having thus contradicted the stock image of unproductive, lazy, and morally decayed Oriental addicts,[23] Ranjitsinhji went on to draw direct parallels between the consumption of opium in India and the use of "herbs and samples as country medicine" in the West, and he observed that even its recreational use was no different from the use of alcohol in America and Europe. For good measure, he added a critique of the moral logic of pinning the blame on production rather than on consumption:

> If you take the total annual consumption per head of population
> in India, what does it amount to? It amounts to two grams
> per head per annum, and that is about the weight of about
> two-thirds of an ordinary lump of sugar. But when you take
> into account the veterinarian use which is made of opium…it
> reduces the two-thirds of a lump to one-third. So you cannot
> rate India as an extravagant consumer of its native equivalent
> of western liquors. In this connection I may further add that no
> one would think of calling that great country, the United States
> of America, an opium consuming country, and yet, no doubt
> for very legitimate and proper purposes, I am reliably told, and I
> believe it, it consumes about twice as much opium as India.[24]

It should be noted that Ranjitsinhji was far from being an unapologetic defender of opium. Although the recreational use of the drug was common in Rajput society, Ranjitsinhji distanced himself from the habit, modulating the distance to indicate his moral and racial location within the overlapping societies of Rajputs, Indians, Europeans, and modern men. He referred to the overall project of regulating narcotics as a "worthy cause" and applauded (in the name of Indian poppy cultivators and with a bare minimum of irony) "the great good that has been achieved" by limiting the drug trade. There is no doubt that he saw opium as an appropriate topic of debate for people like himself in forums such as the League: the issue, he remarked, called for "loyal international cooperation, backed by sustained and expert vigilance by the League."[25] In other words, he wanted the tactical advantage of the enlightened high ground, both for himself as an English-educated Indian and for the Indian elites who might participate, actively or vicariously, in the international gathering of elites that the League manifested. On this high ground, however, he organized a defence of opium production and use that was cultural-relativist as well as rooted in the logic of "Western" cultural practices. Explicitly distinguishing between "legitimate" (Indian) uses and "illegitimate" (Western) abuses of opium, he rejected the moral superiority of the West and simultaneously denied any essential difference between West and East as far as intoxicants were concerned. Thus, he was able to mount a moral counter-offensive: whereas India had made sacrifices by cutting production, America remained a major consumer and was a hypocrite. Logically, the position was entirely consistent: Ranjitsinhji was asserting that opium, like alcohol, is legitimate when used in moderation and that the problem that should be addressed by the League and other international forums was the excessive consumption in America.

This apparently unprecedented assumption of the role of the representative of the colonized, morally vilified, and economically deprived Indian only indirectly challenged British and Commonwealth delegates at the League, although there are suggestions in the India Office records that some of those present (such as the Canadian delegate, Arthur Steele-Maitland) were unhappy with Ranjitsinhji's stance.[26] On the issue of immigration, Ranjitsinhji was more directly confrontational because his particular grievance had to do with restrictions on the right of Indians to migrate to South Africa and other imperial Dominions, and with the disenfranchisement of those already in those countries. His interest in Indian immigration within the Empire was not, of course, unprecedented. At a banquet in Cambridge in 1909, he had declared:

> I think that the British Empire ought to treat all British subjects
> alike. The doors to Indian peoples have unfortunately been shut
> in Australia, and in Canada and South Africa. I cannot but
> regret it, and I think that the Home Government ought to try
> and make out some scheme by which Indians could give their
> labour and trade in our colonies.[27]

One biographer of Ranjitsinhji has suggested that this particular outburst
was brought on by the passage of the Black Act in South Africa.[28] It
is fair to say that as a migrant who had long clung to the view that the
Empire was valuable precisely because it provided a geography of mobility, transformation, and transcendence of the tie between place and race,
Ranjitsinhji's interest in Indian migration was of long standing. Quite
aside from his personal inclinations, Ranjitsinhji would have been aware
that there was great interest and outrage in the native press in India
regarding the status of Indians in South Africa. This outrage was also
explicitly anti-British in the sense that it accused the imperial government of abandoning the South African Indians "to the tender mercies
of the Boers." The *Jam-e-Jamshed* added, in the year that Ranjitsinhji
became the ruler of Nawanagar:

> A greater act of national faithlessness has never been committed
> by any people on the face of the earth than that committed
> by imperial Britain. But there is a Nemesis for nations and
> Governments as for individuals, and Britain may awake to the
> folly of this crime when some of her petted Colonial children
> rise against her, and she feels the need for the help of her Indian
> subjects to maintain her own.[29]

In the same year, the *Mahratta* compared the treatment of Indians in
South Africa to Japanese exclusion in California, and added: "As citizens
of the British Empire, Indians have a right to enter and settle in any
land over which the British flag flies."[30]

This talismanic invocation of imperial citizenship – and the split image of the Empire as a guarantor and a violator of the rights of coloured
migrants, which requires that the images be viewed from within the
protective/abusive structure – is very similar to Ranjitsinhji's own outlook.
It is not surprising, therefore, that he would raise it as an issue when he
was at the League of Nations, representing not only India but the migrant
self in a political geography that both facilitated and punished migration.

As he pointed out in a speech in Geneva in 1923, "I should feel false to my fellow-countrymen in India, and also to my fellow-countrymen in South Africa, were I to neglect this unique opportunity of summoning to the assistance of their aspirations the spiritual power...of your sympathy." Directly addressing the South African delegation, Ranjitsinhji attempted to utilize the "atmosphere of sympathy and good feeling" – not to mention the glare of publicity – of the League of Nations in order to put the Empire in a spotlight that he controlled and to let it squirm under its own discourse of inclusive benevolence. The British mother, he said, had taken under her wing the grizzly bear and the kiwi, the kangaroo and the ostrich, the lion and the tiger, and it was only natural that such a diverse collectivity would occasionally fight. What mattered, he implied, was whether the mother was fair or prejudiced in her response because that would tell whether the Empire was a family or a zoo. Mixing his metaphors eloquently, he added:

> We in this Assembly believe that God made us all men, to
> walk erect on one earth; and we believe in one truth and in one
> justice, universal for all men, and it is to this atmosphere and
> to this faith that I make my appeal. But outside this Assembly,
> there have often been two justices, one for the West and one
> for the East. It is for the League of Nations to engraft its own
> conception, the far higher, and far better conception, upon the
> universal practice of mankind. What is our ideal? What is our
> purpose? What is the very reason of our being? Let us have
> catholic justice and we shall have catholic peace.[31]

The sentiment was not welcomed by the other delegates from the Commonwealth. Joseph Cook, the senior Australian delegate (and former prime minister), dismissed Ranjitsinhji's remarks as "cheap claptrap."[32] Also, Chelmsford had heard a "rumour" that Ranjitsinhji planned to raise the immigration issue in Geneva, and he tried to persuade him to desist. Ranjitsinhji refused, arguing that Chelmsford was a relative newcomer to League protocol and that he, Ranjitsinhji, was a more experienced judge of what topics were appropriate.[33] (He then undermined Chelmsford further by recounting the incident in the Chamber of Princes, protecting himself politically with humour and the usual declaration of loyalty.[34])

The maneuver re-enacted an exchange that Ranjitsinhji had had with the governor of Bombay in 1921. On the occasion of a gubernatorial visit to Jamnagar, he had very conventionally assured George Lloyd about his disdain for nationalist "busy-bodies" and their "sermons of discontent."

If Lloyd was in fact reassured, Ranjitsinhji had poisoned the moment by invoking Woodrow Wilson and the Fourteen Points, specifically "the precious right of self-determination for every community under the sun, of which I am not much mistaken, the world will hear a lot more than the innocent looking formula suggested to its originator."[35] Reciting the Fourteen Points to a colonial administrator, and adding that even Wilson had not grasped the full implications of his most famous doctrine, was hardly a conventional declaration of loyalty. It placed Ranjitsinhji very close to the "busy-bodies" he seemed to deride. Assuming this ambivalent position at the League of Nations served to place the contingencies of his politics before a wider audience that included Indian nationalists.

In 1920 the League of Nations was already under attack in the Indian press as a racist protector of imperial interests and a structure that compelled the colonized to approach the world through their colonial masters.[36] Ranjitsinhji's postures in Geneva should be understood as a nuanced response to these perceptions: as a racially conscious "Indian" who was also something more than a racially determined native, he was happy to articulate in Geneva selected portions of what the true natives articulated in Bombay and Karachi. The League was in many ways the perfect platform for Ranjitsinhji in this mode. He would have been lost in the Congress, not least because of the chronic bad blood between the Congress and the princes.[37] In Geneva, he could tell the assembled delegates that they – an anonymous pronoun that would accuse all, none, and the self-consciously guilty – needed to do more to enforce the mandates that gave colonial powers trusteeship of "primitive peoples." As the delegate of a colonial country with an anomalous status in the League, he could announce that the British were not living up to the spirit of their African mandates; like Ayer, he believed that the League had a moral duty to intervene.[38] Thus, a rather bold anti-colonial position could be phrased in terms of support for an overtly colonial arrangement, with the League superseding the Empire as the imperfect guardian of a moral and political vision.

It is revealing to compare Ranjitsinhji's performances at the League of Nations with his performance as a cricket star. In both cases, he grasped and relished the opportunity to perform on an international stage. In both cases, he represented the British Empire and this affiliation coexisted uneasily with his other identity, which was that of a particular type of Indian. He was able to walk upon the stage precisely because he was colonized, and for this he was genuinely appreciative, yet he constantly threatened to overstep the boundaries of his place in the Empire. The difference between the cricket tours of Australia and America in the 1890s and the diplomatic tours of Geneva in the 1920s is that Ranjitsinhji's location within the Empire had changed. Earlier, he was the Englishman playing the Indian prince who was nevertheless more English than any Australian or American: that is, the insider playing the imperial ornament, coming face to face with the genuine savages on the periphery. In the 1920s, he had lapsed from his old identification and slipped outside, and it was the savages who were on the inside; only he had to pretend he was one of them in order to articulate his critique.

Ranjitsinhji's loyalties matter in the history of modern India, modern Britain, and the imperial encounter because Ranjitsinhji was not merely a modern man. For somebody who was openly enamoured of the methods and monuments of modernity, he was also remarkably ambivalent toward that most central of modern institutions, the nation-state. I do not refer only to the incipient Indian nation-state, but also the British nation-state, with its closed boundaries that were projected into the Empire. Ranjitsinhji's loyalties matter because he manifests a third voice in the politics of imperialism: neither a nationalist nor an imperialist in the conventional sense, but a man whose identities and allegiances were spread widely across the world of nations. Ranjitsinhji was not an exceptional political creature. Many of his positions were shared with the princes of his time, with Congressmen of his time, and with his contemporary colonial administrators, journalists, and members of the public. He was, however, closest to another variety of political agent: the (im)migrant in the modern world, who is frequently opportunistic, who tends to own it all and nothing in particular, who refuses to be monopolized, who is a living denial of the sanctity of the border, and who is therefore liminal and dangerous in every country.

{NOTES}

1 John McLeod, *Sovereignty, Power, Control: Politics in the States of Western India, 1916–1947* (Leiden: Brill, 1999), 39–48.
2 Foreign and Political Dept. c/175-1, 1931; 010c (London).
3 Partha Chatterjee, *A Princely Imposter? The Kumar of Bhawal and the Secret History of Indian Nationalism* (Delhi: Permanent Black, 2002), 375–79.
4 Ashis Nandy, *The Intimate Enemy: Loss and Recovery of Self Under Colonialism* (Delhi: Oxford University Press, 1983), 85–100.

5 Antoinette Burton, *At the Heart of the Empire: Indians and the Colonial Encounter in Late-Victorian Britain* (Berkeley: University of California Press, 1998), 110–51.

6 Roland Wild, *The Biography of Colonel His Highness Shri Sir Ranjitsinhji* (London: Rich and Cowan, 1934), 284–87.

7 David Cannadine, *Ornamentalism: How the British Saw Their Empire* (Oxford: Oxford University Press, 2001), 10, 41–57.

8 Foreign and Political Dept. c/175-1, 1931.

9 Peter Robb, "South Asia and the Concept of Race," in *The Concept of Race in South Asia* (Delhi: Oxford University Press, 1995), 18.

10 *John Bull*, 14 November 1908; *The Daily Mirror*, 19 November 1926.

11 John McLane, *Indian Nationalism and the Early Congress* (Princeton: Princeton University Press, 1977), 49.

12 Political and Secret File 797, 1926; o10c.

13 *Miscellaneous Notes Relative to International Status of India*, December 1927, confidential memo of the India Office; Political and Secret File 797, 1926; o10c.

14 *"International Status of India,"* 14 May 1928, confidential memo of the India Office; Political and Secret File 797, 1926; o10c.

15 Chelmsford and Hardinge were both former viceroys at this stage.

16 Fry, like MacLaren, occasionally worked as Ranjitsinhji's secretary, speechwriter, and all-purpose trouble-shooter. C. B. Fry, *Life Worth Living* (London: Pavilion Library, 1939), 281–305.

17 "International Status of India," 14 May 1928, confidential memo of the India Office; Political and Secret File 797, 1926; o10c.

18 Political and Secret File 797, 1926, o10c; James Mills, *Cannabis Britannica: Empire, Trade and Prohibition, 1800–1928* (Oxford: Oxford University Press, 2003), 152–87.

19 Nawanagar Administration Reports, 1911–12, 1919–20; o10c.

20 Ranjitsinhji pointed the finger directly at the colonial government and extricated princes like himself from the moral dilemma posed by Indian opium. He argued: "Opium is a Government monopoly, and the Indian States, autonomous or otherwise (such as my own) could not export it without the permission of the Government of India. Since the cessation of the Chinese traffic in 1913 no opium produced in the States of the Indian Princes has been exported from India." Ranjitsinhji, speech at the League of Nations, 1923; Political and Secret File 797, 1926; o10c.

21 Ranjitsinhji, speech at the Chamber of Princes, 1924; Political and Secret File 797, 1926; o10c.

22 Ranjitsinhji, speech at the League of Nations, 1923; Political and Secret File 797, 1926; o10c.

23 James Mills, *Madness, Cannabis and Colonialism: The Native-Only Lunatic Asylums of British India, 1857–1900* (London: Macmillan, 2000), 69–90.

24 Ranjitsinhji, speech at the League of Nations, 1923; Political and Secret File 797, 1926; o10c.

25 Ranjitsinhji, speech at the Chamber of Princes, 1924; Political and Secret File 797, 1926; o10c.

26 Ibid.

27 Wild, *Biography*, 106–8.

28 Alan Ross, *Ranji: Prince of Cricketers* (London: Collins, 1983), 153–54.

29 *Jam-e-Jamshed*, 28 March 1907, NNR Bombay 1907; OIOC.

30 *The Mahratta*, 24 March 1907, NNR Bombay, 1907; OIOC.

31 Ranjitsinhji, speech at the League of Nations, 1922; Political and Secret File 797, 1926; OIOC.

32 Wilde, *Biography*, 233–35.

33 Ranjitsinhji, speech at the Chamber of Princes, 1924; Political and Secret File 797, 1926; OIOC.

34 In the same speech before the Chamber of Princes, Ranjitsinhji divulged that he had been approached by other delegates (from outside the British Empire – probably from some of the Latin American delegations, with whom Ranjitsinhji had a good rapport) about a non-permanent seat for India on the League Council. Although Ranjitsinhji had been enthusiastic and had the number of votes required, Balfour had scuttled the idea. Ranjitsinhji concluded his narrative of the incident with "Of course, Lord Balfour's decision was loyally accepted." Political and Secret File 797, 1926; OIOC.

35 Nawanagar Administration Report, 1921–22; OIOC.

36 One journal proposed that the organization change its name to the "League of Masters" or the "League of White Nations." The *Sind Advocate*, 3 and 19 April 1919, NNR Bombay 1919; OIOC.

37 McLeod, *Sovereignty, Power, Control*, 42–43.

38 Political and Secret File 797, 1926; OIOC.

CHAPTER 15

THE EMPIRE ANSWERS:

IMPERIAL IDENTITY ON RADIO AND FILM, 1939–1945

Wendy Webster

IN OCTOBER 1939, A RADIO PROGRAM called *The Empire Answers*
provided a "chronicle of the entry into the war of the peoples of the
British Commonwealth."[1] It emphasized the role of radio in bringing
together an imperial community to hear the British prime minister's voice
announcing war with Germany, as in "thousands of homes" in South
Africa, people "gathered around their wireless sets"; families in Australia
"gathered round the fire after Sunday tea listening for news 12,000 miles
away"; and there were "lights in the houses at midnight and the small
hours" in New Zealand. The program took its audience on a "circuit of
Empire" spanning four continents where the simultaneity of "listening
in," as the program reminded them, could take place in spring, summer,
and winter as well as autumn, and at night as well as in the day. Whatever
the season or the time zone, the voices on the program, from Africa,
South and Southeast Asia, Australasia, the Caribbean, and Canada, all
had the same message: one of loyal devotion and support for Britain.

The role of propaganda in showing the war effort as a "people's war"
has attracted considerable attention from historians. The "people's war"
showed a community united across differences of class and gender as well
as different national identities within Britishness, although Northern
Ireland received scant attention. Most work on this imagery has been
confined to the British war effort. The development of a corresponding
version of imperial identity and the relationship between wartime ideas
of Britishness/Englishness and Empire has received much less attention
within a literature that generally separates the projection of Empire from
discussion of the "people's war."[2] Yet media audiences – in Britain and
the Empire – saw or heard both versions of the war effort, especially on
radio, newsreels, and documentary films.

The idea of a "people's war" was most extensively developed in relation to the home front in Britain, while the imperial war effort was usually shown on the fighting front and emphasized martial masculinity through its most characteristic image of marching troops. Representations of nation and Empire nevertheless converged on common themes – especially from 1942 – and the projection of a "people's Empire" corresponded in many ways to the "people's war." What Stuart Ward has called a "racial community" of Britons was one prominent theme of Empire propaganda, highlighting the role of white Australians, Canadians, New Zealanders, and South Africans as "sons of Empire."[3] This showed the efforts of the common people in the Empire, united with the common people of Britain in a fight for justice and freedom. But Indian soldiers were also acclaimed as courageous sons of Empire and much Empire propaganda projected the Empire as a multiracial community. While the image of a "people's war" showed a homogeneous people pulling together across differences of class and gender, this version of a "people's Empire" showed a heterogeneous people pulling together across differences of race and ethnicity, united in a common cause.

In January 1940, newsreels showed Australian, Canadian, and New Zealand servicemen arriving in Britain; Newfoundland lumberjacks crossing the Atlantic to fell timber in Scotland for Britain's war needs; Indian and Canadian troops arriving in France; New Zealanders living in England forming their own anti-tank unit; South African airmen patrolling "the shores of the British Empire in Africa"; and Australian troops parading through Sydney.[4] Some of these disparate stories – on Australians, New Zealanders, and Canadians – were brought together in early January to demonstrate "the Empire's New Year greeting to the Mother Country." Its greeting – sending "its sons to join the fight" – brought with it the message that "all the Empire stands together in the fight for freedom."[5] These 1940 newsreels projected an imperial identity that, like First World War imagery, showed a devoted Empire coming to Britain's aid at a time of national peril, demonstrating love and support for the motherland. Like *The Empire Answers*, they suggested automatic loyalty.

While Empire imagery remained conservative in the early stages of the war, one link between ideas of nation and Empire was the role the media assigned themselves in bringing together a national and imperial community. Both *The First Days* – the first British documentary film made about the war in 1939 – and *The Empire Answers* converged on a common symbol of unity: the radio.

The First Days offers an image that became recurrent in wartime films about the British home front – people listening to war news on the radio, often in a domestic setting. People who have never met, and are unlikely to ever meet, are shown as connected through the collective and simultaneous act of "listening in." Visual media were thus not only used to represent the nation as a united community, but also to represent aural media bringing the nation into "deep, horizontal comradeship."[6] In its imagery of the reception of the prime minister's radio broadcast announcing war, as in its imagery of people preparing for war, *The First Days* also stresses a common identity across class and gender differences. Class is signified through clothing and housing, as working-class men in cloth caps listen in a pub, a working-class woman in an apron listens in her kitchen, a pipe-smoking man sits beside his wireless set in a suburban domestic interior. All receive the news in calm, grave silence, and the sequence ends in a further silence, against a shot of a cloudy sky. Shots of suburban streets show them completely deserted and quiet while the news is broadcast.

The Empire Answers offered a word picture corresponding to the visual imagery of wartime films. Where *The First Days* focuses on people in Britain hearing the announcement that Britain was at war with Germany, *The Empire Answers* told how the prime minister's voice was heard "in all parts of the British world." The program cast the Empire in the image of radio. However vast the distances, whatever the season or the time zone, the radio's domestic setting of hearth, home, and family unites an imperial community. The familial intimacy associated with radio was also used as an image of imperial unity by George VI in wartime Christmas radio broadcasts. The idea of the King speaking from his home and of the royal family gathered round the hearth at Christmas became an analogy to what the King referred to as "one great family" in 1941, "the family circle" in 1942, and "the family of the British Commonwealth and Empire" in 1943. "Wherever you are, serving in our wide, free Commonwealth of Nations," he told his audience in the royal Christmas broadcast in 1942, "you will always feel 'at home.' Though severed by the long sea miles of distance, you are still in the family circle."[7]

Despite these homely and familial images, the Empire presented problems for the idea of Britain as a tolerant and decent nation embodied in early images of a "people's war." It was not only Nazi propaganda that portrayed British colonial rule as oppressive. There was growing opposition in America to British imperialism in the 1920s and 1930s, fuelled by British responses to Indian nationalism. This was extended before America's entry into the war in American resistance to abandoning a policy of neutrality in order to fight a war in defence of the British Empire. When Allied war aims were defined in the 1941 Atlantic Charter, they included self-determination for all nations, prompting the American under-secretary of state to declare that "the age of imperialism is dead."[8] In 1941 a report based on views expressed by Americans in letters sent to Britain that were intercepted by censors concluded that "few people in England have any conception of the reality of the Empire bogey in the American mind and elsewhere. The Nazi radio keeps at it all the time, and upon this topic it is effective."[9]

Early moves to counter such views drew on what John Mackenzie calls the "peace and economic regeneration" version of Empire that had been extensively developed between the wars.[10] This emphasized that the British Empire had not been founded on conquest or oppression, but on love of liberty and justice. King George VI's Empire Day message in 1940 was heard not only in Britain – where cinema programs were stopped to mark this radio broadcast – and throughout the Empire, but was also carried by American stations.[11] The King stated: "There is a word that our enemies use against us – Imperialism. By it they mean the spirit of domination, the lust of Conquest." But, he countered, "our one object has always been peace – peace in which our institutions may be developed, the condition of our peoples improved."

Sonya Rose argues that a restrained version of exemplary masculinity representing a home-loving, quiet reticence – what she calls the "temperate hero" – was constructed in the Second World War in opposition to the "hyper-masculinity" represented by jack-booted, goose-stepping Nazis.[12] The King's speech produced a similarly temperate Empire against the aggressive masculine conquest and aggression associated with the Nazis. The Colonial Development and Welfare Act, passed in 1940, extended this message and gave some substance to the King's statement about improving "the condition of our peoples."

After 1942, this message was extended further. The fall of Singapore, Hong Kong, Malaya, and Burma to Japanese forces led to increasing pressure to present a modern Empire. American criticism added to such pressure. In a widely reported speech in the wake of the surrender of Singapore, Sumner Welles, President Roosevelt's chief foreign policy adviser, reiterated that "the age of imperialism is ended."[13] The fall of Singapore led the *Times* to argue in an editorial that "misguided conceptions of racial prestige and narrow obsolete interpretations of economic interest" must be surmounted "if democracy is to have any meaning or appeal for the colonial peoples."[14] From 1942, the word insistently used in Empire propaganda to proclaim a modern Empire was "partnership."[15]

Representations of a united nation and Empire dedicated to improving the conditions of its peoples were always in tension with differences between the different groups that were represented. *The Empire Answers* represented India through the voice of Lord Linlithgow, the viceroy, broadcasting to the Indian people and did not mention that eight of the eleven devolved self-governing provinces, established in 1935, resigned after he announced that India had gone to war with Germany without consulting them, or any other Indian.[16] Nor did it mention Eire, a member of the Commonwealth until 1948, which maintained a policy of neutrality throughout the war. In South Africa, where the war issue was highly divisive and the decision to abandon the early policy of neutrality was opposed by many Afrikaner nationalists, the program stressed unity between Afrikaners and Britons "as members of the active citizens forces manning their posts."[17]

The need to address American audiences was a consistent thread in the wartime projection of a "people's Empire." But the audiences for Empire propaganda were highly diverse. The BBC became increasingly aware of the diversity of its audience in Britain and was concerned that jokes about "darkies" would be found offensive. Producers were urged to remember that "there are a lot of coloured people in the country now – Africans, West Indians and Americans, and there is therefore particularly good reason to be careful not to say anything which might be interpreted as showing colour prejudice."[18] In 1942 the monthly intelligence summary argued that people in the Middle East were not won over by images of British decency, while images of Churchill, replete with cigar, did not win over Indians, whose conception of leadership involved the spiritual and symbolic.[19]

In this context, the media began to recognize a need to appeal to non-white audiences to enlist support for the war effort. One strategy used was the production of programs for specific audiences. Before the war, the BBC services had been aimed mainly at the self-governing Dominions, but its services to the rest of the Empire were now expanded. The service to the West Indies, for example, previously reserved mainly for special occasions such as cricket test matches, was now expanded with "morale-boosting talks on West Indians and the war effort."[20] Sometimes the specific audiences addressed were a result of racial segregation. The exclusion of West Africans from Nairobi cinemas was brought to the attention of the Colonial Office in 1941, and, upon inquiry, they were informed by the governor of Kenya that the Kenyan government censored films as "suitable for non-Africans only."[21] The British media showed an Empire united against the Nazi threat, but this exclusion offers a striking example of divisions that were imposed on audiences of such imagery.

If some films were for "non-Africans only," others were specifically addressed to black Africans. The Colonial Film Unit was set up early in the war as part of the Ministry of Information's efforts to mobilize support for the war throughout the Empire. Developing propaganda in conjunction with the Colonial Office, it produced documentaries designed mainly for black Africans and provided mobile cinema vans to take these films into rural areas.[22] The racial hierarchy underpinning ideas about audiences was evident in the assumption that because of the visual illiteracy of their audience, these films should be slow-moving, with their narrative patiently explained in commentaries.[23]

The recognition of a need to address diverse audiences, to counter American anti-imperialism, and to recover from the loss of Singapore meant a continuing need to show unity and loyalty. But such recognition also meant a move to show a modern Empire, emphasizing themes of partnership and welfare. This was an image that advertised the virtues of Britain as a liberal and tolerant nation, and demonstrated common resistance to Nazi Germany by an Empire that was neither racist nor oppressive.

*

In *From the Four Corners* (1941), soldiers from Australia, Canada, and New Zealand who meet in London are greeted by a woman who calls them "splendid fellows" and tells them: "How wonderful you are coming all those thousands of miles to answer the motherland's call to arms." The woman's greeting encapsulates the dominant view of Empire in the First World War: loyal and devoted, answering the call from Britain. But it is a view that makes these Second World War soldiers uneasy, and the woman, who is middle-class and middle-aged, is shown as gushing and patronizing in contrast to their plain-speaking and youthful manliness. These soldiers represent the common people of the self-governing Dominions – privates not officers – on leave in Britain. They are rescued from the woman's clutches by film star Leslie Howard, who takes them off to that classic institution of the "people's war" – a pub, where they drink pints.

Howard was not only a film star but also a prominent broadcaster on the BBC overseas service. His broadcasts identified the temperate heroic qualities of a "people's war" – "courage, devotion to duty, kindliness, humour, coolheadedness, balance, common sense, singleness of purpose...and idealism."[24] In *From the Four Corners*, the soldiers from Australia, Canada, and New Zealand exemplify this temperate heroism and an idealism that links Englishness and Empire. Howard disputes the woman's claim that the soldiers are answering the motherland's call, and they assent to this in characteristic plain speech – "that's a lot of hooey." But he also disputes their own version of why they have enlisted, expressed in equally plain speech – "to kick Hitler in the pants, of course." Howard is prone to eloquence and his voice dominates the film as he treats them to a history lesson – a stirring story of common law and justice, freedom and democracy, taken by British pioneers to the ends of the earth. That is why they came, he tells them, to defend these values – out of idealism.

The trio of soldiers in *From the Four Corners* was one of the most characteristic representations of Empire in the war, foregrounding martial masculinity and a racial community of Britons. Howard plays himself, his status as a film star providing a short low-budget documentary with at least some star attraction. When the Australian soldier tells Howard he has seen him in the movies, he also identifies a more widely disseminated imperial image: "our chaps marching through the streets...the troopship going out." Newsreels of troopships appeared to confirm American fears that the British were fighting in defence of their Empire, as they showed imperial manhood circulating around the Empire, disembarking in various theatres of war that were often imperial territory. And then they marched. *Britain At Bay* (1940), a documentary with a commentary written and spoken by J.B. Priestley, shows a racial community of Britons, like the trio of soldiers in *From the Four Corners*, described by Priestley as "men from the ends of the earth, from our Great Dominions in Australia, New Zealand and Canada," against shots of them marching. But marching was often a metaphor for a wider imperial unity – a multiracial community that marched together. *The Empire Marches* (1941) ends with shots of imperial troops in action and the question: "Is it not significant that men of every race, creed and colour are marching and fighting to the common end?"

Martial masculinity had a long history as a prominent image of Empire that focused on the soldier hero. Imagery of martial Indians had acquired considerable popularity in pre-war Hollywood films of Empire, although their British officers were always the main focus of attention. "Martial race theory," first developed in India, was used in the recruitment of imperial troops by British officers and administrators.[25]

Defining which ethnic groups made good soldiers, it emphasized a martial race as naturally warlike, courageous, loyal, disciplined (when well led), and of considerable physical prowess.[26]

Reporting of the martial masculinity of Indians and Africans lost any subtleties about distinctions between different ethnic groups but repeatedly rehearsed the qualities of courage, loyalty, and physical prowess. Newsreel commentaries on Indian troops claimed that there were "no more fearless fighters in the world," called them "hardy little men from the hills and the plains," and described them as tough as the mules – "fighters from the Punjab and the North West Frontier, men who have spent their lives in the open."[27] *War Came to Kenya* (1942) – retitled *War Comes to Africa* for distribution in Britain – identifies an Indian mounted battery as "men of magnificent bearing and physique."[28] Africans join Indian warriors in the litany of martial masculinity: troops from the Gold Coast are described in a newsreel as "bronze giants of nature, every man strips to display muscles calculated to make Joe Louis look to his biceps."[29] Like Indian soldiers, it is not only their bodies that are a focus of attention but also their loyal allegiance as volunteers: "They are not conscripts, but volunteers who have found the Union Jack worth living under, and worth fighting for."

The loyalty of India to the Empire/Commonwealth, exemplified by the military, was the major theme of media coverage of India throughout the war in imagery that was dominated by British views and British voices. In *Defenders of India* (1941), the voices of General Auchinleck, who provides a foreword to the film, and Robert Stimson as commentator link "India's stalwart troops" to a temperate "people's Empire" – marching, training, and fighting "for the Empire and reasonableness and decency."[30] A 1945 news story of former Indian prisoners-of-war from Germany, visited by royalty in a camp in Norfolk, acclaimed their contribution to the war effort as "warriors of India" receiving a royal tribute for their "heroic contribution to the Allied victory," having fought with distinction "in the honoured tradition of fighting India."[31]

Narratives of India were not always dominated by British voices, and, for the first time, British officers were sometimes nowhere to be seen when Indian military were shown. *India Marches* (1941), sponsored by the government of India and the Ministry of Information, ends with a long sequence of Indian soldiers marching, but this is as much a metaphor of Indian self-sufficiency as of imperial unity, and the film emphasizes Indian membership in the British Commonwealth and not the Empire. Narrated by an Indian – Z. A. Bokhari, who worked in the BBC Empire

Service during the war – the film addresses a Western audience, educating them about India. Bokhari informs them, for example, about sports in which Indians are world champions, including hockey, which "may be an English game, but we have, so to speak, owned it for a bit." Despite the focus on a distinctive Indian identity, emphasizing Indian unity between Hindus, Muslims, and Sikhs, the main message is one of loyalty: an India that is "a member of the mighty British Commonwealth and is proud of it."

The government of India, as well as the Ministry of Information, the Colonial Office, the India Office, and all other bodies involved in decisions about Empire propaganda on India, faced a tangled web of contradictory pressures. The rise of Indian nationalism between the wars made British media more aware of the impact of their productions on Indian audiences, especially in the contexts of popular and official protests in India at Empire films, including those by Hollywood.[32] When war was declared, the need to recruit Indians into the military made the impact of productions on Indian audiences a more urgent consideration. American audiences also had to be considered. Despite Hollywood celebrations of the British Empire in India, American anti-imperialism, like Nazi propaganda, portrayed British rule in India as oppressive. In this context, there was a particular need to portray a "people's Empire" in India – progressive, modern, loyal.

The image of loyalty became especially important in the context of the 1942 Quit India movement, named after the resolution taken by the Indian National Congress in July 1942, which told the British to "purify themselves by surrendering power in India." The mass demonstrations of the Quit India movement in 1942, in the aftermath of the arrest of the leadership of the Indian National Congress, were a serious disruption to the imagery of India that had been developed. Violent British repression of demonstrators did not exactly fit the idea of British rule in India as progressive or of a "people's Empire." The RAF was brought in to machine gun crowds from the air, and it was British statistics which showed that, by mid-September, police firing on rioters and clashes with troops had caused 658 Indian deaths and "large numbers" of injuries: this compared to eleven British troops killed and seven injured.[33] An emergency Whipping Act, introduced in August, allowed whipping to be inflicted on anybody convicted of rioting.[34] American opposition was expressed in an open letter from the editors of the American magazine *Life* to the "People of England," which affirmed: "*One* thing we are sure we are *not* fighting for is to hold the British Empire together. We don't like to put the matter so bluntly, but we don't want you to have any illusions.... In the light of what you are doing in India, how do you expect to talk about 'principles,' and look our soldiers in the eye?"[35]

In this context, the loyal Indian bravely serving Empire became even more important to representations of India. Churchill, speaking in parliament, claimed that the Congress Party was unrepresentative of the Indian majority and attributed rioting to "hooligans and agitators" and "lawless elements." He used India's "martial races" to demonstrate its loyalty and paid tribute to "the bravery of the Indian troops," adding that in two months of Quit India demonstrations, "more than 140,000 new volunteers for the Army have come forward in loyal allegiance to the King Emperor." He went on to praise the "fine work of the Indian Police" in bringing the situation successfully under control.[36] A good deal of the British media followed suit: like Churchill, they attributed the demonstrations to hooligans and agitators, who were unrepresentative of "India's Millions."[37]

Indians, while less widely represented than white Australians, Canadians, and New Zealanders, were a strong focus for images of martial masculinity. The depiction of other groups, like Maori, was sketchy. The representation of the New Zealand armed forces in newsreels focused on white soldiers, with Maori only occasionally visible as part of New Zealand contingents inspected by the King, parading, and marching German prisoners along the road in Cassino in 1944.[38] *Maximum Effort* (1944), a documentary targeted mainly at an audience in New Zealand and with a New Zealand narrator, incorporates a Maori into its narrative of an RAF aircrew, also comprising Canadians and English, flying an air raid over Germany. Such representations, however sketchy, served to present Britain and New Zealand as liberal and tolerant as well as to show the unity of diverse peoples.

Africans were often ascribed the qualities of warriors, but the racial hierarchy of the South African armed forces ensured that black South Africans were even less visible than Maori. Debates about their role in the armed forces provoked very considerable hostility from white South Africans to the idea that they should bear arms. Throughout the war, black South Africans and men of mixed parentage were seen as non-combatants. They served in subordinate roles in white fighting units to release whites for combat duty, under the command of the Non-European Army services – as guards, batmen, latrine-diggers, cooks, waiters, drivers, dispatch riders, stretcher bearers, medical aids, tailors, clerks, and typists. The highest rank open to black Africans was staff sergeant, while that for volunteers in the Coloured Cape Corps was warrant officer I.[39]

The racial segregation of the American armed forces in Britain prompted some media attention, much of it critical, but there was virtually no media interest in the racial hierarchy of the South African armed forces. In debates about the armed forces, Jan Smuts, prime minister of South Africa, identified South Africans in 1940 as a white people, arguing that "I cannot conceive of anything which would have the effect of creating…greater quarrels and greater division among the people than the arming of coloured people or the native population of the Union."[40] Throughout the war, the media followed Smuts in portraying South Africa as white. Its racial hierarchy occasionally emerged in images that showed members of the Cape Coloured Corps leaving for the front and a passing out parade of black African physical training instructors being inspected by the director of the Non-European Army Services.[41]

The racial hierarchy of the South African armed forces potentially disrupted the idea of an Empire of partnership, peace, and freedom where all peoples marched together. But such hierarchy was less apparent in imagery of South Africa, where black South Africans were more or less invisible, than in the focus on white "sons of Empire," who were always more prominent in imagery than those from Asian, African, or Caribbean colonies. As imperial manhood was shown circulating around various theatres of war, white "sons of Empire" moved into the metropolis, and numerous stories showed Canadians, Australians, and New Zealanders, like the trio of soldiers in *From the Four Corners*, receiving a warm welcome in Britain. Emphasis on the ethnic heterogeneity of Empire contrasted strongly with a white metropolis. Indians and Africans served loyally and courageously – on the fighting front, thousands of miles away.

*

"People's war" imagery found its earliest and most extensive development in relation to the home front in Britain. In contrast to the fervent patriotism invoked during the First World War, these images focused on an ability to keep going with the everyday round as a strong symbol of the people's courage. Imagery of the home front in Britain, while often foregrounding the common people, including women, generally maintained racial boundaries between Empire and metropolis, representing "home" as white. But some imagery of other home fronts was developed in newsreels and documentaries. Women's role was highlighted in stories about "Canada's girl-power" – on the land, and in factories and shipyards.[42] Australian women "served the guns," cutting up cordite and filling mines and shells with liquid TNT, and took over from men on lifeguard duty on Australian beaches.[43] *War Came to Kenya* (1942) shows white women taking over the management of farms and the control of African labour, as well as working as nurses. *Arms From India* (1941) shows a predominantly male home front where Indians equipped the forces of the Empire with munitions and clothing – making steel, ammunition, rifles, cotton, woolens.[44] It emphasizes the vast production from India as the "eighth industrial country of the world."

Two contrasting films that unite ideas of a "people's war" and a "people's Empire" are *49th Parallel* (1941) and *West Indies Calling* (1943).[45] *49th Parallel* was the only full-length feature film financed by the Ministry of Information during the war, aimed at an American audience, and very popular in Britain – the highest box-office earner in 1941. *West Indies Calling* was a documentary sponsored by the Ministry of Information and made in two versions – one for a West Indies audience entitled *Hello! West Indies*, and a shorter version with an added introduction for a British audience.[46]

49th Parallel self-consciously portrays Canada as part of an Empire that is ethnically diverse. Telling a fictional story of a Nazi U-boat sunk by the Royal Canadian Air Force on the coast of Canada and the journey made by its Nazi survivors through Canada in their attempt to get to neutral America, it shows their encounters with French-Canadians, English-Canadians, German-Canadians, Inuit, and First Nations people. Indigenous people in the film are not individuated – their main function is to establish that white Canadians are not racist and to demonstrate common resistance to Nazi Germany across ethnic difference. Nazi racism and brutality against the only Inuit character who is named – Nick (Ley On) – is contrasted with his treatment by Canadians, exemplified by Johnnie (Laurence Olivier), a French-Canadian trapper. Nick's brutal treatment at the hands of the Nazi group prompts set-piece dialogue in which white Canadians affirm the humanity of the Inuit against Nazi pronouncements that they are racially as low as Negroes – semi-apes. Once Nick has demonstrated the virtues of white Canadians, in contrast with the Nazis, he makes no further appearance in the film.

The Nazi encounter with Philip Armstrong-Scott (Leslie Howard), an English-Canadian, produces a further contrast between Canadians and Nazis. Armstrong-Scott is a temperate hero, one that the Nazis pronounce "soft and degenerate through and through." An aesthete who collects books and paintings, he is engaged in writing about the customs and culture of the Blackfoot tribe. His writings are among the books that the Nazis burn. Initially ignorant of their identity, Armstrong-Scott offers the Nazis hospitality, and for his pains, not only are his books and paintings burned, but he is ignominiously bound and gagged. A British review of *49th Parallel* worried that this representation of an English dilettante would confirm the idea of "the Englishman as soft and decadent," which, it observed, had been developing over the past decade, especially in the U.S. But it suggested that such a representation might nevertheless be good propaganda, since Armstrong-Scott is revealed as unexpectedly tough.[47] As a temperate hero, Armstrong-Scott can nevertheless fight when roused, and he takes his revenge against his Nazi persecutors by knocking one out with his fists.

West Indies Calling also emphasizes temperate heroism and ethnic diversity, but is highly unusual in showing such diversity on the British home front, disrupting the boundaries between Empire and metropolis where "home" was shown as white. It provides a rare example of imagery that includes black women's active involvement in war. It provides an equally rare example of imagery of a "people's war" and a "people's Empire" that foregrounds black people on active service in Britain.

Set in a BBC studio in London, *West Indies Calling* is dominated by the voices and images of black Caribbeans. The title of the version produced for a British audience is a reversal of the name of one of the major broadcasts on the BBC Empire service to the West Indies – *Calling the West Indies*. It shows a version of this radio program, generally organized as a party and sometimes held in London, sometimes in Glasgow and Edinburgh, with music and guests. But while the main content of the radio program was the messages that guests sent out to relatives and friends in the Caribbean from London, *West Indies Calling* reverses the direction of these messages, as Caribbeans explain their contribution to the war effort to an audience in Britain.

In *West Indies Calling*, the voices of Caribbeans tell the narratives of both a "people's war" and a "people's Empire," and insert Carribeans into these narratives. The compère, as on *Calling the West Indies*, is Una Marson, a Jamaican woman who first came to Britain in 1932.[48] She introduces Learie Constantine, a well-known figure to British audiences as a Trinidadian cricketer who had played in the Lancashire League before the war; Flying Officer Ulric Cross, a bomber navigator; and Carlton Fairweather. They speak about the Caribbean men employed in munitions factories in Britain, some of the ten thousand volunteers for the armed services from the Caribbean, and the foresters in Scotland, recruited mainly from British Honduras. All three speakers, along with Una Marson, are positioned behind a microphone labelled "BBC," with all the weight of authority and truth-telling that label involved, especially in wartime. Narratives and shots of a "people's Empire" emphasize the friendships developed between people from different parts of the Commonwealth – British, Canadians, Caribbeans, New Zealanders – and stress the hope this offers of a "new world," including a better life in the West Indies.

In inserting Caribbean people into dominant narratives, as contributors to the British war effort, *West Indies Calling* studiously avoids any mention of racism in Britain. The widespread practice of colour bars throughout much of the British Empire attracted virtually no public attention in Britain throughout the war. Their practice in Britain was an issue that Constantine publicized in 1944 when he sued a London hotel that had refused him rooms that he had booked in advance in 1943. Questions on the case were raised in the House of Commons.[49] In 1943 Constantine also talked of his experience of racism in Britain in a broadcast to a British audience on BBC radio. His talk was originally intended as a *Postscript* but was rejected for this popular Sunday night slot on the grounds that it was "too controversial." The director of radio talks suggested that "with a British audience I should have thought far more sympathy would be obtained if the speaker identified himself with his audience by describing…some of the joy of first class cricket." However, he saw "no reason why this script should not be accepted for a weekday if Constantine's own Ministry and the Colonial Office will pass it," and the program went out in September 1943 on the Home Service. Rejecting the script for a Sunday *Postscript*, the director of radio talks noted: "You will remember that the object of that series is to stress unity rather than diversity."[50]

Despite its disruption of the racial boundaries between metropolis and Empire and its narrative of Caribbeans on the home front, *West Indies Calling* emphasizes unity as much as diversity. The need to boost morale and to show a united community of nation and Empire offered some scope for self-representation by black Caribbeans who speak on their own behalf and take on the narrative voice and the role of educating their audience. Even so, *West Indies Calling* obscures the issues that Constantine publicized elsewhere to present a wholly positive portrait of West Indians in Britain and of British-Caribbean relations. People of many backgrounds in a diverse Empire are shown pulling together across differences of race and ethnicity, united in a common effort.

When Constantine sued the London hotel that had refused him rooms, the issue of an American colour bar was also highlighted in the reporting. According to the hotel manager, the refusal of rooms was a result of the presence of white American soldiers in the hotel. A witness told the court that Constantine had "stated the fact that he was a British subject, and that he saw no reason why Americans, who were aliens, should have any preference at the hotel over a British subject."[51]

Constantine's claim that he should have preference over Americans as aliens was reversed in much wartime imagery. The self-conscious portrait of ethnic heterogeneity in Canada in *49th Parallel* contrasts strongly with wartime representations of the U.S. when most British films showed British-American relations as a friendship between white nations.[52] Americans were not seen as part of a racial community of Britons, but they were shown on terms that corresponded closely to this version of a "people's Empire," stressing common culture, heritage, and ancestry.

Despite *West Indies Calling*, racially inclusive imagery did not generally extend to the home front in Britain. Nor did it extend to South Africa, which was shown as a white man's country. The practice of colour bars throughout much of the British Empire, notably South Africa, received little media attention, but Britain was shown as tolerant in contrast to the racism of others – including not only Nazi Germany, but also the U.S. because of the racial segregation of the American armed forces in Britain. Since Britain was regarded as a white country, the issue of a colour bar did not arise; it could therefore be represented as an alien practice introduced into Britain by the American armed forces and black GIs. The idea of a geographic separation between metropolis and Empire, white and black, underpinned the association of colour bars with America rather than Britain. Issues of racial difference belonged to the Empire, not the metropolis, and so were largely irrelevant to metropolitan identity.

*

The need to address diverse audiences in Empire and metropolis and to counter American anti-imperialism prompted a considerable shift away from the conservative imagery of imperial identity in *The Empire Answers* and its idea of automatic loyalty from Empire. The impact of the fall of Singapore strengthened moves to emphasize a modern Empire through themes of welfare and partnership. The focus on the martial masculinity of a "people's Empire" gave far less attention to women, civilians, and the home front than imagery of a "people's war," but both showed the common people of Britain and the British World united across vast distances in a common cause. Despite its limitations, the racial inclusiveness of Empire imagery offered a message that echoed that of the "people's war." British imperialism bore no resemblance to Nazi imperialism and was characterized by tolerance and liberty, not conquest and aggression. Britain's decency was demonstrated not only by the kindliness and friendliness of its people, their attachment to democracy, and their qualities of reasonableness and tolerance, but also by its Empire.

After 1945, the idea of a "people's Empire" was developed further, reaching a post-war high-point in 1953 with the coronation of Queen Elizabeth II. Emphasis on welfare and development in Empire, co-inciding with the post-war expansion of the welfare state, once more connected Englishness and Empire. But once the war was over, imagery of the Second World War was subject to very considerable revision. White Australians, Canadians, New Zealanders, and South Africans – the focus of the wartime "people's Empire" – continued to be shown, but the part played by Africans, Caribbeans, Indians, and Maori was generally forgotten.

If a "people's war" and a "people's Empire" marked a twentieth-century high point in inclusive imagery of Britishness, the reworking of Second World War narratives in the 1950s produced a far more exclusive story. Empire and Second World War imagery took opposite trajectories, and the Second World War narrative began to occupy much of the territory that the Empire narrative vacated. Flags, anthems, military displays, and uniforms faded from view in the "people's Empire" and proliferated in imagery of the Second World War, which offered a heroic and masculine narrative of national destiny. Officers and leaders were celebrated in a developing cult of Churchill, in novels, autobiographies, and memoirs, and in films that were often based on this literature. Second World War films took up many of the themes of pre-war imperial films, showing exciting adventure, soldier, and seamen heroes – now joined by airmen – and homosocial worlds where men demonstrated courage, endurance, and humour away from home. The war film became a vehicle for the celebration of the virtues of the old imperial hero – courageous and re-sourceful, but also characterized by emotional restraint and stoicism, and associated with the traditional values of a middle- or upper-class, public school-educated gentleman. The idea of heroic British masculinity was transposed from an imperial to a Second World War setting, providing an image that in many ways resembled older versions of imperial identity. This was an image that enlarged and dignified ideas of Britishness, and associated national strength with white British masculinity.[53]

{NOTES}

1 "The Empire Answers," *The Listener*, 12 October 1939.

2 But see Toby Haggith, "Citizenship, Nationhood and Empire in British Official Film Propaganda," in *The Right to Belong: Citizenship and National Identity in Britain, 1930–1960*, ed. Richard Weight and Abigail Beach (London: I.B. Tauris, 1998), 59–88; Thomas Hajkowski, "The BBC, the Empire, and the Second World War, 1939–1945," *Historical Journal of Film, Radio and Television* 22 (2002): 135–55.

3 Stuart Ward, "The End of Empire and the Fate of Britishness," paper delivered at the British World Conference II, University of Calgary, July 2003.

4 "Australian Airmen Arrive," *British Paramount News*, 1 January 1940; "Making Themselves at Home," *Universal News*, 4 January 1940; "Australia Sends First Instalment," *British Paramount News*, 1 January 1940; "New Zealanders Arrive," *Universal News*, 4 January 1940; "Lumberjacks Cross Atlantic to Help," *British Paramount News*, 29 January 1940; "Newfoundland Lumberjacks Over Here," *Universal News*, 29 January 1940; "Indian Troops in France," *Pathe Gazette*, 18 January 1940; "Indian Troops in France," *Universal News*, 18 January 1940; "First Canadians Swell BEF Ranks," *British Paramount News*, 22 January 1940; "Canadian Commander in Chief," *Pathe Gazette*, 22 January 1940; "New Year Sees Empire Gathering of the Clans," *British Paramount News*, 4 January 1940; "Out with the Dawn Patrol," *Pathe Gazette*, 4 January 1940; "Australian War Efforts," *Pathe Gazette*, 8 January 1940.

5 "Defenders of the Empire," *Pathe Gazette*, 4 January 1940.

6 Benedict Anderson, *Imagined Communities: Reflections on the Origins and Spread of Nationalism* (London: Verso, 1983), 7.

7 Tom Fleming, ed., *Voices Out of the Air: The Royal Christmas Broadcasts 1932–1981* (London: Heinemann, 1981), 33–40.

8 Quoted in Jeffrey Richards, "Imperial Heroes for a Post-imperial Age," in *British Culture and the End of Empire*, ed. Stuart Ward (Manchester: Manchester University Press, 2001), 130.

9 Public Record Office (PRO), CO 875 11/13, Digest of Material Passing through American Division by Censorship in April, based on incoming letters from U.S., 1941.

10 John Mackenzie, "In Touch with the Infinite: The BBC and Empire, 1923–53," in *Imperialism and Popular Culture*, ed. John Mackenzie (Manchester: Manchester University Press, 1986), 183.

11 *Daily Express*, 25 May 1940.

12 Sonya Rose, *Which People's War? National Identity and Citizenship in Wartime Britain 1939–1945* (Oxford: Oxford University Press, 2003), chap. 5.

13 Quoted in Suke Wolton, *Lord Hailey, the Colonial Office and the Politics of Race and Empire* (Houndsmill: Macmillan Press, 2000), 47.

14 *The Times*, 14 March 1942.

15 See Rosaleen Smyth, "Britain's African Colonies and British Propaganda during the Second World War," *Journal of Imperial and Commonwealth History* 41 (1985): 65–82; Rosaleen Smyth, "The British Colonial Film Unit and Sub-Saharan Africa, 1939–1945," *Historical Journal of Film, Radio and Television* 8 (1988): 285–98; Kate Morris, *British Techniques of Public Relations and Propaganda for Mobilizing East and Central Africa during World War II* (Lewiston, NY: Edwin Mellen, 2000), chap. 4.

16 Kathryn Tidrick, *Empire and the English Character* (London: I.B. Tauris, 1990), 250.

17 "The Empire Answers."

18 BBC Written Archives Centre (BBCWAC), R34/306, Policy, Coloured People, 1941–1944, Memo from Assistant Controller of Overseas Services to R.A. Rendall, 1 May 1943.

19 Philip Woods, "From Shaw to Shantaram: The Film Advisory Board and the Making of British Propaganda Films in India, 1940–1943," *Historical Journal of Film, Radio and Television* 21 (2001): 299.

20 Delia Jarrett-Macauley, *The Life of Una Marson, 1905–65* (Manchester: Manchester University Press, 1998), 146–47.

21 Sonya Rose, "Race, Empire and British Wartime National Identity, 1939–45," *Historical Research* 74 (2001): 230.

22 Smyth, "Britain's African Colonies," 77. The Colonial Film Unit's African films were not thought suitable for Indian audiences. See Woods, "From Shaw to Shantaram," 299.

23 See James Burns, "Watching Africans Watch Films: Theories of Spectatorship in British Colonial Africa," *Historical Journal of Film, Radio and Television* 20 (2000): 203.

24 Quoted in Jeffrey Richards, *Films and British National Identity: From Dickens to Dad's Army* (Manchester: Manchester University Press, 1997), 15.

25 Anthony Kirk-Greene, "'Damnosa Hereditas': Ethnic Ranking and the Martial Races Imperative in Africa," *Ethnic and Racial Studies* 3 (1983): 395.

26 Scott Worthy, "A Martial Race? Maori and Pakeha New Zealand Soldiers of the Great War in Imperial Context," paper presented at the British World Conference II, University of Calgary, July 2003; Timothy Parsons, *The African Rank-and-File: Social Implications of Colonial Military Service in the King's African Rifles 1902–1964* (Portsmouth: Heinemann, 1999), 53–103.

27 "Indian Troops in France," *Pathe Gazette*, 18 January 1940.

28 *War Came to Kenya* (Information Office of Kenya, 1942).

29 "Troops from the Gold Coast," *Pathe Gazette*, 20 January 1941.

30 *Defenders of India* (Film Advisory Board, 1941).

31 "Former Indian POWs Cheer King," *British Paramount News*, 28 June 1945.

32 Prem Chowdhry, *Colonial India and the Making of Empire Cinema: Image, Ideology and Identity* (Manchester: Manchester University Press, 2000).

33 *The Times*, 26 September 1942; *The Times*, 17 September 1942.

34 *The Times*, 16 August 1942.

35 Quoted in A. D. Harvey, *Collision of Empires: Britain in Three World Wars, 1793–1945* (London: Phoenix, 1992), 526.

36 *The Times*, 11 September 1942.

37 "The Trouble in India," *Pathe Gazette*, 3 September 1942; *Daily Express*, 12 August 1942.

38 See, for example, "His Majesty Meets New Zealanders," *British Movietone News*, 11 July 1940; "Before and after Crete," *Gaumont British News*, 30 June 1940; "Cassino Close Up," *Pathe Gazette*, 6 April 1944.

39 See Kenneth Grundy, *Soldiers without Politics: Blacks in the South African Armed Forces* (Berkeley: University of California Press, 1983), 63–89.

40 Quoted in ibid., 66.

41 "South Africa's Total Effort," *War Pictorial News*, 22 December 1941; "Transvaal Military Camp," *War Pictorial News*, 30 March 1942.

42 "Canada's Girl War Workers," *British Paramount News*, 4 September 1941; "Canadian Women Shipyard Workers," *Gaumont British News*, 4 February 1943.

43 "Women Who Serve the Guns," *War Pictorial News*, 20 December 1943; "Girl Lifeguards," *British Movietone News*, 27 April 1944.

44 *Arms from India* (Film Advisory Board, 1941).

45 *49th Parallel* (Emeric Pressburger and Michael Powell, 1941); *West Indies Calling* (John Page, 1943).

46 PRO, INF 6/1328.

47 *Documentary Newsletter*, November 1941.

48 For Una Marson, see Jarrett-Macauley, *The Life of Una Marson*.

49 *The Times*, 23 September 1943.

50 BBCWAC, Learie Constantine, Talks, File 1, 1939–62, Memo from the Director of Talks, G.R. Barnes, 8 July 1943.

51 *The Times*, 20 June 1944.

52 These films included *The Foreman Went to France* (Charles Frend, 1942); *San Demetrio London* (Charles Frend, 1943); *Canterbury Tale* (Michael Powell and Emeric Pressburger, 1944); *I Live in Grosvenor Square* (Herbert Wilcox, 1945); and *The Way to the Stars* (Anthony Asquith, 1945).

53 See Wendy Webster, "Reconstructing Boundaries: Gender, War and Empire in British Cinema, 1945–1950," *Historical Journal of Film, Radio and Television* 23 (2003): 43–57.

CHAPTER 16

REHABILITATING THE INDIGENE:

POST-WAR RECONSTRUCTION AND THE IMAGE OF THE INDIGENOUS OTHER IN ENGLISH CANADA AND NEW ZEALAND, 1943–1948*

R. Scott Sheffield

In this favoured land of New Zealand...we have no racial distinctions and, in the years of the past, we have been proud of our Maori people, with whom we have lived on a basis of equality. There has never been, and I trust there never will be, anything that will upset the happy and harmonious relationship that exists between Pakeha and Maori. In this respect I think it can be fairly said New Zealand leads the world in the treatment accorded its native people.[1]

The world today is alive to the vast difficulties involved in re-settling millions of misplaced persons, victims of war and aggression. Canada, too, is doing her part, and Canadians, notably hard-headed and soft-hearted, are anxious to help. Yet such is the paradox in our thinking that we are completely ignoring the same problem here in our own country. We have practically in our own backyard, 125,638 misplaced persons, a ragtaggy, tragic group whose needs cry out for speedy adjustment. I speak of our Canadian Indians, who have been forced to unparalleled levels of degradation and poverty. The sight of these wretched people is a denial of all our high-sounding pronouncements, our Atlantic charters, our San Francisco agreements.... Objects of polite aversion or blatant derision the Indians are mere hangers-on to the fringe of civilisation.[2]

THE PRECEDING QUOTATIONS reveal potent notions about indigenous peoples and their proper place in New Zealand and Canada as these neo-Britians struggled with the transition from war to peace during the 1940s. In different ways, both authors also provide representations of Pakeha

* The research upon which this paper is based was completed with the aid of doctoral and post-doctoral fellowships from the Social Sciences and Humanities Research Council. The author would also like to thank colleagues Whitney Lackenbauer and Karen Duder for comments and suggestions that helped make this a stronger paper.

(Maori word for non-Maori people) and Anglo-Canadian national mythologies. Despite their common British heritage, the tones and claims of the authors suggest a state of relations between the dominant society and indigenous people that could not have been more different. And there is no doubt that there were profound differences. The reasons for these discrepancies were numerous and complex; oversimplified, these grew out of Maori's moderately successful resistance during the nineteenth century, comparatively larger proportion of New Zealand's population, and relative cultural and linguistic homogeneity. But arguably the most important difference in the two national experiences by the mid-twentieth century resulted from the much more cohesive and forceful Canadian articulation of assimilation ideology, legislation, and administration. First Nations never succeeded in slowing or diverting the dominant society's assimilation agenda in the way that Maori did through their political leaders within the Pakeha government system during the first decades of the twentieth century. Yet despite these different national experiences, the Second World War, and especially indigenous involvement, presented challenges to how both dominant Anglo-Saxon societies viewed Maori and First Nations, and to how they viewed themselves. Moreover, in fundamental ways, Pakeha and Anglo-Canadian images of their indigenous others, and their responses to the challenges of this period, converged as a result of post-war reconstruction.

In this paper, I examine how the predominantly Anglo-Saxon societies in Canada and New Zealand represented, discussed, and imagined First Nations and Maori people, respectively. I seek to understand the construction of the indigenous other during the transitional years from war to peace, as Pakeha and English-Canadians prepared to remake their country for a better world and a post-war New Order. In these demanding and emotionally charged years, the image constructed of the indigene provides a useful window into the collective mind of the dominant society. In defining who and what the Indian or Maori were, and where and on what basis they should fit into the future Canada or New Zealand, these neo-British peoples were in essence also defining themselves and the nature of the society that they believed they had built or aspired to create. These images were largely manufactured by the dominant society, for its own consumption and to meet its own emotional, philosophical, and political needs, subject to varying degrees of negotiation.

The following analysis is largely derived from the primary forum of public debate in these societies at the time – the print media. It builds upon previous work on English Canada's image of the "Indian" and is as a result weighted toward the Canadian side, drawing upon an intensive canvassing of a broad selection of periodicals from major urban dailies, to rural weeklies, to popular, conservative, and left-leaning literary monthlies.[3] Against this broad Canadian base is set a more limited examination of the major daily papers in Wellington, New Zealand: the *Evening Post* and the *Dominion*. These are not representative of the breadth of Pakeha discourse, and clearly any conclusions on the Pakeha image of Maori must, therefore, necessarily be tentative. Nevertheless, the contrasts are sufficiently striking to make the exercise worthwhile. Newspapers and other print media, when read deeply and broadly over time, are productive and rich sources from which to reconstruct the dominant society's ways of knowing indigenous people. By layering patterns of content of indigenous stories atop patterns of frequency, salience of placement in the periodical, type of story, and the tone of the language, a remarkably three-dimensional picture of settler-society images of the indigenous other can be crafted. Also importantly, newspapers appear regularly and in a consistent form, providing an essential baseline against which to measure changes over time. Finally, media sources serve not solely as sources of opinions, but also as reflections of the socio-cultural milieu in which they operate. Such publications not only shape and reinforce values and ideas, but also draw from an existing cultural toolbox, containing language and imagery recognizable to their readers. The print media is about communication and to succeed they have to engage their readership in a meaningful and mutually intelligible dialogue.

Prior to the Second World War, Canadians had long discussed and imagined the "Indian," and had developed a complex mental framework of stereotypes, assumptions, and visual impressions that were accessible at the mention of the term. Despite the range and frequent ambiguity in public representations of First Nations, the characteristics coalesced into two seemingly contradictory archetypes. The dominant version was the "noble savage," a benignly historical, romanticized, and usually positive embodiment of a once-great people. Running countercurrent was the "drunken criminal" image: a present-day vice-ridden and loathsome wretch, who, in spite of the benevolent efforts of the Indian Affairs authorities on his behalf, was responsible for his own miserable state.[4] This ambivalent duality functioned effectively to reduce or subvert a latent sense of guilt, almost never explicitly articulated, for the First Nations' dispossession and marginalization. Indigenous people, conditions, and subjects were frequently the object of humour, from condescending bemusement to derisive sarcasm, which served to trivialize them. Constructing the "Indian" as an historical figure also served as a buffer from having to consider the contemporary plight of the First Nations. And even if they did turn their attention to the present, what English Canadians saw was a pathetic drunk with whom they could not empathize. Finally, the still pervasive belief that Native people were a vanishing race provided a last line of fatalistic defence.

To some extent, the same duality of positive historical and negative contemporary indigene was replicated in New Zealand.[5] However, the dichotomous images were not as rigid. The most noticeable difference was the capacity to conceptualize present-day Maori in a positive manner, particularly in the context of politics and the preparations for the 1940 centennial celebrations of the signing of the Treaty of Waitangi.[6] Maori issues were regularly dealt with in detail and Maori quoted at length, lending them a degree of legitimacy unimaginable in Canada,[7] where First Nations people were rarely even named, let alone allowed to speak for themselves, and the relevance of their issues was undermined at every turn. Overall, the Pakeha image of Maori betrayed little of the mechanisms to manage guilt, arguably because there was none. Indeed, the dominant impression is of an almost smug contentment with the country's race relations and the place of Maori in New Zealand society. In part, this was a product of a unique time period in Maori-Pakeha relations. Capable Maori political leaders like Apirana Ngata were pressing for Maori people to acculturate in some ways, while fostering the maintenance of their *Maoritanga*, or their culture and identity. Pakeha, for the most part, heard what they wished to hear in this message and gained confidence that Maori were keenly advancing toward full assimilation. In addition, the Labour government of the late 1930s was gradually extending measures of social welfare and improved health care to Maori. The perception of movement from both sides arguably created a sense of confidence between Maori and Pakeha greater than at any other point in the twentieth century. The Waitangi Centennial celebrations in 1940 powerfully reaffirmed for Pakeha the salience of the relationship with, and progressiveness of, Maori in Pakeha nationalist mythology.

The Second World War proved a significant catalyst in bringing both First Nations and Maori into wider public notice and creating pressures for policy and legislative reform. In Canada, the eagerness of many First Nations men to enlist drew media attention to these long-neglected people. In excess of four thousand would eventually serve, dispersed among the million-plus other Canadians in uniform, despite calls for an all-Indian unit.[8] The vast majority served in the Canadian Army, as racial, health, and educational barriers made it difficult for Native men to enter the Royal Canadian Air Force or Royal Canadian Navy.[9] Thousands more worked in forestry, fishing, and agriculture, or left the reserve and moved into cities to work in wartime industries. However, First Nations communities also made other, frequently well-publicized, contributions to the national war effort: foregoing their treaty money so that it could be sent to the King for the war; holding an otherwise illegal Sun Dance for victory; donating ambulances and money to patriotic and humanitarian agencies from band funds; purchasing victory bonds; or making their meagre reserve lands available for defence purposes.[10] The result of First Nations' wartime profile was post-war recognition and a climate ripe for policy reform. Demands for a review of Canadian Indian policy flooded into government from religious, civil liberty, veterans, and Native rights groups and led to the creation of a Special Joint Parliamentary Committee to consider the Indian Act, which sat from 1946 to 1948, and eventually to a new Indian Act in 1951.

In New Zealand, similar factors combined with the Maori involvement in the 1940 centennial celebrations of the Treaty of Waitangi to expand massively their interaction with Pakeha society. The exploits of the 28th (Maori) Battalion with the 2nd New Zealand Division in North Africa and Italy were especially important in garnering media attention. The all-Maori combat unit, recruited and organized at Maori request along tribal lines, earned a reputation, both among Allied forces and at home, as a first-rate unit with an impressive combat record.[11] On the home front, Maori began moving into urban areas for war work, and, despite the expectations of officials, they stayed once hostilities ended. Maori also sought and gained control over their contributions to the New Zealand war effort in the form of the Maori War Effort Organisation (MWEO), which was set up in 1942. Initially designed to enable Maori control over recruitment for the Maori battalion, it grew into an extensive structure of over three hundred tribal committees and dozens of regional executives working under the direction of Maori parliamentarians. Its responsibilities expanded to include encouragement of Maori primary production, co-operation in the placement of Maori workers, and by war's end, involvement in Maori social welfare. As early as 1943, some twenty-seven thousand of an estimated ninety-five thousand Maori had either enlisted in the armed forces or been placed in essential industry through the efforts of the MWEO,[12] which was maintained for the duration of the war, even once its military utility had disappeared, at the request of Maori leaders. The tribal committee structure was eventually incorporated into the Ministry of Maori Affairs by the Labour government's Maori Social and Economic Advancement Act (1945).

In both countries, the war and indigenous engagement in the national war effort fostered changes in the way the dominant society construed the "Indian" and the "Maori." English Canadians had some difficulty accommodating First Nations military service and support of the national crusade within their existing dualistic imagery of the "Indian." A new, dynamic, and highly patriotic archetype, the "Indian-at-war," emerged that encapsulated the positive contemporary nature of these unaccustomed activities. This image became the dominant representation after the fall of France and provided reassurance that the First Nations population was loyal and doing its bit. This was no trivial matter, as anxious Canadians shed the pretense of a limited commitment to war and confronted a total war in which they were now Britain's largest ally. English Canadians experienced a process of social tightening: rallying around the flag, determining who was with them and who was against them, as well as clarifying what they were fighting for and against. The result for the image of the "Indian" was a transition from an external and marginal other to a more inclusive part of the "we" group, albeit on the fringe.

Pakeha had far less difficulty incorporating Maori contributions to the war than did their Canadian counterparts. They already had a capacity to comprehend Maori in a relatively inclusive, positive, and modern guise. New Zealanders threw themselves into an "all in" war effort from the very beginning and went through a more gradual process of culturally, socially, and emotionally girding for war. But interestingly, this focused on ensuring sectoral, class, and political unity, with issues of race or ethnicity all but absent. Nevertheless, the Pakeha's "Maori" did change as a result of Maori war service and especially the institution of the Maori War Effort Organisation. Whereas English Canadians were forced to recognize and construct the "Indian" in a more inclusive sense, Maoridom's seizure of proprietorship over the nature and extent of their contributions to the war effort led to a greater degree of segregation in Pakeha representations. Alhough undeniably pleased by Maori activities, the Pakeha press rarely mentioned the Maori in stories about the national war effort.[13] Instead, discussion was compartmentalized in coverage dedicated to Maori contributions: in a sense, "their" war effort was aiding "ours," but was not a part of it.

By 1943 Allied forces had seized the initiative from the Axis powers and were driving them back in every theatre of war. Though no one argued that victory was imminent, the spectre of defeat had been banished, and many began at long last to ponder seriously the nature of a post-war world. Canadians, enjoying the wartime economic prosperity, overwhelmingly longed to create a New Order rather than return to the uncertainties of the pre-war status quo.[14] Essentially projecting Anglo-Canadians' national mythology onto the future, they aspired to create a kinder, gentler society free from the privations of poverty, social unrest, and war that had marred much of the previous generation. By 1943 post-war reconstruction was gaining centre stage on the national agenda. As one returned soldier stated in a letter to the editor, "Next to winning the war, there is nothing of more urgent importance than that we, on the home front, shall have taken some definite steps toward winning the peace before the boys return."[15] This manifested itself in major political victories for the social democratic Co-operative Commonwealth Federation and a swing to the left by the mainstream Tories and the Liberals. The reconstruction agenda developed a tremendous momentum during the war's final years. The federal government had actually begun planning for peace almost from the outbreak of hostilities in 1939, and by 1943–44 had developed an extensive system of agencies and committees to plan for, and make policy on, every imaginable issue connected to social policy, demobilization, and the transition to peace. With two key pieces of the social welfare net in place – Unemployment Insurance (1940) and generous Family Allowances (1945), and the maintenance of government economic controls – Canada negotiated smoothly into its New Order without the sharp recession and social unrest that had marked 1919–20.

Within this broad context of imagining the future, Native people and subjects continued to be publicly discussed; indeed, such debate accelerated and diversified. Trivializing comedy had largely disappeared, and a more respectful tone was evident throughout the English-Canadian media. This was evident in the coverage of a large conference of Native leaders in Ottawa in the fall of 1943.[16] Coming together to institute a national political organization to make First Nations voices heard, the delegates also took the opportunity to protest the imposition of conscription and wartime taxation on their people.[17] What immediately becomes apparent is a total lack of recrimination for First Nations' desire to be exempt from compulsory service and income tax. Earlier in the war, jingoistic Canadian journalists might well have reproached Native leaders for shirking and potentially undermining the war effort, but the grievances, presented in a detached fashion, appeared reasonable, and their assertions of full support for the war effort were accepted at face value. With the war going well, and the highly documented efforts of the "Indian-at-war," it was possible for Canadians to accept the legitimacy of First Nations protests and to see Natives as contemporary human beings.

From 1944 onward, English Canadians increasingly began calling for Indian policy reform and an improvement in the living standards of the country's First Nations. The House Committee on Reconstruction and Re-establishment, the main parliamentary body on post-war matters, even dedicated several sittings to the conditions of Canada's Native population in May 1944.[18] Shaping the renewed interest in finding a solution to what was usually termed the "Indian problem" was the inescapable fact of Native military service. An article in the *Saskatoon Star-Phoenix* noted that "some 3000 Canadian Indians were serving in the armed forces, a fact that has injected the problem of Indian policy directly into the field of postwar plans."[19] The stark inequity of accepting and even compelling the military service of people bereft of the rights of full citizenship was uncomfortably obvious. But more, Native war service demonstrated their potential to be a positive contributing force in the country and marked them as worthy for such consideration. A letter written to the Committee on Reconstruction and Re-establishment encapsulated a sentiment frequently found in the public debates on the "Indian problem":

> There are Indian men and boys in the Services who will not want to come home to Reserves. They are making sacrifices on a par with the "Whites" for Freedom, they are fighting for a freedom they never had. One of the first places where we could well begin to dispense the "Four Freedoms" is right in our midst: to the Indians.[20]

The link was clear in the minds of English Canadians, and the not inconsequential national will and energy dedicated to post-war reconstruction would subsequently also be focused on the plight of the Native population and Canadian Indian policy.

Although First Nations' wartime activities in the war's early years had forced English Canadians to re-evaluate their images of the "Indian," as the war drew to a close the dominant society began increasingly to turn this examination inward upon itself:

The truly sad picture these Indians present today is a direct reflection of our unjust administration. They are wards of the government in the fullest sense of the word, and we, the citizens are responsible for the actions of our government. What the Indian is today we have made him through neglect…[and] in criticizing the Indians, we are but criticising ourselves.[21]

And English Canadians found much to criticize. In particular, Canadian Indian policy and administration drew fire for the "centuries of tutelage [that] have robbed the Indian of his independent spirit and self-reliance…a heavy indictment against us in our treatment of a once proud people…and we have meant so well."[22] But many went further to decry the existence of "that complacent racial superiority that we dislike so much in other people that we're willing to fight a war with them about it."[23] Driving this self-castigation was a profound desire to make the post-war New Order match the principles of equality, freedom, and democracy for which the country had sacrificed so much blood, sweat, and treasure. When they then turned their gaze on their own country, the poverty, marginalization, and wardship status of Native people presented the most glaring contradiction to these ideals. Such a challenge demanded action, for to do otherwise diminished the sacrifices of the war and threatened to undermine the New Order Canadians hoped to erect.

Increasingly in the debates on the "Indian problem," English Canadians emphasized the poverty and plight of First Nations people and communities, and they consistently stated that the blame for the often wretched living conditions on reserves did not lie with the "Indian." Rather, the First Nations were portrayed as powerless before the smothering combination of an indifferent, racist society and an autocratic administration "so far removed from their daily lives as to be beyond reach."[24] This "Indian victim" came to dominate public representations of Natives from 1944 into the post-war period. It inspired pity among members of the dominant society and mobilized public support for legislative and policy reform. There are indications that this support was quite broad and that a multiplicity of English Canadians were thinking about the "Indian problem" and sufficiently moved by it to make their feelings known to the government.[25]

In 1946 the federal minister responsible for Indian Affairs, J.A. Glen, responded to the pressure and informed the House of Commons that a Special Joint Parliamentary Committee (sjc) would be set up to review

Canadian Indian legislation and administration.[26] In the course of its investigations over more than two years, the SJC held 128 meetings, heard 122 witnesses, collected 411 written briefs, and amassed a total of 3,211 pages of evidence.[27] For the first time at such a high level, First Nations leaders were able to present their diverse views of the "Indian problem" and their visions for the future. The SJC's activities, and especially the presentations by indigenous delegations, received continuous media coverage by the Canadian Press wire service and by the Ottawa correspondents of the major urban dailies. The SJC's Final Report, released in June 1948, recommended the repeal or revision of virtually the entire Indian Act and some significant changes to Canadian Indian policy, including some increases in autonomy for Indian band councils. However, it was far from revolutionary, largely ignoring the demands of Native delegations and, in line with most Anglo-Canadians' views, reaffirming assimilation as the only proper and moral goal for the indigenous population. Its findings would eventually form the foundation for a new Indian Act, although it would not become law until 1951.

By largely ignoring the input of the First Nations, the SJC was simply continuing a trend evident throughout the public discussion of the "Indian problem" from 1943–48. Little thought was given to Native peoples' vision of the "problem," their ideas for reform, or their hopes for the future. First Nations voices were increasingly evident in the post-war years, both in the media and through their delegations to the SJC. Nevertheless, indigenous contributions to the national dialogue were still rare and scattered. Canadians often heard only what fit their preconceptions or assumed that they knew what the "Indian" wanted. Overwhelmingly, this was a debate among English Canadians about what the dominant society had to do to solve a problem it had created.

In the forum of the SJC and in the pages of the country's print media, English Canadians struggled to make the square peg of Native assimilation fit the round hole of the post-war New Order. In the wake of the Second World War, the cavalier championing of assimilation on the grounds of perceived racial superiority was simply not possible. Moreover, the longstanding assumption that assimilation was both natural and inevitable combined with the gross inadequacies of the country's treatment of First Nations people and the real indigenous contributions during the war to breed a buoyant optimism about the future of the "Indian." Nothing in the existing repertoire of "Indian" images was reconcilable with the confident, positive, forward-looking representation of Native people prevalent from 1946 to 1948. A new image was needed to encapsulate the heady mixture of lofty ideals, hope, and assimilation that drove Anglo-Canadians and the SJC. Father J. O. Plourde, a member of the Catholic delegation to the SJC, summed up much of this sentiment when he stated,

> The Indian is not a lazy fellow by any means. He will work for his living. He is not a dissipated man either. He will behave properly if given a chance, police protection and so forth. He is not an immoral man. He is a family man. He likes his wife and children. In other words, he is what I would call, at least in prospect, a very good Canadian citizen.[28]

The "potential Indian citizen," then, had some temporary, correctable flaws but was worthy of citizenship, readily assimilable, and someone who could be just like everyone else, given the opportunity. This conceptual retooling enabled English Canadians to overcome the challenge that First Nations contributions in wartime had presented to their nationalist mythology and post-war aspirations. The reconstructed "potential Indian citizen" rehabilitated assimilation as "the gradual transition of Indians from wardship to citizenship," a guise that fit with Anglo-Canadians' idealistic sense of themselves, their country, and their future.[29]

New Zealand was also booming by 1943, its human and financial resources fully committed, and in some cases over-committed, to the war effort.[30] With the war well on its way to final victory, New Zealanders began to talk about and plan for the coming peace. Here too, discussion was of a New Order and of claims that it "was the responsibility of every citizen in the British Empire to see that those [four freedoms of the Atlantic Charter] were attained and preserved."[31] Jamie Belich recently argued that with victory, "the clouds of doom lifted; the clouds of uncertainty did not. Postwar New Zealand was torn between two strong trends: a sense of irrevocable change, a world shattered and rebuilding in different shapes; and a desire to restore – to restore a past that, ideally at least, was more familiar and secure."[32] But the Pakeha media showed little of the angst about losing the peace so prevalent in Canada. In part this was probably due to the fact that most of the social security provisions and post-war changes that English Canadians sought in order to allay their fears had already been initiated in New Zealand by the Labour governments of 1935 and 1938. For this reason, Pakeha undoubtedly were much less inclined than English Canadians to yearn for a profoundly changed post-war society. Overall, the public discussions in the Wellington papers reveal a quiet confidence, in part growing from pride in New Zealand's wartime achievements. As Prime Minister Peter Fraser proclaimed at the Labour Party's Annual Conference in November 1945, "It is doubtful whether any country made a greater contribution to the war effort than New Zealand in relation to its size and population."[33] Such assertions have remained prominent in Kiwi popular memory of the conflict.

This self-assurance about the future was also apparent in stories about Maori. In broad strokes, material on Maori subjects appeared relatively infrequently in 1943 but grew through the last years of the war before declining slightly to a moderate level in peacetime. This suggests a waxing of interest in Maori matters up to the passing of the Maori Social and Economic Advancement Act in the spring of 1945 and a gradual waning thereafter. In the swelling interest in the future of Maoridom that marked the transition to peace, there was some questioning of Pakeha's supposedly supportive relationship with Maori. In August 1945 the Bishop of Waiapu declared:

> The Maori problem is the problem of the minority. What are
> we going to pay the Maori? The country was his; it is now
> ours. What have we given him in return? Have we given him
> Christianity? The Christian way of life is extremely attractive
> to the Maori, but do not some pakehas in their daily lives cause
> the Maori to imagine that the religion of Jesus Christ is being
> ignored?[34]

However, such concerns and criticisms were rare. Assimilation was assumed and rarely explicitly articulated. More typical by far was the following post-war editorial:

> In no other country of the British Commonwealth of Nations is
> there greater freedom for its original inhabitants to go forward
> in harmony with others towards the full development of its
> resources. Maori and pakeha mingle and co-operate in local
> and national service, in employment, in sport and indeed, in all
> departments of our social life.[35]

Indeed, this editor was prepared to accept that Maori maintenance of their culture would be beneficial, not only to Maori, but to the Dominion as a whole. Arguably, this was flirting with the kind of proto-biculturalism being advocated by Sir Apirana Ngata and other Maori leaders at the time.[36] Conveniently overlooking Ngata's persistent fostering of Maori cultural activities and autonomy, Pakeha heard with pleasure the part of Ngata's message encouraging Maori adoption of Pakeha ways. This amplified Pakeha confidence already founded on assumptions that Maori were assimilable, eager to do so, and already well on the road to that goal. Although it seems doubtful that most Pakeha would have gone very far in engaging biculturalism in the immediate post-war period, if the backlash against the Maori cultural resurgence of the 1970s and 1980s is any indication, the degree of comfort with the idea of a culturally distinct Maoridom speaks volumes for Pakeha aplomb. Perhaps nothing so clearly divided the public debates in Canada and New Zealand over the future of the indigene than the relative lack of self-evaluation and recrimination evident in the latter.

Maori voices might have made a difference here, but the impact of their contributions to the dialogue does not appear to have significantly affected the dominant society. Certainly the media continued to print more Maori perspectives, activities, and views than was the case in Canada. Senior Maori politicians like Paraire Paikea, Eruera Tirikatene, and Apirana Ngata were all heard through the text of their speeches at public events, but in letters to the editor and in news stories, the views of other Maori added their weight. And some were willing to poke pins into Pakeha's complacency, as did a returned Maori battalion officer who, in a speech to Auckland's Rotary Club, stated that the colour bar was more pronounced in New Zealand than it had been in England.[37] Other Maori often leaped quickly to deny such claims. Mr. O. T. Haddon, secretary to the Maori Advisory Council, insisted that

> to assert, or even to convey the impression, that the pakeha
> majority in New Zealand entertains a definite prejudice, a
> unified prejudice connoting a colour bar, in respect to the Maori
> people seems to me a rash proposition.... It is true that the
> Maori people as a whole have not attained the highest pursuits
> in the community, specially in the professions, but who would
> dare to say that they have been deliberately blocked, in the
> exercise of a colour bar, from more consequential activities?[38]

Amidst the diversity of Maori perspectives, Pakeha could find what they needed to support their own preconceptions.

While neither Maori, nor the Maori war effort, had forced Pakeha to re-evaluate themselves, they did spark a renewal of discussion about the "Maori." What becomes increasingly obvious as one reads through the collective conversation about Maori subjects between 1943 and 1948 is Pakeha's almost fetishistic concern with the major flaw they saw remaining in their indigenous population: a lack of what was usually described as responsibility, initiative, or self-reliance. A fine exhibition of this trend can be found in the coverage of the major conference of Maori leadership in October 1944.[39] Among the preliminary addresses, one church representative stated that

> it was his experience that the Maori did not want to be regarded as a race to be humoured, but to be invested with responsibility. It was his experience that the Maori could assume responsibility, and if there was anything that preserved the democratic way of life it was the self-reliance of the individual, the family and the race. That self-reliance must be aspired to, attained and held.[40]

In his speech before the nearly four hundred Maori delegates at the assembly, the minister of agriculture opined that the

> first essential for the Maori race was to supply their own domestic needs.... It was entirely wrong that Maoris should be providing labour to assist in Chinese, Hindoo or pakeha gardens.... Maori should be concentrating on their own scheme for growing their own supplies. However, this could only be achieved if they showed leadership and ability to accept responsibility.[41]

Nor had this abated in the wake of the war when Sidney Holland, leader of the opposition National Party, spoke to South Island Maori. He praised at length their many wartime exploits and other achievements, before saying that if Maori were granted "equality of privilege with the pakeha, they must also accept equality of responsibility in the new world."[42] Here was that crucial missing ingredient to complete the assimilation of Maori, an ingredient that the Maori war effort seemed to have finally unmasked.

For this reason, the MWEO became the focus of attention from 1943 to 1945, as both Maori and Pakeha sought a way to retain and harness its dynamism for the post-war New Order. Many prominent Maori wanted to maintain the organization in some post-war capacity for fear of losing the autonomy and unity of Maoridom that the war had helped create. But while Pakeha were happy to preach Maori initiative, they were less interested in the autonomy and collectivism that had been key components of the MWEO's success. To have acknowledged these aspects would have presented a challenge to Pakeha mythology of racial utopia where Maori were happily progressing on the road to becoming individuals within a single New Zealand race. As a result, the public discussions proved unwilling to credit the MWEO's accomplishments to the fact that it was Maori-led, communally structured, and segregated from the Pakeha war effort. Therefore, Pakeha interpreted the Maori war effort more narrowly and simply as evidence of initiative and responsibility at long last unleashed. This conceptual view of Maori wartime participation was eventually ensconced in the Maori Social and Economic Advancement Act (1945), which maintained the tribal structure under the umbrella of the Department of Maori Affairs, but without any role for Maori direction and control beyond the local level.[43] Able to conceptually circumvent the potential problem of indigenous military contributions, and content that a solution had been obtained, Kiwis got on with the post-war business of making money and babies.

This exploration of the public image of indigenous people in the neo-British societies of New Zealand and Canada reveals the degree to which their participation in the Second World War threatened core elements within the dominant societies' sense of self. Contributing to the defence of the nation in Western, and especially British, democracies carries important connections to citizenship, or at least to belonging. Military service was the most symbolically powerful contribution, creating a moral obligation on the part of the society concerned. Indigenous military service and aid in the national war efforts of Canada and New Zealand in fighting for democracy, equality, and freedom served to highlight the anomalies, inconsistencies, and contradictions of those ideals and principles evident in the status and day-to-day experience of First Nations and Maori people. In this way, indigenous wartime contributions actually threatened the New Order that Pakeha and particularly Anglo-Canadians hoped to attain.

This occurred in quite different ways in the two Dominions. English Canadians suffered through a painful re-awakening to the deplorable neglect of First Nations people, a neglect that they had willfully ignored for decades. The concern for the "Indian problem," especially once it was incorporated into the agenda of post-war reconstruction, played into the larger environment of concern for winning the peace, with the ambivalent mixture of hope and anxiety. But while the First Nations were only a small percentage of the national population, their low standard of living and wardship status stood, for Anglo-Canadians, as a mockery of the latter's wartime rhetoric, their sense of being the embodiment of good old-fashioned British justice, fairness, and democracy. Conversely, Pakeha maintained their smug complacency regarding their relationship with

Maori in spite of the Maori contributions to the war effort. Although the communal nature, tribal structure, autonomy, and separateness of Maori service and achievements had the potential to undercut Pakeha delusions of a happily assimilating minority, confident assertions of assimilation nearly attained were central to the myth of racial utopia that Pakeha had long utilized to distinguish the unique Kiwi brand of Britishness. Where the "Indian" had presented an external threat to the philosophical foundations of Anglo-Canadians' sense of self, the "Maori" was itself a central element of Pakeha's sense of self. And they needed it in order to maintain their careful balancing act of identity in which Kiwis constructed themselves as British, but different from and better than the other strains, particularly their trans-Tasman cousins. Thus in a subtle but more direct way, the indigenous war effort also struck at the very stuff of Pakeha conceptualizations of self.

Yet despite the differences of process, the two neo-British societies converged significantly through the mid-1940s in the way they constructed the indigene and in their ability to reconstruct the meaning of indigenous wartime contributions to match the nationalist mythologies they had set themselves as templates for post-war reconstruction. The linking factor, and the solution that English Canadians and Pakeha agreed upon, was assimilation. Arguably, the only real difference between the processes in the two Dominions was Pakeha confidence that Maori were nearly there and that the dominant society had done all that was required to aid the indigene. English Canadians held few such illusions about the First Nations, yet they shared with their neo-British antipodean cousins the same abiding faith in the logic, morality, benevolence, and inevitability of assimilation. But perhaps more fundamentally, what the two peoples shared was a fundamental confidence in the superiority of their own racial, cultural, and social virtues. In interpreting the Maori war effort narrowly as evidence of initiative, or in reconstructing the "Indian" as the "potential citizen" and reimagining the "Indian problem" in liberal-democratic terms, Pakeha and English Canadians were dusting off an old British imperial birthright – the white man's burden.

{NOTES}

1 "Maori All Blacks, South African Tour," *The Evening Post*, 2 September 1946.

2 "Blueprint for the Redman," *The Canadian Forum* 25, no. 300 (January 1946): 233.

3 See R. Scott Sheffield, *"The Redman's on the Warpath": The Image of the "Indian" and the Second World War* (Vancouver: University of British Columbia Press, 2004). The Canadian publications examined include six prominent urban dailies: *The Globe (and Mail* by the late 1930s), the *Winnipeg Free Press*, the *Halifax Chronicle*, the *Calgary Herald*, the *Saskatoon Star-Phoenix*, and the *Vancouver Sun*. The papers of four smaller communities were also canvassed: two dailies, the *Prince Albert Daily Herald* and the *Brantford Expositor*; and two weeklies, the *Kamloops Sentinel* and the *Cardston News*. In addition, several weekly and monthly journals were included in the sample: the conservative weekly magazine, *Saturday Night*; the popular weekly *Maclean's*; and the left-leaning literary monthly, *Canadian Forum*. To the core sample has been added two files of newspaper clippings of Indian stories forwarded to the Indian Affairs Branch by its field personnel. Most of the stories are from publications not included in the main survey groups and thus broaden the source base.

4 The public articulation of the "Indian" was almost invariably masculine, though there were feminine counterparts to each archetype that appeared from time to time.

5 Examples of historical noble savage imagery include "The Maori Wars," *Evening Post*, 19 January 1938; "Cook Strait's Ilse of Romance – Kapiti's Wild Past – Burial Caves Recall Te Rauparaha's Day," *Dominion*, 23 February 1938, and "'A Very Busy Woman' – Ancient Maori at Home," *Evening Post*, 23 March 1939. For instances of negative contemporary imagery, see "Morals of Maoris," *Dominion*, 5 February 1938, or "A Wild Ride – Maori's Offence," *Evening Post*, 3 March 1939.

6 A good example of this phenomenon can be found in the *Evening Post's* serious discussions of Maori politics around the election in October 1938, "Western Maori Seat," *Evening Post*, 4 October 1938, and "Maori Elections," *Evening Post*, 15 October 1938. On Maori and the Centennial, see "Native Race's Part in Centennial," *Dominion*, 10 December 1938, and "Standing Out – Waikato Maoris – Waitangi Celebrations," *Evening Post*, 3 February 1940.

7 For instance, the experiences of Maori witnesses of a flash flood receive extensive space in "Plucky Maoris – Vivid Stories Told by Survivors," *Dominion*, 21 February 1938. Also see the measured, thorough, and sympathetic tone in assessing Ngai Tahu efforts to obtain the compensation recommended by the Royal Commission almost two decades prior in "Native Claim, Lands in South – Purchase in 1848, Maoris want £354, 000," *Evening Post*, 6 January 1938.

8 For instance Chief Joe Dreaver, a prominent Cree from Saskatchewan made such a call in 1940: see "All-Indian Battalion Suggested," *Saskatoon Star-Phoenix*, 5 July 1940. Another point worth mentioning is that most First Nations communities across Canada strongly endorsed voluntary enlistment while opposing with equal vigour their liability for conscription. For more on Native responses to conscription, see Michael Stevenson, "The Mobilisation of Native Canadians during the Second World War," *Journal of the Canadian Historical Association* 7 (1996): 205–26, and R. Scott Sheffield and Hamar Foster, "Fighting the King's War: Harris Smallfence, Verbal Treaty Promises and the Conscription of Indian Men, 1944," *University of British Columbia Law Review* 33, no. 1 (1999): 53–74.

9 The exact figure of Native service personnel remains contentious, with some estimates exceeding six thousand. See Olive Patricia Dickason, *Canada's First Nations: A History of Founding Peoples from Earliest Times* (Toronto: McClelland and Stewart, 1992). The Indian Affairs Branch official figure of 3,050 is often quoted but was based on inadequate record keeping and did not include Natives conscripted under the National Resources Mobilisation Act (1940). The figure given is based on systematic recent work done by Veterans Affairs Canada from their case files, compiled as part of the National Round Table on First Nations Veterans Issues: see R. Scott Sheffield, *A Search for Equity: A Study of the Treatment Accorded to First Nations Veterans and Dependents of the Second World War and the Korean Conflict. The Final Report of the National Round Table on First Nations Veterans' Issues* (Ottawa: Assembly of First Nations, 2001). Both the RCAF and the RCN maintained a racial ban, or colour line, in official recruiting when the Second World War broke out, requiring recruits to be "of Pure European Descent and of the White Race." The Air Force made an exception for "North American Indians," and both had abandoned the restriction by 1942 and 1943, respectively. This combined with the poor health care and meagre education provided to First Nations, which prevented them from enlisting in these two services in any numbers. See R. Scott Sheffield, "'Of Pure European Descent and of the White Race': Recruitment Policy and Aboriginal Canadians," *Canadian Military History* 5, no. 1 (Spring 1996): 8–15.

10 P. Whitney Lackenbauer, "Vanishing Indian to Vanishing Military: Military Training and Aboriginal Lands in Twentieth-Century Canada" (PhD diss., University of Calgary, 2003).

11 The Maori Battalion has been the focus of Wira Gardiner's recent *Te Mura o Te Ahi: The Story of the Maori Battalion* (Auckland: Reed, 1992). Unfortunately, Gardiner's book reflects the limitations that so often afflict regimental histories. A broader and more systematic historical examination of the Maori battalion and the Maori war effort on the home front is badly needed.

12 Claudia Orange, "The Price of Citizenship? The Maori War Effort," in *Kia Kaha: New Zealand and the Second World War*, ed. John Crawford (Melbourne: Oxford University Press, 2002), 241.

13 For instance, weekly recruitment figures that provided detailed breakdowns by region never included Maori figures, *Evening Post*, 3 July 1940. In some cases, mention of Maori was almost lost within the larger national story, as in the designation of the 2nd NZ Division, "Second New Zealand Division – Designation of the Special Force," *Dominion*, 28 October 1939. More commonly, Maori participation was discussed as a distinct topic in separate articles like "Maori Battalion – Registrations Total 411 – 267 in Special Force," *Dominion*, 18 October 1939, and "Maoris and War – Full Participation," *Evening Post*, 18 September 1939.

14 An early opinion poll in October 1943 showed that 71 per cent of Canadians wanted post-war reforms rather than a return to pre-war conditions: see *Public Opinion Quarterly* 7, no. 4 (1943): 748. This figure was much higher than results to the same question in either the United States or Great Britain, where only 32 per cent and 57 per cent, respectively, demanded a significantly different new order.

15 G. Cairns, "What of New Order? Soldiers Want to Know," *Globe and Mail*, 7 October 1943.

16 "Indians Ask Exemptions," *Prince Albert Daily Herald*, 23 October 1943; "Indians Ask Tax Exemptions," *Vancouver Sun*, 21 October 1943; "Indian Petition Was Presented," *Brantford Expositor*, 23 October 1943; "Indians Press Gov't To Grant Exemptions,"

Calgary Herald, 23 October 1943; "Indian Deputation Preparing Written Argument in Museum," *Globe and Mail*, 21 October 1943.

17 The conference was organized at the request of the radical and abrasive Jules Sioui from the Huron community of Lorrettville, Quebec, with aid from John Tootoosis, a Plains Cree leader and the flamboyant Andrew Paull from the west coast. The result of the this conference and another in 1944 was the North American Indian Brotherhood, Canada's first national Native organization, under the leadership of Paull. For more on indigenous politicization, see E.P. Patterson, "Andrew Paull and Canadian Indian Resurgence" (PhD diss., University of Washington, 1962); Hugh Shewell, "Jules Sioui and Indian Political Radicalism in Canada, 1943–44," *Journal of Canadian Studies* 34, no. 3 (Fall 1999): 211–41; and Jean Goodwill and Norma Sluman, *John Tootoosis* (1982; Winnipeg: Pemmican Publications, 1984).

18 See Canada, House of Commons, Special Committee on Reconstruction and Re-establishment, Minutes of Proceedings and Evidence, 18, 24 May 1944.

19 "The Canadian Indian," *Saskatoon Star-Phoenix*, 25 September 1944.

20 National Archives of Canada (NAC), Record Group 10 (RG 10), vol. 8585, file 1/1-2-17, Winifred Paris to the Committee on Reconstruction and Re-establishment, 6 August 1944.

21 "Champions Native Indians," *Kamloops Sentinel*, 4 April 1944.

22 "Where Rivers Run North," *Winnipeg Free Press*, 19 April 1945.

23 Kathleen Coburn, "The Red Man's Burden," *Canadian Forum* 24, no. 285 (October 1944): 153.

24 "Question Medical Care Given to Indians in North," *Globe and Mail*, 17 April 1945.

25 This is clearly demonstrated in the letters, motions, petitions, and briefs received either by the Indian Affairs Branch or by the Special Joint Committee on the Indian Act, including the Dock and Shipyard Workers Union of Vancouver and District; the Alberta-based Committee of Friends of the Indians; the municipal councils in Fredericton, New Brunswick and Sudbury and Sault Ste. Marie, Ontario; the Canadian Federation of Home and School; and the Social Security Council of Canada. Beyond these, other correspondence was received from religious groups of numerous denominations, political associations of various affiliations, veterans' organizations, professional societies, youth groups, and social clubs such as the Calgary Branch of the Canadian Authors' Association. See the appendixes of the Reports of the Special Joint Committee on the Indian Act and the following archival files: NAC, RG 10, vol. 6811, file 470-2-3, pt. 11, NAC, RG 10, vol. 6811, file 450-3-6, pt. 1; and NAC, RG 10, vol. 8583, file 1/1-2-16, pt. 3.

26 Canada, House of Commons, *Debates*, 13 May 1946: 1446. Though not the Royal Commission that many were demanding, the SJC could hear witnesses and gather evidence, and its broad mandate was a virtual *carte blanche* to delve into any aspect of the "Indian problem."

27 SJC, Minutes of Proceedings and Evidence no. 5, April–June, 1948, 186. See also John Leslie, "Assimilation, Integration or Termination? The Development of Canadian Indian Policy, 1943–1963" (PhD diss., Carleton University, 1999), 177.

28 SJC, Minutes and Proceedings no. 27, 27 May 1947, 1484.

29 SJC, Minutes and Proceedings no. 5, 13 April to 21 June 1948, 187.

30 In particular, the decision to field an additional Infantry Division for the Pacific theatre would prove too great a burden for the country's already heavily mobilized

population, though John Martin has argued that in fact the Labour government never really pressed the extension of working hours or attempted any radical reorganization of the nation's workforce in "Total War? The National Service Department and New Zealand's Manpower Crisis of 1942," in *Kia Kaha: New Zealand and the Second World War*, ed. John Crawford (Melbourne: Oxford University Press, 2002), 221–35.

31 "Maori Conference Addressed by Ministers – Housing and Land," *Dominion*, 21 October 1944.

32 James Belich, *Paradise Reforged: A History of the New Zealanders from the 1880s to the Year 2000* (Auckland: Penguin Books, 2001), 297.

33 "N.Z.'s War Effort," *Evening Post*, 13 November 1945. Interestingly, this story also falls into the pattern of segregating Maori from the national war effort. Almost a full column was dedicated to meticulous coverage of the statistics provided in the prime minister's speech, before the final tersely worded sentence gave notice that the "Hon. E. T. Tirikatene presented a report on behalf of the Labour Maori Advisory Committee."

34 "More Tolerance to Maoris," *Dominion*, 23 August 1945.

35 "Maintenance of Maori Culture," *Dominion*, 12 June 1947.

36 Jeffrey Sissons, "The Post-Assimilationist Thought of Sir Apirana Ngata: Towards a Genealogy of New Zealand Biculturalism," *New Zealand Journal of History* 34, no. 1 (April 2000): 47–59.

37 "The Colour Bar – Considered More Obvious Here Than in England," *Dominion*, 17 October 1944.

38 "Pakeha and Maori – Existence of Colour Bar in New Zealand Denied," *Dominion*, 18 October 1944.

39 See, for instance, "Maori Welfare," *Dominion*, 21 October 1944.

40 "Welfare of Maori – 30 Tribes Represented at Conference," *Dominion*, 19 October 1944.

41 "Maori War Effort – Desire to Retain Existing Organisation," *Dominion*, 20 October 1944.

42 "As of Right – Equality for Maoris," *Evening Post*, 11 September 1946.

43 Orange, "The Price of Citizenship?" 242–45.

CHAPTER 17

AUSTRALIA'S COLD WAR:

BRITISHNESS AND ENGLISH-SPEAKING WORLDS CHALLENGED ANEW

David Lowe

ONE OF THE STRONGEST MESSAGES to emerge from a number of scholarly explorations of Australian political culture and overseas policy-making in the 1950s is that the decade was more dynamic and contradictory than popular interpretations have often suggested. In his book *Imagining the Fifties*, John Murphy argues that the expansion of middle-class ideals into the public realm produced sharp contradictions of sentiments and virtues: for example, between the responsible citizen and the avid consumer; between religious definitions of social relations and new streams of thinking about youth, sexuality, and psychology; between promised prosperity and seemingly uncontrollable economic instability; and between a mode of post-war beginnings and the prospect of another global war. Such tensions surfaced in both private and public realms, and running through the debates they generated was often a contest between tradition and modernity.[1] This chapter is an attempt to insert the identity-shaping consequences of the Cold War during the 1950s into this general picture of contradictions and contests within identity-related debates in Australia. I suggest that looking at Australia's Cold War merely as a case study of the history of post-war international relations risks overdrawing it as a new, modern, history-rupturing or path-to-Vietnam-charting type of struggle. Instead, the Australian experience suggests that the challenge posed by the Cold War in the 1950s was also an opportunity for Australians to revisit more familiar, more stable means of interpreting events, and many, especially conservative, politicians seized the chance to do just this. In fact, the Cold War invited Australians to identify themselves again as part of the British World or as part of Winston Churchill's increasingly used collective, "the English-Speaking Peoples."

The approach here is to tease out some of the recent suggestions to emerge from research on the 1950s over the significance of the Cold War for Australians. I am interested in those ideas that emerged publicly, and I am especially interested in those that emerged in the arena of the federal parliament. There are two related reasons for this focus on parliament. The first is that it is an undervalued resource for historians of Australia in the world. Speeches in parliament may not fit neatly into causation chains establishing the formation of foreign policy, but they provide invaluable glimpses into how the reactive responses met the more imaginary and visionary elements of thinking about Australian destiny in world affairs. More than other Australians, parliamentarians tended consciously to locate themselves in the historical streams of continuity and change. They looked back and sometimes forwards in their efforts to navigate through the currents of world affairs; they drew on historical markers for guidance and, especially in the middle of the twentieth century, on both past and possible future world wars. In the pages of *Hansard*, there is a strong sense of members, especially backbenchers, publicly processing the various sources of information shaping their contributions to debates relating to the state of the world. Indeed, a second reason for focusing on parliamentarians is that they tend to tell us which books, reports, newspapers, or international statesmen they are relying on for their authority, and they are also sometimes confessional, or indeed brazen, about prejudices and experiences informing their comments.

The other main reason for concentrating on parliament is that as Australia was increasingly drawn into a modernizing, globalizing world, Australians were increasingly forced to imagine how others saw them. The self-consciousness of Australian parliamentarians, their sense of how they were being identified, even how they were being listened to on the radio (an innovation in parliament legislated in 1946), was a growing theme during the decade. The parliamentary chambers encouraged performance to an unseen listening public as well as the articulation of ideas. Given the similarities between the white settler Dominions in the format and reporting of parliamentary debates, this is one line of inquiry that might be applied elsewhere with the potential to flesh out the idea of the British World and to explore its changing nature over time.[2]

Two features of Australia's federal parliament in the 1950s need comment in the context of the following arguments. The first is that it was full of old men. The decade began with a new Liberal/Country Party coalition government and with many men in federal parliament who had served considerable time either there or in the armed forces before winning their seats. In the 1950 parliament some 63 per cent of members were over the age of fifty (in other words, nearly two-thirds, or 115 of the 183 members, had been born before the turn of the century).[3] For the purposes of comparison, in 1978 only 39 per cent of members were over fifty.[4] Although it is tempting to invoke the wizened figure of Billy Hughes as a representative example (at least up to late 1952), the more appropriate figure might be a Liberal member such as Eric Harrison (a veteran of the First World War) or Athol Townley, to choose some examples from members of the Cabinet whose parliamentary career had been delayed by military service in one of the two world wars. Or perhaps Wilfrid Kent Hughes, if we want an example of someone who had served in both world wars. These members, therefore, took up their seats somewhat older than they might have otherwise done. And this is the second feature of parliament. Some 45 per cent of new members joining the chambers after the December 1949 election were ex-service-men, and roughly two-thirds of all new Liberal members during the 1950s were ex-servicemen.[5] Although the decade did not see a significant number of British-born sitting in parliament it might be worth noting that in the early 1950s, around one-third of members claimed Church of England religious faith, the highest figure since the first decade of the Commonwealth.[6]

Labor members were, then, at a disadvantage in debating matters of wars, both past and future. On many occasions they took issue with government policy. They mounted impressive arguments against over-reliance on the Cold War as a means of explaining change in Asia; they argued the need for faith in the United Nations and for resisting Cold War polarity, pointing to speeches by Indian, Ceylonese, Indonesian, and other Asian leaders; and the best speakers stressed both the desirability and the complexity of decolonization. With such arguments, they could not draw on the powerful narrative of Australian involvement in wars in an affirming way. But there were some more consensual ideas, not only in parliament but also in the broader realm of public opinion. Two oft-repeated themes were (1) that Britain had set a noble and selfless example on the world stage during the Second World War, holding back the tide of fascist darkness at the cost of exhaustion and (2) that the British civilizing mission overseas, a project in which Australia played its part, was incomplete. There was plenty of room for debating the full meaning of these general tenets of Britishness, and I suggest that conservatives (*i.e.*, Liberal/Country Party members) were able to bring the Cold War to bear in ways that enabled them to dominate the debate.[7]

In particular, they were able to mobilize the growing number of apparent links between the present Cold War and the British World's involvement in the two previous world wars in ways that rendered the Cold War more explicable and familiar than some of Labor's more challenging ideas about the new world order.

Because the Cold War was another global war and because many politicians determinedly emphasized its continuities with the Second World War, discussions of the Cold War invited historical excursions and comparisons and tapped into narrative frameworks that had often been generated in Britain, or at least had Britain as their starting point. This trend was detectable at the start of the 1950s, when parliamentarians often incorporated or anticipated a British revival in world affairs from the blows suffered during the Second World War. Conservative politicians, back in power in Australia from the end of 1949, led the way in stressing British endurance in world affairs and British genius. Having blasted Labor interlopers for placing too much faith in the new United Nations (too quasi-contractual and experimental for most non-Labor politicians), they drew again on the stock images of organic unity with the Commonwealth/Empire and of Britain as an exemplar in world affairs. External Affairs Minister Richard Casey, for example, praised Britain in 1952 as "an anvil that has worn out many hammers." Britain was the heart of the Commonwealth, "a modern miracle" and a multinational, multiracial "example to the world as a whole."[8] In the early years of the decade, the seemingly real prospect of global nuclear war reinforced an Anglocentric way of viewing of the world – not least because most members assumed, correctly, that Australia's role would be again to provide an expeditionary force to a location of crucial Commonwealth strategic responsibility, such as the Middle East. And contemplating a third, probably atomic, world war also meant, for some members, contemplating the end of Western civilization, in which Britain stood out again as the basis for the Australian project.[9]

The atomic theme was especially strong in the 1950s. This was the decade of spectacular discoveries of uranium ore in northern Australia, fuelling overblown optimism about the country's industrial future and enhanced standing in world affairs. Moreover, the parliamentary debates took place against the backdrop of British atomic bomb testing in Australia between 1952 and 1963, and some considerable thinking about the possible development of Australian nuclear weapons.[10] The atomic bomb and, from 1953, the hydrogen bomb were revolutionary. Members imagined that a third world war would make the earlier two "pale into insignificance, almost nothingness."[11] Mortality hung in the air when members occasionally referred to the prospect of nuclear holocaust. Noting ever more frightening developments in the testing of bigger, more powerful bombs, members from both sides of the House looked into the abyss of civilization destroyed. Labor giant Dr. H.V. Evatt, commenting in 1955 on reports which suggested that there was no defence against atomic weapons, declared that "the present crisis of humanity must colour every question of international policy."[12] The debate of March 1956, which took place in the wake of abortive disarmament talks in the United Nations, was extraordinary for its apocalyptic qualities. No one was more doom-laden than Liberal member Billy Wentworth, who prided himself on his knowledge on matters atomic,[13] but some of his strongest warnings were echoed on the other side of the House as well.[14] It had already been pointed out that the prospect of Britain's rapid obliteration through hydrogen-bomb attack might also leave Australia with new responsibilities in what remained of the British World.[15]

Yet the fears of atomic bombs did not quite dislodge more historical ways of reading international affairs. The bombs could be considered evolutionary as well as revolutionary, for the world was again divided into two hostile camps; it was only their immensely increased destructive power that was different. Often, especially in the hands of government members, the bomb was also a dark saviour, a necessary evil holding back the Russian hordes.[16] When members spoke fearfully for their children and of the legacy that they hoped to leave them, Britain often loomed large. Hugh Roberton (Country Party), for example, urged his colleagues in March 1950 to re-establish the strength of the British Empire, "for the sake of all good people, and for the everlasting good of mankind, and in order that the right honourable member for Barton [Evatt] and I may leave to our children, if to no one else, the same degree of security and liberty that he and I have enjoyed for so long."[17] What we decide in relation to the threat of atomic war, said his colleague Magnus Cormack in the Senate, "will shape events for our children and grandchildren."[18]

Cold War defence planning and history-based appreciations of Australia in world affairs were mutually reinforcing. A key defence-planning episode in 1950–51 illustrates this effectively, as well as demonstrating that the history-based narratives running through parliamentary debates were also strongly present in top-secret discussions. On 21 June 1950 Australia's Council of Defence assembled in Canberra for a conference with Britain's chief of imperial general staff, Field Marshal Sir William Slim. The Council of Defence was a combination of leading

Cabinet members and Australia's top defence personnel, and it met with Slim to consider the gravity of the Cold War crisis and its implications for Australians. Slim wanted agreement from the Australians that Europe and the Middle East were the most crucial theatres to hold in the event of a war with the Soviet Union. More specifically, he wanted the Australians to send an expeditionary force to help defend British air bases in the Middle East. Interestingly, he prompted something of a collective excursion into the history of Australia at war. The Australian prime minister, Robert Menzies, pointed out that "the Middle East has been an Australian theatre now in two wars. We raised and sent the 2nd AIF to it and it was our primary preoccupation until Japan entered the war." His chief of general staff, Sidney Rowell, added: "We did right to help out in [the] M[iddle] East in [the] last war, and [the] situation now resembles this," while another Cabinet member suggested that the situation was in fact "more comparable to [the] first world war than to [the] second."[19]

From the detailed notes taken of this meeting, Slim seemed both pleased and surprised at the historical turn the conversation took. He encouraged the Australians to assume that war with the Soviet Union would be global, and he pointedly reminded them that the British Empire might unravel should the Middle East not be held. If this happened, he said, "it may open the route to Africa, finish cooperation by Pakistan and India, cut the sea route through the Mediterranean and deny to us oil resources which may be essential to the prosecution of this war." Menzies agreed, adding that the Russians were also students of history: "If they take note of the lessons of past history their aim must be to knock us out in the early period of the war."[20] Later, as Menzies tried to gear up the economy for war preparedness, Rowell made ambitious promises about how many troops would be available to travel to the Middle East on the basis that national service trainees had joined up in droves when the First World War had broken out. The new national service trainees of the early 1950s would surely do the same.[21]

For the first three years of the 1950s, there was a strong strategic basis, according to British and American defence planners, as well as the Australians, for Australian preparations for another world war. The logical corollary was to assume a traditional role for an Australian expeditionary force sailing quickly to an area of Commonwealth strategic responsibility such as the Middle East. Significantly, the United States State Department seemed happy with this way of viewing Australia, declining in a 1950 review to take Australia away from the desk of British

Commonwealth Affairs in their European Bureau and put it in a more Asian designation. Only in 1954–55 did the State Department decide on a partial redesignation for Australia to the Southeast Asia Desk. Planning and preparing for another world war – even if such efforts amounted to little in the way of actual transfers or action overseas – kicked into action an historically powerful default setting for seeing Australia as part of the British Empire/Commonwealth and for expecting Australians to raise a force to send to a theatre in the British sphere of Anglo-American responsibilities.[22]

In parliament, debates concentrating on international affairs and the Cold War were irregular during the 1950s, but they attracted voluble contributions. Members were not shy about confessing a lack of expertise in international affairs before launching into world history writ large and the current risk of war. Many of these surveys had Britain as their starting point. Other huge historical surveys featured gloomy realism from both sides of the House (nations had always been fighting each other for booty)[23] and sagas of empires and civilizations. It seems likely that Toynbee's *Study of History*, widely discussed in the middle years of the decade, lay in the background to some speeches. Evatt drew on Toynbee's *Civilization on Trial* early in 1951, as well as on Winston Churchill, to argue the potentially catastrophic consequences of both sides facing off in the Cold War.[24] But there were also more positive assessments of how history had shown that it was the quality of people that counted, in terms of their influence in world affairs, rather than their quantity. Labor member Gordon Bryant emphasized how Britain had punched above its weight over the course of the previous three hundred years.[25] Others emphasized the British achievements in Australia. In 1954 Henry Turner (Liberal) declared that

for hundreds of years, the existence of Australia was known to the people of South-East Asia, but they made no attempt to populate or develop it. Our indefeasible title to Australia is based upon the enterprise of British seamen, upon the ingenuity and perseverance of our settlers and colonists and the sweat and toil of our ancestors. We raised Australia from a state in which nobody else was able to develop it, and so our title to it is indefeasible.[26]

Those who commented directly on the changed position of Britain in world affairs covered a spectrum of views ranging from fierce determination to restore Britain to its rightful leading role to wanting to preserve the best of the Empire in a new alliance of English-speaking peoples in which the other major actor was the United States.[27] The sense of belonging to an English-speaking people was arguably one of the most consensual ideas in parliament, one step removed as it was from the more contestable history of Britain in Australia and of Britain and Australia during the war. To government members, it was also racially consoling, allowing for ties to the British Empire to rejuvenate while Australia established itself as a bastion for Western civilization in the Pacific. Allen Fairhall (Liberal) pondered optimistically in 1955: "It may well be that we are cast in the historic role of a catalyst to produce the great union of the English-speaking peoples of the world which I believe is necessary and which alone can check and balance the upsurge of communism."[28] "English-speaking peoples" became a favourite phrase of several politicians, including Liberal member Alexander Downer, Sr. and the breakaway anti-communist Labor member, John Mullens.[29]

During the first half of the decade, External Affairs Minister Richard Casey was often joined by his colleagues in highlighting the success of Australia's evolution from colonial origins to sophisticated nationhood.[30] His colleagues also pointed to the benefits of enlightened colonial rule as a counter to communism in places like Malaya and India.[31] Labor members were often happy to praise Australia as the product of a well-charted colony-to-nation story, but remained inclined to give imperialism elsewhere a mixed report card and, in the case of the far left of the party, to dismiss imperialism as a grubby capitalist plot.[32] On Malaya, for example, Dr. Evatt loudly proclaimed that the more critical published studies of British policy by such authorities as Victor Purcell, Vernon Bartlett, and United States Justice William Douglas were "a thousand times more important" than the information about that colony provided by Casey.[33]

Members from both sides of the House and Senate occasionally revealed that their reading tended toward a British perspective on world affairs. As historian David Cannadine has emphasized, Churchill, the prolific writer and crafter of speeches, armed legions of admiring contemporaries with potent words, phrases, and rhetorical strategies.[34] He always had his critics in Australia, especially in the left wing of the Labor Party, but his special blend of practicing and preaching history ensured him popularity beyond memories of his wartime leadership. During the 1950s, his volumes on the Second World War were eagerly devoured by Australians, who were thereby helping fulfill his prophecy that history would treat him well because he intended to write it. There were many direct references in parliament to his published works[35] and probably many examples of their unacknowledged use in the preparation of speeches. The message in the first volumes on the need for preparedness rather than appeasement of dictators was favourably received in a climate increasingly sensitive to the hardening of lines in the Cold War. In November 1950, in the wake of Chinese intervention in the Korean War, Menzies' first minister of external affairs, Percy Spender, went so far as to proclaim that avoiding appeasement was one of the "principles" of Australian foreign policy – even though, by this stage, Churchill was arguing that appeasement from a position of strength could be "magnanimous and noble" and the way to peace.[36]

Churchill's style of historical narrative lent itself easily to parliamentary thrusts and parries. Churchill hung "the chronicle and discussion of great military and political events upon the thread of the personal experiences of an individual,"[37] and his practice of interweaving his narrative with quotations from his wartime correspondence and parliamentary speeches was a style that was easily and often adapted to parliamentary debate. Historically founded arguments boasting chunks of direct quotation – sometimes even those recorded thoughts of the current speaker that seemed prescient in the light of subsequent events – took on Churchillian shape in their aspirations toward participant history. Dr. Evatt, the Labor leader for most of the decade and a published historian/biographer himself, was especially disposed toward Churchill-like contours in his parliamentary performances.[38]

Prime minister again from the end of 1951 to 1955, Churchill did more than anyone else to promote the idea of the "English-Speaking Peoples" as a moral-cultural-strategic force in the post-war world. Churchill, himself the product of a trans-Atlantic union, had been a strong promoter of the English-Speaking Union created in the aftermath of the First World War to disseminate knowledge, especially across the Atlantic, and inspire reverence of common traditions among English-speaking peoples. In turn, by the 1950s, the English-Speaking Union was a strong promoter of Churchill, and with good reason. Between 1956 and 1958, Churchill's four-volume *A History of the English-Speaking Peoples* was published. Having begun the project in the mid-1930s but delayed it due to war and more pressing and lucrative publishing opportunities, Churchill believed that its original theme was still valid. "Vast numbers of people on both sides of the Atlantic and throughout the British Commonwealth of Nations have felt a sense of brotherhood," he wrote in the preface to volume one. "A new generation is at hand. Many practical steps have been taken which carry us far."[39] Despite the lack of elaboration on the nature of the task or where the new generation was being carried, the sense of rallying was strong. ·

Earlier, in his "iron curtain" speech at Fulton, Missouri in 1946, the speech so important to his re-emergence as a statesman and seer, he had argued that even if the United Nations were to become an effective world court, the "fraternal association of the English-speaking peoples" would have to act as its sheriffs. In the aftermath of the speech, Soviet observers certainly took him seriously enough to view Canada and other Dominions with new wariness.[40] Earlier still, in 1939, Churchill wrote that the English-speaking peoples had been the authors and trustees, and should now become the champions, of a core package of ideals "of the growth of freedom and law, of the rights of the individual, of the subordination of the State to the fundamental and moral conceptions of an ever-comprehending community."[41] His history of the English-speaking peoples was serialized in Australian newspapers in the mid- to late 1950s, just as his history of the Second World War had been earlier in the decade.[42]

Menzies, ever Churchill's public champion in Australia despite his bruising contest with him in the early 1940s, took up some of the Churchillian challenges for the Australian public. He was particularly quick to seize on the Fulton address as a call to Australians too, and as a reminder that those common attributes of English-speaking peoples – racial stock, love of freedom, language, religion, political institutions, and educational development – constituted the real stuff of international co-operation.[43] When visiting Churchill at Chartwell in 1948, Menzies was given the full charm treatment and treated to Churchill's verbal and pictorial depictions of the essential connections between Britain and its colonies, the United States, Western Europe, and the English-speaking world, which included Dominions such as Australia.[44] Menzies admired Churchill for his powers of prose and his capacity to loom large in history. He seemed to be thinking of the post-war Churchill when he recorded that Churchill wrote his speeches "partly because he knew that he was a man of destiny and that the world, in its anguish, was reading him and listening to him, and getting fire from him; and partly because he conceived them as literary exercises."[45] In fact, it might not be going too far to suggest that Churchill inspired in Menzies a distrust in professional historians of recent events and a desire to match Churchill's sense of being at the centre of contemporary stories. In 1956 Menzies wrote:

When I was a schoolboy, I read, learned and inwardly digested a British history which ended, forty years before, in 1867. This created in me an idea (still prevalent in many minds) that history is something written about the past. It has taken a concentrated adult experience to teach me that history is always in the making, that Winston Churchill probably made more history that he has ever written and that, in fact, we have in the last forty years lived with more revolutions that the world produced in its previous three hundred years.[46]

Throughout the first half of the 1950s, Menzies' colleagues were still drawing on Churchill's Fulton speech to defend the need for unity among English-speaking peoples and the logic of negotiating with the communist world only from a position of strength.[47] Labor politicians, too, continued to quote Churchill; they even fought over his imprimatur, as when he and Anthony Eden took seriously the rallying call of the new non-aligned nations in the mid-1950s for "peaceful co-existence." If Churchill and Eden could bring themselves to face this new movement squarely, argued a young Labor member, Gough Whitlam, then why couldn't Australian conservatives?[48]

Other British military authorities and participants in the Second World War added to the Churchillian story – Sir William Slim's book *Defeat into Victory* (1956) was all the more topical for Slim's having become governor-general of Australia in 1953, and Liddell Hart's *The Other Side of the Hill* (1951) and Australian Chester Wilmot's *The Struggle for Europe* (1952) were regarded as authoritative in parliament.[49] In 1958, for example, when Labor members were calling for a great power summit between Khrushchev, Macmillan, and Eisenhower, some government backbenchers reached for their well-thumbed Churchills and Wilmots in order to remind the House of how the early "big three" diplomacy – Churchill, Stalin, Roosevelt – of the Second World War was very different from what was being proposed by Labor.[50]

Less exclusively focused on the Second World War, Purcell on Malaya,[51] Lord Tedder writing on *The Shape of War to Come*,[52] and A.J.P. Taylor in *New Statesman and Nation*[53] provided fuel for debate. Norman Angell, who prophesied in 1933 that countries waging war would destroy themselves in the process, was a sage recalled for parliamentary purposes; in 1958 he provided more food for thought with his book *Defence and the English-Speaking Role*.[54] American writers were also drawn on; memoirs and works on China and Japan, and on recent American battles or disasters, such as the Japanese attack on Pearl Harbour, were among the most popular.[55] Contemporary American leaders provided plenty of fuel for debates, but the imperial publishing house legacy was strong in Australia and ensured British stories pride of place. And recollections of the recent war were enlivened by a recurring struggle between Labor and government members for the greatest share of the credit in successfully prosecuting the Second World War, a contest sharpened by the publication in 1952 of the first of Paul Hasluck's two-volume official history of Australian politics and society during the war. As Hasluck had become a minister in Menzies' government by this time, the basis for dividing on political party lines seemed all the greater.[56]

The circulation of works on the Second World War and world history emboldened a few of the more adventurous members into truly remarkable *tours de force*. In March 1956, David Henry Drummond, Country Party member for New England, provided a survey of human history that went back four thousand years and speculated about the future up to ten thousand years hence. In the space of minutes, he moved from the United Nations to the exploits of Napoleon and the advent of the atomic bomb, with a glance at *Alice in Wonderland* to smooth the transitions. Drummond was a great enthusiast for the British system of government as one that offered the maximum sense of fair play and justice, and he lamented the decline in Britain's stature in world affairs. In fact, he declared that the current situation was comparable to that of the decline of the Roman Empire: the overstretched British faced a terrible time, as did those countries that had previously enjoyed British protection but were now subject to the "grasping ambitions" of men and nations. It is worth quoting one of his key passages:

> We have come to one of those periods in the history of mankind
> in which we see a reshaping of the whole scheme of things, and
> some of things that we see, as descendants of British, are not
> very comforting to us. We in Australia are predominantly and
> overwhelmingly a British people, in the British tradition. We
> have seen the effects of World War I. We have seen the titanic
> struggle waged by Great Britain to retain the strength of the
> position which it held. We have seen Great Britain plunge into
> World War II, and throw everything it had – every asset, all its
> defences, all its capacity to endure which it had built up over
> centuries of free government – into the pool so that the greatest
> challenge to freedom which has yet appeared, that of Hitler and

his Nazis with their infamous doctrines, should not gain control over mankind and, of course, Great Britain. But the price which has been paid has completely altered the whole approach to foreign affairs.[57]

The price paid, noble self-sacrifice for the sake of the world, was a common way of describing the impact of the Second World War on Britain, especially among Liberal and Country Party members. Sometimes it was followed by references to a transfer of responsibilities – from weakened Britain to maturing Australia. There was even quite a strong undercurrent of mission in these declarations, especially regarding Australia's new role in Asia. In 1955 Henry Pearce (Liberal) told fellow members of the "tremendous job" they had to do in the world: "We do not know, and we cannot gauge, just how much people in the Asian countries are looking to Australia; because Australia is to them the most recent copy book, as it were, of a country that has gained self-government for itself and is working out its own destiny."[58]

Australians' active imagining of their role in world affairs was central to the tensions of the period and is a theme worth teasing out further. Some of the contrasts and contests between tradition and modernity were played out in special events that forced Australians to think hard about how they were seen by others. The 1954 Royal Tour, for example, featured both affirmations of Britishness and the heralding of Australia's new modern age. The stories of Australian progress drew straight lines from imperial traditions to supercharged technological feats; the headline "Redcoats to Atom Bombs" captured the public mood. The stories seemed to be partly directed at Australians of British Isles descent and partly at the significant number of post-war immigrants beginning to arrive from continental Europe.[59] Two years after the Royal Tour, as Graeme Davison has shown, the organizers of the 1956 Olympic Games, to be held in Melbourne, were divided between traditionalists, intent on linking the Melbourne games to a familiar image of the sportsman as God-fearing and peaceful warrior, versus the modernizers. The modernizers, those entrepreneurial businessmen who stressed growth and successful implementation of American models for productivity, eventually won out in the promotional images of Melbourne developed for overseas visitors.[60]

The last in the series of Marten and Carter's Histories, used in Australian high schools in the 1950s, captured the juxtaposition pithily. In Book IV, published in 1955 and taking readers up to contemporary times, the two English historians admire the spate of post-war activity in Australia: the expansion of manufacturing and great developmental projects such as the Snowy Mountains scheme and long-range weapons testing, the ambitious immigration program and the extension of social services, and the active role by Australians in United Nations activity and the Colombo Plan. Then, the final paragraph begins: "*In the midst of all this activity*, Australia has also found time to remember that she is a member of the British Commonwealth of Nations with ties of loyalty to Great Britain." And, of course, it ends with the "tumultuous scenes" of welcome for the Queen in 1954, the stabilizing and rejuvenated core of Empire that would act as a counter to rampaging modernization.[61]

This is not to imply Australian uniqueness in experiencing a tension between tradition and modernity. In 1953 Britons themselves had revelled in a juxtaposition of the two. They promoted a conflation of a new or renewed "Elizabethan Age" and the dawn of a new multiracial Commonwealth with the coinciding coronation of their young Queen and the ascent of Mt. Everest by Edmund Hillary and his Sherpa guide, Tenzing Norgay.[62] Arguably, too, a similar tension was notable in British perceptions of their great, ascendant ally, the United States. The British Labour Party could be horrified, for example, at the departures from civil society wrought by McCarthyism and some of Eisenhower's and John Foster Dulles's atomic-laden expressions of foreign policy in the 1950s; yet revisionists such as Anthony Crosland could also applaud the exemplary commitments to social equality in American public policy that could still point the way for British socialism.[63]

Interestingly, in the mid-1950s, there was also a change in emphasis in the "story of Australia" generated for overseas consumption and particularly aimed at Asian countries. It seems likely that Australian involvement in the Colombo Plan for aid to South and Southeast Asia, and the elaborate fine tuning that accompanied efforts to maintain a distinctly Australian angle on the benefits of Australian aid had something to do with it. But the shift may have also stemmed from the cool reaction to Australia's minister for external affairs, Richard Casey, when he sermonized in Asia about Australia's wonderful colonial legacy.[64] At the end of 1955, he sent a long telegram to all posts suggesting that they accentuate the positives in the Australian story, such as the advantages of voluntary co-operation in economic development and the vigour of democratic institutions and methods. Australians were, of course, playing a vital role in the Colombo Plan, providing aid without strings and gaining much in return from increasing human and cultural contacts with Asian countries.

The recommended approach was to say that Australians appreciated that their own welfare was tied up with the development of the Asia-Pacific area and that they also knew that Australia too had its development challenges ahead: "In seeking to extend Australian influence among Asians we should lay suitable stress on our relatively advanced development but at the same time indicate that we have many economic and development problems in common with neighbouring Asian countries."[65]

This last theme was one that began to appear more often in Australian public information and diplomacy. In parliament, members' reminders that Asian peoples were listening, or would discover soon what was being said on the floor, were more common from the middle of the decade.[66] Casey, in particular, acknowledged on several occasions that Asians and Australians had economic and development concerns in common. His sense of mission in Asia and his affinity with at least some of Asia's problems led him to write in 1954, in a book entitled *Friends and Neighbours*: "We [Australians] share the anxieties of our Asian friends because, though our exports are largely different from theirs, we know what it is like to be dependent on the export prices of raw materials."[67] Other ministers, in their briefs on Australia, presented the country as a model of successful development when welcoming Asian students and trainees to Australia, often in the context of a history lesson on "progress" that had many Asian countries in the same position now as Australia had been in the immediate aftermath of white settlement. The story of Australia as a model for Asia in terms of successful modernization began to overtake the story of Australia as a successful case study of enlightened imperialism.[68] The tone was often patronizing, but the idea of identifying with Colombo Plan recipient nations in this way built on the earlier self-proclaimed Australian distinctiveness in their approach to the Colombo Plan. It was also easily grafted onto the prevailing modernization theory informing American plans for the development of Asia, courtesy of Walt Rostow, David Lilienthal, and others.[69]

What conclusions can we draw from this study of Australia's Cold War in federal parliament? The first is that parliamentary efforts in the 1950s to make the Second World War meaningful in the context of the current situation were to be expected. With Churchill at the helm of government in Britain and offering plentiful spoken and written words with which to make sense of the last war, these efforts and the debates they provoked were a major sub-theme running through many debates on international affairs. More importantly, for historians, the debates provide a new cultural texture to the history of Australians' thinking

David Lowe   375

about their role in the world; perhaps they even enable us to incorporate something of the life story-telling style of historian Manning Clark, whose work is generally ignored by historians of Australian foreign policy. Clark's attention to the contests between the main actors (admittedly, mostly male and white) in his account of struggles over which of the different strands of European inheritance should triumph in Australia makes the most of visions publicly expressed in journals, newspapers, parliamentary debates, and other sources.[70]

In general terms, the parliamentary debates on wars past and anticipated blended easily with the sense of emergency and fears of a third world war in the early years of the 1950s; they tended to reinforce an Australian sense of Britishness or intimate involvement in British civilization, and they were buttressed by the Churchillian rhetoric on the need for unity among the English-speaking peoples. The related conclusion is that, like the contests between tradition and modernity being played out in Australian public and private spheres, the Cold War was thus made familiar at the same time that its revolutionary qualities, chiefly the prospect of a nuclear holocaust, loomed large.

At a pinch, we might even point to a coincidence between a Cold War-inspired renewal of Britishness in Australia and Churchill's trajectory in British life. During his "Indian Summer" in government again (1951–55), he devoted much time and energy toward holding a summit meeting between himself and the Soviet and American leaders – another "big three" meeting like those in the latter part of the Second World War. It was an idea that looked more possible after Stalin's death in 1953, but it never gained enough support in Moscow or Washington and then it faded with Churchill's own dotage.[71] From 1955, the lessons digested or learned and the rhetorical battles fought over the Second World War among Canberra's politicians also began to fade, and Churchill's shadow seemed to give way to greater space for consideration of the non-aligned movement at Bandung, nation-building in Asia, and other themes. Australians' sense of Britishness had diverse and strong roots, many of which were still very strong in the second half of the 1950s, but one of the more powerfully constructed ways of imagining Australia in world affairs, a line between the Second World War and the Cold War, drawn with the help of Churchill and his rallying of the English-speaking peoples, was giving way to new ways of seeing.

{NOTES}

1 John Murphy, *Imagining the Fifties: Private Sentiment and Political Culture in Menzies' Australia* (Sydney: Pluto Press, 2000); see also special issue of *Australian Historical Studies* 28, no. 109 (October 1997), edited by John Murphy and Judith Smart, on "The Forgotten Fifties: Aspects of Australian Society and Culture in the 1950s."

2 Historians have begun exploring this theme; see Carl Bridge and Kent Fedorowich, eds., *The British World: Diaspora, Culture and Identity* (London: Frank Cass, 2003).

3 Joan Rydon, *A Federal Legislature: The Australian Commonwealth Parliament 1901–1980* (Melbourne: Oxford University Press, 1986), 49.

4 Ibid.

5 Ibid., 107–8.

6 Ibid., 133.

7 For discussion of the British World, see P.A. Buckner and Carl Bridge, "Reinventing the British World," *The Round Table* 368 (2003): 77–88.

8 *Commonwealth Parliamentary Debates* (CPD), House of Representatives, vol. 216, 22 February 1952, 272.

9 These are themes developed more fully in my book, *Menzies and the "Great World Struggle": Australia's Cold War 1948–1954* (Kensington: University of New South Wales Press, 1999).

10 On these themes, see Alice Cawte, *Atomic Australia 1944–1990* (Kensington: University of New South Wales Press, 1992), and Wayne Reynolds, *Australia's Bid for the Atomic Bomb* (Melbourne: Melbourne University Press, 2000).

11 Senator Benn, CPD, Senate, vol. 7, 9 April 1957, 382–83.

12 CPD, House of Representatives, vol. House of Representatives (H of R) 6, 27 April 1955, 193.

13 Ibid., vol. H of R 9, 13 March 1956, 733–35; and see remarks by Percy Joske, ibid., vol. H of R 4, 17 August 1954, 329.

14 Bruce's speech, ibid., vol. H of R 9, 15 March 1956, 887–89.

15 Ibid., vol. 6, 4 May 1955, 419.

16 Ibid., vol. 9, 14 March 1956, 785.

17 Ibid., vol. 206, 22 March 1950, 1090.

18 CPD, vol. 216, Senate, 27 February 1952, 407; and see Bruce Wight's comments, ibid., vol. 6, 4 May 1955, 424.

19 Brigadier Rourke's notes of Council of Defence Meeting, 21 June 1950, Commonwealth Record System (CRS) AA1971/216, National Archives of Australia (NAA).

20 Ibid.

21 Rowell memo for McBride, "Citizen Military Forces – Survey," 28 February 1952, CRS A5954, item 2291/4, NAA.

22 Lowe, *Menzies and the "Great World Struggle,"* 71–72.

23 Bruce, CPD, House of Representatives, vol. 9, 15 March 1956, 887–88.

24 Ibid., vol. 212, 14 March 1951, 492–93. In fact, Evatt returned to Churchill's warning throughout the decade. See, for example, ibid., vol. 14, 2 April 1957, 426.

25 Ibid., vol. 18, 1 May 1958, 415–17.

26 Ibid., vol. 4, 17 August 1954, 300–301.

27 For examples of the first view, see Charles Russell, ibid., vol. 206, 21 March 1950, 964; and for examples of the second, see contributions by Keon and Eggins, ibid., 21–22 March 1950, 986, 1070.

28 Ibid., vol. H of R 6, 5 May 1955, 478.

29 Ibid., vol. 206, 21 March 1950; vol. 208, 8 June 1950; and vol. 209, 4 October 1950, 274.

30 Ibid., vol. 217, 4 June 1952, 1373.

31 Senator McCallum, CPD, Senate, vol. 216, 27 February 1952, 413; Kent Hughes, CPD, House of Representatives, vol. 208, 8 June 1950, 4037.

32 Fred Daly, CPD, House of Representatives, vol. 4, 17 August 1954, 327.

33 Ibid., vol. 6, 5 May 1955, 499.

34 David Cannadine, In Churchill's Shadow: Confronting the Past in Modern Britain (Oxford: Oxford University Press, 2003), 85–113.

35 For example, Senator Wordsworth, CPD, vol, Senate 4, 11 August 1954, 163; Senator Wright, ibid., vol. 216, 27 February 1952, 418.

36 CPD, House of Representatives, vol. 211, 28 November 1950, 3165–3166. The first of Churchill's volumes, The Gathering Storm, was published in the United States in June 1948 and in Britain in October 1948. See David Reynolds, "Churchill's Writing of History: Appeasement, Autobiography and The Gathering Storm," Transactions of the Royal Historical Society, 6th ser., 11 (2001): 221–47; Churchill quoted in John W. Young, Winston Churchill's Last Campaign: Britain and the Cold War, 1951–5 (Oxford: Clarendon Press, 1996), 9.

37 Winston S. Churchill, The Second World War, vol. 1, The Gathering Storm (Sydney: Cassell & Co., 1948), vii.

38 See, for example, Evatt's reply to Menzies, CPD, House of Representatives, 19 September 1957, 801–7.

39 Winston S. Churchill, A History of the English-Speaking Peoples, vol. 1, The Birth of Britain (London: Cassell and Co, 1956), vii–viii.

40 Denis Stairs, "Realists at Work: Canadian Policy Makers and the Politics of Transition from Hot War of Cold War," in Canada and the Early Cold War, 1943–1957, ed. Greg Donaghy (Ottawa: Canadian Department of Foreign Affairs and International Trade, 1998), 104–6.

41 John Ramsden, Man of the Century: Winston Churchill and His Legend since 1945 (London: Harper Collins, 2002), 160, 330–31, and see 325–413 for extended discussion on Churchill and the English-speaking peoples.

42 Herald (Melbourne), 31 October–13 November 1959.

43 Ramsden, Man of the Century, 493–94.

44 Ibid., 495–97.

45 Sir Robert Gordon Menzies, The Measure of the Years (London: Coronet, 1970), 17.

46 Robert Menzies, "The Ever-Changing Commonwealth", written for the Times, 11 and 12 June 1956, and reprinted in his Speech Is of Time: Selected Speeches and Writings (London: Cassell & Co., 1958), 21.

47 For example, see Turner's remarks in CPD, House of Representatives, vol. 6, 4 May 1955, 405.

48 Ibid., vol. 4, 12 August 1954, 276; ibid., vol. 6, 28 April 1955, 307. See also Evatt on Churchill's warnings about the catastrophic effects of war with the Soviet Union, ibid., vol. 206, 913.

49 Sir Wilfred Kent Hughes, ibid., vol. 15, 1033, and Henry Drummond, 8 May 1957, 1186–1188.

50 Ibid., vol. 19, 1 May 1958, 1370–73.

51 Ibid., vol. 6, 28 April 1955, 291.

52 Ibid., 5 May 1955, 463.

53 Ibid., 28 April 1955, 305.

54 See comments by Holloway, ibid., vol. 207, 9 May 1950, 2262; Norman Angell, *The Great Illusion 1933* (London: Heinemann, 1934) and *Defence and the English-Speaking Role* (London: Pall Mall Press, 1958).

55 See, for example, CPD, House of Representatives, vol. 4, 10 August 1954, 130, 144; ibid., 11 August, 180; CPD, vol. Senate 4, 9 September 1954, 274. Kent Hughes's 1952 list of recommended reading on the Second World War is probably a representative guide for reading in the early years of the decade: Churchill's volumes; Grenfell's *Main Fleet to Singapore*; James's *Rise and Fall of the Japanese Empire*; and Utley's *Last Chance in China*.

56 Paul Hasluck, *The Government and the People, 1939–1941* (Canberra: Australian War Memorial, 1952). Hasluck was, by 1952, minister for territories in the Menzies government.

57 CPD, vol. H of R 9, 8, March 1956, 682–84.

58 Ibid., vol. H of R 6, 4 May 1955, 417.

59 This is a theme I developed in "1954: Australia and the Queen in the World," *Journal of Australian Studies* 46 (September 1995): 1–10.

60 Graeme Davison, "Welcoming the World: The 1956 Olympic Games and the Representation of Melbourne," *Australian Historical Studies* 28, no. 109 (October 1997): 64–76.

61 Sir Henry Marten and E.H. Carter, assisted by H. de Havilland, *Histories*, Book 4, *The Latest Age* (Australian Edition; Melbourne: Macmillan & Co., 1955), 232–37 (my italics).

62 Peter H. Hansen, "Coronation Everest: The Empire and Commonwealth in the 'Second Elizabethan Age,'" in *British Culture and the End of Empire*, ed. Stuart Ward (Manchester: Manchester University Press, 2001), 57–72.

63 Stephen Fielding, "'But Westward, Look, the Land is Bright': Labour's Revisionists and the Imagining of America c.1945–64," in *Twentieth-Century Anglo-American Relations*, ed. Jonathan Hollowell (London: Palgrave, 2001), 87–101.

64 See John Murphy, "Vietnam and Conservative Imagination in the 1950s," in *Australia and the End of Empires: The Impact of Decolonisation in Australia's Near North, 1945–65*, ed. David Lowe (Geelong: Deakin University Press, 1996), 90–91.

65 External Affairs Guidance sav. 19 to all posts, 10 November 1955, CRS A5462 2/4/2, NAA.

66 CPD, House of Representatives, vol. 6, 4 May 1955, 416–17, 421.

67 R.G. Casey, *Friends and Neighbours: Australia and the World* (Melbourne: Cheshire, 1954), 94; and see Casey's lecture on Australian foreign policy, printed in *Current Notes on International Affairs*, 23, no. 9 (Sept. 1952): 477–78.

68 For example, see Sir Philip McBride's welcoming comments to visiting Asian journalists in September 1955: McBride's speech, 6 September 1955, CRS A1838/294 2048/2 pt 7, NAA.

69 Modernization theory and American plans for development in Asia are discussed in Jonathan Nashell, "The Road to Vietnam: Modernization Theory in Fact and Fiction," in *Cold War Constructions: The Political Culture of United States Imperialism, 1945–1966*, ed. Christian G. Appy (Amherst: University of Massachusetts Press, 2000), 132–54; and David Ekbladh, "'Mr. TVA': Grass-Roots Development, David Lilienthal, and the Rise of the Tennessee Valley Authority as a Symbol for U.S. Overseas Development, 1933–1973," *Diplomatic History* 26, no. 3 (Summer 2002): 335–74.

70 Of Clark's six volumes recording the history of Australia, the one that comes closest, chronologically, to the period under examination here is volume 6: C.M.H. Clark, *A History of Australia*, vol. 6: *"The Old Dead Tree and the Young Tree Green," 1916–1935* (Melbourne: Melbourne University Press, 1987). See, for example, 493.

71 This is a major theme of Young's book, *Winston Churchill's Last Campaign*.

CHAPTER 18

HISTORY WARS
AND THE IMPERIAL LEGACY
IN THE SETTLER SOCIETIES

Stuart Macintyre

IN THE EARLY SPRING OF 1914, a South African mining engineer took up residence in London. He was a man of leisure, having made his pile at Bulawayo, and had long dreamed of returning to the Old Country he left as a young boy in the 1880s. But this colonial found himself at a loose end. The weather made him liverish, the amusements palled, the locals took very little interest in his stories. He was not wholly lacking in invitations, however. "Imperialist ladies" asked him to tea "to meet schoolmasters from New Zealand and editors from Vancouver, and that was the dismalest business of all."[1] It was just as well that the American adventurer Franklin P. Scudder sought refuge in his flat with the story of the Black Stone spy ring and its plan to assassinate the Balkans statesman Karolides, for otherwise Richard Hannay would have cleared out and returned to the veld. Without Hannay's dogged heroism, Britain's naval defences would have been revealed to the Germans for a pre-emptive strike in 1914, the Middle East would have been stirred into a general rising in 1916, German intelligence would have assisted the enemy to break through the Western Front in 1918, and we would not be meeting regularly in the Old Dominions to ponder the legacy of the British Empire.

John Buchan's British World is served by a remarkable variety of heroes. There is Sir Walter Bullivant, the Foreign Office man and director of British intelligence who has his home in the Cotswolds and whose son Harry sacrifices his life as an undercover agent in Iraq. There is Harry's friend Sandy Arbuthnot, who passes as a local from the Albanian mountains to Samarkand. There is the Border radical and Clydeside shop steward, Andrew Amos; the fiercely independent Peter Pienaar, who like many of the great hunters took the British side in the Boer War; the dyspeptic engineer, John Scantlebury Blenkiron, proud of his American republic and yet admiring of the Old Country; Launcelot Wake, the pacifist intellectual who finds his manhood on the front; and Mary Lamington, who possesses a wisdom beyond her years and has that other quality of Buchan's heroines – she is as beautiful as a boy.

All of them serve the Empire by their actions. Their code of masculine valour is marked out by deeds rather than words, and their imperial patriotism is a deeply ingrained loyalty that needs no declaration. During his flight through Scotland in *The Thirty-Nine Steps*, Hannay enjoys the hospitality of Sandy Arbuthnot's father, Sir Harry, who is a Liberal politician. Sir Harry had arranged for "the Colonial ex-Premier fellow, Crumpleton" to address a campaign meeting on the virtues of free trade (this sounds suspiciously like Sir George Reid, the former premier of New South Wales and leader of the Free Trade Party in the first Commonwealth parliament, who was Australian high commissioner by this time), but Crumpleton has sent a telegram saying that he has influenza.[2] Sir Harry therefore presses Hannay into service as "a trusted leader of Australian thought," and Hannay does his best:

> I simply told them all I could remember about Australia,
> praying there should be no Australian there – all about its
> Labour party and emigration and universal service. I doubt if I
> remembered to mention Free Trade, but I said there were no
> Tories in Australia, only Labour and Liberals. That fetched a
> cheer, and I woke them up a bit when I started in to tell them
> the kind of glorious business I thought could be made out of the
> Empire if we really put our backs into it.[3]

Hannay judges his effort a success, though he observes that the chairman of the meeting, a weaselly minister with a red nose, described him as having "the eloquence of an emigration agent."

Hannay's familiarity with the British World is clearly limited. He seems to have had no contact with the Australian troops who fought alongside him in the South African War or the substantial numbers of Australians who worked with him in the mining industry. His knowledge of this Dominion is restricted to its political parties, the system of compulsory military training it had introduced in 1910, its assisted migration scheme and the role it might play in a Greater Britain. His British World is configured by a set of unilateral relationships between Britain and each of its Dominions, like spokes on a wheel. The Dominions take a close interest in the imperial homeland but not, it seems, in each other. Hence Hannay's dismay with the tea parties of the imperialist ladies.

The idea of the British World posits a community of transplanted Britons in distinctive local settings and working out their destinies with a common ancestry, institutions, language, culture, and traditions. The maintenance of such a community required an informed appreciation of each other's efforts, familiarity with their distinctive character, and recognition of their common heritage. This need was served by formal machinery that originated in the late nineteenth century with the Colonial Conference and survives as the Commonwealth Heads of Government Meeting; it was fostered by elite organizations such as the Round Table that reported regularly on local matters of common concern and was popularized in imperial literature that provided vivid descriptions of how life was lived in the Dominions.

Yet the realization of such a British World was circumscribed by the form of the British Empire. The insistence on a common foreign policy meant that the Dominions directed their diplomacy through Whitehall and their dealings with each other through High Commissions in London. An imperial division of labour made Britain the manufacturer and financier, the Dominions providers of commodities. As such, they were competitors rather than partners. Trade and investment flows from London far outweighed business between the Dominions, even between Australia and New Zealand, and the same was true of migration. Britain sent vice-regal representatives, executives, professionals, and experts, and ambitious children of the Dominions returned to Britain to pursue their careers; but there was far less lateral movement, especially at the official level.

Richard Hannay's homely American friend Blenkiron suggested a further separation. In *Mr. Standfast*, he rebuts a British newspaper's suggestion that there is a natural affinity "between Americans and the men of the British Dominions":

> I don't understand them one little bit. When I see your lean, tall
> Australians with the sun at the back of their eyes, I'm looking
> at men from another planet. Outside you and Peter, I never got
> to fathom a South African. The Canadians live over the back
> fence from us, but you mix up a Canuck with a Yankee in your
> remarks and you'll get a bat in the eye.

He goes on to suggest that these settler societies are too similar, and yet too unfamiliar with each other, to be easy in their dealings.

You'll find us mighty respectful to other parts of your Empire, but we say anything we damn well please about England. You see, we know her that well and like her that well, we can be free with her.... It's like a lot of boys that are getting on in the world and are a bit jealous and stand-offish with each other. But they're all at home with the old man who used to warm them up with a hickory cane, even though sometimes in their haste they call him a stand-patter.[4]

It is worth noting that these observations are prompted by Blenkiron seeing a company of American troops on the Western Front and asking Hannay for a frank assessment of their quality. War, it seems, stimulates the need for national affirmation in the eyes of others. It gives added intensity to the working out of feelings about other English-speaking peoples, turns an historical relationship into a familial one.

The current interest in the British World is marked by an appreciation of the imperial dimension in the national histories of these former white Dominions. It is properly comparative because the treatment of British heritage as some peculiar relic retarding the progress toward full autonomy has bedevilled their national historiographies. Interest in the British World also draws on the comparatively recent restoration of Empire back into British history and provides a helpful corrective to the continuing assumption that this history finds authoritative expression in Cambridge, London, and Oxford, or from British television history series. The spirit and setting of the British World conferences challenge the outworn model of metropolis and province. The reconfiguration of relations between the settlers and the original inhabitants gives added force to the exercise.

Alongside the academic interest in the British World, however, there are other versions of national and imperial history that work in a different register. They arise out of the uses of the past for commemoration or display, affirmation or challenge. This form of public history is increasingly prominent: its practitioners appeal to sentiments grounded in formative national events and binding traditions. They apply such lineages to issues arising out of contemporary politics to show how they are true to national honour and to impugn the patriotism of their opponents. Such uses of history have become a regular means of resolving the competing claims of cultural identity that vex the settler societies of the British World.

Let me suggest how this practice took shape in my own country. Late in 1991, Paul Keating replaced Bob Hawke as the leader of the

Australian Labor Party. From 1983 until he resigned earlier in 1991 to mount his challenge, Keating had been an iconoclastic modernizer. He was the treasurer who removed the props that supported the national economy and pushed through a program of radical liberalization of trading, financial, and industrial arrangements. Becoming prime minister at a time when economic deregulation afforded little comfort to the victims of a severe recession, he took a new tack and began painting what he would refer to as his Big Picture. It depicted a nation that was committed to reconciliation with its indigenous peoples, comfortable with its multicultural diversity, generous in its social provisions, secure in its cultural identity, fully engaged with its Asian neighbours, at ease in the new world order.

The Big Picture of national modernization was also a history painting. Aided by his speechwriter, historian Don Watson, Keating told a story of a people who had suffered but overcome. They triumphed over their tribulations to create a fully independent nationhood that would be sealed with the transition to a republic. Keating told this story in speeches that commemorated national anniversaries: the Queensland town of Winton for the centenary of "Waltzing Matilda," the Murray River town of Corowa for the centenary of a conference on the path to federation. There were also anniversaries of Australians abroad: the seventy-fifth anniversary of the opening of Australia House in London, where he spoke of the republic, and the fiftieth anniversaries of the Kokoda Trail and the Burma-Thailand railway, where Australians had served and died in a war that began as an act of imperial service and became a battle for national survival.

Implicit in this story of national redemption was a final abandonment of British ties. When Keating spoke in London, he argued that the friendship between the two countries would be stronger if the relationship were more mature. When he addressed the Queen and the Duke of Edinburgh in Canberra in 1992, he again emphasized that "our outlook is necessarily independent."[5] It was on this occasion that Keating had the temerity to guide the Queen with his arm and the tabloid press in Britain dubbed him "The Lizard of Oz." The Australian opposition sought to capitalize on the British criticism, and Keating responded with a broadside against its lack of national pride. The British had left Australia to defend itself against the Japanese advance in 1942, he declared, yet these local Tories remained British to their bootstraps.

It was Robert Menzies, the Liberal prime minister from 1949 to 1966 and a fervent monarchist, who had declared himself to be British to his bootstraps, and much of Keating's assault was directed at that era of Liberal supremacy, when the country had missed its opportunities, timorously shielding itself from the changing post-war order behind a tariff wall that protected inefficient domestic industries and a White Australia policy that caused widespread resentment in the region. The concentration on the immediate post-war period was an adroit move. Industrial protection and maintenance of the living standards of a White Australia had been the basis of Australian national policy since the establishment of the Commonwealth fifty years earlier, and Labor had been fully wedded to the insular and defensive arrangement created then until it was dismantled in the closing decades of the last century. Keating, who had broken with this component of the national heritage, attached responsibility for it to his opponents. In a characteristically rhetorical flight, Keating suggested that the present leaders of the Liberal Party should be placed in a museum in the old Parliament House. They could be installed along with other icons of suburban life in the 1950s: the Morphy Richards toaster, the Qualcast lawnmower, the Astor television console, the AWA radiogram, an armchair, and "a pair of heavily protected slippers." As for himself, Keating declared, he had acquired self-respect and respect for Australia, and learned not to cringe to Britain. "Even as it walked out on you and joined the Common Market," he concluded with a final thrust, "you were still looking for your MBEs and your knighthoods and all the rest of the regalia that goes with it."[6]

This was not the first time that Australia's historical relationship with Britain had been the subject of political debate. In the long preparation for the bicentenary of Britain's colonization of Australia, there were complaints that the commemorative program gave insufficient acknowledgement of the First Fleet. The initial planning began in 1979 under a Liberal government, and Prime Minister Malcolm Fraser was conscious of the need for an inclusive treatment that would negotiate sensitivities. From the beginning, he referred to 1988 as the anniversary of European settlement rather than British colonization.

The 1938 sesquicentenary had involved an elaborate re-enactment of the landing of Governor Phillip and drawn protest from Aboriginal organizations, which declared it a day of mourning. Despite such criticism, Aboriginals were brought from inland settlements on that occasion to perform a threatening ceremony before a party of marines advanced with fixed bayonets to allow the landing of the governor, who in turn delivered a fictitious imperial oration.[7] The organizers of the bicentenary appreciated from the beginning that such a re-enactment would be inappropriate in 1988. In its place, they settled on the idea (taken from the American bicentennial of 1976) of a fleet of tall ships from all around the world that would gather at Sydney harbour to symbolize the many journeys that had created a diverse society. The bicentennial slogan, "Living Together," emphasized this idea of multicultural inclusiveness, with which was associated a program of activities designed to be "serious and broadly educational and cultural in nature."[8] The chief executive officer of the Bicentennial Authority spoke of the anniversary as an opportunity for "re-dedicating ourselves to the immense task of solving the problems that still confront us as a people – racism, philistinism, materialism, lack of national pride, widespread inequalities of opportunity, desecrated historic sites, polluted streams, ignorance of our collective past."[9]

This went too far for Malcolm Fraser, who altered the bicentenial slogan from "Living Together" to "The Australian Achievement." The Labor government, which had taken office in 1983, restored the original slogan until increasing criticism persuaded it to retreat to the safer theme of "Celebration of a Nation." One of the early and most persistent critics was a journalist and amateur historian, Jonathan King, who was a direct descendant of one of the officers on the original First Fleet. King conceived the idea of a re-enactment of that voyage from England to Australia and could only interpret the Bicentennial Authority's lack of enthusiasm for his scheme as evidence of "a nation ashamed of its past."[10] To promote his scheme, he and his friends began dressing up in costume on Australia Day and acting out the first landing of Governor Phillip. These masquerades drew Aboriginal protest, yet King persisted with his First Fleet re-enactment project as a private venture with commercial sponsorship. Hence on 26 January 1988, more than a million Australians were confronted with the spectacle of the tall ships gathered in Sydney harbour, and also of a replica First Fleet entering the Heads with its flagship flying a red spinnaker advertising Coca-Cola.

Government ministers condemned King's First Fleet re-enactment as a "tasteless and insensitive farce." Historian Geoffrey Blainey hailed it as "the most moving event" of the entire bicentennial program and a "triumph of the silent majority" over the politicians and bureaucrats who had devised the "lickspittle slogan," "Living Together."[11] But Blainey had by this time become embroiled in a parallel argument over the government's immigration and multicultural policies. In 1984 he warned that the level of Asian immigration was straining public acceptance and went on to allege discrimination against British applicants for entry. The Department of Immigration and Ethnic Affairs, he claimed, "could well be called the department of immigration and anti-British affairs."[12]

In 1985 a business think-tank initiated a campaign against the Bicentennial Authority, which had recently released its program for 1988. The Authority was accused of sacrificing tradition to the fashionable concerns of a minority, of slighting the achievements of the past and denigrating "the core values and sources of pride of most Australians." Among the themes ignored by the bicentenary were Christian traditions, the work ethic, private enterprise, the monarchy, the British Commonwealth and the American alliance, and "the British contribution to Australia's heritage."[13] It is perhaps worth observing that in the course of the bicentenary, Britain was represented by the Queen and Duke of Edinburgh, the Prince and Princess of Wales, the Duke and Duchess of Kent, the Duke and Duchess of York, and Margaret Thatcher. The most memorable speech on Australia Day in 1988 was delivered by the Prince of Wales.

Even so, a number of episodes during the 1980s fed an apprehension that the British contribution to Australia's heritage was at risk. In 1984 the banal song "Advance Australia Fair" was proclaimed as the national anthem, to the chagrin of many monarchists. In the same year, the Commonwealth government established a royal commission into British nuclear tests in Australia during the 1950s, and it encountered a singular lack of co-operation from the British government as it assembled a story of perfidious Albion laying waste to Australian land with reckless disregard for the welfare of its Aboriginal inhabitants.[14] In 1985 a row broke out when an English economic historian took exception to the suggestion by an Australian one that officers of the First Fleet might have deliberately infected Aboriginals with smallpox.[15]

In 1986 the Australia Acts severed the last remaining links of law and government with the United Kingdom. In the same year, the British government sought to prevent the publication in Australia of a book by a former officer of MI5, Peter Wright, and dispatched the cabinet secretary to Sydney. He was surprised to discover that the Supreme Court of New South Wales was not prepared to accept his claims, and an aggressive young Sydney barrister subjected him to a humiliating cross-examination. Sir Robert Armstrong's dissembling and equivocation provided an irresistible spectacle. His admission that his government was "perhaps being economical with the truth" seemed to apply not just to the operation of the British Official Secrets Act but more generally to the accepted record of relations between the United Kingdom and its Australian Dominion.[16]

These and other episodes unsettled the conservative version of Australian history. They removed familiar landmarks and brought back troubling episodes from the past. They allowed Paul Keating to make political capital from his own reinterpretation of Australian history. In the end, the conservatives found an effective response. They were assisted by Geoffrey Blainey's invention of the Black Armband (a device that suggested the historical revisionists had rejected an excessively celebratory view of the past for an excessively gloomy one).[17] They drew also on the American neo-conservative invention of political correctness to demand that the people be liberated from the tyranny of historical thought police, and they learned from American precedents in 1994 over the National History Standards and Smithsonian Museum's exhibition to mark the fiftieth anniversary of the end of the Second World War. Both these exercises were portrayed as hateful exercises in national denigration and both were successfully discredited. From a book on the Smithsonian controversy came the term "History Wars," which has been taken up more widely as an international phenomenon.[18]

It was the present Australian prime minister, John Howard, who assembled these components into a successful political strategy. Having won office in 1996, he immediately declared that "the balance sheet of Australian history is a very generous and benign one," and deplored "the endless and agonised navel-gazing about who we are, or as seems to have happened over recent years, as part of a 'perpetual seminar' for elite opinion about our national identity."[19] More recently, he has claimed that "we no longer navel gaze about what an Australian is. We no longer are mesmerised by the self-appointed cultural dieticians who tell us that, in some way, they know better what an Australian ought to be than all of us."[20]

The History Wars are fought over national identity, over the capacity and willingness to confront painful episodes in the national past that touch the national conscience, over the treatment of minorities and the recognition of cultural difference, and over the reputation and responsibilities of historians. It is a distinctive characteristic of History Wars that national traditions have to be defended from internal threat of subversion and betrayal. This gives them the quality of a civil war. The History Wars are also an international phenomenon, conducted as fiercely in Japan or Argentina as in the United States or Australia. They are a legacy of the violence and trauma of the twentieth century, its processes of national formation, its wars, its ideological conflicts, its enforcement of loyalty by terror and extermination, its ethnic cleansing and displacement.

It is not easy to follow other countries' History Wars from afar. They are typically prosecuted in the press and on talkback radio, and operate across a wide front of local reference points. When the history profession responds to such outbreaks, it is on unfamiliar terrain, and attempts to provide a more coherent account in its own house journals trail some way behind the action. The *Canadian Historical Review*, for example, has published a number of articles dealing with what one historian has described as "our own thinly Canadianized 'History Wars North.'"[21] Yet Jack Granatstein's *Who Killed Canadian History?* set hares running, and many are still loose. There have also been large conferences of Canadian historians and history educators in an effort to counter the alleged crisis of Canadian history. Yet the Dominion Institute seized the headlines with its survey of a knowledge deficit; as a media commentator suggested, the "Dominion Institute knows which buttons to push."[22]

The founder of the Dominion Institute resurrected an old name for a new purpose. He has explained that the Institute has "a singular and straightforward mission: to reclaim Canadian history and in particular to make English-speaking Canada aware of the rich and important past it has." But this is not a simple exercise in heritage conservation. It is a response to what Rudyard Griffiths sees as "the rebranding of the country; the rubbishing of 'dominion,' the renaming of traditional departments, the debunking of past historical heroes, the whole downsizing of the national story." He defends the monarchy as "one of the great historical touchstones of Canada."[23] It is one of the links with Canada's British past that he claims has been removed to placate French Canadians, one of the ways that the British World figures in the History Wars.

I have suggested already how Australian traditionalists defended their country's British past in the lead-up to the bicentenary during the 1980s. The argument between national separatists and imperial loyalists is a longstanding and familiar one; it can be traced in the historiography of every part of the British World. The advent of the History Wars, however, gives it a new inflection. History warriors appeal with particular insistence to national honour: they claim to defend the nation and its past from detractors who would impugn its reputation and attack its legitimacy. And as Paul Keating's polemics suggested, their earlier insistence on British origins and character was vulnerable to allegations of a lack of confidence in the nation. As the argument over the British legacy was subsumed into the History Wars, the traditionalists reformulated their position.

This can be seen in John Howard's treatment of the issue. During the 1980s, he had been the most constant defender of Australia's ties with Britain and the anglophile legacy of Menzies, the chief critic of republicanism and multiculturalism. He never failed to react to Keating's taunts and he was duly cast as yesterday's man, consigned to the museum along with other artefacts of the 1950s. When Howard assumed office in 1996 and promulgated the new regime, he denounced his predecessor's "attempt to rewrite important parts of Australian political history" and especially his "sustained, personalised and vindictive assault on the Menzies legacy." But in delivering the Sir Robert Menzies Lecture in 1996, Howard emphasized that "Australia today is very different to the Australia of the Menzies era." The Menzies he celebrated was forward-looking and intensely Australian. Howard took pains to rebut the "perverse myth" of Menzies' "alleged subservience to Britain," stressing his assertion of national priorities and protest against "British indifference to Australia interests."[24]

One of Howard's achievements in office was to defeat the campaign for an Australian republic that Keating had encouraged and exploited so effectively. Howard did this by corralling the self-appointed cultural dieticians into a carefully managed constitutional convention where the differences between the republican majority were exploited. He then put a minimal republican proposal to a referendum, along with a draft preamble of his own (which declared that "Australians are free to be proud of their country"), and both were duly defeated.[25] But the minimal republican model, changing nothing more than the head of state, could only be defeated by a minimal monarchism. Far from defending the role of the Queen as an enduring affirmation of the link with Britain, the Australians for a Constitutional Monarchy insisted that her role was merely titular and that Australia already had its own head of state. He has since demonstrated his claim by elbowing the governor-general aside at the Sydney Olympics, displacing him from ceremonies to honour the armed forces as they leave or return from foreign duty, and upstaging him at any public event likely to yield electoral advantage. This was surely a pyrrhic victory for the British World. Howard himself recognized the new dispensation when in London during 2000 to mark the centenary of the enactment of the Commonwealth constitution by the British parliament: he declared to London journalists that "Australians no longer think of themselves as a British country." As Stuart Ward suggests, the published response of one of them to this "arcane Commonwealth anniversary" indicated that the feeling was entirely mutual.[26]

Of all the former white Dominions, Australia is the one where the neo-conservative strategy that spawned the History Wars has had greatest political effect. The country's multicultural agencies have been disbanded, its feminist initiatives replaced by familial ones; the peak indigenous body is abolished; and Australia's incarceration of refugees has attracted world attention. The Labor government pursued partnerships within Southeast Asia; the conservative coalition government declares that Australia is now the region's "deputy sheriff." In its resolute support of the United States during the invasion of Afghanistan and Iraq, Australia has embraced a new martial alliance of the British World. This time, however, the dependencies gather in Washington, not London. John Scantlebury Blenkiron's puzzled admiration of "your lean, tall Australians with the sun at the back of their eyes" is surpassed by President Bush's acclamation of a short, dumpy, and anxious "man of steel."

It might seem that this outcome settles the longstanding argument over the British heritage. But the ghosts of the past are not so easily banished. Paul Keating drew on history to transfer the evils of colonialism to the imperial master. In his Big Picture, it was the British who had claimed possession of Australia and disregarded the rights of its original inhabitants, the British who worked the land with convict labour and planted it with exotic species of flora and fauna regardless of the damage to the native environment.

To this refusal of guilt, there was a conspicuous exception. In a memorable speech delivered in 1992, Keating declared: "We took the traditional lands and smashed the original way of life. We brought the diseases. The alcohol. We committed the murders. We took the children from their mothers. We practised discrimination and exclusion. It was our ignorance and our prejudice." When the prime minister delivered this speech at Redfern Park in inner-city Sydney, the Aboriginal audience was barely attentive. An undercurrent of conversation is audible in the recording. As he reached this passage, a hush fell, as if the listeners could scarcely believe their ears, and when he finished the confession, they burst into applause. Here was a frank acknowledgement of the past, for Keating insisted that "there is nothing to fear or to lose in the recognition of historical truth."[27]

All of the propositions put forward in the Redfern Park speech have since been denied. The past decade has seen a circumscription of Aboriginal land rights, campaigns to discredit the integrity of claimants, refusal to accept the findings of an inquiry into the stolen generations of Aboriginal children taken from their mothers, attacks on Aboriginal self-determination, and denial of frontier violence. The last of these denials has been especially significant since it strikes at the new understanding of settler history that had been shaped by historians during the 1980s and was generally accepted before the onset of the History Wars.

Keith Windschuttle, the chief prosecutor of this campaign, accuses the history profession of inventing massacres, misreading sources, exaggerating the number of Aboriginal casualties, covering up each other's mistakes, and suppressing dissidents. He calls this "The Fabrication of Aboriginal History." There was no frontier war, he claims, because the Aboriginal inhabitants were incapable of waging war. So far from defending themselves from invasion, they were a primitive and doomed people who engaged in criminal violence. The colonial authorities acted with restraint because they were "Christians to whom the killing of the innocent would have been abhorrent" and Britons who were guided by the rule of law. The British, he asserts, "regarded their settlements as peaceful exercises, mutually beneficial to both colonist and native."[28]

In Australia, and I suspect in other former white Dominions, the History Wars are now concerned principally with the colonial past. The fiercest disputes arise from the status of these countries as settler societies superimposed on pre-existing indigenous ones. The neo-conservatives insist that there is no need for apology and that the British legacy is good. This is no longer an argument about relations with Britain so much as an argument over Britishness. Donald Akenson sees the establishment of a British World in settler societies producing a British culture that was new and synthetic, a merging of the distinct Anglo-Celtic cultures brought from Britain into a recognizable form that was shared throughout the British World and yet coterminous with the creation of new national identities.[29] In the early years of the twenty-first century, when those national identities are no longer new and are challenged by the assertion of other cultural and ethnic identities, the history warriors invest new significance in foundational history. Their British World provides the nation with its legitimacy.

This can be illustrated in one of the latest episodes in Australia's History Wars. Earlier this year, an inquiry was established into the country's new National Museum. Even before the museum opened in 2001, a member of its council, who was also the friend and biographer of John Howard, had protested against its "reworking of Australian history into political correctness" and submitted a long list of objections to particular exhibits and texts. He did not object to its gallery of Aboriginal Australia. Rather, he condemned the treatment of European Australia.[30] Similarly, when Keith Windschuttle turned his attention to the issue, he said that the display of Aboriginal and Torres Strait Islander culture was "by far the best part of the museum."[31] He did criticize the presentation of frontier massacres and also claimed that the museum's building incorporated the symbolism of the Jewish Museum in Berlin to signify that the indigenous people had suffered the equivalent of the holocaust, but his chief criticism was aimed at the non-indigenous galleries. He described them as "a repository of nothing more that the intellectual poverty of the tertiary-educated middle class of the post-Vietnam era."[32]

Particular criticism was directed at the trivialization of white Australia with exhibits of popular culture, the mockery of suburban life by hanging a lawn mower and a clothesline upside down, the disrespect for sacred episodes such as the Anzac sacrifice with a bleached statue of a digger. The underlying message, wrote a tabloid columnist, "is one of sneering ridicule for white Australia. It is as if all non-Aboriginal culture is a joke."[33] The juxtaposition of indigenous exhibits, treated with respect, and non-indigenous ones, treated with postmodern playfulness, increased the offence.

Similar responses were evoked in New Zealand as it developed its national museum, Te Papa. Here there was a conscious endeavour to "express the bicultural nature of the country, recognising the mana and significance of the two mainstreams of tradition" and "providing the means for each to contribute effectively to a statement of the nation's identity."[34] It was recognized from the beginning that "traditionally held views of New Zealand are being scrutinised" and that many New Zealanders found the reappraisal disturbing, but it was "an essential part of the nation's growth towards maturity."[35] There had indeed been a remarkable historiographical revolution in New Zealand in the 1980s, accompanying the country's transformation of Maori-Pakeha relations, but in the 1990s there were clear signs of resistance that employed the tactics of the History Wars.[36] The disturbing consequences of the reappraisal were apparent when the museum opened a preliminary exhibition in 1993, designed by a curatorial team of four men and four women, four of them Maori and four Pakeha. The gender balance was acceptable; the bicultural balance brought angry complaints. Among the entries in the visitors' book was the charge that the museum was "filled with Maori junk, it's a kiss and make up to the natives."[37]

When Te Papa opened in 1998, there was particular criticism of the way that it jumbled objects together in the Pakeha galleries, juxtaposing household items, industrial design, signs, and videos with paintings and sculpture. As in Australia, I suspect it is the comparison of the treatment of Maori and Pakeha pasts that aggravates such criticism. The richness, depth, and authenticity of the one points up the uncertainty of the other. "Where has New Zealand's museum gone, it's now the Maori museum" was another of the comments made by visitors to the earlier 1993 exhibition. In the same year, Jane Campion appended a note to the published version of the screenplay of her film *The Piano* and declared, "It's a strange heritage I have as a pakeha New Zealander.... In contrast to the original people of New Zealand, the Maori people, who have such an attachment to history, we seem to have no history, or at least not the same tradition."[38]

The History Wars work on such anxiety in Australia, Canada, and New Zealand. As these three parts of the British World have worked out their nationhood, they have also reworked their British histories. As the formal links disappeared, the British legacy still generated passion, and during the 1980s it was a recurrent point of contention in Australian public life. But Britain itself ceased to be the principal point of contention as Britishness became a signifier of an old Australia thought to be under threat from multicultural diversity and an indigenous renaissance. The History Wars provided such sentiment with a language and strategy.

In 1917, as the United States finally entered the Great War, a senator warned that the first casualty when war comes is truth. The History Wars respect few of the conventions that govern historical debate. They caricature their opponents and impugn their motives. They appeal to loyalty, hope, fear, and prejudice. In their intimidation of the history profession, they act as bullies. In submitting history to a loyalty test, they debase it. Our own academic exploration of the British World is no idle enterprise, and I hope we will not shirk its challenge.

{NOTES}

1 John Buchan, *The Complete Richard Hannay* (London: Penguin, 1992), 5.

2 Ibid., 38.

3 Ibid., 40.

4 Ibid., 541.

5 Mark Ryan, ed., *Advancing Australia: The Speeches of Paul Keating, Prime Minister* (Sydney: Big Picture Publications, 1995), 151, 172.

6 *Commonwealth Parliamentary Debates*, House of Representatives, vol. 182, 374, 27 February 1992, quoted in Geoffrey Bolton, "Two Pauline Versions," in *The Menzies Era: A Reappraisal of Government, Politics and Policy*, ed. Scott Prasser et al. (Sydney: Hale and Iremonger, 1995), 33.

7 Julian Thomas, "Heroic History and Public Spectacle: Sydney 1938" (PhD diss., Australian National University, 1991); Gavin Souter, "Skeleton at the Feast," in *Australians 1938*, ed. Bill Gammage and Peter Spearritt (Sydney: Fairfax, Syme and Weldon Associates, 1987), 13–28.

8 *Australian*, 25 August 1980, quoted by Peter Cochrane and David Goodman, "The Great Australian Journey," in *Celebrating the Nation: A Critical Study of Australia's Bicentenary*, ed. Tony Bennett et al. (St. Leonards, NSW: Allen & Unwin, 1992), 182.

9 Denis O'Brien, *The Bicentennial Affair: The Inside Story of Australia's "Birthday Bash"* (Sydney: ABC, 1991), 38.

10 Jonathan King, *The Battle for the Bicentenary* (Milsons Point, NSW: Hutchinson, 1989), 1.

11 Geoffrey Blainey, "Triumph of the Quiet Majority," *Australian*, 30–31 January 1988.

12 Geoffrey Blainey, *All for Australia* (North Ryde, NSW: Methuen Haynes, 1984), 155–56.

13 Ken Baker, "The Bicentenary: Celebration of Apology?" *IPA Review* 38, no. 4 (Summer 1985): 175–82.

14 James McClelland, *Stirring the Possum: A Political Biography* (Ringwood, Victoria: Penguin, 1989), chap. 16.

15 N.G. Butlin, *Our Original Aggression: Aboriginal Populations of South-eastern Australia 1788–1850* (North Sydney: Allen & Unwin, 1983); Charles Wilson, "History, Hypothesis and Fiction: Smallpox and Aboriginal Genocide," *Quadrant*, 29, no. 3 (March 1985): 26–33; Noel Butlin, "Reply to Charles Wilson and Hugh Morgan," *Quadrant* 29, no. 8 (June 1985): 30–33.

16 Malcolm Turnbull, *The Spy Catcher Trial* (London: Heinemann, 1988), 75.

17 Geoffrey Blainey, "Drawing up a Balance Sheet of Our History," *Quadrant* 37, nos. 7/8 (July/August 1993): 10–15.

18 Edward T. Linenthal and Tom Engelhardt, eds., *History Wars: The Enola Gay and Other Battles for the American Past* (New York: Metropolitan Books, 1996).

19 Howard in *Commonwealth Parliamentary Debates*, 30 October 1996, 6158, and Sir Robert Menzies Lecture, 18 November 1996. I draw here on Stuart Macintyre, *History Wars* (Melbourne: Melbourne University Press, 2003).

20 *Age* (Melbourne), June 9, 2003.

21 Ian McKay, "The Liberal Order Framework: A Prospectus for a Reconnaissance of Canadian History," *Canadian Historical Review* 81, no. 4 (December 2000): 61.

22 John Fraser, "...And the Rest Is History," *National Post*, 6 June 2001.

23 Ibid.

24 Sir Robert Menzies Lecture, 18 November 1996.

25 Howard's draft preamble to the Constitution appears in Donald Horne, *Looking for Leadership: Australia in the Howard Years* (Ringwood, Victoria: Viking, 2001), 271.

26 Stuart Ward, *Australia and the British Embrace: The Demise of the Imperial Ideal* (Melbourne: Melbourne University Press, 2001), 3.

27 Ryan, *Advancing Australia*, 228.

28 Keith Windschuttle, *The Fabrication of Aboriginal History*, vol. 1, *Van Diemen's Land* (Paddington, NSW: Macleay Press, 2002), 32, 360. See also "The Myths of Frontier Massacres in Australian History," *Quadrant* 44, nos. 10–12 (October–December 2000): 8–21, 17–24, 6–20.

29 Don Akenson, "The Historiography of English-Speaking Canada and the Concept of Diaspora: A Sceptical Appreciation," *Canadian Historical Review* 73, no. 6 (September 1995): 377–410.

30 "Howard's Man: 'These People Are not My Heroes,'" *Sydney Morning Herald*, 5 June 2001.

31 Keith Windschuttle, "How Not to Run a Museum: People's History at the Postmodern Museum," *Quadrant* 45, no. 9 (September 2001): 19.

32 Ibid.

33 Miranda Devine, "A Nation Trivialised," *Daily Telegraph*, 12 March 2001.

34 A Concept for the Museum, 1989, quoted in James Michael Gore, "Representations of History and Nations in Museums in Australia and Aotearoa New Zealand" (PhD diss., University of Melbourne, 2002), 223–24.

35 A Plan for Development, 1985, quoted in Gore, "Representations of History," 220.

36 Lorenzo Veracini, *Negotiating a Bicultural Past: An Historiographical "Revolution" in Aotearoa/New Zealand* (Treaty of Waitangi Research Unit Occasional Paper Number 7, Stout Centre, Victoria University of Wellington, 2001), who cites Stuart C. Scott, *The Travesty of Waitangi: Towards Anarchy* (Dunedin: Campbell Press, 1995).

37 Gore, "Representations of History," 233, quotes excerpts from the visitor's book for the exhibition, Voices, which were broadcast on Radio New Zealand on 1 March 1993.

38 Quoted by P.G. McHugh, "Australasian Narratives of Constitutional Foundation," in *Quicksands: Foundational Histories in Australia and Aotearoa New Zealand*, ed. Klaus Neumann, Nicholas Thomas, and Hilary Ericksen (Kensington, NSW: University of New South Wales Press, 1999), 104.

CHAPTER 19

WORLDS APART:

THREE "BRITISH" PRIME MINISTERS AT EMPIRE'S END

Stuart Ward

THE BRITISH WORLD PRESENTS A CHALLENGE to historians as they unravel the many overlapping layers of ethnic, cultural, and material aspirations that this eclectic grouping comprised. The concept itself is fraught with ambiguity. Charles Dilke coined the term "Greater Britain" in 1868, but he used this interchangeably with "Saxondon" and "greater Englands across the seas," while others have employed related phrases such as "Britannic nationalism" and "British race patriotism."[1] Whatever the nomenclature, historians have now begun to take seriously the task of understanding how the settler-colonial world was imagined as a singular community of Britons, bound by kinship, loyalty, and experience to a common racial destiny.[2] Fundamental to this new research agenda is an appreciation of the limitations of that sense of community and an understanding of how and why Greater Britain failed to resonate meaningfully into the post-imperial era. I have argued elsewhere that it was primarily changes in the material relations between metropole and Dominion in the post-war era that determined the pace and character of the demise of Britishness as a credible object of civic pride, loyalty, and identity in settler-colonial communities.[3] That is to say, profound shifts in the political, economic, and strategic foundations of British power and influence in the world gave rise to acute conflicts of interest between Britain and Commonwealth countries, conflicts that were difficult to reconcile with the idea of a worldwide community of Britons. The issues that precipitated these conflicts are familiar ones: the Suez crisis of 1956, the rapid decolonization in Africa from 1957 to 1964, the withdrawal of South Africa from the Commonwealth in 1961, Britain's attempt to gain EEC membership in the 1960s, the unravelling of Commonwealth trade preferences and Sterling Area co-operation, the demise of the concept of imperial defence, and the controversy over white majority rule in Rhodesia. As Bill Schwarz argues in the case of white Rhodesians, the era of decolonization signalled a critical failure of mutual trust – or as Schwarz terms it, "a critical moment in the process of decolonisation, when the differences between the settler communities and London intensified into outright antagonism."[4] Throughout the post-Suez decade, deeply ingrained assumptions about mutual identification and mutual assistance in times of crisis were put to the test and found badly wanting. Often, this crisis was understood (both in Britain as well as the Dominions) in terms of a failure of will on the part of the mother country – an abrogation of duty to the wider Commonwealth ideal, leaving communities of abandoned Britons scattered around the globe.

Although most of the research to date has looked at how these problems affected bilateral dealings between the United Kingdom and the individual Dominions,[5] it is worth examining how this crisis might have cut across the ranks of the abandoned Britons themselves. To what extent was there a common feeling of disillusionment among the white Commonwealth countries – a shared sense of betrayal at the hands of a British government that seemed indifferent to the needs of fellow Britons overseas? Did the material consequences of the unravelling of the British World tend to unite these countries under the banner of their mutual grievances? Or did the crisis of mutuality resonate more widely, exposing even further cracks in the façade of Greater Britishness?

In this admittedly impressionistic survey, I will examine this problem in terms of the personal and political relations among three self-styled "British" prime ministers – Robert Menzies of Australia, John Diefenbaker of Canada, and Roy Welensky of the Central African Federation. Each of these political leaders played key roles in this crucial phase of decolonization, and each are widely regarded as the last bastion of Britishness in their respective countries. An examination of their mutual dealings, correspondence, and perspectives on the unravelling of Empire and Commonwealth reveals only a limited capacity to view their problems from a common standpoint, and far more fundamental differences about the meaning of being British.

It is not at all difficult to find broad similarities in outlook among these three otherwise very different political leaders. They all viewed Britain as the taproot of their respective cultures and communities, and drew on the language of family, kinship, and community of interest to describe what they regarded as a unique bond uniting the British family of nations. Each saw himself as somehow embodying the core beliefs, values, and aspirations of the people he represented, holding the line against those who would seek to undermine the special intimacy and sureness of the British connection. London formed the centre of their mental landscape – a place to which they would each gravitate to act out the time-honoured performance rituals of Greater British community. Robert Menzies' diary records the feelings of reverent awe that accompanied his first visit to England in the 1930s, and over the next thirty years, his periodic journeys retained a special, almost spiritual significance.[6] Roy Welensky, too, recalled his first attendance at a Commonwealth Prime Minsters' Conference in 1957 as something far more than a mere overseas trip: it was "an impressive gathering to a newcomer. It still preserved the pattern of an older epoch in which we were all members of the Commonwealth family, with a trust and understanding of each other transcending any differences there might be between us."[7] And one of John Diefenbaker's closest advisers, Basil Robinson, recalls: "Travelling to London with John Diefenbaker, one always felt caught up in the aura of a pilgrimage. A dimension of the man had survived from childhood – a sense of excited wonder – and it emerged afresh whenever he revisited the sacred places, Buckingham Palace, Windsor Castle, No. 10 Downing Street, and the Mansion House in the City of London."[8] His June 1957 visit, coming so soon after his election as the first Conservative Canadian prime minister since 1935, was occasioned by such unbridled euphoria that one London-based Canadian commented: "One would think that Canada had not only re-joined the Commonwealth, but was almost going to amalgamate with the United Kingdom."[9]

It was precisely during state visits to London that these British sensibilities received their fullest expression. Robert Menzies was by far the most lyrical in style, equipped with a seemingly endless array of metaphors to describe the inner substance of Australia's ties to Britain and the monarchy: a "common and all-powerful human emotion," "a warm and inarticulate instinct," a "living, breathing and everlasting unity," a "fusion of the heart and the mind."[10] Menzies drew unapologetically on racial language and imagery to describe the essence of the British World. As he explained to an audience at the Savoy Hotel in 1959, "I belong to those millions of people who like to feel that when we think of our own country, Australia, we think of the British world; we think of the ancient homes of our race."[11] Welensky was more straightforward in his utterances, but no less insistent in reminding British listeners that "being British is our pride. We know no other way of life and we want no other."[12] Diefenbaker rarely, if ever, spoke in explicitly racial terms, having imbibed the civil libertarianism of the age, but he was no less anxious to establish his British credentials. On returning from his 1957 London visit, the Canadian prime minister announced, in a now infamous display of pan-British exuberance, his intention to divert 15 per cent of Canada's imports away from the United States and toward the United Kingdom. This undertaking, made without consulting any minister or official, proved to be hopelessly impractical and not a little embarrassing for the Canadian government.

The rapid dissolution of Empire and the transformation of the Commonwealth from a cosy white man's club into a multiracial debating society was bound to be problematic for these three exemplars of the Greater British patriot. While each had his own distinctive interests to defend in the political and economic evolution of the Commonwealth, none were immune to the sentimental hankerings that inevitably occasioned the conceptual unravelling of the organic British family. At different times and for varying reasons, all three were forced to grapple with the unpalatable realities of a Conservative government in Britain that was either unwilling or unable to uphold the traditions and conventions of the "old" Commonwealth. And all three increasingly focused their resentment on the man whom they saw as the chief engineer of the breakup of the British World – British Prime Minister Harold Macmillan. By the end of his seven years in office, Macmillan had achieved the singular distinction among British prime ministers of being disliked, distrusted, and bitterly resented by virtually all of his white Commonwealth counterparts.[13]

John Diefenbaker's problems with Macmillan were as much personal as political. Despite his initial high hopes that he might restore the close personal relations between the two governments in the wake of the dramatic split over Suez, the simple fact is that Diefenbaker became an object of ridicule and scorn in British government circles, from the prime minister downwards. From their initial encounter at the 1957 Commonwealth Prime Ministers' Conference, Macmillan regarded Diefenbaker as something of an oddity, and by 1960 this view had hardened into out-and-out contempt.[14] For Macmillan, Diefenbaker was a narrow political opportunist, unfailingly provincial in outlook and incapable of taking a position on any issue without considering its likely impact on the Canadian voter. As he recorded in his diary during the 1960 Commonwealth Prime Ministers' Conference: "Diefenbaker is very disappointing – deaf, ignorant, and little more than a 'tub thumper.'

He never forgets 'party' politics and talks of little else."[15] Diefenbaker, for his part, was highly sensitive to Macmillan's slights, both real and imagined. Difficulties frequently arose, for example, over the planning of Macmillan's periodic visits to the United States. As far as Diefenbaker was concerned, Ottawa was the natural stopover for any British prime minister en route to Washington, whereas Macmillan intimated on a number of occasions that he would ideally prefer to bypass his Canadian counterpart. British High Commission officials in Ottawa advised repeatedly against this, warning Macmillan of Diefenbaker's "feminine temperament" while acknowledging that "if we were dealing with rational people," then it might not be necessary to call in to Canada every time he crossed the Atlantic. But clearly, as far the British government was concerned, this was not the case.[16]

The real differences of substance, however, arose over Diefenbaker's decision, after much soul-searching, to weigh in against South Africa's continued membership in the Commonwealth as a republic. Diefenbaker has often been commended for his principled stand at the 1961 Commonwealth Prime Ministers' Conference, both at the time and since, but he might just as easily have taken a different line.[17] The last thing he wanted was to be seen as the wrecker of an institution that he regarded as Canada's prime guarantor against American domination, and he had been strongly advised by both the Department of External Affairs and the Canadian High Commission in London to adopt a conciliatory tone toward South Africa. The trouble for Diefenbaker was that the climate of press opinion in Canada was turning rapidly against the kind of extreme racialism represented by the apartheid regime, a trend that he did not welcome and that placed him in a far more awkward position than his Australian and New Zealand counterparts. Ironically, he blamed Macmillan's highly publicized "winds of change" speech in Cape Town in February 1960 for turning up the political heat over South Africa. As Basil Robinson recalls, Diefenbaker "would frequently complain about the 'winds of change' speech, which he felt had brought the situation facing the Commonwealth to a crisis he had hoped to avoid." On the eve of the 1961 Prime Ministers' Conference, Diefenbaker confided in his closest staff members that his "emotional reactions" were in favour of keeping South Africa in the Commonwealth, citing as his reasons "South Africa's wartime record and its historical connection with other Commonwealth countries."[18]

As the 1961 conference unfolded, however, Diefenbaker was drawn firmly into the opposing camp. Two factors proved decisive: South

African Prime Minister Hendrick Verwoerd refused to offer any kind of concession that might ease the political pressure, and Macmillan's position seemed to Diefenbaker to represent a backing away from the "winds of change" speech. Some months prior to the conference, he complained to the British high commissioner in Ottawa that he felt "let down by Macmillan," having been compelled by Macmillan's own rhetoric to adjust to the political realities of the "new Commonwealth." Macmillan's transparent attempts to mollify Diefenbaker with sentimental appeals to Commonwealth unity were resented by the Canadian prime minister and probably strengthened his resolve not to be cajoled into a position that might well hurt him politically at home.[19] Although Diefenbaker's role in forcing the withdrawal of South Africa has at times been exaggerated, it remains clear that by siding with the Afro-Asian opposition to South African membership, Diefenbaker helped to frustrate Macmillan's hopes of holding the opposition at bay. This was certainly how Macmillan saw it.[20]

For Robert Menzies, the departure of South Africa from the Commonwealth also created a deep and long-lasting rift in his personal and political relationship with Harold Macmillan. Like Diefenbaker, Menzies viewed Macmillan's "winds of change" speech as a damaging assault on the integrity and harmony of the Commonwealth. Unlike Diefenbaker, however, he endeavoured to do everything within his power to prevent South Africa's expulsion, arguing that it was contrary to the spirit and tradition of the Commonwealth for members to discuss each other's internal affairs. In this, he assumed he was of one mind with Macmillan, and in the lead-up to the 1961 conference he worked closely with the British prime minister to devise a strategy that might head off the mounting pressures for South Africa's exclusion. But the outcome of the conference was a source of profound disillusionment. Not only did Macmillan fail to hold the agreed line against South Africa's vocal opponents – a fact that Menzies put down to dissembling and double-dealing on Macmillan's part[21] – but he also seemed prepared to go to any lengths to appease the African and Asian members.

In one telling incident when Macmillan was temporarily called away from the conference chair, Jawaharlal Nehru was invited as the most senior prime minister in attendance to take control of proceedings. While Nehru certainly had the longest unbroken record in office (since 1947), Menzies had been prime minister on two separate occasions (1939–41, and again from 1949), which, as far as he was concerned, clearly earned him the mantle of senior Commonwealth statesman. To be overlooked in favour of Nehru infuriated Menzies. As his high commissioner in London, Eric Harrison, explained to the Commonwealth Relations Office a few weeks later, Menzies was "much put out by Mr. Macmillan's apparent preference for a brown face." He elaborated on this analogy by pointing to "the sooty faces on the statues" around the quadrangle of the Commonwealth Relations Office, which stood as "an omen of where [Britain's] friendships now lay."[22] Clearly, there was more to Menzies' misgivings than the protocols of Commonwealth seniority – the slight cut right to the quick of his sense of belonging to the inner circle of ethnically British Commonwealth statesmen.[23] He recorded his indignation in his private correspondence with Harrison: "I have a feeling that the 'Winds of Change' are blowing a little too strongly."[24]

But if Menzies was despondent at South Africa's exclusion from the Commonwealth, he became deeply resentful in the immediate aftermath of the 1961 conference when the United Kingdom delegation at the United Nations changed its vote on resolutions critical of apartheid without consulting the Australian government. Until this time, the British had voted down these attacks on South Africa in the U.N., while Australia had abstained as a show of sympathy. By switching their vote to outright opposition to apartheid, the British government caught the Australians completely off-guard, confronting them with the difficult choice between taking a lone stand in their continued abstention or making an embarrassing last-minute change of policy to fall in line with the new British vote. Coming so soon after Menzies' vigorous defence of South Africa at the Commonwealth conference, this proved difficult to stomach. As Menzies viewed the situation, "The choice was therefore one between my own personal position, which became one of humiliation, and in fact exposed me to considerable ridicule, and the general repute of my country." In the end, he decided to change Australia's vote, but he complained bitterly to Commonwealth Secretary Duncan Sandys: "I should make it clear that I deeply resent the way in which these circumstances arose. I can see no possible excuse for the failure to consult us." In a further telling remark that was edited out of the final draft, Menzies gave full voice to the deep personal nature of his misgivings: "If, in the result, my position as PM is imperilled, as it may well be, you may conceivably regret the treatment accorded to us. After all, in my fashion, I have been a good friend."[25] For Menzies, the entire issue boiled down to unrequited loyalty – to the failure of the Macmillan government to live up to the underlying tenets of Greater British fraternity. Or, as Menzies more succinctly put it in a letter to his wife, "The simple fact is that Harold is much more concerned to be right with Nehru than to be right with me."[26]

Roy Welensky's grievances with the Macmillan government had a similar personal quality. What was at stake for Welensky was not only the survival of the Federation of Rhodesia and Nyasaland but the more fundamental question of whether "the Union Jack will cease to fly in Africa within ten years."[27] His instinctive distrust of British intentions can be traced back to the very beginning of his prime ministership in 1956, but it was in 1960, in the context of the "winds of change" speech and the activities of Colonial Secretary Iain MacLeod, that his relations with the Macmillan government began to unravel. The Federation of the three central African colonies had been established in 1953 on the basis of self-government with a predominantly "whites only" franchise but without formal independence from Great Britain. Thus, while the Macmillan government retained the ultimate authority to determine when and on what basis the Federation should be granted full "Dominion" status, these powers had to be delicately negotiated with an almost aggressively "British" federal government. The key point at issue was the rights of the disenfranchised black majority in an independent Federation, and specifically whether the territories of Northern Rhodesia and Nyasaland, where the white population was notably thin, should have the right to secede from Southern Rhodesia, which had a more established white settler community. Despite repeated British assurances to Welensky ruling out secession or any looser form of federation, by the early 1960s it was becoming clear that Macmillan's resolve to bind Northern Rhodesia and Nyasaland to the Federation against the wishes of the black majority was waning fast.

There thus ensued three years of the most extraordinary wrangling and recriminations between the Macmillan and Welensky governments, culminating in the formal dissolution of the Central African Federation in December 1963. Throughout that time, Welensky, an inveterate letter-writer, corresponded freely with former Conservative government ministers in Britain in whom he found a sympathetic audience. For example, during the climactic phase of negotiations that sealed the Federation's fate in the spring of 1963, he confided in Anthony Eden: "The one thing that stands out like a sore thumb is the fact that this last act of betrayal is, to me, convincing proof that the present Government consider we whites on this Continent, as well as those Africans who've stood by us, as expendable."[28] His feelings fluctuated up and down a scale of defiant anger, cynical resignation, and sheer incredulity that "the last White bastion that believes in Britain and the British connection" could be treated so shabbily by its own kith and kin. As he confessed to the former colonial secretary, Alan Lennox-Boyd, "I just find it impossible at this stage to believe that everything we started out to achieve in 1953 has been wrecked, and wrecked by the action of a Conservative Government in the United Kingdom."[29] He reserved his deepest antipathy for Macmillan and Macleod, or "the two Macs," as he disparagingly referred to them. By 1961 he had become convinced that "the policy of Macmillan, aided and abetted by that excellent bridge player, is to liquidate what is left of the British Empire as quickly as possible."[30]

In this he was not wide of the mark, but what is significant is the way he viewed Macmillan's objectives and methods in terms of the most unspeakable treachery. He vented his feelings freely on this subject with his favourite British sympathizer, Lord Salisbury, bitterly indicting Macmillan for "presiding at the liquidation of the Commonwealth, for being really responsible for the loss of South Africa, and for the betrayal of the white man."[31] When Salisbury, himself a constant thorn in the side of the government on colonial issues, countered that Macmillan was more a misguided idealist than a scheming traitor, Welensky would hear nothing of it: "This man has been an actor for the whole of his political life and I don't believe that even today any of us know what his real feelings are about any subject."[32] For Welensky, the one true constant about Macmillan was his unbridled political opportunism – sufficiently in tune with the sensibilities of Greater British patriotism whenever it suited his conniving political purposes but perfectly capable of turning his back on his fellow Britons abroad in their hour of need. Macleod, too, was "completely and utterly dishonest politically," in Welensky's view, and seemed equally determined to bend over backwards to meet the demands of African nationalists at the expense of loyal British subjects.[33] Thus Welensky shared Menzies' sense of *ethnic* betrayal at the hands of the Macmillan government: "It's an amazing world when you realise that Southern Rhodesia was represented at the Prime Ministers' Conference before India, and look where we are today. Our trouble is, of course, that our skins are white and that is the greatest mistake in the world."[34]

Taken together, the shared animosities of Welensky, Menzies, and Diefenbaker provide vivid insight into the highly emotional and fractious landscape of the British World under siege. One issue that brought these churning resentments to a head, and in which all three prime ministers shared a common interest, was the Macmillan government's attempt to seek membership in the European Economic Community (EEC) in 1962.

What was at stake here was far more than the reversal of imperial trade preferences in favour of "foreign" producers of commodities traditionally supplied by the Empire and Commonwealth. These economic problems were certainly significant, but at a deeper level lay the cultural symbolism of Britain taking full part in the political and economic integration of Europe – a move that seemed hardly compatible with leadership of the Commonwealth family of nations. And it was largely on these grounds that Commonwealth prime ministers vehemently objected to Macmillan's European ambitions. According to Basil Robinson, Diefenbaker "could never quite overcome a sense of mystified grievance" that Macmillan had decided to "marry into Europe."[35] The fact that Macmillan's push for EEC membership received the firm backing of the Kennedy administration made it all the more suspect. During discussions with Macmillan in April 1962, Diefenbaker wondered out loud why the Americans were so keen for Britain to merge with the EEC but were "not prepared to join it themselves." He surmised that they "were in the mood, as they had sometimes been in the past, to try to determine Canada's destiny."[36] Diefenbaker remained wary of Macmillan's blandishments about preserving the vital interests of the Commonwealth and became convinced that Britain was prepared to "write off the Commonwealth" as the price of EEC membership.[37] British officials in Ottawa were understandably anxious, particularly in the wake of the South African episode, that the Canadian prime minister might seek to rally Commonwealth support and "outchampion the rest in the role of chief objector."[38]

Menzies, too, saw the EEC as the final straw in a series of intolerable burdens on the viability and integrity of the Commonwealth. Following Macmillan's announcement of his EEC membership application in July 1961, Menzies bluntly announced that Britain was faced with a "dilemma the like of which was never seen before in peaceful history": the dilemma of choosing between Europe and the Commonwealth. Britain, he claimed, was faced with "a terrible choice, an historic choice, a disastrous choice," which threatened to ruin the age-old fabric of Commonwealth unity, kinship, and co-operation.[39] Privately, he revealed his anguish to Winston Churchill: "You must feel just as puzzled as I am about some of the modern developments in the Commonwealth. Perhaps we are paying too great a price for the doubtful advantage of retaining some countries as nominal members of what used to be a splendid crown Commonwealth."[40] Welensky's reaction was basically the same, only conditioned by bitter experience and his customary cynicism. "I see all the plans are now being lined up for the big sell-out," he remarked to

Lord Salisbury. "I frankly believe that if Britain goes in, it's the beginning of the end, if it has not started already."[41]

To what extent, then, did the various grievances of Welensky, Diefenbaker, and Menzies provide the basis for a common, pan-Britannic perspective on the Macmillan government's shifting priorities? How far could this wide-ranging acrimony and ill-feeling be harnessed to a collective effort to resist Macmillan's challenge to the interests and identities of Britons overseas? All three prime ministers insisted that their misgivings derived not merely from their own selfish concerns but embraced the future viability and prosperity of the Commonwealth as a whole. And Macmillan certainly feared that a united Commonwealth voice might cause him electoral difficulties and perhaps even thwart his EEC membership bid. In assessing the potential damage at home, he recognized that "sentiment towards the Commonwealth is really centred on the old Commonwealth countries" – in other words, it was the prospect of white Commonwealth leaders appealing directly to the Greater British instincts of British voters that was the real cause for concern.[42] It is therefore worth considering whether there was ever any basis for this prognosis – whether the "old" Commonwealth prime ministers viewed their respective difficulties with the Macmillan government as part of a singular crisis of Britishness.

Perhaps the first thing to bear in mind here is that Diefenbaker, Menzies, and Welensky were troubled by different aspects of Macmillan's disengagement from the Commonwealth. Diefenbaker's overriding concern was that any weakening of the Commonwealth would undermine Canada's ability to resist American domination, politically as well as economically. Menzies' strident defence of South Africa's right to remain in the Commonwealth was always conditioned by his fear that Australia's racially selective immigration policy might be the next item on the Commonwealth hit list if apartheid were to be ruled out of court.[43] And Welensky was fighting not only for the preservation of the federal state that he represented, but by extension, for the very way of life of British settlers in southern Africa. Thus, there was a visceral quality to Welensky's rhetoric that was less apparent in the speeches and correspondence of the Australian and Canadian prime ministers. This was particularly true of Welensky's racial outbursts. He frequently spoke of his "nausea," "loathing," and "contempt" for the cordial reception accorded to African leaders by the British government.[44] On the elevation of Jomo Kenyatta to the presidency of Kenya, for example, he dictated a torrent of abuse: "Some people can stomach this stuff but I can't, and when I think that Kenyatta will attend the next Prime Ministers' Conference and will sit at the Queen's table it makes me want to spew."[45] Similarly, his criticisms of the British were heavily tinged with imperialist and racist imagery: "I'm satisfied that the present Government have no more guts in them than one would find in an Indian baboo."[46] Such thinking was completely out of bounds in Canadian political culture in the early 1960s and was neither to Diefenbaker's personal taste nor political inclinations. Menzies was more in tune with Welensky's basic instincts, as his resentment of Nehru indicates, but he would never have committed these feelings to print in such lurid terms. Thus, while sharing a common sense of grievance toward the Macmillan government, the prime ministers of Australia, Canada, and the Federation occupied considerable uncommon ground.

And it was precisely these divergent perspectives that exposed subtle cleavages in their respective philosophies of the meaning and utility of "being British." From the moment he came to office, Diefenbaker was on the lookout for dramatic gestures to make good his electoral promises to repair Canada's Commonwealth links after the breakdown over Suez. He arrived at the 1957 Commonwealth Prime Ministers' Conference fresh from his electoral victory, armed with an ambitious proposal to stage a Commonwealth Finance and Economic Conference in Ottawa for the purposes of establishing new ways of promoting Commonwealth economic unity, "harking back to Bennett's Ottawa Conference of 1932."[47] He sought a tangible, dynamic, and above all, visible program of action that would demonstrate Canada's freedom of economic manoeuvre outside the American orbit.[48]

This approach, however, was anathema to Menzies, who did not share Diefenbaker's fear of the United States and who abhorred the trend toward formalizing Commonwealth meetings into large convention-style gatherings with delegations, resolutions, and expectations of concrete political and economic outcomes. It was precisely this tendency that was wearing away at what he saw as the intrinsic quality of the Commonwealth – the small, intimate family gathering where mutual problems and perspectives could be discussed in an informal, non-combative, and above all, non-binding manner. As he declared in his 1960 Smuts Memorial Lecture in Cambridge, "We are not a court. We are brothers in a special international family. That is why I can sit in a Prime Ministers' Conference and feel instantly as much at home as if I were sitting in my own Cabinet."[49] Menzies, therefore, poured cold water on Diefenbaker's grand scheme, which, according to Macmillan, left the

Canadian looking "first puzzled, then pained, then indignant."[50] To make matters worse, Menzies was rumoured to have made disparaging public remarks characterizing Diefenbaker as a Johnny-come-lately espousing unrealistic views about what the Commonwealth might achieve. As Basil Robinson recalls, "It must be said...that Diefenbaker and Menzies, though both staunch Commonwealth loyalists, were anything but soulmates."[51]

These underlying personal differences came to the fore over the problem of South Africa, where Diefenbaker and Menzies found themselves arguing in opposing camps at the 1961 conference. Diefenbaker deplored the subtle indications that Macmillan and Menzies had concerted their positions in advance while assuming his own acquiescence. Basil Robinson's diary records Diefenbaker's "intense dislike" for Menzies, who had "created...the impression that he is the old pro whose savvy puts him in the position of helping Harold Macmillan solve the thorniest problems."[52] Menzies, for his part, regarded Diefenbaker's performance at the 1961 conference as the ultimate betrayal of the old Commonwealth ideal and a reckless breaking of ranks with the fellow British countries of the "inner" Commonwealth. While he never made his views public, he was scathing in private, recounting to Lord Salisbury some months later:

> If Nkrumah and company had received no encouragement from
> Diefenbaker, I do not think they would have launched such a
> vigorous attack. Some of them at least would have realised that
> it would be fatal to the Commonwealth to have divided it on
> colour lines. But of course, as you know, Diefenbaker arrived
> heavily pledged to strenuous action and in a highly emotional
> fashion took the lead. This gave the "all clear" to the others, and
> left me extremely apprehensive about the result.[53]

According to Menzies' logic, Diefenbaker's failure to vote with his natural constituency broke the spell of white solidarity, enabling the African and Asian members to gain the upper hand. In Menzies' mind, the Commonwealth Prime Ministers' Conference had become a microcosm of the fractured colonial world, with uncertainty and mayhem proceeding in step with the weakening of white racial cohesion and the dissipation of British resolve.

Against this background, it was unlikely that Menzies and Diefenbaker would put up any concerted opposition to Macmillan's EEC aspirations. On the contrary, from the earliest intimations of a British membership bid, Diefenbaker suspected that Macmillan had secretly secured Menzies' acquiescence in advance as a means of undermining any united Commonwealth protest.[54] He therefore distrusted Menzies' every utterance on the subject, informing his Cabinet in July 1961 that he found it "hard to understand the attitude of the Australian Prime Minister" because of the apparent conflict between his public statements and the views he had communicated directly to Diefenbaker himself.[55] In reality, there was no special arrangement between Macmillan and Menzies, nor any substantive discrepancy between Menzies' public and private remarks on the subject (as one of Diefenbaker's own ministers pointed out in Cabinet), but the fact remained that there existed no basis for any concerted action. When Harold Macmillan convened a Commonwealth Prime Ministers' Conference in September 1962 to discuss the terms of British EEC membership, the instincts of Diefenbaker and Menzies could not have been further apart. Diefenbaker, who had been urging Macmillan for months to assemble the prime ministers for this very purpose, saw the conference as a fitting occasion for a "great collective debate" at such a critical moment in Commonwealth history.[56] Menzies, by contrast, was horrified at the thought of another prime ministers' conference after the experiences of March 1961 and initially intimated to Macmillan that he would not be able to attend. "I am completely sceptical," he confessed, "about a meeting of fourteen Prime Ministers, few of whom have trade problems in common, achieving concerted views upon such complex matters." Rather, he put it to Macmillan that he would "attach much greater practical value" to a smaller gathering of "the old Brigade," who might meet up in London in advance of the conference and discuss their common problems "without benefit of Ghana and Ceylon, but with all the benefit of old and tried comradeship."[57] But Macmillan was quick to see the dangers in this, reminding Menzies that the task of preserving Commonwealth harmony "would not be eased if the impression were created that the old Commonwealth were ganging up."[58] Thus, Menzies' half-hearted scheme to regroup the Commonwealth around the Crown was never even put to Diefenbaker. Not so much as a telegram, let alone a phone call, passed between the two in preparation for the conference, and when the prime ministers finally convened in London, they each pursued their own separate agendas. Macmillan noted in his diary with some satisfaction that Menzies had "reverted to his favourite sport of teasing Diefenbaker."[59]

Welensky, for his part, was dismayed by the lack of solidarity among the white "British Commonwealth" (as he persisted in calling it) over the South African and EEC problems, but he declined to take sides or to blame Diefenbaker for the loss of South Africa. Rather, he typically saw the devious hand of Harold Macmillan at work, claiming that he "had it from a very good source" that Diefenbaker had taken his stand over South Africa at Macmillan's express request. As he recounted the tale to Salisbury, "I know this may sound completely haywire but when one has a mind as machiavellian as Macmillan I'm not so certain." He remained convinced that Diefenbaker, having earlier signalled his agreement with the principle of non-intervention in the domestic affairs of Commonwealth countries, would not have altered his stance without coordinating his position with Macmillan in advance.[60] Diefenbaker was not among Welensky's long list of correspondents, and he knew very little of him personally. While his suspicions of Macmillan's "divide and rule" subterfuge were almost certainly groundless, they nonetheless reveal the depth of his belief in the common plight of fellow Britons around the world, cast adrift by the most implausibly cynical and devious British government in London. Similarly, over the EEC question, Welensky ascribed the failure of Menzies and Diefenbaker to put up a united front not to their mutual enmity or divergent interests but to the fact that both were politically vulnerable at home with precarious parliamentary majorities. For Welensky, it was "one of the tragedies that, at this hour, neither of the two older Dominions will have a government that will be in a position to act."[61]

If Diefenbaker was regarded as having strayed from the herd – whether by conscious design or as the dupe of the British government – what then of Menzies and Welensky? Here the issue becomes more complex, because the two did strike up a warm and lasting friendship, and there is ample evidence in their correspondence of a shared sense of grievance. From their earliest encounter at the 1957 Commonwealth Prime Minsters' Conference, Welensky identified Menzies as "a far-sighted statesman of the highest possible calibre who, in the tradition of Jan Smuts, strove to make the transition from Empire to Commonwealth practicable, honourable and dignified."[62] Although their correspondence was intermittent, they were both extraordinarily frank in exchanging views on the sorry state of the Commonwealth. Welensky, for example, confessed to Menzies in the aftermath of the 1960 Prime Ministers' Conference, "If I may say so, Bob, the thing that frightens me about the Prime Ministers' Conference, almost more than anything, is the possibility that some day you won't be there."[63] Welensky had every reason for seeing Menzies as a kindred spirit in the Commonwealth forum, and received occasional letters of support from the Australian prime minster reassuring him that "you and I are friends and that we have all our basic Commonwealth ideas in common…my heart is with you in your vicissitudes."[64] In a further exchange during the dying months of the Federation, Menzies was even more forthcoming:

> Is all lost? Are there any means by which the people within the
> allegiance to the Throne could get together? I know that this
> cannot be done in any formal way because it would appear to
> divide the Commonwealth. But I am giving a lot of thought
> to how far the Crown Members can keep up their bridges with
> each other without public formality but with a gain on the
> substance…. These are matters on which reactionary old Tories
> like you and me might find it useful to discuss.[65]

Menzies, however, knew full well by this stage that the prospects of a revival of the old white Commonwealth were almost nil, and it is more likely that these musings were merely a nostalgic flourish to console Welensky in his moment of defeat. Welensky, too, concluded his official correspondence with Menzies with a wistful backwards glance at what might have been: "I don't suppose I shall ever set eyes again on you in this vale of tears, Bob…. I only wish that circumstances had been such that you had been Prime Minster of Great Britain and that Macmillan had been Prime Minister of Australia, if of course destiny felt that he ought to be Prime Minister at all."[66] Although tinged with a heavy irony, this was no mere fantasy – rather it contained an inner kernel of logic, deriving from Welensky's unswerving belief that the United Kingdom had been hijacked by a thoroughly un-British government. For Welensky, there were "better Britons" at hand, both in the "home" country and abroad, whom fate had excluded from influence during the British World's hour of need.

But even here, there were subtle differences that placed fundamental limitations on the scope for mutual assistance. While Menzies was far less sensitive to racial issues than Diefenbaker, he had nonetheless come in for some stinging criticism over his defence of South Africa's right to remain in the Commonwealth, and could ill-afford to sympathize openly with Welensky's strident racialism. The irony here is that it was precisely because Britain had given up on the Empire that the Menzies government had taken steps to place its relations with the new post-colonial states in Southeast Asia on a new footing. This had become a major priority of the Australian Department of External Affairs and involved a careful reconsideration of Australia's image as one of the last bastions of white racism in the region. Rhodesia, therefore, posed an intractable dilemma for Menzies: "a horrible problem, in which my sympathy and my realism find themselves in conflict."[67] His warm and sympathetic correspondence with Welensky was thus punctuated with all kinds of qualifying phrases and escape clauses. He frequently cautioned against any drastic action to preserve white supremacy in the Rhodesias, reminding Welensky that "we are now dealing with 'the art of the possible.'" "Our real trouble," he explained in July 1963, "is that now that the 'winds of change' have blown us into the new Commonwealth, we are…rather at the mercy of the new members." It was "for this reason alone" that Menzies confessed that he had felt bound to speak out publicly about the need for Southern Rhodesia, in the post-Federation era, to progress within "measurable time" to majority rule.[68] Welensky, however, was clearly unimpressed. In a tart rejoinder, he informed Menzies that "we Rhodesians of European stock relish this prospect about as little as Australians would welcome a handover of government to the Aborigines."[69]

This was perhaps the most telling remark of all. Although designed to remind Menzies which side he was on, it merely served to underline the world of difference that separated their respective problems and perspectives. For all his genuine sympathy for Welensky's treatment at the hands of the Macmillan government, the realities of Menzies' own post-imperial predicament rendered him no more able to assist the Rhodesian prime minister than Macmillan himself. This tendency became even more pronounced following the dissolution of the Federation and Welensky's retirement from active politics. One of Menzies' parting gestures as Australian prime minister in December 1965 was to reject Harold Wilson's repeated calls for assistance in holding the line against African criticism of Britain's handling of the rebellious Smith regime. Menzies wanted no part of the Rhodesian crisis and certainly had no wish to harm Australia's international reputation by defending "a country remote from us and our immediate problems."[70]

In his memoirs, John Diefenbaker wrote of his "deep and abiding emotional attachment to the Commonwealth," which he had nurtured while in office by adhering to "the principles that bring about the best of relations within families: recognition of differences, but the recognition also that the unity of a family is not destroyed by differences."[71] This formula had been a favourite standby among Commonwealth leaders for generations and was frequently invoked by Menzies and even Macmillan as a means of keeping family disputes within the family. But the end of Empire opened up a whole new set of problems that challenged the very integrity of the greater British ideal: the arrival of non-white members at family gatherings, the departure of an integral member of the "old brigade," the refusal to allow white Rhodesians to claim their majority as a fellow white Dominion, and the apparent willingness of the United Kingdom to leave the nest and join up with Europe created rifts and resentments that could not easily be reconciled with the traditional conception of kinship, camaraderie, and community of interest. The experience of Macmillan's dealings with his fellow "British" prime ministers shows that the underlying sense of "family" could indeed be destroyed by the sheer scope and intractability of internal discord. But this crisis was not merely a bilateral conflict, with Britain ranged on one side and the disgruntled Dominions on the other. Although the cries of alarm that reverberated around the British World were invariably couched in terms of shared experience, closer examination reveals that there were as many conceptions of the British World as there were British interests at stake.

The divergent perspectives of Menzies, Diefenbaker, and Welensky speak volumes about the inner contours and outer limits of the imagined British World in the age of imperial decline. The common denominator binding British communities overseas had always been the sentimental ties to a shared ancestral homeland. The unravelling of those ties not only removed the basis of their mutual identification but also opened up material and political disputes that drove them steadily further apart. This process was generally unselfconscious. As each prime minister adopted divergent positions, the others looked on aghast at what seemed to them a betrayal of the core tenets of British community. Thus, Diefenbaker was angered and hurt by Menzies' refusal to support his grand design for a new Commonwealth economic pact; Menzies, in turn, was embittered by Diefenbaker's fraternizing with the "new" Commonwealth; and Welensky was completely bewildered by Menzies' insistence on the principle of majority rule in Rhodesia. In each instance, all three were responding to their own specific needs within their own distinctive contexts, the very contexts – African, Canadian, and Australian – that had informed the evolution of their respective British sensibilities. In other words, the breakup of Greater Britain in the early 1960s unmasked fundamental differences about the raison d'être of being British. As Roy Welensky once remarked, in contrasting his own "imperialism" with that of the British government, "It once again proves the old story that one word can have a hundred different meanings."[72]

{NOTES}

1 Charles Dilke, *Greater Britain* (London: Macmillan, 1868), vii–viii.

2 See most recently Carl Bridge and Kent Fedorowich, eds., *The British World: Diaspora, Culture, and Identity* (London: Frank Cass, 2003); Carl Bridge and Phillip Buckner, "Re-inventing the British World," *The Round Table* 368 (2003): 77–88; Simon Potter, *News and the British World* (Oxford: Oxford University Press, 2003).

3 Stuart Ward, *Australia and the British Embrace: The Demise of the Imperial Ideal* (Melbourne: Melbourne University Press, 2001).

4 Bill Schwarz, "'The Only White Man in There': The Re-racialisation of England, 1956–68," *Race and Class* 1 (1996): 69.

5 On Australia, see Ward, *Australia and the British Embrace*; David Goldsworthy, *Losing the Blanket: Australia and the End of Britain's Empire* (Melbourne: Melbourne University Press, 2002); On Canada, Phillip Buckner, ed., *Canada and the End of Empire* (Vancouver: University of British Columbia Press, 2005); José Igartua, "L'autre révolution tranquille: Le canada anglais," *Possibles* 23 (printemps 1999): 41–52. On New Zealand, James Belich, *Paradise Reforged: A History of the New Zealanders*, vol. 2 (Auckland: Penguin, 2001). On South Africa, Peter Henshaw and Ronald Hyam, *The Lion and the Springbok: Britain and South Africa since the Boer War* (Cambridge: Cambridge University Press, 2003).

6 See, for example, A.W. Martin, *Robert Menzies: A Life*, vol. 1 (Melbourne: Melbourne University Press, 1993).

7 Roy Welensky, *Welensky's 4000 Days: The Life and Death of the Federation of Rhodesia and Nyalasland* (London: Collins, 1964), 78.

8 Basil Robinson, *Diefenbaker's World: A Populist in Foreign Affairs* (Toronto: University of Toronto Press, 1989), 60.

9 Graham Spry (Agent-General for Saskatchewan) quoted in J.L. Granatstein, *Canada 1957–1967: The Years of Uncertainty and Innovation* (Toronto: McClelland and Stewart, 1986), 43–44.

10 See Judith Brett, *Robert Menzies' Forgotten People* (Sydney: Pan Macmillan, 1992), 146–48; Gerard Henderson, *Menzies' Child* (Sydney: Allen & Unwin, 1994).

11 Menzies, quoted in Ward, *Australia and the British Embrace*, 39.

12 National Library of Australia (NLA), Menzies Papers, MS4936, 421/1. Address by Roy Welensky, "The Federation and the Commonwealth: A Challenge to the West," delivered on 8 November 1961 at the Royal Albert Hall to the Annual Conference of the Institute of Directors.

13 This is certainly true of Hendrick Verwoerd of South Africa, but less so in the case of Walter Nash and Keith Holyoake of New Zealand.

14 See Macmillan's diary entries published in Macmillan, *Riding the Storm* (London: Macmillan, 1971), 377.

15 Bodleian Library Oxford, Macmillan Papers, Diaries, d.39, 12 May 1960.

16 Public Record Office (PRO), DO182/69, Memorandum by Joe Garner (Ottawa), "Canada: Visit by the Right Hon. H. Macmillan," 9 May 1961. See also Edward Heath, *The Course of My Life* (London: Hodder and Stoughton, 1998), 221–22.

17 His biographer, Denis Smith, has described it as "a high point of his Prime Ministership" in *Rogue Tory: The Life and Legend of John G. Diefenbaker* (Toronto: Macfarlane, Walter and Ross, 1995), 366. See also contemporary accolades in the

Vancouver Sun, 16 March 1961; the *Toronto Daily Star*, 16 March 1961; the *Globe and Mail* (Toronto), 17 March 1961.

18 Robinson, *Diefenbaker's World*, 123, 177–80. Denis Smith, in *Rogue Tory*, 361, also emphasizes that Diefenbaker flew to the 1961 conference "with no fixed position…fearful of failure, hoping for postponement, and with no desire to take to the barricades."

19 Robinson, *Diefenbaker's World*, 174–78.

20 Horne, *Macmillan* (London: Macmillan, 1989), 2:394.

21 As Menzies reported to his deputy prime minister, John McEwan, "I can only assume that this change in approach by Macmillan came from the meeting he had last night at Chequers with Nehru" (quoted in Goldsworthy, *Losing the Blanket*, 113).

22 Ibid., 104.

23 See Menzies articles in *The Times* on 11 and 12 July 1956, where he argued for the idea of an inner and outer Commonwealth.

24 NLA, Menzies Papers, 14/122, Menzies to Harrison, 30 May 1961.

25 Ibid., 27/221, Menzies to Sandys, 3 May 1961.

26 Quoted in Martin, *Robert Menzies: A Life* (Melbourne: Melbourne University Press, 1999), 2:428.

27 Rhodes House Library (RHL), Oxford, Welensky Papers, 665/2, Welensky to Salisbury, 4 October 1960.

28 Ibid., 587/6, Welensky to Eden, 18 April 1963.

29 Ibid., 592/8, Welensky to Lennox-Boyd, 8 April 1963; the reference to the "last White bastion" appears in an earlier letter to Lennox-Boyd in the same file dated 27 June 1956.

30 Ibid., 665/3, Welensky to Salisbury, 7 October 1961.

31 Ibid., 665/5, Welensky to Salisbury, 27 July 1963.

32 Ibid., Welensky to Salisbury, 24 June 1963.

33 Ibid., 665/3, Welensky to Salisbury, 27 February 1961.

34 Ibid., 665/4, Welensky to Salibury, 1 August 1962.

35 Robinson, *Diefenbaker's World*, 210.

36 PRO, DO 182/74, "Record of a meeting held in the Cabinet Room, Parliament buildings, Ottawa," 15 April 1962.

37 PRO, PREM 11/4016, Amory (British High Commissioner, Ottawa) to Macmillan, 23 March 1962.

38 PRO, DO 159/55, Amory to Sandys, 2 October 1962.

39 *Sydney Morning Herald*, 9 August 1961; see also Menzies, *Commonwealth Parliamentary Debates*, vol. 32, 16 August 1961, 134–41.

40 PRO, PREM 11/3331, Menzies to Churchill, 21 October 1961.

41 RHL, Welensky Papers, 665/3, Welensky to Salisbury, 7 June 1961 and 3 July 1961.

42 PRO, CAB133/262, Memorandum by the Prime Minister, "Commonwealth Conference," 4 September 1962.

43 He made this explicit in his report to Deputy Prime Minister McEwen immediately after the 1961 conference: "In view of our plainly discriminatory immigration policy we have a good chance of being next in line" (quoted in Martin, *Robert Menzies*, 2:426).

44 RHL, Welensky Papers, 665/3, Welensky to Salisbury, 18 August 1961.

45 Ibid., 665/5, Welensky to Salisbury, 12 November 1963.

46 Ibid., 665/4, Welensky to Salisbury, 3 February 1963.

47 Smith, *Rogue Tory*, 252.

48 Robinson, *Diefenbaker's World*, 12.

49 Quoted in Martin, *Robert Menzies*, 2:415–16.

50 Macmillan, diary entry 5 July 1957, quoted in *Riding the Storm*, 377.

51 Robinson, *Diefenbaker's World*, 81–82.

52 Ibid., 175.

53 NLA, Menzies Papers, 27/221, Menzies to Salisbury, 15 January 1962.

54 National Archives of Canada (NAC), RG2, vol. 6177, Cabinet Conclusions no. 68/61, 15 June 1961.

55 Ibid., Cabinet Minute, 13 July 1961.

56 Robinson, *Diefenbaker's World*, 279.

57 PRO, PREM 11/3665, Menzies to Macmillan, 18 April 1962; PREM 11/4017, Menzies to Macmillan, 11 July 1962. Menzies explained to Macmillan in his July letter: "The relations between Britain, Canada, Australia and New Zealand are to me the most important things in the Commonwealth, and we must work hard to maintain them."

58 PRO, PREM 11/4017, Macmillan to Menzies, 20 July 1962.

59 Macmillan, diary entry, 19 September 1962, quoted in Macmillan, *At the End of the Day* (London: Macmillan, 1973), 136.

60 RHL, Welensky Papers, 665/5, Welensky to Salisbury, 28 May 1963.

61 Ibid., 665/4, Welensky to Salisbury, 21 June 1962.

62 Welensky, *4000 Days*, 78.

63 NLA, Menzies Papers, Welensky to Menzies, 30 May 1960.

64 Ibid., Menzies to Welensky, 27 June 1963.

65 Ibid., 421/1, Menzies to Welensky, 27 July 1963.

66 Ibid., 421/1, Welensky to Menzies, 16 July 1963.

67 Ibid., 421/4, undated handwritten memorandum by Menzies, "Rhodesia – my story of what turned out to be my problem."

68 Ibid., 421/1, Menzies to Welensky, 27 June 1963; 27 July 1963.

69 Ibid., Welensky to Menzies, 16 July 1963.

70 Ibid., 22/187, Menzies to Harold Wilson, 24 December 1965.

71 Diefenbaker, *One Canada*, 52, 187.

72 RHL, Welensky Papers, 665/4, Welensky to Salisbury, 25 February 1962.

NOTES ON CONTRIBUTORS

JAMES BELICH holds the Keith Sinclair Chair in History at the University of Auckland, New Zealand. His previous books include *The New Zealand Wars* (1986); a two-volume history of the New Zealanders: *Making Peoples* (1996); and *Paradise Reforged* (2001).

FRANK BONGIORNO is a Senior Lecturer in History at the University of New England, Armidale, Australia, and has published widely on the history of Australian labour. He is a member of the Australian Fabian Society.

BETTINA BRADBURY is a feminist family historian. She is a member of the History Department of the Faculty of Arts and Glendon College at York University, as well as a member of the School of Women's Studies and a long-time member of the Montreal History Group. Her past publications have focused on working-class families during the nineteenth century and on aspects of marriage and widowhood. Current projects include: a manuscript entitled Wife to Widow: Lives, Laws, and Politics in Nineteenth-Century Montreal; a study of debates about marriage in the white settler societies of the nineteenth century British Empire; and research into the 1832 by-election in Montreal.

PATRICK H. BRENNAN is Associate Professor of History and Fellow of the Centre for Military and Strategic Studies, University of Calgary.

PHILLIP BUCKNER is Professor Emeritus of the University of New Brunswick and a Senior Research Fellow at the Institute of Commonwealth Studies, University of London.

ELIZABETH ELBOURNE is an Associate Professor in the Department of History, McGill University, where she teaches British, South African, and British imperial history. Her publications include *Blood Ground:*

Colonialism, Missions and the Contest for Christianity in the Cape Colony and Britain, 1799-1853 (Montreal & Kingston: McGill-Queen's University Press, 2002). She is currently working on a transregional history of struggles across the British white settler empire over settler-indigenous relationships in the early nineteenth century.

R. DOUGLAS FRANCIS is a Professor of Canadian History at the University of Calgary.

JEFFREY GREY is a Professor of History at University College, Australian Defence Force Academy.

CATHERINE HALL is the Professor of Modern British Social and Cultural History at University College London. Her most recent book is *Civilizing Subjects: Metropole and Colony in the English Imagination, 1830–1867.*

JOHN LAMBERT is an Associate Professor in the Department of History, and Director of the School of Arts and Humanities, at the University of South Africa in Pretoria. He has published widely on the socio-economic and political history of the Colony of Natal. He is presently working on the history of white English-speaking South Africans.

DOUGLAS LORIMER (PhD, UBC) is professor of history at Wilfrid Laurier University, Waterloo, Ontario. He is the author of *Colour, Class and the Victorians* (1978) and of articles and essays on the status of black slaves in eighteenth-century England, Victorian anthropology, race and popular culture, and black resistance to racism in the late Victorian period. He is currently working on a study of racism, the language of race relations, and resistance in the late Victorian and Edwardian period, 1870–1914.

DAVID LOWE is an Associate Professor in History at Deakin University, Australia. He has published widely on the history of Australia in the world, including *Menzies and the 'Great World Struggle': Australia's Cold War, 1948-54* (UNSW Press, 1999).

STUART MACINTYRE is the Ernest Scott Professor of History at the University of Melbourne and currently the Dean of the Faculty of Arts. He has published books on aspects of British and Australian history. With Anna Clark, he wrote *The History Wars* (2003).

ADELE PERRY teaches history at the University of Manitoba, where she holds the Canada Research Chair in Western Canadian Social History. She can be reached at *AdelePerry@ms.umanitoba.ca*

PAUL PICKERING is Senior Fellow, Humanities Research Centre, The Australian National University, Canberra.

SATADRU SEN teaches South Asian history at Washington University in St. Louis. He is the author of *Migrant Races: Empire, Identity and K.S. Ranjitsinhji, and Disciplining Punishment: Colonialism and Convict Society in the Andaman Islands.* He is currently working on a book on childhood and children's institutions in colonial India.

R. SCOTT SHEFFIELD is Assistant Professor at the University College of the Fraser Valley in British Columbia, Canada.

PAUL WARD teaches British history at the University of Huddersfield. He has written three books: *Red Flag and Union Jack* (1998); *Britishness since 1870* (2004); and *Unionism in the United Kingdom, 1918-1974* (2005). In 2005–2006 he was Fulbright-Robertson Visiting Professor of British History at Westminster College, Missouri, USA.

STUART WARD is an Associate Professor in the English Department at the University of Copenhagen. His main research interest is the impact of the end of empire on British and settler-colonial communities since 1945. He has published *Australia and the British Embrace: The Demise of the Imperial Ideal* (Melbourne 2001), and edited *British Culture and the End of Empire* (Manchester 2001) as well as a variety of essays and articles on the break-up of "greater" Britishness.

WENDY WEBSTER is Reader in Contemporary British History at the University of Central Lancashire, UK. She has published widely on questions of national identity, imperialism, "race," ethnicity, gender and immigration in the post-1945 period, and her publications include *Imagining Home: Gender, "Race" and National Identity* (UCL Press, 1998), and *Englishness and Empire, 1939-65* (Oxford University Press, 2005). She is a review editor for *Women's History Review.*

INDEX

A

A History of the English-Speaking Peoples, 396

A Short History of Australia, 225

Aaron, Isaac, 91

Aberdeen, Lady, 268

abolitionism, 22, 29–30, 62, 70, 110–11, 112–13, 119, 123, 126. *See also* emancipation; slavery

Aboriginal people. *See* indigenous people

Aborigines Protection Society (APS), 60, 62, 78–79, 112, 113, 119, 120, 121, 127

"Aborigines' Friend, The," 79, 80

Aborigines, Australian
  and Australian bicentenary, 386, 387
  and Australian national museum, 394
  and claims to land, 138, 147–48, 149, 236
  and labour, 23
  and racism, 225–26
  and self-government, 415
  history of, 388, 392–93

Acoose, Janice, 173

Active Citizen Force, 287

Adams, Philip, 224

Adelaide, 211

"Advance Australia Fair," 388

Afghanistan, 392

Africa
  and the British World, 10, 14
  and the civilizing mission, 110
  colonist-formed militias in, 236
  commerce in, 119
  East, 296, 298
  evangelization of, 73, 74
  German troops in, 287
  indigenous people of, 60. *See also* Khoekhoe
  North, 345
  partition of, 114
  South West, 298, 311

Afrikaners
  and military service, 289–90
  and nationalism, 125, 243, 246, 298–99, 300, 325
  and patriotism, 286
  and South Africa, 16, 236
  and South African Indians, 314
  and the British Empire, 287, 289, 291
  and the First World War, 239, 240, 285, 292
  and violence, 71

Against Race, 117

Airey, E., 270

Akins, Sir James, 193

Alberta, 46, 278

alcohol, 312, 313, 392

Ali, Sir Imam, 311

Alice in Wonderland, 372

American Revolution. *See* United States, War of Independence

American Settler, The, 54

Amiens, 257

Among the Peoples of British Columbia: Red, White, Yellow, and Brown, 163, 166, 167

Amos, Andrew, 381

"An Appeal to the British-born to Promote the Sense of Canadian Nationality within the British Empire," 192

anarchism, 210, 216, 217

Anderson, Benedict, 141, 183

Andreski, Stanislav, 234

Angell, Norman
  Defence and the English-Speaking Role, 371

Anglobooms, 42–44, 46

Anglophilia, 223, 251, 311, 391

Anne, Queen, 77

Anthropological Society of London, 113

anthropology, 111, 112, 113, 127, 140, 143, 149

Anti-Corn Law League, 92–96, 101.
    See also United Kingdom, Corn
    Laws
anti-slavery movement. *See* abolitionism
Anti-Slavery Society, 112, 127
Antigua, 33
Anzac Day, 246, 247, 394
ANZUS Treaty, 220
apartheid, 403, 405, 409
Arbuthnot, Sandy, 381, 382
Arbuthnot, Sir Harry, 382
Archer, William, 128
Argentina, 50, 389
Argus, 278
Armistice Day, 196
Arms From India, 332
Armstrong, Sir Robert, 388
Arrons, L., 296
Asquith, Herbert, 113
assimilation, 35, 161, 342, 344, 350–51,
    352–53, 354, 356
Atholl, Katherine, Duchess of, 276
Atkinson, Alan, 102
Atlantic Charter (1941), 324, 341, 351
Atlantic Provinces in Confederation, The,
    198
Attlee, Clement, 218, 219, 221, 223
Auchinleck, General, 328
Auckland, 46, 353
Aurobindo, Sri, 307
Australasian League Against
    Transportation, 87, 88, 89, 92–97, 98,
    100, 101
Australia
    and British identity, 12, 26, 182, 185–86,
        201, 375, 401
    and military activity, 236, 246, 392
    and national identity, 252, 277, 278
    and South Africa, 405
    and the First World War, 240, 241–43,
        286, 297
    and the History Wars, 393
    and the Second World War, 244, 245,
        321
    and trade, 383
    bicentenary, 386–87, 390
    Defence Act, 239
    Indian immigration to, 314
    indigenous peoples of, 23, 161.
        See also Aborigines, Australian;
        indigenous people; Torres Strait
        Islanders

Section 92 of the Constitution, 221
Western, 42, 51
White Australia Policy, 227, 386
women in, 137, 138, 148, 268
Australia Day, 387, 388
Australia House, London, 385
Australian Army, 243
Australian Association for Cultural
    Freedom (AACF), 223
Australian Defence Academy, 18
Australian Department of External
    Affairs, 414
Australian Imperial Force (AIF), 240, 241
Australian Institute of International
    Affairs, 225
Australian Labor Party (ALP)
    and Australian history, 387
    and Australian military activity, 392
    and Paul Keating, 385–86
    and socialism, 211, 216, 219, 220, 221–22,
        223
    and the Australian labour movement,
        212, 218
    and the Cold War, 363, 365, 369, 371–72
    and the First World War, 242
    Victorian, 213, 214
Australian Legend, The, 225
Australian Observer, 218
Australians for a Constitutional
    Monarchy, 391
Auxiliary Missionary Society, 64
Auxiliary Societies, 64, 66
Ayer, Sir Sivaswamy, 311, 316

B

Baden-Powell, Robert, 189, 197
Baker, Charles, 140
Baker, Richard, 141, 144, 146, 147
Balfour, A.J., 9
Bandung, 376
Bannister, Saxe, 77–78
Barbados, 26, 33, 122
barbarism, 36, 140, 141, 166, 213
Barman, Jean, 164
Barrow, John, 71
Bathurst, Lord, 78
Bawtree, Viola, 271
Bederman, Gail, 141
Belgium, 51, 287
Belich, James, 14, 17, 18
Bellamy, Edward, 210–11
Bennett, R.B., 410

Berger, Carl, 182–83, 185, 187, 190
Berthon, C., 310
Bethelsdorp, 67, 69, 76
Bevan, Aneurin, 219, 220, 221
Bevin, Ernest, 218
Beyers, General Christiaan, 289–90
Bicentennial Authority (Australia), 387, 388
Big Picture, 385, 392
Bigge, J.T., 61
Billig, Michael, 269
Bird, Christopher, 68
Birdwood, Sir William, 241
Birthright, The, 192
Bishop, Billy, 185
Bismarck, Otto von, 211
Black Armband, 389
Black Week, 237
Blackfoot tribe, 332
Blackwood's Magazine, 53
Blainey, Geoffrey, 387, 389
Blair, Tony, 223
Blatchford, Robert, 210–11
Blenkiron, John Scantlebury, 382, 383–84, 392
Blitz, Jack, 222
"Blurred Image: The Australian Identity at Home and Abroad, The," 224
Board of Control for India, 32
Boer War
    and Australian national identity, 242, 246
    and British imperialism, 172, 189–90, 215, 237
    and John Buchan's British World, 382
    and racial exclusion, 123
    Canadian participation in, 181, 185
Boers. *See* Afrikaners
Bokhari, Z.A., 328
bomb, nuclear.
    See nuclear weapons
Bombay, 315, 316
Bonaparte, Napoleon. *See* Napoleon I
Booy, Willem, 69
Borden, Sir Robert, 191, 241, 252, 256, 260
Botany Bay, 39
Botha, General Louis, 286, 288, 289, 290, 292
Bourke, Richard, 61
Boy Scouts, 189, 197
Boy's Own Annual, 198
Boyd, Archibald, 138

Boyd, John, 194
Boys' and Girls' League of South Africa, 271
Brant, Elizabeth, 78
Brant, John, 77–78, 80
Brant, Joseph, 77
Brant, Molly, 77
Brazil, 26
Brennan, Pat, 17
Bridge, Carl, 17, 278
Bright, John, 93
Brighton, 307
Britain At Bay, 327
Britain, Greater, 10, 11, 13, 49, 382, 399, 416
Britains, Better, 15, 41, 52, 186, 278
British Army, 255, 260, 294
British Banner, 95
British Broadcasting Corporation (bbc), 325, 326, 328, 333, 334
British Columbia
    and Chinese immigration, 167
    and first-wave feminism, 169
    and Frances Elizabeth Herring, 159, 162, 166, 174
    and interracial marriage, 172
    and marriage law, 136, 143
    and transportation, 42
    colonial history of, 160, 163–65
British Columbia Commonwealth, 163
British Columbia Teachers' Convention, 162
British Commonwealth Affairs, 366–67
British Commonwealth Air Training Plan, 243
British Commonwealth of Nations, 199
British Commonwealth Office, 202
British Empire League, 186, 288, 289
British Empire Service League, 195
British Expeditionary Force (bef), 256, 260
British General Headquarters, 259
British High Commission in Canada, 202
British Honduras, 334
British Imperial Army, 245
British News in Canada, 191
British 3rd Army, 255
British Women's Patriotic League, 272
British World Conferences, 13, 17, 18, 234, 286
British World: Diaspora, Culture, Identity, The, 18

Britishness
    and British imperialism, 19, 21, 49
    and masculinity, 337
    demise of, 399, 400, 409
    in Australia, 186, 210, 214, 221, 227
    in Canada, 191
    in India, 26
    in New Zealand, 356, 395
    in the West Indies, 28
    national identities within, 13, 321
Britons: Forging the Nation, 1707–1837, 12
Bromley, B.M., 296
Brougham, Henry, 31
Bruce, Stanley Melbourne, 243
Bryant, Gordon, 367
Bryce, James, 122, 124, 128, 129
Buchan, John, 299, 381
Buckner, Phillip, 17, 18, 260, 278
Buenos Aires, 14
Buffalo, 194
Bulawayo, 381
Bullivant, Sir Walter, 381
Burgmann, Verity, 213
Burma, 244, 324
Burma-Thailand railway, 385
Burnham, Lord, 192, 193
Burrow, J.W., 113
Burton, Antoinette, 159
Burton, Richard, 112, 113
Burton, William, 61, 80
Bush, George W., 392
Butte de Warlencourt, 295
Button, John, 221, 224
Buxton, Sir Thomas, 62, 75, 78, 79, 81
Byng, Sir Julian, 241, 253–54, 255
Byron, Lord, 91

C
Cairns, Jim, 220
Caledon, Earl of, 68
Caledonian Societies, 288
Calgary, 286
California, 43, 145–46, 150, 162, 314
Calling the West Indies, 333
Cambrai, 255
Cambrian Society, 288
Cambridge, 384, 410
Cambridge History of the British Empire, 9–10
Cameronians, 297
Campbell, John, 72–74
Campbell, Robert, 99
Campbell, Thomas, 78

Campion, Jane, 395
Canada
    and confederation, 163, 235
    and national identity, 12, 23, 247, 253,
        254, 262, 278. *See also* national
        identity, Canadian
    and the "History Wars," 390
    and the Boer War, 238
    and the Commonwealth, 401, 410
    and the First World War, 240, 270, 286,
        297
    and the Second World War, 321, 332
    and the Statute of Westminster, 242
    and the United States, 408
    Canadian Militia Act, 239
    colonization of, 41, 42, 46, 49, 52, 236
    Durham Report of 1839, 53
    ethnic heterogeneity in, 335
    Family Allowances Act, 347
    Indian Act, 345, 350
    Indian immigration to, 314
    indigenous peoples of, 60, 62, 161
        (*See also* First Nations; indigenous
        people)
    Military Voters Act, 277
    Quiet Revolution, 202
    Unemployment Insurance Act, 347
    Upper, 44, 61, 77
    Wartime Elections Act, 277
    women in, 137, 162, 268, 272
    women's property rights in, 138, 144,
        145, 148
Canada Food Board, 272
Canadian Air Force, 197
*Canadian and British News in Canada,
    The*, 191
Canadian Army, 253, 260, 345
Canadian Camp Life, 163, 164, 170
Canadian Cavalry Brigade, 255
Canadian Corps, 193, 240, 241, 251–53,
    254, 256–57, 259–62
Canadian Expeditionary Force (CEF),
    239, 240
Canadian flag, 200–201, 202
Canadian Headquarters in London, 255
Canadian Historical Association, 181
Canadian Historical Review, 390
Canadian Legion, 195–96, 200–201
Canadian Overseas Ministry, 241
Canadian Pacific Railroad, 163
Canadian War Contingent Association,
    268

Canadian, The, 191
Canberra, 18, 245, 365, 376, 385
Cannadine, David, 183, 307, 368
Cape Colony, 23, 59–61, 62, 63–64, 65, 81,
    145, 291
Cape Times, 299
Cape Town, 65, 102, 234, 295, 403
Cape Town Highlanders, 291
Caribbean. *See* West Indies
Carlyle, Thomas, 111, 113, 211
Carpenter, Edward, 213
Carter, E.H., 373
Carter, Sarah, 18, 169
Casey, Richard, 364, 368, 374–75
Cassino, 330
Catholics, 11, 16, 31, 91, 172, 190, 213, 233,
    240, 351
Censor Headquarters, 256
Central African Federation, 400, 406,
    410, 414, 415
Central Intelligence Agency (CIA), 223
Ceylon, 412
Chakrabarty, Dipesh, 22
Chamber of Princes (India), 310
Chamberlain, Joseph, 13, 119
Champion, 212
Champion, Henry Hyde, 211–13
Chartism, 90, 91, 93, 94, 95, 98, 99, 101,
    103
Chatterjee, Partha, 22, 306
Chelmsford, Lord, 310, 311, 315
Cheshire, 94
Chicago, 43, 45
China, 311, 312, 371
Chinook Jargon, 165, 167, 168
Christianization, 60, 72–73.
    See also missionary movement
Chums, 198
Church of England, 363
Churchill, Winston
    and "the English-speaking peoples," 13,
        361, 369, 376
    and Anglocentrism, 40
    and British Policy, 219
    and Canada, 190, 194–95
    and India, 330
    and the Cold War, 367
    and the Commonwealth, 408
    and the Second World War, 244, 325,
        336, 375
    Fulton speech, 370–71
Cincinnati, 42, 43, 45, 46, 47

citizenship, 31, 54, 79, 116, 124, 126, 269,
    277, 307, 351
Civilization on Trial, 367
civilizing mission, 110, 111–12, 115, 118,
    363
Civilizing Subjects, 110
Clapham Sect, 29, 30, 31
Clark, Manning, 376
Clark, Reverend Andrew, 273
Claus, Daniel, 77
Cleburne, Richard, 88
Co-operative Commonwealth Federation,
    347
Cobden, Richard, 93, 94, 95, 101
Cole, Doug, 182–83
Cole, G.D.H., 210, 220
Colley, Linda, 12, 49, 99, 233–34, 247
Collini, Stephan, 115
Colombo Plan, 374, 375
Colonial Conference, 383
Colonial Defence Committee, 237
Colonial Film Unit, 326
Colonial Office
    and convict transportation, 97
    and humanitarianism, 61
    and immigration legislation, 124, 125
    and India, 329
    and indigenous people, 79, 119, 120,
        121–22
    and marriage, 136
    and race relations, 126, 128, 326, 334
Colonial Times, 87, 88, 92, 95, 97, 103
Colonial Times and Tasmanian, 93
colonization, explosive, 41, 43–46.
    See also hyper-colonization
colour bar, 335, 353.
    See also discrimination; racial
    exclusion; segregation
Coloured Cape Corps, 331
Columbus, Christopher, 122
Commonwealth Division in Korea, 245
Commonwealth Finance and Economic
    Conference, 410
Commonwealth Heads of Government
    Meeting, 383
Commonwealth Prime Ministers'
    Conferences, 401, 402, 403, 407, 410,
    411, 412, 413
Commonwealth Relations Office, 405
communism, 216, 218, 223, 368, 371
Communist Party (Australia), 217
community, imagined, 64, 183, 271

Companion in The Most Distinguished Order of St. Michael and St. George (CMG), 259
Companion of The Most Honourable Order of Bath (CB), 259
Confidential Print on the Native Races in the British Empire, 125
Congo Reform Association, 120
Congress Party (India), 330
conscription, 239–40, 243, 297, 328, 347
Conservative Party (United Kingdom), 402, 406–7
Conservative Party of Canada, 190, 198, 251, 347, 401
Constantine, Learie, 333–35
constitutionalism, popular, 98, 99–100, 103
Cook, Capt., 295
Cook, Joseph, 315
Cook, Ramsay, 188
Copp, Terry, 198
Cormack, Magnus, 365
Cornwall and York, Duke of, 185
Corowa, 385
Cotton, G.W., 143
Council of Defence (Australia), 365
Cowper, Charles, 89, 101, 102
Crean, Frank, 218, 219–20
creolization, 22, 23, 25, 26, 27, 36, 165
Creswell, Colonel, 288
Cromwell, Oliver, 24, 32
Crosland, Anthony, 221, 222–23
Cross, Flying Officer Ulric, 333
Crow, Jim, 124
Crowther, Samuel, 75
Cuba, 39
Cubs, 197
Curran, John, 98
Currie, Sir Arthur, 193, 195, 241, 254–61
Curtin, John, 214, 244
Curtin, Philip, 111
Custom of Paris/Civil Code, 145
Cuyler, Jacob, 68, 70

D
Dafoe, John W., 188, 189, 193, 195
Daily Mail, The, 112, 191
Daniel Deronda, 24
Darwin, Charles, 113, 115
Darwin, John, 17, 234–35
Davies, Alan, 219
Davin, Anna, 161

Deakin, Alfred, 242
Dean, Misao, 160
decolonization, 14, 15, 110, 306, 363, 399–400
Defenders of India, 328
Delville Wood, 286, 295, 296, 297, 298, 299
Delville Wood Day, 246, 247
democracy, 97–98, 126, 127, 129, 294, 324, 349
Denison, Sir William, 89, 90, 99
Denoon, Donald, 49
Denver, 46
Department of External Affairs (Canada), 200, 403
Department of Immigration and Ethnic Affairs (Australia), 388
dependency, 21, 22, 33, 260
Depression, Great, 201
determinism, biological, 115, 116, 129
Diefenbaker, John, 400, 401, 402–4, 407–8, 409, 410–13, 414, 415, 416
Dieppe, 244
Dikkop, Paul, 73–74
Dilke, Sir Charles, 9–10, 13, 49, 119–20, 399
Diocesan College, 293
discrimination, 124, 388, 392. *See also* colour bar; racial exclusion; segregation
diversity, 169, 308, 333, 334, 385, 395. *See also* multiculturalism
domesticity, 30, 167, 275, 279
Dominion, 343
Dominion Institute, 390
Donnelly, Ignatius, 211
Douglas, William, 368
dower rights, 137, 138, 149, 150
Downer, Alexander, Sr., 368
Downer, John, 142
Drummond, David Henry, 372
Drury, E.C., 193
Du Bois, W.E.B., 122
Dubinsky, Karen, 164
Dublin, 215, 256
Duffy, Charles Gavan, 92, 103
Duguid, Fortescue, 258
Duke University, 235
Dulles, John Foster, 374
Dunedin, 46
Dunmore Lang, John, 91, 93, 97, 99, 100
Durban, 289, 299

Dutch Reformed Church, 66
Dutton, Geoffrey, 224

E
East African Brigade, 292
East India Company, 33, 34, 119
Eastern Commissioners of Inquiry, 61
Economist, 96
Eden, Sir Anthony, 219, 371, 406
Edinburgh, 73, 278, 333
Edinburgh Missionary Society, 72
Edinburgh Review, 31
Edinburgh, Duke of, 385, 388
Edmonds, James, 257
Edmonton, 46
Edward VIII, King, 196
Edwards, Bryan, 27
Eggleston, Fred, 216
Egypt, 295
85th Battalion (Nova Scotia), 261
Eisenhower, Dwight D., 371, 374
El Alamein, 244
Elder, Sir Thomas, 212
Elgin, Lord, 125
Eliot, George, 24
Elizabeth II, Queen, 200, 202, 336, 388
emancipation. *See also* abolitionism;
    slavery
    and Jamaica, 111, 114
    and marriage, 137, 147
    and the United States, 120
    and the West Indies, 25, 28, 29, 119
    Catholic, 32, 91
Empire Air Training Scheme, 243
Empire Answers, The, 321, 322, 323, 325, 335
Empire Day, 271, 324
Empire Exhibition, 197
Empire Marches, The, 327
"English-Speaking Peoples," 13, 40, 120,
    368, 369, 370, 376, 384
Epic of Vimy, The, 196
equality
    and Australian Aborigines, 119
    and colonization, 25
    and First Nations, 349
    and indigenous people, 76, 121
    and Maori people, 341, 354–55
    and post-war New Order, 349
    and race, 117, 122–23, 126, 128–29, 308
    and the Khoekhoe, 76, 80
    in the West Indies, 61
    social, 374

Esher, Lord, 239
esprit de corps, 255, 259
Essex, 273
European Economic Community (EEC),
    201, 223–24, 399, 408, 409, 411–12,
    413
evangelicalism, 22, 30, 62, 63, 66, 72, 80,
    115, 119. *See also* Christianization;
    missionary movement
Evangelical Magazine, 63
Evatt, H.V., 365, 367, 368, 369
Evening Post, 343
Everest, Mt., 374
exclusion. *See* racial exclusion
Exeter Hall, 112, 113
Expansion of England, 125
Expeditionary Lodge, 293
export rescue, 42, 46–49
extermination, 121, 390
Eyre, Governor, 112

F
Fabian Autumn Lectures, 224
Fabian Bullitin, 220
Fabian News, 222
Fabian Society, 210–11, 214, 216–20,
    222–23, 224–25
Fairhall, Allen, 368
Fairweather, Carlton, 333
Federation of British Daughters of the
    Empire, 190
federationism, imperial, 182, 186, 189, 237
femininity, 160, 165–66, 267, 277
feminism
    and imperialism, 165
    and marriage, 135–36, 138–39, 147, 150
    and maternity, 170
    and race, 173–74
    and the "History Wars," 392
    and the Colonies, 166
    and the suffragist movement, 275
    first-wave, 169, 170
Fenianism, 111, 189, 236
Ferreira, Thomas, 70
Field, Dudley, 144
Finch, George, 92
1st Army, 255
1st Canadian Brigade, 251
First Days, The, 322–23
First Fleet, 386, 387, 388
First Nations
    and assimilation, 356

and claims to land, 138, 149
and the Orange Lodge, 186
and the Second World War, 332, 342,
    345, 346, 351, 355
in British Columbia, 162, 165, 167, 170
protests, 348
public representations of, 343–44
women, 136, 168, 172–73
1st South African Infantry Brigade, 291,
    292, 295, 297, 298
First World War
    and Anglo-Dominion relations, 235,
        242, 247
    and Australia, 243, 372
    and Canadian national identity, 182,
        184, 185, 195, 203, 251–52
    and imperial identity, 17, 49, 190, 194
    and Kumar Shri Ranjitsinhji, 306, 309
    and patriotism, 331
    and socialist organizations, 211, 216
    and the British Empire, 240, 322, 326
    and the Cold War, 366
    and the Dominions, 238
    and the History Wars, 395
    as a global conflict, 244
    Canadian participation in, 197, 198
    Last Hundred Days, 255–56
Fitzroy, Sir Charles, 99, 100
Flanders, 291, 292, 293, 294
Forbes, Lt., 299
Foreign Office, 124, 381
Forster, William, 142
Fort Frederick, 67
Fort Langley, 162
49th Parallel, 332–33, 335
Foucault, Michel, 114
Fourteen Points, 316
4th Australian Division, 241
4th Canadian Division, 255
4th (Scottish) Regiment, 291, 296
Fox Bourne, H.R., 127
France
    and colonialism, 143
    and imperialism, 120
    and Kumar Shri Ranjitsinhji, 305, 307
    and marriage law, 144, 145, 150
    and the British Empire, 32, 49, 233
    and the First World War, 270, 291, 295,
        299
    and the Industrial Revolution, 51
    and the Second World War, 322, 346
    and the Vimy Pilgrimage, 196

Francis, Douglas, 18
Franklin, John, 61
Franklin, Lady Jane, 61
Fraser, Malcolm, 386, 387
Fraser, Peter, 352
free trade, 111, 382
Free Trade Party (Australia), 382
Freedom and Independence for the Golden
    Lands of Australia, 97
Friends and Neighbours, 375
From the Four Corners, 326–27, 331
Fry, C.B., 310
Fuller, J.G., 294
Fulton, 370–71
Furse, Michael, 295

G
Gallagher, John, 10
Gallipoli, 242, 277, 285, 286
Gascoigne, John, 98
Genadendal, 64
gender relations, 140, 149, 172
gendered identities
    and British citizenship, 114
    and colonial India, 305
    and dower rights, 138
    and indigenous people, 113, 121
    and marriage, 135, 137
    and national identity, 12
    and racial discourse, 109, 111, 167–68,
        173–74
    and The First Days, 323
    and the Second World War, 321, 322
    and white settlers, 25
    and women's patriotism, 273, 275
    traditional, 269, 275
General Headquarters, 253
Geneva, 309, 310, 311, 312, 315, 316, 317
"Gertrude of Wyoming," 78
George III, King, 236
George V, King, 271
George VI, King, 323, 324
George, Lloyd, 238, 241
Georgia, 43
German Army, 255, 257
Germany, 215, 243, 276, 286, 296, 321, 323,
    325, 326, 335
Ghana, 412
Ghandi, Mahatma, 307
Giaour, The, 91
Gilroy, Paul, 117
Girl Guides, 189

Girls' Friendly Society, 187
Gladstone, William Ewart, 119
Glasgow, 279, 333
Glasgow Sentinel, 95
Glasgow University, 116
Glen, J.A., 349
globalization, 59, 62, 117, 129, 362
Globe, 163
God Save the King, 286
"God Save the Queen," 87, 89, 101, 103
Godley, Sir Alexander, 241
gold, 43, 45, 95, 97, 101, 136, 170, 217
Gold Coast, 328
Gold Miners: A Sequel to the Pathless West, The, 168
Gordon Highlanders, 270
Governor-General's Fund (South Africa), 289
Grahamstown Journal, 65
Grainger, M. Allerdale, 170
Granatstein, Jack, 198, 203, 390
Great Lakes, 40, 42
Great War, the. *See* First World War
Greater Britain, 119
Greenland, 64
Grey, Earl, 88, 89, 97, 99, 101, 102
Grey, Jeff, 17, 18
Grey, Sir George, 61
Griesbach, Brigadier-General William, 251
Griffiths, Rudyard, 390
Gronlund, Laurence, 211
Gullace, Nicoletta, 277
Gurney, Anna, 74–75
Gurney, Anna (née Backhouse), 75
Gurney-Buxton circle, 75, 78

H
Haddon, O.T., 353
Haig, Field-Marshal Douglas, 195, 240, 258, 259, 260
Haldane, Robert, 73
Halford, H.J., 194
Halifax, 39
Hall, Catherine, 11, 18, 110–11
Hamilton, 194
Hannay, Richard, 381, 382–84
Hansard, 216, 362
Hardinge, Lord, 310
Harkness, David B., 199
Harpin, Helen, 272–73, 276
Harris, Cole, 160

Harris, Rev. John, 127
Harrison, Eric, 363, 405
Hart, Liddell, 371
Hasluck, Paul, 372
Hasting, Brother, 64
Hawke's Bay, 147
Hawke, Bob, 384
Hawkes, Arthur, 191–92
Hawksley, Edward, 91–92, 96, 97
Hay, A., 146
Hello! West Indies, 332
Herring, Arthur May, 162, 163
Herring, Frances Elizabeth, 159–60, 162–74
Hertzog, General, 286, 288, 291
Heyck, T.W., 111–12
Higgins, Esmonde, 215
Higgins, H.B., 215
Higgs, W.G., 211
High Commissions, 202, 383, 403
High Court (Australia), 216, 225
Hill, Father Eustace, 294
Hillary, Edmund, 374
Hindus, 329
Hipkiss, Richard, 91, 93
Hirst, John, 97
Histories, Book 4, 373
History of England, 29, 35, 36
Hitler, Adolf, 327, 372
Hobart Technical College, 225
Hobart Town, 87–90, 93, 94, 96, 97–98, 99, 102
Hobart Town Advertiser, 90, 99
Hobart Town Courier, 88, 89
Hogg, Adelaide, 212
Holland, Rob, 17
Holland, Sidney, 354
Hollywood, 329
Home Service, 334
Hong Kong, 244, 324
Horne, General, 255–56
Hottentots. *See* Khoekhoe
House Committee on Reconstruction and Re-establishment (Canada), 348
House of Commons (Australia), 217, 365, 367, 368, 371
House of Commons (Canada), 200, 349
House of Commons (United Kingdom), 31–32, 33, 93, 95, 97, 334
House of Commons Select Committee on Aborigines (British Settlements), 60, 62, 74, 75, 78, 113, 119, 143–44

House of Lords (United Kingdom), 31–32, 143
How Britain's Weakness Forced Canada into the Arms of the United States, 203
Howard, John, 391, 393
Howard, Kenneth, 299
Howard, Leslie, 326–27, 332
Howard, Nellie, 299
Howay, F.W., 164, 165
Hughes, Billy, 363
Hughes, Sam, 241, 252, 253–54
human rights, 67, 129
humanitarianism, 30, 61, 67, 71, 79–81, 112, 118, 126–27, 218
Hunt, James, 111, 113
Hunt, Nancy Rose, 161
Hunter, P., 291
Hurrah for Merry Sherwood, 197
Huttenback, R.A., 123
Hutton, E.T.H., 237
Hyndman, Henry, 211
hyper-colonization, 41–42, 50. *See also* colonization, explosive

I
Ibsen, Henrik, 128
identity. *See* national identity
Illinois, 49
Image of Africa, 111
Imagining the Fifties, 361
Imperial Bureau of Ethnology, 113
Imperial Conferences, 238, 243
Imperial Defence, 237, 238
Imperial Federation League, 186
Imperial General Staff, 240
Imperial Light Horse, 290, 291, 292
Imperial 9th (Scottish) Division, 291
Imperial Order Daughters of the Empire (IODE), 187, 190, 196, 201, 268
Imperial Press Conferences, 192–94
Imperial 2nd Division, 291
Imperial War Cabinet, 238
imperialism
and democracy, 129
and racial discourse, 117, 118, 126, 129
and reproduction, 161
and the Cold War, 368
and women, 173
Australian, 416
British, 10, 11, 19, 181, 202
Canadian, 182–83, 186, 187, 190, 194, 197
feminist analyses of, 165

liberal, 189–90, 203
modern meaning of, 120
South African, 298
In Place of Fear, 220
In the Pathless West with Soldiers, Miners, and Savages, 163, 167, 173
India
and British media, 325
and immigration, 313
and language of instruction, 35
and marriage law, 146
and racial discourse, 110, 114, 119
and self-government, 34
and slavery, 23
and the British Empire, 9, 26, 120, 305, 308
and the civilizing mission, 110
and the Cold War, 366, 368
and the Commonwealth, 10, 407
and the League of Nations, 310
and the Second World War, 244, 327–30, 332
Indian Mutiny, 113, 123
nationalism in, 306–7, 308–9, 316, 317, 323, 329
opium cultivation in, 311–12
India Office, 310, 311, 313, 329
Indian Affairs (Canada), 343
Indian National Congress, 306, 309, 329
"Indian problem" (Canada), 348, 349–50, 356
Indiana, 49
indigenous people. *See also* Aborigines, Australian; Blackfoot tribe; First Nations; Inuit; Iroquois; Khoekhoe; Maori; Métis; Mohawk; Six Nations; Torres Strait Islanders
and Australia, 385, 392
and Canada, 332
and colonization, 50, 62–63, 119, 120–21
and land claims, 42, 80, 149, 159, 161
and marriage, 137, 173
and modern imperialism, 120
and patriarchy, 169
and racial exclusion, 114
and South Africa, 15, 67
and the British Empire, 10, 59, 60, 62, 71, 78–79
and the civilizing mission, 110
Christianization of, 72, 81
exploitation of, 160
women, 174

Indochina, 245
Industrial Revolution, 51
Inglis, Ken, 220, 246
Innis, Harold, 43, 49
Institute of Commonwealth Studies, 17,
    18
International Barbers' Union, 194
Inuit, 332
Iraq, 381, 392
Ireland, 22, 32–33, 48, 100, 111, 141, 247,
    268, 325
Irish Association, 288
Iroquois, 77
Italy, 145, 345
Ivanhoe, 197

J
Jacobinism, 32
Jam-e-Jamshed, 314
Jamaica
    and slavery, 114, 122
    and Thomas Babington Macaulay, 29,
        33
    colonization of, 24, 25–28
    Morant Bay Rebellion, 28, 31, 111, 113
James Cook University College, 225
Jamnagar, 315
Janssens, J.W., 70
Japan, 244, 366, 371, 389
Jebb, Richard, 187–88
Jews, 31, 33
Jocks, the, 298
Johannesburg, 294
Johnson, Sir Guy, 77
Johnson, Sir William, 77
Jones, J.P., 214
Jones, Peter, 80
Journal of Imperial Commonwealth History,
    18
Jupp, Jim, 222

K
Kalk Bay, 296
Karachi, 316
Kat River, 76
Keating, Paul, 384–85, 389, 390, 392
Kemp, Johannes van der, 70
Kemp, Sir Edward, 87, 89, 257
Kennedy, John F., 408
Kent Hughes, Sir Wilfrid, 363
Kent, Duke and Duchess of, 388
Kent, Susan Kingsley, 267, 275

Kenya, 311, 326, 409
Kenyatta, Jomo, 409–10
Kercher, Bruce, 138
Khoekhoe, 32, 60, 61, 64–69, 71, 73, 75, 76
Khrushchev, Nikita, 371
Kidd, Benjamin, 116
Kidd, Colin, 183
Kimberley Company of the 1st Regiment,
    291
King, Jonathan, 387
Kingsley, Mary, 127
Knight Commander in The Most
    Distinguished Order of St. Michael
    and St. George (KCMG), 259
Knox, Robert, 111, 113
Kokoda Trail, 385
Kondratieff, Boris C., 49
Korean War, 369
Kraal, Hooge, 73
Krygier, Richard, 223
Kuester, J.A., 64
Kuznets, Simon, 49

L
Labor Party (Australia). *See* Australian
    Labor Party (ALP)
labour
    African, 332
    and marriage, 137, 138
    and racial discourse, 127, 128
    and slavery, 122
    colonial, 120, 159, 170
    convict, 392
    free, 89
    movements, 126, 190, 212
    of indigenous peoples, 26, 68, 116
    relations, 221
Labour Party (New Zealand), 344, 346,
    351–52
Labour Party (South Africa), 288
Labour Party (United Kingdom), 217, 219,
    220, 221–22, 223, 374
Labrador, 64
Ladies' Working Part of the Good Hope
    Red Cross Society, 274
Laidlaw, Zoe, 60
Lake, Marilyn, 166, 277
Lamb, John, 100
Lambert, John, 17
Lancashire, 23, 94
Lancashire League, 333
Land Court (New Zealand), 148

land rights. *See* property rights
Lant, Antonia, 267
Laotian crisis, 246
Laqueur, Thomas, 30, 71
Latham, John, 216
Latin America, 39, 48, 50
Launceston, 92, 94
Laurier, Sir Wilfrid, 189, 238, 239
Lectures on Colonies and Colonization, 120
Legionary, 195, 196
Legislative Council (Australia), 100
Lemoyne, Colonel, 67
Lennox-Boyd, Alan, 407
Lester, Alan, 60, 65, 136
Levyns, J., 294
Liberal Party (New Zealand), 217
Liberal Party (United Kingdom), 116,
    119, 270
Liberal Party of Canada, 190, 198, 347
Liberal/Country Party (Australia),
    362–63, 365, 367, 368, 373, 382, 385–86
liberalism, 23, 32, 63, 115, 122, 187, 217, 218,
    270
Life, 329
Lilienthal, David, 375
Lilley, Charles, 145
Linlithgow, Lord, 325
Lintott, Harry, 202
Liverpool, 195
Liverpool, Lady, 268
Lloyd, David, 196
Lloyd, George, 315–16
Lockwood, Florence, 270, 275
London Missionary Society (LMS), 62, 63,
    64, 68, 72–73, 76, 112
London School of Economics and
    Political Science, 209, 217
London, City of
    Address of the Pan-African
        Conference in, 122
    and *Calling the West Indies*, 333
    and export staples, 47–48
    and racial discourse, 125
    and the British World, 22, 49, 385
    and the Commonwealth, 391, 412
    Commonwealth Prime Ministers'
        Conference in, 401–2
    First Imperial Press Conference in, 192
London, United Kingdom government in
    and British Fabian socialism, 222
    and British imperialism, 11
    and the Australasian League Against
        Transportation, 94

and the Dominions, 236–37, 247, 400,
    413
and the Second World War, 243–45
Canadian Headquarters in, 255
High Commissions in, 383, 403
Long, Edward, 26–27, 123
Loomis, Major-General Frederick, 257,
    258
Lord Strathcona's Horse, 237
Lord's, 307
Lowe, Robert, 94, 97
Lowry, Donal, 103
Lucas, Sir Charles, 124, 125–26
Luderitzbucht, 288
Lugard, Lord, 127
Lukin, Brigadier-General Henry, 295
Lusitania, 289

M

MacAdams, Sister, 278
Macaulay, Colin, 30
Macaulay, Henry, 29
Macaulay, Thomas, 30
Macaulay, Thomas Babington, 21, 27,
    29–36, 308
Macaulay, Zachary, 27
MacBrien, James, 258
Macdonald, John A., 186
Machell, Percy, 184
Macintyre, Stuart, 15, 18
Mackenzie King, William Lyon, 193, 198,
    203, 243
Mackenzie Wallace, Sir Donald, 184
Mackenzie, John, 324
Mackie, Jamie, 220
Macleod, Iain, 406, 407
Macmillan, Harold, 371, 402–16
Macmillan, Rev., 295
Madagascar, 74
Mahratta, 314
Malaya, 324, 368, 371
Malik, Kenan, 117
Malthus, Thomas, 40–41
Manchester, 74, 101, 211
Manchester Examiner, 101
Manchester Guardian, 191
Mandler, Peter, 115
Manitoba, 191
Manitoba Free Press, 193
Mann, Tom, 214, 216
Maori
    and claims to land, 138, 149
    and marriage law, 147–48, 150

and New Zealand, 341
and New Zealand national museum,
     394–95
and settler colonialism, 42, 121
and the First World War, 276
and the Second World War, 330, 336,
     346, 355–56
and the Treaty of Waitangi, 345
media representation of, 352
Pakeha relations with, 342, 343, 344,
     353–54
Maori Advisory Council, 353
Maori War Effort Organization (MWEO),
     345–46, 354–55
Maoritanga, 344
"Maple Leaf Forever, The," 184
Maritimes, 190, 198
Maritz, Colonel Manie, 290
Maritzburg College, 293
Markey, Raymond, 211
Marlborough, Duke of, 233
marriage, 16, 121, 135–50, 171, 172
Marson, Una, 333, 334
Marten, Sir Henry, 373
Marwick, Arthur, 274
Marx, Karl, 210, 211, 216
Mary, Queen, 279
masculinity
     and marriage, 139
     and national identity, 31
     and settler colonialism, 170
     and the First World War, 294
     and the Second World War, 324, 337
     martial, 322, 327–28, 330, 336
Mathematical Philosophy, 198
Mathews, Race, 211, 213, 222–23
Maximum Effort, 330
McCalla, Douglas, 44–45
McDonald, Nina, 270
McGuire, Ada, 276
McInnis, Marvin, 43
McKay, Ian, 190
McKenna, Mark, 102
McKenzie, Francine, 199
McLachlan, Noel, 224
McLaren Brown, Mrs. George, 268, 273
McLaren, Angus, 170
McLaren, Barbara, 275
McLeod, John, 306
McNaughton, Andy, 253–45
Meaning of Race, The, 117
media
     and racial discourse, 331, 335, 351

and the Second World War, 322–23,
     325
British, 326
coverage of India, 328, 329, 330
representation of indigenous people,
     342–43, 344, 345, 347, 350, 353
Melbourne
     and Fabian socialism, 210, 211, 213, 214,
          217, 218, 220, 225
     and the Australasian League Against
          Transportation, 95
     and the British government, 101
     colonization of, 45, 46
     1956 Olympic Games in, 373
Melbourne Round Table group, 216, 218,
     220, 226, 383
Menzies Centre for Australian Studies,
     17
Menzies, Robert
     and Australian national identity, 385,
          391
     and Fabian socialism, 220, 224
     and Harold Macmillan, 404–5
     and John Diefenbaker, 410–12
     and marriage law, 145
     and Rhodesia, 415
     and Roy Welensky, 413–14
     and the Cold War, 366, 369, 370–71
     and the Commonwealth, 407, 408–9,
          416
     and the Second World War, 243, 244,
          372
     political dealings of, 400, 401
Merivale, Herman, 120–23
Métin, Albert, 219
Métis, 42, 121
Mexico, 39
Meyer, Willem, 69
Meyer, William, 310
MI5, 388
Michels, Jamie, 69
Middle East, 10, 244, 325, 364, 366, 381
Midlands, the, 23
Military Cross, 295
military participation ratio, 234
Mill, James, 31
Mill, John Stuart, 28, 115
Miller, Carman, 189
Miller, Ian, 190, 198
Miller, Kirby, 52
Mills Committee, 236, 242
Ministry of Information (United
     Kingdom), 326, 328, 329, 332

Ministry of Maori Affairs, 346
Minute on Education, 35
missionary movement.
  See also Christianization
  and British imperialism, 126
  and Canada, 184, 187
  and indigenous people, 72
  and Jamaica, 28
  and slavery, 112, 118
  and the Cape Colony, 59
  international, 63
  networks, 62, 66, 68, 78, 80
Mississippi River, 42, 43, 47
Missouri, 370
Mitchel, John, 102, 103
Mohawk, 32, 77
monarchism, 98, 102, 103, 109, 390, 391
Mons, 239, 256
Montagu, Edwin, 310
Montgomery's 8th Army, 244
Morel, E.D., 120, 127
Morgan, William, 146
Morning Chronicle, 95
Morris, William, 210–11
Morrison, Mrs. Arthur, 279
Mort d'Arthur, 197
Morton, W.L., 191
Moscow, 376
Mr. Standfast, 383
Mullens, John, 368
Muller, Ignatius, 69–70
multiculturalism, 117, 129, 391. *See also*
  diversity
Mumford, Lewis, 51
Munro Ferguson, Lady Helen, 268
Murdoch, Walter, 216
Murphy, John, 361
Murray River, 385
Murray, Gilbert, 122
Murrell, Jack Congo, 61
Muslims, 146, 150, 329

N
Nairobi, 325
Nan, and Other Pioneer Women of the West,
  164, 167
Napoleon I, 372
Napoleon III, 120
Nasson, Bill, 17, 247
Natal, 291
National History Standards, 389
national identity
  and gender roles, 269

and marriage law, 144
and the British imperialism, 185, 193,
  196, 278, 306
and the Dominions, 12, 15, 16, 23–24,
  54, 160, 187–88
and the First World War, 270, 286
Australian, 224, 227, 242, 361, 389. *See
  also* Australia, and national identity
British, 11, 15, 99, 109, 118, 184, 233
Canadian, 181–83, 189, 191–92, 194–95,
  199, 201, 203–4, 255, 256, 259–61. *See
  also* Canada, and national identity
South African, 247, 299. *See also* South
  Africa, and national identity
National Museum (Australia), 393
National Party (New Zealand), 354
National Party (South Africa), 286, 287,
  288, 291, 297, 299
National Service League, 240
Navy League, 288
Nawanagar, 305, 307, 308, 310, 311, 312, 314
Nazi Party, 243, 323–24, 326, 329, 332–33,
  335, 373
Nehru, Jawaharlal, 404–5, 406, 410
New Brunswick, 53
New Fabian Essays, 220
New Order, 342, 347, 349, 350, 351, 354,
  355, 385
New Orleans, 42, 47
New South Wales
  and Corn Law repealers, 93
  and indigenous people, 60, 61, 80
  and self-government, 97
  and the Australasian League Against
    Transportation, 96
  colonization of, 42, 51
  exports from, 43
  marriage law, 138, 139, 149
  memorial for volunteers, 246
  property rights of women in, 142, 143, 144
  Supreme Court of, 217, 388
New South Wales Constitutional
  Association, 91
New Statesman, 221
New Statesman and Nation, 371
New Westminster, 162
New York City, 42, 47, 48, 49
New York State, 77, 194
New Zealand
  and British imperialism, 185, 201
  and national identity, 277, 278
  and the Boer War, 238
  and the First World War, 270, 286

and the Second World War, 244, 245,
321, 330
and the Statute of Westminster, 242
and trade, 383
colonization of, 23, 52
exports, 43, 48
indigenous peoples of, 62, 80, 121, 161,
394. *See also* indigenous people;
Maori
Maori Social and Economic
Advancement Act, 346, 352, 355
marriage law, 142, 147, 149
Married Women's Property Bill, 141
New Zealand Wars, 236
property rights of women in, 137, 138,
143, 145
Treaty of Waitangi, 344, 345
women in, 140, 268, 276
New Zealand Division, 240
New Zealand Expeditionary Force, 241
New Zealand Legislative Council, 148
New Zealand Military Forces, 241
Newfoundland, 9, 39, 246, 322
Ngata, Sir Apirana, 344, 352–53
Niger, 111
Non-European Army Services, 330, 331
Nonconformist, 95
Nongqai, The, 288, 290, 292
Norfolk, 328
Norgay, Tenzing, 374
North American Treaty Organization,
245
North West Frontier, 328
Northern Ireland, 321
Northumberland, Duke of, 77
nuclear weapons, 364–65, 372, 376

O

O'Connell, Daniel, 33, 91
O'Dowd, Bernard, 213–16, 219
O'Dowd, Eva, 214
Offer, Avner, 49
Ohio, 49
Ohio Canal Board, 44
Oklahoma, 52
Olivier, Laurence, 332
Olivier, Sydney, 128
Olympic Games, 373, 391
Ontario, 43, 50, 77, 143, 193, 199
Ontario Military Hospital, 278
opium, 311–13
Orange Free State, 291
Orange Lodge, 186, 187, 197, 201

Orpington, 278
Otago, 43
Other Side of the Frontier, The, 226
Other Side of the Hill, The, 371
Ottawa Conference of 1932, 410
Ottawa Journal, 200
Ottawa, Canadian government in, 241,
253, 257, 347, 403, 404, 408
Ottawa, City of, 189, 192–93
Ottoman Empire, 48
Ourson family murders, 67–71
Owram, Doug, 12
Oxford, 220, 384
Oxford English Dictionary, 24, 115
Oxford History of the British Empire, 12
Oxford University, 17

P

Paardeberg Day, 189
Paarl, 66
Pacalt, 73
Pacific War, 244
Paikea, Paraire, 353
Pakistan, 366
Palestine, 296
Pan-African Conference, Address of the,
122, 127
Papua, 244
Parkes, Henry, 91, 92–94, 95, 96, 100, 103
Parkes, Joseph, 93
Pascoe, Peggy, 170
Passchendaele, 260
patriarchy, 148, 149, 167, 169, 174
Patriotic League, 288
patriotism
and conservatism, 234
and nationalism, 182–83
and religion, 294
and the First World War, 286, 331
and women, 270–75, 277
British, 219, 233
British race, 216–17, 224, 278
Canadian, 194, 252
imperial, 382
Paulton, Abraham, 93, 101
Pearce, George Foster, 239, 241
Pearce, Henry, 373
Pearl Harbour, 371
Pearson, Lester B., 202
Peel, Mrs. C.S., 275, 276
Pelling, Henry, 211
"people's Empire," 322, 325, 329, 332, 333,
334, 335, 336

"people's war," 321–22, 323, 326, 331, 332, 333, 336
Periodical Accounts Relating to the Missions of the Church of the United Brethren Established among the Heathen, 64
Periodical Accounts relative to the Baptist Missionary Society, 63
Perry, Adele, 136
Peterloo, 31
Philip, John, 75, 76
Philipton, 65
Phillip, Governor Arthur, 386, 387
Phillips, Dr. Marion, 217
Phillips, Jack, 213
Phillips, Theresia, 26
Piano, The, 395
Pienaar, Peter, 381
Pilcher, Charles, 139, 144
Platje, Hendrik, 70
Playne, Caroline, 275
Plourde, Father J.O., 351
Pocock, J.G.A., 12
Policies for Progress, 219
Ponsonby, Tom, 222
Poona, 211
Pope, Jessie, 274
Port Philip, 80
Port Philip Herald, 138
Postscript, 334
Pratt, Mary Louise, 165
prayer, international, 64, 65
Preston, Dave, 221–22
Pretoria, 293, 295
Pretoria News, 289
Pretorius, Andries, 69
Priestley, J.B., 327
Problems of Greater Britain, The, 120
Proceedings of the Church Missionary Society, 63
Progress Industry, 44–47
property rights, 63, 79, 80, 81, 135, 137–39, 141–43
Protestants, 15, 50, 63, 109, 186, 190, 233, 240, 246
Pugh, Martin, 268
Punch, 274
Punjab Frontier, 328
Purbrook, Annie, 271
Purcell, Victor, 368, 371
Purkiss, William, 88
Push, 217

Q

Quebec, 137, 145, 200, 202
Queen Mary's Needlework Guild, The, 275
Queensland, 42, 138, 142, 145, 225, 385
Quit India movement (1942), 329, 330

R

race relations
    and the British Empire, 322, 336
    Australian, 225–26
    colonial, 113
    language of, 114–15, 122–24, 125, 128–29
    New Zealand, 344
Races of Man, 111
racial exclusion, 314, 392. *See also* colour bar; discrimination; segregation
racial typologies, 116, 125, 129
racism
    and Australia, 225–26, 387, 415
    and colonialism, 110
    and democracy, 126
    and gender, 168, 173
    and slavery, 123
    and the apartheid regime, 403
    and the British Empire, 114, 316, 334, 335
    and Victorian racial discourse, 111, 113, 119
    Anglo-Saxon, 119
    history of, 129
    Nazi, 332
    nineteenth-century, 109
    terminology of, 124–25
radicalism
    Australian, 210, 213, 214
    British, 93, 94, 95, 99, 102, 127
    colonial, 91, 92, 100
rail systems, 44, 51. *See also* Burma-Thailand railway; Canadian Pacific Railroad
Rajputs, 313
Ramsay, J.G., 142
Rand Light Infantry, 291
Ranjitsinhji, Kumar Shri, 305–17
Razack, Sherene, 161
Read, James, Jr., 65, 75–76, 80
Read, James, Sr., 64–65, 67–70, 75–76
Reading Society, 65
recolonization, 41, 45, 47, 49, 50
Red Cross, 268, 277
Red River Colony, 121, 236
Red Sky Woman. *See* Acoose, Janice

Reeves, Amber, 217
Reeves, John, 222
Reeves, William Pember, 217
Regina, 46
rehydration, 45–46
Reid, Sir George, 382
Relations of the Advanced and the Backward Races of Mankind, The, 124
Remembrance Day, 196, 247
republicanism, 97–98, 99, 101, 102, 103, 120, 298, 391
revisionism, 221, 223, 374
Reynolds' News, 95
Reynolds, Henry, 79, 224–27
Reynolds, Margaret, 225, 226
Rhodesia, 291, 400, 407, 415–16
Rhodesia and Nyasaland, Federation of, 406
Richmond, James, 140–41, 145
Rickard, John, 185
Riley, Denise, 277
"Rise of the Angloworld: Settlement in North America and Australasia, 1784–1918, The" 14
Robb, Peter, 308
Roberts, Morley, 212
Robertson, Hugh, 365
Robinson, Basil, 401, 403, 408, 411
Robinson, Ronald, 10
Roe, Michael, 220
Roosevelt, Franklin Delano, 244, 324, 371
Rooyen, C.J. van, 70
Rooyen, Piet van, 67, 69–70
Rose, Sonya, 324
Rosebery, Lord, 116
Ross, Alex, 254
Rostow, Walt, 375
Round Table group. *See* Melbourne Round Table group
Rowell, Newton W., 188
Rowell, Sidney, 366
Royal Air Force (RAF), 329, 330
Royal Australian Navy, 243
Royal Canadian Air Force, 332, 345
Royal Columbian Hospital Women's Auxiliary, 162
Royal Engineers, 162, 167
Royal Flying Corps, 285, 294
Royal Irish Rifles, 270
Royal Military College Duntroon, 241
Royal Navy, 48, 285, 294
Royal Scots Fusiliers, 297

Royal Tour (1954), 373
"Rule Britannia" (song), 92, 184
Ruskin, John, 211
Russell, Bertrand, 198
Russell, Lord John, 88
Russia, 51, 365–66. *See also* Soviet Union
Rutland, 92

S
Said, Edward, 110
"Saints, the," 29, 30
Salisbury, Lord, 407, 409, 411, 413
Salute to Valour, 196
San, 60, 71
San Francisco, 96, 167
San Francisco agreements, 341
Sandys, Duncan, 405
Saskatchewan, 46
Saskatoon, 46
Saskatoon Star-Phoenix, 348
Saturday Review, 274
Save Our Sons Movement, 225
Scates, Bruce, 275
Schwarz, Bill, 400
Scotland, 24, 52, 73, 74, 278, 322, 334
Scott, Andrew, 223
Scott, Ernest, 216, 225–27
Scott, Rose, 171
Scouting for Boys, 189
Scudder, Franklin P., 381
2nd Australian Infantry Battalion, 366
2nd New Zealand Division, 345
2nd South African Infantry Brigade, 291
Second World War
    and assimilation, 350
    and Australia, 217, 372, 375, 376
    and Canada, 197, 199, 200
    and masculinity, 324
    and the British Empire, 326, 363, 373
    and the Cold War, 364, 370
    and the Dominions, 17, 243, 245
    and women, 268
    as a global conflict, 244
    imagery of, 336
    indigenous involvement in, 342, 343, 344, 355
Secord, Laura, 185
Seddon, Richard, 238
Seeley, John, 125, 255
segregation, 122, 124, 325, 331. *See also* colour bar; discrimination; racial exclusion

Selborne, Lord, 277
self-government
    and Australia, 89, 91, 97, 98–99, 209,
        373
    and Canada, 53, 187
    and India, 325
    and New Zealand, 236
    and the Aborigines Protection Society
        (APS), 127
    and the Central African Federation,
        406
    and the Dominions, 10–11, 22, 53, 123,
        286, 326
    and the West Indies, 24, 25
    colonial, 122, 129, 159, 188
Sen, Satadru, 14
Senate (Australia), 221, 365, 368
*Sense of Power: Studies in the Ideas of
    Canadian Imperialism, 1867–1914,
    The*, 182
Sentinel, 197
separatism, 98, 101, 103, 202
Serle, Geoffrey, 218–19
Seven Years' War, 237
Shah, Nayan, 167
Shanghai, 14
Shann, Edward, 216
Shape of War to Come, The, 371
Sharp, Granville, 123, 127
Shaw, Flora, 119
Shaw, George Bernard, 210, 211
shirkers, 292–93, 297, 348
Siberia, 50
Sicily, 244
Sierra Leone, 29, 30, 35, 73
Sikhs, 329
Sinclair-Maclagan, Major General E.G.,
    241
Singapore, 324, 326, 335
Singapore strategy, 235, 243, 244, 246
Sir Robert Menzies Lecture, 391
Six Nations, 77
Skinner, Constance Lindsay, 164, 171
Slater, Francis Carey, 287
slavery. *See also* abolitionism;
    emancipation
    and Africa, 66, 67, 73, 75, 127
    and Australia, 91
    and colonization, 52
    and marriage, 139, 147
    and the United States, 111, 120
    and the West Indies, 22, 25–28, 122

and Thomas Babington Macaulay,
    29–30, 32
    and Victorian racial discourse, 112, 113,
        114, 118, 123
    chattel, 79
    sex, 171
Slim, Field Marshal Sir William, 365–66
    Defeat into Victory, 371
Smartt, Sir Thomas, 288
Smith, F.B., 220
Smith, Ian, 415
Smith-Dorrien, Lady, 275
Smithsonian Museum, 389
Smuts Memorial Lecture, 410
Smuts, Jan, 286, 291, 331, 413
Smyth, Paul, 221
Snowy Mountains scheme, 374
Social Democratic Federation, 211, 217
Social Questions Committee (SQC),
    211, 214
socialism, 99, 128, 374
Socialist, 214, 215
Socialist League, 211, 288
Solomons, the, 245
Somme, the, 246, 285
Sons of England, 187, 288, 293
Sorabjee, Cornelia, 307
South Africa
    and Afrikaner nationalists, 243, 325
    and English common law, 137
    and national identity, 185, 286. *See also*
        national identity, South African
    and racial hierarchy, 125, 330–31, 335
    and republicanism, 102
    and slavery, 127
    and the British media, 321
    and the Commonwealth, 246, 399,
        403–5, 407, 409, 411, 413
    and the First World War, 238, 239, 240,
        247, 270
    and the Statute of Westminster, 242
    and women's patriotism, 276, 278
    Black Act, 314
    British World Conference in, 17
    Indian immigration to, 313–15
    indigenous peoples of, 15, 126. *See also*
        Khoekhoe
    1912 Defence Act, 289
    Ordinance 50, 61
South African Brigade, 240, 297, 299
South African Commercial Advertiser, 65
South African Defence Force, 246

South African Field Artillery, 291
South African Infantry Brigade, 239
South African Party (SAP), 286, 288, 300
South African War. *See* Boer War
South Australia, 140, 142, 143, 146, 147
Southeast Asia Desk, 367
Southeast Asia Treaty Organization
    (SEATO), 245
Southern Cross flag, 96
Soviet Union, 219, 366, 370. *See also*
    Russia
Soward, Frank, 199
Spain, 51, 145
Special Joint Parliamentary Committee
    (SJC) (Canada), 345, 349–50, 351
Spectator, 273
Spender, Percy, 369
Spigelman, Jim, 217
Springboks, 285, 296, 298
St. Eloi, 257
St. Lawrence River, 41, 42
St. Louis, 43
Stalin, Joseph, 371
Steele, Sam, 185
Steele-Maitland, Arthur, 313
Steevens, George, 112
Stent, Vere, 289, 290, 293
Sterling Area, 400
Stoffels, Andries, 75–76, 80
Stoler, Ann Laura, 161
Story, Judge, 140
Struggle for Europe, The, 371
Study of History, 367
Suez crisis, 202, 399–400, 402, 410
suffragist movement, 95, 111, 162, 270,
    275, 277
sugar, 25–26, 29
Sunday, John, 80
Supreme Council (India), 33, 34
Supreme Court (Australia), 213
Sussex, 271
Sutton, Catherine, 80
Swakopmund, 288
Sweden, 233
Sydney
    and Australian Aborigines, 392
    and Chartism, 91
    and the Australasian League Against
        Transportation, 94, 96, 97, 98–99,
        100
    and the Australian bicentenary, 387
    and the Second World War, 322

Australian Socialist League in, 211
Fabianism in, 217–18
Olympics in, 391

T
Tasmania, 42, 87, 93, 96, 99
Taylor, A.J.P., 371
Te Papa, 394–95
Tedder, Lord, 371
Thanksgiving, 196
Thatcher, Margaret, 388
3rd New Zealand Division, 245
3rd South African Infantry Brigade, 292
Third Way, 223
Thirteen Colonies, 40–41
Thirty-Nine Steps, The, 382
36th Ulster Division, 246
This Nation Called Canada, 199
Thomas, Nicholas, 161
Thompson, E.P., 89
Thompson, Walter, 197
Thorn, George, 142
Thorne, Susan, 112
Thornton, Henry, 29
Through Afro America, 128
Times, The, 224, 234, 272, 324
Tirikatene, Eruera, 353
Tolstoy, Leo, 211
Toronto, 45, 78, 163, 190, 191, 193, 198, 246
Torres Strait Islanders, 225, 394
Tory Party (Australia), 211, 212, 382
Townley, Athol, 363
Townsville, 224–25
Toynbee, Arnold, 367
Trades Union Congress, 221
Trades' Union, 87, 89
Transactions, 63, 68
transportation, 42–44, 47–48, 50–51
Transvaal, 124
Transvaal Scottish, 290, 291
Treatise in Equity Jurisprudence, 140
Trevelyan, George Otto, 30
Tritton family, 273
Tshatshu, Dyani, 75–77, 80
Turner, Henry, 367
28th (Maori) Battalion, 345

U
Uitenhage, 68
Ulster, 213, 246–47
Union Defence Force, 289
Union Jack, 185, 195, 201, 328, 406

Union Jack Flag Day, 279
Unionist Party, 252, 288, 300
United Action crisis, 245
United Brethren, 64
United Empire Loyalists, 39, 53, 185
United Kingdom
    Act of Union, 32
    Australia Acts, 388
    British Official Secrets Act, 388
    Coercion Bill for Ireland, 32, 33
    Colonial Development and Welfare
      Act, 324
    common law, 137, 138, 140, 147
    Constitution, 98, 100
    Corn Laws, 95, 101, 102. *See also* Anti-
      Corn Law League
    1870 Elementary Education Act, 275
    English Married Women's Property
      Acts, 139, 142
    Ilbert Bill, 123
    India Bill of 1833, 33
    People's Charter, 102
    Reform Act of 1832, 32, 91
    Second Reform Act of 1867, 111, 116
    Statute of Westminster, 196, 242
    Whipping Act, 329
United Nations, 219, 245, 363, 364, 365,
    370, 372, 374, 405
United States
    and anti-imperialism, 326, 335
    and Australia, 209, 246, 392
    and Canada, 194, 195, 200, 402, 410
    and capitalism, 219
    and Harold Macmillan, 403
    and opium, 311, 312
    and religion, 233
    and segregation, 124, 126, 331
    and the "History Wars," 389
    and the Cold War, 368
    and the First World War, 395
    and the Progress Industries, 47
    and the Second World War, 245
    bicentennial, 387
    Civil War, 49, 111, 236
    colonization of, 11, 40–41, 42, 43–44,
      51–52
    emancipated slaves in, 120
    indigenous peoples of, 121
    marriage law, 145, 150
    Northwest Ordinance, 53
    War of Independence, 13, 23, 39, 100
    women in, 147

United States State Department, 366–67
University of Auckland, 17, 18
University of Calgary, 18
University of Cambridge, 31, 307
University of Cape Town, 17
University of London, 17, 18
University of Melbourne, 18, 213, 216, 221
University of New Brunswick, 17, 18
University of Sydney, 217
University of Tasmania, 220, 225
Upington, 290
Utilitarianism, 31, 119
utopianism, settler, 51–52

V
Valenciennes, 255, 257
Valentyn, Willem, 68–69
Van Diemen's Land, 61, 88, 96
Vance, Jonathan, 190, 252
Vancouver, 170, 381
Verwoerd, Hendrick, 404
Victoria, 42, 43, 92, 96–97, 138
Victoria Cross (vc), 295
Victoria League, 187, 288
"Victoria 1906," 214
Victoria, Queen, 87, 92, 94, 101, 102, 120,
    123, 234
Victorian Labour College, 222
Victorian Socialist Party (vsp), 216
Vietnam War, 225, 361, 394
Villiers, C.P., 101
Vimy Day, 246, 247
Vimy Pilgrimage, 196
Vimy Ridge, 242, 251, 285
Vincent, Henry, 95
violence
    and colonial British Columbia, 170
    and imperial loyalty, 100
    and men, 171
    and settler-indigenous relations, 66–68,
      70–71, 78, 79, 173, 225–26, 236, 393
Virginia, 53

W
Waiapu, Bishop of, 352
Wake, Launcelot, 382
Wakefield, Edward Gibbon, 53, 136
Wales, Prince of, 388
Wales, Princess of, 388
Wallas, Graham, 113, 126
"Waltzing Matilda," 385
War Came to Kenya, 328, 332

War Comes to Africa, 328
War of 1812, 185
War of Independence. *See* United States,
     War of Independence
War Office, 238, 253, 260
War Peace Committee, 225
War Savings Card, 271
Ward, Pat, 17
Ward, Russel, 225
Ward, Stuart, 224, 278, 322, 391
Washington, D.C., City of, 392
Washington, D.C., United States
     government in, 244, 245, 376, 403
Waterhouse, George, 141, 145
Waterloo, Battle of, 234
Watson, David, 256
Watson, Don, 385
Webb, Beatrice, 209–11, 214, 219, 223
Webb, Sidney, 209–11, 214, 219, 223
Weekly Dispatch, 278
Welensky, Roy, 400, 401, 406, 407,
     408–10, 413, 414–15, 416
Welles, Sumner, 324
Wellington, 244, 343, 351
Wellington, Duke of, 32, 233
Wells, H.G., 210, 217
Wells, Ida B., 128
Wentworth, William Charles, 99
Wentzel, Eric, 294
West Indies
     and free trade, 111
     and independence, 29
     and national identity, 24, 25, 36
     and slavery, 22, 110, 119, 120, 122
     and the British Empire, 14, 21
     and the British media, 321, 325
     Britishness in, 26–28
     women in, 147
West Indies Calling, 332, 333, 334, 335
West, G.M., 277
West, John, 88, 89, 90, 93
Western Front, 257, 272, 296, 297, 298,
     381, 384
*"What is my Country? My Country is the
     Empire. Canada is my home."*, 184
Whig Party (United Kingdom), 31, 32,
     50, 95
Whitaker, Frederick, 142
Whitlam, Gough, 210, 218, 220, 223, 224,
     371
Who Killed Canadian History?, 390
Why Weren't We Told?, 225

Wilberforce, William, 29, 70
Wilhelm II, Kaiser, 257
Williams, Shirley, 222, 223
Wilmot, Chester, 371
Wilson, George, 92
Wilson, Harold, 223, 415
Wilson, Kathleen, 26
Wilson, Woodrow, 316
Win the War Cookery Book, 270
Windeyer, Richard, 93
"winds of change" speech, 10, 403–4, 405,
     406
Windschuttle, Keith, 393, 394
Winnipeg, 46, 195
Winnipeg Free Press, 200
Winter, J.M., 183
Winton, 385
Wolfe, Patrick, 160, 161
women
     Aboriginal, 112
     active participation of, 61, 112
     and British imperialism, 187, 190
     and indigenous people, 61, 128
     and marriage, 136–41, 144–47
     and slavery, 25, 27
     and the First World War, 293, 331–32
     and the Second World War, 333
     and the vote, 210
     British imperial identity of, 31, 112,
          115–16, 137
     property rights of, 135, 142, 148–50
Woodbine Pomare, Miria, 276
Woods, Edith, 278
Woodsmen of the West, 170
World War I. *See* First World War
World War II. *See* Second World War
Wright, Gilbert, 97, 101
Wright, Peter, 388
Wrong, George M., 191

X

xenophobia, 124, 128
Xhosa, 60, 75, 76, 77

Y

York, Duke and Duchess of, 388
Yorkshire, 94
Ypres, 257

Z

Zwartkops River, 69